SERMONS ON
GENESIS

SERMONS ON
GENESIS

∿ CHAPTERS 11:5-20:7 ∿

John Calvin

Forty-eight sermons delivered in Geneva between
24 January 1560 and 15 May 1560

Translated into English by
Rob Roy McGregor

THE BANNER OF TRUTH TRUST

THE BANNER OF TRUTH TRUST
3 Murrayfield Road, Edinburgh EH12 6EL, UK
P.O. Box 621, Carlisle, PA 17013, USA

∾

Translated from *Supplementa Calviniana,* volume XI/2,
edited by Max Engammare, published by
Neukirchener Verlag, 2000

First Banner of Truth edition, 2012

© Rob Roy McGregor 2012

ISBN: 978 1 84871 154 9

∾

Typeset in 11/15 pt Adobe Caslon Pro at the
Banner of Truth Trust, Edinburgh
Printed in the USA by
Versa Press, Inc.,
East Peoria, IL

CONTENTS

v

Contents

INTRODUCTION
by the Translator

*A*LL OF HIS LIFE, James was marginally acquainted with a Christian congregation and was minimally informed about biblical teaching. He would have easily fitted the category of those who think that, to go to heaven, all you have to do is die. For most of his years, he dabbled broadly in science and scientific theory, which likely prompted his query. 'Rob Roy,' he asked me one day, 'where is heaven? I know how to get there. You can get there through wormholes. I just don't know where it is.'

'James, I know people talk about "going to heaven," as if it were a place somewhere out there where you can go and live comfortably with God, but you would do better to think of it as a condition, a spiritual condition." Our conversation ranged on for a while. When it was over, I was not sure he had understood my point that heaven is a place 'in which righteousness dwells' (*2 Pet.* 3:13).

Be that as it may, given his propensity to refer to sinners as earthworms (*vers de terre*), Calvin might have thought it appropriate to view the cross of Christ as a 'worm' hole by which believers could enter the kingdom of God. One thing is certain, though. He speaks at length about the human condition that distinguishes us from the spiritual condition that characterizes the kingdom of God, and he underscores the biblical teaching that the spiritual condition of suitors of the kingdom which is not in harmony with the spiritual nature of the kingdom is unfit for the kingdom. Is it, then, unorthodox to suggest that believers must now be in preparation for the kingdom of heaven, bringing themselves into line with God's mind and will through glad and engaged obedience before entertaining the hope that they are ready to occupy the place, wherever it may be?

Calvin, when preaching on Genesis 11:31-12:2 and speaking of Abraham's difficulty in leaving his own people and possessions in faithful obedience to God, provides a partial summary of his preaching, for he always understands that the Old Testament serves to instruct the Church: '[L]et us learn from this passage… that when we serve God, our lives will be filled with many struggles. If we do not sense them right away, they will come eventually. So if hypocrisy is not to get the best of us, let each of us enter into ourselves, to the deepest part, and consider the things that are required for obedience to God and the obstacles the world provides, those things which are in our very selves, for no greater resistance is to be found than the resistance found in our inner selves' (pp. 52-53). Those words show Calvin is aware that as we confront the internal and external problems of ordinary life, our resident self is in a very real sense our worst enemy and that our success in Christian living depends upon sincere and intentional obedience to God's will and call, irrespective of the material, physical, and emotional demands that are made, 'for we will never serve God without a struggle' (p. 79).

He reminds us that 'when we come to preaching, we are not to seek to be soothed or stroked or have our ears tickled with quaint speculations, but [we are] to allow the preacher to get under our skin so we will be pierced, cut to the quick, and deeply wounded, and have to take the bitter medicine and sometimes pass through fire and searing reproaches so that everything will be shut off from the corruption in us; otherwise, there would be no Christianity in us' (p. 406). Such rigorous preaching is the purpose of the pulpit, 'the place for teaching about faith and the fear of God' (p. 642).

These sermons will burden and challenge any spiritually-minded person. In them the reader will encounter a passionate and skilful Calvin who delivered sermons that offer the water of life for transforming sinful and redeemed creatures so that they, repentant, forgiven and cleansed, may worship more freely and gratefully the God of grace and mercy and serve him more devotedly and perceptively.

Calvin did not preach as one who lived in an ivory tower, but as one who experienced the persistent struggles and battles of daily existence. He preached as one who deeply cared for his people, analyzing for them and warning them of the wiles of Satan, the temptations of the world, and the traps hidden in their human nature. He exhorted them to allow the gospel to penetrate their hearts through increasing and persevering obedience. He nourished with the truths of Scripture God's hungry pilgrim people, fortifying them to resist all the trials, tribulations, and temptations that work to turn them from the heavenly kingdom, the ultimate goal, the awaiting reward for diligence.

Their various teachings are still relevant and demanding for the dynamic correction and growth of the Body of Christ until God 'has made us completely like himself and his righteousness, to which he calls us every day by his word' (p. 777).

These sermons will provide Christians at all levels of spiritual development with important insights and emphases for preaching, teaching, and living the truth of God's Word as revealed in the book of Genesis and beyond.

A hasty but attentive reading of any of John Calvin's sermons reveals that the Reformer understood the struggle Christians are obliged to engage in as he encourages them to press on to attain 'the prize of the high calling of God in Christ Jesus' (*Phil.* 3:14), that struggle which will eventually confirm all believers in their readiness to enter into the presence of the Triune God and enjoy him forever.

After reading but a few of Calvin's many sermons, I am convinced that the time is ripe for all those who claim to be of the Reformed tradition to restore the integrity of the first Reformation, an integrity that is more than being confessionally 'theologically correct.' The Reformers had to restore both confessional integrity based on Scripture and personal integrity based on the moral principles established in Scripture. Some in the Reformed tradition have arrogated the authority, through its forms of government and assemblies, to modify the standards for theological correctness and for moral behaviour, lenient standards that condone gross sin in its clergy and membership and that grant easy absolution for perfunctory public confession of sin, confession that is without genuine repentance and determined intention and effort to correct personal moral deficiency. The original Reformation recognized that kind of failure in the Roman Catholic Church and acknowledged the inherent tendency toward that failure among its adherents. Was it not said during the battle to correct (reform) the Church on the basis of Scripture that *'ecclesia reformata semper reformanda est'* ['The church, having been reformed, is always having to be reformed.']?

∽

My preference is to repeat verbatim the Translator's Preface to Calvin's *Sermons on the Acts of the Apostles 1-7* (Banner of Truth, 2008) and Calvin's *Sermons on Genesis 1-11* (Banner of Truth, 2009), but will forbear and refer the reader to those sites for a statement of appreciation for my wife's and son's indulgence and patience during the translations of Calvin's sermons.

It is difficult to find words adequate to thank Dr Terry L. Eves, Professor of Old Testament and Hebrew at Erskine Theological Seminary in Due West, South Carolina. His training in Semitic languages and the depth of his commitment to the Reformed tradition fitted him ideally for the task I asked him to undertake. I deeply appreciate his gracious acceptance of my invitation and his many apposite observations.

A word of overdue appreciation goes to the Banner of Truth editors of the *Acts* and *Genesis* volumes, whose trained and vigilant eyes saved the printing of the text from many an oversight.

∾

Preached in Geneva from Wednesday, 24 January 1560 through Wednesday, 15 May 1560, Calvin's *Sermons on Genesis 11:5-20:7*, numbered 50 through 97, translated here into English for the first time, are collected in the *Supplementa Calviniana*, volume xi/2, edited by Max Engammare, and published by Neukirchen-Vluyn: Neukirchener Verlag in 2000. For readers of French and Latin, the editor's introduction and notes afford much scholarly information of use and interest. To this translation have been added only notes considered useful for the rectification of certain of Calvin's references and for the elucidation of obscure points in the sermons, points a modern reader might need explained for hearing the sermons, had he been present at their delivery. The choice of Engammare's notes (initialed *M.E.*) is, of course, arbitrarily mine, as are the titles added to the sermons. The scriptural references, given in Engammare's footnotes, have been placed within the text of the translation.

∾

My prayer is that these and all other of Calvin's sermons will convict of sin, prompt effective repentance, and strengthen believers as they participate in the works laid out from the foundation of the world for the glorification both of the Lord Jesus Christ and, in the Last Day, the Church Triumphant.

ROB ROY McGREGOR
Anderson
South Carolina
USA
November 2011

50

God's Judgment Eventually Strikes the Mighty and Arrogant and Rewards the Humble

*And the L*ORD *came down to see the city and the tower, which the children of men builded. And the L*ORD *said, Behold, the people is one, and they have all one language; and this they begin to do: and now nothing will be restrained from them, which they have imagined to do. Go to, let us go down, and there confound their language, that they may not understand one another's speech. So the L*ORD *scattered them abroad from thence upon the face of all the earth: and they left off to build the city. Therefore is the name of it called Babel; because the L*ORD *did there confound the language of all the earth: and from thence did the L*ORD *scatter them abroad upon the face of all the earth* (Gen. 11:5-9).

*T*O TAKE ADVANTAGE of what has already been recounted, we need to remember what we dealt with yesterday, namely, that those who wanted to build the city and the Tower of Babylon were driven to do so by a foolish excess of pride, for they had forgotten their condition and wanted to make a name for themselves here below. God puts us here to crawl around for a while, as mentioned in Psalm 90 (cf. *Psa.* 90:3). It is our lot to live and rush about hectically and then return to dust. So inasmuch as we are created and born in this condition wherein we pass quickly through this world like strangers (cf. *Heb.* 11:13; *1 Pet.* 2:11), we show contempt for God and nature when we carve out some bit of immortality for ourselves. Now as those mentioned here had such a disposition, so the prophet points out in Psalm 49 that those who were supposed to aspire after the kingdom of heaven tried to make their nest here and snuggle down in it forever (cf. *Psa.* 49:12) and shared in a persistent vice which has continued to reign in every age. So what we need to note first is that God, when confusing human language, declared once and for all that he is the enemy of all excessive pride and will not permit the great to exalt themselves without knocking them off their high horse. Now, as we said, that story was not written for the people who lived then, but for our instruction.

We come now to what Moses recounts. Since God punished those who exalted themselves beyond measure and did not want to be scattered abroad lest they have no memorial to give them renown, it is said that the Lord God came down to see the building the children of men were constructing. Now God does not have to change his location to look at and consider what men are doing or even what they are thinking, for he fills all things with his infinite being, as we know. But Scripture, well aware that we cannot attain the exalted and incomprehensible majesty of God, advises us of our lack of learning and our weakness. In short, it shows that God seems not to pay attention for a while but finally appears and executes judgment, as it says in Psalm 34: his eyes are on all evildoers to cut off their name from the earth (cf. *Psa.* 34:16). Thus God stands watch to maintain and preserve his people and those who find rest and refuge in him; on the other hand, all evil deeds must reach his desk, as they say, and be recorded before him, and men must finally be called to account. It is true that the wicked harden themselves when God exercises patience and does not immediately show his arm and power to punish them. As a result, they deceive themselves into believing that they have escaped his hand. In fact, God rightly shows himself to be long-suffering and does not immediately act to confound his enemies (cf. *Jon.* 4:2; *Nahum* 1:3; *Eccles.* 5:4). Even so, we must bear in mind that God sees and knows all.

However, because we do not understand and will have no visible experience with God, it is said that he comes down when he demonstrates by deed that men err when thinking they accomplish their undertakings and practices in hiding. That is why the prophet Isaiah says, 'Woe to you who hide your plans from the Lord' (*Isa.* 29:15), for men think they are so subtle and clever that God will not notice their intentions. And when they conspire among themselves like a knot of vipers, they think God will not see a jot of it. How very mistaken they are!

Therefore, let us take note that when God allows the wicked to abandon themselves to their own wills and lets them run free, it may seem that he has withdrawn. It is not that he is slothful at that time or has forgotten his office, for he is always this world's Judge, but he is waiting for the right time. He does that to make even worse the rebellion of those who will not be corrected and abuse his goodness and kindness. On the other hand, he comes down, that is, in a moment of time he shows that everything must come before his judgment seat and that everything has to be made known and that those who have scorned him for a time must become aware that they have to be crushed under his majesty because they did not choose better. That is why Scripture so often says that the condition of rebels and despisers of God is like childbirth, which comes upon a woman unexpectedly (cf. *Job* 15:35; *Psa.* 7:15; *Isa.* 30:13). They will make merry and sense no displeasure. Likewise, when the wicked say peace and assurance, as Isaiah also says, and make a covenant with death and the grave and think that neither God nor the devil can do anything against them and mock, saying that even if floods engulf the whole world, they will not be affected (*Isa.* 28:15). Suddenly, suddenly, when they are having a good time and are full of themselves, God will bring them down.

So let us pay close attention to this statement, that God came down to see the building the sons of men had begun. And let us learn again that he does not chastise us forthwith as we deserve, but that he seems to close his eyes and stop his ears so as not to be aware of our sins so that we, for that reason, will be emboldened with greater audacity to do evil. Let us be careful, I say, not to abuse God's enduring patience by deceiving ourselves into finally believing that he wishes to forgive us; but when he supports us, let us know that he is giving us an opportunity to return to him and that he even wishes to draw us to himself in that way. That is how we will anticipate and avoid his judgment. Let us be aware of that.

In addition, let us not envy those who act fearless in this world, who make everybody tremble and take their pleasure in being dominant and celebrating their victories. Let us wait for the time that God will descend, that is, will manifest himself as Judge, and we will not be disappointed when we walk in fear of him and always attribute to him the honour which is his. In other words, all creatures are under his hand and guidance, and he will not guide the world with an absolute power, but his justice is joined to it in such a way that he is the protector of the good and the innocent. And at the same time he is capable of striking down the haughty look of the proud, as another psalm says (cf. *Psa.* 101:5). Yet Moses informs us about what we ought to know rather well, although he declares that nothing will go unpunished before his face even if he does not lash out immediately (cf. *Exod.* 20:7; *Deut.* 5:11; *Prov.* 11:21; *Nahum* 1:3; etc.).

And there is another point to note here. God does not strike without thinking or haphazardly, but he knows what we deserve before he puts his hand on us. So let us be aware of this: although God makes us feel his rigor when we sorely offend him and obstinately fight against him, he has nevertheless supported us over a long period. So much for that point.

For the other point, let us admit that we are guilty immediately upon receiving some punishing blow, knowing that we will gain nothing by resisting. It is certain he always uses equity and uprightness in such a way that all his judgments are flawless. We can grumble about him, even vent our blasphemies, accusing him of cruelty and injustice, but he will easily be able to absolve himself by his own authority. In any case, when the text says he came down, it shows that he has always condemned men justly before applying his hand to make them feel his corrections. That, I say, is what we must use from this passage.

On that point, Moses introduces God speaking as though it were very annoying to remedy that licence and audacity that men had taken upon themselves. He says, 'What! What do I have to do here? There is a great conglomeration of people here. They are empowering one another'—as we saw yesterday that they were encouraging one another— 'and now we have a people who have banded together. Moreover, they have a single language and can agree together; they have made a decision about their project; they have even begun; they are making a real effort; every one is trying very hard. With such great audacity, with such enthusiasm, seething with their great longings and desires, what would they not be able to do in this place? Who could hold them back?' Now God, speaking that way, derides men for not taking their own measure, for not taking a good look at themselves, as we say, when they presume to undertake one thing or another which exceeds their ability. Consequently, men think they do not have to take God into consideration, and they occupy themselves with the things that surround them. It is as if he meant nothing to them, and that is why God mocks them. What is the significance of that? They are so blinded by presumption that they do not think anything can resist them. Why? They see there is a great multitude of them, and that puffs them up with pride and overweening confidence. And then, after conspiring together, the decision they make gives them even greater confidence. They are a sturdy people! Each one makes up his mind and resolves to put his hand to the task because they limit themselves to what they see and know, and they convince themselves that they will not be prevented from accomplishing what they have begun.

Now this is a passage which deserves much attention, for one of our much too common vices is that our minds do not go beyond the world's mediocre means when we get something into our heads and seek advice. All the more, then, must we value what is said here about God's mocking from on high our failure to think about him and realize that he controls us and that we cannot take a single step or lift a finger unless he gives us leave. James mocks those who deliberate for a year or two and say, 'Now this year I will go abroad and engage in commerce.' 'How,' he asks, 'can you be sure of your lives just for one day?' (cf. *James* 4:13-14). People who talk that way without entrusting themselves to God and his providence do not fight as openly against God as did those who endeavoured to build the Tower of Babel, but they still diminish God's honour by taking greater license than they should. That is also what Solomon means when he says that the heart of man plans his ways, but God directs the tongue (cf. *Prov.* 16:1). Nonetheless, he mocks that foolish boldness and fearlessness characteristic of men when they discuss their plans and imagine various things and say, 'This is the way we have to get things done without asking about God's will or acknowledging that our lives depend on him.' Now is that the way they went about it?

Did they build castles in the air with their foolish undertakings and their opinions and fantasies? God governs their language. In other words, they cannot utter a word, as we will soon see, unless God gives them the freedom to do so. To utter words is an insignificant thing, for we see that what tongues say evaporates into the air and that their boastings are like smoke. And still men could not move their tongue to make their boasts without God's permission. And what does that have to do with taking counsel and firming up plans and then setting to work and executing the project? That is the common vice I spoke of. What is the reason men are so bold, indeed so crazy that they break loose and let themselves go, as if they were horses set free and running in every direction? It is because they consider only themselves and what they are focusing on and what is close at hand. If a man has a good reputation and authority, if he is well off and well connected, he thinks he is like an idol and will then say, 'I can. How so? Because I have the means. What do I need God for? Oh, he does not make a big to-do about it.' So that is how people of the world become hardened in their pride. They are attached to the world by all their senses, and they become insensitive at will, such that this is their only consideration: 'And who is this fellow in comparison with me? Oh, I will come out all right. After I deal with that fellow, will he want to face me? Oh, he will find out who he has to deal with. And then that other fellow. Will he want to take me on? Oh, I will have to get even one way or another.' So, according as men are blind that way in their upcoming undertakings, they challenge God and his sovereignty. But still let us note that God is mocking on high, and that is what the second psalm says about the enemies of the gospel and about those who fight against the kingdom of our Lord Jesus Christ: that God does not immediately want to take arms and avenge himself on their godlessness and scorn, but he mocks them for a time (cf. *Psa.* 2:4). Did he mock them? Oh, but later he works with purpose when the occasion arrives.

In that way, let us learn to look to God in everything we have to do. In the first place, let us realize that our lives depend completely on him and that they are sustained by his power. Otherwise, they are only like puffs of air that evaporate every minute. And even though he gives us circumspection and vigour and everything we need, he still always preserves for himself the right to guide us and keep us from undertaking anything he does not permit. Let us keep that fixed firmly in our minds and not undertake anything that has not been placed in his hands, and let us add to all our deliberations the condition that nothing will be done which has not been granted by his grace. That is the first thing we have to observe here.

And even though our Lord does not overturn all our plans, yet if we are foolhardy and overweening, he will mock us for a while, and then his mocking will take effect, and there will be only confusion in everything that we, trusting our own good sense and foolish imagination, thought was perfectly well planned and arranged.

Moreover, although God does not employ that kind of chastisement every day as it is here recited by Moses, we have to gather from this story a general teaching, such as is found in holy Scripture, namely, that God's responsibility is to confound and upset all the plans of the wicked, as Solomon says: 'There is no wisdom and no understanding and no counsel that can stand against the Lord' (*Prov.* 21:30). And even through Isaiah he scorns the great kings and peoples when they have plotted carefully together, thinking they have won the day: 'Oh, take counsel together, consider together, consult and deliberate, and then make your decisions, and they will come to naught; all will be vain, for I stand opposed and will break to pieces everything you plan to build' (*Isa.* 8:9-10).

So what we have to gather from this story is that when it seems we can do anything, our Lord will mock our foolishness unless we remove the blindfolds which obstruct our sight, and let us be aware that all the means we think we have in hand will soon disappear, and that even what we think gives us an advantage will work against us until we learn to humble ourselves under God's strong hand. Oh, it is certain we could be the wisest and most capable people in the world and he will make us all, to the smallest child, ridiculous, and we will be taken by surprise, like poor animals. When we think we have everything under control, it will slip away in a moment, for God has limitless ways to reduce men to confusion and make them ashamed of their arrogance. But even so, the wicked will always persist in confronting him in their fury. As for us, let us learn both from holy Scripture and the testimonies that God gives us in it that we experience what an enemy he is of the proud and that he will bring down all pretensions to grandeur. Let us learn, I say, to walk humbly and modestly when we see tyrants and God's enemies conspiring together. Have they engaged in countless intrigues? They will all crumble away. It will be said that such a thing has existed and that they trusted in it, but it is certain God is at work in it. So, on the one hand, let us realize that when we have many enemies and everyone has agreed to exterminate us, if God is on our side, he is powerful enough to destroy and bring to nothing all of the enraged audacity of those who dare to rise up against him that way. On the other hand, let us be warned not to throw off God's bridle and yoke, but to yield to our God's guidance.

There, then, are two points we have to note about this teaching, that is, the purpose to which we must apply it. We have said that there is no council to deliberate against God and that when the wicked consult together and make their decrees, he will bring everything to naught. How will that be of use to us now? As I have pointed out, we must first place ourselves under our God's protection, for if we want him to extend his hand and preserve us (cf. *Psa.* 138:7), ward off the blows and thwart everything our enemies contemplate against us, we must place ourselves under his protection and yield to his guidance, being thoroughly persuaded that we are his people, that he watches over us as he promised he would (cf. *Psa.* 100:3), and we must have hardy contempt for everything that is against us. And when men think they will consume us with a sprinkling of salt, as the saying goes, even though they do not have the power to do so and we are nothing in comparison with them, let us not fail to entrust ourselves to our God. Why? He mocks their presumption. The more they try to exalt themselves and abandon themselves to their excesses without moderation or modesty, the more they affront God. It is certain the person who exalts himself ever so little will always affront him. Now Scripture says that God's hand is against the proud (cf. *Dan.* 4:37). They cannot praise themselves a penny's worth without bumping up against God. And then, on the other hand, we are in his safekeeping, and whoever touches us, touches the apple of his eye, as he declares (cf. *Zech.* 2:8). Therefore, let us be boldly confident that he is powerful enough to defeat the machinations and intrigues, the very efforts and preparations directed against us. Although those who think they are a hundred times more powerful than they are give it their best shot, everything they do will vanish into thin air and dissipate like smoke. And whatever they do and conspire to do to destroy us, God will work to see that we land on our feet, as they say. That is a part of what we have to remember.

And the other part we need to remember is that we must not forget what kind of people we are and what our condition is. Therefore, seeing how weak we are, let us not undertake anything rashly, but let us entrust our steps to God, as Jeremiah says: 'Lord, I know that it is not for man to direct his ways, but that you have kept for yourself that authority' (cf. *Jer.* 10:23). In that way, let us grant God the pre-eminence which he demands and which belongs to him. And in that way, walking in simplicity, let us allow him to reign over us, and let us receive no counsel except what we have sought from his mouth, that is, what we have considered as permitted by his word, and then let us call upon him at the same time, and entrusting ourselves to him, let us wait for him to bring our affairs to a good conclusion. And may he direct them so well that the outcome will be better than if the entire world favoured us.

In addition, as I have already said, God has an infinite number of ways to use as he pleases to reverse the course of those who rise up against him. He will route their plans even if he does leave them one language, as we see in the case of Ahithophel, who was well understood when he employed the ruse of following David quickly even though he thinks his counsel is to be approved, as it usually was. God blinds those who listen to him, and the plan comes to naught. Now sometimes he will permit counsel to be accepted and approved and even be carried out. And yet everything will be dashed to pieces, and those who think they are making a lot of headway will lose ground. In short, it is with good reason that God says his counsel is incomprehensible, but he still testifies that he will not allow men's pride to remain unpunished when they forget who they are, as we have already pointed out, and usurp what he reserves for himself alone and make of themselves idols. That, in short, is what we need to remember in addition to what was mentioned earlier, namely, that we will all be blinded by some foolish ambition which will turn us into God's enemies until we learn to long for heaven and walk simply in this world and be like newly weaned children who are doing no wrong.

In addition, we see hidden in that mockery what leads men astray. It is that sense of greatness and exaltation that they have, and they think God no longer has any usefulness for them. The more those who are held in honour and have a good reputation and have means in hand, the more they have to be on guard for

fear that the devil will intoxicate them in such a way that they
will begin to battle against God without being aware that they are
doing so. That has caused the ruin and confusion of the greatest
and most renowned people in the world, for they have abused
what God was giving them, whether it was reputation, or power,
or people and lands. So when they reached that point, they had
to feel God's hand when they tried to confront him. We even see
that the saints have stumbled in that kind of situation, and if God
had not had pity on them, they would have been destroyed forever.
David himself makes that confession. When he saw himself
flourishing and having everything he wanted, he was like a brute
beast, as he says in Psalm 49 (cf. *Psa.* 49:12): men, when they are
held in honour, do not realize the kind of people they are. And yet
God visits them. And that is reason enough to abase them. Some
people will always think that God is making sport of humankind
when those who are raised on high are brought low. And because
man cannot be content with their condition, the wheel of Fortune
is brought into play. The kinder God shows himself to be by
raising them to some dignity and giving them power, the more
they become like wild animals and think they are permitted to
do anything, measuring, as they do, all things by their power and
ability, without considering that God is always in charge of his
vineyard and that they must govern themselves in accordance with
his good will. Inasmuch as we see that those of small estate know
that God rightly humbles them so that their pride will not destroy
them, and inasmuch as we see that the great also do not think of
attempting anything that is not permitted to them and continue
to walk in lowliness and simplicity, he does not, although he has
raised them up, wish to diminish his place of honour when he is
pleased to show that he is kind to the great and small and is their
Judge. But all those who exalt themselves under the pretext of their
greatness are all the more inexcusable, and they must be punished

more severely for abusing God's goodness, which was supposed to give them an opportunity to walk in fear of him and obey him and bring themselves completely into line with his will.

On that point, Moses adds that God stirs into action: 'Come, let us go down and see if we can hold them back. Yes, all we have to do is to divide their languages and they will no longer be able to understand one another. And that will be the end of the building. They will no longer be able to place stone upon stone, brick upon brick'—for we said yesterday that they were building with bricks. 'They will not be able to lay a single brick when their languages are confused that way.' Moses had earlier introduced God as being astonished, as we have said, mockingly, as when he said, 'How will it be possible to restrain them, seeing that they have begun, are working very hard, and are so dead set to get the job done? How will we be able to stop them?' And he shows that without moving from the spot, he will be able to disperse them. God certainly had the power to strike them with lightning from heaven, if he had been so disposed, or he could have set that great multitude to flight. But he found a different way that put them to greater shame and subjected them to greater reproach. If they had been scattered by some storm or tempest and God had shown his dreadful power that way, there would not have been such shame and infamy as when they became incomprehensible babblers and thought they were communicating with their neighbours but were stammering and bellowing like oxen to one another, like baying dogs, or like a grunting pig, incapable of being understood. So when God abandoned them in that kind of reproach, they were repaid as they deserved, for we have already seen that the thing that had persuaded them to build the tower was a memorial that would gain them immortality: 'We have descended from that people, and it is they who built this!' So in order to exalt themselves, they undertook that work (cf. *Gen.* 10:10-12).

We have already seen that Nimrod was the leader in Babylon. He ruled there and was indeed satisfied with nothing, but usurped everything by tyranny, oppressing those near and far, devouring everything like a bottomless pit. God, as I have said, does not now punish them so terribly that you would say, 'Well, they are done for! They have been wiped out! And it was done by the strong hand of God!' Oh, God has employed his strong hand here. But in appearance it looked weak, for God has only gently exhaled: 'Stand forth! You think you are well on your way. You think you are coming to the end of your undertaking. But all I will do is confuse your languages. I will leave you your arms and your legs; you will have an unbridled and evil desire to continue zealously. I will not put in your way heaven, or earth, or the elements. I will send no wounds, no storms, nothing to hinder you, and yet you will be able to accomplish nothing, knowing neither why nor why not, but only confusion.' That is how God crushes the pride of those who exalt themselves beyond measure and heaps shame upon them, as if he were putting them on a scaffold to be despised, mocked, and rejected by everybody.

Seeing that, let us be determined all the more by that teaching to use restraint and not move forward without thought and deliberation. Rather, let us acknowledge our weakness and always be cautious and concerned, and may our boldness be founded on our God's grace, kindness, and help. And let us not find it strange that our Lord reduces the proud to confusion, for, as we have said, they not only oppress their neighbours with extortion, physical injuries, and violence, but they also rebel against God and rise up against heaven. Now they will think they have a very strong case against God; they will not say so and will even protest to the contrary: 'What? You say we are rising up against God? God forbid!' Yet, all of their acts and plans, all of their manoeuvrings show they have contempt for God, resist him, deprive him of his honour, show no fear of his power, and set themselves up in his place, as if they were idols. So we must not be astonished if they are brought low in this manner. That is what we need to observe when we hear that punishment fell upon those who were building the tower.

Besides, when God deliberates that way in himself, he shows us he is not proceeding hastily, as we hear every day this kind of comment: 'So? We cannot commit even a tiny sin without having God's wrath fall on us immediately.' But here we are told the opposite, that God never extends his hand to punish men's iniquities and transgressions without awareness of our sins. Not that he needs to conduct investigations or inquests or conduct lawsuits the way earthly judges do, but that is said to accommodate our incapacity and lack of knowledge, as we have already mentioned. So much for that point.

In addition, here God sets his judgment over against all those foolish opinions men deceive themselves with. That is what clouds their vision, for the first thing we note is that the great of this world burst with pride and are not only intoxicated, but even bewitched by Satan to the point that they do not recognize themselves and consider their condition but place themselves, in a word, above other men. And then when people applaud them and even fear them and hold them in awe, they are doubly bewitched and delude themselves with these signs of flattery even as they see people laughing on all sides. Now our Lord is giving us another lesson here, namely, that when we are honoured to high heaven and people want to carry us on their shoulders, so to speak, and we are partially worshipped as small gods, let us not fail to be embarrassed before him. Let us learn to hold our heads up, not in presumption, but in faith, and look to God. And even though there are many who can do much in this world, let them realize that all their achievements are as nothing.

And let us weigh well this word that God says: 'Come, let us go down.' He is not here taking men's counsel, for there is nothing ordinary here, but a difference as great as between fire and water. The interpretation of those who formerly declared that he consults with his angels is limited in scope and forced. There is no doubt that God is counselling with himself here, as we have dealt with the point. We are obliged to return to this point when men think they have done exceptional things, boast that they have achieved everything, for God will never relinquish his authority, and his freedom to act will remain fully intact, and men will not prevent him from breaking and scattering all their undertakings when he pleases. That, in summary, is what we have to remember.

It is true that we can also gather from this passage that in the nature of God exist both the Word, which constitutes his eternal wisdom, and his Spirit, which is his truth. That is how God deliberates within himself because in his nature there is a distinction of persons. Nonetheless, with these words he distinguishes himself from men and shows that their counsel is but pure vanity and folly. And in whatever they presume, they puff themselves up and embolden themselves against God and, in so doing, fall heavily to their ruin and such shame that their everlasting infamy will be evident. So let us learn to make the best of that teaching.

In addition, if for a time the great and powerful of this world, the giants, scorn us and trample us underfoot, let us be content that God sustains us with his hand and that we will never fall except into his hand. And if the wicked have their triumphs, if they are great, strong and powerful, and cause the earth to tremble, well, let us nonetheless remain at peace under our God's hand. And let us be content with the reward that the memory of the just will be blessed forever and that the pride of those who think too highly of themselves and are completely attached to this corruptible life will not only perish and vanish away, but their corruptible lives will be turned into such shame that the hair on their heads will stand up when they hear mention of God's judgments, which will, as a result, be despised by all those who oppress unjustly.

That, then, is how we must be instructed and admonished to walk in all lowliness and so remain within our status that God will rule over us and guide us and we will not think so highly of ourselves that we will turn things to our praise, but let us wait until it pleases him to exalt us after humbling us for a time. And when it seems we are at our lowest point, may he lift us up again and restore us according to his promise.

Now let us bow before the majesty of our gracious God in acknowledgment of our sins, praying that he will cause us to feel them so strongly that we will be increasingly compelled to repent sincerely and turn to him as our only recourse so we will receive pardon in the name of our Lord Jesus Christ. And may he so sustain us in our weakness that he will continue to hold us as his avowed children, even though we fall short in many ways. So let us all say, Almighty God, heavenly Father...

51

God Protects and Increases the Church

Thursday, 25 January 1560

These are the generations of Shem: Shem was an hundred years old, and begat Arphaxad two years after the flood: And Shem lived after he begat Arphaxad five hundred years, and begat sons and daughters. And Arphaxad lived five and thirty years, and begat Salah: And Arphaxad lived after he begat Salah four hundred and three years, and begat sons and daughters. And Salah lived thirty years, and begat Eber: And Salah lived after he begat Eber four hundred and three years, and begat sons and daughters. And Eber lived four and thirty years, and begat Peleg: And Eber lived after he begat Peleg four hundred and thirty years, and begat sons and daughters. And Peleg lived thirty years, and begat Reu: And Peleg lived after he begat Reu two hundred and nine years, and begat sons and daughters. And Reu lived two and thirty years, and begat Serug: And Reu lived after he begat Serug two hundred and seven years, and begat sons and daughters. And Serug lived thirty years, and begat Nahor: And Serug lived after he begat Nahor two hundred years, and begat sons and daughters. And Nahor lived nine and twenty years, and begat Terah: And Nahor lived after he begat Terah an hundred and nineteen years, and begat sons and daughters. And Terah lived seventy years, and begat Abram, Nahor, and Haran. Now these are the generations of Terah: Terah begat

Abram, Nahor, and Haran; and Haran begat Lot. And Haran died before his father Terah in the land of his nativity, in Ur of the Chaldees. And Abram and Nahor took them wives: the name of Abram's wife was Sarai; and the name of Nahor's wife, Milcah, the daughter of Haran, the father of Milcah, and the father of Iscah. But Sarai was barren; she had no child. And Terah took Abram his son, and Lot the son of Haran his son's son, and Sarai his daughter in law, his son Abram's wife; and they went forth with them from Ur of the Chaldees, to go into the land of Canaan; and they came unto Haran, and dwelt there (Gen. 11:10-31).

WE SAW YESTERDAY that those who seek to acquire fame on earth gain a great deal. In part, they get what they ask for, but it is not what they expect, for God works in such a way that their name is made known everywhere, but it is with disgrace. They claim to make themselves noble and outstanding and perpetually honoured after they die. But God exposes them to such ignominy that they are spoken of with shame until the end of time, just as those who built the tower are still remembered today. How? The name 'Babel', or 'Babylon', carries with it the idea of confusion and disorder, as if God were making them abhorrent. That is the way it is with those arrogant people who have tried to acquire great renown by tyranny and violence, as we have already seen in the case of Nimrod, who was the top man in Babylon (cf. *Gen.* 10:10-12). So there he is, humbled personally along with his confederates, who are likewise defamed. But God shows he has a higher regard for his church than for all those who gain a reputation for themselves that way, for Moses again recounts Shem's lineage. He had already given it in the preceding chapter (cf. *Gen.* 10:22-31). Why does he now recount it again except to show that God had separated that family from the others and had privileged it so that in his eyes its members are held in honour and dignity while the others are set apart from that family and banished? So that is what we must first consider as Moses speaks of Shem's line here.

Now, it appears God is considering the adoption he had made when choosing that line as sacred. Shem had begotten other children and they had multiplied into such a great number that there are a great many people who have issued from him and filled the lands and nations. Moses moves from Shem to Arphaxad and is content to deal with just one person. From Arphaxad he comes to Salah. From Salah it comes to Eber, and the rest are buried, so to speak. So we see that God is looking toward his elect inasmuch as he had determined to establish his church in the person of Abraham and in his descendants, as we will see later (cf. *Gen.* 12:1-3). Now that is not to say that the children of Shem did not deserve to be completely cut off and that their names were not held in contempt, as were the names of Ham's children. Even so, God wanted his kindness to overcome the disposition to evil and ingratitude that existed among them. Among them are Abraham's father and grandfather, who worshipped idols. It is not likely that they were the first, but that line was already corrupted. Now, let us keep in mind that that could have been the case with others, but we must place our emphasis upon those who are spoken of here, for God wanted to inscribe them in his book as a holy lineage which he had set apart from the rest of the world. They are like the flowers that were to possess more holiness than all those around them and to be reserved as the choice offering to be made to God. They, too, break away and get lost in their superstitions. They do not know God and they even despise him. Consequently, God had to remain constant in his election in order to be successful against such a determined will to evil. If he had treated them as they deserved, it is certain he would have totally eradicated them and their name would no longer exist. And let us see in that how God disregarded all merit inasmuch as he calls to himself those

21

whom it pleases him to call and adopt as his children. For from the beginning, what can God find in them but every abomination? But after he has placed his mark upon them and acknowledged them as his own, to the extent that they can be his, they still go astray and alienate themselves from him; yet he clings to them and reserves them for himself. As a result, we quickly see that we cannot achieve salvation unless God wages a miraculous battle against our vices.

In addition, we also need to note the kinds of hardships endured by Noah and his son Shem, who feared God as his father did. Noah was still alive and there were already millions of people, in a manner of speaking, who were his descendants and filling the earth. For Peleg, who is of the fourth generation, indeed a direct descendant, bears this name because men were scattered here and there, not as a result of the destruction of the Tower of Babel, but because God had blessed the human race so the earth would be inhabited again. Since there were fourth-generation descendants of Noah, what could that mean subsequently? He sees how completely perverse and wicked and rebellious his descendants are against God, as if they had never had the Flood to instruct them. Noah cries out, for it is not without cause that he is called a preacher of righteousness (cf. *2 Pet.* 2:5). He does his duty, even with burning zeal, in order to maintain the purity of the worship of God. He was to have authority over his children. Even his age was to acquire for him the kind of reverence that inspires everyone's respect. If an 800-year-old man were to speak today, even if we had no connection with him, his age would induce us to listen to him. Now here is Noah, who tries with all his might to hold in check, not strangers, but his own blood. What good does it do him? He sees them filled with the devil. He sees a madness that possesses them. They are totally beyond correction. They disobeyed God, and among them there is only cruelty, violence, and the like. Now there is no doubt that this holy patriarch endured many occasions of great sadness and was in relentless torment as he saw men's exorbitant wickedness, which he could do nothing about.

To get the most out of this story, we must first note how God wanted us to know the length of time between then and the Flood and then the length of time between Noah and the kingdom of David, and the time between the kingdom of David until the people were taken into captivity in Babylon. That is useful because we need to know how long the church has existed on earth. If we did not have this chapter from Moses, we could possess all of the pagans' books with their many scribblings and languages and whatever else, and we would still be unable to find a single word of truth in them about how the world was restored after the Flood or anything about the first creation, for their books talk about only fables and things imagined. And the very person who told the boldest lie was the most heralded, as if he surpassed the others in ingenuity and great knowledge. God did not want us to be ignorant of his grace in these matters. Many things happened back then that it would be profitable for us to know today. But it is true that we still have sufficient instruction in this brief account which Moses followed. In fact, God did not want to burden us with large, verbose volumes so that we would have fewer excuses for our laziness at those times we do not deign to receive the teaching of what is written, seeing that we must not waste a lot of time! That is enough about that.

The point is that after learning the power and effect that God's blessing had upon multiplying the human race, we may know how long the world lasted from the Flood until God called Abraham out and, in his person, set up his church. And from Abraham to the Law; and from the Law until the time we have mentioned. Now the preparation for the church is odd, for if we compare Abraham with all his relatives, not one of them had a large family or even a few members. And what about Abraham? His wife is sterile! Not only does God allow him to languish without seed, but he also knows that he is like a man who is used up and that no one will descend from his line. That is why I said the preparation for setting up and establishing the church is very different from what human understanding would expect.

In fact, if someone back then had known that God had chosen Abraham, that he would be the father of all believers, that he was ordained for that purpose, that God wanted to honour him that way, that he would be like the fountain producing those who were destined to be dedicated to God as his own people, what would that person have said upon seeing Abraham without lineage? And not at thirty or forty years of age, as those who have been mentioned and those who began to increase their line at the age of thirty and thirty-two and increased in such a way that each one of them saw people coming from them that would fill the villages and towns. With that information, what could people have thought but that the choice of Abraham was a wasted effort? But God works that way intentionally by his wondrous counsel so that we may know our salvation must be attributed to him. For if the church arose and multiplied in the ordinary way, the way we see peoples and kingdoms increase and sustain themselves, we would think people, by their industry and power, or by their good fortune, would end up as children of God. But when we are blind to and confused by God's work, and when we are compelled to be astonished at what he does because it goes against our sense of reason, we must indeed come to the conclusion that God garners for himself all the praise for our salvation and that we can contribute nothing and must be totally emptied and humbled so that God will be exalted as he deserves to be.

Along this same line, we need to note that we should not seek, from the world's perspective, great solemnity or ostentation in the church. And if on occasion the church is hidden and seems to be trodden under foot and we do not know where to find it, we must not be troubled or offended by that. Why not? Let us allow God to work in his own way. And let us not doubt that he will always keep for himself some people in whose midst he will be worshiped and served. This story is recorded and this catalogue, or roll, is written down so we will know that Shem, with his small handful of people, has always persevered in the fear and obedience of God, as did his father, Noah. It is true he lived a long time with him and remained with him to strengthen him. Shem survived and protected those who continued to have some good seed in themselves and caused them to be steadfast in following the right path. Therefore, God maintained his church and preserved it in such a time as that, and if we think about their situation, we would think that there was no hope for the church. There was such great dissipation that everything was deformed and no one would have thought: 'There is a church. There is a people that worships God in purity.'

Therefore, let us put that teaching into practice when it pleases God to let the world go its way, and all are like wild animals, when all reject both bridle and yoke, when rebellion is the order of the day and they even throw themselves wildly into evil as if wanting to wage war against God and serve Satan. When we see all those things taking place and we do not know where to look for faithful believers to keep company with, let us always be convinced that God will take care of his church. So, let us not linger among the vast majority. Let us not seek out what looks good; rather let us be content that God will not permit the church to be completely wiped out and that he will preserve some remnant for himself.

It is true that if God spreads his truth abroad, extends his grace to many to receive it and they are gathered in in his name and profess to be his servants, he will be even more glorified for offering the riches of his goodness to us. And that will also serve to give us greater assurance. Even so, we will still have to make progress when ruin and confusion are all around us and it seems the church is completely laid waste. We must, I say, overcome such obstacles and fight mightily against that discouragement and remain firm and constant in the service of our God, following the example of the holy fathers who are spoken of here.

Shem could indeed be disturbed when seeing himself, except for the small flock he is leading, practically alone after the death of his father. The rest were depraved and could not accomplish what needed to be done. He could indeed throw up his hands in despair, were it not for his relentless steadfastness. On the one hand, the Flood was always before his eyes to make him tremble. On the other, he was always restrained by the inestimable grace that God had made known to him. In addition, he was well aware that the fullness of his joy lay in following God's will and that there was a reason he had been preserved from the waters of the Flood. And since God had saved his life, he had done so not only for his sake, but so that he might serve the Master and Teacher and be the patriarch of the entire church at that time. So when we see the world going through difficult times, experiencing storms and tempests, and everything seems to be in upheaval, let us always find strength and support on the foundation of God's truth, which he wants to undergird our faith. That is the way we have to repel all the troubles which could turn us away and completely alienate us from God if we were not armed from on high.

And we also have to groan when we see that men's malice is so great, and we have to peel away our nature when we see that it is so disposed to evil. And on the other hand, we have to bless God for being pleased to guide us by his Holy Spirit and draw us to himself and give us perseverance so we will not fail. For when we see the world yielding to its excesses, we have just that many mirrors to show us what kind of people we would be if our Lord were not having pity on us. All the diseases that befall us, are they not to point out our weakness? For what happens to our neighbours can also happen to us unless God protects us against them.

The same is as true of the soul as it is of the body. All of the vices and all of the transgressions that are committed are witnesses to the fact that in the whole of the human race and in the entirety of Adam's line there is perversity and only perversity. And as long as we entertain fantasies, longings, appetites, plans, opinions, practices, thoughts and desires of the heart, we harbour just that many enemies for making war against God and provoking him to vengeance against us. Consequently, we have many opportunities to be displeased with ourselves, to cast our eyes down, and to refuse to acknowledge the inestimable goodness of God in the fact that he holds on to us by his Holy Spirit and prevents us from being depraved like others. We would tend in that direction and give ourselves completely to those things, were he not pleased to take us under his guidance and show us the effects of that kind of life. He does that not just for a day, but he will continue until we die. That, in short, is what we still must remember.

Now Shem's line is particularly mentioned here. And although Moses does not say that those who came from him were idolaters, we still must admit that such is the testimony elsewhere, namely, in the last chapter of Joshua (cf. *Josh.* 24:2). Here we need to continue to be armed against such stumbling blocks as the men we see who yield freely to every iniquity, but also those who had previously been set apart, to whom it seemed God was saying, 'This is my flock. It is among them that I wish to live as if I had chosen them as my dwelling place. I have set them apart and adopted them as my children.' When we see those very ones fall away, let us not be shaken and abandon the path that is set before us in God's holy calling. That is a powerful temptation for us to go astray. When we see people give themselves over to evil that way, but especially when we see those who belonged to the house of God, those who bore his mark, those whom he himself had reserved for himself and his service, when they fall into evil ways, it is sure our faith would experience terrible shocks if we had not been fortified by the Holy Spirit with shield and helmet and breastplate so that we might be steadfast in every call to arms and prevail. That, then, is what we have to remember.

Now, as I have said, God chose his church and nourished and sustained it in an incomprehensible way, which cannot enter into men's way of thinking. We must take that into consideration and learn to give God the glory which belongs to him so as not to defraud him of the glory of our salvation as though we were the authors of it and not he. God must be recognized as the sole author of our salvation. Men and created things had nothing to do with it. So let us acknowledge that it is his work, which he alone initiates and perfects. That, I say, we must acknowledge as much in what is written about Shem as in what will be written about Abraham.

Now I also said that Shem's line was more inexcusable than Ham's because God had given them more goods and honour. And because God deigns to bring us near unto himself, it is certain that if we do not come to him and enter into his obedience, we are more than guilty. Likewise, we see in Shem's line how those who should show the way to others have become perverted, and from that we have to conclude: if God has called us into his church, we must walk with great solicitude and make every effort to make our calling secure, as Peter exhorts us to do (cf. *2 Pet.* 1:10), so that our lack of gratitude will not cause us to fall away from the honour God is calling us to. It is certain that if we make a comparison between ourselves and those who have preceded us, it is certain they were considered a holy root, just as Paul says about Abraham's line (cf. *Rom.* 11:16-17). For although Abraham was not called, we have heard what was said about Shem: 'Blessed be the Lord God of Shem' (*Gen.* 9:26). There we have God, willing to be allied with that man and all his offspring. So it is certain that those people preceded us in worth, and we are allied with them because God granted us the grace to live in their pavilions, just as it is said that Japheth served Ham and Shem. That is how we are reckoned as believers. That is how we have hope that God will gather us into his kingdom. It is because we have been brought into union with Shem. Now if it is thus that those who were the natural heirs, who had the promise of the blessing of God and his grace, were not only driven out but were more worthy of damnation, and still are, than those who were far from God, so to speak, let us consider our situation carefully and see to it that we walk so carefully in our calling that when God extends his hand to us, we will not fall away and be intractable, thus showing by our evil disposition our contempt for him and our rejection of his grace. That, again, is what we have to remember about this passage.

Now after the point has been made that everyone begat sons and daughters and that there is only an honour in each degree and each line mentioned here and that the process continues until the house of Abraham, we see in that even better, as I have said before, that the number of God's children is small. Consequently, we must not be surprised if our situation today is apparent in our Lord Jesus Christ's parable that the seed is hidden under the straw but not seen. And then the number of seed is small and the straw covers it deeply and forms a large pile. So has it been from the beginning. And the holy fathers who lived at that time were probably much more troubled than we ought to be today, for they had the testimony of God's wrath in the Flood. They had also known and experienced God's grace, so that it served them as a double restraint. Be that as it may, as I have said, the teaching was very obscure to them. Today we have so many warnings and admonitions that we have no excuse if we do not serve our God. All the more, then, must we continue to have before our eyes and remember to meditate on the fact that God is content to have a small number of people, which has been normal for him in all times and in all ages. Why so? Even if we had not known why, we would have had to humble ourselves and worship his counsel which is hidden from us and unknown. But it is certain he wishes to give greater lustre to his grace. Consequently, we will see most men go to hell while we are nothing by comparison. Nevertheless, God recognizes us and acknowledges us as his children. Therefore, his special grace must be more highly prized since he sets us apart for himself this way, seemingly against nature. That is what we have to remember in connection with Shem's line.

Many have been rejected. They were indeed called God's elect and a blessed people, but there was only a small number who shared in that blessing. So let us be consoled when we are despised by those who scorn God, for we see that their pride has no limits and they think we are not worthy to lay our eyes on them. Now that could anger us and cause a lot of bitter feelings if we had not been armed against them beforehand, since those who have gone before us and with whom we must be one were cast out, so to speak, since they were given no consideration and were mocked for their simplicity as if they had been poor witless fools. It is certain that the apostates and those who had revolted against God thought of themselves more highly than they should have, and those who have remained obedient to God are now the judges of those who condemned them previously. Therefore, let us make an effort to be approved by our God, for when we are despised and slandered in this world and people spit in our face, so to speak, that will not keep us from being judges of the world, as Paul calls us (cf. *1 Cor.* 2:15).

We also need to note this point. Although men are so proud that no way can be found to subdue them and although they are so set in their vices that there is no medication that can heal them, we must not, insofar as possible, abandon our efforts to draw them to the way of salvation. In Noah's case, he could have abandoned everything when he saw he was making no headway in exhorting his children. He sees himself despised by his own blood, yet he is God's prophet. And then he testifies that God appeared to him and made himself known privately as if an angel had descended from heaven. He sees in all that that he has no authority, yet he continues to do as he is told. The same is the case with Shem. Now when we see that these holy personages were steadfast in resisting men's evil disposition, let us, when we seem to be facing despair on every hand, do what God shows us in order to bring to salvation those who are going to hell.

Moreover, if God's word does not always bear fruit, let us not be discouraged, for we have already stated that man's disposition to evil is so outrageous that it cannot be restrained by bridles, ropes, or yokes. Not even chains are strong enough for that. Even so, let us sow, and our Lord will cause our labour to bear fruit according to his good pleasure. Even though his word does not always produce its fruit in those who hear it, let us not doubt that God will keep some, use them, and make them ministers of the salvation he has reserved for those whom he has chosen, even though we do not know who they are until he points to them when he is pleased to call them. That is another thing we have to remember about this passage.

At this point, some insignificant questions arise. Yet we can mention them in passing. Moses says that Arphaxad was begotten by Shem two years after the Flood (*Gen.* 11:10), and yet in the preceding chapter he was said to be the third child. That would seem to be a contradiction. Now let us note in the first case that Moses did not, curiously, retain the order when he gave the number of children descended as much from Shem as from his two brothers. And then we cannot judge for certain whether he had a twin brother, for we have already seen that God multiplied and increased the human race in an unusual way (cf. *Gen.* 10). That was extraordinary. We cannot judge that situation by what we see today. Even so, Arphaxad could have been Shem's second or first son even though he is named in the third place because that was stated briefly and the order, as I have said, was not maintained. It must be enough for us that God has always kept someone to show that his church was not yet completely dead, even though it was hidden from the world and was in shame and despised by everyone. And inasmuch as we have a witness of that in Shem's time and thereafter, we must use it until the end of the world, according as it is said that as long as the sun and the moon are in the heavens (cf. *Psa.* 89:35-37; *2 Sam.* 7:16), they will be faithful witnesses that David's race will not perish, that is, his spiritual children, whom God regenerates by his Holy Spirit under the head he established, our Lord Jesus Christ.

Now, it is also stated that Nahor begat Terah. And Terah begat Abraham, Haran, and Nahor. Here Moses did not consider the dignity of the persons, for if the other of Shem's children were already treated as if they were cut off and God had not done them the honour of being considered as his or of being inscribed on that sacred roll, as if they were listed in God's register, if, then, they were not already excluded, it is certain Terah deserved the same treatment as Nahor. In other words, Moses has something else in mind, namely, God's free goodness, because he had predestined Abraham to be the root whose lineage of the faithful was to follow. So then we have already said that beginning with Terah and Nahor, that is, both Abraham's father and grandfather, idolatry was dominant in that entire line. Therefore, to the extent it depended upon them, they deserved to be placed in the bottom of hell. So much for that.

But because Lot came with Abraham, his father is mentioned. And because Sarai descended from Haran's other brother, he is named here. In short, we see how God shows us, as in a mirror, that when there is some good, it proceeds from him alone and that, as for men, they are completely lost because they are filled only with corruption. That, then, is what we have to observe.

Now, Abraham, who is the true image of the church, is also included, as we shall see later (cf. *Gen.* 12:1-3). And his name is there because those who are close to him are honoured here because, as I have already said, God wanted to have mercy on a part of that line.

Now it is said that Terah begat Abraham, Nahor, and Haran, and that Haran died in the presence of his father, indeed in Ur of the Chaldees. And that was the land in which Abraham lived, rather near Babylon. It was a very fertile land, if one ever existed in the world, and for that reason it cost him even more to leave everything behind. When a person has lived in a very large place with an abundance of good and delightful things, everything a man could wish for, it is certain he does not pull up his roots willingly. A powerful motive is required, so Abraham's country is especially brought to our attention so that when his calling is spoken of later, we will be better aware of his zeal to obey God, since he had to give up his very desirable possessions.

Now the Jews, according to their custom, have invented fables and tried to make people believe against Scripture that Haran had been martyred. Now the word 'Ur' in their language means 'fire'. They do not understand it to be a city or a village, and they say it was burned because he did not want to serve idols. Now this passage clearly gives the lie to the Jews, as I said about Joshua (cf. *Josh.* 24:2), for there God shows them that their father Abraham was not better than the rest or well prepared when he chose him. In short, he shows that Abraham was not preferred because of his merits, for men delude themselves into believing that they are somehow prepared to approach God. That is shown to be totally false, for it is said that God drew Abraham out, as from a cavern of curses, because his house was polluted and infected with many forms of idolatry. How, then, was Haran a martyr for not wanting to worship the idols of Chaldea? But Ur of the Chaldees is mentioned elsewhere. So it is certain that the Holy Spirit's intention was only to show the land of Abraham's birth so we would know that he was not a vagabond who had left some deserted mountains and some barren and almost inhabitable place, but that he was established in a land of plenty. Its fertility was immeasurable. Therefore, we may assume that when he left there, God had to have provided well for him and that he had to have forgotten self-interests somewhat and all of his comforts and conveniences.

In addition, we always have to remember that it was said that his is a small line and that they are afflicted with many hardships. Nonetheless, here is our Lord, who has watched over his church as if it had been buried in the ground in a small and very narrow grave. So when we understand that, let us endure being closely confined, provided we are in our God's hand. Let us be satisfied with that whenever it seems we are piled together here in a small grave. Provided God continues to sustain us when it pleases him, that is enough. His church will grow larger in every direction. Even so, let us always be persistent in his holy calling, and let us not grow weary when we see that the wicked are held in honour and respect in this world, and when they have wealth and many advantages over us, let us not lose courage. May our faith not grow weak because of that, but let us realize that our Lord wants to magnify his power in our weakness.

And in addition, when it also pleases him to elevate his church and make it prosper, he will employ such means that he will not require a lot of time and resources gathered from here and there to do so, for his power, as I have said, exceeds the usual order of nature when it comes to the status of the church. That is how we have to put this teaching into practice.

Now let us bow before the majesty of our gracious God in acknowledgment of our faults, praying that he will be pleased to receive us in mercy, however unworthy we are, praying also that he will not only forget the offences we have committed, but also take us under his holy guidance and cleanse us of all our wicked affections and desires and give us such power by his Holy Spirit that we will be victorious in all the combats Satan places before us. And let us persevere until the end in those struggles, striving to advance along the path of salvation with such determination that we will approach our goal more closely until we have laid aside all our earthly corruptions and finally attain it. May he grant that grace not only to us but to all the peoples and nations on earth.

52

Obedience: The Key to Spiritual Progress

Friday, 26 January 1560

And Terah took Abram his son, and Lot the son of Haran his son's son, and Sarai his daughter in law, his son Abram's wife; and they went forth with them from Ur of the Chaldees, to go into the land of Canaan; and they came unto Haran, and dwelt there. And the days of Terah were two hundred and five years: and Terah died in Haran. Now the LORD had said unto Abram, Get thee out of thy country, and from thy kindred, and from thy father's house, unto a land that I will shew thee: And I will make of thee a great nation, and I will bless thee, and make thy name great; and thou shalt be a blessing (Gen. 11:31-12:2).

U P TILL NOW, Moses has expounded the creation of the world, after which men became corrupted and perverted. At that point, he introduced the horrible judgment God provided in the Flood and showed how men had again abandoned themselves and that there was only godlessness, contempt for God, rebellion against his majesty and his word, and that he had kept apart only a small seed. Moses now enters into another part of the narration which is one of the principal parts of the book. It shows how God chose in the person of Abraham a particular people whom he dedicated to himself so that from them the Saviour of the world might descend.

Now in order to show us that, he says Terah took his son Abraham because God had spoken to Abraham. These chapters are incompetently divided. That is the reason this very excellent passage has been corrupted and wrongly interpreted. As a result, the general understanding is that Abraham followed his father, Terah, as far as Haran and was then called from there. Those expositors had to be blind and totally obtuse inasmuch as God had said to Abraham, 'Leave your country and the land of your birth.' If he had already left, why would that have been said to him? That would have been ridiculous. In short, they understood nothing about it, as is evident. And whoever divided these chapters was an idiot.

So we must now follow the unbroken story which Moses recounts here. He says, in the first place, that Abraham left his country to live in the land of Canaan. It is as if he were saying that Abraham followed God, not that he knew, as we will see later, in what land he was to live. He had no address. He was proceeding like a poor blind man. The fact is, Moses is saying that Abraham's intention was to obey God. So much for that point.

Then he tells us why so that we will not think that Abraham departed without a reason and unadvisedly, or that he was angry, like many people who throw up their hands and huff and puff irrationally. Moses says God commanded him to leave the land of his birth, to leave his father's house and forget everything in order to enter the country which would be shown to him. That, in short, is what we have here.

Now we need to explain things in detail. When it is said that Terah took his son Abraham, it does not mean he was the principal initiator of this voyage, for it is easy to conclude that God did not honour Terah by calling him and that he was addressing his son Abraham. Now it is certain that the father joined his son and that Moses, realizing the superiority God gave fathers over their children, says that Terah took his son (cf. *Exod.* 20:12; *Deut.* 5:16; *Eph.* 6:1-3; *Col.* 3:20). So that is how the passage is to be understood.

Now the first thing we note here is that even though God will grant more outstanding favours to children than to their fathers, he still wants to maintain the dignity the fathers have over their children. So the order of nature must take its course and not be broken or completely done away with even though God will, as I have said, bestow his blessings and goodness on the children in a more excellent way. He works that way so the children, despite their better minds and greater industriousness and achievements, will not grow proud under any circumstance but will always live with appropriate modesty, realizing they are debtors because the obligation God placed in nature must not be effaced or broken.

On the other hand, this passage advises us that we must not seek approval among men when we follow God, even though we are preferred over many others. Abraham has a revelation expressly from heaven. His father does not. Yet Moses recounts that he followed his father and that his father took him along, saying, 'Come', as if he had the authority. So we see that when God made himself known to his servant Abraham, he did not do so to give him an opportunity to prize himself, for that would conceal his purpose and give the impression that he was walking in his father's steps. Therefore, although the calling of God is devalued by the generally accepted opinion, let us be content with his approval, knowing that he does not wish to make us great in the world's eyes, but that our full nobility, our full worth, our full joy and glory reside in aspiring to the heavenly kingdom, to which he invites us. That is another point we need to note here.

At the same time, we have to consider that Terah, although a poor idolater, did not fail to be touched when hearing that God called his son Abraham. There was in him some touch of godliness even though he was insensitive because of many superstitions and no longer knew who the living God was. Yet he is moved when seeing that God spoke, indeed the God who remained unknown to him even in his old age. He was already ancient, totally decrepit, and did not know what true religion was, for he had gone astray with the others, as we have said. Knowing that, we can conclude what condemnation will befall those who have greater intelligence and to whom God opened his truth, but yet are disinterested and cold, those who know God's will but are content to wallow in their filth. Terah will certainly be their judge in the last day! For having received a hint through his son's experience that he had been misguided up till then and had been on the wrong road, and having reached his old age, with one foot in the grave and his strength failing, he is obliged to depart like a pitiable, confused old man, not knowing where he is to go, yet not refusing. We see in that how God strengthened him.

In the first place, there had to be in him an old-fashioned innocence, for we know that old people will ignore listening to the young, thinking it belittles their age. They think, because they have lived a long time in the world, that they have acquired more prudence and that others should not presume to teach them. In fact, you always hear this from them: 'A father cannot allow his child to serve as his master and teacher.' But the fact is that Terah agreed with what his son told him. Let us see in that fact that he was modest and not influenced by an attitude of pride and ambition.

Now what caused him to be humble and a willing disciple of his son? There is no doubt that Abraham lived in such a way that his father, Terah, had already formed a good opinion of him. Consequently, because he knew that he was of a good reputable character and moral, he trusted what he said. As a matter of fact, if Terah had not been convinced that the matter came from God, he would not have been so easily persuaded to agree to the wishes of his son, who was still young and robust in comparison with himself. So that is how God revealed to his servant Abraham that he did not wish to exclude his father, Terah. But that was a second stage of revelation, and he tested the obedience of his faith when he wanted him to be instructed only by his son, and even without giving him full instructions. Abraham himself was caught by surprise, and God did not communicate with him intimately at first by making him acquainted with everything required for his salvation. We will see that when they arrived in the land of Canaan, they were often given assurance because his faith was still very simple and lacking in knowledge. So Abraham can no longer share with his father what he received. He is like a novice, still dealing with his ABCs, so to speak. He only experienced by revelation that there is a living God, from whom he was previously separated. Even so, God wants him to be his father's teacher and at the same time touch his father's will in such a way that he no longer questions or contradicts his son but leaves the land of his birth.

Now, if Moses were only recounting that Terah trusted his son's word, had humbly received it and shown some sign of worship, that would not have been small praise for him inasmuch as he had been hardened in his superstitions for a long time. For when a young man has been brought up on lies and in the midst of idolatry, it is certain that, before he becomes a man, if he is only fifteen years old, he will retain his former way of thinking and his mind will be closed to all good teaching. What does that mean for old people? They have that obstinacy and, as I have said, that foolish presupposition that because they have been in the world for a long time, they are wiser. Consequently, Terah already had the great virtue of listening innocently to his son; but when the poor man, already worn and broken with age, since we see he died on the journey, leaves his home, that is something incredible. So we must pay even closer attention to that example so that no one will seek a way to avoid following God when he is called, and we must not use those pretexts we have been accustomed to offering, thinking that we are excused if what God requires of us is difficult or is an obstacle or that if some situation hinders us, God is obliged to give us a free pass. In Terah, we have a contrary example.

And let us join that example with what our Lord Jesus Christ proposes when he mocks the excuses that men make when they reject God's calling (cf. *Luke* 14:16-20; *Matt.* 22:1-6). As he points out there, one will claim an inconvenience, another a different one, and few will be found who obey promptly, as would be required. For that reason, he compares that apathy and procrastination which is seen in the preaching of the gospel with a solemn banquet. If someone invites his friends to a wedding, one will say, 'I am to get married'; another will say, 'I must go see after my barn and lands'; another will say, 'I have bought some oxen and must go try them out'; and another, 'I have business affairs to handle.' That is how the man who was hoping to have good company is disappointed. Thus, when God exhorts us to come to him and even wishes to have his only Son's sacred marriage with us, each one of us finds something to serve as an excuse.

Now what is recounted here about Terah is enough to condemn everybody. Thus, as I have already said, let everyone find a way to correct that apathy and indifference which are so deeply rooted in us. And let the young people realize, because they are in the flower of their age—and may God grant them its vigour—that they must step lively, and let not the old people think that they are without responsibility, claiming that they are already slow, that their bodies are worn out, and that they do not think God will be satisfied with something so worthless and will grant them an exemption. Therefore, let them all move forward when God but gives them a sign and they realize that the one who created and formed them is the one who is seeking them. May they not hide from him and withdraw when he wants to advance them, but let them hear his voice and follow and be ready to listen to one another. When it is a matter of coming to God, let us not refuse instruction. That is the first thing we must remember when it is said that Terah took his son Abraham, his daughter-in-law, and his nephew Lot to go live in the land of Canaan in obedience to God without knowing how or where he intended to lead them or cause them to settle.

We also have to remember what we touched on yesterday, namely, that Terah did not leave behind a sterile land or a life that was difficult. It was a land as fertile and productive as any in the world and eminently pleasant. So when he leaves that place, we see that he fought well and valiantly against his preferences and deep-seated desires, for we can be pleased with a little bit of nothing. When we have a very modest possession, we are attached to it, even glued to it, so firmly that we cannot be torn away from it. So when Terah left a country that was so agreeable, let us realize it was not without a struggle. To be sure, he worked very hard to break all his bonds and ties in order to go willingly where God was calling him.

In the same way today, let us learn to repulse all of this world's delights that the devil offers us when it comes to whether or not we will follow God and go to the trouble of imitating the example of Terah, who put behind him everything that might hinder him or hold him back. And may we not to be grieved by letting go of what we find desirable as we seek what is incomparably more excellent: God's guidance and protection, for that is our sovereign good, the blessing we must aspire to. Therefore, may those who have left something or other behind have no regret and say, 'Oh, I had a house in a beautiful location. I had this and that and many conveniences. My income amounted to this. I had much to eat and drink.' Leave those things in the past, for they are just so many of Satan's illusions and delusions to turn the heads of those who are already on the right path and to keep them fixed on their earthly attachments and concerns.

Let us now move on to do what Moses adds. He says that Terah and his son Abraham came to Haran—which is commonly called Harras by historians and secular people—and there, he says, Terah died at the age of two hundred and five. The Jews, since they are crammed full of lies and imaginings, have come up with the notion that Abraham lived in Haran with his father for a period of sixty years. Now that works fine to invert, maliciously or impudently, what Moses wrote, for he does not say that Terah, and even less Abraham, changed his mind. If they had lived in Haran for what would have been a lifetime, they would have failed in mid-journey. What would it profit us if we started out and only went halfway and were called to go a hundred or two hundred miles and only went five and remained put? We would have done as well to stay at home. That was a fabrication the devil put in their heads to obscure God's truth and deprive us of the usefulness we are to receive from this passage.

The long and short of it is that Terah died on the journey. In other words, worn out with age, he is at the end of his strength, but he nonetheless left the land of his birth. His age takes its toll, for when he reached Haran, he was two hundred and five years old and died. His death shows he was not able to bear the hardships of the journey. And even though he dragged along until then and completely broke down, we see that he did not consider what he could do and did not take a measure of himself to determine his strengths and weaknesses, but that he resolved to serve God not only in life but in death. It is as if he were saying, 'Alas, Lord, all of my life I have been a poor stray animal. I have lived more than two hundred years serving idols, renouncing you, you who were my God and my Creator. What can I do now? I am no good for anything. Well, I will die in your service, and at least with my death I will affirm my regret that I have lived badly.' That, in summary, is what Abraham's father felt.

In addition, we have to conclude from his example that when our Lord calls us, we must not enter into a dispute about what we are able to do. Since there are many who will make excuses for their indifference, indeed their rebellion, saying, 'What good can I be? What can I do in this place?' If someone were to tell them they were useless, oh, they would get their hackles up and think they had been highly offended. But if God must be served, everyone will confess hypocritically and with lies that he can do nothing, as if his arms were broken and he did not know what good he could do or where to begin or how to go about it. That is a very commonplace excuse. Terah's example, on the contrary, shows us that even though we think we are only flailing the water by serving God, we are nonetheless moving forward and overcoming all trials, and that it is enough for us to live and die for the one who created and formed us and has prepared a much better life for us than we have here, which is but a shadow that is passing away. That again is what we have to remember from this story.

On the contrary, we see or can imagine that Abraham was deeply grieved upon seeing his father die this way in mid-journey. On the one hand, since we are inclined to be distrustful, it is possible he murmured against God and might even have spoken abusively to him because he had not given his father the joy of the blessing he was calling him to. He could have thought in his heart, 'If that calling by God were definite, why has he now not permitted my father to know the good thing he was doing for me and that would have assured him? Since my father was so devoted to serving him, there was good reason to let him taste his grace, but it seems that he wants to take him from the world out of spite while he is only seeking to approach him.' So Abraham could have become distrustful.

On the other hand, he could have been reproached: 'You murdered your father! You had to go and drag that poor old man out of his house! You killed him when you abused him by dragging him along on that journey! It is as though you had cut his throat!' So we have Abraham surrounded by terrible perplexities from God and men. On the one hand, as I said, he could have harboured doubts: 'What does this mean, that my father was cut off from among the living?' And then on the other hand, he could have endured the reproaches the world can deal out. Those are two abuses which could trouble him till the end, even repel him, so that he might have been turned aside from the right path. Whatever it might have been, he endures it all patiently and survives all such trials. And even though his father died, his faith is not dead. He rejoices and perseveres, concluding that the beginning is meaningless if he does not obey God until he comes into the land he will be shown.

He cares nothing for all the rebukes, reproaches, and calumnies that could be thrown in his face and is satisfied with God's approval. Despite being unjustly condemned by men, he has no concern for his reputation. But when they all look down on him, it is enough for him that God calls him into the service he is rendering. So when things do not turn out the way we would like and God sends difficult times as if he were showing us that what we do displeases but does not disturb him, let us realize that it is not an occasion for us to go astray, as those who wish to follow God will fall into some misfortunes, and when they think they find a way out and God is extending to them a helping hand, that is like the onset of a sudden storm and they will be heavily afflicted either in their persons or in their possessions, and they will be tested in another way. They will endure some hardship and loss or they will experience some other misfortune that will make them back away. When that happens, let us remember what we are told about Terah for our instruction, namely, that if we have God's word to assure us he approves what we are doing and that we are doing nothing without thinking ahead, but that, by obeying, we are always proceeding steadily.

Also, let us scorn this world's reproaches, and let us not be hindered or discouraged, as are some who are so touchy that, when someone asks them to follow God, they will make excuses: 'Well, if it were only a matter of the loss of possessions, I would not care so much, but shall I dishonour my relatives that way?' That is how they will bring in their relatives. One will say, 'My father will die of grief if he learns that I have converted and will be considered a heretic.' Another will say, 'It will hurt my children because I will lose all respect.' Such are the excuses people usually make. And people who talk like that think they have a good excuse for rejecting God's calling. It is a waste of time to proceed that way, but let us learn to live the way Paul exhorts us to by his example, both with a good reputation and being reproached (cf. *1 Cor.* 4:11-13; *Eph.* 4:1-4; *Phil.* 3:16-18). And if God should test us to the point that we suffer reproach when we desire to please him, let us not be grieved by it. That, in brief, is what we have to remember about this passage.

Now everything Moses records would be of little value if more were not said. That is why he adds that 'the Lord said to Abraham.' In that phrase we see the purpose of the story: Abraham was not a fickle person, as is the case with many vagabonds who wander from place to place in search of their fortunes, as we say. Others move about because of coercion or necessity, and then when they come into a foreign land, they will make certain assumptions about this and that. Others flee because their crimes have been discovered and they fear being punished. They will drop out of sight. So that we will know that Abraham was not fickle and worldly-minded and that there was nothing sinister that caused him to leave the land of his birth, particular note is made that God had spoken to him. It is as if Moses were saying that Abraham did not leave for personal reasons or was moved by some fanciful dream. In short, he did not set out rashly but was obeying God. That is the true basis for everything we do. That is also why we have been placed in the world: to honour God in all our plans, in all our thoughts, actions, and undertakings. For that to be so, the man of faith must most certainly not proceed without knowing that God approves what he does. That is what Paul says when speaking of eating and drinking: Everything must be done in faith (cf. *1 Cor.* 10:23-31). For if we doubt or have a twinge of conscience, we cannot take a single step without offending God. Let us realize, then, that God's will is our only and unchallenged rule, and especially when it is a matter of undertaking an enterprise or a journey and determining the direction of our lives, which is knowing what we must hold sacred, let us realize that we walk in confusion if God's word does not go before us to light the way. If we walk in confusion, we will only distance ourselves from the right path, and we will only trip up at every turn. We will wander around without purpose, alienating ourselves completely from the life of heaven, and then we will take heavy falls and break our necks. That is the outcome for all those who follow their own teachings, who trust in their own power, who think God has to hold in high regard everything that comes into their heads. All they do is stay busy and, after much effort, make no progress.

Moreover, as I have said, we will only stumble and fall if we do not adhere to God's path. So let us pay close attention to what Moses says: 'The Lord said to Abraham,' and may we be able to stand firm like sturdy trees, and may all our thoughts, affections, and pursuits be dead until God, in his own good time, makes known to us what pleases him, and let us follow his counsel and accept what he teaches, and let our obedience to all that be the source of our wisdom. And then may he, at the same time, rule over and guide all our desires and affections, and may we consider nothing good but what pleases him. And then, when it comes to putting into practice what he commands, let it all be in obedience to him. That, then, is what we have to remember about the saying 'God said'.

At this point, let us think about the inestimable good that God has done for us when he was pleased to receive us into his school, instruct us inwardly about his will and show us the path of salvation. And we see the poor papists; we see the Muslims, who have no enlightenment. It is true that they make great efforts, for the papists burden themselves endlessly with mumbling, hovering around altars, and in sparing no money to redeem their sins, or so they think. And then they go on pilgrimages. They fast. They get up in the night. There is no end to it. But have they done everything? Still, after concluding that God is obliged to them, all they have done is heap upon themselves his vengeance because they have stolen his honour and given it to idols. And that is what they have achieved, they and all those who are destitute of solid teachings. Therefore, seeing that our Lord has removed us from such an abyss of confusion, let us acknowledge the good he has done for us, and let us make a special effort to honour him for it and in that way enjoy the privilege of scorning Satan and everything that might engage our fanciful imaginings, and in so doing say, 'If God has spoken, I am satisfied. And since he has done me the honour of instructing me, I cannot fail, and by following him I will hold to the right path, and the final outcome will prove it.' That, then, is how God's word must serve us as our protector, our defence, our everything.

Let us now consider the form Moses gave his account: 'Leave your country, the land of your birth, and your father's house.' It seems that that could be said briefly. Would it not have been enough to say, 'Leave your country,' or 'Leave the land of your birth'? That repetition seems to be useless, for sometimes we use circumlocutions when the point is obscure or when the precise words do not come to mind. Now when the subject is clear and apparent and there are no obscure words, why say more than is necessary? But let us consider how nimbly and promptly we follow God if he does not nettle us and plead with us and add commandment upon commandment. Has God spoken? How many become active? I am talking about those who are not at all rebels and who do not reject good solid teaching but seem to seek it. Even so, they continue to remain unchanged. So it is not without reason that God adds commandment upon commandment, each one pointing in the same direction, for nothing new is added. The first means the same as the second and the second means the same as the third. But as I have already said, because a single command will not be enough to wake us up and encourage us and convince us to be always ready to obey God, we always need him to nettle us and plead with us. So when the Lord said to Abraham, 'Leave your country, abandon the land of your birth, and leave your father's house,' he does so to show us that we need to be exhorted many times, that it is not enough for us to be told once what God commands and requires of us, but we must be assured by that and reminded often of what he has said, and it must be drilled into us, as little children, whose memories are short or who do not immediately understand what they are shown.

There is yet another vice in us, for we will come across some who will put up excellent defences, as we say, and when God calls them, they become active. Come now, since that is the truth, we must hold to it. So we will see an appearance of great zeal in some who will be bubbling over when they hear a word from the gospel and become aware that they were mistaken: 'Oh, we must go in a different direction. When it comes to God, we must not procrastinate.' That will be amazing to see. Now the next day they are changed. Talk about a fire that soon goes out! That is why we need to be assured every day, indeed every hour. And when our Lord grants us the grace to be resolved to conform ourselves in all obedience to his will and then presses that disposition even more deeply into our hearts and then resumes the process, and when we grow more and more in the faith and are always cultivated, like a vine that is often dug around, cut back and pruned, God must, in a word, always be in pursuit of us to make us persevere; otherwise, we would easily fall away. Since we see from experience that the majority, after beginning well, go astray, it is a wonder that we see so few persevering.

Therefore, let us realize there was good reason to say to Abraham, 'Leave,' and a second time: 'Leave,' and then a third time: 'Leave.' Let us apply the same practice to ourselves. The simple steps of perfecting the teaching of the gospel is to renounce ourselves. It is not enough to be told once that we must slough off our old skin, put the old man to death and, as Scripture says, die to ourselves in order to be sacrifices unto God (cf. *Rom.* 12:1). It is not enough, as I said, to hear that once, but let it be our constant meditation. Let it be our daily pursuit. And when it seems to us that we have made good progress, let us realize that we must be made even stronger. That, then, is what we have to remember.

Now these matters could be drawn out at length, but it is enough that each of us has an opportunity to think more about them at leisure. This does not require great eloquence. The main thing to know is that it is God who is speaking and that not a word or a syllable is to come out of his holy mouth without being received by us with all humility, weighed seriously, and inquired into diligently to discover what he commands. When we realize that, each of us can then profit from what has been touched upon only briefly.

Now there is more, for God not only says, 'Leave your country,' but he then also says, 'Leave the land of your birth,' and then, 'your father's house.' That had to be excruciating for Abraham, for we know that we all want to keep to our nest. Even savages, when promised wonderful opportunities by honest and sincere people, still prefer to scratch in the ground and eat roots over going into a distant land, for they have that natural love which leads them to remain in their land, and they do so, as I have said, except for the ones who are unstable or who conceive some fantasy or who are compelled to throw their hands up in despair. But if a man is not driven by extreme feelings, it is certain he will always gladly remain where he was born.

Now God stayed after Abraham, and it grieved him when God said, 'Leave,' but when he adds 'the land of your birth,' it is as if he wanted to cut him more deeply and, if he had at first given him a flesh wound, plunge the lance between his ribs down to his heart and test everything that was in him. But when he continues speaking and adds 'from your father's house,' it is as if he were saying, 'I must tear out your entrails, and you must be like a poor man torn in two.' For when Abraham has to leave his father and all his relatives, that is certainly more bitter for him than it would be for a person to leave the land of his birth if he had no family or friends or ties to hold him there. But Abraham was living in the midst of his own people and possessions, and when he had to leave them, it was like having his inward parts torn out. So we see how God is here testing the faith of his servant Abraham.

Therefore, let us learn from this passage—because we cannot say everything—that when we serve God, our lives will be filled with many struggles. If we do not sense them right away, they will come eventually. So if hypocrisy is not to get the best of us, let each of us enter into ourselves, to the deepest part, and consider the things that are required for obedience to God and the obstacles the world provides, those things which are in our very selves, for no greater resistance is to be found than the resistance found in our inner selves. Let us acknowledge all those things and, following Abraham's example, let us be so strengthened that when the devil uses many devices to turn us from the right path and employs his stratagems to deprave us, we will nonetheless overcome and determine once and for all that we must follow God. Even if it should ever be a question of being torn to pieces, we must remain dedicated to him, and the worship which he seeks and approves must be given to him. So if we should have to be divided that way, let us be content that, having God's word, we must yield to it totally and not consider what can happen to us, what we can bear with difficulty, and what can produce moments of anguish, pains, regrets, torments and the like. And after thinking about those things carefully, let us have no concern for them. That, in short, is what we must conclude and remember while we wait for what comes next.

> Now let us bow before the majesty of our gracious God in acknowledgment of our faults, praying that he will make us so repentant of them that we, being led by his Holy Spirit, will learn to condemn ourselves in his presence. And since that cannot happen unless we renounce ourselves, may he give us the strength to do that, and may he bury our past faults and, in the future, endure our weaknesses until he has purged and cleansed us completely. May he grant that grace not only to us but to all the peoples and nations on earth.

53

Confidence in God:
Resting on His Promises

Saturday, 27 January 1560

*Now the LORD had said unto Abram, Get thee out of thy country,
and from thy kindred, and from thy father's house, unto a land that
I will shew thee: And I will make of thee a great nation, and I will
bless thee, and make thy name great; and thou shalt be a blessing:
And I will bless them that bless thee, and curse him that curseth
thee: and in thee shall all families of the earth be blessed* (Gen.
12:1-3).

WE SAW YESTERDAY how Abraham readied himself to
obey God, and then we pointed out that the rule for
ordering our lives well is to inquire carefully where
God is leading us, what purpose he intends for us, and what path
he wants us to take.

It is true that we will receive no command exactly like the one
given to Abraham our father. For to be faithful and to be used in
God's service, no one of us is required to move away from the place
of our birth and be vagabonds throughout our lives in a strange and
distant land. So that will not be required of us indiscriminately, but
what is common to us all is that we must get out of ourselves. It

would not have been enough for Abraham to leave his father's house if he had not renounced the things he was attached to. One even depends on the other, for he would have otherwise remained comfortable and at peace in his own bed. So when he leaves, and without knowing where he is going, he is obliged to have forgotten all his material aspirations, to have left behind his natural disposition, and to be changed in such a way that he allows God to guide him. So we must all follow his example, as Psalm 45 says: 'Hearken, O daughter, and lend an ear. You must forget your father's house and all your kin' (*Psa.* 45:10). That is said using the figure of Solomon's wife, but it refers to the church. And at that point it is added that the king will honour his wife when she leaves all her kin (*Psa.* 45:11). That shows us in a few words that we cannot to be Christians, that we cannot be disposed to serve God, and that we can in no way please him until we renounce everything that belongs to the world.

Now in the meantime we must also imitate our father Abraham and be pilgrims here below, not, as I have said, that we must trudge through different regions, but we must be ready and not be attached to the earth, but rather be citizens of heaven even though we must live a while here below. That, then, is what we need to observe in the second place in order to be strengthened by Abraham's example.

And then, in the third place, we must, if it pleases God to make us more aware that we are strangers in this world, bear it all patiently. As today, we see many who must leave the land of their birth because of the horrible captivity there and because they are not permitted to worship God simply and unconditionally but are forced to participate in the Papacy's abominations. So when our Lord wants us to imitate what we are told about our father Abraham, we must be resolved to follow and to learn not to be so given to our appetites and the things that please and delight us that we do not always prefer God's calling over everything else.

Those, then, are the three things we must strive for if we are to be Abraham's true spiritual children. In short, we must overcome all our desires and all our lusts as if we were getting out of ourselves; and then let us not leave a place that our hearts are not attached to here below, but let us be ready to depart, as birds on a branch. And finally, when God is pleased to put us to that kind of test, let us be vagabonds, as Paul speaks of his time (cf. *1 Cor.* 4:11), and since we see today that many of the faithful are forced to do that, may it not be difficult for us.

Another test of Abraham's faith follows. God tells him to go into a land he will show him but does not tell him where he is to dwell. So Abraham leaves his country without knowing where he is going. God keeps him in suspense, toying with him, so to speak. It is as if he were saying: 'I am assigning you to a certain place to live and you will inhabit it,' as if to alleviate his concern a little. But when God removes him somewhat forcefully from his country and throws him to the wind, the poor man does not know what is to become of him. That is a very difficult and harsh trial to endure, but he overcame it. So we have to evaluate that situation in order to be able to tell ourselves, when God calls us, that we must be wise when it comes to discussing what might happen and realize that it is enough to obey his word. It is true, as I have already said, that we will not have a special revelation about what is recounted here, and our situation will not all be like Abraham's, but we need to note the similarity which exists between him, as father of the church, and us, who are members of the body.

Here, then, in short, is what we have to remember. In order to bring ourselves into line with God's will, we must bring to heel our wariness and not inquire too cautiously into various situations as we think and talk and make plans. For there are those who will never make a move until they know where they are to go, what they are to do, and what the good outcome will be. Now we must not make deals with God this way or make agreements that suit our preferences and fantasy, but we must allow ourselves to be governed by him. To say again plainly and briefly what is involved here, we must see clearly on the one hand and be blind on the other. The worldly minded are wide awake when it comes to seeking their own advantage and security. They flip from one side to the other, and if they perceive some danger, they say, 'Oh, we have to avoid that'; if they experience some doubt, they say, 'Oh, we will do well to stay quiet'; if they encounter a problem, they say, 'Oh, we have to avoid that.' So we see how the children of this world are very perceptive and ingenious and that is why God cannot overrule them, for he has to deal with them and manage them in accordance with their will or they will back away. Now, as for us, we must be blind in that particular. In other words, we must leave in God's hand all those things we have doubts about, for he will provide, as we will see shortly when Abraham was commanded to sacrifice his son (cf. *Gen.* 22:8). So we must honour God by depending on his wisdom, assured that he will give us good results in everything we do, provided we undertake nothing without following his word. That, then, as we understand the ways of this world, is the way we have to let God hold us by the hand like poor blind people and lead us, turn us, wheel us about, prod us on, and tug at us as he wishes.

Now in the meantime we have to see differently and more clearly than the children of this world. We must see using the eyes of faith (cf. *Heb.* 11:1). Those who are so given to their own needs that they are concerned only for their comforts, for their own peace and quiet, for providing for themselves, and for avoiding all inconveniences—those people do not know what it is like to be guided by God. They cannot understand how his word is the light that shows us the way (cf. *Psa.* 119:105). And this is how we have to see: we must not wander about like poor lost people, those who wander aimlessly, in a state of perplexity and indecisiveness. We must adhere strictly to the straight path as it is shown to us in the word of God. That, then, is the teaching we must gather from this passage where it says that God drew Abraham out of his father's house without stating where he wanted him to dwell.

And it is not just for a single day that we must hand ourselves over that way to God and his guidance. As when we ask him for our daily bread, it is the same as if we declared solemnly that he nourishes us from day to day. That is what 'daily bread' means: from day to day. Now if we speak that way from our hearts, it is certain that by letting go of a great and burdensome concern, we would be freeing ourselves up to make plans further ahead. Consequently, there are some who are like paralytics, and God pays them according to their deserts, for they would like to carve out for themselves an inaccessible niche away from their enemies and be guaranteed certain things and lack nothing. In a word, they have no idea what it means to commend themselves to God.

And that being true, they tremble, wherever they are, and just like the sick, they move from bed to bed, turning now to the right, now to the left, now on their backs, now from head to foot, then back to the head, never feeling any better. Why not? They have an inner disturbance which torments them. So that is what we see in those who are 'foresighted' and do not, in their simple-mindedness, open themselves to uncertainty. For one reason or another, they will never stop being nervous. Meanwhile, the children of God will sleep at night because they realize that God is protecting them and fortifying them with his power, which will be for them a fortress and rampart. Although they encounter fears and apprehend the dangers involved, that does not keep them awake, for they are confident that God is powerful enough to keep them safe. And we see those who are wise in their own eyes and want to be secure for a hundred years after they die, but who will always be uncertain, flipping from one position to another, always on the move. They are not comfortable here now. They have to go somewhere else, and after changing place, they have to move on if they find themselves again uncomfortable. They are always moving from place to place, but God brings them down slowly and finishes them off in the end. All the more, then, must we remember this lesson: we must turn a blind eye to the many cares which could interfere with our obeying God, allowing him to govern us, and moving forward as soon as he calls us (cf. *Isa.* 48:17). And when we are uncertain about what is to take place tomorrow and the days following, let us always be confident that God is wise enough to provide for and remedy everything that might harm us. That, in short, is what we have to remember about this teaching which says that God did not want to specify to our father Abraham the land he was to inhabit.

It is true he said, 'I will show it to you,' as if he were saying, 'I will be your wisdom.' Though, when all is said and done, what will be better for us: to use all our five senses and be the cleverest people in the world or to be like blind people and have God being vigilant for us? Who has better eyes? So we still have a lot to learn from that statement when we do not know right away what might happen, although God will eventually show us he was our guide (cf. *Psa.* 48:14). Then let us wait patiently. Now when I say we must wait patiently, it is not so that we can wonder whether what we do is good or bad, for God will always give us understanding through his word, but whether, from the perspective of our external enemies, we will be assailed, subjected to some scarcity and famine and pestilence. In short, we will be threatened by many things. But at times like that, as I said, we must remain captive to our Lord and wait for him to show us that he has a reason for taking us under his care and commanding us to renounce ourselves and all the world holds in order to devote ourselves fully to him.

At that point Moses relates the promise made to our father Abraham. The point is well worth making. It is true that we saw the same thing in the story of Noah earlier, for God not only commanded him to build the ark; he also promised him that he would not work in vain. The command and the promise must always be joined together. That is, God commands what he wants us to do, what is good for us to do, and at the same time he assures us of his grace. Why? It is certain we will never be inclined to obey his will unless faith leads us to do so. So if faith is the mother of all the obedience that we render to God, and faith cannot exist apart from the promises, let us conclude that we will be useless, as those completely dead, until God quickens us by testifying that he will not fail us. Consequently, we must first be convinced and persuaded that God loves us and is on our side and will reveal himself as our Father until the very end and that he would take such good care of us that we will be helped and supported by his grace in time of need. That is the place we need to begin, for the first thing we understand about ourselves is that we have no zeal. How quick are we, pray tell, when it comes to abandoning ourselves completely to God and renouncing our natural disposition? So if God only gave commands categorically and precisely: 'That is what you must do,' and exerted his superiority, what would be the result? It is true we would be sufficiently convinced of our duty, but at the same time it would not be enough to make us get up and go and provide us with the incentive of a free will to go where he calls us and the steadfastness to persevere until the end. So, in short, our Lord must draw us gently and his promises must give us life. That is the source of all the strength and courage we possess in our hearts and in all the members of our bodies. That, in short, is what makes us able and fit for service to our God.

So there is good reason that God said to Abraham, 'I will make of you a great nation.' Now he was very pleased for a time with the revelation he had heard. Even so, if he had not had anything else, he would have been angry within himself, and after a time of bitterness, he would have rebelled against God. But when he sees that God deigns to show that he is being like a father to him and assures him of his grace and that it is for his welfare and his salvation that he is taking him from the land of his birth—that is what breaks all the ties that could hold him back. That is what assures him and even excites and inflames a desire and ardent zeal in him to obey God.

Therefore, since that is a matter of reining in our lives and dedicating ourselves to God's service, let us now focus all our attention to the promises he gives us. That is why Paul, in the first chapter of Colossians, when praising their faith and the gifts they possessed, says: 'That is because of the hope that his laid up for you in heaven, which you have heard through the doctrine of truth, that is, the gospel' (*Col.* 1:5). So we must continue in that truth, knowing that God does not need us and can receive from us no service which is useful to him; yet he seeks us. Why? For our welfare and salvation. And with that he certifies that he will always keep us as his children (cf. *Deut.* 14:1; *Rom.* 8:16) and grant us the inestimable privilege of being able to claim him as our Father (cf. *Isa.* 63:16; *2 Cor.* 6:18) and of finding our refuge in him (cf. *2 Sam.* 22:3; *Psa.* 9:9), while he adds that he will always be reaching out to help us (cf. *Psa.* 80:17; 119:173). Moreover, if we fall seven times in a day, as the psalm [sic] says, that is, if we are oppressed with many misfortunes, he will raise us up until the end (cf. *Prov.* 24:16). Therefore, we must apply all our attention to appreciating God's promises and meditating upon them often and taking strength from them to walk in his way and say: 'Oh, whatever happens, we will not go wrong by walking in the path God shows us.' Why not? The outcome is in his hand, for it could only be good and to our advantage, for that is what he promised us, and it is not some fantasy we have conceived, but something he has witnessed to with his mouth.

So we see how the Holy Spirit in the person of Abraham set before us a mirror, or a living image, to show us how we are to be governed if we are to reach the kingdom of heaven. That, then, must be our certainty even though we have to be doubtful and uncertain about everything that might happen. Even so, we must remain confident that when God commands us to go, he does so to bring us to a safe harbour. Now it is true that not everyone will hear these words: 'I will make of you a great nation, and I will bless you,' but it is enough that we, in general, can lean upon God, certain that since he has lifted us up and adopted us, we possess the sum of our felicity and that that must also be the height of all our desires. Abraham was given a higher rank because he was established as the father of the church, as we will see later. As for us, we must be content even though God does not raise us to such an honour and dignity. Yet we have more than Abraham did. He did indeed see the day of our Lord Jesus Christ and rejoiced (cf. *John* 8:56), but it was from afar, in a shadow. Now we do indeed have another declaration of it that he did not have. But for all that, if we have but a small portion of what was given to him, we must not seek for or desire more than pertains to our salvation, and we must say with the prophet that it is much better to live in the courts of the Lord, withdrawn into a corner, than to dwell in the tents of the wicked (*Psa.* 84:10) and exult and boast with them. So what I mentioned earlier is what we have to observe even though we are not individually fathers of a great nation. It must be enough for us to be children of God and heirs of his everlasting kingdom (cf. *Rom.* 8:17; *Gal.* 3:29).

Now it is said at the same time that God will bless him and that he will be a blessing. That statement is equivalent to saying he was to seek all his prosperity in God. Since he has the hope that he will not be wronged, but even that he will be an example of felicity and that it will be evident that God favours him and wishes to shower his blessings upon him—that is the meaning of the word in the language.[1] That must be especially noted again, for it is an assurance common to all the faithful that God's blessing will be upon them and that the wicked will realize how God has pity on them and is well disposed toward them because he was pleased to choose them. So let us learn to seek all our well-being in God's grace alone. Whereas the people of the world think that they will, by their cunning and deceit, their intrigues and practices, always exist on earth and make progress in such a way that some of them will give themselves over to violence and fraud, and others will hang their consciences in the closet, as the saying goes, so that, if they have one, it will be of no use to them. And others will be completely heartless and like ravenous wolves, as the psalm says, or like rabid dogs running about biting and snapping at one another (cf. *Psa.* 59:14-15; also *Ezek.* 22:27). We see that is how the world works. We are called to be the opposite and seek our prosperity in God. And although our prosperity is not apparent, let us wait patiently for the outcome that he will be pleased to grant us. In the meantime, may a small taste of his grace satisfy us more than if all our extravagant appetites were sated and we possessed all that the world has to offer.

In fact, our father Abraham, although he was blessed by God and represented a pattern and mirror to say to us: 'May God bless him just as he blessed Abraham' (cf. *Gen.* 28:4), and although everyone would like to be in this situation, he did not forgo enduring many occasions of anguish. And that blessing which is spoken of here did not appear immediately, as we shall see later. When he entered the land of Canaan, famine chases him from it for a while (cf. *Gen.* 12:10). And then the people deal with him so harshly that the poor man shifts from one place to another (cf. *Gen.* 13:7-12, 18; 14:12;

[1] The Hebrew word is *berâkâh*, translated unanimously as '*benedictio*' [benediction, blessing] in the dictionaries of the sixteenth century.—*M.E.*

20:1). He is not looking for a palace. He is satisfied to have a place to set up and live in his tent. His cattle are there in the fields. He asks only to rent a place like a poor stranger. But look. He has no water to drink, and even when he digs a well, he is not allowed to draw water from it, and it is filled in so that he cannot use it (cf. *Gen.* 21:25).[2] And again another famine drives him to another region, and he is persecuted everywhere, and his wife is even taken from him (cf. *Gen.* 12:15). He sees himself disgraced. He sees himself enduring such sorrows that he would have preferred to die a hundred times, yet he is blessed by God. Yes, but as I have already said, the blessing God gives his children is not always visible and cannot be perceived by human sensitivity.

So our father Abraham had to cling solely to the word which was announced to him, for he is told: 'I will make you a great nation.' But his wife is sterile and he is a poor decrepit old man, and his wife has passed the flower of her age! He knows she cannot conceive. Yet he will become a great people. And then he is told, 'I will bless you,' and there you have a poor pitiable fellow. So Abraham could say that God was mocking him in all sorts of ways. If he had opened the fleshly eyes of his understanding and stopped there, as we have said the wise of the world did when engaging in their great discourses and intrigues, it is certain he would have thought God was mocking him. But he closed his eyes to all those things and rested completely on the promise, knowing that God is faithful. That, then, is what we must do.

Moreover, let us note what I have said. If there is but a single drop of God's grace, it must satisfy us better than if we died, in a manner of speaking, full of wealth, honours, pleasures, and delights, and all the things men seek according to the flesh. For the wicked can be rich and opulent. They can be highly exalted. They can explore their sensual pleasures thoroughly. And the result? They in

[2] This episode happens to Isaac, cf. Genesis 26:15.—*M.E.*

no way taste of God's grace. And when we experience some small sense of it, however small, that must be enough for us. And when we are thus brought low, let us take courage and bear patiently the afflictions which are mixed with his gentleness until we arrive at our goal, which we must reach despite the fact we are weak and weary of body. God will give us the strength to arrive at the end if we are grounded in him that way.

At that point, Moses makes even clearer the favour God showed his servant Abraham when he says he is making a covenant with him such as men have been accustomed to do when making agreements among themselves. God descends so low that he becomes like Abraham's equal and companion. For when men want to make alliances, they especially state that each one will be a friend of friends and an enemy of enemies (cf. *Exod.* 23:22). That is the way God speaks. It ought to pierce our hearts when we see God lowering himself to the level of making a covenant with us, as we make them among ourselves, as if he wanted to obligate himself, he who owes us nothing and cannot owe us anything. We are completely his, and if we could do a hundred thousand times more than we are able to do, even all of that belongs to him. Now, from his perspective, what can he owe us, as I have said? All that we have comes from him. And by what law can we bind him? How can we impose an obligation on him? What can we require of him? Truly, by his own good pleasure he has obligated himself to us. If an earthly father were to do that for his child, he would be showing him a great kindness. If a father said, 'I will be obligated to you for that,' we would recognize an act of great generosity. What are we in comparison with God? If an earthen vessel is esteemed for his kindness when doing what his child wishes (cf. *Rom.* 9:20; 2 *Cor.* 4:7), what will the honour be for the one who formed the heavens and the earth? Now we understand that God is just that kind and benevolent when he makes a very personal covenant with

Abraham: 'I will bless those who bless you and curse those who curse you,' as if he were saying: 'I want to be so allied with you that all those who are friendly toward you will feel that I am also favourable toward them because of you. On the other hand, when you are unjustly troubled and afflicted and when someone rises up against you, I will be there as if he had taken me on personally, and I will treat your cause as if it were mine. And the wrongs he does to you will be done to me, as if he had violated my own majesty.' That, in short, is the import of Moses' word.

Now there is no question that that includes the entire body of the church and is not limited to Abraham in particular. We see the promises which are not addressed to two or three individuals but to everybody in general without exception. Scripture says that God will keep us as the apple of his eye (cf. *Psa.* 17:8). There is nothing more tender in man than his eye. If you cut off his arms and legs, you are far from hurting him more. Our Lord says that he loves us with such a tender love that if someone hurts us, it is like gouging his eyes (cf. *Zech.* 2:8). And although these promises have existed from all time and the fathers under the law prayed this way: 'Keep us as the apple of your eye,' as the psalm says, we today have an even greater certainty of it. So since God joined himself to us in the person of his only Son, we are to be confident that we cannot be separated from him and that he who is our Head wants to be united to us. That is why he says, 'Saul, Saul, why are you persecuting me?' (*Acts* 9:4) And Paul says that he is suffering what is lacking in the afflictions of our Lord Jesus Christ (cf. *Col.* 1:24).

So we see in summary that what Moses says is not restricted to Abraham alone, but that it is a teaching which is to be received by all the faithful and upon which they can boldly lean, confident that God is so kindly disposed toward them that he wishes to obligate himself willingly to them and be the friend of their friends and the enemy of their enemies. Consequently, confident that God holds us in such favour, let us realize that when someone does something good for us because of who we are as God's children, he will consider that good deed as done to him, just as Solomon says that the one who gives alms to those in need lends to God (cf. *Prov.* 19:17). How do we do that? What can we lend him? Everything is his, but God accepts it and enters it into his accounting.

So let us not doubt that our Lord sends us what we need, not as we might like, but as he knows to be good and expedient, and let us not doubt that he will provide for us in all our situations, seeing that he takes it upon himself to reward those who do good for us. On the contrary, when it is said that he will be the enemy of our enemies, do we not indeed have occasion to be submissive when we are wrongly persecuted by men and they rise up against us? Seeing that God wishes to take our side, do we not have occasion, I ask, to exercise patience until we see the result of what he has promised? So let us prepare ourselves, in accord with this passage, and when the wicked rise up against us and become so furious that it seems they are going to eat and swallow us whole, let us wait for our Lord to lift his hand to help us, and let us be assured that he will do so, for he said he would. And let us not be envious of those who feel triumphant today after oppressing the church with their high-handed violence and cruelty, for in the end they will discover that God is in the enemy camp and has always had us under his protection and will show that it is he that they have done violence to and wronged when coming against us unjustly. Now it is true that that will not be evident at first, but let us wait, as I have said, for in the end they will be made to feel it.

Moreover, let us note that although we may be the most peaceable people in the world, we will not be able to exist here without anger. Why not? The devil is called the prince of this world (cf. *John* 12:31; *Eph.* 6:12), and he also has a great multitude of henchmen whom he urges on. And because we must live among the wicked and the devil is our mortal enemy, is it possible that we can flee their acts of violence and oppression and excess? We must then submit to that situation. If ever there was a man who could acquire grace and favour in the eyes of others because of his kindness, his virtues and patience, it was Abraham, as will be shown extensively later, and yet God does not promise him without cause that he will be the enemy of his enemies. Consequently, we presuppose that there will be those who will make war on him and nettle him and provoke him and cause him many torments and hardships. And where will all that begin? With the devil, as I have said, who is against all of God's children and has at his disposal his underlings, whom he prods to vent their rage on us. Yet we must take note that Paul says we are to pursue peace with all men insofar as it depends on us (cf. *Rom.* 12:18), which is in keeping with the psalm: 'Seek peace and pursue it even though it seems to flee from you' (*Psa.* 34:14). But it is noteworthy that Paul adds this correction: 'as far as it depends on you.' That means that, after doing everything we should, we are not to pick quarrels with anyone or to cause others to be angry despite the fact we will not always be successful.

Therefore, let us pay close attention to the teaching that we are to be fortified like an invincible fortress when it comes to enduring, and let us never fail since we have from God's mouth the word that in the end he will take up our cause as his own because he is joined to us in an unbreakable bond (cf. *Sir.* 2:3; *Rev.* 3:8-10). And at the same time that is to teach us to do good and to try hard, even beyond our ability, to comfort God's children, to please them, and to help them in times of need, and to abstain from all wickedness and violence. In face of all the godlessness in the world, when we try to do good and we are repaid evil for good, or when all our good is forgotten, or when the poor people we serve have no means to show their gratitude, even though it seems our efforts are wasted when we work to fulfil our duty toward our brothers and neighbours, we ought to be adequately encouraged when God says that he will be the friend of the friends of his people. Therefore, let us not doubt that he considers as done to himself everything we do to those who are entrusted to us and to his cause. In that respect, as I have said, let us be aflame to share with God's children everything he has given us, sparing nothing, for it is from God that we are to await our reward. And likewise, to the contrary, let us be advised not to take the license to do evil, for if we oppress the poor, who cannot protect themselves and are, from the world's perspective, helpless, God will be our adversary. For he says that he will be the enemy of the enemies of all his people, as it is said that a cup of cold water will not be forgotten when it is given in his name (cf. *Matt.* 10:42). Likewise, on the contrary, if we touch with our little finger those whom he has taken under his care, it is certain we will not go unpunished. So let us learn to refrain from all violence, all harm, and all fraud, and to live with our neighbours in such a way that we will not provoke God's wrath against us, and let us not engage in hostile actions against members of his body. That, in brief, is what we have to keep continually in mind.

Now to conclude, it is said that all the families of the earth will be blessed in Abraham. That does not limit this manner of expressing oneself that we have recently seen, where it is said that Abraham would be a mirror of blessing, but here God is making him a special promise to bless all the nations of the earth through him. The Jews give this point meagre treatment. They say that when someone wants to ask God for prosperity, Abraham is put forth as an example: 'And may God do for me as he did for Abraham.' Now it is true that holy Scripture says that when someone pronounces a blessing upon himself in a certain way, he will also pronounce a curse in a certain way (cf. *Gen.* 28:4). To pronounce a curse, one will say: 'May it be done to you as to Sodom and Gomorrah' (cf. *Deut.* 32:32).[3] That is how, as an example, Sodom and Gomorrah are a curse, but we also see in Scripture that this is taken not just as an example, but as a cause for blessing in God's name (cf. 2 *Sam.* 6:18; *Psa.* 129:8). How is that to be understood but that the name of God is taken as the source and cause of all blessedness and of all that we can desire? That, in short, is how this passage is to be faithfully expounded: all nations of the earth will be blessed in Abraham, and not as regards him but as regards the seed which has descended from him, namely, our Lord Jesus Christ (cf. *Gal.* 3:16).

In fact, Paul faithfully explains this passage when he says that four hundred and thirty years before the law was given, that free covenant on which the salvation of the world is founded had already been made (cf. *Gal.* 3:17). Now when we have counted out the time, we will come to what Moses recounted here, namely that God introduces Abraham as already in possession of the promise that all the nations of the earth will be blessed in him.

Now Jesus is descended from him. So it is at that point that we must stop if we wish to be Abraham's spiritual children. And our faith must not depend upon Abraham's holiness (cf. *John* 8:33; *Gal.* 3:7; *Heb.* 2:16) or on any merit that was in him, but on Jesus Christ. For if Abraham did not have that blessing and did not draw from that fountain, it is certain that misfortune would be upon him and also upon us, for all of Adam's kind are cursed and God's enemy. So Abraham had to be in possession of his free blessing on the seed that was to descend from him, as we are sharing in it today. That is how he is called our father (cf. *Rom.* 4:1, 12, 16). This will be dealt with more fully on another occasion. That is why I have touched on it only briefly.

Moreover, when Moses said that God had already called Abraham in Chaldea (cf. *Gen.* 11:31), he adds that he left Haran.

[3] But there exists in the Bible no curse such as Calvin reports here.—*M.E.*

At this point he returns to the thread of the story to show that the death of Abraham's father did not discourage him and cause him to abandon his mission, but he pursued his calling until he reached the land that God told him about. Thus, in short, on the one hand, Moses informs us that Abraham was not at all foolhardy and, on the other, that he not only began to obey God when he left his country, but that he did not give up in mid-journey, but continued. And although his journey was interrupted for a certain period of time because of the illness and death of his father, yet God awakened him and showed him that he had to persevere; whereupon he gathered new strength and pursued his course not only to come into the land of Canaan but to live there and be a stranger until God gathered him into his rest.

> Now let us bow before the majesty of our gracious God in acknowledgment of our faults, praying that he will be pleased to touch us with such repentance that we will groan and ask him for forgiveness and seek it diligently. May he also help us by his Holy Spirit to overcome all the assaults the devil can direct against us. And let us valiantly resist all our self-serving impulses and do battle under his banner while we live on earth so that we will attain that victory which we are promised. And may we also enjoy the accompanying triumph when it pleases him to transfigure us into his immortal glory. May he grant that grace not only to us but to all the peoples and nations on earth.

54

The Anatomy of Patience: Hope, Confidence, Resistance, and Endurance

Monday, 5 February 1560

So Abram departed, as the LORD had spoken unto him; and Lot went with him: and Abram was seventy and five years old when he departed out of Haran. And Abram took Sarai his wife, and Lot his brother's son, and all their substance that they had gathered, and the souls that they had gotten in Haran; and they went forth to go into the land of Canaan; and into the land of Canaan they came. And Abram passed through the land unto the place of Sichem, unto the plain of Moreh. And the Canaanite was then in the land. And the LORD appeared unto Abram, and said, Unto thy seed will I give this land: and there builded he an altar unto the LORD, who appeared unto him (Gen. 12:4-7).

W E HAVE SEEN how Abraham left the land of Chaldea, where he was born and brought up, to go into a strange country to which God was calling him without knowing, however, the place that could be assigned to him as a dwelling place. In that fact, as we have said, he demonstrates admirable faith by allowing himself to be guided by God without knowing where he was going or what the outcome of his journey would be.

We learn here that he was seventy years old when he left Haran, for he had lived in that city for a while and had not soon or on first effort reached the place where God wanted him to go. We have seen that he was delayed by his father's illness and death. Now some commentators imagine that he remained there for sixty years and settles down in what at first appears to be an excellent place that is now empty. For it is said in the preceding chapter that Abraham's father was seventy when he fathered sons and daughters, whose names are given, with Abraham's being placed first (cf. *Gen.* 11:26). Now if his father was seventy at the time, it follows that sixty years have been omitted, for the text says that Abraham is seventy when departing after his father's death. And his father was two hundred and five years old when he died. So we see that Abraham had to be older if he had already been born at that time. Now the solution to the problem is quite easy.

But we note in the first place that Moses did not want to say at what time Abraham was born. He simply mentions how long his father lived, that he was already an old man, and that he had no children at that time. And, as we have already pointed out, that was to show that when God wants to establish his church in this world, he employs unusual and unused means to underscore his power more effectively. But the fact remains that Abraham's father was older, according to the text, for it would not be acceptable to say that the Holy Spirit concealed sixty years for no reason and that there was some confusion. Add to that the fact that Sarai was only sixty-five years old at the time Abraham was seventy-five. She was, then, only ten years younger than her husband. Otherwise, Abraham's father would have been younger than he. And how would that have played out if she had been only ten years younger than he? She would have had to be as old as his father. So we can calculate for certain that Abraham was born when his father was a hundred and thirty years old and that

Abraham's age of seventy-five is mentioned for the reason I have already stated.

Now with that problem solved, let us consider what Moses shows us that is useful for the instruction of our faith. It is said that Abraham left Haran in accordance with God's command. His doing so confirms his constancy and shows that he was not motivated by a fleeting zeal, as are many people when it comes to repenting, and that he was resolved to obey God until the end with relentless perseverance. It was the death of his father which could have been, as we have said, a grievous trial for him. It seemed that God was mocking when he permitted that poor old man to leave his country and give up his home and then in the middle of the journey die. And why is it that he did not at least see the place where God wanted his son to dwell?

Furthermore, one could, judging from the world's perspective, accuse Abraham of murdering his father by dragging him out that way and shifting him from place to place in his final old age. Now, however you look at it, he does not stop obeying God and he does not quit in the middle of the journey because of lack of commitment and zeal. That is particularly why it is noted that he left Haran in accordance with God's command. Now Moses is considering the fact that Abraham, as we saw earlier, did not leave the land of his birth on a whim but because he knew God wanted him to. He did not know why, but it is enough that God has authority over him. That, then, is why he yields to what is taught him by revelation.

Now we must observe here that the Holy Spirit, not without reason, always places the word of God before us as the rule for governing our entire lives so that we may know, should we be esteemed overmuch by men, that all our virtues will still be only filth and trash unless our lives are founded on obedience to God, which is for him more precious than many sacrifices, as he said in the first book of Samuel (cf. *1 Sam.* 15:22). Therefore, the first thing we have to bear in mind is that we must undertake nothing that is not approved by God and that we do not clearly know to be his will. That much for that point. As Abraham was in fact a pattern of true holiness, so he will be called thereafter 'father of all the faithful' (cf. *Gen.* 17:4–5). So we must conform ourselves to his example or we will only wander throughout our lives and be like poor lost animals. And even though we put a lot of effort into wanting to serve God, it will be a waste of time unless we adhere to his word, as we have said.

The second thing we need to bear in mind is Abraham's constancy, for even though he survived many misfortunes after God appeared to him, he does not forget the command he received but fulfils it at an opportune time when he has the means and the leisure. By that we are instructed and warned that when the devil has thwarted us and placed before us all kinds of hindrances and it even seems that God has given us some leeway because we are unable to obey his word, we must not abandon him. And we must not lose courage, but we must do as commanded, if we cannot today, then tomorrow, and we must persist until the end without wearying. That, then, is what we have to remember about this passage.

Now it appears that Abraham was in Haran for a few years, seeing that the text says he carried with him the substance he had acquired there, including 'the souls,' that is, his servants. Since that was the case, he had to have remained there not for a day or a year, but possibly for three or four, and his father lingered there until God took him from the world. And yet Abraham continues to have this command engraved in his heart and memory; this word of God always resounded in his ears: 'You must leave the land of your birth and your father's house and all your kindred' (cf. *Gen.* 12:1). So Abraham keeps that within himself until God gives him an opening and he can continue his journey until he reaches the land of Canaan.

Now with the mention of slaves, we have to note that theirs was a much broader servitude than we know today among ourselves. It is true we hear a good bit of talk about it, for it is employed not only among the Turks and in barbaric countries, but in Spain, where slave traffic goes on, where they take poor captives who will be held as slaves. Now it seems that that state is in violation of God's order and that there is no doubt that it came about because of confusion caused by sin. For when God created human beings in his image and likeness, it is certain he ennobled them so much that their condition was not to be like that of poor horses or oxen to be tormented at the pleasure of their masters and even beaten and killed. That is a corruption of the order God had set up for humankind, but that servitude was not disapproved by God so that men's pride might be humbled. Thus Abraham was allowed to acquire slaves and use them as the custom of the time permitted. And even the gospel, although it teaches us to be perfect in all things, does not order masters to dismiss or set slaves free, but he orders them to treat them humanely and exhorts them to realize that there is a God over us all who is above both great and small and the father of us all, in consequence of which there must be a brotherhood between masters and slaves (cf. *Col.* 4:1; *1 Tim.* 6:1-2; *Philem.* 15-18; *1 Cor.* 7:20-24).

So it was possible for Abraham to acquire slaves in accordance with what custom allowed. But it is quite certain he asserted his right in keeping with God's instruction, that is, he did not practice rigor or cruelty toward those who were subjected to him. In fact, we will see later how prompt and willing they were to obey him in every respect and at all times (cf. *Gen.* 13:1; 17:23); and they did not abandon him even though he was a poor vagabond, for those who belonged to him could indeed find ways to escape if they had wanted to because they were living among wicked and ill-intentioned peoples and because he was an unknown quantity and frequently changed his location. Nonetheless, the fact is that he maintained a peaceful household. How did he do that? By being upright and fair.

We still need to observe in passing that Abraham was rich, and we will see more about that later (cf. *Gen.* 13:1-2). Yet he realized that those who have some authority over others must not oppress them on the pretext that they could do so without being rebuked. But the first thing Abraham did was to follow the order of nature, and knowing that men are created in God's image, he showed that in reality he was seeking only to exercise fraternity with those who were in subjection to him. And that is how they dealt with him, and God blessed them increasingly. It is certain that those who wish to exercise their position using fear and tyranny will always receive their reward. And because they want to be feared, they will necessarily be troubled and apprehensive, and God will hold them in that torture-like state; and those whom they deal with so severely will rise up against them. So what we need to remember here is that the subservient do not become angry at staying in their place and honouring and obeying those whom God has set over them. On the contrary, those whom he has raised to positions of honour and dignity do not forget who they are but always remain humble and modest so that if they ever have the license to do evil, to torture one person, to wrong another, the sense of justice which is rooted in their hearts will serve to restrain them more than all the laws and all the restrictions in the world.

Let us come now to what Moses adds. He says that Abraham, after arriving in Canaan, went through the country from one end to the other. And again Abraham's faith is profoundly tested, for he had been told: 'Go into a land that I will show you' (cf. *Gen.* 12:1). Abraham is like a poor blind man. He does not know which way to turn if he is not moved along by God, as if carried along by the wind. But then when he came into the land of Canaan and God tells him this is the place where he wants them to dwell, he is disappointed that he has to pull up stakes repeatedly and continue as a vagabond, moving not just twenty-five or fifty miles, but throughout the entire country without finding a place to settle. At that point he could conclude that God had mocked him since he was not keeping his promise. He had now completely fulfilled his duty and fully acquitted himself. He had left his country and his kindred behind. And although his father follows him, he nonetheless sees him die, but that does not prevent him from reaching the land of Canaan. So it seems that Abraham finished his course without failing in any respect.

Now it remained for God to show him by deed that he had not spoken empty words when he said, 'I will assign you a country in which you will dwell.' And when he arrived, he is still moved from place to place, and God does not give him a small corner where he can find rest, but he keeps him constantly on the move. Abraham had to have an admirable faith since he remained steadfast the way he did, undeterred by his hardships, never losing courage as he waited patiently for what God would be pleased to send him. This was indeed written to praise him as well as to instruct us.

Therefore, let us realize that we will find no excuse when we claim we have been hindered for one reason or another and been diverted from our good intentions and encountered this or that difficulty and, because of our weakness, have had to remain uninvolved. When we propose all such reasons, it is certain we will be condemned, for we will never be able to serve God without a struggle. We must always keep that in mind. Why so? The devil, who is our mortal enemy, will always be engaged in battle and apply all his efforts to turning us in the opposite direction or to making us wander so far afield that we lose our way. Consequently, because we have to resist many of Satan's assaults when we desire to serve God, let us follow what we learn here about our father

Abraham and remember that he was driven hard from one end of the land to the other.

In addition, we must also remember what we discussed earlier, namely, that when God withdrew Abraham from the land of his birth, he wanted him to practice what Scripture teaches about our needing to be strangers in this world (cf. *Heb.* 11:13). It is true that not everyone will be expressly commanded to leave the land of his birth, but we must always have our bags packed, so to speak, and be ready to go at God's pleasure. And if he gives us no rest, such as we would like, let us not be displeased. Sometimes the church will be disturbed by storms and tempests, as Paul says of his time that Christians had no stability or certainty and had to be on the move, tossed like straw in the wind (cf. *Eph.* 4:14), but finding occasional rest. But in the meantime, we must not let our affections be attached to the earth and ask God to give us a stable world, but we must endure being vagabonds in accordance with his pleasure. And if he gives us respite, let us continue to look heavenward, and even when he is pleased to disturb our situation, either our finances or our location, let us know that he wants us to be conformed to our father Abraham, and let us be consoled and strengthened by that and not be unduly afflicted.

Let us come now to the verse that says the Canaanite was now living in the land. That is not a superfluous statement, for Moses is now pulling together all the troubles and vexations of body and mind that Abraham was able to endure, problems that would have led him astray if he had not been strengthened by an invincible patience and had not resolved to continue to serve God even though everything worked to counter his effort and expectation. We will see later that the Canaanites were removed, a dishonest, insincere, and untrustworthy people given to robbery and plunder and vicious cruelty and all kinds of evil, and contemptuous of God. In short, it is as if Moses were saying that that land was inhabited by marauders and thieves, lawless and inhumane people.

Now it is curious that God removed Abraham from the land of his birth to bring him to a land of marauders. It seems that he wants to plunge him into the depths of the abyss when he places him in the midst of such corruption. It is true that the Chaldeans were not better, for we see that idolatry was rampant there, but it is likely there was more uprightness in Chaldea than in this country Moses is talking about. For Shem's line was living there, and Shem was still alive, or he had very recently died. So there is the likelihood that there was more fear of God in Chaldea. Despite the fact that everything was perverted, instruction could still have some value. So when Abraham was taken from his country, where the people were so wicked and perverse, it seems that God wants him to be filled to overflowing with evil, as if he were saying to him, 'You will be in this land associating with the world's most wicked people, and if you grow up to be like them, you will experience neither remorse nor scruples.' For that is the way it often happens when everyone observes his companions; each one blackens the other, like bags of coal, as the saying goes. If we live in a well-regulated environment, we will be ashamed of not having some appearance of uprightness, but when whoredom and drunkenness, other acts of indiscretion, all types of loose living and acts of violence are in vogue, each person will think he is an angel when he is not worse than all the others.

So it seems that God was knowingly making an effort to corrupt his poor servant Abraham. Moreover, where does he place him? At least he gave him some respite. He tore him out from among all his relatives and friends as if he were tearing out his entrails, in a manner of speaking, and he leads him into an unknown country where he finds no support and wanders throughout the land. He does not have a foot of land he can call his own. Wherever he goes, everything he has is borrowed. He has no house or possession. He has some small leather tent to shield him from the rain. And did he still have to be persecuted by such wicked people and live like a poor sheep among wolves? Now there was a reason for that. For because we are very delicate, as soon as God makes a request of us we think that we have to take leave of him and that our excuses will be acceptable when we claim that we were willing but that he placed too great a burden on us. Now we must learn to be on our guard against that kind of fanciful thinking when it comes to what is recited concerning our father Abraham. When those who are today among the more severely tested compare all their hardships and vexations with those of Abraham, it is certain they will be far out of his league.

So let us take someone who is tested by God by all kinds of trials. It is certain he will be a long way from enduring a tenth of what the Abraham had to face. His example still ought to serve as a general rule, as we have dealt with it. So let us apply that teaching for the purpose it was given, which was so that we might learn to try hard consciously and not be so tender and delicate, as is our custom, that we withdraw from serving God and become weaker, but that when our situation becomes very difficult and hard, we will fight against those kinds of trials. And even though things do not happen as we would like and we are disappointed in our expectations and desires, let us always take the bit in our teeth, as they say, and plod ahead. But why does God not take pity on our weaknesses? Why does he allow us to be beaten down at every turn? It seems that he wants to discourage us and turn our lives upside down to make us abandon his calling. Now if he is pleased to put us to the test, he will do so in accordance with his good will. And because our faith, as Peter points out, is more precious than gold and silver, which are corruptible metals, it must be tested by fire to be completely purified (cf. *1 Pet.* 1:7). And that is so we will know it is a live root in us and that we do not hypocritically claim to worship God, but when we demonstrate we are truly his, totally dedicated to him, it is not to serve him as a pastime in our ease and leisure and when he satisfies us in every way we can imagine. But when we have to undergo many conflicts and attacks and be bound as captives in all our senses, let us pass through those trials. So let us note that if Abraham suffered many wrongs and much violence from the Canaanites, we must always be ready, wherever we are, to bear God's yoke whenever he wants us to experience whatever it may be, and let us be armed with patience (cf. *Col.* 3:12; *2 Pet.* 3:15), for therein lies our victory.

In addition, it is said that God appeared to him and comforted him, saying that he would give that land to his seed. Here we see that even though God deals rigorously with his own and seemingly wants to overwhelm them, he has in hand at the same time everything that will console them, and he will not fail to alleviate their sadness in order to mitigate the bitterness of their hardships and deliver them from all fears and cares. That is how God provides for his servants so they will always have something to comfort them in the midst of their trials. Now we cannot engage combat unless we are armed, and we will not find our armour here below (cf. *Eph.* 6:13-17). We must find it in God, for our arms and our legs and our entire body will fail us. So how will we be able to resist our enemy, who is so strong? For it is said that Satan is the prince of the world (cf. *John* 12:31; 14:30; 16:11; *Eph.* 6:12). So God has to give us his power to resist such force and violence. That is why it is said here that when Abraham was engaged in such great and difficult struggles, God did not fail him or forget him. So much for that one point.

For the second, we are also shown the true power that fortifies us until we finish our course and attain the goal God is calling us to. It is his word that guides us in our journey! Here are two points that are well worth noting. One is that we must so hope in God that when we are at our wits' end and are so overwhelmed by extreme circumstances that we see only dark shadows everywhere, and when it seems we are excluded and banished from life and salvation, we remain confident that he remembers us and will help us at the right time, for he knows how to deliver us because the outcomes of death belong to him, as the psalm says (cf. *Psa.* 68:20). When we are dead and buried, God has the outcomes of death in his hand. That is when we have to follow our father Abraham and be strengthened by what is said here about him, namely, not to doubt that when God wants to test our faith, he will prove himself faithful, as Paul says, and not allow us to be tested beyond our strength and ability, and he will provide a good and blessed outcome for all our trials (cf. *1 Cor.* 10:13). Why? It is he who places in the grave and removes from it. It is he who puts to death and restores to life, as is stated in the first book of Samuel, the second chapter (cf. *1 Sam.* 2:6).

Now that is the teaching we must put into practice when it seems that all is lost and that God has shunted us aside, when it seems all the elements are against us and the clouds of heaven are about to fall out of heaven to overwhelm us and men are planning our ruin. Let us not doubt that God will provide, for he is faithful and has shown us in the person of Abraham that he never forgets his own. That is not a teaching especially for Abraham, but for all the faithful, and it is in keeping with what Paul says: that God will bring all our hardships and trials to a good conclusion and we will never be disappointed in the hope and undergirding we are to expect from him even though we must withstand brutal assaults.

Now the means we are to use is quite specific: the word of God. So let us be satisfied that we have his promises to sustain us when everything else fails. For if we expected God to appear visibly to us from heaven, it is certain we would be disappointed, for he wishes to test our faith. What kind of test would it be if God were always there present with us and his favour had been quite obviously known? We would always be able to go to him with our heads lifted up. But when God conceals himself and his power seems to be absent and far removed, and when many kinds of evil present themselves, there we find the true test of our faith if we do not fail. Why? Because we have the word. It is our sword and shield, our helmet and breastplate (cf. *Eph.* 6:16-17). In other words, being certain of God's truth and knowing that he has received us and adopted us as his children, we have confidence in his promise to be a good father to us (cf. *Gal.* 4:5; *Eph.* 1:5) and be near all those who call upon him in truth (cf. *John* 6:32; 8:41; 16:27; *1 John* 3:1). Since we have our refuge in him, that ought to be like an invincible fortress for us. We will always be assailed, but we have an impregnable fortress when God's word strengthens us and we attribute to it the authority it deserves. If a man is assailed by his enemies and threatened and often alarmed but is in an impenetrable place and supplied with everything he needs, he will defy his enemies. He must nonetheless be vigilant and on the defensive and work to repulse the attacks. But in the meantime he is secure, for we will not find in this world a better fortified fortress than God's truth.

Let us emphasize this point again. If we are to persist in the midst of all our struggles and never fall short until God gathers us into his rest, we must be content with his simple word and adhere to it. Although he may be hidden for a time and seem to have turned away from us, let his word be for us a light (cf. *Psa.* 119:105) to overcome all the darkness that could surround us and prevent us from obtaining the kingdom of heaven.

We will even be able to see that better in the way Moses recounts it, for he says that God appeared to Abraham and said to him, 'I will give this land to your seed.' That appearance Moses talks about was like a seal that ratifies a promise. If Abraham had simply heard a voice and had been uncertain about its origin, it is certain that would not have been a basis for repeatedly confronting the many obstacles he had to overcome. His word had to be ratified and Abraham had to know it was God who was speaking. Now we will not have the kind of particular revelations Abraham had, but God has nonetheless approved his law and his gospel so that all the visions and ecstatic prophecies we might receive today cannot be more powerful or effective than what we have in holy Scripture and keep us from holding strictly to it. Is it not enough that God shook the world when the law was given (cf. *Exod.* 20:18), that trumpets resounded, that everything was filled with thunder and lightning, that there was a dark cloud and signs and wonders, and is it not enough that God always held the people in obedience to himself until the advent of our Lord Jesus Christ? And at that time, as the prophet says, heaven and earth were shaken (cf. *Joel* 3:16). Must not the miracles that were performed to confirm the gospel serve today? So when it is said that God appeared to Abraham, it was done to show that the word will never be useful to us and we could not apply it properly for our instruction if we did not know that it was God who spoke. So we must be instructed that God is the author of all the promises contained in the law, the prophets, and the gospel, and that must bear a permanent signature engraved in our hearts, one that cannot be eradicated.

Now we do not have to have new visions and prophecies every day, as we said, but even so we need to come and present ourselves to God to be instructed in his school, and we must come with such reverence that we are prepared to receive what will be made known to us. And since our faith bears the witness that we are taught by God and is founded not on men's wisdom and worth, as Paul says, but on the power of the Holy Spirit (cf. *1 Cor.* 2:5), as the Holy Spirit is called the seal of the pledge God gives us to certify the inheritance he has promised (cf. *2 Cor.* 1:22). But what has to proceed that is that we do not doubt that holy Scripture contains God's pure and certain truth, which can never deceive or lie to us.

Now, whatever the situation, God is not speaking here to satisfy Abraham as a man, that is, to satisfy his carnal affection, for it seems that he is revising and correcting what he said. He had promised him a land, and he now says to him, 'Oh, this will be for your successors and those who come after you.' Now that is obvious capriciousness, for God appears to contradict himself and withdraw his hand, and after giving his servant Abraham a sprinkling of hope, he leaves him empty-handed, there is a great difference between the promise of Abraham's being lord of the land and enjoying it and its postponement until after his death. So Abraham could again conclude that God had mocked him.

Moreover, when he speaks to him about his seed, children, lineage, what does he have in mind? Abraham is already an old man. He has been married a long time and lived beyond the flower of his age. Sarai herself is sixty-five years old and has never conceived. God showed that she was sterile. Abraham is without lineage and yet God says to him, 'It is for your seed that I am reserving this land.' So it seems that in many ways God wanted to pierce Abraham's heart, not only to test him with a spear, but to wound him mortally to the depths of his being. Now where is the consolation we have been talking about? Now it was a matter of having to remedy those sorrows and hardships that had tormented Abraham. On the one hand, he sees himself wandering in the midst of a nation as wicked and perverse as no other, and on the other hand, he is left without a place to rest and expect to find help. God was at least obligated to remedy that situation. But it appears that he wants to aggravate the situation even more when he says, 'Be of good courage. I will do nothing during your lifetime, but after your death.' 'But may I have some peace during my life?' 'Not at all! But wait until you have died.' 'Then that promise is no good.'

'You will not enjoy it as long as you live. It will be for your seed.' Now, as I have said, instead of remedying his situation, it seems that God wants him to be like a foreigner here and that he wants to exacerbate his wounds instead of salving them. And then again, if he had given him offspring, Abraham would still have had some expectation: 'Well, if this is not for me, it will be for my children.' But now he could not even hope to have any children following the natural process!

Thus we see how we must give place to the word of God so that it will reach far and wide throughout the entire world. In other words, what good would it do if we tried to keep it enclosed in our minds and God spoke in conformity with our imaginations, our desires, and fantasies? So let us be careful not to limit God's word. It is worth noting that the Jews have been reproached for confining God within nets and drawing circles around him as if to tell him: 'This is what you will do. You will give us thus and so.' There is nothing more contrary to faith than assigning certain limits to God by wanting him to act in accordance with notions we come up with. All of that must be rejected. So what remains? We must extend our faith beyond the world and suppress all our thoughts, all our reasons, all our desires, and conclude that God's will must take precedence over anything we might conceive that would turn us away from him. And that will happen when we do not ask God to grant everything our carnal appetites seek, but let us be content that he speaks to us, and let us remember that he has not forgotten us and will provide for us in all our troubles as he sees fit, and not as we would like. That, then, is what we have to remember.

It is true that these things will not be said to us today word for word, as it was to our father Abraham, but we nonetheless have here a living picture that shows us how God's word is to cause us to rejoice (cf. *Psa.* 119:162) in all our sorrows, how it is to ease the heaviest of the world's burdens, how it is to enlighten us (cf. *Psa.* 119:105) in the midst of our deepest and darkest moments, how it is to quicken us in death. Thus, when we get into an argument and it seems there is something absurd about what God says and does not conform to our understanding and the way we think, let us say, 'Oh, God knows what he has to do.' We can certainly wish, but we must restrain ourselves in every case. And when it does not please him to give us what we ask, let us always return to this conclusion: 'Your will be done' (*Matt.* 6:10; *Luke* 11:2). That teaching is one we must practice every day of our lives. Whenever we get it into our heads we can manage what God has promised, if it is escaping us and we sense no experience of it, let us continue to wait patiently for the moment he will have us experience it. And then when we become discouraged and have endured an evil another person has survived and God does not let us sense his help and support but keeps us in suspense until we think we cannot continue, let all the promises he has given us keep us steadfast, and let us say, 'If it does not happen today, he will not long delay. And if he does delay, it will come in his good time.' The effects and fulfilment of the prophecies were hidden. It seems that when God spoke, it was only a sound that struck their ears, but, no matter, we know everything was fulfilled, for he is faithful, and we must consider what has proceeded from his mouth as certain, for it is not ours to bring to reality what he says, but we must fight against all trials and hardships by struggling with the power of faith until God fulfils his promises at a time he knows to be right. It is not for us to determine when it will be. So that is what we have to remember about this passage. Tomorrow, God willing, we will deal with the altar Abraham set up.

Let us now bow before the majesty of our gracious God in acknowledgment of our faults, praying that he will be pleased to move us to such repentance of them that we will make an effort throughout our lives to withdraw from them. And let us resist them so that it will be known that we desire to serve our God despite the fact that things do not turn out the way we would like and so that we will be able to rejoice with Paul that we have not only finished our course but have fought the good fight (cf. *2 Tim.* 4:7), not being disappointed with the reward for our victory. And what pleasure this good Father has in supporting us in our weaknesses until he has cleansed us of them all! And in proportion to the trials he sends us, may his help be provided, may he give us the remedies he knows to be appropriate and suitable until he delivers us from all the miseries of this world and all the perplexities that we encounter in it as he makes us participants in the rest that was so dearly acquired for us by the blood of our Lord Jesus Christ. May he grant that grace not only to us but to all the peoples and nations on earth.

55

The Meaning and Function
of Abraham's Altar

Tuesday, 6 February 1560

*And Abram took Sarai his wife, and Lot his brother's son, and all
their substance that they had gathered, and the souls that they had
gotten in Haran; and they went forth to go into the land of Canaan;
and into the land of Canaan they came. And Abram passed through
the land unto the place of Sichem, unto the plain of Moreh. And
the Canaanite was then in the land. And the LORD appeared unto
Abram, and said, Unto thy seed will I give this land: and there
builded he an altar unto the LORD, who appeared unto him. And
he removed from thence unto a mountain on the east of Bethel, and
pitched his tent, having Bethel on the west, and Hai on the east:
and there he builded an altar unto the LORD, and called upon the
name of the LORD. And Abram journeyed, going on still toward the
south* (Gen. 12:5–9).

WE SAW YESTERDAY that when God appeared to his
servants, he added some mark so that their faith would
not be hesitant or uncertain, but that they would know
it was he who had spoken so that they could lean on his truth
and power and be fully and firmly resolved not only that what he
declared to them is a truth which would not fail, which they could

trust completely, but that he would also fulfil everything they had heard from his mouth.

Abraham, then, is fortified and ready for all encounters because he knows that 'God is all powerful,' that he has experienced his mercy, and, third, that he is assured God will keep his promise. These three things are always required when it comes to standing firm against Satan. For that we must put forward God's name and the three things I mentioned if we are to be able to say: 'If God is for us, who can be against us?' (cf. *Rom.* 8:31). He will overcome all our enemies and everything that threatens our salvation. And then he shows he will be kind and gentle toward us when he condescends to come and make himself known to us personally so that we may take refuge in him. And on the other hand, he does not change his purpose, and when he speaks, there is immediate fulfilment.

That is why the text now says that Abraham built an altar as a testimony that he was grateful for the alleviation which had been granted him,[1] for we have seen the afflictions he could have been hard-pressed by up until the time God appeared to him. He is so satisfied with that appearance that he even declares before men how obligated he is to God for considering his needs and helping him the way he did.

It is true that Abraham was able to bless God's name and acknowledge that he was obligated to him without setting up an altar, for we know that the worship of God is spiritual (cf. *1 Pet.* 2:5). But Abraham did not neglect the secondary aspect of worship while remembering the main one. If we want to offer God worship which is acceptable to him, it is certain we must not waste our time with ceremonies and gestures that men find pretty and impressive, but our faith must be founded upon him. We must acknowledge

---

[1] Calvin imagines great hardships for Abraham, hardships about which the biblical text is silent.—*M.E.*

him as the fountain of all good things and put all our trust in him. We must also offer him sacrifices of praise for his benefits. That is the true worship of God such as it is spoken of in Psalm 50, where God rejects everything the hypocrites present as fine appearance (cf. *Psa.* 50:8-13). And below that he adds: 'You will offer me a sacrifice of praise. In that I will be honoured. Call upon me in the day of your trouble and I will answer you and you will bless me' (cf. *Psa.* 50:14-15). In the meantime, since God created the body as well as the soul, he seeks to be honoured both on the outside and on the inside. Therefore, when we worship God on the first level, we must add at the same time the confession of our faith and the external worship he requires.

That is why Abraham built the altar Moses talks about here and thus gives us an example of what Paul says, namely, that as we believe with our hearts unto righteousness, so must we make confession with our mouths unto salvation (cf. *Rom.* 10:9-10). In other words, we are, at all times and everywhere, to show in our bodies and in our souls, that we are dedicated to God. As he says in another passage, we are to contain him (cf. *2 Cor.* 4:7) and then make an effort to be pure and clean of all pollution because God has chosen us to be the vessels of his temple, for he wants to dwell in us (cf. *1 Cor.* 3:16; *2 Cor.* 6:16). That is reason enough for us to be cleansed of all defilements and filth. So we have to gather from what Abraham did that it is not enough to honour God and trust him in secret, but we must follow that with a declaration of the honour we give him. We must do that because we are totally his, as I have said, and because he created our bodies and our souls. He redeemed them, for they will be reclothed in his glory and the heavenly life we hope for (cf. *2 Cor.* 5:2). It is also not without cause that our Lord Jesus Christ took on our nature, doing so in order to sanctify our bodies. And that is also why our bodies participate in the sacraments even though they are spiritual, that is to say, the sacraments aim at things higher than this world. Nevertheless, we must receive their testimony in our bodies because their fruit and power will be demonstrated in our bodies everywhere until the last day. That ought to motivate us to honour God before men.

Above and beyond that are these reasons: we must try to attract our neighbours and move them to do as we do, for it is not enough for each to do as he should in secret, but we should also have a burning desire for God to be worshiped by all people with common accord and harmony. So we must try to build up those who need building up and encourage the lukewarm by employing verbal persuasion as well as showing by deed everyone's responsibility and duty toward God. That, in short, is the meaning of Abraham's altar.

Now that teaching is to be practiced and especially today because there are many people who keep the knowledge of God inside themselves. It is true they cannot have faith or love of neighbour unless it is shown outwardly, but they convince themselves that it is enough to worship God in their minds. And yet they defraud him of his right, for they will make excuses for themselves. Otherwise, the world cannot tolerate them if they wish to follow the truth of the gospel and adhere to it. So, for them, it is enough to confess in their closet that God's word provides the rule for living right. But at the same time they will continue to give themselves over to godlessness before men and will give no consideration to glorifying God in any way. And because we see that kind of negligence, we must all the more follow what the Spirit of God teaches us, namely, that since our hearts are dedicated to God, our tongues must likewise respond, and our hands and feet, our whole bodies.

But if one charges that the world is so wicked today that it is not permissible to serve God, Abraham was indeed in that very kind of peril. For, as we said yesterday, he was living in a region that was as corrupt as any that ever existed. The Canaanites were a people filled with pride and arrogance, faults surpassed only by cruelty and malice. In short, they lacked no wickedness. That situation was to cause Abraham grief, as if he had intended to set a fire to enrage them all. Yet that did not prevent him from building his altar, as if he were proclaiming that his religion was different and that he did not want to be polluted by the superstitions of those who worshiped idols and forged their own gods and worshiped them when necessary. It is true it was not his place to reform his neighbours, for he had no jurisdiction over them. Even so, he wanted his house to be pure and God to be worshiped as he should be.

Therefore, let us not think that that reason has no merit inasmuch as we claim it is not possible for us to worship God as we ought if we live in the Papacy, in the midst of the enemies of faith, for they will straightway rise up in fury, and we see how they are prepared to exterminate all those who are unwilling to consent to their iniquities and abominations. When all of that is said, it can be reduced to a simple concept: Abraham, who was the father of the faithful, showed us another way, which is set before us to follow. He was not exempt from persecution or hardship or affliction when he set up his altar to God. But he overcame all those things that could discourage him and completely corrupt him.

So what are we to do when we dwell in the midst of idolaters? It is true we cannot reclaim them except insofar as God gives us the means to. We may be able to exhort them and make an effort to deliver them from the confusion that is in them, but we have to allow them to pursue their own superstitions. And when we see God being dishonoured among them, we cannot correct that. Even so, we must each keep ourselves pure of all such defilements and follow what has already been proposed with respect of dedicating ourselves to God since he is calling us. And at the same time we have to avoid polluting the temples he has chosen and elected, which are our bodies, as Paul says in another place (cf. *1 Cor.* 6:19).

In short, since we have the inner desire to serve God and honour him, let us show it outwardly insofar as we can, and as the occasion arises and the ability is granted to us, let us demonstrate in the presence of men that we are temples of God. That is one point: each person is to keep himself unpolluted.

Now for the second point: each person is to maintain such order in his family that he does not allow the worship of God to be subverted and corrupted—insofar as possible. For a wife could disagree significantly with her husband and fight against the true faith, but all heads of household must nonetheless make an effort to set up an altar to God so that his name may be purely invoked. When each person wishes to be honoured and served in his own house, must God be forgotten and his honour rejected? Is it appropriate for mortal creatures, who are but worms, to be preferred over the one who created all things, who guides and rules over all things? So this is what we must do today. Wherever we are, even though those among whom we live may be the greatest imaginable enemies of God's truth and worship, we must continue to reject all of their idolatries in our personal lives and at least show that we do not consent to them and accept them in any way soever.

Yet we could ask who gave Abraham permission to set up an altar, for we know God wants to be worshiped with obedience (cf. *1 Sam.* 15:22) and does not accept what men think is good. So we must come to this point: Abraham did not take it upon himself to build that altar to God but was instructed to do so. Even though that instruction was not written down, obedience is better than sacrifice (cf. *1 Sam.* 15:22), and God, who does not change and is unchangeable (cf. *John* 1:11), has always had his command, and those who have wanted to worship him have followed it, as we saw previously in the person of Noah.

Abraham, therefore, was not, properly speaking, the originator of that altar. In other words, he did not build it in response to his own thinking. How do we know? From Moses own words: 'He built an altar to the God who had appeared to him.' There we have two bits of inseparable information. Abraham did not have some random representation of his faith, but he followed the revelation which was given to him. Therefore, it is now rather well known that Abraham did not worship some God who was unknown to him and, likewise, he did not follow something he could not explain, for idolaters will have their religious scruples, and that is all they will be able to say when they become deeply upset if they are rebuked and shown that they worship in vain and that everything they do is meaningless. What will be their answer? 'Oh, everything that is done with good intention is well done.' So why does God not approve it? Those people think that that answer negates God's right and that God, like it or not, has to consider good and worthy everything they think is.

Now that is not the way Abraham went about it. When Abraham built an altar, he built it to the God who had appeared to him. So he knew that that was God's will and that he was following the revelation which had been given to him. In short, he did not start out aimlessly and did not have an absurd zeal that did not distinguish between good and evil, but he knew what God's will was and conformed himself to it completely. That too is very noteworthy, for we are shown in this passage that we cannot call upon God or honour him appropriately unless his word is always before us like a lamp in the darkness (cf. *Psa.* 119: 105). That is also why Paul says in the tenth chapter of Romans: 'How shall they call upon him whom they have not known? And how shall they know him about whom they have not heard?' (Cf. *Rom.* 10:14.) Consequently, the gospel has to be preached, and after it is received by faith, it must be a true guide to those who want to call upon God. That is another point that is well worth noting.

We often see men urged on by boldness and audacity in matters of serving God. They will, in that enterprise, be even more daring when they undertake unreasonable projects, whereas when it comes to something simple, they will seek advice for the most insignificant of matters. If the thing is useful, going about it that way might be advisable. In short, a thousand things will have to be taken into consideration for things which do not require the word. But in matters of serving God, they close their eyes and strikeout with such audacity that you would think they have the situation under control. We see that everywhere today, and it is a vice that has ruled from ancient times. So let us note that it is impossible for us to offer God worship which he approves or accepts unless we have previously known him. And how will we know him? It is certain we cannot rise to that level by our own efforts, but he must extend his hand and come down to us and lift us up to himself, which he does by means of his word. So we will be well prepared to serve God when we have carefully learned from the law, the prophets, and the gospel that he is God, what he demands and requires of us, and what meets his approval. Then we will be well disposed to worship him.

Consequently, we must conclude with Paul that faith comes by hearing and hearing comes by the word of God (cf. *Rom.* 10:17), and as a result, we must be guided by doctrine in the matter of making formal presentations and prayers and everything that concerns God's honour. So that is how we are to understand this passage about Abraham's erecting an altar to the Lord, as it was revealed to him by the Lord. For if he had had no revelation and had known nothing, it is certain he would have worked hard without results. Why? For if we follow our own plans, we will be lost and wandering, and the faster we run, the farther we will go from the right road, and we will stumble and fall. So we must allow ourselves to be guided by God, who calls us to himself, and we must respond simply: 'Here I am, Lord, and since you asked of me this and that thing, I come to offer them to you, as is my duty' (cf.

Gen. 22:1; *Exod.* 3:4; *1 Sam.* 3:4; *Isa.* 6:8; *Heb.* 10:7). That, in short, is what this passage means.

And to be noted also is the fact that that altar presupposes sacrifice. Abraham did not erect an altar without also sacrificing. Now sacrifices were not invented on the spur of the moment or to satisfy man's purposes. God commanded them. Therefore, we must consider the end our father Abraham had in mind. It was because he intended to offer sacrifices to God. Let us now consider whether God was ever pleased to have animals burned to him after they were killed, their blood poured out and their fat burned. In other words, did he take pleasure in all those things? In the first place, as we said of the psalm we quoted, he neither eats nor drinks (cf. *Psa.* 50:9-15). Later we learn that he created everything and that all riches are in his hand. Nothing can be taken to him then, but we must learn the spiritual truths of these figures which were before and under the law.

So God intended for people to sacrifice to him. Why? So that they might pay him homage for everything and declare that all they possessed that was good proceeds from him and his pure liberality. That was the purpose of the prayers and offerings. And that also was the purpose of all the sacrifices even though God provides all good things for our use while retaining ownership of them—not for any advantage he may receive from them, as we said, but so his name will be blessed and exalted, as he deserves. That much for that point.

Now men confessed that they were indebted when brute beasts were killed, for all that was like declaring they were guilty and deserved death. And every time they offered sacrifices, it was like a legal document placed before God admitting: 'Lord, here we are, poor evildoers. We deserve death. Here we offer an innocent animal to answer for us.' Not that the sacrifice itself pleased God, but its purpose was to instruct men so that they might be touched with a true feeling of repentance and learn to yield humbly to God. But that was not the whole story, for at the same time, men needed to know how God's wrath could be appeased among poor sinners. In that was a testimony of the suffering and death of our Lord Jesus Christ in all the former sacrifices. For what would men gain by offering God a sacrifice and declaring they were like condemned and lost men? They would have been men without hope, but they had taken into consideration how God was appeased by the sacrifice that was to be offered to him as it was when our Lord Jesus Christ, who is the spotless lamb of God (cf. *1 Pet.* 1:19), stooped to take our curse and our sins upon himself and was made a curse, as Paul says, so that we might be sharers in God's blessing (cf. *Gal.* 3:13), which he provided for us and of which we have just spoken and will necessarily speak again at length. That is, I repeat, a brief account of Abraham's intention when building his altar.

Today the papists will, it is true, have some semblance of comparison with Abraham, and yet what they do is detestable in God's sight. Why so? The reason is very diverse, for under the law, these figures and shadows were necessary because of the absence of our Lord Jesus Christ, as Paul says in the second chapter of Colossians (cf. *Col.* 2:17). Now that Jesus Christ has appeared and fulfilled all that the ceremonies of the law prefigured, it is certain that when a person still wishes to hold to what was in use for that time, he does so to bury the Son of God along with his power and the grace which is to shine everywhere today by the preaching of the gospel. Therefore, when the papists set up altars today, it is certain they blaspheme our Lord Jesus Christ and do all they can to show contempt for God his Father. For altars, that is, material altars, existed before the coming of Jesus Christ. What now is our altar? There is no other altar than the Son of God. He is the altar and the sacrifice. He offered himself. He removed the priest who sacrificed to God. He is all three together: altar, sacrifice, and priest.

Therefore, the more the papists waste their time and open their purses to establish chapels, to set up altars and chant masses, the more it is certain they only increase their condemnation because they openly blaspheme God. Why so? The coming of the Lord Jesus Christ, as we have said, brought to an end all the shadows of the law. And whenever one wishes to sacrifice today in the former manner, it is as if they were saying that they are not satisfied with the suffering and death of our Lord Jesus Christ, that that is not sufficient, and that they are not seeking in his sacrifice reconciliation or the cleansing of sins. Each sacrifice at the altar is a blasphemy against him. So let us note closely that we must not randomly and without consideration follow what those holy fathers did, but we must consider the difference between their situation and ours. Before Jesus Christ was manifested in the flesh, died, and was resurrected, they had to have some figures to fill in for his absence. Today we contemplate him face to face in the gospel, and, as Paul says to the Galatians, he is crucified in our midst so that we see more than a dead painting (cf. *Gal.* 3:1). But every time the death of our Lord Jesus Christ and the fruit that it brings to us are declared to us faithfully, it is as if Jesus Christ were being shown before our very eyes as crucified for us and his blood as being poured out for our washing and cleansing. That is what we have to continue to remember about that altar.

And there is more. Moses adds in the second place that Abraham called upon the name of the Lord. Here he shows us both the substance and the form of the worship of God, both of which we have touched upon. Consequently, we must give close attention to what the worship of God consists in as regards its pure nature. It consists in, as Psalm 50 tells us, taking refuge in him and placing our confidence completely in him so that we may engage in prayers and offer him sacrifices of praise when we experience his goodness and help. That, I say, is the substance of the true worship of God.

As for the form of worship, we have aids and means given in his word to assist us in our worship because we are weak as well as remiss and negligent. Hypocrites always rip apart what God has unified. They will utilize only one part and leave aside the other, which is worse. They will spend their time trifling over unimportant matters and put the cart before the horse, as we say. In short, hypocrites in every age have done that when they make a big to-do over exterior formality and create pomp to please men for their applause, but they do not consider God's intention, but circumvent it. In that way, the Jews, under the law, have always been diligent in bringing their sacrifices to the temple and engaging in elaborate and flashy ceremonies. Yet their hands were bloody and their hearts full of ungodliness. They were bursting with pride while filled with contempt for God. They rebelled against his word and refused correction from the prophets but responded like rabid animals when their faults were rightly pointed out. That is the kind of people they were, and the same is true today.

If we take a good look at the most devout in the Papacy, it is certain that those who trot from altar to altar, mumble a lot, and go through the motions of the mass are those who have the least faith and loyalty and are filled with pride, betrayal, cruelty and ill will, and often among them will be found even vile and shameful lechers who give themselves over to every kind of filthy behaviour. But after making many signs of the cross, beating their breast, hearing mass, and performing all their other empty rituals, they think they have appeased God, but all they do is whitewash themselves, imagining they have done what is necessary. Seeing that kind of behaviour, let us follow the procedure the Holy Spirit provides, which is to worship God by putting our faith in him and letting it abide in him, knowing that our well-being lies with him and our felicity is found in clinging to him. We must be able to say with David: 'Behold, my sovereign good is that I am joined with my God' (cf. *Psa.* 16:2). And then there is this passage: 'And my portion has come due because God is my possession and I am content' (cf. *Num.* 18:20). With those words, may our faith not be asleep, but may it be awakened by prayers and thanksgiving. That must be our starting point.

The other aspects of worship are not superfluous, such as what we do out of respect when we remove our hats, kneel, and lift up our hands, affirming that we are seeking godliness. It is good to do those things when we are assembled in his name to confess our faith. In short, we must not neglect all the ways and means given to us because of our frailties, but we must be especially careful not to neglect what God demands of us. In that respect, let us imitate our father Abraham, for when Scripture tells us he set up an altar, it immediately adds that he called upon the name of the Lord. What do hypocrites do? They come and trample his courts and put on fine airs, as our Lord mocks them through the prophet Isaiah: 'I have this against you: you come and wear out the courts of my temple. Stay at home, every one of you; do not bring your abominations and mingle them with my holiness' (cf. *Isa.* 1:12-13). They thought that when they had fulfilled their outward duties, they had done all. When they had performed their elaborate rituals, as I said, they thought that God was obliged to leave them alone. Now as for us, when we come to the sanctuary, let us read holy Scripture; let us lift our hands to heaven; let our hearts take charge, and let us truly call upon the name of the Lord.

Now that comment means two things, as we have stated elsewhere, and it will suffice to mention them briefly here. That is often why when Scripture speaks of calling on the name of God, it is a reference to praying to him (cf. *Gen.* 4:26; 13:4; 21:33; 26:25). But sometimes the meaning is broader, as when the name of God is called down upon us, that is, when we proclaim that we are his people, consider him to be our Father, and that we are his children, inasmuch as he has adopted us and gathered us into his church (cf. *1 Chron.* 16:8; *Psa.* 105:1; *Isa.* 12:4). Also, to call upon the name of God, when understood that way, is to take a part for the whole. In truth, as we have already said, the worship of God consists principally in dwelling completely in him, seeking in him the fullness of our lives and all the good things we are to wish for, and declaring that they come from his unlimited bounty and that all the good things we enjoy are just that many blessings he bestows upon us. That is the highest level of what the worship of God consists in.

And that is why Scripture, when speaking of calling upon the name of God often and insistently, understands that if we call upon him in truth and in sincerity, it is then that we worship him, and the rest follows naturally (cf. *1 Kings* 8:43; *Psa.* 116:17; *Jer.* 14:9), for there is an inner connection between calling upon God in sincerity of faith and then dedicating ourselves to him, bringing ourselves into obedience, and offering ourselves to him as a holy offering. That, in summary, is what we have to remember.

Now we must keep in mind that Moses does not just say that Abraham set up an altar in one place, but when he changed locations, he always set up another altar.

As for these changes in location, we have to note how thoroughly God tested his servant's faith. As we saw yesterday, he had him come into this land of Canaan, and then he caused him to move from place to place from one end of the country to the other without knowing where his dwelling place was. But did he set up his tent? Did he set up some order in his household? He has to make a sudden change and go in another direction. Is he urged on by some impulse or anxiety? He certainly is not. Does he have some curiosity that incites him to move from place to place, like many people will live the lives of pilgrims and move from day to day? Now it is quite certain that Abraham would have preferred to be at peace and govern his household if he had had some small corner where to settle down. So when he pulls up stakes, he does so out of necessity and against his will. That too is a new test of his faith, for that is not the only time God tested him that way, as we saw yesterday that he kept him in suspense by not letting him know what was to become of him. But when he saw he would be able to rest, God suddenly moved him, as if a blast of a trumpet signalled that he had to change places. And that did not happen just once, but twice and even more times. Moses tells us Abraham changed lodgings in a short time, in no time at all, not just a short distance away, but he left one region for another, an unknown region, and not every time the mood struck him. He was not like many who, on a whim, change everything. Today one job, tomorrow another. And then there are others who want to change locations every minute. They say, 'What am I doing? I am wasting away here. I have to go somewhere else to see if I can find my place.'

Abraham experienced nothing like that, as we have said. That being the case, if it pleases God for us to be pilgrims all of our lives and subject to every wind of change, let us learn not to be shaken. We Christians must be characterized by these two things, on the surface seemingly contradictory, but in fact complementary: in the first place, our faith remains strong and is so firmly rooted that if God plays with us as with a ball tossed about in the air, the steadfastness of our faith never varies. Yet, let us be ready to depart, like a bird on a branch, and if God is leading us, may he not grant us a place of repose, but may he dislodge us. When we think we have reached some dwelling place, let us still endure being pilgrims, vagabonds, as we quoted yesterday in the passage from Paul, who gives us that teaching (cf. *Heb.* 11:13). That, I say, is what we must remember first.

And everything is confirmed for us by Abraham's example. Scripture does not say simply that he went from one place to another, but that, in the second place, he also set up an altar (cf. *Gen.*

12:8). And that was enough since he had a revelation proclaiming solemnly that God's appearing to him was a special blessing. But after dedicating his house to God, which was like a sanctuary and a temple in which God is honoured, he is sorely tried when he is chased from it and not allowed by God to worship him in it. Yet he continues to persevere unerringly. Although he is unable to enjoy any respite, he still shows that he does not distance himself from God. When he leaves a place, he does not do so to change his religion or to forget God, but he always does so to draw nearer to him.

What is more, it is very likely that Abraham, although it is not stated, was chased out by his neighbours because of their hatred of scruples, for we know that men become angry when someone refuses to agree with them on how to worship. So it is possible that Abraham was chased away for that reason and that his outward worship was a clear challenge to their idols because he was making it known that he did not want to be like the Canaanites and all the others who had corrupted the worship of God. Knowing that his actions made him odious, he still continued his practice. Why? He prefers God's honour to his life and is well aware that we must not take the liberty of exempting ourselves from God's commands. Whatever danger we may perceive and whatever threat Satan and the world pose for us, the worship of God takes precedence over all else. So it is not without cause that Moses repeats that Abraham did not forsake the worship of God and continued to proclaim that the living God had appeared to him, that it was to him that he was adhering, and that it was because of him that he renounced all the idols men had fashioned and invented. That again is what we have to remember.

Finally, he says that Abraham was not only constrained to move from one region to some unknown place, but that he had to leave Canaan completely. And the reason for that was certainly to make him renounce God a hundred thousand times, had he not been fortified with a wondrous power. For God caused him to leave the land of his birth. He said to him, 'Come and inhabit the land that I will show you.' He goes into the land. He inhabits it. He goes and comes. Thus, as God shifts him from one side to another, he endures it all patiently and would even tear himself to pieces in order to remain obedient to God. And although he experiences some periods of severe difficulty, he attributes it to the anxiety of his flesh and to God's delay in showing him why he had called him. When he is living in the land, he is peaceable and he labours. He endures a great deal. He is tormented. He is chased out. He is rejected. And by faith he overcomes it all. But when he is forced to leave the land to which God had led him, it seems that he had to leave God behind because he had abandoned him. That is the way people could have judged the appearance that God had intended to deceive Abraham and give him an empty hope when he took him from the land of Canaan.

Now we will have to put this into practice until the end. Let us consider how vulnerable we are and how easily we fall into temptation. If we encounter the slightest obstacle in the world, we think all is lost, and immediately this wrongheaded notion pops into our mind: 'What does God mean? Why did he promise me that? Is this now the reward I expected? Why does he say that he will be near all those who call upon him, but I am gaining nothing even though I have sought him diligently?' We will never suffer a trial without having such diabolical notions that show that unbelief is so deeply rooted in our hearts that we will never be freed from them as long as we are in this world. And there will not be just those kinds of thoughts that the devil puts into our heads, but there will be grumblings and expressions of contempt. Now let us consider a trial like the least of those experienced by Abraham. It is sure that we will not find one, not a hundredth part of one, and yet we see he overcame them all.

Subsequently the text says that Abraham went to Egypt to sojourn there (cf. *Gen.* 12:10), that is, to live for a while. Again we see how it appears that God intended to annul all the promises he had made to Abraham, although he remains in Canaan in the integrity of his faith, steadfast, a pilgrim in the land. And even though he understands that famine is chasing him from that place, he always remains confident that God did not intend to disappoint his expectations. Now the rest of the story cannot be explained at this time.

Let us follow that example so closely that when we have many opportunities to stray from the narrow road, we will always have our eyes fixed on God and aspire to the heritage he proposes for us, and let us make every effort to draw nearer to it until he completely gathers us in.

Now let us bow before the majesty of our gracious God in acknowledgment of our faults, praying that he will be pleased to cleanse us of them and forget them so that they will not count against us. And may he so mortify us in all our thoughts and feelings that, after renouncing all our lusts and all that is repugnant to his holy calling, we will be governed by his Holy Spirit so that we will walk in this world in such a way that we will hold steadfastly to the path he sets before us without deviating from it to the left or to the right. And let us have such strength and constancy that we will always continue in his service and overcome all the hindrances which confront us, those times when he will hold our hand, and may he lift us above the entire world so that we may say truly from our hearts that we are citizens of heaven, that it is there that our treasure lies, and that our whole soul is given to that pursuit. May he grant that grace not only to us but to all the peoples and nations on earth.

56

Weakness and Humiliation, Troubles and Dangers: God's Invitation to Depend on and Follow His Guidelines

Wednesday, 7 February 1560

And there was a famine in the land: and Abram went down into Egypt to sojourn there; for the famine was grievous in the land. And it came to pass, when he was come near to enter into Egypt, that he said unto Sarai his wife, Behold now, I know that thou art a fair woman to look upon: Therefore it shall come to pass, when the Egyptians shall see thee, that they shall say, This is his wife: and they will kill me, but they will save thee alive. Say, I pray thee, thou art my sister: that it may be well with me for thy sake; and my soul shall live because of thee (Gen. 12:10-13).

Yesterday we saw the kind of trial that Abraham might have had when God snatched him almost by force from the country to which he had called him and which he had assigned to him as a place to dwell, for it was the same as if God had changed his mind, in appearance, and had reversed everything Abraham had expected. There we have a poor old and decrepit man who, because he had been commanded to do so, left his country with at least the hope that after his death, God would make the change of countries worthwhile. Although he is a foreigner all his life, he rests in what he is told, namely, that his seed will possess the earth even though he has no children (cf. *Gen.* 12:7). But his faith overcomes all that might have come to his mind and caused him to reverse his course. But when famine forces him to go into Egypt and leave the country to which God had led him as if by the hand, it seems that he has reached such an extremity that there is no longer a way to obtain what God had promised him before.

But the fact remains that he continues to hold fast the promise which is given to him despite the fact it seemed to have been completely withdrawn. But we can surmise from this comment which Moses makes that he came into Egypt to be a foreigner, for it is not his intention to return to his country, but his heart remains attached to the land of Canaan because he knows that God wants him to live there. Nevertheless, it is impossible for him to live there at the time, for otherwise he would die of hunger and want. So he goes into Egypt with the confidence that that country is like a pledge that God will not default on his promise. Now it is true that this pledge slips from his hands and he is deprived of it, but he is content with the simple word, just as our faith can be approved only if we are content with God's simple truth even if all else fails.

In addition, we also have to note that this trial was all the more grievous and bitter because he had left a fertile and abundant land if there ever was one, even according to the pagans who wrote about it. Furthermore, he was not at all poor there, for we have seen that he had some possessions and substance. He had family. He had menservants and maidservants and animals (cf. *Gen.* 12:5). Consequently, because he was well-to-do there and had advantages in the country of his birth, he must have been all the more distressed when he sees himself besieged by death, so to speak, because of the famine, for he was not accustomed to suffering poverty. We even see that the inhabitants of the country stay close together for mutual assistance. The one who used to have animals and a lot of people has no intermediary. Even though he has money, he nonetheless enjoys no sense of calm, for we know that in times of scarcity, each person keeps to himself. There is such distrust that if someone has wheat in his granary, he keeps it well hidden and locked up, for it seems that death threatens the richest.

So there we have Abraham pressed by extremities beyond all others. Consequently, he had to be armed in every situation with superhuman power and strengthened by God's Holy Spirit, or he would have failed a hundred times. That is especially worth noting because, as we mentioned before, we are such delicate creatures that we can endure almost nothing. And when we encounter some difficulty, we think we deserve some exemption in God's sight because he ought to excuse us from more since he knows our frailty. That is the way we react. But the fact is that we must follow Abraham if we are to be considered children of God because he is the father of all believers (cf. *Gen.* 12:3; 17:4; *Rom.* 4:11). So we must conform ourselves to his life when he shows us the way to obey God; otherwise, boast as we will that we are believers, we will be denied by God and his angels unless we keep fellowship with our father Abraham and follow his example according to the measure of our faith. And if we cannot reach his level of attainment, we must still work at achieving it.

Therefore, although men find themselves under constraints after living bountifully and God so cuts back on their rations that they subsist on scanty fare, whereas they had been accustomed to enjoying a table well furnished with all the trimmings, let them learn to control themselves with such restraint that they can thank God with will and spirit as if they had all the abundance and variety in the world. And even if we should have to endure poverty and want, let us be aware that we are not more privileged than our father Abraham. All the more reason, then, that those who have always been of low estate and little influence should not be grieved when they experience great difficulty in earning their bread and, often finding the cupboard bare, do not know what they are to eat. For if Abraham, after enjoying many comforts, was not overcome by dearth, what will be the lot of those who are surely thoroughly accustomed to hard times because God has long held them on a short leash? So let us learn from that example not to miss what we have left behind.[1] There are some in that situation. Even though they have nothing, they continue to have affections for a native land. 'Oh everything was nice there. We had so many conveniences!'

We have a picture of our father Abraham, for he was in an earthly paradise, so to speak. The land of Chaldea was rich and fertile from one end to the other and very pleasant. In fact, when we look at everything closely, that was the place of the earthly paradise in which God placed the first man. Yet Abraham is taken out of it. So when we make a comparison between one country and another, we will be greatly distressed, for there are those who are easily angered and incensed against God and bitter, for they could be easy-going and peaceable depending on the situation in which God placed them. So they could eat the bread provided for them and thank God, but they take pleasure in talking about what they remember: 'We had this, and we had that.' Some will be able to remember enough about all that, and yet they will not be troubled about it. If they talk about one thing, it will be to say, 'For a while, God showed us his grace in this way and provided for us and treated us very gently, but now, if he is pleased to cut back on our provisions, well, we have to bear it patiently.' That, I say, is how some will recommit themselves to God even though life is not as

[1] Once again Calvin is surely addressing the French refugees who were fleeing repression and seeking haven in Geneva. Cf. a letter of Calvin's to Ambroise Blaurer dated early February and contemporary with this sermon. In it Calvin speaks of the French situation and the repression. See CO, letter 3161, col. 15.—*M.E.*

easy as they were used to. But others will take pleasure in suffering an unpleasant situation and chafing about it: 'Oh, I used to have such and such, and now I am much worse off. Life was easier then; now I am enduring a great deal.' Now let us note from what we are told about our father Abraham that such destructive thinking must be put out of our minds. Whatever our situation may be, let us follow the path God sets before us. And even though we sometimes encounter storms that uproot us in some way or another, may we always be restored to the right path, and may our affection never grow cold so that we turn away from what God proposes for us. That, in brief, is what we have to remember.

It is true Abraham was a stranger in the land of Canaan, as he was in Egypt, as Jacob states later.[2] Even so, he acknowledged the land of Canaan as his proper dwelling place. Egypt was a foreign country to him. Why so? Did he have lands or possessions in the land of Canaan? No. Did he have kinsmen or friends there? We know that he was unknown and that, in that land, he was like a person lost. After leaving the land of Chaldea, he renounced and practically forgot the place he was born. Why? Because God no longer wants him to be there. So Abraham puts out of his mind any thought which could turn him from God's calling. In the meantime, since the word was given to him, he will be lord of the land of Canaan, or his seed after him will be. That word is a bond which cannot be broken, a bond that is for him more powerful than all the ropes and chains in the world. He remains there like a captive in freely accepted and voluntary servitude. Inasmuch as God assigned that land to him, Abraham does not doubt that God will fulfil his promise. That, then, is how Abraham conducts himself among the Canaanites as if he had been born there. In fact, the word which was given to him is like a second birth. He had to

---

[2] The closest reference is in Genesis 47:28-30, where Jacob asks Joseph to bury him outside of Egypt, in the land of his fathers.—*M.E.*

become a new man and renounce both himself and everything he might cling to in Chaldea. So, because of the word, he possesses the land of Canaan as if he had been born there. As for the land of Egypt, good and productive as it was, where he might have been able to live in complete comfort, the fact is that he understood that God is calling him elsewhere. And that is why, despite the fact that necessity forces him to go into Egypt, he concludes that it will not be forever and that he will forthwith be able to have a way to live in the land of Canaan, that he will return there, and that Egypt will mean nothing to him. In that way, as I said, we are sufficiently taught and exhorted to close our eyes to every distraction that might turn as from the true path God is directing us to or that could cause us to stumble or impede our progress. Let none of that influence us, and let us be firmly resolved to obey God not for a day or a month, but with perseverance until the end.

And even if we can find many ways to rationalize our failings before men and they accept our pretence and outward appearance, and even if they have pity on us and forgive us because of our weakness when our trials are great, let us not think that, as a consequence, it will go easier for us before God. As we have seen previously, when things are difficult for us and even seem to be completely impossible, it is then that God is examining us and testing whether we have an unfaithful and hypocritical heart or whether we are walking in truth and integrity before him, preferring his will above all else. So much, then, for the point Moses makes about Abraham's withdrawing into Egypt.

And Moses even repeats his point to show the virtue of Abraham's faith better, for when he says that the famine was grievous, it is as if he were saying Abraham was not raised up for an insignificant event. So, many people today will convince themselves that there is a famine when they only have white bread to eat and wine to drink. For them, everything is lost. That is when they go take their chances elsewhere. So

Moses shows us that Abraham did not pull up stakes on a whim and that he suffered hunger and severe lack before departing, but it was only after he reached the end of endurance and was no longer able to do more and there was nothing left for himself or his animals, as if a whirlwind had snatched everything away. That was the circumstance that drove him to Egypt. From that we understand how difficult that trial was for him, but the hardest part was when Abraham had to depart from this country which had been assigned to him by the very mouth of God. We must always remember what was shown earlier, namely, that although God does not dislocate all believers and transfer them to another country, we must not settle down and make ourselves comfortable anywhere as if we were to stay there forever, but we must go and come according to God's pleasure. And that attitude must be practiced by those who would like to stay in one place, where some have to work the fields while others are engaged in other kinds of activities. Well, Abraham does not have that kind of choice. Even so, God always advises his people that they are not to cling to the world as if they were attached to it (cf. *Heb.* 11:13), but they must always be poised to depart, whenever it pleases him to have them go through open fields, facing the wind and the rain, not for just a day or a month, but throughout their lives, if they happen to be harassed by all nations and tossed from pillar to post, so to speak. May they learn to endure it.[3]

We come now to what Moses adds when Abraham is approaching Egypt. He says to his wife, 'I see that you are beautiful and will be desired by these people. Someone will want to have you and will kill me because of you if it is known that I am your husband. Then say that I am your brother so that they will leave me alone and favour me for your sake.' Moses here shows us that there is a flaw in Abraham's perfection. He was like an angel among men,

[3] This sermon could touch the numerous French refugees who had reached Geneva in the course of recent months, struggling through the countryside in bad weather—we are in February, let us remember—and who were facing the possibility of continuing their journey.—*M.E.*

but, even so, his weakness was revealed. This does not show us that his faith was overwhelmed or destroyed, but that the most perfect still harbour some vice and stain such that if God wanted to judge them rigorously, they would be condemned along with all their virtues. But in order to understand the end of this story and learn from it the lesson it contains, let us note that Abraham, as I have already said, was not overcome, nor was his faith, but he stumbled along the way. He did not go astray; he did not turn from the way; he always followed his calling; he always strove for his goal. But as a man who is walking can stumble along the way, if he comes upon a bad spot or is wearied beyond measure so that he can scarcely drag his feet, there is always the possibility, as I said, of a jarring encounter. Yet he continues to hold to his path. That is what happened to our father Abraham.

Now that is worth noting for several reasons. Those who have contempt for God, who are like vicious dogs which can only bark when they cannot bite, reproach Abraham for being a pimp for his wife in order to save his life. What kind of coward is he? Would not a courageous man prefer to die a hundred times than to expose himself to the shame of having a wife who is a prostitute, of seeing it with his own eyes, and of living with it? How is it, then, that anyone can prize so many virtues in that man? That is how Satan unleashes poisoned tongues to obscure the favours God has showered down on Abraham, as many as on any other living creature. But it is quite certain Abraham possessed love, which is incomprehensible to such scoundrels, for they have only their rotten lives and are so wrapped up in them that all their senses are in a stupor.

Now Abraham, as we have seen, did not waste his time with this world, its pleasures, its sensuality, its wealth, its ease, or anything else. In short, as we have said, he was truly passing through this world and aspiring after heaven. And how is it that he is now fearing so much for his life? It is not out of concern for his person. We have already said that all of Abraham's senses were collected and focused on the word which was given to him. He was a complete captive to that and did not wander from it a single step. He did not make the changes in his life, as do the wise of the world who want to arrange everything a hundred years after their death. Abraham was like a poor blind man who was allowing himself to be led by God's hand and, as I have mentioned, did not allow himself the liberty of letting his imagination go and wondering what might happen and what would become of one thing or another. The entirety of Abraham's wisdom, therefore, lay in obeying God, depending on his promises and taking refuge in them.

Let us now look at what God promised him: that that land would be given to his seed and that in him all the nations of the earth would be blessed (cf. *Gen.* 12:3). We see here an Abraham who realized he was wretched because he and all the rest have been corrupted in Adam. So he knows there is a curse upon him and all men because all are enemies of God and cut off from his righteousness (cf. *Rom.* 5:10). Now God cannot renounce himself, and we are filled with sin and corruption. Thus God cannot love us and, as we have seen, he disavows us because we are not worthy of being considered among his children. Abraham, realizing that, has the promise by which he is removed from the general confusion of the entire human race. Now God told him that in his seed all the nations of the earth would be blessed. Consequently, if his trust is in God's word, his life is necessarily more precious to him than the whole world. We are not talking about a life of thirty years or even forty that might remain to him when he might have lived five hundred more, but about God who, when he withdraws him from this world and the earthly pilgrimage, shows him that his inheritance is in heaven. How? By that hope he had given him that in him all nations of the earth would be blessed. So he sees that his life involves the redemption and eternal salvation of the world, as much for himself as for others. With that understanding, he is not concerned for redeeming himself for a short period of time and prolonging his days for an unknown period. He does not spend his time on anything transitory, but he knows that if he is killed, all will be lost and the Redeemer of the world, in whom his hope for salvation lies, will be lost at the same time.

So that is why Abraham prizes his life so highly and why he is content to suffer the shame of having his wife taken from him when someone abuses her as a prostitute. Yet it is quite certain that Abraham was not excused in the least. His faith is good and holy. And even in that it is clear that his faith was tested better. It is certain that if he had had a different consideration than this life, he would have preferred to have himself killed and even suffer a hundred deaths, had it been possible, than to endure the degradation of having his wife snatched from him, who is even a kinswoman. If there had been only the matter of kinship, it would have been unbearably distressing. But if he had been cut off from the other half of his person and had suffered such dishonour and shame that his wife was a prostitute, and if he had been exposed to mockery as a consequence, it is certain that, had he been attached to this world, he would not have valued his life more highly than his wife's chastity. Consequently, when he wants to redeem her, it is certain he does so because of the affection and zeal that he has for obtaining the fulfilment of God's promises. So we see in this fault and this weakness which befell him the strength of his faith, which is indeed admirable. It is as if he renounced what was dearest and most delightful to him in the world in order to acquire what he expected and hoped for from God.

When the meaning of the word faith is discussed and how it can be recognized, we will always come to this point, namely, that we will disregard everything that is present and we will not be deluded by all of the enticements of this world and led from the path God shows us. Abraham had that kind of faith.

We already see in that an act worthy of great praise, wherein Abraham is ready to leave his wife in order to redeem his life. As we have said, we must not imagine that Abraham was held back at this point because he loved the earth, but that he was waiting until God raised up seed for him and accomplished what he had said. So this is the point where Abraham failed: that was only one way. And that is why I gave the example of a man who will follow his path, even though it is painful. A man will be obliged to take a trip. The road is long. There will be many hardships. The road will be difficult. In addition, he will have to jump over hedges and walk among thorns and brush. The road will be rough and he will be more exhausted after a half mile than he would have been after a dozen miles on an open road. That is Abraham's situation. Even so, although the road was very difficult and he encountered many obstacles and hardships, his goal was always before his eyes, and he never wavered.

In addition, he stumbled, as I said, in this particular, but he did not fall and then say, 'What am I to do? I have to go back and start over again.' So he was not in a hurry to go astray, but after falling, he was immediately put back on his feet, and God had a hand in it, as we will see, for he had pity on his servant's weakness since he never permits his own to remain in their fallen condition, but he lifts them up even though they stumble and fall hard. Even so, Abraham held fast to God's promise. Yet, having that, he has a lot. And then Abraham always had his eyes on what God was calling him to and he followed his course. He failed only by creating for himself a procedure which was not allowed. He was supposed to place everything in God's providence. If we ask, 'What should he have done since he found himself in such a perplexing situation?' It is clear he would have been killed. And what would have happened to the promise he had been given? At that point, as I have said, he should have had recourse to God and closed his eyes, as he had done at the outset, and said, 'Oh Lord, you have to reach out to me, for what will happen if you do not help me? Here I am on the edge of a cliff. Even your promises will be blotted out. And I am helpless. And because I hoped in you, I will have worked in vain while wanting to obey you. So, Lord, since I find myself in such a hard place, show that you never forget and abandon your people.'

So Abraham had to pray that way and adhere to what God had impressed upon his heart previously: that he was powerful. For this attribute which God had declared of himself was to mitigate those times of anguish and distrust which tested Abraham. In fact, we have to follow the same rule, namely, that as often as God calls himself all powerful (cf. *Gen.* 17:1; *Exod.* 6:3; *Rev.* 1:8), he is judging the world and, with all knowledge, is disposing of all things in accordance with his will. He did not say that just to magnify himself and give lustre to his glory, but so that we may be sustained by his power. And although we see everything in confusion in the world, let us not at the same time relinquish our rest in him. Why not? Because God has means at his disposal that we do not know about. Therefore, Abraham was not to wonder how he could preserve his life, but he was to place all of that in God's hand and surrender everything to him. It is God's responsibility to pull us back from abysses when we are about to fall into them, pull us back in such a way that it is like a dream, just as the psalm says when its speaks of the restoration of the church, that the faithful were as in a dream, for God thus overcomes all their experiences (cf. *Psa.* 107:26-28). Such must be the experience of each particular individual when God delivers us from an unusual situation which we would never have imagined or understood.

So then we see Abraham's fault. It now remains for us to profit from this story. In the first place, let us learn not to be pleased, as if our faith were perfect, when we virtuously obey God, when we valiantly struggle against many attacks, and let us not be so filled with pride that we convince ourselves that we have arrived at some level of perfection, for if we could achieve a hundred times more than anyone else, Abraham has still surpassed us all. And yet we see in his stumbling that there was still something to criticize, that he was weak, and that he was not so cleansed of what belonged to his flesh and his nature that there was no remnant of it in him. He himself would never have thought that he had wandered in that way from God's will. He did it indirectly. That, then, is a shortcoming so deeply hidden within him that he is not aware of it but is suddenly caught off guard by it.

So let us not pat ourselves on the back, but let us always examine what is in us, and then we will see clearly that we are very far from our goal and that the powers that God has placed in us are mingled among the many vices by which we are still marred. And when we recognize our faults and are humbled and displeased by them, let us learn to practice what David says, for when he says, 'Blessed is the man whose transgression is forgiven and whose faults are covered, and whose iniquities are pardoned', he adds, 'and in whose spirit there is no deceit' (cf. *Psa.* 32:1-2). Now it would seem on the surface that that comment was superfluous or that David suddenly changed horses in midstream, as they say. But when saying that, he shows us that we sense how indebted we are to God, how we need his mercy and his support throughout our lives, that is, whenever we willingly acknowledge our vices. Otherwise, why is it that men are without hope and God's mercy means nothing to them? The reason is that hypocrisy so blinds them that they do not recognize their need. So that is where we have to begin: there is no deceit in our minds, that is, our senses are not so deadened that we deceive ourselves and convince ourselves that we are what we are not. So much for that point.

Thus, when our hypocrisy has been purged and our eyes have been opened and all our senses have been awakened so that we know what kind of people we are, we will indeed be aware, as I have said, that many weaknesses and imperfections remain in us. And even though we do not recognize them, God knows them, for he sees incomparably more clearly than we do.

What we have to remember, then, is that if Abraham, who had an angelic faith, that is, a faith that is more than human, since he is the pattern of all of God's children—if he fell short, what will happen to us? So let us learn to back away from such a danger and not be too wise and be unduly curious about what is to happen and consequently seek consultations and make our plans based on imaginative thinking. There is nothing more at variance with faith than when men let themselves consult together and think, 'We will do this, and then we will do that.' They are, I say, preoccupied with their own notions. It is as if they are possessed when they think they can arrange everything. So when men discuss their speculations among themselves and say, 'This is what will happen, and that will follow,' then they are ready to deliberate. And when they engage in their deliberations, they are closing the door to God. They want to be wise in their own thinking. And unfortunately, as a consequence, they have to stumble and fall. It is true that Abraham only stumbled, as we pointed out, but even so God helped him miraculously. Yet let us be careful not to abuse God's patience. So the real remedy for remaining steadfast and not weakening and not stumbling from the right path, is not to resist when we find ourselves in difficulties, in times of discontentment and worry and care, but to commend it all to God's providence because everything is in his hand.

It is true that when we realize God is vigilant in our behalf and has taken us into his care, he will sustain us until the end, but we must not, as a consequence, let that keep us from utilizing the means he has placed in our hands and permits us to use. Faith does not make us unfeeling or stupid, but God joins the spirit of counsel and discretion with faith and will show his servants how they are to walk, and when they are perplexed, they will see more clearly than all those who have a broad experience in the world. Still, let us be careful not to become involved in enterprises and deliberations that conform to our senses and notions. Whenever we do so, as I have said, we will plunge into an abyss we will never be able to get out of. In those times we will immediately look for unacceptable means, for it is not for the entire undertaking that our intention is good and that the act itself is approved by God. I am talking about the main undertaking. There are also incidental and accompanying acts. So when we want to follow the path that God proposes for us, we must not follow just any path, but we must let ourselves be completely guided by him. And, as I said, we must find our rest in God's providence, where there is no lack of acceptable means.

So if we are at our wits' end, as we say, and if we have looked for solutions, if we do not find that God gives us a way to escape the continuing danger which holds us back, we must return to what Abraham will say later after learning in God's school: 'The Lord will provide' (cf. *Gen.* 22:8).

Here, then, is the second thing we need to remember about this passage: if it falls our lot to be terrified and discouraged in the face of troubles and dangers, as we all must pass that way, God wants to humble us by those circumstances and at the same time draw us to himself so that we will learn to surrender our entire lives to him. Whenever we do that, let us not try to be too ingenious or clever, and especially let us be on guard against putting God's word to the test in any circumstance, and let us not be bold and foolhardy like those who are always adding to what God declares with his mouth, but let us realize that God is restraining us and does not wish to let our appetites run free but wishes to keep us in his embrace when we are deprived of means which are in conformity with his word and are clearly given to us by him. When we realize that, God will be appropriately honoured. As for us, we will experience that there is nothing better than to cling to him and thank him that all the wisdom in the world does not come close to his counsel, which we cannot comprehend and which he employs in such a way that we will be transported with admiration and confess that he has always surpassed our faith, great as it may have been, and that our hope was empty in comparison with the outcome which he has made known to us. That is how we must walk, in part, in accordance with the example of our father Abraham and, in part, in the knowledge that his failure, which cannot be excused, warns us so that we will be the more encouraged to call upon our God and let his word and Holy Spirit guide us.

> Now let us bow before the majesty of our gracious God in acknowledgment of our faults, praying both that he will make us so aware of them that we will be brought to a true repentance and that we will work every day to withdraw from our fleshly affections and everything that keeps us from obeying his holy word. Let us take more and more advantage of our faith and our fear of his name until we finish our course and are gathered into his eternal kingdom, where we will enjoy the fruit of the victory he has promised us and which we will obtain by his power, provided we do not fail along the way. So let us all now say, God Almighty, heavenly Father, we acknowledge and confess as true that we are not worthy of lifting our eyes to heaven to present ourselves before your face.

57

Humility: Holding Desires and Impulses Captive

Thursday, 8 February 1560

And it came to pass, when he was come near to enter into Egypt, that he said unto Sarai his wife, Behold now, I know that thou art a fair woman to look upon: Therefore it shall come to pass, when the Egyptians shall see thee, that they shall say, This is his wife: and they will kill me, but they will save thee alive. Say, I pray thee, thou art my sister: that it may be well with me for thy sake; and my soul shall live because of thee. And it came to pass, that, when Abram was come into Egypt, the Egyptians beheld the woman that she was very fair. The princes also of Pharaoh saw her, and commended her before Pharaoh: and the woman was taken into Pharaoh's house. And he entreated Abram well for her sake: and he had sheep, and oxen, and he asses, and menservants, and maidservants, and she asses, and camels (Gen.12:11-16).

YESTERDAY WE SAW that Abraham preferred to abandon his wife rather than to lose his life because he was waiting for the blessing God had promised him and he knew that his life was more precious. So his intention is good and holy, for there was a singular value in him that was worth suffering the shame which he subjected himself to and dying a hundred times for, but he still fell short in respect of how to proceed. For as we have shown, he did not show God the honour that belonged to him at all times and in all places. That is, when depending on God's providence, he was ready for any situation that might occur. So that is how Abraham acted too hastily when trying to fix the situation with an illicit solution. He was nonetheless guilty on that point, even though he did not go completely wrong and his faith tended in the right direction.

And since one evil attracts another, there is deceit, which cannot be excused, for he tells his wife, Sarai, to say that she is his sister or kinswoman. For these words 'brothers' and 'sisters' in Hebrew signify other degrees of kinship, such as uncles' relation to nephews, nieces, and first cousins. In that way, it is quite true that Sarai, as we saw in the preceding chapter, was Abraham's sister, for she was a rather close relation, but the response Abraham puts in her mouth is not without fiction, that is, it is not without trickery or deceit. It is not a lie, if we wanted to define it as knowingly putting something forth as false. We will not say that, in that sense, either Abraham or Sarai lied, for what she says about being his sister is not against the truth, for she was his kinswoman. Still that equivocation is not without some vice, for we must not dispute about words as do the sophists, who think they deceive God with their crafty and deceitful ploys, but we must always deal with the substance of the matter.

Speech is given to us so we can communicate with one another. Consequently, the language of pagans is called the heart's image. And the truth is that we also experience it. When some speak to others, they have means by which to express their emotions and thoughts, which were hidden and unknown. Since nature shows us that God endowed us with speech so that we can express what is in our hearts, it is certain the person who pretends to be what he is not abuses the gift of language and rejects the order of nature.

Consequently, Abraham, in that situation, failed again. All the more must we learn to keep ourselves on a short leash because as soon as we veer slightly from the path, one evil attracts another, and another, and another, endlessly, and vices become so entangled that the person who thought he glimpsed a very small and insignificant sin in himself finds himself enveloped in a much greater one, and he will finally be convicted of heaping evil upon evil. That is what happened to our father Abraham.

Now when we look at such a patriarch, a man outstanding in all virtues, who is presented to everyone as a mirror of holiness and perfection, and see that he forgot who he was, what will happen to us by comparison? At this point, it is not a matter of using Abraham as an excuse, as do many who think they are at least halfway absolved when they point out that the most saintly were not without vices. But the Holy Spirit shows us the opposite is true. We have to be on our guard and walk even more carefully. In short, that example shows us how necessary it is for us to adhere to the teaching in which Paul condemns all lies and adds that we are to speak the truth with one another (cf. *Eph.* 4:25). In other words, there is to be no pretence and deceit. And Scripture, not without reason, speaks of a double tongue when we do not speak plainly and sincerely (cf. *1 Tim.* 3:8). But that is not the whole story, as I have said. Words cannot be blamed, but if the heart does not respond and there is no conformity between our inner thoughts and our speech, we are already condemned. And then, when our language is doubtful and distorted, people do not know what to make of it because of ambiguity, for it sometimes happens that a person will not be able to express his thoughts clearly. But when we intend to speak knowingly and willingly with a double tongue and no one can make heads or tails of what we say, that too is an inexcusable vice. Therefore, let us realize that Moses is testifying that Abraham is condemned here so that we may know that no one is so perfect that he does not go astray, that he is without shortcomings, and that he does not need God's mercy.

In addition, Moses is also teaching us to be more diligent to walk in fear and apprehension, for if the most saintly of those who have set out to dedicate themselves completely to God are still held back by some weakness or other, how will we manage, we who are far removed from their zeal and can scarcely follow in their footsteps at a great distance? That ought to motivate us not to think highly of ourselves.

Also, for the future, let us be advised not to forgive ourselves of a vice, however small, for the moment the devil finds a very small opening, it is certain he will make it larger and gain entrance when we are not thinking about him. So we must pay even closer attention to what we are told here.

It is true that some have gone to a great deal of trouble to excuse Abraham and, as I have already said, if we do not give attention to simple statements, we will not say that Abraham's response contained the substance of a lie. And we will likewise see that that is the way he answered Pharaoh. Yet he did not try to justify himself completely. As for us, because God does not engage in clever debates and the kinds of subtleties we invent, let us consider what he requires of us. In other words, let us not misrepresent situations, and let our words serve to converse plainly and simply with men.

Let us look now at what induced Abraham to misrepresent his relationship with Sarai. It was a fear that arose from distrust. There are two things to note here. One is that we must not have too great a fear, but we must walk as our Lord guides us while not carelessly creating for ourselves many perils, as is our tendency. All of us do indeed seek rest, and we avoid cares, troubles, and displeasing and perplexing things to the extent we can; yet we bring them upon ourselves. Each of us is glad to do so; each of us engages in them;

each of us plunges into them; in a word, each of us drowns himself in them (cf. *Rom.* 7:19). Therefore, because God cares for us, let us learn to be confident that he will provide many things for what could happen to us.

Now that is not to say we must not be completely unaware, like logs of wood, of what is happening, for our Lord, as we mentioned earlier, has many reasons for wanting us to experience some concern that will wake us up. It is all for our training, for we are not to live here below without some feeling or concern. So God wants men to apply themselves and use the abilities he has given them. And that is why he gives them opportunities to think about them, to take counsel, and to provide for their own undertakings. In that way he counsels us to acknowledge what our state and condition are and realize that we are always surrounded by dangers and need his protection, that we must be encouraged to call upon him and always hasten to him for aid and give him the glory for it, that our lives are suspended by a thread unless they are sustained by him, and that we would be immediately defeated without his power. That is why we said we must be keenly aware of the dangers which threaten us.

And then there is the matter of restraint, which means that we must heed our Lord's exhortation not to worry about the next day (cf. *Matt.* 6:34). In other words, we must avoid our customary concern about changing situations, those times when we say, 'What is apt to happen? What will become of this? What will be the result of that?' When we are disturbed by such fears, it is certain we are guilty of a lack of faith. We are miserable enough when we think only of living through a day, for we cannot reach midnight before something else angers and torments us. And what will happen when we take note of all the annoying things which might happen to us afterward? What kind of burden will that be? Is that not enough to break our backs? So let us learn to be calm and peaceful and to be in fear, not frightened like those who are afraid of their shadow or at the sound of a falling leaf. And if a storm arises, they are so frightened they cannot be comforted. Let us to be wary of such fear, but if we experience fear, let it be directed toward remedying an evil, as God gives us the means.

And then, distrusting our wisdom and the things that come to mind, let us make God our principal refuge, and let us make it our primary prayer that he will guide us with his counsel and wisdom. In addition to that, although he guides us in such a way that he does not permit us to help ourselves, may he supplement our deficiency with his strength, and may he so work in us that we will know that while we slept, he was being vigilant in our behalf (cf. *Job* 29:4; *Psa.* 31:23; *Psa.* 141:3). That, then, is a very useful point to note so that we will not be unduly disturbed by fear,[1] for it is then that we know we are pitiable.

Then we need to observe that the fears which torment men often come from doubts they fashioned in their own minds, truly on the spur of the moment, when they distrust one another. It is true that until God remakes us, a hidden malice will remain in those who think they are more upright and sincere. It is also true that we will see a very great difference in men's dispositions. Some men will be so inclined to evil and so filled with deceit that they will always have their nets cast to trap those who deal with them. In a word, we will always encounter in our own experience people who are totally given to that kind of evil. Others have more integrity. We can trust their word a little bit. When we deal with them, we can trust what they say. Even so, the root of pretence and lying is hidden in men's hearts until God purges them. And since there is still some integrity around, that is a special gift of God because he does not want men to be crafty and deceitful. What would that be like? What kind of confusion would we have if every

[1] Man cannot find rest apart from God, a leitmotif of Calvin.—*M.E.*

one of us had an evil and perverse spirit, as we see in some people? It is certain it would have been better for us all to be exterminated on the first day, for only despicable animals think of nothing but entrapping and deceiving. But those who are upright and maintain some sense of integrity are honest because God keeps a bridle on them. In any case, we would do well to distrust all men until God has put his hand on them, that is, until he guides them with his Holy Spirit and we can recognize that they have been renewed and are governed by the grace of our Lord Jesus Christ than by Adam's corruption. That much for that point.

But that distrust must also be moderated, even corrected, for it is said that love is not suspicious.[2] So when we are inclined to judge unfavourably and have great doubt, we always imagine: 'Now there is someone who might do me harm. And this fellow might have a grudge and do me some dirt.' So when we imagined such things, it is certain we wrong our neighbours. And if love is the perfect bond of unity (cf. *Col.* 3:14), as Paul calls it, it is certain we do a grave injustice when we are suspicious. For this passage that I quoted from Paul cannot lie (cf. *1 Cor.* 13:5). So if we do not wish to be unduly fearful of what others might do to us, let us learn not to judge others wrongly. Let us learn, I say, not to judge wrongly, but let us interact with people in such a way that we consider that they, for their part, walk uprightly and honourably among us, for these suspicions often come from the fact that the wicked think others are like themselves. And in fact we will never see people more suspicious than those who lie, cheat, and defraud. For people like that think everyone is like them. And in this way they are never taken in, and they find fault with everything and everyone.

[2] Cf. 1 Corinthians 13:5. The spelling of *'soupçon'* [suspicion] and its derivatives varied greatly in this passage. This word must have seemed strange to the copyist. In his commentary, Calvin does not speak of suspicion; he even picks up Erasmus, who translates *'non est fastidiosa'* [is not disdainful].—*M.E.*

But there will be some who are sincere, yet they continue to be suspicious because they see that the world is perverse and that they do not know what they can depend on. As a consequence, this vice is much too common. That is why we need to look for a remedy, for we also see the bad consequences which result from that vice, as we see in this passage. In short, we make great progress when we learn to commend ourselves to God and pray that he will protect us from all the craftiness and subtle deceptions of the wicked, among whom we are. And while we walk in simplicity, let us be careful not to entertain suspicions unless someone gives us a reason to do so, and let us not project that wrong on those who have been trustworthy and honest with us, at least not until we experience their malice, their betrayals, their lies or deceptions. So let us not condemn those whose vices we have no knowledge of, and let us remember this admonition of our Lord Jesus Christ: 'Judge not, that you be not judged' (cf. *Matt.* 7:1; *Luke* 6:37). For he shows us that when we rashly condemn those who have given us no reason to, we well deserve to be condemned just as rashly.

And there is this too: judgment without mercy will be accorded the person who is not kind and gentle toward his brothers (cf. *Matt.* 7:2; 18:23-35), for when we judge adversely, it is certain we provoke God's wrath and are not worthy of his granting us his clemency and benevolence to help us along.

That, then, is what we can learn from what happened to our father Abraham before he says, 'I know you are a beautiful woman; and when the Egyptians see you, they will kill me.' He is thinking he will be killed. Why? There is no doubt that he had heard bad reports about that country. And it was not when he was forced to go there because of the famine that he asked what kind of nation it was. And the fact remains that that did not completely excuse him. Whatever report he received before hand, he should not have condemned those he did not know. We will see later that there was good reason for him to doubt and distrust the Egyptians, but he still cannot, in this passage, be excusable, but he has to be partially excusable because he had to become guilty. If he had frankly confessed that Sarai was his wife, that fact would have been a veil of chastity to protect her, in the same way Abimelech speaks of it later (cf. *Gen.* 20:16). So when Abraham experiences fear and misrepresents the situation, it is as if he removed the veil of chastity from his wife and left her there exposed and available. Consequently, the evil arose because of him, his excessive fear, and the unjust suspicion which manipulated him. That much, then, for that.

At this point, we can ask how Sarai could be considered beautiful at that time. Although a woman may possess the most outstanding beauty possible, she still has to be getting wrinkled since she is over sixty years old, and at that age you would not find beauty to say that you desired it. So it does not seem that she had such a great appearance that Abraham feared that his wife's beauty might be the cause of his death, for she was, as we have already said, over sixty. But we can easily conclude that God had kept her beautiful. Even though that is not seen as ordinary, it is true that a woman without children will remain in vigour longer than one who has been fertile. We know that women decline a great deal through multiple child births, so much that their strength wanes, and their face also shows they are no longer what they used to be. That is widely observed to be true. Even so, we must not doubt that it was a special gift of God that Sarai retained her beauty.

There is this also, that at that time, because men and women lived longer, God also gave them greater strength and energy, as if he refreshed them every day. How does it happen that today a man would appear old at the age of fifty?[3] It is because our lives

---

[3] Calvin had had his fiftieth birthday on July 10 of the preceding year.—*M.E.*

are growing short. Consequently, every division of life must play its part and God has to give less to the first quarter and less to the second quarter until we come to the fourth. That accounts for the deterioration that we see today, that men are brought low in short order.

Now we must not be astonished if men had a greater vigour at that time than today, but still, beyond that, we must remember what we have already touched upon, namely, that God had preserved Sarai in her beauty just as he renewed Abraham in such a way that, after his wife's death, he was as robust as a young man who will beget a great lineage, as we will see later (cf. *Gen.* 23:1-25:4), and yet it is certain that he was previously decrepit. Sarai also demonstrates it, for she thinks it is a dream and a fable that she is to conceive inasmuch as she was no longer living with her husband (cf. *Gen.* 18:12). By that I mean the bed and that they were, because of their old age, like a couple living apart. Nevertheless, as we have said, Abraham was rejuvenated by a special gift of God. So let us conclude that beauty was maintained in Sarai. We do not know why unless God still wanted to nourish the hope he was giving his servant so he would not wonder about his wife's sterility and would wait patiently to have a lineage in accordance with the promise. Now although that beauty resulted from God's pure liberality and showed that he was favourable to his servant Abraham, we see that her beauty cost him dearly.

So let us note that all of the evidences of God's love have something unknown mixed in with them, that is, some temporal evidences of his love in this earthly life are always accompanied by something bitter. And that is so the faithful will not become intoxicated with their delights when our Lord provides them with some advantage, gives them some prosperity, and causes them to rejoice in one thing and another. Let them not overly congratulate themselves and, as I have said, let them guard against that spiritual intoxication that Scripture condemns so roundly (cf. *Luke* 12:16-21). That is why our Lord allows his gifts to be often mixed with trying experiences.

We particularly note here how Sarai's beauty served to comfort Abraham in his affliction, as it was not at all incomprehensible that it would, but the fact is that it would have been much better for him not to have a wife who was so beautiful and so highly regarded. All the more, then, are we taught to be satisfied with mediocrity. There are those who would like for God to be a painter and fashion women for them the way they like them, but they will never be satisfied. This feature will be too big and that feature will be too small. And sometimes men will even precipitate their own filthiness and lechery by giving great attention to dressing and beautifying their wives and wishing they had what they do not have: 'I wish my wife had more of this and less of that.' Because our appetites are thus excessive, let us learn from this example to be satisfied with mediocrity. Let those who have wives love them chastely in loyalty to their marriage vows. When that love exists, it is certain men will not be overly stimulated by their capricious appetites and will not be displeased by their wives, for, as the saying goes, there are no ugly loves. But when men and women are filthy minded and when the husband does not love his wife and the wife does not love her husband, they are already perjured because they do not maintain the faithfulness and loyalty that they promised each other. So let us note that point once again.

And whenever we happen to have lustful desires and ask God to do this or that, let that bridle immediately restrain us. Indeed, when God gives me everything I wish for, what will happen? He will make me pay dearly for it. That is how our desires and wishes are tempered. In other words, when we know that, we could soon envy our own selves if our Lord gave us everything we fancy and followed our directions precisely and at our whim. It is certain we would be carried away and not know when to stop. That, then, is why we must remember this procedure.

Now Moses adds that the princes of the court, that is, the lords and the king's favourites, as they are called, after seeing the woman and finding her beautiful, come to Pharaoh and praise her. We can surmise from that what we have already mentioned, namely, that Sarai's beauty was singular. For in the kingdom of Egypt, there were also beautiful women. And every time a woman comes from a strange and unknown land, the news immediately comes to the king's ears. So some excellence had to exist. But this praise brings with it the suggestion of a pimping service. It is certain that the lords and great favourites at the court[4] did not prize Sarai's beauty except to gratify their king.

Now here we see that this corruption did not begin to reign in the courts, for princes want to be fawned over above all, and they want even more to be indulged and satisfied to the full extent of their desires. They also want everyone to bring them some device to excite them and provide them matter for indulging themselves even more. They want more than having their own lusts; they want someone to set those lusts on fire and fan them from every direction, and then they want to be presented with objects that excite them even more. Their passions are already at a fast boil, and they want the fire turned up a notch. A prince who is addicted to avarice and robbery will want someone to devise for him some new deceitful manoeuvres to garner more of the people's substance for himself and to come up with more fees and taxes. A prince who is given to gross sensuality will want everyone to talk to him about it

---

[4] The expression *'mignon de cour'*, used to characterize a royal favourite, is recent in the sixteenth century (cf. [the dictionaries of] Godfroy, Huguet, von Wartburg 6/11, p. 141, Littré). Calvin already uses it in 1544 in 'Excuse de Jehan Calvin à messieurs les Nicodemites', ed. Francis Higman, (London, 1970), p. 138. I thank the editor for communicating that reference.—*M.E.* French: *'grands mignons de la court.'*

and find ways to blunt the distinction between good and evil and remove all shame so that it seems normal and ordinary for women to be violated and so that lewd, vile, and filthy acts may be rampant everywhere. That is the way of kings.[5]

On the other hand, those who are against them never think about anything else than to get ahead, and as ambition drives them, they also prostitute themselves in every way possible. They do not care, provided they gain favour and advance themselves. That is the reason the ears of kings and princes are filled with every kind of enticement, whose purpose is to tempt them to indulge to excess, for they seek out evil and find it, especially, as I said, those who are trusted, those self-centred people who are led by ambition because they always want to rise higher. That is why they cast aside any thought of integrity and close their eyes to it. And the result of so much bowing and scraping in the courts of princes is the creation of disorder and confusion.

So since we see that this evil is ancient, let us not find it strange today if kings incline their ears to these flatteries which please and gratify them shamelessly. And even if the toadies make them believe that black is white so that they become increasingly hardened, let us not find it strange. It is true that that is a deplorable situation, but the fact remains that we are strengthened against such offensive behaviour. That, then, is what we have to remember from this passage.

Now it is immediately added that the woman was taken into Pharaoh's palace. Here we see that it is because of the lusts of those who are not restrained by the law or any legal authority. For a king will think he is exempt from every law. It is true that if kings were aware of their purpose and to what God calls them, they would

[5] Once again, Calvin deals more severely with princes and kings in his sermons than in the *Institutes* or in his commentaries. That critique of evil counsellors can, at the beginning of 1560, likewise refer to the Guises, who surrounded the young king François II.—*M.E.*

have to be a law even for their own lives. In other words, they would have to be very satisfied that their example serves as a standard for everybody, and they would not, moreover, have to entertain this thought: 'That is forbidden. And yet there is a punishment for that, and I am king. So I must order my life in such a way that the laws and ordinances are reflected in my life, and my life must be in accord with them.' The thought of God's purpose and call should guide all kings and all princes. But they think they do not possess authority and pre-eminence unless they reject limitations and any kind of submission. That is what they make themselves believe, and in that way they withdraw from the rank of men as if they were not creatures. And they immediately forget God as if they were never to come before him. That diabolical pride exalts them above and beyond being the best regulated of people, and they take such licence that they think they are permitted to do anything.

Consequently, when we learn from this passage that Abraham's wife was taken from him, let us first realize that God has blessed us inestimably by delivering us from a tyranny where everything is permitted and where there is such excessive self-indulgence that there are no scruples about taking possession of a woman, acquiring another's substance, and even killing and oppressing the innocent. In a word, let us realize that God grants us a special grace by not allowing the strongest to win, but that all men are held in check by some restraint. And let all those who are in some position of authority be aware that they are under the law. Therefore, let them not put forth their hands indiscriminately to engage in violence and extortion. And because we are not oppressed by tyranny, let us be quick to magnify God's grace.

And above all, whenever we compare ourselves with the many poor people who are despoiled of their substance, who are chased from their homes, pillaged and robbed, and even when seats of justice act like highway robbers and the throats of the weak and helpless are cut, let us realize that we have good reason to thank God when he is pleased to provide a better and more pleasant situation for us. Let us remain in subjection to him and thus avoid giving him the occasion to expose us to those kinds of excesses. And when kings take the liberty to become loose cannons, it is because of the people's sins, as Scripture indicates (cf. *Isa.* 3:1-5; *Isa.* 10:5-6; *Jer.* 27; *Dan.* 9). If we allowed ourselves to be governed by God and he ruled over us, it is certain he would so lead those who have judicial authority that we would see that they are acting as his hands and, in this way, he is presiding over us. That would not be apparent. But he threatens us that, if we act like ferocious animals and cannot submit to well-ordered governance but consume one another and engage in quarrels and betrayals and violent revolts, it is then that he shows us he will send us masters to chastise us in another way. In other words, he will permit another to put his foot on our necks and visit us with all kinds of cruelty.[6]

All the more then must we give attention to this passage inasmuch as it is clearly evident today that restraint has been loosened for the many outrageous excesses committed by kings and by princes and lords. Let us, then, always walk in modesty so that God will always be in the midst of us to guide us with sovereign authority. Those who enjoy greater privilege and renown than others must also pay close attention to this example. For if in this passage the Holy Spirit condemns the king of a great country, what will be the lot of those who do not have such eminence and yet abuse their power under the pretext that they possess some high position and dignity. So let each of them refrain from cruelty and exercise the equity God commands to be written in their hearts, and let us not wait for laws that force us to do good out of the fear of punishment for our noncompliance, but let us act out of

---

[6] It is God who allows tyrants. Such is the teaching that Calvin gives at the end of his *Institutes*. Cf. *Institutes* IV, xx, 27-29.—M.E.

conformity to God's will and keep our desires under control. For it is certain that as long as our desires are in control, they will drive us, we will act irrationally and without good judgment, and we will not distinguish between good and evil. Consequently, if we wish to exercise equity and integrity and live together in mutual love, we must hold our desires captive, even with an iron fist, so to speak. That, then, is what we must remember about this passage.

Subsequently, the text says that Pharaoh dealt liberally with Abraham, giving him sheep and oxen, male and female asses and camels, and a larger household than he had had previously, for he had not arrived in Egypt completely poor (cf. *Gen.* 12:5), as we have seen. Thus, it would seem at first glance that Abraham had gained a great deal with that pretence he had contrived to hide his marriage with Sarai, for he had escaped death, the thing he feared most. We have already mentioned why his life was so precious to him, but, in the main, here he is free, having endured no hardship because of his wife.

But there is more. He is treated humanely, the king is kind to him, and more wealth comes to him than he expected. In Scripture, all of that is called God's blessing. So it would seem that Abraham had greatly profited from that dissembling and pretence which were condemned earlier. But we must, on the other hand, consider how God preserved him miraculously. And if he spared him again in this case, as in all the others, as we will point out at greater length tomorrow, let us be aware that if God provided for him so humanely, he did not do so to lessen his fault. For God does not always punish us as we deserve. But does that mean our faults are virtues? Not at all. But we are all the more obliged to humble ourselves before him and realize how pitiable we are, even though he does not compensate us in accordance with our merits.

Therefore, although it seems that Abraham found a good and effective way to save his life, to be received with kindness in Egypt, and to live there peacefully and at ease, let us not fail to judge as evil what he did against God's word. So let us not engage in deceitful deeds under the pretext that we are influenced by a worthy hope, for every day we will have occasion to say, 'And if I do this thing, will it be so bad? I will accomplish a greater good.' That will be a daily temptation, but we must resist, realizing there is contentment and well-being only in what God teaches us and in what we can do with a good conscience. In other words, let us be able to state forthrightly that we have not offended God as we seek our own welfare and advantage.

> Now let us bow before the majesty of our gracious God in acknowledgment of our faults, praying that he will be pleased to renew us by his Holy Spirit so that we will not be more encased in our fleshly desires, which are that many acts of rebellion against him and his righteousness. And after he buries all our sins, may he be pleased to grant us the grace of walking in his presence with such approval that he will consider us as his children when we are guided by his Holy Spirit. And let us take advantage of that guidance as we struggle against all our weaknesses, which are always many, and by acknowledging them, let us learn to groan until he completely cleanses us of them. May he grant that grace not only to us but to all the peoples and nations on earth.

58

God's Punishments Serve to Instruct and Guide

Friday, 9 February 1560

And he entreated Abram well for her sake: and he had sheep, and oxen, and he asses, and menservants, and maidservants, and she asses, and camels. And the LORD *plagued Pharaoh and his house with great plagues because of Sarai Abram's wife. And Pharaoh called Abram, and said, What is this that thou hast done unto me? why didst thou not tell me that she was thy wife? Why saidst thou, She is my sister? so I might have taken her to me to wife: now therefore behold thy wife, take her, and go thy way. And Pharaoh commanded his men concerning him: and they sent him away, and his wife, and all that he had* (Gen. 12:16-20).

*I*F WE FIND an expedient way to get out of some difficulty and danger, that blinds us, and we no longer consider whether God is offended by it. Rather, we think that bad counsel is all right with him if it succeeds. That is how men often become conscienceless, for they are playing games with God. And if he does not react, they take advantage of his patience. Even the most saintly are mistaken that way sometimes. They do not intend to mock God or take advantage of his patience, but they are not aware that they are provoking his wrath unless someone hits them on the head, so to speak. To the contrary, if God does not react, they think their sins have been buried or that they have done no wrong. That is why the psalm says it is good to be chastened by the hand of God (cf. *Psa.* 94:12). If we were well disposed to receive instructions, we would find enough in God's word, but because of our remissness, he has to add corrections. And that must be closely noted, for Abraham would never have recognized his offence if God had not apprised him of it, even at Pharaoh's expense. He pardons his folly for a while, but he makes it quite clear that his act was wicked. That is why he finally reproves him by the mouth of Pharaoh, who was a pagan and an unbeliever. So when it is said that Abraham's livestock and household are increased, let us not think that God did not impute to him the sin he had committed by exposing his wife to an immoral situation. But that is how he spares his own in his infinite clemency whenever it seems good to him, until he chastens them in a different way.

We come now to what Moses adds. God struck Pharaoh and his house with grievous plagues. We can find it strange that God dealt with him so rigorously for taking Sarai, not as a concubine but as a wife. We would say that it was a great virtue for a powerful king of a great country to look so favourably upon an unknown woman that he honours her by marrying her. That would be a mark of great humility, and we would not say that Pharaoh was either proud or violent, or lascivious for that matter. Yet he is chastened by God's hand, indeed harshly and bitterly, for it is said that the plagues were great. So we could say that God did not use restraint and even that he wanted to advise Pharaoh not to become blind to and obstinate in his vice. Still some people will not understand why he employed such extreme severity. And they will find it even stranger that his entire family was afflicted. For, as we say, those whose fault it was not have suffered the consequence of it.

On that point, we have to note that human judgment cannot be depended on to give a true evaluation when it is a matter of judging between good and evil. So God alone must be dominant and we must all yield to what he knows. For example, if a sentence is to be handed down in closed chambers and everyone on the street can put in his two cents' worth, would it not be foolhardy of them to speak without knowing the merits and arguments of the case? Let us now consider whether God's judgments are not incomparably wiser and more profound than all of men's judgments. So whenever we think God has been excessive when punishing sins or has been unduly rigorous toward the innocent, let us be humble and not intrude our two cents' worth as if we wanted to oppose him if cases on appeal should come before us. What sacrilege that is and what blasphemy that we would want to judge the one by whom we are to be judged!

That is why Paul also declares we must all appear before God's judgment seat to give an account of our lives (cf. *2 Cor.* 5:10). Our duty, then, is to humble ourselves. Will we then take arms against God? Let us note this passage well, more so because today there are many modern-day extremists who would like to deprive God of his right on the pretext that they cannot understand how or why he does what he does. What diabolical arrogance! They experience no shame when saying, 'That seems to me unreasonable. It is repugnant to me.' And with that they conclude that the situation cannot be as it is since they are unable to approve it. And there are even those who will seek an opportunity to doubt God's majesty when they cannot comprehend his judgments, analyze the depths of them, or confirm their opinion about what God has declared or done. As for us, although we are commanded to exercise restraint and moderation at all times, let us nonetheless strongly reject the audacity to question God's judgment, and let us confess that everything he does is good and just even if we do not immediately understand the reason.

In fact, that is the way God often tests the humility and obedience of our faith. He will work in a way that we would consider bad or unreasonable. It is then that we must be like little children and not seek to be wise beyond our ability. In short, let us always declare, even if we are confused, that God does not forsake being just. Indeed, our ignorance, or the inability of our minds, can in no way diminish his dominion and his inherent impartiality, which is unknown to us.

In addition, we must simultaneously agree with the prophet: 'Lord, how wondrous are your judgments and especially the manner in which you govern the sons of men. Your thoughts are hidden from us, indeed because contemplating them and determining their number is like counting the hairs of our head. And how would we achieve such a high goal since the very things which are before our eyes and should be familiar to us because of their nearness overwhelm all our senses so that we understand nothing' (cf. *Psa.* 19:9, 11). That much for that point. What we need to note here is that if we judge that Pharaoh does not deserve such severe correction, we must remember his judgment is rightly in God's hands and that we assume a role that is not ours when we seek to sit in his seat and claim his authority as our own. Therefore, what Moses recounts here must satisfy us. In other words, we must be completely convinced that when God corrected Pharaoh, he did so with good reason, and that even though his family seems innocent in our eyes, God knew quite well why he extended his hand over the small as well as the great.

Moreover, may that instruction not only restrain us and keep us from judging badly, but may it also teach us to be patient in all our adversities and to confess that God deals with us equitably and rightly even though we often do not know why we are beaten and struck by his hand. When men experience some affliction or other, it is difficult for them to examine their situation because they are preoccupied with their misfortune. And inasmuch as we are sense-oriented, we do not look beyond what hurts us and weighs down upon us. In addition, when we think God visits us because of our offences and transgressions, we will not be able to take note of all our personal evils, and we will examine only some mischief that everyone condemns. And if we find that we are 'not all that bad', we quickly absolve ourselves in accordance with our simplistic thinking. Then we grumble: 'Why is God so hard on me? I do not feel I deserve such severe punishment.' It is true we will all confess we are poor sinners, but we still do not understand why God has to deal so harshly with us. And what is the reason? Hypocrisy! We want to unseat God and take his place. That would not be tolerable among men. We say that no one is a good and competent judge in his own case, but we want to be, and we want to oust God from his jurisdiction.

So when the text speaks of the blows that Pharaoh and all his house felt, let us realize that God will sometimes chasten us for faults we do not know about and that we will then think he is being excessive. Nonetheless, we must say nothing, and when we do speak, let it be to condemn ourselves and acknowledge God's justice even if it is beyond our comprehension for a while, for his incomprehensibility is unfathomable, as we have already said.

Also to be noted in this passage is how much whoredom and concubinage displease God. With men that is a game and something to laugh about. It is not just in our day that the debauched have given themselves great license by making jokes to make light of their sin. Even in the time of Paul, such moral laxity was rampant. 'Let no one', he says, 'by vain words or deceitful talk, for the sexually immoral will not enter the kingdom of heaven' (cf. *Eph.* 5:3-6). Therefore, since the devil has from all ages intoxicated men to make them believe that sexual immorality is an insignificant venial sin, we find that today people give themselves even greater license than ever to make game of sexual immorality and become so insolent that they think they are hoodwinking God when they remove every thought and scruple concerning this sin. Seeing that the devil has blinded poor sinners that way and that their blindness is the reason they are completely cast into the abyss, let us learn from this passage that we are not to disregard God's judgment, but that when he indicates that something displeases him, we are to condemn it, and that in accordance with the chastisement he wants us to receive from it.

Paul also advises us in the tenth chapter of 1 Corinthians what the sin is and how egregious it is. He makes particular mention of sexual immorality as well as other sins. He speaks of rebellions, murmurings, wicked cravings, and idolatries. And he also speaks of fornication. 'Let us realize', he says, 'how detestable it is before God, seeing that he punished it so severely among his people' (cf. *1 Cor.* 10:6-11). Paul presupposes that God is well aware of the punishments that sins deserve. And since God punished them that way, he concludes that it is a despicable crime deserving of God's vengeance. In fact, in the passage we have just quoted, he says, 'Let us consider God's punishments.' And when we see that unbelievers are not spared, let us lower our heads in shame and not think it does not matter if we jest and make game of what is so detestable in God's eyes. That, then, is how we are to profit from the example which Moses cites here.

Pharaoh did not intend to take another man's wife forcibly. He did not intend to take Sarai as a concubine. He protests that he was taking her as his wife and had taken her as such. He does not know she is married. Ignorance could serve as his excuse, as is widely believed.[1] Nonetheless, God does not forgo punishing

---

[1] For a long time the sin committed in ignorance had been more excusable than it was for Augustine or Isidore of Seville. Cf. Pierre Lombard, *Sentenciae:* lib. II, dist. xxii, chapt. IV, 11; lib. II, dist. xxxvi, chapt. VI, 4. Thomas Aquinas makes many distinctions between the different forms of ignorance. Cf. *Summa Theologica*

him and his household severely, and not with one blow, that is, not with one kind of punishment, as the text indicates. What will happen to a fornicator who knowingly gives himself to every impurity and debases women and girls? And especially what will happen to an adulterer who repudiates and violates the marriage vow? So let us note that God, in this passage, wanted to condemn all of the jests and lax attitudes that blind men to any fear of his judgment.

Moreover, if we possess a drop of prudence, that ought to strike us with horror and contempt for the evil which God punishes that way, seeing that his wrath is thus provoked. Indeed let us remember that Pharaoh was a poor, blind pagan. Consequently, he was more excusable than we would be because we are instructed in God's school. Even so, if the sin were exactly the same, it is nonetheless certain that our guilt would be greater when we offend God. Why so? We have his word, which is to serve us as a leash to hold us back, and in it are many admonitions which come continually to our ears. If all of those helps are useless to us, what kind of gratitude is that? It is obvious that we knowingly have contempt for God. That is also why it is said that the servant, knowing his master's will and doing it not, will be severely beaten, and he will deserve it (cf. *Luke* 12:47; *Matt.* 25:26-30).

There we have a point of teaching, which is that God has declared to us, as it were in a painting or in a living image, that sexual immorality is execrable to him and he will pass judgment on it. Moreover, because he has shown his severity to a poor blind and ignorant man, let us learn to walk with greater care since he has shown us this special kindness to know through his word what has already been determined, namely, that marriage will always be

---

1/2 q. 76, 2 to 5, and 4 and 3; 1/2 q. 19, 6c; q. 73, 6c; etc. Calvin, however, in the name of the natural law which is written in everyone's heart, refuses to admit sin by ignorance. Cf. *Institutes* II, ii, 22.—M.E.

honourable in his eyes. He is the judge of the sexually immoral and adulterers, who will not escape his hand and will finally give an account. That is the instruction we have to gather from this passage.

We must not be astonished in our day that God sent such plagues into the world because of sexual immorality. We see that many people have rotting bodies. We see a contagious disease like the pest, like the pox, and many other impurities and contagions. We are rather well aware of that. But let us think about the hand which is striking. There is nothing new about that. The blows are seen and felt, but God's hand does not come into play. The prophet laments about such brutishness that men cannot understand when God punishes them (cf. *Isa.* 26:11). And that is why evil continues, indeed because people give themselves over increasingly and shamelessly to every excess. What is worse, we will see these poor wretches who are falling to pieces continue to mock God and scoff at the punishments he sends them, as if they were making a manifest effort to scorn him.

Now let us consider what the prophet Isaiah says about that, for God swears by his majesty that that sin will be unforgivable if a person cannot submit to him (cf. *Isa.* 3:7-9), and he adds other similar admonitions. Even more then must we weigh what we find in the story Moses recounts, namely, that because shamelessness has infected the entire earth and because people, both men and women, have taken the extravagant liberty of giving themselves to every excess, God had to apply his hand. It is a miracle that again he has restrained himself with great patience up until now, seeing that iniquity rushes forth like a flood and people seem to have conspired to corrupt everything and launch their filth to the heavens, as if they were trying to defy the hand of God. In any case, following Paul's exhortation, let us profit from all the chastisements God sent long ago and which he shows us for our instruction today (cf. *1 Cor.* 10:11). Let us not wait for him to redouble the blows. Let us learn from the experience of others, even the experience of unbelievers: 'Since God punishes rebels in this way, do not provoke him further, but let him give us the opportunity to return to him, and let the evil which you sends upon those who despise his majesty serve you and be profitable to you' (cf. *1 Cor.* 10:8-10, 22). That is also something we must remember from this passage.

In addition, let us note what is said in Psalm 105, namely, that God wanted to testify that he keeps his own in his care and that his hand is always ready to help them in time of need, yes, even though the world views them as contemptible. That point is touched on there, and it is said that when Abraham and the other fathers were small in number, they wandered from place to place and were foreigners among the peoples and nations, a fact which made them doubly despised. Yet God protected them, and for their sakes he did not spare even kings and chastened them saying, 'Touch not my anointed, and do my prophets no harm' (cf. *Psa.* 105:15). In recounting that story, Moses also applies it to our instruction and shows, as in a mirror, that God is representing himself as the guardian of those who call upon him and trust in him.

That, then, is how we must adhere to the assurance of his protection. That is, if we encounter many abuses and extortions so that it seems we have no support, being completely without relatives, friends, and good will, and it seems we are being pillaged, he will extend his hand to help us (cf. *Ezra* 8:22; *Psa.* 80:17). Why? He has given us good reason and witness in Abraham and people like him. Here we have Abraham, who has come into Egypt as a poor starving man. Because he does not have bread to eat, necessity forces him to go into that country. Because of that, men do not esteem him highly. Who offends him? The king. Now when that royal majesty comes forth, it seems rather like God has to remain still. But yet the king himself has no support and had fallen short as a result of Abraham's guilt rather than his own. That is true, but God chastens him anyway and speaks severely to him in favour of Abraham. It is true we will not even come close to the holiness of this holy person so we can have God near to help us. But the prophet says notably that in this way God maintains and protects all his anointed and prophets (cf. *Psa.* 105:15).

Now, by this means of anointing, the psalmist points out those whom God has marked and imprinted with his seal to indicate that he reserves them as his own, in just the way earthly princes put their coats of arms on a house or in a field to protect it or give grants and charters to a person. In this way God calls his servants 'anointed' (cf. *1 Sam.* 12:3; *Psa.* 18:50; *Lam.* 4:20). There was at the time no visible anointing. Abraham was not a priest established by the law. So he was not anointed with a visible anointing. Nonetheless, God had marked him. And then he calls him his prophet because he had revealed to him his secrets. The poor world was at that time plunged into horrible darkness. There, then, is Abraham, who has God's word like a burning lamp to protect him.

Today we are rightly called Christians and do not think this word is empty of substance. The word 'Christian' comes from the word 'anointing', for Christ means 'anointed.' Now the Son of God was anointed, and that for our advantage and salvation, as is mentioned in Psalm 45 (cf. *Psa.* 45:7) and the first chapter of John (cf. *John* 1:41) and elsewhere (cf. *Acts* 4:27; 10:38). Let us mark well that claim that we are members of his body, and let us not make a false claim of belonging to him. And at that time, it is certain, God will uphold us and we will be protected by his power, as was our father Abraham.

We will also bear the title of prophet when we become God's true schoolchildren. It is true we will not all be teachers, yet Joel, speaking of the knowledge that will be given by the gospel at the

Redeemer's coming, says they will all be prophets, both men and women, both young and old (*Joel* 2:28). Thus, after we profit from our God's school by leaning on him and taking refuge in him, he will honour us by keeping us as his prophets.[2] Even though we are like dregs of the earth and people despise us and spit in our face, and those haughty people who occupy the courts consider us as less than nothing, God will still take care of us.

In fact, he has demonstrated that well up until now, for those who could have eaten us with a grain of salt, as the saying goes, how were they restrained? Do we think that if God had not watched from heaven and kept us in his care, we could have persisted until now? We would have perished more than a hundred thousand times. So if we were thus deprived of help and fully destitute and exposed to all kinds of wrongs, and if it would not have taken much to destroy us, but we remained strong, we know that God's hand was on us.

Now understanding by experience how God has sustained us, let us learn at the same time to have confidence in him and come to him and find refuge under the shadow of his wings (*Psa.* 17:8; 36:7; 57:1; 63:7). In acknowledgment of our weakness, let us also learn to have no confidence in ourselves and fully despair of ourselves even to the point of being brought to nothing. Yet, since God has granted us the grace of giving us his gospel and since Jesus Christ shows that he is our head (cf. *Rom.* 12:5; *1 Cor.* 12:27; *Eph.* 5:30) and declares that he wants to gather us into his body, since we also have the same teaching by which God instructs us inwardly of his will and declares to us his secrets, since we can be considered prophets, indeed the most idiotic, who have only tasted the worth of our Lord Jesus Christ and his power and known the summary account of the gospel within the limits of their ability,

[2] In 1 Corinthians 12:28 and Ephesians 4:11, only some are prophets, not all.— M.E.

since we have reason to boast of being prophets because we are faithfully taught in the gospel, let us always follow that holy calling and be assured that God will always display his power against all those tyrants who wish to exalt themselves in that way. For whatever grandeur there is in them and although they are feared by the world, it is certain that they will also discover in all that how God is able to limit their actions, the way he controlled Pharaoh. That, then, is what we have to remember.

And since we see that, according to means available here below, tyrants cannot be withstood, that they do not breathe fire, as is said, and they do not vent all their fury, let us consider how God dealt with Pharaoh. Where are Abraham's people to receive help from? He is waiting there in silence. The poor man is enduring the wrong being done to him, and he is not even employing the freedom that he should. For as we pointed out earlier, he had to maintain his wife's chastity more openly. Even so, God does not withhold his hand from Pharaoh. Thus those who are seemingly given great leeway because they remain unpunished by men, since there is no judge here below to condemn them, yet they will feel the God who is in heaven, whose hand they will not escape, for he has other messengers and ministers of his justice than men.

It is true that God established the order of justice here below, that those whom he appointed to that responsibility are his ministers, but when they cease or are remiss or are unable to resist evil, God is able to do the job. Plagues and diseases are called not only his rods but also his messengers (cf. *Exod.* 15:26; *Deut.* 28:59; 2 *Chron.* 21:14-15). He makes them hasten on their rounds in accordance with his will. So let kings become as proud as they please in their haughtiness, and let them look down upon us as if we were nothing, God will show that he has received us and adopted us as a people, that our lives are more precious to him than anything else in the world, and at the same time he will show there is neither kingdom nor principality that keeps us from being maintained and protected by his mighty hand. That is the kind of confidence we must have as we walk with him, seeing that God deigns to take charge of all our conflicts, for he has once received us unto himself. That, then, is one more thing we need to remember.

Now since we are told that Pharaoh had already taken Sarai as his wife, we could ask whether God punished him too late. We could conclude from that that Pharaoh had already wronged her and that she had been prostituted and shamed for her entire life. It is true that on the surface it would seem so, but we can easily judge that God miraculously preserved her. For as we shall see later, when Abimelech, king of Gerar, took her the second time, she remained intact and God did not allow her to be violated at that time (cf. *Gen.* 20:4). Why would God have wanted to preserve her that way after abandoning her once before to sexual immorality, and why would he not have caused her to remain a chaste and unpolluted woman? Moses does not answer that, but all things in Scripture are not said in words and syllables. We have to judge from subsequent events what has been omitted here.[3] And even when the text says that God punished the kings in favour of his faithful, it does so to show that he had pity on Abraham. And then the text says that Pharaoh was stricken with grievous plagues because of Sarai. If it was because of Sarai, it is certain that God

[3] Calvin's biblical hermeneutic is not limited to a simple inerrant literalism. It is based on accommodating the biblical text to the people's 'obtuseness' and on a useful and necessary God-given knowledge of salvation. That knowledge does not have to be exhaustive. This principle makes room for the interpreter, who is to decide not by himself, but inspired by the Spirit of God what is good for the people. In this sense, only certain persons, teachers and prophets (with the meaning we defined above), can decide what has been omitted, restore it and explain it. In fact, in Geneva, almost Calvin alone could interpret so freely. Cf. Ganoczy, *Hermeneutik,* pp. 90-187, who did not point out the liberty Calvin takes to complete Scripture. Remedying what has been omitted is, however, a perilous practice.—M.E.

had not forgotten her and had not submitted her to the act itself. And as for what is said about Pharaoh's taking her as his wife, it is not because he cohabited with her, but because he had taken her apart and had designated her as his wife. There was even much greater integrity back then than there is today, for here we have reached the pinnacle of audacity, for the devil is more prevalent today than ever. Therefore, even though Moses does not recount that Sarai was preserved, we can nonetheless easily judge from the story which we will see in another passage that she was (cf. *Gen.* 20:3, 8).

In addition, when the text says that Pharaoh, after calling Abraham, complained about him because he had concealed from him the fact that Sarai was his wife, we can see that God not only struck him and beat him with his rods, but that he also made him feel why it was something like a special grace. We will see later that Abimelech had a revelation (cf. *Gen.* 20:3-7), which Pharaoh also might have had. In any case, that is omitted, but the situation shows that if he had only been afflicted, he would not have guessed that it was because of Sarai. Why not? He had no sense of remorse for having taken her, for he was doing wrong to no one, he thought. So how would he have thought that God punished him for something that was not reprehensible? Consequently, God had to review to him the cause or he had to sense it, whatever the situation was.

That is worth noting. God will often strike not just a man or a house, but an entire people. Yet no one will know why. It is true that men will always be condemned as incorrigible when they do not repent, even though he does not sound an alarm and assure them of how or when they offended him. For we have to follow this general rule: that afflictions are not accidental or do not happen by chance, but it is God who is making himself known as Judge. So we must acknowledge our sins in general without any warning or reproof from him. Whatever the case, men will always remain soaking in their filth when our Lord strikes them, unless he favours them by overcoming them so that they will groan. After receiving the blows, let them examine themselves, acknowledge that they are poor evildoers, present themselves before their Judge, and ask his forgiveness. God must, I say, work in that kind of situation to prepare men for patience. Sometimes we will see that God's rods will be attached not only to the backs of those who were debauched, but that they will be in their entrails, as it were, that there is no bone or marrow that will not feel them, and yet they will continue to be rebels, seemingly unfeeling as they add offence upon offence. That is evident everywhere. So let us learn, as I have already said, that God grants us an inestimable blessing when he is pleased to show us why he punishes us: so that we will think about ourselves and be prepared to return to the good road we have wandered from.

We can now make a comparison between the Pharaoh whom Moses is talking about and the one who succeeded him a long time afterwards, about four hundred and thirty years.[4] It is the one who, after receiving correction from God, humbles himself, calls Abraham immediately, and returns his wife to him. So that is the fruit of the chastisement he received after he reacts so quickly that he does not expect Abraham to come plead his case, but anticipates it. He does not delay until the next day. He does not use pretence in an effort to deceive God. He does not wait to see whether the plagues will continue or increase, for it is enough for him to feel but once that God is unhappy with him and is displeased with his behaviour. There, then, we have Pharaoh, the first to yield under God's hand.

Now the second Pharaoh does not receive just one plague, but he sees that God thunders from heaven, that the evils and the plagues

---

[4] Calvin is thinking about the Pharaoh whom Moses will oppose and then about the plagues of Egypt.—*M.E.*

he is sending on his country are so monstrous that they would make the hairs of the heads of all those who hear about it stand on end (cf. *Exod.* 7-9). Still he continues to struggle consciously against God, and as soon as he finds some respite, he goes from bad to worse. So when we see such a difference between two kings of the same country, let us realize God has three ways to chastise men.

One is to strike with severe blows without speaking a word. He will not tell them why. And that is why they do not profit from his rods and always continue to give him new reasons to exercise his severest and harshest vengeance.

Sometimes he will warn them with words, but their hearts will remain hard and obstinate, and their plagues will grow more numerous. Those who harden themselves willingly that way are assured of a greater punishment.

But the third way is when God causes those who affect others to feel the hurt, so much so that they are not informed by words so much as they are touched in their hearts, become pliable, and submit of their own will.

In such a case, we have to pray to God continually that when he beats us with his rods, he will not allow us to be like brute beasts. When a dog is struck with a stick, he feels it, barks, and whimpers, but he comes back immediately because he does not understand. May God not allow us to have that kind of animal-like understanding, but let us understand and think diligently about our sins and ask his forgiveness.

Moreover, when he brings us to that point, he does so to touch us with his word and at the same time touch our hearts more to the quick. We will, to be sure, see many who cannot stand to have their faults pointed out without immediately gritting their teeth and venting their fury against God. So let us be all the more moved to pray that he will give us such a gentle and patient disposition that we will conform ourselves to him and be responsive when he touches us with his hand and, by his word, adds corrections at the same time, in proportion to our need. That, then, is another point.

Now, when we are told that Pharaoh rebukes Abraham, there is no doubt that God wanted to shame his servant by sending him such a schoolmaster. Abraham had sinned upon being seized by fear. It is true that fear so preoccupied him that he did not think he was doing anything wrong when thinking he would be able to save his life by pretending that Sarai was his sister. He did not want to go against God's will intentionally, but he should have examined his situation more closely. As we have pointed out, it is certain he did not allow God the honour that belonged to him, for he did not depend enough on God's providence and find refuge in it in his predicament. So Abraham cannot be completely exonerated.

Now, it is possible that he later condemned himself when seeing what had happened to him, and he must have thought: 'Alas. What have I done by exposing my wife to such shame? God blessed me by choosing me and declaring that my lineage would not only be blessed, but that I would also be a blessing for the whole world, and now I have put a black stain on my house, which was the temple in which God was to be worshiped, and I have made of it a house of prostitution.' That is what Abraham must have thought, and yet his eyes are covered. And in that event we see that when God loosens the bridles on his own, they become hardened. But look. God remedies that right away, as we see that he shames Abraham by condemning him through the mouth of an unbelieving king who rebukes his foolishness. So let us note first, to bring this to conclusion, that we do not give enough attention to our sins. And even though God chastises us, he is good to us when we do not have the kind of feeling and apprehension we should, and he urges us on like beasts of burden. And when that happens, let us not find it strange.

Moreover, whenever we endure some ignominy in the presence of men because of our sins, let us know that God is rightly leading us to that point because we have not profited in his school. He blesses us every day with instruction. And what an honour it is to have God speak to us face to face, as it were! May we be gathered in, and may he be pleased for us to know that he is not only like a master among his servants (cf. *John* 13:13-17), but also like a father among his children (cf. *Isa.* 22:21; *Jer.* 21:9; *John* 16:27). Indeed, our Lord Jesus Christ places himself here in our midst, speaking as to his friends, just as he says in the seventeenth [sic] chapter of John (cf. *John* 15:14-15). So when we do not keep to all his teachings which are presented to us this way every day, does our Lord not need to proceed beyond that and send us other instructions, namely, by bringing us to shame, allowing the youngest of children to judge us, and giving those who are less than we something to rebuke us for and mock us about? When that situation arises, let us know that it comes from God's hand, and let us not be astonished if he deals with us the way he dealt with his servant Abraham. Let that humble us doubly and drive us back to his school, led by his hand so that we will not be reproached by the wicked, who seek not only to mock us but also to blaspheme the holy name of our God because of our offences.

Now let us bow before the majesty of our gracious God in acknowledgment of our faults, praying that he will chastise us in such a way that we will always understand his paternal goodness. And let us not be like defeated and bewildered people, but let us return to him, not doubting that he is kind and compassionate when we seek him in truth. And may he touch us with such sharp repentance that we will be especially displeased with his anger toward us. But, being grieved by that, let us be led to yield completely to obeying his will and conforming ourselves to it unstintingly. Let his name

God's Punishments Serve to Instruct and Guide (Gen. 12:16-20)

be truly glorified in us, and let us give full rein to our Christian faith by allowing his word to be our guide, to restrain us, to draw us away from all the corruption and wickedness and lusts and rebellion of our flesh, and also to lead us to the right path. May he grant that grace not only to us but to all the peoples and nations on earth.

59

Hardships and the Blessings of Wealth and Poverty; the Prudence of Being Alert in the Presence of One's Mortal Enemies

Saturday, 10 February 1560

And Abram went up out of Egypt, he, and his wife, and all that he had, and Lot with him, into the south. And Abram was very rich in cattle, in silver, and in gold. And he went on his journeys from the south even to Bethel, unto the place where his tent had been at the beginning, between Bethel and Hai; Unto the place of the altar, which he had made there at the first: and there Abram called on the name of the LORD. And Lot also, which went with Abram, had flocks, and herds, and tents. And the land was not able to bear them, that they might dwell together: for their substance was great, so that they could not dwell together. And there was a strife between the herdmen of Abram's cattle and the herdmen of Lot's cattle: and the Canaanite and the Perizzite dwelled then in the land (Gen. 13:1-7).

$\mathcal{W}$ E HAVE TO CONSIDER now God's grace toward Abraham, and then his goodness toward him, for all the riches Moses speaks of show that God wanted to deal favourably with his servant in order to give him some occasion for rejoicing or some relief in the midst of the many troubles which he had already endured and which had prepared him for the future. And we see the riches which witness to God's blessing of Abraham. Now, we know how the goods of this world corrupt hearts to the extent that there are very few whose heads are not turned by them when they are great. Some are corrupted by magnificence and profusion. Others are completely besotted by pleasures. Others become haughty and proud. Others are insatiable, and the more they have, the more they want. And then from pride and greed come tyranny and assaults and plundering. In a word, you will have a hard time finding one out of a hundred who is rich but not corrupt and who walks an upright life of integrity before God.

Consequently, Abraham's integrity is all the more praiseworthy when we learn that he with his wealth was not held back or prevented from serving God, for he was able to find an occasion to return to Egypt. And when it is said that the king commanded him to be taken from the country (cf. *Gen.* 12:20), it is not to expel him from the country, for it would have been permissible for him to live there, but that is considered from the perspective of Abraham, who spent a long time in Egypt because of the famine, but his heart was still attached to the land of Canaan because that was his habitation. It is not that he would have had no heritage or that his personal ease enticed him, but because God had assigned it to him as his dwelling place. So he leaves Egypt and, as we have said, his wealth could certainly keep him there, for moving a multitude of people and animals is problematical and troublesome. Consequently, he was in a position to live in a foreign land, and it takes a little bit of nothing to hold us back, even though we have good intentions to follow God when our endeavour is small, but when we see hardship, we are, as I said, immediately discouraged. And the good thing we undertake to do changes.

Therefore, let us note that it is said Abraham left Egypt to return to the land of Canaan, from which the famine had driven him. That was very difficult for him. He had had to take with him a large company and his animals, but he overcame it all. Thus, although his riches are compared to thorns, although the good seed of God's word will be choked by the cares and pleasures of this world when men dedicate their habits of life to it, let us rather follow our father Abraham and not abuse God's blessing when he is pleased to prosper us, for we are far from being incited to love God more ardently and serve him and dedicate ourselves completely to him when he shows us his liberality and we turn our backs on him and riches produce in us either rebellion or ingratitude, or such stupidity that we are completely enveloped in this world and do not think about heaven. As a result, although this vice is far too common and men use the occasion of their riches to become corrupted themselves, we must nonetheless consider the fact that God gives them for a very different purpose, namely, to show that he is a good and merciful father and that he supports us in our weaknesses so we will be more motivated to seek him and cling more completely to him.

Moreover, riches in themselves are not things to be preserved, according to some extremists who think only the poor can reach the kingdom of heaven. If men do not take advantage of the gifts God pours out upon them, that is not to say they are to be condemned because of their nature. We see that in the person of Abraham. The purpose of that is to remove that excuse from those who make that claim under the pretext that they have possessions. Now it seems to me that I have on my shoulders a burden which presses me down to the ground while they are careful to give up nothing. It is certain that those who wish to trust their wealth instead of God would not like to part with a penny of it. Those who condemn them would like to snatch it up for themselves. Now when Abraham is proposed to us as an example, we see a man who, although possessing great wealth, continues to serve God sincerely as if he were completely free of it. And that is why the psalm exhorts us not to set our hearts on it (cf. *Psa.* 62:10).

And Paul also makes a similar exhortation when he says that the rich of this world must not be haughty, which is too often the case, but that they should hope in the living God and not in uncertain riches (cf. *1 Tim.* 6:17). When Paul speaks that way, he shows that a man of faith, when he is thinking right, will be able to have fields and possessions, money and merchandise, and similar goods, and still hold his course. As he says in another passage, we must, even though we possess things, act as if we possessed nothing, and we must always bear in mind that the image of this world is passing away, that it is only a shadow, that nothing is stable.

So let us learn from the story of Abraham that if men are proud because of their wealth or if they risk their good reputation, if they become excessively haughty and draw everything to themselves like a magnet, that is not the result of their wealth but of their vice and perversity because they cannot attach God's name to the purpose for which they are destined.

And as for these extremists who condemn all the rich people in the world without distinction and who do not consider whether they misuse the good things which are placed in their hands, we see how Abraham, who is the father of the faithful (cf. *Gal.* 3:7), stops their mouths and reproves their rashness.

Now it is true that the poverty Luke speaks of concerning Lazarus did not keep him from coming to God (cf. *Luke* 16:19-31). Lazarus is poor, indeed in such dire straits that only dogs have pity on him. Men have no concern for him. We have there a living example of those who endure their poverty patiently and yet are acceptable to God even though they are scorned by the world. The rich man, after being buried, was plunged into hell, and Lazarus was taken up by the angels. But where do they take him? To the bosom of Abraham (cf. *Luke* 16:22). There, then, is the poor man, among the number of God's children. So whatever may be required for achieving the heavenly inheritance, he takes his place with Abraham. And what is Abraham's condition? Rich, Scripture says (cf. *Gen.* 13:2). Therefore, as I have said, we understand that the goods of the world are not to turn us from God or from the hope of the life to come, but let us consider ourselves. For it is not without cause that our Lord Jesus gives us that parable to show that the rich walk among thorns and that there are very few who are not affected and suffocated by them and that riches would extinguish any drop of pity or ray of faith's enlightenment in them (cf. *Matt.* 13:22; *Mark* 4:18-19; *Luke* 8:14). So let us be vigilant. And they who are poor, let them be content with their condition, however small and despised they may be, knowing that God preserves them and that they would be in danger of being totally corrupted if he gave them a longer leash. And they who have possessions, let them keep well in mind that they are not the owners of what they possess, but that they have to give an account of it to God and to alleviate their neighbours' need and share with them in accordance with God's command (cf. *1 Tim.* 6:18). And more than that. They are to use their possessions wisely, without being given to gluttony or intemperance, abstaining from all kinds of ostentation and excessive abundance, and then they are not to allow what they have to spark an avidity to grasp more and more, and they are to maintain that degree of moderation so that if God blesses and increases them, they will be even more motivated to serve him, knowing what good use to put their worldly possessions to.

It is then said that Abraham journeyed until he reached Bethel and again set up his tent where he had built another altar between Bethel and Hai. Here Moses shows that Abraham continues to worship God. We have already explained what it means to call upon God's name. That worship is not limited to praying to him, for that was Abraham's regular practice, as it ought to be of all believers. If we do not have recourse to God morning and evening, we must certainly be beyond insane, for we cannot wiggle a finger without his guidance, and we have to be protected by his power night and day. We need to bear that in mind not only for our bodies but also for the needs of our souls, which are much greater.

So we have to pray to God without ceasing, as Scripture says (cf. *1 Thess.* 5:17). But the invocation Moses speaks of here means only that Abraham is making known that he was not associated with the superstitions of all the peoples among whom he was living and that he was worshipping the living God, the very one who had manifested himself to him and had said that he was his very great reward (cf. *Gen.* 15:1) and had commanded him to walk uprightly before him. That, then, is what we have to remember, as it was explained above.

It is noteworthy that Abraham again called upon God in that place to show he did not waste his time with the ceremonies hypocrites go through the motions of to satisfy God, but they do not have the truth and the substance for the worship of God, which is spiritual and proceeds from true faith in him, worship that cannot exist apart from reverence for his majesty. So Abraham did not participate in those empty motions engaged in by those who put on fine airs, desire to pass as good Catholics, but yet are filled only with scorn for God, dissembling, lying, ingratitude, and rebellion. But Abraham truly called upon God's name when he worshipped him outwardly, for in that way he declared before men that he belonged to him. There is no doubt that he followed Paul's recommendation despite the fact it was not yet written down. That is, whoever calls upon the name of God, let him depart from all iniquity (cf. *2 Tim.* 2:19).

Here again is what we have to remember from this passage. First, we have to note that Abraham's faith was not hidden, as is the case in our day when many want to give no evidence of their piety. Why not? Because it is odious in the eyes of the world to worship God sincerely and thereby preserve superstitions. Death lies therein, as the world thinks. That is how many deaden their feelings in order to defraud God of the external worship he commands. Abraham confessed God's name with his mouth (cf. *Rom.* 10:9) and, in order to edify his neighbours and draw them to the way of salvation, he worshipped the living God. Since he had no compunctions about drawing upon himself the ire of the unbelievers by challenging them, for he had to demonstrate that he had a spiritual devotion, and since God had drawn him to himself in this way, he remained unequivocally in his service. So much for one point.

The second point, as we have said, is that Abraham did not fulfil all his obligations by means of external signs, but he did fulfil the one indispensable sign, that is, coming to God and humbling himself before him, seeking all his welfare in him, and then praising him, while remembering that he was nothing, could do nothing, and had nothing except from God's pure, free goodness. So that is how Abraham, above and beyond the witness that he rendered before men, set up the primary altar to God in his heart, where he worshipped him spiritually, as Scripture teaches (cf. *Psa.* 51:17; *1 Pet.* 2:5).

Then there is perseverance. Abraham never wearied of calling upon God. He did not make a commitment, as will many who are adventurous for a day or a short time and then see that the world threatens them with some danger as they press along on the right path and immediately fall away. So Abraham shows that he was not just a flash in the pan, but that he was so rooted in the fear of God that that root always produced fruit. That is why it is now said that he again invoked God's name at the altar he had set up in Bethel.

In addition, since it is said that Abraham reached that place after his journeys, Moses is showing us that he was put to the test so that his patience might be better confirmed. God not only called him back into the land of Canaan, but he had to get there by a long road. It was not the prospect of an easy road that impelled him, as we have pointed out. So there is no doubt he did not find a little corner where he thought he would live at peace, for God was moving him from place to place as if he wanted to keep him in suspense and test him thoroughly to determine the depth of his commitment. It is likely Abraham was often vexed because he had no respite. It was at least enough that God should be content that he had a foothold in this land that God had assigned to him. Even so, he still has obligations and must move from place to place and endure hardships until reaching his final objective. All of these painful journeys have been diligently recorded so that we will struggle not just against a single trial, but when they are many. And if God tests our faith in ten or a hundred or a thousand ways, let us not think that that is too harsh inasmuch as we are not better than our father Abraham. That is something else we need to remember from this passage.

At that point, Moses says that Lot had great substance, so much that one locale could scarcely contain it because of the multitude of their animals and their households. We will see later that Abraham had three hundred servants whom he could arm (cf. *Gen.* 14:14), in addition to children and women servants. There, then, we have a household which is like a small nation. And Lot—although his substance is not as great, it is nonetheless noteworthy that God multiplied him. On the surface, everything appears to be well and good.

But at that point Moses adds that there was strife and contention among them, along with great dissension, because Abraham's herdsmen were not getting along with Lot's. They were even destitute of good sense, and their disputes put them in such turmoil that they were blinded to the danger they were exposing themselves to as they were fighting with one another that way, seeing that the Canaanites and Perrizites were in that land and occupied it. That shows us that when God blesses his servants with some ease in this world, he does not do so without adding a bit of vinegar, as is good for us. I have already said that wealth, by its nature, is not given to turn us from God; it is rather to lead us to him, for he is extending his hand to us as a father extends to his child what he is asking for. So when a father extends his hand to give his child something to eat and drink, must the child, for that reason, strike his hand or trample on the good thing that has been offered him, turn his back on his father, or kick against him? The child is to be drawn to the father, even if he did not know it, for this sign that he receives is to induce him to come to him. So what will happen when God extends his hand to us that way and feeds and nourishes us? Must we not be drawn to him in the same manner? Now, even though wealth is not supposed to corrupt us, the fact is that our evil disposition inclines us to misuse it, as we misuse all other of God's gifts, even those which are to serve the church. There exists no knowledge or aptitude for teaching which our personal ambition does not corrupt at some time. Indeed, if God's Spirit does not guide us, it becomes evident that even the most scholarly apply their minds to wicked inventions. That is what causes troubles, divisions, and factions in the church.

Now if God's spiritual gifts are misused, it is certain that wealth will most likely tend toward evil. All the more, then, must we note this passage because it shows us that God always stirs in some trouble or other, some bitterness, with this world's passing goods, as if he were putting vinegar in the honey. For honey will strangle us. It suffocates us, as we see in the case of those who are addicted to sweets and stuff themselves with them to the point of bursting. Consequently, our Lord, seeing that the abundance and pleasures of wealth will destroy us, adds a bit of vinegar into the mix. And there is no doubt it was by God's singular providence that Abraham and Lot disputed among themselves, not as individuals, but because of their herdsmen.[1] It is true that that vice is present there, but our

---

[1] Even quarrels are foreseen in God's providence. Jerome Bolsec, followed by others, opposed such a concept of Calvinian providence. Cf. *Registres de la compagnie des pasteurs de Genève,* vol. 1, ed. by J.-F. Bergier (THR 55), (Genève,

Lord saw to it that his servant Abraham did not become insensitive to it because of the great wealth he had received. For since he is rich and opulent, he can spurn those who confront him. And he is even able to redeem himself because he has gold and silver in abundance, as the text says, so that he could enhance his prestige and renown throughout the land and at the same time make himself feared. And then he could acquire the good favour of many by giving to the poor and associating with the rich. Well, if he had been content to do that, what would have become of the promise God had given him that he or his seed would dominate that land? It is certain he would have made alliances with the Canaanites and yielded to all influences. In short, he would have lost all his value. He would have done better to remain in Chaldea, in the land of his birth, than to have mixed with such wicked nations, as we will see later (cf. *Gen.* 14). He would have thought only about having an easy time. In a word, God would have been forgotten along with his special blessing, which he was charged to bear. Consequently, God has to keep him alive so that riches will not blind him, for he sees that they are a great inconvenience to him, for he would have preferred to possess little and live with his nephew Lot, whom he considered as his own child, than to separate from him. For there you have an old man without lineage; his wife is old and has no hope of ever conceiving. Of all his relatives, the only one left is his nephew, who is like an adopted son. In him lies his only hope, and yet he has to part company with him. Think about how hard that was for him. He knows that God does not wish to leave him indifferent under the pressure of riches, but that he is giving him an opportunity to use his wealth in such a way that he will not become overly attached to it.

Now that was not written for his instruction but for ours. So let everyone take his own inventory of what he possesses in this

1964), pp. 80-118.

world. He will certainly find some difficulties and cares in addition to troubles. When God sends us a lot of possessions, we become preoccupied and it seems we are in an earthly paradise and are to be free from all unpleasantness and every care. But experience then shows us that we are more harried than before, for those who have possessions and inheritances will always find this old proverb to be true: 'Possessions invite aggressions.'[2] And those who deal in merchandise will have bad experiences. They will be defrauded or go without profit; they will lose business, not knowing how well those who work with their hands and have a skill will always prosper. God will cause their enterprise to retreat or advance. And even though God provides all the world's goods and some people have them running out their ears, as the saying goes, with others having gold and silver and others, commodities, our Lord still gives them annoying problems which are often bitter, and as a result they would prefer to possess half of what they have in order to live quietly at peace, for in that way God provides for their well-being. But let us take note that we are so disposed to evil that we cannot stand to have God see to our welfare, if we could ever avoid it, even though he is ready and able. That attitude shows us the extent to which sin controls us, for when God gives to one fine possessions and to another enough to live comfortably, it is the same thing as his extending his hand to show that he is their Father and telling them of his goodness, his love for them, and his concern for their salvation. Is there anything more desirable than to see God's hand? He reveals himself to us inwardly and gently.

Now why does God not give us purely and simply what he knows is good for us, but always mixes bitterness, even stinging bitterness, with it? Because we cannot, as I said, stand it when he does good things for us. For if we were provided for in our ease, our lack of gratitude would make us forget God. Then we

[2] French: *'Qui terre a guerre a.'*

would become like unfeeling animals. And then we would come and, in rebellion, give free rein to all our wicked desires. Our pride would rise against God. Eventually our violence, our assaults and robberies would break loose upon our neighbours, along with our arrogance and vainglory. From that we can judge that we are so infected with Adam's sin that we are corrupt and defiled to the core, seeing that we profane all of God's good gifts and cannot receive them without corrupting them. That is quite enough to humble us.

In addition, let us know that God is always working for our welfare and our salvation. When he sends us troubles and cares and when we discover among his blessings some painful goad, let us know that he gives it because it is useful for us. Therefore, when the rich have their worries, are envied by some and conspired against by others, and are pillaged and devoured and begrudged, let them know that our Lord applies some health-giving remedy, so to speak, so that wealth will not be overly pleasant and so that they will not take in so much of it that they will burst wide open.

And let the poor bear in mind that God knows the extent of their capacity and does not want to give them wealth because they would abuse it and not know how to conduct themselves in his goodness and moderation. For if a man does not have possessions, it is easy for him to become bitter, complain against God, and quickly grow impatient. But if it is a great virtue to bear poverty patiently, it is certain that knowing how to conduct oneself in the midst of abundance is an even greater virtue. For when men are well off, they grow blind in their rivalry and self-interest (cf. *Phil.* 2:3), or their appetites will be so inflamed that their only focus is on grasping everything insatiably, and the more they become engulfed in them, the more their covetousness is inflamed and their greed becomes a real sickness.

Therefore, let one and all realize that they need to be directed in that same way by God's hand so that the rich will be brought under control, that their pride will be crushed, that they will not become puffed up in their riches, and so that they will realize that God has moved them further along. Let the poor know that if they had what they want, it would do them more harm than good, and that God knows what is most advantageous for them. In this way he keeps them partially hungry so they will rely on him and more diligently ask him for their daily bread, and think realistically, for if they had the means, they would ruin themselves in self-indulgence. God knows those kinds of vices, but men do not think about them. The person who possesses the greatest sense of reality while earning his living from day to day—if he were in the place of the person who lives on income from properties—would, it is certain, live to greater excess than all the others. So God has the means to keep us for himself, under his yoke. That, then, is what we have to learn from this passage.

On the other hand, we see what it is to have a large family. I do not mean having a great multitude of children. It is true that, given the perversity of the entire human race, if there are many children in a house, there will be a great deal of squabbling and brawling, but I am going to talk rather about those people who desire to have a great following, like these people of the world who want it said of them, 'There is a gentleman who has a large retinue; many people depend on him; he provides a great table.' That is the way those who are given to this world make a show, and they think they are like angels, in a manner of speaking, so great is their suite and long their train. Many people are fed at their expense and bow and scrape for a crumb. Now we see the fruits of such ambition, for it is impossible, when many mouths are to be fed in one house, to have none going hungry, and everyone will not share as well as he would like. So envy raises its head. As a result, whereas servants should obey their master with common accord and seek his well-being, they band together against him.

Then people become very angry. Each one out of resentment for his partner throws dishes on the floor, and the master hears a great din. A servant comes to make a complaint, another defends himself, and the master sees that he has a war in his house. Then those who acquire large houses also try to spew their venom at one another in order to acquire some advantage, and those who think they are snatched up into paradise when they can possess large houses and large companies of people see that it is just one grief after another, and all of that is fatiguing and wearying—although the torment does not appear at first.

That is what happened to Abraham and Lot. Yet Abraham did not wish to take advantage of his superior position, as the worldly minded do. God had given him a large family, and he must endure vexation because of his great company. So what will happen to those who are thus torn by rivalry and want to be carried on the shoulders of others, as it were, in order not to appear to belong to the rank of common men. That, then, is what we have to remember here.

Yet those who are restrained in their own houses, one having a manservant, the other a maidservant, or none at all—let them realize that peace is an inestimable blessing, as everyone will admit, a great blessing which our Lord grants when he removes from us the things and situations that cause such troubles, dissensions, and squabbles that they do not know which way to turn. That is why we will not be envious of those who extend their wings and fly high because they have a multitude of people in their house. Why not? They pay a high price for their desire to appear great, which is the first thing we have to remember.

Moreover, we are admonished to stay on guard since the devil has so many tricks to lead us astray. Here we have Abraham, who had only his nephew Lot, and neither one ever had a quarrel with the other. They lived in unity, and as a result, even if everybody else had been up in arms, they would have remained at peace, even though they must now separate. And for what reason? Their servants. Thus it is not enough for each one to live in harmony with his own, as a husband with his wife, as a father with his children, as the master with his servants, as relatives and neighbours with one another, but we must close off all of Satan's entrance ways so that he cannot slip in through some crack or crevice and create divisions among us. We know from experience that if two brothers are living in harmony, it takes only one woman to kindle strife, and then follows a deadly enmity. The same is true for a servant when he is clever enough to get the best of his master. Then there is trouble in the house, trouble that cannot be calmed, and everyone sees it and thinks, 'No one is doing anything about it.' But that sounds like we want to help Satan so he will have cracks and crevices for creating divisions among us. Therefore, let us learn from Abraham and Lot's example to be so well prepared that when occasions of alienation arise, love will restrain us and we will realize that God has united us and requires nothing more of us than to maintain our fellowship inviolable so that each of us will help his neighbours (cf. *John* 13:34; 15:12; *1 John* 3:1). And let us devote ourselves to one another in such a way that all the distractions that the devil places before us will have no effect on us. There again is what we need to remember.

Now we must note the circumstance Moses indicates: that the Canaanites and Perrizites possessed that land. For even though there is no fear of God among them, the fact is that those who are like cats and dogs will find common ground in the presence of a third party. We see nations which are full of lies and subterfuge, even full of bitterness and gall, which would like to devour each other and in fact seek only to destroy each other. Now when some enemy arrives and threatens them, it is certain they will cooperate out of necessity even though there is no sincere affection between them. God draws them together as if by natural inclination.

Now we see Abraham and Lot, who for their part are experiencing no contention, but they cannot control their herdsmen and domestics. With them now are the Canaanites and Perrizites, who are cruel people and want nothing better than to rush upon Abraham and Lot: 'These dogs and foreigners who have come here are fighting among themselves.' Consequently, those people could take the animals, kill everything, and then cut the throats of the two masters. Since Abraham and Lot are not considering that and are preoccupied with their intense feelings, which the presence of their mortal enemies, who are surrounding and besieging them, cannot dissipate, we have to say there is a terrible conflict raging.

Let us realize, then, that since these contentions are erupting, there is no end or holding back. Whenever there is some dissension, some discord, it often seems that there will inevitably be a rupture and God in his grace will reconcile us when strong feelings get out of hand and we become like animals. God in his goodness has to intervene, for Satan will soon gain control. And especially if the bad feeling remains, the devil will gain the upper hand and we will not soon be able to get out of his nets. That is why Paul exhorts us not to make room for him and let malevolence remain in us and not to let the sun go down on our wrath and passions (cf. *Eph.* 4:26). For if the sun goes down, the devil has won the day, and we cannot, as I said, escape. And in fact it is frightful to see in Abraham and Lot the kind of blinding we see here, namely, that they were more stupid than the pagans and idolaters, who do not have God's instructions but are necessarily held back by their own instincts. That is something neither Abraham nor Lot had.

Let us learn to anticipate Satan's clever devices and so avoid giving him any access. When he tries to put turmoil and discord between us, let us know that that is a mortal plague, and when the fire is kindled, there is nothing in us to extinguish it. If the Canaanites and the Perrizites are not near us, not far away is the devil, who is an even more mortal enemy than those nations. So let us watch and always be on the alert. In a word, let us realize that the devil seeks only to win us over today and to bring us into conflict with our enemies and those who lie in wait for us. Let that knowledge restrain us, and even if our passions have moved us to come against one another, let the situation be brought under control not by force, but by a willing fear of God.

In addition, to conclude, this is also added so that we may know that God had pity on his servant Abraham and, for his sake, on Lot also. For what might have happened? They were there in the midst of people who hated them mortally. And yet they fight among themselves. What might have happened if God had not hidden them under his shadow? So we see that God worked in that situation in such a way that they would have been exterminated if God had not had pity on them in their weakness, not because he approved their vices, but because he spared his servant Abraham along with Lot again despite the fact that the fault was in Lot rather than Abraham, as we will see later. Abraham had to yield (cf. *Gen.* 13:8-9).

So let us note that God must indeed support us in our weaknesses and not allow us—although we may be deprived of good sense and counsel—to be cast aside, despised, and thrown into a pit (cf. *Prov.* 22:14; *Isa.* 24:17). We much need him to restrain us and protect us. But even so, let us not take the licence to do evil on the pretext that our Lord is piteous toward us and will sustain us, but let us submit to him out of gratitude and in acknowledgment that we are alive because he is pleased to spare us. For there is no one who does not realize and who is not thoroughly convinced that he would be destroyed a hundred times over if God did not preserve him and protect him with his hand. So when we realize that, let us return to this living image which is placed before our eyes to magnify God's goodness and praise him not only because he has created us and taken us up to protect and guide us, but also because he has to overcome our vices and imperfections by his goodness, and, in a manner of speaking, he must fight against us, since we have no enemies worse than ourselves (cf. *Rom.* 7:18-24). He has to heal all our diseases, which would otherwise lead us to total confusion.

Now let us bow before the majesty of our gracious God in acknowledgment of our faults, praying that he will be pleased to touch us with such repentance that we will be truly humbled and seek all our refuge in his mercy, implore his grace and the help of his Holy Spirit so that we will have the means to fight against all our lusts and the vices which live in us and by which we would be plunged into confusion without the healing of his Holy Spirit. Therefore, let him guide us in such a way that his name will be glorified in us and that, being preserved in his hand and by his power, we will know we owe a great debt of gratitude to his goodness as we move to fulfil the purpose for which he calls us, namely, that we pay him homage for our lives and all the good things we receive from him. May he grant that grace not only to us but to all the peoples and nations on earth.

60

Sodom: The Destructive Consequences of Yielding to Ease, Personal Desires and Self-Interest

Monday, 19 February 1560

And Abram said unto Lot, Let there be no strife, I pray thee, between me and thee, and between my herdmen and thy herdmen; for we be brethren. Is not the whole land before thee? separate thyself, I pray thee, from me: if thou wilt take the left hand, then I will go to the right; or if thou depart to the right hand, then I will go to the left. And Lot lifted up his eyes, and beheld all the plain of Jordan, that it was well watered every where, before the LORD destroyed Sodom and Gomorrah, even as the garden of the LORD, like the land of Egypt, as thou comest unto Zoar. Then Lot chose him all the plain of Jordan; and Lot journeyed east: and they separated themselves the one from the other. Abram dwelled in the land of Canaan, and Lot dwelled in the cities of the plain, and pitched his tent toward Sodom. But the men of Sodom were wicked and sinners before the LORD exceedingly (Gen. 13:8-13).

WE ALL ADMIT that peace is a good thing and beyond price. But when it comes to avoiding squabbles, disputes, and controversies, no one is willing to give up what belongs to him, not even the point of a straight pin, for he wants to be in control. So we must not be surprised if there is a great deal of discord between people and they are like cats and dogs, as the saying goes. The Lord has impressed it on the hearts of everyone that we must maintain ourselves in a way that is not too difficult (cf. *Matt.* 5:39-42), namely, that each of us forgo his right rather than, by obstinacy, start a fire he cannot extinguish later. God is therefore justified in rewarding us according to our deserts. While everyone should serve his neighbour, there is such enmity between us that we walk a thorny path.

For that reason, Paul, exhorting the Philippians in the second chapter to live in harmony and brotherhood, tells them to do nothing through strife and vainglory or haughtiness (cf. *Phil.* 2:3). He had said previously that they should be like-minded and of one accord (cf. *Phil.* 2:2), but because men are dominated by their own ideas and desires to the exclusion of all else, he adds: 'Let nothing be done through strife and vainglory, but through lowliness of mind.' In other words, he admonishes them not to bicker too much. Many people will create a storm at the drop of a hat and declare open war over nothing. How then can we keep people from behaving that way? Paul says we can avoid being that way if we are of a lowly mind and do not seek to put ourselves on display. The word which he uses means that. In short, we understand that Paul's remedy is the opposite of ambition. In other words, everyone wants to win, put himself first and pursue his own advantage or importance. That is the cause of all the conflicts and all the wrangling and hostility that rule throughout the world. All the more, then, must we remember that admonition. That is why he adds that no one should seek only his own interests but also those of others (cf. *Phil.* 2:4), for if we could do that, we would be able to look after one another's interests. It is at least certain that, under those circumstances, a great part of our self-promotion would be defeated in us. When that kind of brotherhood exists, it is impossible for us to be ill-disposed toward our neighbours, for the person who promotes his own interests has to trample on others to advance himself at the expense of others. In short, ambition, self-promotion, so blinds men that they lose all sense of what is just and upright and merciful. It makes no difference to them as long as they reach their goal.

Now in order to be more disposed to forgo our right when the occasion arises and we are required to re-establish peace and harmony that way, we have in Abraham a noteworthy example. For even though he is standing in as a father for his nephew Lot and has provided for him as a small child and brought him along with him, he takes the lesser role. And seeing that there would be contention in his household which could not be allayed, he says to him: 'Choose what seems good to you. I give you your choice. You have a free hand. Your choice precedes mine even though I am like your father. You go the way you choose, for the choice is yours, as if I were obligated to you and you owed me only what seemed good to you.' In other words, it is as if Abraham were saying to him that he had been defeated and that Lot could do with him as he pleased. Now, as I have said, when we are able to imitate our father Abraham in that way, it is certain we have the means to remedy the many disputes and dissensions that surround us.

But everyone is inflexible. When we find ourselves faced with some controversy or disagreement, we want to have the upper hand, come what may. But when the devil interjects himself and poisons our hearts, our hearts are so venomous it is impossible to pacify them. What Paul says in another passage should persuade us, and at that time it is certain we would be more on guard. Is there anyone who wants to open the door to Satan and let him take control? That would horrify us. And yet Paul declares that if the sun goes down on our wrath, the devil has taken such control over us that we no longer have the power to reject him (cf. *Eph.* 4:26-27). And even though we deeply hate being involved in controversy, we cannot escape his grip because we have opened the door to him through anger.

So the first thing we need to do is to prevent all controversies and differences, which would be easy to do if each of us would look at our own vices, as Paul says (cf. *Eph.* 4:28-31). For there is an anger which is good and holy—for example, when we examine ourselves and then work against the evil that is in us. But who of us does that? We are blind to our own shortcomings. Each of us wants to be complimented and applauded even if we strongly condemn ourselves. We do not want to change. Even when convinced of doing wrong, we want to be spared and forgiven. Now if we would consider ourselves, it is certain we would discover traits that would anger us and make us our own enemies. Then we would truly have something to exercise our wrath against and not have so much time to engage in disputes with one another. Let us rather consider the danger that all those who become angry and enraged with one another incur. In addition to opening themselves up to Satan, they cause the name of God to be shamed and blasphemed, as indeed happened in the case of Lot and Abraham.

It is true that guilt cannot be attributed to either one of them because it was their herdsmen, as we have already seen, who started the quarrel. However, they are not to be totally blamed for holding God's name up to shame, for they were mixed among the Canaanites. What was likely to happen? Even though they were afflicted, they were nonetheless allowed to live in one place or another in that country. Now the Canaanites have to tolerate them and can get along with them in some way or other, but they cannot remain at peace. They were likely to say, 'Here we have a pack of dogs which lay claim to the name of God. It is not enough for them to live among us; they have to have their own altar. They have to proclaim a separate God and have a religion that is better than ours. They are so occupied with their own interests that they do not act like ordinary, reasonable people. The nephew stands up against his uncle, and the whole outfit acts like two gangs of devils fighting among themselves.' That is how God's name was exposed to mockery. And that will happen every time, for the wicked are always ready to make fun of the gospel we profess when they see us quarrelling among ourselves. The weak will be disturbed and find it scandalous when they see those who wish to be considered Christians acting like mortal enemies and fighting among themselves. If we took that into consideration, it is certain we would not so quickly engage in quarrels and controversies, as has been our custom.

In addition, if our strong feelings get the best of us sometimes or if we cannot control ourselves at first, as we would need to do, let us at least, as a second step, humble ourselves and not pursue our own interests, but let us realize we are obliged to yield to our neighbour so that all haughtiness in us may be overcome, for it is certain all controversies will then come to an end. And especially let us avoid wilful obstinacy, for this vice is much too common. Indeed our refusal to yield is the height of evil. For if there has been some controversy, deep bitterness will surely remain. Once evil has hatched, the heart is filled with venom. And obstinacy is the result, and disdain grows stronger. So when that abscess produces its poison in the heart, it is then impossible to heal the evil. All the more then must we pay attention to this example, for that is what it proposes to teach us.

So when it is a matter of restoring peace during the disputes and controversies Satan creates among us with his clever strategies, let each of us remember we must not be too obstinate in maintaining our right and our position. It is not even a matter of saying, 'What obligates me to him?' What obligation did Abraham have to his nephew Lot? More often than not, those who have quarrels among themselves are just alike, and that fact ought to induce them to reconcile. But when one party can offer many reasons why the other ought to forbear him and yield to him, that is not to say that his reason is adequate or valid. Lot was obliged to honour Abraham as his father, and yet Abraham yields to him. And it is a wonder one person will know how to behave that way in respect of the other, but neither one even begins to master and instruct himself in this particular so that he is able to admonish himself. We will say, 'Show me you are wiser than I am.' When we are discussing a question and dealing with a harebrained windbag, we will say, 'Well, you will have to show you are the wisest.' That will be said even when a father is dealing with his child: 'Alas, you are not old enough to understand, and it is something that has to be endured.' Now when we are obliged to practice that teaching which we all talk about, there is no one who does not want to get the best of his adversary. As a result, all these ways of talking will make us inexcusable before God. And let us apply to our advantage what would otherwise serve for our condemnation, and let us learn to use good sense and fairness in such a way that, even though we think we are being wronged and would be inclined to return evil for evil, we will repel the devil, who is urging us on, and let that accursed plague not take root in our hearts and produce decay, that is, let us not be obstinate in our malice and contempt. That is the first thing we need to put into practice.

Now the reason that motivated Abraham is special: he and Lot were kinsmen. Although one of them had been a Canaanite and the other a native of Chaldea, they were obliged to continue to associate and live in harmony with each other, for there is a universal kinship with the entire human race. The pagans have known it and nature even teaches it: we are one and all of the same flesh, and the most alien person in the world is a mirror in which I contemplate myself. Thus there is next degree of kinship in us all. And when the law says: 'You will love your neighbour' (cf. *Lev.* 19:18,

34), it does not mean neighbours and private friends, but everyone in general. Our Lord Jesus expresses the same thing in the parable of the good Samaritan (cf. *Luke* 10:29–37). And there is an even greater shame and the evil doubles if those who are joined together in a closer relationship rise up against one another and break all unity and are like enraged animals that cannot be restrained. If there are two men who have no other relationship except that they are men, they are to be condemned if they kill each other, for it is engraved in their hearts that the one is obliged to live with the other without offense or injury. But if there are two neighbours God has brought together, it is certain that that relationship condemns them even more strongly. If they are kinsmen, the closest relationship, it can be said that there exists no restraint capable of holding them back and that they have completely forgotten they are related.

Now it is true you will often observe squabbles only between neighbours and kinfolks, and there is a reason for that. For if they were distant from one another, they would be having little to do with one another. And that is why we have the proverb that says when brothers and relatives have to share, that makes them enemies and drives them to consume one another.[1] Even so, it remains true that they forget who they are if kinship cannot bind them together. We will see kinsmen remain kinsmen in severe quarrels with one another against a third party. But that is because no one wishes to yield to his neighbour. Consequently, we have principles in nature which are good, but they are corrupted by our carnal affections because we cannot submit to God's will (cf. *1 John* 3:10), as is our duty. In short, we can tolerate no restraining bridle, but, as I have said, even if that reason did not exist, the fact remains that God created us and put us

[1] Cf. Plutarque, Moralia 31, 'De fraterno amore' 11, 483a-f. Cf. also Aristotle, Politique VII, 7, 8, 1328a; Erasmus, Adages 150 (col. 90; Opera-Amsterdam: II/1 p. 266); Gilles Corrozet, Hecatongraphie (Paris: Dednis Janot, 1544), emblème 32.—M.E.

in the world to live together and try to serve one another. More is required of us than to abstain from every wrongful act as we interact with our neighbours according to our ability.

Moreover, beyond the fact that we are to be united as men, let us also consider the kinship that was consecrated through the blood of our Lord Jesus Christ (cf. *Eph.* 2:13-22; *Heb.* 10:19-25; *1 Pet.* 1:18-22). Is that not to be of greater value than all the earthly relationships that we could have among ourselves? God has adopted us as his children (cf. *Eph.* 1:5), and we cannot call upon God unless brotherhood exists among us (cf. *1 Pet.* 1:16-17). Now if we place dividing walls between ourselves to the extent we can, we tear God and our Lord Jesus Christ to pieces inasmuch as there is no unity in God unless, as I have said, we live in harmony with brothers. We cannot call upon God and boast of being his children unless Jesus Christ is our head (cf. *Eph.* 4:15; 5:23). And can we be members of his body and remain mortal enemies (cf. *Eph.* 5:30) by engaging in every possible evil against a neighbour?

It is monstrous that those who call themselves Christian are quarrelsome and contentious, and yet that is what everybody sees, and it appears that it is a rare gift of God when we can reconcile differences. It is monstrous that we do not completely fulfil our duty and use all our energy whenever possible, as we are obliged to do, in an effort not to harm anyone. That is such a rare virtue that it is almost impossible to find an example of it. Even though wars do not always break out, there will be squabbles, suspicions, ill will, and discontentment. In other words, our hearts will never be completely cleansed of all evil feelings. Even so, that fact will not excuse us before God and will not diminish our guilt. Since God alone is Father of the faithful and has honoured us by adopting us as his children, let us take counsel then and at least live in harmony and fraternal unity with one another. Let us resist when the devil eggs us on and encourages us to become angry and create discord. Let us remember this: 'Jesus

Christ has created between us a unity that he wishes to be inviolable. Indeed, he created it with his own blood.' So let us take counsel not to dishonour and disgrace the blood of God's Son and trample it underfoot, so to speak, by our haughtiness and pride. Let each of us, then, not give in to himself and his own interests. That is what we have to remember from this passage.

Now when Abraham says, 'If you wish to go to the right, I will go to the left, and if you choose the left, I will go to the right,' we understand that with those words, as we have already seen, Abraham is redeeming peace. And pagans also realized that to sustain loss at the right time is to gain much,[2] and that is true. What good would it be to us if we owned everything in this world and did not have peace and rest? It would only be torment and trouble. So it would sometimes be useful for those who are overly rich to lose half or a third of what they possess as long as they have enough to be content and maintain themselves with little. The fact is that even though that has been verified for us, we have become so accustomed to it that when we are inflamed by enmity and rancour, the disease becomes completely incurable. Why do squabbles and controversies continue to control men? If we checked out all the reasons for quarrels, we would find that some people become riled because of some little word said at random and that others are riled because a child gives another a fillip, or a housemaid taunts a child, or a woman taunts a neighbour, or else there is envy over a bauble of no value or someone is haggling over a straw, so to speak. A few trifling things like that are enough to stir up quarrels and disputes that lead to offences that open the way for the devil to create irreconcilable hatred.

That is what starts quarrels for the most part—a little bit of nothing. That tells us a lot about man's perversity. If it were a matter

[2] Cf. Plautus, *Captivi* 327: '...*est etiam ubi profecto damnum praestet facere quam lucrum.*'—*M.E.* ['Sometimes it is better to lose than to win.']

of someone's being deprived of everything he owns, we should not be surprised if he happened to be overemotional if someone else in his life had been affected. Well, if that hurt him and if he had been angered beyond measure, we would say he was justified even though he is still guilty before God. But if we become angry over nothing, it is like gathering straw to start a fire when there is no wood. That is what we do when we are so easily roused to anger. And then the height of evil is reached when obstinacy is added and harmony and friendship cannot be restored. All the more then must we put greater effort into destroying that evil emotion in our hearts, for when it is excessive, it almost blinds all of us so that we abandon what would be useful for obtaining peace and harmony.

Moreover, when Abraham says to Lot, 'Let there be no strife between you and me,' he provides a teaching we need to note because it was the herdsmen who developed the faction among themselves. Abraham did not stop loving Lot as his own son, and he asks that there be no strife between the two of them. It is not that the faction was between them as individuals, but the purpose of the incident is to show us that quarrels and squabbles so anger those who are neighbours that it is a very rare virtue that they will be able to be fair judges and put an end to their quarrel without being motivated by a strong feeling. For example, let us take two brothers who are neighbours. Let us suppose some anger between the wives or between the menservants and maidservants. The neighbours have a quarrel with each other, whereas they were previously brothers. When the dispute gets under way, they are able to restrain themselves only with great effort and avoid combat. They do not enter into the dispute, and neither one wants to support their respective sides. And if the problem were presented to them, they would condemn both sides. And that is what happens, as I have said, when the devil poisons people's hearts. As soon as some quarrel arises, the air stinks with the infection. A fire is set which spreads in all directions and cannot be stopped from spreading. That is just the way it is. We must be even more vigilant when we see that the devil has subtle devices, and experience also shows us that we are set against one another by a little bit of nothing and that when a quarrel is involved, nothing can quash it.

Now as we see in our father Abraham great considerateness, which the Holy Spirit lays down for us as a rule for living, so also we see Lot's lack of considerateness. For he lifts his eyes, and with that Moses indicates he was preoccupied with his own advantage and dominated by greed, as a result of which he chose a good region where he could live comfortably. When he sees that his uncle Abraham gives him the option of choosing the best for himself, he should at least say, 'Since you are my superior, it is right that I defer to you the honour and advantage of choosing first.' But we see in that how inconsiderate the young are.[3] That is why I said that those who ought to have priority must often forbear just as fathers bear with their children, following Abraham's example. And those who could push others aside and take the biggest piece of the pie, as the saying goes—let them learn to yield with such humility that when they have to deal with hare-brained and irrational people, they are careful to redeem the peace insofar as they can.

Moreover, we have here an example for all young people who please themselves, for there will always be fretting and fuming at that age—an example for those who are the most worthy and think they are worth a hundred times more than they will later come to realize they are. Consequently, because those of that age are so inclined not to be submissive and humble, let them follow Lot's

[3] Calvin was often severe with youth, as he realizes in a letter to Jacques de Bourgogne: 'Young people think I am hard on them. But it would be a pity if they were not held on a tight leash. Consequently, we must work hard for their welfare, in spite of them.' (Cf. Calvin, *Falais:* letter 37, pp. 158ff.). In a passage in the *Institutes,* on the other hand, he asks for gentleness and not undue rigor when dealing with young people (cf. *Institutes* II, viii, 46)—*M.E.*

example and realize that his fault is for their instruction inasmuch as he was so covetous and ungrateful as to choose before his uncle and push him aside as if it was his duty to dislodge him from his rightful place. Since that point is made for us, there is no doubt the Holy Spirit wanted to shame Lot so we would have a useful example today when we need it.

But what Moses adds immediately is to confirm this teaching even better, for Lot, who is overly concerned for his own advantage because his excessive greed is getting the best of him and he thinks he is entering paradise, leaps into the pit of hell, as it were. It is said that he looked at the plain of Jordan, which was like an earthly paradise and well watered like Egypt, a land fat and fertile. Beholding that, he thinks he has acquired everything, and he is no longer concerned for his uncle Abraham. Now particular note is taken of the men of Sodom, who were very wicked and perverse before the Lord, to show that it cost Lot dearly to seek his earthly advantage. For he came to live with the devils, and it is a wonder that he was not completely corrupted, as we will see later.

The first thing we need to note here is that avarice blinds us as much as our other desires as we seek our own welfare and often fall into misfortune. That was not peculiar to Lot, for there is no one who is not aware that when we are so set on acquiring our own advantage, it is certain our Lord is mocking us and we are disappointed from one day until the next. Since many people work hard to lay the groundwork for something that will eventually bring them down, this noteworthy example is placed before us to make us think twice.

Consequently, Lot has no other goal or desire than to dwell comfortably and profitably and to enjoy all that makes life easy and convenient. But does he have that? The main thing is lacking and he is not looking for it. So let us learn not to be so influenced by our desires and tantalized by Satan's and the world's allurements that we forget what is to be preferred and given the highest priority. Since we are told we are to seek the kingdom of God and the rest will be added to us (cf. *Matt.* 6:33), we put the cart before the horse if our concern is only to be at ease, to enjoy some convenience or other, to avoid some difficulty, or to take care of our affairs better. That is where we start. So we must not be surprised if God disrupts our expectations, for we pervert every kind of order.[4] Therefore, it is inevitable that we get the disruption that follows since that is what we are looking for.

So the first thing we have to remember is not to be so preoccupied with our strong desires and the things that make our lives easy and convenient and provide for our earthly rest; but we must order our lives in such a way that we direct them toward the goal to which our Lord calls us. And we have to do that because it takes next to nothing to distract us. When a person has a very minor convenience, he makes of it a miniature king and gives it such a high place in his heart that he is quick to express his regrets if he has to forsake I-know-not-what for God's honour. And people even become perplexed with themselves and make occasion to say they are 'having a hard time of it' when they could be content and thank God with a joyous heart.

All the more then must we note that when we are living in a fat and fertile land, when we have water at our disposal, when we are in effect living in an earthly paradise, we still do not have the main thing. Why not? If people are filled with malice and iniquity and are contemptuous of God, would it not be better to live in a desert? Even though our zeal for God does not move us to go to that extreme, we will all still naturally say unhesitatingly and

[4]Whether it is the heavenly order (cf. *Institutes* I, xiv, 2), order in the church (cf. *Institutes* IV, x, 27), or the social order (cf. *Institutes* II, ii, 13; IV, x, 5), Calvin, as his contemporaries, is strongly attached to the idea of order. The idea that men are to admire and imitate the world's order by their restraint and moderation is found perhaps in Cicero. Cf. *De natura deorum*, II, 15-16; 37-38; *De divinatione*, II, 148.

unapologetically that it would be better to be on some barren mountain or in some desolate place and have peace than to live in a paradise where there is always bickering and controversy and quarrelling. Everyone will think that and say it, but no one avoids the evil we are forced to condemn. So let us be admonished by this story to seek the company of people who can be in harmony with us, with whom we can be in conformity, and with whom we can cultivate peace and friendship. We should do that even if we had no zeal for God. But the main thing for us to know is that by keeping company with the wicked, we will be corrupted by their example. We are already so weak that even though we do not create a scandal which perverts us, we corrupt ourselves individually. So what will happen if we become sacks of coal and foul one another up by association? So let us know we have gained a lot even when we do not have half enough bread to eat if we can live in a place where we are not turned aside from the right path. That is even truer if we are in the place God takes us to, that place where he incites us to come to him after he gives us the word which is preached to us daily and invites us to approach him and yield ourselves to our salvation. So when we have things like that to help us, must we not prize those things more highly than the world's goods? Therefore, we must not long for the trifles and meaningless things that the devil presents to us to make spiritual things distasteful, spiritual things we can enjoy in this life if he did not cling to us and make us forget the kingdom of heaven and become insensitive to things of real value. That, then, is how we have to profit from this passage.

Now when it is said that the men of Sodom were wicked and sinners before God, it is to say that they were not only corrupt and astray like the others, but that they were also a wicked and detestable nation. The Canaanites were not worth much, as we will see more clearly. They were people filled with pride and greed. They were tyrannical and fraudulent and filled with other similar vices. Even so, it is said that the people of Sodom surpassed them, which shows they were not like their neighbours, who were already worthless, but those who had engaged in excesses were even worse than devils.

And when Moses adds 'before the Lord', it is not to lessen their guilt. On occasion it will happen that those who are indeed honest and upright before men will continue to be wicked before God. But here Moses wanted to intensify Sodom's iniquity by saying they were wicked before God, as if he were saying that even though the world approved them, God hated and despised them. That in short is what he wanted to say.

We are admonished by this passage to walk in such a way that our senses are always being lifted up to God, who is our judge and to whom we will have to give an account of our entire lives. And if our iniquities are not revealed at the outset to bring shame and reproach upon us, let us not think we have gotten away with a great deal. For here we have the people of Sodom and Gomorrah, who are living on a high scale. They are bathing in their pleasures, and it even seems that God is favouring them because everything is coming to them lavishly. So what if it is? The judgment Moses pronounced on them by the authority of the Holy Spirit is that they were wicked before God. So let us learn to order our lives in such a way that we gravitate toward God, knowing that we cannot flee from his presence and that it is his approval we must seek and not that of men.

And that will be made even clearer when we observe what the prophet Ezekiel says about Sodom. When he compares Judea with Sodom, he says, 'There is your sister Sodom' (cf. *Ezek.* 16:46). He is speaking to that people God had chosen and who were the sacred lineage of Abraham, and he calls them 'your sister Sodom'. 'It is true that you are the elder sister, even as two prostitutes are both vile, yet one is more clever, more wicked and corrupt. Consider', he says, 'what the sin of your sister Sodom was. They lived in a land of abundance. They had their fill of bread and wine. Pride followed, as did the cruelty they displayed of not giving alms and showing mercy toward the poor. Consider now', he says, 'whether your vices are much different from those' (cf. *Ezek.* 16:49). It is clear that the people of Sodom were addicted to other gross sins, but in them we have the source. And when it is said that they were perverse and wicked before God, we must not look at a simple act as being condemned before men that must be held in horror today,[5] but we must note the prophet's principle: they were filled with bread and wine and meat.

By noting that, we observe the ingratitude in ourselves, which shows we do not know how to employ the good things God does for us. Since God is so lavish with us that we can eat and drink to our heart's content, we should demonstrate whether we can use moderation and restraint. And even as we use more liberally the good things God gives us, we should be encouraged to praise him even more, and we should immediately be caught up in his love. His goodness should be so pleasant to us that all our senses should respond to it. The proverb 'good land, bad people' has been around a while.[6] Why so? It did not come about by chance. In other words,

---

[5] In Geneva at that time, sodomy was almost always punished by death. Cf. William Monter, 'La sodomie à l'époque moderne en Suisse romande', in *Annales, Economies-Société-Civilisation* 29, (1974), pp. 1,023-33; also, 'Crime and Punishment in Calvin's Geneva, 1562', in *Archiv für Reformationsgeschichte* 64, (1973), pp. 281-286, here p. 283, taken up again in *Enforcing Morality in Early Modern Europe,* (London, 1987), III. A few years later Henri Estienne consecrated a chapter (the 13th) to the sin of Sodom in his *Apologie pour Hérodote (1566),* ed. P. Ristelhuber, (Paris, 1879, reprint Genève: 1969), t. 1, pp. 174-78.— M.E.

[6] This proverb [*'bonne terre malle gens'*] is not found in Otto, Walter, Erasmus, Estienne, Nicot, Cotgrave, etc., but the meaning Calvin gives the expression is easily understood. It can be compared with *'Bonne terre mauvais chemin'* ['Good land, bad road'] or *'De grasse terre meschant chemin'* ['From fat land, bad road'], proverbs collected by Le Roux de Lincy (*Proverbes français,* t. 1. p. 86.)—M.E.

people who are too much at ease rebel like well-fed horses that even bite their master and cannot be tamed. And such are we, but that cannot be blamed on the fertility of the land; it is because of the vices of men, who become heavy eaters when the goods are available. It is not a matter of nourishing oneself, but of gorging oneself. Now is that not the nature of intemperance? Pride plays a role at the same time, for men are still not content to abuse God's gifts and waste them in intemperance, but they must make an ostentatious show to demonstrate how important they are, and if they cannot have a parade to show off their vice, that is all right. Now with the ostentatious show comes scorn, for a proud man will never remain in his rank and be like the little people despite the fact that is the way to foster harmony, which is, as Paul teaches, to descend so that we can live in one accord with them (cf. *Phil.* 2:2–3). All haughtiness must be subdued. And when we want to prove who we are, cruelty follows along. And what happens? It is Sodom all over again. Horrible confusion. All the more then must we note what is said here. And every time God displays his largesse and we are enticed to enjoy many earthly pleasures and conveniences, let us look at the example Sodom provides. There is a paradise of God, and yet it is a vast hole opening into hell. It is a place where vice is heaped upon vice, when all is said and done. So let us be on guard and repress all our covetousness and strong desires.

Moreover, if God deals with us meagrely and we do not have the variety of foods we would like, let us bear that patiently, and let us come look at ourselves in this mirror which is provided for us and conclude: if God released our bridle and we had everything at our disposal, what would happen to us? Sodom!

Therefore, since our Lord knows what we need and cuts back on our share, so to speak, to keep us from destroying ourselves with intemperance and subsequently forgetting its effect, let us bear patiently our meagre condition, and let us admit that we are so guided by our God's hand that when we have laboured much in this world, we will enjoy that eternal rest in which we will experience the full joy to which we aspire.

Now let us bow before the majesty of our gracious God in acknowledgment of our faults, praying that he will be pleased to make us so aware of them that we will fight against them while asking him to forgive them so that we will continue seeking his help despite the fact we are not what we should be and are far from doing everything we should. And at the same time may he mortify us day by day so that we will withdraw from this world, from ourselves, and from all our vices, so that we will approach him more and more and conform ourselves to the righteousness he shows us and to which he daily invites us by his word. May he grant that grace not only to us but to all the peoples and nations on earth.

61

The Demands and Expediency of Obeying God's Word

Tuesday, 20 February 1560

*And the L*ORD *said unto Abram, after that Lot was separated from him,*
Lift up now thine eyes, and look from the place where thou art north-
ward, and southward, and eastward, and westward: For all the land
which thou seest, to thee will I give it, and to thy seed for ever. And I will
make thy seed as the dust of the earth: so that if a man can number the
dust of the earth, then shall thy seed also be numbered. Arise, walk through
the land in the length of it and in the breadth of it; for I will give it
unto thee. Then Abram removed his tent, and came and dwelt in the plain
*of Mamre, which is in Hebron, and built there an altar unto the L*ORD
(Gen.13:14–18).

THE PSALMS, speaking as if God were a surgeon who binds
and bandages wounds, say about him, among other things,
that he heals those who are afflicted and have a broken
heart (cf. *Psa.* 103:3; 147:3). We need that teaching very much.
As soon as we are grieved and displeased, we feel like our faith is
beaten down and we cannot show its effectiveness. Consequently,
it is impossible to glorify God and find rest in him and his goodness if we do not have the assurance that he and he alone can
lessen all our sadness. We have an example of that in Abraham (cf.

Gen. 17:8–13), for the separation we have spoken of brought him great distress and could not do otherwise since he was constrained to move away from his nephew.

And let us always remember he was in a foreign land. He had no lineage. Lot was the supporting staff of his old age and the only source of his comfort. So when one had to be separated from the other, it was as if Abraham's inward parts were torn out and his inexpressible sorrow would completely alienate him from God. It takes only a very small problem to discourage us to the point that we can no longer trust God or his promises. But Abraham was assailed from every side and experienced no end of assaults and hardships. In that situation he could have been a man lost, whose faith was completely dead within him, if God had not helped him in such a time of need.

And that is particularly why it is said that God spoke to Abraham after Lot was separated from him. The circumstance of the time is noted so we will know God intended to grant a suitable and convenient remedy for his servant at this very difficult time. At this point he said nothing new to Abraham, for he already had the promise Moses repeats at this time, namely, that God would give him the land of Canaan, in which he was living as a foreigner (cf. *Gen.* 12:7). That had already been said to him, but now God sees him as a man forsaken and adds a new confirmation because of his current difficult and perplexing situation. Up until this point, it is all right that he had no children to succeed him, but now since his nephew, who was like his own son, has departed, he had to be extremely grieved, for he could have thought: 'Alas, God has removed me from the land of my birth. He wanted me to renounce all my relatives and friends. I have come into an unknown land. I am surrounded on all sides by wicked people who are snapping at my heels like barking dogs. I had only a nephew to depend on, and now I must be deprived of him.' We see then how God has said nothing new to Abraham, but he has made application of the promise he had given him for his particular use in the time of need.

That point is very useful, for God's promises, seized out of the air, so to speak, are cold and have no great power over us. But when we see them turned to our use, they take on significance. Example. When it is said that God's children are heirs of this world (cf. *Rom.* 8:17), we receive it generally, but it does not touch us to the quick unless we are going through a time of need. Sometimes we will be led from one place to another and not know where to plant our feet before we are immediately chased away and can find no small corner in the world to receive us. At that time, then, upon seeing we are thus rejected everywhere, we can appreciate both the meaning of the promise that we are heirs of the world and the fact that God is bringing us—if we are patient—to the reality and letting us enjoy his promise. That is how it will become meaningful for us. That is how it will exercise its power over us.

The same is true when we are oppressed by poverty and are despised and shamed by the world, for it is then that we must be all the more aware of the value of God's promises inasmuch as it is said that our Lord Jesus Christ has come to give us by his grace everything we lack (cf. *1 Tim.* 1:15; *1 John* 5:20) and that he is the living image of God his Father (cf. *2 Cor.* 4:4) so that we will be transfigured into his celestial glory (cf. *Phil.* 3:21). That will cause us to bear more easily all the poverty and scarcity this world provides. Since we will be deprived of the means which are at the disposal of unbelievers, we will extend our senses and our minds to the life which is still hidden from us. In that way we will pass through all the torments which can otherwise corrupt us and even cause us to be displeased with God to the point of blasphemy. If the prideful people of this world reproach us and spit in our face, so to speak, let us remember that God imprinted his mark on us when he was pleased to regenerate us by his Holy Spirit so that once and for all his majesty would be shed on us so we can participate in his glory and be conformed to his nature, as Peter says in his first letter (cf. *1 Pet.* 4:14). That is how we are affected by what would not have greatly benefited us generally, and we see how our Lord gives it value at the appropriate time.

Let us weigh carefully what Moses said, namely, that God spoke to Abraham after Lot went his separate way. And when we read in holy Scripture passages that can build up our faith, passages that can make us rejoice in times of sadness, that can console us in our difficulties and give some relief to our griefs and anxieties, let us apply them when we need them. For what good does it do a man to have his weapons hanging on a wall unused and rusty, as the saying goes? And at the call to arms, when we have to enter into combat, if the armed man says, 'I am armed and fully equipped,' but has neither sword nor shield in hand, he still remains unarmed. What good will that do him? That is the way it is with us. For we will be strengthened by and armed with God's word, provided it does not remain idle within us (cf. *Eph.* 6:17). In short, in proportion as each person needs to apply the general teaching to a specific situation, let him also utilize that wisdom and discrimination. That is also why Paul says that God's word is profitable not only for teaching the way we are to go, but also for reproving us whenever we are remiss or fall short, and for encouraging us when we are too cold and indifferent, and for rebuking and threatening us. That is how we must know how to divide God's word and realize why he has given it to us and why it does not serve us in just one way. But depending on the different ways we are tested, may God always help us find in his word a suitable and expedient way to overcome. In sum, that is what we have to remember.

Now it is true God will not give us visions today such as Abraham had, for we have what he was lacking because he had neither written law nor prophets such as we have that would have given him such instruction. Nor was there a gospel. In other words, things were not revealed the way they have been since then. At that time God had to supply what was lacking, but today we need only open our eyes and ears and God will speak whenever there is need to. As Paul shows us in another passage, everything that is written about Abraham and all the fathers is for our instruction so that we will be patient and have information to console us (cf. *2 Cor.* 10:11; *Rom.* 15:4) whenever we are in urgent need. Consequently, when we feel laziness and indifference, let us always turn to holy Scripture, and we will experience incentives to encourage us and correct our indifference. Whenever we are angry and annoyed, God will give us something to make us glad, and we will find sufficient consolation in holy Scripture. Whenever we feel we have become hardened, let us remember the threats God has made, and they will awaken us and pull us from Satan's bonds and snares. So whenever we are attentive and listen to God, it is certain we will have everything we need to build up our faith, to strengthen our endurance, and to help us resist all temptations and deliver us from all our hardships and perplexities. That is what we need to remember about this passage.

Let us come now to what I have mentioned, namely, that God promises his servant nothing here that he was not already informed about, that is, that the land belonged to him, but God shows him he knows how to change evil into good. And the reason that made Lot leave his uncle Abraham was not good. If Lot had been thoughtful and humble as he should have been, it is certain he would have left everything he had rather than abandon his uncle, to whom he was so obligated. That, then, is a great misfortune that Abraham also realized he could not avoid. In any case, it was a bad situation that caused them to separate.

Now God turned that into good, for it is his office to draw light out of darkness (cf. *Psa.* 18:28). Abraham would have had to share the land if Lot had remained with him, and Lot's lineage would not have had to be excluded from that country, for they were relatives. Besides, he also left his father's house. So both groups would have been mixed together. Now God's decree tended toward the opposite. In other words, there had to be only one people to descend from Abraham's race to possess that land. God wanted to have his church there and reside in it. He wanted his grace and his goodness to be enclosed within it until the coming of our Lord Jesus Christ, for the promise of salvation was like a deposit placed in the hands of Abraham and his lineage. So that is how God finds the way for Abraham to dwell in it alone so that his lineage possesses the land without there being a mixture. Therefore, when Lot is cut off from him, the cause, as I said, was unfortunate, but God works in such a way by his wondrous counsel that he changes the bad into extraordinary good.

Now that is very noteworthy because many people enter into contention when something happens that is contrary to their intention and they think everything is irremediably lost, indeed because they think God's power is limited to their imagination, which is the greatest dishonour they could do him. For the characteristic of faith is that men, who are blind in themselves, rise above the entire world, above all their fears and everything visible in it. Otherwise, faith will come to nothing if we try to measure God's power by our understanding. So what we especially need to note in this teaching is that God is well able to use what is evil in itself in such a way as to draw good from it. That is strange to us, but in the end we know from experience it is true.

There are also dogs which growl against God when there is talk about his providence and people say he disposes of everything in such a way that nothing is done unless he has decreed it. And then he holds his secret bridle so that neither devils nor the wicked can do anything unless he gives them leave. They then come and argue that all iniquities that are committed would have to be imputed to God. Indeed! As if he could not use bad tools to make his work good and praiseworthy! So let us learn on the one hand, when God brings good out of evil, not to excuse men who fail, but, by condemning them, to justify God by admitting that he possesses incomprehensible wisdom, which we must revere because we cannot attain to it. And whenever we see things going badly, let us not grow weary, but let us pray for God to rectify the situation so that what seems to us to be confusion and failure within the church will be turned to our good, to our advantage and salvation. Whenever we see something threatening us, well, God controls the issues of life and death, and, not only that, he will change for our good and welfare those things which seem to be working against us. 'Therefore, may you work in your way, Lord, and may we be before you as silent people,' not that he does not need to watch over us, not that we are to be unconcerned about our fears and difficulties and fail to call upon God more ardently, but whatever the situation, may the outcome be such that we remain calm until our Lord has stretched out his hand and worked, not in accordance with our will and desire, but in accordance with his way, which is strange and unknown to us. That is something else we need to remember about this passage.

Now when the text says, 'Lift up your eyes and look in every direction, for I will give you the land that you see,' we understand that God did not console his servant Abraham except by simple words. And that was to teach us, as we were shown above, that we are to honour God by simply believing what he said and by depending entirely on everything from his mouth when he does not show us specifics, for faith must also be a vision of things invisible, as Scripture says (cf. *Heb.* 11:1), and as Paul says: there would be no hope if our salvation and all the good things we expect from God were not hidden (cf. *Rom.* 8:24), for we do not hope for what we have in our hands, but for what is far from us and what seems to be beyond our command. So when we are living in expectation, we are living in hope.

Now for that reason, let us note that God did not help his servant Abraham by putting him in possession of the land that he had promised him, for from man's perspective Abraham could rejoice in that because he would have possessed the land and would then have had a lineage, and because he would have seen with his eyes that he had heirs to succeed him after his death. But he had none of that. God said, 'Lift up your eyes. Look at the land.' But what good does it do him to contemplate it? He is still a foreigner. He is chased from one place to another, and that only intensifies his desire, for the object we want stimulates us even more. When we do not see the thing we want, we are not so tormented by it, but the desire always increases and we have greater incentive when we are enticed by our desires, seeing what is desirable, but deprived of it. It seems that God is not content that Abraham is languishing, but that God wants to excite him and whet his appetite but still leave him in suspense when he says, 'Lift up your eyes and look at the land.' Moreover, when Abraham has looked at the land and considered his offspring, he will find himself alone. It is true he has a large group of servants, but his wife is old and decrepit and he has one foot in the grave by all appearances. So when he sees his house empty and he is in possession of nothing he has been promised, what can he think but that God has mocked him and is still holding him at bay without giving him a foothold or a beginning? In other words, it seems that he is farther away than ever.

Now that is to teach us to add faith to God's pure and simple word and to be bound to it so we can keep control of all our emotions and all our desires so we will not go astray but so that when God speaks, we will remain firm, for it is enough for us to have the word from his mouth inasmuch as we will not be disappointed because of our hope in him. That, then, is the sum of what we have to remember here.

Now it is noteworthy that Abraham's seed is spoken of again, for without that, what would he be? It had already been pointed out that he was to be a foreigner (cf. *Gen.* 15:13). And we will see later that his seed and his lineage will be held in servitude. But in the matter of the land, if everybody had paid him homage and he had received dues and fees, what would it have profited him? He was a poor condemned soul without hope of salvation in God. In addition to that, he was already old and broken, as much from age as from being harried from place to place over a long period, and he had suffered great hardships. So if he had had all the riches, delights, and honours in the world, they would have meant nothing to him if he had not expected that blessed seed (cf. *Gen.* 12:7), of which he had already been told and which will be dealt with further (cf. *Gen.* 15:18; 17:8). It is not without cause that God repeats that his seed will be multiplied like to dust of the ground.

There are those who wish to deal with this passage subtly and say that the simile means God's church is like dust, is of no great significance, is not raised to great honour and dignity. And on the surface that could be considered amusing, but when dealing with holy Scripture, we must always be reverent and sober minded when seeking the Holy Spirit's intention[1] and remain so and even avoid all those fanciful speculations which could titillate us because we have itching ears when it comes to Scripture. It is true the church will be trampled underfoot like dust. It is true people will not see great lustre in it, and even when unbelievers are fashionable and the poor faithful are crouching on the ground, we nonetheless see that God has revealed himself, for he says to Abraham, 'Consider

[1] Calvin adopts the old hermeneutic principle of the *intentio auctoris* ['author's intention'] in the biblical text, whose author is admitted to be the Holy Spirit. Cf. Ganoczy-Scheld, *Hermeneutik,* pp. 90-94.—M.E.

the dust of the earth. If it can be counted, so will your seed be.' That is what that simile means, that Abraham's seed will be multiplied, even though at the time he was only one man. We will also see later that God compares Abraham's line with the stars of heaven (cf. *Gen.* 15:5; 22:17; 26:4). Now those kinds of speculators who are always seeking subtle interpretations also say, 'Oh the church, from one perspective, will be like the dust of the ground and, from another, like the stars of heaven.' But we must consider the simplicity of what God intended to show: that Abraham's lineage would be so great in number that it could not be counted.

In fact, that was fulfilled in part, for we see what a great multitude of people came out of Egypt. It grew in a short time in an incredible way (cf. *Exod.* 12:37). God had to work above the ordinary course of nature in order for twelve tribes to descend from Abraham's lineage when four hundred years had not passed since his death. Between the promise given to him and the law, there were only four hundred and thirty years (cf. *Gen.* 12:40), and he lived a long time. And we also see that when Jacob went down into Egypt, there were only seventy individuals. And when he leaves with as many as a hundred thousand (cf. *Gen.* 46:27), we clearly understand that God extended his arm and his power beyond man's comprehension, as in a dream, so to speak. That was demonstrated when the people left Egypt. We see further how God continued his blessing increasingly. What was the situation in David's kingdom and Solomon's?

Therefore, seeing that God did not speak to Abraham in vain, we ought to be all the more strengthened in all the promises which are given to us today. The same God who spoke has not changed his language. He is unchangeable and will demonstrate his truth to us as Abraham experienced it, and we will know it today as he declared it after Abraham's death. Although he was not able to observe with his eyes what is said to him here, he did indeed see it by faith, as if he had touched with his hand the things which were still far off (cf. *Heb.* 11:13). So we have affirmation of God's faithfulness when we see by virtue of that word spoken to Abraham that he continued to demonstrate his faithfulness after Abraham's death. And Abraham died after receiving the promise. Yes, but that does not mean God's word is mortal. So if we die a hundred thousand times, God's word will remain permanent, and even though heaven and earth complete many revolutions and everything changes, God's word will still remain firm and in force (cf. *Isa.* 40:8; 54:10). So that is what we have to remember.

Yet God diminished Abraham's seed miraculously, and especially in respect of the church. For it was unimportant for Abraham to have such a great and well-populated lineage, for there had to be an initiator of lineage, as we mentioned above and will mention again later, for he spoke of a seed. It is true that this word 'seed' means offspring, whether a hundred, a thousand, or many more. But it is not without reason that Paul takes note of the word 'seed' (cf. *Rom.* 9:7; *2 Cor.* 11:22; *Gal.* 4:29), for there had to be a unity of Abraham's lineage. And that unity depended on the head, namely, our Lord Jesus Christ. Abraham had other children. He had Ishmael before Isaac, as we will see (*Gen.* 16:15). He had many children by his wife Keturah when God renewed him and gave him vigour, as if he had been another man (cf. *Gen.* 25:1-2). But all of them were not reputed to be of his lineage. It is in Isaac that his seed is called, and we must always come to the unity.

Consequently, concerning the church, Abraham's seed was not only diminished sometimes, but almost completely abolished. That is why God, speaking through Isaiah, says, 'When you are like the sand of the sea or the dust of the earth, there will only be a remnant' (cf. *Isa.* 10:22). The presumption of the Jews was such that they thought God was obligated to them. And that is the way hypocrites act. It is true they have neither faith nor trust and that they will never be able to lean on God's word. No matter. They will be puffed up with presumption and pride and boast this way: 'What? Do we not have the unfailing promises that our seed will multiply as the sand of the sea?' Now it is true their seed was great, but there was only impiety and scorn for God. It was a cursed seed and they had gone badly astray from their father Abraham to such an extent that the prophets rightly call them bastards and sons of harlots and send them to brothels to seek their origin (cf. *Isa.* 1:21; *Jer.* 2:20; 3:1–2; 13:27; *Ezek.* 16:15; *Hos.* 2:4; 4:13; *Nahum* 3:4), not because they had not actually descended from Abraham, but because they resembled him in no way. For that reason, Isaiah says to them: 'Do not boast of your lineage, for you are totally profane. Only rebellion and complete infidelity reside in you. Therefore, you must not only be diminished in number, but almost completely abolished (cf. *Isa.* 10:22). God will indeed keep some small number of seed, and of that seed he will again perform a new miracle. For God will cause that seed to slip away from the surface of the earth, as if a stream were gently watering both the rising and the setting sun. Even so, your seed will not always be such as you think.'

When the text speaks of Abraham's seed as being like the dust of the ground, what we have to remember is that God showed himself to be faithful after the Jews' unbelief and wickedness forced him to obscure his promise, as if he had forgotten it, but he still re-established Abraham's seed by his unseen and infinite power when it seemed that the seed had completely perished. We must now apply that point to ourselves, for it is certain that everything that happened until the coming of our Lord Jesus Christ was only the initiation of the perfection that followed. And that is also why we have the fullness of time today, as Scripture speaks of it (cf. *Gal.* 4:4).

In fact, when it is said that God will give the land to Abraham's seed forever, it does not mean that it was actually accomplished.

Although it is true that the Jews are vagabonds today and instead of flourishing and prospering in the land of Canaan, they are, so to speak, rejected by everybody, for this 'forever' is to refer to the coming of our Lord Jesus Christ because he fulfilled all the figures of the law and the world was at that time renewed, in a manner of speaking. It is in that respect that the Jews were again mistaken, for their promise was that the land of Canaan would be the Lord's resting place, that is, his eternal dwelling. Now they thought they would never be driven from it, in the same way the blood of the prophets was shed because it seemed they wanted to make God a liar when the prophets threatened that the Jews would be carried away from the inheritance they had been assigned and that God would violently remove them far away, for they would reply: 'Did God lie when he said that his place of rest would be here and that we would dwell in it forever?' Now they were mistaken in two ways, for they thought that after breaking God's covenant, he was nonetheless still obligated to them. Now God was able to preserve Abraham's seed even though it was a small remnant. Moreover, the Jews were not considering the head we spoke of, that is, the Lord Jesus Christ, and it did not occur to them that at his coming they were to be restored as his spiritual kingdom. So they had conceived false expectations and continued to kill and murder the prophets.

But from our perspective, seeing that they misunderstood God's promises and that that resulted in their confusion, let us be true expositors of what is said here. In the first place, we know that we are heirs of the world, not that God wishes to handle us with kid gloves, for that would not be good for us, but he parcels out our difficulties, since he knows our limits and that the promise is certain and unfailing as it concerns us, but he wants us to bear the trials with patience so he can put our faith to the test. And when we suffer from hunger and thirst and heat and cold and grow faint and weary, let us not fail to hold firm to the foundation that the inheritance of the world is ready and waiting for us at the appropriate time. After realizing that that is the way we are like our father Abraham, let us also realize that it is enough for us to be members of our Lord Jesus Christ (cf. *1 Cor.* 6:15; *Eph.* 5:30), for it is in him that all the fullness and perfection of felicity lie (cf. *Col.* 2:9). Let us desire nothing more since we possess it and belong to him. Let that satisfy us.

Moreover, let us realize that the holy fathers who lived from the creation of the world until the Flood, from the Flood until Abraham, and Abraham until the coming of our Lord Jesus Christ, and from the coming of our Jesus Christ until now and the end of the world are all brought together at that time, and us with them, by virtue of that seed which is spoken of here. That, then, is how we must use that promise to build up our faith not only so we can always rejoice in God, but also so we will realize that even though the world considers us miserable, we will continue to be happy, provided God is always our Father in the name of our Lord Jesus Christ.

Now when it is added that God commands Abraham to go up and down in the land, we see another testing and trying of our father Abraham, which is that the word that caused him rejoicing also caused him new hardships, for was not God to grant him some small corner of the land because he was an old man who was living off his animals without a foot of land to call his own? He had to buy all the grain he ate. We will see later it was like a miracle that Isaac sowed (cf. *Gen.* 26:12) on borrowed land, so to speak. At least God allowed him to stay there in his own tent, for he did not have a constructed house. He possessed no stones to build a lodging for himself. He had only some leather to stretch out. And why does not God sustain him in some place?

Since God's word promises us rest, we need to learn from this passage that that rest was not according to the world, as our Lord

Jesus Christ also taught his disciples when he said, 'I give you my peace, not the peace the world desires, not the peace that can be found by lesser means' (cf. *John* 14:27). It is a peace, as Paul says, which surpasses all human understanding (cf. *Phil.* 4:7). So let us note that God's word brings us a rest which we do not understand, for it is spiritual, and we have to renounce ourselves, as I have said, and keep our desires in check so that our passions will be subdued if we wish to rest in all of God's promises. But what is more, in proportion as God strengthens us by his word, he tests us even more and sends us troubles and struggles, for our faith must not be idle. That is the way it was with our father Abraham.

We have already pointed out that God wanted to alleviate and heal the anguish that was holding him back. But when he says to him, 'I give you this land; your seed will possess it,' he also adds, 'Go and walk about it in its length and in its breadth.' That cannot be done without great effort. If all we have to do is move from one house to another, we still find it very hard. It costs a lot, and it is very annoying. Here we have Abraham endlessly moving about throughout the whole land of Canaan without finding lodging. He has to sleep on the hard ground unless he sets up his tent. And after being in one place, he has to go to another. It is not enough that he goes from one end of the land to the other, but now he has to go its length and its breadth. God makes him keep moving as if he were mocking him without pointing out a definite way, as if to say, 'You are now in such and such a place; now go to the place over against you,' and he says, 'When you arrive there, go on beyond, and then backtrack.' In all of that there seems to be only confusion. But, as I have already said, all that is written is for our instruction. When our Lord instructs us by his word and tells us where to go, he will guide our steps (cf. *1 Sam.* 2:9; *Psa.* 119:105), and he will be our shield (cf. *Gen.* 15:1; *2 Sam.* 22:31; *Psa.* 3:4), our wall and rampart (cf. *2 Sam.* 22:2; *Psa.* 18:3), and he will be our help in every time of need. So since we have all these promises, let us know that it is because he wants to test our obedience and does not want us to be at ease in this world for fear that we will go to sleep in it. But when he visits us with afflictions and problems and other troubles to which we are subject, he gives us his word at the same time to strengthen us so we will never grow weak. That, then, is what we have to observe about this passage, in which it is said that Abraham goes and walks from one place to another at God's command.

Now since God ordered Abraham to do that, Moses also informs us that Abraham was ready and able to go where he was called. So he sets out, inasmuch as God wills it so, and it is said that he goes to the oaks of Mamre, for there were oak trees planted there, which is in Hebron, where he again set up an altar to the Lord. Yet, we, as he, must not procrastinate when God shows us what pleases him, for we must immediately be disposed to obey him. And even if he is pleased to move us from one place to another, let us not have any regrets about that. It would be an easy task if we were pushed along by the wind, but we must move along exactly when it pleases God to withhold this world's rest from us. We will see a lot of criminals who are fugitives and will always be on the move. We will see others who are footloose, who will throw caution to the wind and take long trips. Now that must not be attributed to some praiseworthy trait, for some are forced to leave, and others travel because of their own folly and lack of stability. But when God dislodges us and we have no rest and endure it patiently, we are following in our father Abraham's footsteps. So let us note that Moses not only relates what God says to Abraham, but that Abraham immediately followed through, without delay and without faltering or making empty excuses, as we are accustomed to doing.

In order to confirm that better, he says again that Abraham built an altar unto the Lord. From that fact we have to gather that he was grateful to give thanks to God inasmuch as he offered him sacrifices of praise everywhere he went. That is an indication that he submitted himself to God's good will and had so renounced himself that he found that everything God commanded him was good. That is what Moses had in mind. However, let us remember what we touched on earlier, namely, that even though that land was profane, he did not become a part of it, but he always kept himself pure and unpolluted in God's service. For he held his altar apart, an altar which he did not fashion in his head. He was indeed carrying God's altar in his heart. In other words, he was worshipping God spiritually, for at the same time he wanted to make known before men that the God he had called upon was the sovereign God and that there was no other and that he did not have a self-made procedure for worshipping God, but that God had instructed him how he wanted to be worshipped. That, then, is how we must endure patiently all the hardships that God sends us and how we must always be ready to receive the blows, provided we are always ready to bless his holy name and show that we have nothing better or more desirable than to be governed by God's hand so that when he approves our service, we will arrive at that inheritance which he promised us when he was pleased to adopt us for himself in the name of his well-beloved Son, our Lord Jesus Christ.

> Now let us bow before the majesty of our gracious God in acknowledgment of our faults, praying that he will cause us to be more aware of them than ever before and that we will be so touched by them that we will be displeased with them and groan to obtain his mercy and approach his righteousness, from which we are still far removed, and to profit from our fear of him and from all that his word teaches us. And let us be strengthened by it to fight against all the temptations, all the challenges, all the stumbling blocks, and against all the obstacles that Satan places before us to turn us aside from the right path. May he grant that grace not only to us but to all the peoples and nations on earth.

62

Profiting from Being Corrected by Our Merciful Father for Our Sins

Wednesday, 21 February 1560

And it came to pass in the days of Amraphel king of Shinar, Arioch king of Ellasar, Chedorlaomer king of Elam, and Tidal king of nations; That these made war with Bera king of Sodom, and with Birsha king of Gomorrah, Shinab king of Admah, and Shemeber king of Zeboiim, and the king of Bela, which is Zoar. All these were joined together in the vale of Siddim, which is the salt sea. Twelve years they served Chedorlaomer, and in the thirteenth year they rebelled. And in the fourteenth year came Chedorlaomer, and the kings that were with him, and smote the Rephaims in Ashteroth Karnaim, and the Zuzims in Ham, and the Emims in Shaveh Kiriathaim, And the Horites in their mount Seir, unto Elparan, which is by the wilderness. And they returned, and came to Enmishpat, which is Kadesh, and smote all the country of the Amalekites, and also the Amorites, that dwelt in Hazezontamar. And there went out the king of Sodom, and the king of Gomorrah, and the king of Admah, and the king of Zeboiim, and the king of Bela (the same is Zoar;) and they joined battle with them in the vale of Siddim; With Chedorlaomer the king of Elam, and with Tidal king of nations, and Amraphel king of Shinar, and Arioch king of Ellasar; four kings with five. And the vale of Siddim was full of slimepits; and the kings of Sodom and Gomorrah fled, and fell there; and they that remained fled to the mountain. And they took all the goods of Sodom and Gomorrah, and all their victuals, and went their way. And they took Lot,

Abram's brother's son, who dwelt in Sodom, and his goods, and departed.
And there came one that had escaped, and told Abram the Hebrew; for he
dwelt in the plain of Mamre the Amorite, brother of Eshcol, and brother of
Aner: and these were confederate with Abram (Gen. 14:1-13).

HEARING THE PRESENT story read would be rather meaningless if we did not gather some fruit from it, but we know it was not written to no purpose because we see that Lot was punished for seeking his advantage too enthusiastically and for leaving his uncle Abraham and dwelling in a fertile land. Moreover, we also see how God punished him with restraint, as a father would. He did not rigorously prosecute the wrong he had committed, but it was enough for him to warn him so he would not corrupt himself further and would know he needed to be smitten by God's hand so he would not corrupt himself along with the rest of the people. For we know it is easy to become corrupted when we live in a fat land, in the midst of all kinds of pleasures and delights with plenty to eat and drink. In that kind of situation where there is no fear of God and no uprightness, it is easy for us to become corrupted. Consequently, it was necessary for Lot to be awakened so he would not sleep comfortably in the midst of the inhabitants of Sodom, among whom he was living. Now the deliverance he received from his uncle Abraham shows also that God sometimes spares the wicked because of the good people who are mixed among them. He does not allow them to escape completely, as we will see, but he postpones visiting his vengeance upon them for a while. So we need to consider all those things in order.

In the first place, let us note that there is a double danger in surrounding ourselves with people who have contempt for God and yield to excess, for they can easily lead us astray, and we know how weak we are. So we must do everything we can to flee from those who disregard God and give themselves over to every evil and iniquity. We must flee from them as from deadly plagues, for we will soon be infected by their corruption unless God preserves us by some kind of miracle. But we must not knowingly throw ourselves into the fire, for that would be testing God. And we often see that he punishes the foolhardiness of those who are convinced they are so strong and powerful that no one can lead them astray or corrupt them. So our Lord often mocks such presumption (cf. *1 Cor.* 10:12). Thus, seeing our weakness and how easily we are corrupted, let us be on guard. And especially let us do our best to distance ourselves from the wicked, who seek only to win us to their side. And when we cannot be completely separated from them and are obliged to walk carefully as among thorns, let us remain steadfast in the fear of God on the right path. For if we close our eyes ever so slightly, we will immediately be taken by surprise. And because we do not have the power within us to resist, let us be quick to call upon God and place ourselves anew under his guidance so that we may be strengthened by his hand as we continue to follow the right path even as the devil places before us many stumbling blocks to make us reverse our course or go astray in many directions. So much for that point.

There is yet another danger. It is when our Lord eventually punishes those who have abused his goodness, being rebels to the end, and have persisted in their evil. If we are with them, we will also have to feel some of the blows of the rods. And let us not think that God will go about it haphazardly and strike indiscriminately without considering who deserves it, for he will always find a just reason for chastising those who seem to be and are in fact the least guilty. Daniel, whom the Holy Spirit named among three righteous men and who was like a living example of all saintliness (cf. *Dan.* 1:6, 17), was nonetheless carried into Babylon, and he confesses that it was for his sins. He especially did not join his sins with theirs for appearance sake in order to excuse himself under the pretext of shared guilt, as hypocrites are accustomed to do, but he confesses his own sins in particular and then the sins of all the people (cf. *Dan.* 9:5-7, 20). So we see that, even if we should approach angelic perfection, our Lord Jesus Christ will always be a just and equitable judge when it pleases him to chastise us. And the fact is that he sustains his people by his goodness and does not impute to them their faults without striking them on occasion along with those whom they live among.

That was the case with Lot. We have the testimony that God afflicted his soul. He was so far from being an accessory to or an accomplice in Sodom's iniquities that he was in continual torment and had no peace. There is no doubt that he rebuked the people of Sodom as much as he could and had the means to.

Moreover, as we have said, Lot receives his payment for being too concerned for his own welfare and ease, for he lifted up his eyes and cast them upon the plain of Sodom and Gomorrah. There his covetousness draws him, and he is not concerned for the main thing so long as he, his family, and his animals have enough. That is the limit of his interest. Now because he was preoccupied with his covetousness and because his temporal ease blinded all his senses, God sends him the recompense he deserved. Therefore, let us pay particular attention when we are similarly fixed on our advantage and have no regard for anything but eating and drinking and enjoying our delights and pleasures, for our Lord will teach us that we must not be like brute beasts, which have only their natural appetites to urge them to do what they must in accordance with this fragile life. So our Lord will use reality to show us we have been ill-advised to forget what we must seek first, namely, to love and serve him. Therefore, whether we want to order our lives and assume some status and condition, whether some wish to marry, whether others have to choose a place to live, let them consider the place where they can best give themselves fully to God's service. For if we forget that, it is certain God will show he cannot tolerate such confusion, namely, that we disregard him. And as long as men are as unaware of God as brute animals are, they have no hope of a better life in this world. That, in short, is what we have to remember. And if Lot was not spared, what will become of us?

Moreover, let us note that in that situation God procures our salvation and that it is better for us to be corrected that way by his hand than for him to pardon us completely, for it is certain we cannot become worse ever so little without completely falling all the way. And even though God raises our chin forcibly to look higher, it is with great difficulty that we apply our efforts toward the heavenly life and what everybody ought to prefer. Therefore, instead of raising our heads on high, we will point our snouts toward the ground, like animals, and spend all our time sniffing out something to eat and drink and yielding ourselves to every kind of intemperance. And what good will come of that in the long run? When our Lord sees that we are leaning over to the point of falling, he is required to lift us up again and force us to look at him and aspire to his spiritual kingdom. So let us note well that when God chastises the faithful and they endure afflictions, he is in that way declaring his grace and the care he has for their salvation. For if he supported them too much, it is certain they would immediately become lost.

And let us receive patiently those kinds of admonitions that God sends us. Although they are hard to bear, let us nonetheless consider them and allow that sentence of judgment to soften all the hardships we can imagine. God works that way because he knows it is not good for us to be too much at ease because we would otherwise quickly forsake the kingdom of heaven if he did not forcibly draw us to it. And let us examine what we have done when our Lord sends some severe illness to one individual and to another some hardship that results in the loss of half his possessions or diminishes him in some way or another, and let us ask, 'How have we gone about serving God? How hard have we tried to disentangle ourselves from the encumbrances of the world?' We have preferred to think about other things, about being held in honour or esteem or about amassing things for ourselves and our children, or we have abused our health (we enjoy it by his grace) or we have been so besotted that we no longer have any of that sense which drew us to heaven. We were so deeply sunk in a grimy bog that only filth remained in us.[1] So because we were pre-occupied with the world and turned our backs on God, he had to show us that he still does not want us to perish like poor straying animals but wants to bring us back to the right path. That, then, is what we have to remember whenever the example of Lot is set before us.

Now the text says that five kings waged war against four. The reason given is that those of Sodom and Gomorrah had paid tribute for twelve years and in the thirteenth year revolted, and war followed. One might find it strange at first blush that the world had thus multiplied, for the Flood had consumed everything, and it had not yet been long enough for so many peoples to appear and inhabit cities and even have kings.[2] On that point, we need

[1] Calvin presents a causative concept for the troubles of human existence: the problems man encounters in the matters of health and possessions are a consequence of his sin and occur as a result of divine punishment. Man remains responsible for the evil that befalls him. Cf. *Institutes* III, vii, 10; III, viii, 2; and his *Epistre contre un certain Cordelier suppost de la secte des libertines, lequel est prisonnier à Roan* (1547), CO 7, col. 354f. Calvin's discourse resembles that of Job's friends (cf. perhaps Zophar in Job 11 or Elihu in Job 33), even if God is able to use troubles and calamities to lead man back to the right path.—*M.E.*

[2] Here Calvin asks another completely rational and modern question, one that he has already asked in the commentary. Cf. *Commentarii*, col. 196; *Commentaire*, p. 161. This question is ignored by the ancient commentators: Ambrose of Milan (*De Abraham* I, 3, 14f.), Augustine (*Quaestiones in Heptateuchum, sub voce*); John Chrystome, (*Homélie* 35, 3), Bède, (*In Genesim* III, 14, 1ff.), Nicolas de Lyre

to note what was stated before concerning God's restoration of the human race in an unusual way. Therefore, we must not compare how the population grows in our day, for God worked at that time in an extraordinary way because he wanted to show how the population could be renewed quickly by his power, just as it had been quickly annihilated. It was an incredible event, one that surpasses our imagination: the Flood exterminated both people and animals. Since that is beyond our comprehension, let us also know that when God wanted to replenish the earth, he worked in such a way that his blessing surpassed everything our minds can conceive. That, I say, is what we need to note in order to resolve the question that could be asked.

As for the kings mentioned here, they were only rulers of cities and villages, but this title of honour[3] is attributed to them by the people even though it was not a large country, if they chose a leader and called him king so that he would have more dignity and be more highly revered. We must not waste time over this title, so let us consider those who had it as lords and rulers. And their armies ought to be considered in the same way, for at that time kings did not gather ten thousand or thirty thousand men, but only as many as they could.

Yet we see that ambition had already taken the upper hand with violence and bloodshed. We have seen that giants existed before the Flood (cf. *Gen.* 6:4) and that they were in fact terrifying and tyrannizing others. And God abolished them, and that vengeance was to be a perpetual reminder to restrain men so that they would govern themselves humanely, with moderation and in brotherhood. But immediately the desire to dominate takes charge. It

---

(*Postilles*), etc. Nor does Luther ask such a question. Calvin wants to give an account of the least scriptural detail by asking a rational question, a question which receives God's providential action as a response.—*M.E.*

[3] The Hebrew word used to designate these personages is always *mélék.*—*M.E.*

could be a repeat performance of Shem and his two brothers and all of their relatives of the same race devouring one another. There is no question that in each town there was a head, for that was necessary for the common good because men can never do without order and government, but it is outrageous for one person to subject the others to paying tribute. We cannot say that that arose from a good or just cause. If a king wanted to take authority over others, it was because of overweening desire. Each city needed to have its head for the exercise of justice so that the strongest would not be dominant. But when one person encroaches upon another, that, as I have said, is perverse corruption. Even so, that is what happens almost everywhere.

Let us realize then that that accursed arrogance is so deeply rooted in all men that everyone desired to be a master until God brought his people under control, indeed with the spirit of humility. It is true that not everybody has the fantasy of being a king or a prince, but it does mean that there is an abundance of pride and malice in all of us and that God has kept us in subjection in order to preserve the human race. And when we see those who are born to serve and who think only of being in subjection, let us note that that is not so much a virtue in them as God working so quietly in them and restraining them that they are not motivated to rise too high. Now that is the case of those who are restrained by true humility, for if everyone were always highly active and ambitious, what would happen? What horrible times of confusion would there be in the world? It is certain the earth could not endure us for a day, not even for an hour. Consequently, many remain in their condition and rank without aspiring higher, but as I said, that is not a virtue, for it is God who is keeping a bridle on them without their being aware of it.

Moreover, presumption will always characterize them until God brings his faithful believers into line. He gives them that gentle spirit I spoke of so that they are, as David says of himself, like little children who have been recently weaned, who do not consider exalted matters (cf. *Psa.* 131:1-2), a thing Paul also forbids, especially if we try to exceed our capacity and seek lofty things (cf. *2 Cor.* 10:4-5), for doing so will ruin us and break our necks. There are very few magnanimous people, that is, people who have a zeal for priority of service to God and for dealing rightly with their neighbours. But everybody has such pride and arrogance that he will forget his place and duty and even God himself in order to ascend the ladder of self-interest. Even more must we keep up our guard when we realize that this vice has reigned for all time and that our drawing others into it is like a deep-rooted contagious disease that only the Spirit of God can eradicate. That, then, is what we have to remember.

But let us not be surprised if we see the princes of this world today who are insatiable gulfs and seek only to heap piece upon piece and continue to increase their country.[4] Nonetheless, let us learn to remain in our place in our personal situation, however small and abject it may be.[5]

In addition, even though we are poor, let us not think we will be cleansed of our arrogance unless God works in us by his Holy Spirit. If that were to happen, we would be immediately transported if God did not hold us back by his grace. That, then, is how we must have our refuge in him and humbly beseech him to guide us with a spirit of humility so that we will walk like little children under his guidance and avoid the high positions, honours and dignities of this world. And if it pleased him to elevate us, let us be even smaller and humbler in our own eyes, knowing that if our

---

[4] Once again the criticism of monarchs is sharper in the sermons than in Calvin's other writings.—*M.E.*

[5] Man cannot change his condition, for it is willed and given by God. To disparage it is to attack the order of the world established by God.—*M.E.*

hearts are haughty, we are in the process of being humbled, and by stumbling and falling from a higher place, we would be brought down even further. So let both great and small remain humble, and let us all focus our attention on nothing but how we can apply ourselves to the service of God and our neighbours in accordance with our particular calling.

Yet we see that the inhabitants of Sodom were punished rightly. Although their neighbour wronged them by demanding tribute, the fact remains that they were, for their part, guilty, and God punished them justly. For if we wanted to search out the sources of all principalities, we could claim the following: one principality usurped something or other; another became great because of a certain illegal procedure; another engaged in a wicked practice; another used force and violence against those who were not associated with it in anyway. We could have many excuses for rejecting the whole lot of them so that they all would have to be changed and each principality would have to be put underfoot. That is why we must return to Paul's teaching that there is no dominion that is not from God (cf. *Col.* 1:16), not that he approves the principles behind principalities, for there is evil in them. Moreover, in the course of time, those men who were princes and legitimate chiefs forgot their role, exercised tyranny, and suppressed their subjects' freedom. Well, that evil continues to exist in them, but we must yield our necks and bear the yoke peaceably, for it will never be good and will never receive God's approval if those who are subjected to some authority of whatever sort wish to revolt. It is certain that God will apply his hand and be against them. It is not without reason that Paul says that all those who rise up against the governing authorities make war on God and will sense that he is their adversary (cf. *Rom.* 13:1-8).

Consequently, let us note well in this passage that when we are in subjection, we must bear it, knowing that God receives that humility as if it were service offered to him. Why? He ordained authorities. Therefore, out of honour for him they must remain inviolable and unchanged. So if we are the peaceable subjects of those who have a level of pre-eminence over us, it is certain that we serve God and that he approves that obedience as if it were given to his own majesty. On the other hand, if we want to resist and cannot endure the subjection but want to make some change in our condition, we will have to confront God's strong resistance.

That, then, is in summary what we have to note again concerning the sudden defeat of the king of Sodom and his companions even though it was in their own country that the battle took place. It was such a horrible defeat that some jumped into tar pits out of despair, and others fled into the mountains and their possessions were pillaged and carried away with their women, and nothing was left. So when we see that it was not just a small defeat to flee from and remain hidden nearby but that they jumped into tar pits and were able to save with great difficulty some small portion in the mountains—when we see that, let us note that God was their enemy and corrected their rebellion when they tried to revolt and refused to pay tribute to the one whose subjects they were (cf. *Matt.* 22:21; *Mark* 12:17; *Luke* 20:25).

Yet God has pity on his servant Lot, and as a favour to him he helps the people of Sodom and Gomorrah and their neighbours even though they were unspeakably despicable, and even though he had already severely judged and condemned them, he postpones the execution of his sentence until another time and supports them. So we have to note here, as we have said, that God punishes his own in such a way that he moderates the blows and subdues his harshness in order to confound them completely, but he admonishes them like a father punishing his child. The concern of a father, although he shows himself to be harsh and bitter when he is angry with his son, is certainly not to make him worse and drive him away, but to restore him and give him the opportunity to do better in the future. And as a father does not punish his son to make him worse, as Paul says when exhorting fathers: 'Be careful not to provoke your children, for that would alienate them from you' (*Eph.* 6:4). That, then, is the way prudent fathers deal discerningly with their children.

Now God, who is the fountain of all wisdom and goodness (cf. *Sir.* 1:5), employs incomparably better restraint. So when he is pleased to correct the faults of the faithful he has elected and adopted, it is certain that he proceeds with restraint and that it is with a man's hand that he strikes them, as is stated in holy history, according to the promise made to Solomon and all his lineage (cf. *Jer.* 30:10-11). For God says he will visit their iniquities when they fail, but he will do so with a man's hand. It is as if he were saying that he would not send forth his power to bring us to nothing with the first blow, for how will we, poor frail creatures that we are, hold up against God's hand if he wanted to send it against us? But he will take man's hand, that is, which will serve as his own, not to strike us down, but to punish us the way fathers do.

Now that is how God behaves toward us, and we see a notable example in Lot. For although he receives his due payment for greatly desiring the fertile land of Sodom, with its ease and rest, God nonetheless has pity on him. It is true he did not do so at the outset, for he was able to keep his enemy from wreaking havoc on him. And it is not likely he was in the battle inasmuch as Moses adds that he was taken with the rest, that is, when the cities were pillaged and the women and children taken, Lot was also taken. So God had a way of preserving him, seeing that he had not taken up arms, but he wanted him to be taken captive with the others.

So we need to note that even though God shows us he pities us and never exercises his extreme rigor to correct the sins we have committed, although he does not want us to be so insensitive that we are not well aware of the blows when he applies them, let us not be paralyzed temporarily into inaction, for Lot was in no way different from the people of Sodom. Here we see prisoners dragged away like slaves. Here we see women and children stripped of all their goods and carried away into slavery. Lot has nothing left to his name. Everything has been pillaged, and his enemies have carried everything off. It is not enough that he is poor and totally destitute, but he is obliged to remain in servitude all of his life. He who had a full household must now be like a donkey or a horse and serve at the pleasure of another, beaten and tormented without any means to resist. His condition is worse than wretched, but God wanted to humble him this way. Even though he had already provided for ways to help him, he does not show it at first. So let us weigh all the circumstances and realize that God never forgets his mercy. Although he shows us his angry face and punishes us for our sins, he will always be a father to us and will never turn away from loving and helping us. Since we are persuaded of that and have those promises in Scripture (cf. *Psa.* 89:26; *Isa.* 22:21; *Jer.* 31:9; *John* 6:32), if we apply them later and are destitute of help, let God remain hidden. And since we have our place of refuge, we will cry out, 'Alas, how will this turn out? What will become of me?' Let us continue to persevere in faith and with patience, and let us never be weary of calling upon him, for he has in his hands the times and the seasons that are unknown to us (cf. *Dan.* 2:21). So we must not press forward in accordance with our desires, which are too fervent, but we must rather put everything in his hand and in his providence. And when it seems that we are completely lost, let us know that he has the issues of death in his hand (cf. *Psa.* 68:20) and that it is he who gives life after he has killed, as we read in 1 Samuel (cf. *1 Sam.* 2:6). That, then, is what we have to observe when it is said that Lot was taken by his enemies, taken captive, and that all his goods were pillaged.

It is true, as the story shows and as has already been stated, that God had pity on him and also that for his sake alone he still wanted to preserve the five cities which were there. Nevertheless, the fact is, that did not happen. One could offer here, if one were disposed to judge according to human understanding, the following argument: 'What good did it do Lot to live uprightly and walk in integrity and agonize in his heart when he saw that God was offended and that iniquities were so egregious in Sodom? What did all that profit him?' The people of Sodom were put to flight, as were he and the others. So one could say God no longer spared him, but let us learn that God has his way to help us at the right time, which our understanding and imagination cannot grasp. So let us place ourselves entirely in his hands and allow him to let us languish as long as he pleases, and provided we always lean on his promises, we cannot fail. And when we call upon his name, it is certain we will never be disappointed. That is another point that we have to note.

We now have to observe that although God supported the people of Sodom and Gomorrah and, because of Lot, withdrew them from the hand of their enemies and restored their possessions, that still did not mean they have finally given a reckoning. What is more, that was to make them more inexcusable because they remained incorrigible and the warning did not restore in them some fear of God.

Here is how we must profit from this story. In the first place, when there are some good servants of God among the wicked, let us know that sometimes God, in order to preserve them, will still have pity on those who have no use for him and would be worthy of extermination the first day. The fact is, the good will sometimes suffer, as I have said, along with the wicked, even though there will be some delay before God executes his judgments because there will be a small number of people who fear him. We will in fact see later in the eighteenth chapter that although God had been provoked by the evil deeds committed in Sodom and neighbouring cities, he nonetheless promises that if he found ten or even five righteous people,[6] he would spare all the rest for their sakes (cf. *Gen.* 18:22-33). Whatever the reason, God often delays the rigor of his judgments because he does not want to manifest his severity on those whom he has chosen and to whom he has granted the special grace of being disposed to doing good and yielding to his word. That much for that matter.

As a result, the people of Sodom and Gomorrah were preserved with Lot and delivered out of the defeat which they had suffered. Yet God eventually brought them to account in time and space, as we will see, and what they were spared for a time did not increase their situation at all. But what is more, that iniquity was aggravated even more, for we know men must humble themselves before God when he reclaims them with afflictions. And if the afflictions do not help them, it is a sign their diseases are incurable. For whenever a doctor has hopes for a sick person and all the necessary remedies are applied, but none of it does any good, oh, there is no more hope. So when the medicines, that is, the corrections, God sends us are useless for us, it is certain we are in complete despair and our sins must grow even worse. For our Lord is rightly angered when he sees we are asleep, indeed in a profound sleep, and are not aroused by any warning he gives us to bring us again under his strong hand and acknowledge him as our judge so that we will take refuge in his mercy and ask him for forgiveness.

So that is how the people of Sodom were preserved for Lot's sake. But God kept them in suspense until their iniquity was so ripe that it had only to rot. So let us note how sometimes we will be sustained because of good people, although we are not worth it and must not put confidence in that fact or find comfort in it. God will always find enough reason to punish us, and two or three times over. So let us not think that our situation is much better

[6] Abraham's argumentation stops at ten, not five.—*M.E.*

because we will not be eaten with the first fruits, as it is said in the prophet Jeremiah, for the fruits which are gathered first are eaten immediately, but those that are preserved do not escape.[7] So let us not put confidence in God's not punishing us today or waiting until tomorrow or being long-suffering toward us, and may that not give us occasion to go to sleep, for we will only increase the store of his vengeance until our condemnation is much more horrible. But let us use his goodness and patience in another way, using the spare time to return to him since he invites us gently, and let us pray that he will put to death all those wicked affections which lash out against him. That is how we must let every situation teach us to come into line with our God and place ourselves under his control when he invites us to walk in fear of him, and if he corrects us, let us wake up and come to him, and if he deals with us gently, let us seek only to cling to him, knowing that he is the fountain of all good things and the source of every joy.

That, I say, is how we must profit both from the corrections God sends us and from his gentleness and fatherly kindness, by which he sustains us until he obtains the remission of our sins and gathers us into his eternal rest, where there will be no more struggling against thousands of trials.

Now let us bow before the majesty of our gracious God in acknowledgment of our faults, praying that he will be pleased to touch us with them more effectively than before so we will make a greater effort to strip ourselves clean of all our carnal appetites and be reclothed in his righteousness. And in every circumstance may he govern us in such a way that his Holy Spirit will always have dominion over us and mortify all that is contrary to his service and allows us to abuse his patience and prevents us from profiting from being docile children who submit willingly and gladly to their father when they see he deals with them mercifully. May he grant that grace not only to us but to all the peoples and nations on earth.

63

First Sermon on the Story of Melchizedek, Which Treats of Abraham's Deliverance of Lot[1]

Thursday, 22 February 1560

And there came one that had escaped, and told Abram the Hebrew; for he dwelt in the plain of Mamre the Amorite, brother of Eshcol, and brother of Aner: and these were confederate with Abram. And when Abram heard that his brother was taken captive, he armed his trained servants, born in his own house, three hundred and eighteen, and pursued them unto Dan. And he divided himself against them, he and his servants, by night, and smote them, and pursued them unto Hobah, which is on the left hand of Damascus. And he brought back all the goods, and also brought again his brother Lot, and his goods, and the women also, and the people. And the king of Sodom went out to meet him after his return from the slaughter of Chedorlaomer, and of the kings that were with him, at the valley of Shaveh, which is the king's dale (Gen.14:13–17).

E NEED TO CONTINUE the story begun yesterday with the deliverance of Lot. First, we see how God declared his goodness and favour toward Abraham when he gave him a way to go to Lot's rescue. And that is why Moses says

[1] The title of this sermon and those of sermons 64 and 65 are supplied in the French text. *Translator.*

233

in particular that one who escaped came to Abraham the Hebrew. Now it is true that was not said in reproach, for Eber's lineage bore that epithet, and Eber was descended from Shem (*Gen.* 10:21), as we said before, such that Abraham was, so to speak, already separated by God so he would not be polluted among the Canaanites. In any case, Moses attributed to him that epithet as if to say he was a foreigner and had come to live in a distant country in the land of Canaan. Now we know he could be scorned because he had neither relatives nor friends there. Yet God granted him the favour and privilege of being advised of the devastation which had befallen his nephew so he might help him.

Moses adds that Abraham was allies with his neighbours. We saw earlier that he had to move from place to place because he was not well received. Wherever he went, he was chased away. It is true God commanded him to travel the land from one end to the other to put him to the test, but before that he had to move because of necessity. So there is no doubt his integrity had gained him some authority, with the result that he was accepted and those who were chiefs in that region received him as their friend and made an alliance with him for mutual support. It is often true that all the virtues in the world will not end that well, but there are two supporting factors. One is that those who conduct themselves uprightly and with integrity will seek to conform their lives to God's will, and while serving God, they will also demonstrate a considerate disposition toward their neighbours, who will often make peace and remove the ill will of those who would otherwise be ready to cause them trouble. In fact, Peter introduces that argument when he exhorts servants to do well and to serve those to whom they owe service. He says that in this way they will be able to avoid abuse and assaults. And he says, if you must endure hardship while doing good, you have to glorify God that way so that your conscience will not rebuke you (cf. *1 Pet.* 2:18-20). That, then, is what we have to note.

The second supporting factor is that God blesses those who walk uprightly and mollify men's hearts. So when it says that Abraham had allies, it is certain he was seen as one whose friendship was desired by those very people who previously bore him enmity or who might have wanted to devour and pillage him. They were now inclined to join with him. But that alliance was only temporary. For it is certain Abraham never associated with those whom God had already condemned, although he postponed the execution; and that would also have been contrary to the promise, so that as a result Abraham always retained his integrity so as not to diminish the blessing he had been promised. Even so, he did not refuse to ally himself with them so that he might live in peace without being an open prey and vulnerable. That admonishes us, as I have said, to live among men in such a way that, even if they have spurs to ride us hard with and we are deeply offended by them, we will try to defend ourselves in such a way that if there is some malice and hard feeling in them, we will ward it off when they learn that we seek only peace and their welfare. Even though they try to harm us and deal unjustly with us, let us pray that God will change their venomous and malicious hearts or restrain them in such a way that if we are sheep, we will continue to be guarded and secured in the midst of wolves by the hand of this heavenly Shepherd. That, then, is what we have to remember.

Now the cause of the war is immediately noted in the fact that Abraham, seeing that his nephew was a prisoner, took arms. Earlier he had been given many opportunities to skirmish, but all the inconveniences and all the losses he endured did not lead him to make war. He puts up with all that. Only his nephew's captivity impels him. We could ask here whether it was permissible for Abraham to take up arms. For even though blood cannot lie,[2] as the proverb says,[3] and even though he could have such an affection for

---

[2] The French text: *'le sang ne peut mentir.'*
[3] Not in Erasmus, but cf. R. Belleau, *La reconnue*, acte 5, scène 5: *'Le vray sang qui*

his nephew to deliver him and even though taking up arms to do so was not attributed to him as a fault, we must nevertheless follow this as a general rule: no man is permitted to take up arms.[4] God alone must give them. It is he, as Paul says, who arms kings and princes. And when he asserts that they have the right and authority to punish the wicked, he says, 'That is why they bear the sword' (cf. *Rom.* 13:4). It is not that they usurped their position and hold it by human desire. God has to be its author. That is why I said no one can utilize force and violence unless he has acquired authority from the one it belongs to. On that condition, only kings, princes, magistrates can bear arms along with those under their command. That is a matter which has to be resolved, for what would happen if everyone took up arms if some wrong were done? There would be dreadful confusion everywhere.

Moreover, Paul, in order to keep us restrained and to exhort us to patience, cites what is said in the Song of Moses: ' "Vengeance is mine," says the Lord' (cf. *Deut.* 32:35). Thereupon he concludes that we must give place to wrath. God keeps for himself the office of avenging in the event of some excess and some offense, as it is God's office to punish. If at this point everyone wishes to get involved in a situation and an unofficial individual intrudes in order to object, it is certain he deprives God of his honour and his right as if he wanted to throw God out of office. So that we may

---

ne peut mentir'; Cotgrave, [under '*Mentir*'], '*Le bon sang ne peut mentir.*'—*M.E.* (Randle Cotgrave's *A Dictionairie of the French and English Tongues,* London, 1611, provides this equivalent: 'A noble nature will not yeeld unto base conditions; or cannot, when occasion is offered, conceale it selfe.'—*Translator.*)

[4] Calvin strictly limits an armed uprising against a magistrate. Men owe obedience to those set over them, 'whoever they may be'; they must wait patiently if their king is wicked and look for the reason for that wickedness in the offenses they have committed against God. Furthermore, vengeance belongs to God alone. Cf. *Institutes* IV, xx, 29-32. Moreover, Calvin's thought on the sixth commandment is spiritual: to conceive evil in one's heart is already to kill a man. Cf. *Institutes* II, viii, 39f.—*M.E.*

give place to wrath—that is, so that God can show that he is our protector, chastises our enemies, and takes our war in hand—we must remain quiet on the sidelines. For the one who takes up arms takes from God, as I said, the authority which is his for the defence of his people. In short, unofficial individuals must not only abstain from all violence, but they must also have a patient heart to endure when it pleases God to humble them, and they must at the same time, as Peter exhorts us, entrust their souls and their lives to the one who protects and possesses them (cf. *1 Pet.* 4:19).

We see nevertheless that Abraham was approved, for Melchizedek, while blessing him, says it was by God's guidance that the victory was given to him (cf. *Gen.* 14:20). Abraham, however, was an unofficial man. He was neither a king nor a prince and was even living in the land of Canaan as a foreigner. But we have to note first that he had already been established as lord and master of that country. And even though he had not yet been given possession of it, the right to it still belonged to him, for God had already declared it: 'This land belongs to you and your posterity' (cf. *Gen.* 12:7; 13:15). So Abraham is not to be placed in the same category with the others because God witnessed to him that he was giving him possession of that land, even though he is not enjoying it. That distinction already belongs to Abraham.

If one answer is that it is not enough that he had the right in the future, we still need to note that the example we read here is like the example of Moses. When Moses killed the Egyptian (cf. *Exod.* 2:12), the time for the people's redemption had not yet come. It was still forty years away, and yet Moses performed an execution by sword, and that not because of rashness or foolishness, for he had God's approval. Notably, Stephen mentions that Moses thought his brothers understood that God had ordained him and assigned that office to him (cf. *Acts* 7:25). So Moses was making known that he had not intruded presumptuously. In fact, when God calls him forty years later, Moses makes excuses. He offers all the reasons he can possibly think of in order to escape the commission (cf. *Exod.* 3:11, 13; 4:1, 10, 13). That shows he had not killed the Egyptian out of foolish audacity, and it shows that God had reserved his servant by having him commit that act alone in order to use him later for greater things when the time came.

Thus God was able to give his servant Abraham permission and freedom to exercise the power of the sword once, although he was still not given possession of the land he had been promised. And then we also have to note that God often gives his servants singular initiatives which are not to become precedents. The book of Judges is an excellent example of that, for as often as that book tells about people God raised up to help his people, just that often do we have examples to show us there is not always manifest election when someone is armed with the sword and authority. Was Gideon *elected*? Certainly not. Nor was Samson and all the others. We do not need to point out three or four examples, for, as I said, all those mentioned there were *chosen* by God,[5] indeed without their being aware of it. There is Gideon, who doubts and is in great perplexity (cf. *Judg.* 6:37-40). God has to provide him with an obvious sign of his calling, and then he has to repeat when Gideon, still not satisfied, received what he was asking for. So we see he was very fearful, but God chose him and equipped him to deliver his people, so that with three hundred men he put to flight a large and powerful army (cf. *Judg.* 7:7, 22). All that is recounted for us there is not to serve as a general rule.

It would be foolish to argue and it would be a joke if we said, 'There God has redeemed his church from the tyranny of wicked and unbelieving men by using Jephthah or Samson or Gideon, or someone like them. So that is the way it will be. If we see the

[5] Calvin makes a distinction between 'elect' and 'choose', which no-one would find subtle.—*M.E.*

children of God being unjustly oppressed, we will be permitted to take up arms to help them.' That argument is too fanciful, for we would have to have the wit of those we are aiming at, that is, we would have to be certain that God calls us to do that. Why? As I said, they had singular initiatives like the privileges of the general law. Therefore, we must note in all things that when God works outside the general rule, which is based on his word, it is his privilege and we must not usurp it. It is the authority of a king or a council to give certain privileges to someone without my knowing the reason for it. If I wish to do the same thing as the person who has the privilege, it is like attaching myself to the one who had wanted to separate it from the general public. But it is necessary to allow kings and magistrates the authority to do what they know to be good for the body politic, and that is only reasonable. Consequently, every time we see in Scripture that God wanted to help his church by using those whom he ordained and provided as ministers of redemption and salvation, let us realize that they were singular acts from the hand of God and that those who were chosen by him were armed with his authority and his power. But to say that everyone may proceed to do the same thing would, as I said, end in horrible confusion.

What we have to remember then concerning Abraham is that God had already wanted to give him some sign it was not in vain that he had established him as lord and master of the land of Canaan. In that victory he also gave him a small indication that his posterity was to enter that land and that they would not be prevented from having victory, no matter what force might oppose them. For although the army of those kings we spoke of yesterday might not be thirty or forty thousand men strong, the fact is that Abraham had only those of his household, 318 servants. Now to say that they were not trained for war would be ridiculous. Just because Abraham had never been at war does not mean he did not know what it was to handle a sword or shield. As for his allies, his alliance with them was far from giving him greater confidence. It was to give him greater fear. For they could say, 'This foreigner will end up ruining everything for us, for those four kings have been victorious. They have pillaged Sodom and Gomorrah and the neighbouring cities, and here we are taking them on? That is like saying we wanted to perish intentionally.' So in the general opinion of many, Abraham ought not to get involved because he saw himself as alone and without support. On the surface, it would be very foolish of him to arm 318 servants inasmuch as he was a poor old man taking the role of a commander without ever having been in a war or even a battle or even wanting to know what it was like, and yet there he is throwing himself into it with abandon. So we must even more pay attention to what I said, namely, that God wanted to use that to show him that when the time came to give the land to his successors, there would be no difficulty since he was now giving him such a notable victory, which no one would ever have believed, judging from a human perspective. That, in brief, is what we have to remember at this point when the text says that Abraham armed his servants.

We see how God gave him wisdom, even though he was not practised in arms or in any way crafty. He nevertheless takes his enemies by surprise and attacks them at night at the very time they were at ease after eating and drinking and gluttonizing, thinking they were secure after plundering Sodom and Gomorrah. Now we know that after such victories, much unbridled and deplorable behaviour occurs. Consequently, Abraham was very astute in taking his enemies by surprise, and he must have been astonished by what had happened and by the victory his enemies had had. And when he arrives there suddenly and moves quickly, the outcome is not achieved without tumult, but God guides him by his Holy Spirit. That shows us that God wanted to work through him not only for Lot's sake, but so that he might know that God's promise to give him the mastery and upper hand over the entire country of Canaan was not vain or frivolous. That, in brief, is what we have to remember.

Subsequently, the text says that the king of Sodom came before him, which magnifies God's grace toward Abraham. We have already cited the passage from Ezekiel in which it is said that the people of Sodom were filled with pride and that that was the source of all the enormities which called forth God's vengeance to exterminate them completely (cf. *Ezek.* 16:49). Whatever pride the king of Sodom might have had, he nonetheless came to pay homage to Abraham, knowing that he owed his entire life and country to him. That shows us how God conducted that entire matter and blessed his servant Abraham. It is true Abraham would have preferred not to stir from his tent or subject himself to such peril, but God extended his hand to him, wanting him to experience his power and help in time of need. That subsequently was a great advantage to Abraham, for if he had remained in his house without knowing of such defence by God, it is certain he would not have been as strengthened as he was later. So when God sends us afflictions, as difficult and painful as they may be to bear in the beginning, we see in the end that the outcome is useful and advantageous for our salvation. For perseverance produces character, Paul says (cf. *Rom.* 5:4), so that we may know from experience that God has helped us at that time, and when we know that, our hope in him is increasingly strengthened (cf. *Isa.* 49:23). Hope never makes us ashamed, for those whose refuge is in God will never be confounded. We see then that we will never be able to remain still and peaceable until God shows us why he has afflicted us, and may he cause us to realize that it is for our welfare and that, consequently, we have the opportunity to bless him and call upon him with greater conviction. That is what we need to note on that point.

Now Moses says that the king of Sodom came before Abraham and then adds that Melchizedek king of Salem also offered bread and wine. And because he was a priest of the sovereign God, he blessed Abraham, and Abraham gave him the tithe of all the spoils. Here is a noteworthy story, if there is one in holy Scripture, and not only a story but the living image to represent our Lord Jesus Christ, as Psalm 110 speaks of him (cf. *Psa.* 110:4), for it is not without reason that it is said there that God swore and will not repent that the solemn oath that he made will be unchangeable, namely, that Jesus Christ is a priest after the order of Melchizedek. If we had only the story, we would have Melchizedek the well-known priest of God, but he would still not be the equal of Abraham. Far from it. For it will be said later that Abraham is the father of all the faithful (cf. *Gen.* 17:4) and of the entire church and that all of the children of God must be his spiritual children (cf. *Rom.* 4:12). So Melchizedek had to be somewhat inferior to him. Yet Moses attributes to him a dignity above Abraham's, as the apostle deals with the subject, as we will see (cf. *Heb.* 7:4-7).

Some have judged that Melchizedek was Shem, but it is not likely that that is the case. But let us suppose it is. Would Abraham have waited so long to see the patriarch Shem, from whom he was descended? There is no doubt that at the outset he would have gone straight to him and lived in company with him, for he was king of Salem. And Abraham could have gone and placed himself under his protection, but he moved from place to place throughout the land, and yet there was no mention of Melchizedek.

In addition, it is not without reason that the apostle notes that Melchizedek was without father and without mother, without beginning and without end, like a man who would have descended from heaven and been immortal (cf. *Heb.* 7:3). Not that Melchizedek was not of the rank and number of men, but the apostle wants to indicate that he is introduced as if he had

had no birth. We do not know who his father was or from what mother he descended. We know nothing of his lineage or his life. And then there is no mention of his death, but it is particularly stated that he is a priest of the living God. Yet he appears and then passes out of sight and is buried, and it is not known how or when. With that the apostle shows he was a figure of our Lord Jesus Christ (cf. *Heb.* 7:17), who, although he is the Son of the everlasting God, nevertheless does not have a father by ordinary means because his divine essence is spiritual and eternal, having been miraculously conceived by the Holy Spirit beyond the natural order. And even though he died, yet is his life permanent, and especially he acquired life for us all when he died willingly for us. Consequently, he is without beginning and without end. Without beginning, because he is eternal God; and without end, because we have eternity in him, as the prophet Isaiah asks: 'Who will declare the lineage that will come from him?' (Cf. *Isa.* 53:8.) The church is immortal by virtue of our Lord Jesus Christ, a greater reason then for him to be everlasting. But that will be dealt with further later on. Right now we are dealing with it briefly to show the text is not talking about Shem. And that is why David particularly equates the Redeemer who was to come with Melchizedek (cf. *Psa.* 110:4).

Now before moving along, let us note that it was an admirable grace of God that Melchizedek maintained his purity that way, seeing that the whole earth was filled with idolatries at that time, for the house of Abraham's father was a den of idols, as we said before, and the Holy Spirit testified to that by the mouth of Joshua (cf. *Josh.* 24:2). Inasmuch as everything was corrupted the way it was in the land of Chaldea, which was closer to Noah's dwelling place, where he had always lived, as had Shem and his people, and inasmuch as the devil had already perverted and defiled the worship of God with many pollutions, how is it possible that in the land of Canaan, there where the people are wicked, there where only impiety and scorn for God and rebellion existed, where only iniquity, deceit, fraud, cruelty, and violence held sway, there still exists one who sacrifices to the living God? In all of that we see how God sometimes hid his church underground, so to speak, and that his church is unknown to men's minds, but it is enough that God knows it. So we have a testimony of that in Melchizedek. One might have thought there was not a single man at that time who worshipped God in purity and simplicity, for if Abraham's grandfather and all his kin were devoted to diabolical errors and served idols, where did that leave the rest? They might have judged that God's church was thoroughly abolished, but we see how God kept for himself a small seed when he made Melchizedek a priest, especially in a land which was more deeply plunged into every kind of iniquity than the others.

We must apply this for our use, for it is a very perilous temptation to think that God no longer has a church in the world, for his promise would have to be empty and impotent. And then if a man thinks he is alone, he loses his sense of purpose and grows despondent until he falls into despair. We see that in Elijah, who is nearing that condition when he said, 'What more can happen? They have killed your prophets and set up their idols everywhere, and I alone am left' (cf. *1 Kings* 19:10). There he was, a poor frightened man on the point of tripping and falling into a pit. But what happens? God consoles him and says that he still has seven thousand men, that is to say, a large number, whom he has reserved for himself, who have not bowed the knee before Baal (cf. *1 Kings* 19:18). So, as I have said, our faith would be shaken, even completely demolished, if we were convinced that God had so abandoned the world that the church no longer existed. That being the case, let us learn not to judge by human sight whether or not there is a church, but let us rather renounce any such consideration because we have been advised that God will have a few seed of it hidden somewhere, for a single seed does not appear when there is a large pile of straw that covers the small number. Consequently, sometimes it will seem that all the faithful have been exterminated here below, but God has incomprehensible ways to maintain his people because he must always be worshipped and served, not that the church has to be large in number, shining and majestic, but we must be content that God knows who his people are. So let us forsake all iniquity so we will be able to call upon his name and be bound together with those who are our brothers, even though they do not know who we are, for it all depends on adoption by God, since he testifies by the Holy Spirit that he has a large number of believers we do not need to know. For that reason, he wants them to be scattered here and there, without renown before men. He wants them to be disregarded and unnoticed. In a word, he wants no one to know anything about them, no more than if they were put underfoot. So much for that point.

And we need to be exhorted by this passage not to follow the largest crowd. Melchizedek could have devoted himself to idols, as others did, if he had had regard for what they were doing. All around them there was nothing but defilement of the worship of God, yet he continues doing what he knows to be good and upright, according as God instructed him. He had no written law, but God had given him knowledge, as he did for Noah and Shem, of what was necessary for salvation. Now if as little instruction as Melchizedek had could have constantly sustained him and the purity of religion, what will be our excuse when God reminds us often that the law shows us how he wants to be worshipped and served, that the prophets have expounded it to us, and that the gospel trumpets it in our ears and pierces all our thoughts and feelings? So since God has so many ways to keep us and the purity of his service, if we fall away and men lead us from it, and if it is received and accepted under the influence of some current popular but corrupting trend and we end up associating with unbelievers and idolaters, what will be our condemnation, seeing that Melchizedek persisted in his faith with such constancy and determination? Let us then fix our eyes on God, attune our ears to his word, and be fully alert so that we will never be turned aside, even though we are tossed about here below like ships on the sea, driven by winds and storms. And until there are a people who uphold religion and a great king who wants people to govern themselves rightly, let us learn to cling always to God alone, and let him suffice for us to keep us from straying from the path that he shows us in his word, and let the clarity of the law and the gospel be always before us, and let us not wander inasmuch as we know God is our guide. So that is what we have to remember from the example of Melchizedek.

Now let us come to the text where Moses says that Melchizedek king of Salem offered bread and wine, was a priest of the living God and blessed Abraham. We have to resolve this text which says that Melchizedek, a king, received Abraham and gave him bread and wine as food for him and his company, and Melchizedek, as a priest, blessed him, and Abraham gave him the tithe of all the spoils. Now here we have Melchizedek presented as a king and a priest. In order to look at the different acts in their separate function, we must distinguish between his being a king and exercising liberality toward Abraham by feeding him and his troupe, and his being a priest and blessing Abraham. Now it was rather common among the ancients for a king to be a priest, for that was common practice among ungodly people in many countries. Kings were not content to be kings. Because of their ambition, they wanted to be priests because they thought the priesthood held a dignity more sacred than that of royal majesty. And that is often why they made themselves priests. In fact, we see that that office was sought by means of intrigues and that those who had renown and reputation always wanted to move into that position. Even so, Moses recounts that about Melchizedek as being singular.

Yet we see that God made a distinction between the one and the other in his law and did not want one individual to have both offices. Moses was as outstanding in every perfection of virtues as any man ever born into the world, and yet God will not want him to be a priest, but his brother Aaron (cf. *Exod.* 28:1), because Moses was occupied with the government he was overseeing. In fact, we see how Uzziah was punished, for he, the king, was motivated by foolish arrogance to usurp the role of sacrificing priest (cf. *2 Chron.* 26:16). And just for perfuming the altar he was stricken with leprosy and cut off from the house of the Lord for the rest of his life (cf. *2 Chron.* 26:21). And yet it seems there is some worthy devotion, or at least he was excusable. Yes, but God does not punish only what appears, for he knew king Uzziah's pride. And then it is said that obedience is better than all sacrifices (cf. *1 Sam.* 15:22). Because he went against God's injunction and disrupted the vocation and the order that was to be inviolable, he was punished. As he was not content with his rank, he must be placed among the infamous and detestable and separated from the company of men.

So we see that in the law these two things, kingship and priesthood, are incompatible. Since that is the case, we must conclude that this is a singular example that does not pertain to the law. It is true that at that time the law had not yet been written and Levi's lineage was not yet in the world to have the right to the sacerdotal dignity, but this example is given for our instruction, so that the law retains its force and the church is edified by it, as it appears in the psalm that we cited (*Psa.* 110). We must then conclude that the reference is not to Solomon or to any other king descended from the race of David, for if they were kings, they had to refrain from being priests or they would have otherwise been apostates.

Yet when it is said that there will be a king in the likeness of Melchizedek, according to his order and state, we see that there is no talk of David's entire race, which descended from him according to the flesh, until we come to the sovereign Priest, who is our Lord Jesus Christ. It is true he is son of David and of his seed, but there is in him a special, even unique, aspect: he puts an end to the legal priesthood because his kingdom is spiritual, which also brings to an end the priesthood's earthly authority, which was established for a time until his coming. Now when it is said that it is forever, it is because it continued in the person of the Redeemer. So that is what we have to observe concerning Moses' comment that Melchizedek was king of Salem and at the same time a priest.

Those two offices belong only to our Lord Jesus Christ according to the regulation given by God in his law. Consequently, we must not doubt it was the priesthood of Jesus Christ which was already shown to Abraham so that his faith might be sealed and strengthened in that way. For since the body did not appear, it at least had to have some shadows. Therefore, the fathers had that to support their faith while waiting for Jesus Christ's appearance. They had, I said, images and figures. Even though that is not common with them, it is nonetheless useful for us. We can conclude from it that Jesus Christ was not sent on the spur of the moment and that God did not take under advisement for a single minute whether to give him to us as our Redeemer. He was already the true Redeemer, even though he had not been clothed in our nature, even though he had not yet been manifested and even though the gospel had not yet been made known. From that we understand that the faith we have today extends far and wide, and we also understand that the gospel has existed from all time, so that the ancient fathers were founded on our Lord Jesus Christ and the hope of their salvation was there. In short, it is a help which is not to be scorned. But when we compare the figures with the body, we will see that our condition is more desirable than that of the fathers (cf. *Luke* 10:23-24). That is why it is said that blessed are the eyes which see what the disciples saw, for many kings and prophets had an ardent desire to enjoy such a vision and did not receive what they asked for but were content to have a confident trust that God's promise would be fulfilled at the appropriate time, as we will see later when Jacob says when dying, 'I will see your salvation, Lord, and I trust in it' (cf. *Gen.* 49:18, 33).

So when we make that kind of comparison, we have a lot to be strengthened with and a lot to help us reject everything that the devil can throw up against us to turn us from the purity of the gospel. And we ought to be even more encouraged to embrace our Lord Jesus Christ because he brought the full and perfect truth of what is figured in the law. That is how we must profit from this passage. As for Melchizedek's seat, it was very likely Jerusalem, which was so named later. But there was the compound word Jebusalem because of the Jebusites, who had occupied that place (cf. *Gen.* 10:16; 15:21; *Josh.* 18:28). Be that as it may, it was the city where Melchizedek was, where also Jesus Christ exercised his priesthood not only while preaching the gospel, but when he was crucified for us and was offered as a sacred oblation to God his Father to reconcile us forever and cleanse us of all our sins.

Now let us bow before the majesty of our gracious God in acknowledgment of our faults, praying that he will receive us in mercy. And seeing that we are condemned in our own eyes, may we, through the one he has given us as our Redeemer, be removed from the curse in which we would be plunged if he had not cured us by his infinite goodness, and since he has extended his hand to draw us to our Lord Jesus Christ, may he strengthen us more and more in such perseverance of faith that we will cling to him and never be turned aside by any of the temptations of this world. Rather let us struggle against all the traps Satan places before us until we reach the eternal kingdom which was prepared before the creation of the world and was acquired for us at such great cost. May he grant that grace not only to us but to all the peoples and nations on earth.

64

Second Sermon on Melchizedek Wherein It Is Shown How He Was a Figure That Jesus Christ Was to Be Eternal King and Priest at the Same Time

Friday, 23 February 1560

And Melchizedek king of Salem brought forth bread and wine: and he was the priest of the most high God. And he blessed him, and said, Blessed be Abram of the most high God, possessor of heaven and earth: And blessed be the most high God, which hath delivered thine enemies into thy hand. And he gave him tithes of all (Gen. 14:18-20).

WE HAVE UNDERTAKEN to show that Melchizedek, who is mentioned here, was a figure of our Lord Jesus Christ. And so that we may be more attentive to this teaching, we have to remember what we stated yesterday, namely, that God swore by a solemn oath that the one who was to be king over the people would also be a priest.

Now it is certain that God is sparing with his name and does not throw it about carelessly inasmuch as he wants us to reverence it and take it only when necessary on occasions worthy of his holiness. He gives us an example. So we must conclude that it is very important and useful to know how the one who was to be the redeemer of the people also bore the title of king and priest. In fact, if we separated the two, our faith in the Lord Jesus Christ would be very weak and would not be a certain and firm foundation. For two things are required for our salvation. On the one hand, God accepts us as righteous and even acknowledges us as his children; on the other, we are led by his hand and are sustained and secured by his invincible power.

If we wanted to take just one of those points, it would only be half sufficient. Here is how. Let us take a case in which God is propitious toward us and does not impute our sins to us. If, however, the devil had power over us and we were exposed as prey to all the assaults he directs against us, what would happen except that we would be pitiable, lost people? On the other hand, if God only displayed his power to defend us and we were not reconciled to him and reputed to be righteous, it is certain we would always have to be called to account. And woe to us should we be judged without mercy. But we know that all our righteousness consists in God's pity on us and burying all our faults. So our Lord Jesus Christ had to appear as king and priest. In other words, he made peace between God and us so that we can come with uplifted heads when taking refuge in him and be assured that he acknowledges us as his children. We possess all of that through the benefit of the suffering and death of our Lord Jesus Christ. For he shed his blood to wash and cleanse away all our blemishes (cf. *Acts* 22:16; *1 Cor.* 6:11). He was made the sacrifice for satisfaction and by it we are acquitted of all our debts, and the bill of indebtedness of our salvation was torn up and shredded, as Paul says in Colossians (cf. *Col.* 2:14).

That then is what was accomplished in the person of the Son of God when he was sent into the world. By suffering for the forgiveness of our sins, he made us righteous. Not that we are completely so in truth. Far from it, but God does not want to judge us according to our deserts. On the contrary, because of his infinite goodness, he sustains us, and the obedience that Jesus Christ offered up is appropriated to us as if someone were paying our debts: 'I am debt-free.' Thus did our Lord Jesus Christ make himself the chief debtor and, in that way, set us free before God. And the devil himself has nothing to accuse us of when we place our trust in the satisfaction which has been borne for us by the Son of God. It is not without cause that he is called a priest.

On the other hand, we have to consider carefully the advantage we are to receive from that office. For it is not only for himself but for our use and salvation that the Father gave him that status and dignity with a solemn oath. Now let us note that he is called an everlasting priest so that that honour is reserved for him and not transferred to another. If this point had been considered as it should have been and as the apostle demonstrates it incomparably well in the Epistle to the Hebrews (cf. *Heb.* 7-10), the abomination which was introduced into the world and still reigns today would never have existed. For the Pope creates his priests on the condition of appeasing God. Here are the very words he uses when he consecrates them by his sorcery: 'I bestow on you the power to offer to God the host that is to appease him.' That is detestable blasphemy. For that is equivalent to making God a liar and destroying the solemn oath that he swore with his mouth and spoke of in Psalm 110, which we have quoted, where God says that Jesus Christ and he alone will be an everlasting priest after the order of Melchizedek (cf. *Psa.* 110:4), who has no equal. Yet we have priests in the Papacy who boast of offering up Jesus Christ and of being priests to God to make reconciliation for sins for both the living and the dead. They are not satisfied to be redeemers of those who have redeemed themselves with their hands, hands like those of thieves and robbers, but they even want their sorcery to extend to the dead. We see there is a very evident limitation between that decree uttered by the sacred mouth of God and what that Antichrist invented and continues to maintain today.

So let us note carefully not only that Jesus Christ offered himself one time in order to appease the wrath of God his Father toward us and pay for all our sins, but also that the power of the offering he made lasts forever and will be permanent. That is why the apostle says the way provided for us has been made fresh and living by the blood of Jesus Christ our Lord (cf. *Heb.* 10:20). It is as if he were saying that the blood which was shed once for our salvation will never become dry but will flow daily over our souls by the power of the Holy Spirit, who sprinkles us with it, as Peter says in the first chapter of his first letter (cf. *1 Pet.* 1:2). That is also why Jesus Christ says at his Supper, 'This is my blood of the new covenant and thus perpetual' (cf. *Matt.* 26:28). It is as if he were saying we must not think that he brought about a reconciliation which lasts only for a day or a year, but that he still exercises his priesthood today because he is the Mediator between us and God his Father by virtue of the suffering and death he endured one time, because he so intercedes for us that we are assured of being pleasing to God when we come to him in the name of our Advocate, and because we are founded on and sustained by the sacrifice offered once, so that it is serving us today and will be until the end of the world.

Now I said that it would not be enough for us to be reconciled to God that way and for our sins to be pardoned unless we had been defended and preserved at the same time by God's protecting hand. For that reason, Jesus Christ had to have also been king. For the full salvation we hope for from God must be sought in our Lord Jesus Christ. We do not have to rise high into the air and search for what we need in far places, for he gives himself to us and presents himself before us. So we must find in the person of this Redeemer the fullness of what is required for our salvation. That is why our Lord Jesus Christ is called king. The anointing given to him belongs to his kingdom so that we can be enriched by all his possessions and defended against all our enemies and have an invincible fortress. And although we are assailed, the victory always remains ours. So those are riches of the kingdom of heaven which are showered upon us because Jesus Christ was filled with them to perfection and we are completely destitute of them. In us is only severe poverty. So we must come beg from him, and he must sustain us with his generosity. That is what he does when he shares with us the gifts of his Holy Spirit so that we can remake ourselves in his image. And then the devil must be repulsed. And what power do we possess? The least temptation in the world can defeat us, and even our shadow makes us faint. But it is said that when Jesus Christ takes us under his protection, we are in such a fortress that all our enemies will have no power over us. We now see more clearly that God had a good reason to swear an everlasting oath when he established our Lord Jesus Christ as king and priest after the order of Melchizedek (cf. *Heb.* 5:6, 10; 6:20; 7:2, 17, 21).

Now the apostle continues, putting emphasis on the name, for Melchizedek signifies both king and righteousness (cf. *Heb.* 7:2).[1] He shows us that the kingdom of the Son of God is not ordinary and must not to be thought of as being like others because it has the ability to justify us. Earthly kings can still be just because they use their offices faithfully. They will abstain from excesses, from tyranny and cruelty and do their duty by everyone. In that way they will be called just. But there is a quite different justice in the Son of God, which is the one in which we are made participants. A man could be like an angel in all virtues, but that will serve only

[1] In the Romance languages, words deriving from the Latin *iustitia, iustus, iustificare* (respectively, 'justice', 'just', 'to justify') are translated into English as 'justice' or 'righteousness', 'just' or 'righteous', 'justify' or 'make righteous', depending on the context. The French in these cases is *justice, juste, justifier*. A king, for example, is not 'righteous' but 'just' when he does right. Jesus is both just and righteous when he does right.—*Translator.*

for his person. He will be able to be a good example to others, punish those who fail, see to it that people live uprightly and in good order, but he cannot make others just, for that exceeds all human ability. However, our Lord Jesus Christ has a justice, or righteousness, which is not enclosed within himself and which he possesses not only for himself but to share with us, so that we are made righteous before God through him. And how does that happen? We have already seen that God considers us righteous and innocent when it pleases him to bury our offenses and iniquities. In addition, according as he has regenerated us by the spirit of our Lord Jesus Christ, he has reclothed us in his righteousness. It is quite true this is only done in part. While we live in this world, our sins are pardoned fully and without exception, but we are not remade in such a way that we do not have many weaknesses and vices. Thus we must have our refuge in that righteousness, that is, in the forgiveness of our sins. Even so, we see how our Lord Jesus Christ makes us participants in his righteousness. That is the first point we need to note.

The second concerns the place of Salem. Salem means peace, and it also shows us that in addition to the righteousness we receive from our Lord Jesus Christ, we enjoy at the same time a peace which he alone gives and which we cannot obtain in any other way. And even though the wicked and despisers of God try to find rest, God awakens them in such a state of mental agitation that they are almost paralyzed. For the wicked try to find rest by forgetting God to the extent they can, and then they become stupid like animals. With contempt for their rage, God still remembers, and when he appears to them, they tremble as they would before their judge. And at that time they have a hundred thousand witnesses, for their consciences are better than all the arraignments in the world. They must even condemn themselves. And even if God pretends to be silent, the wicked cannot absolve themselves. They are forced to be aware of their curse. So there is no peace for the wicked, as Isaiah says (cf. *Isa.* 48:22; 57:21). But Jesus Christ is our peace, says Paul to the Ephesians (cf. *Eph.* 2:14), because he joined us with and united us to his Father. That is also why in the fifth chapter of Romans he says that being justified by faith we have peace with God (cf. *Rom.* 5:1). He makes a distinction between the peace of the wicked, that is, the peace they seek but cannot find, and the peace of believers. The wicked will turn their backs on God and distance themselves from him as far as possible, but believers present themselves before God and acknowledge him as their Father, knowing that he does not impute to them their sins because Jesus Christ has absolved them of them. In that way they have peace and rejoice in the infinite mercy he has granted them. Hence, Jesus Christ is rightly called the king of peace.

And there is more. Believers not only have assurance in the present but also for the future. They know God began his work in them with the intention of bringing it to conclusion (cf. *Phil.* 1:6). Consequently, they hope he will never fail them and will guide and govern them more and more until they come into his kingdom. That, in a word, is how we achieve peace and will possess it in Jesus Christ because without him we are necessarily God's enemies, and since we make war with him by our vices and rebelliousness, he must be armed against us.

It is also noteworthy that he was the eternal priest when Melchizedek is introduced as being without beginning, without end, and without genealogy. That is so we will know that our Lord Jesus Christ, although he was sent in the fullness of time, is nonetheless the eternal Son of God and was even established as Redeemer before the foundation of the world. For he is the firstborn of all creatures because it is in him and through him that everything was made (cf. *Col.* 1:15-17) and because, according to the wondrous counsel of God, he was to restore all things because dissipation was rampant everywhere after the fall of Adam, who wreaked havoc on all creatures along with himself. But our Lord Jesus Christ restored everything. So let us realize, as the apostle says in the last chapter of Hebrews, that Jesus Christ not only today is but was yesterday, that is, he is for all time (cf. *Heb.* 13:8); his power has been demonstrated just as it will be until the end. So that is how we must take full refuge in his power, which the fathers themselves felt and experienced before he was manifested in the flesh (cf. *Heb.* 11:13), not doubting, even though we are absent from him and there is a great distance between heaven and earth, that we will always be made alive by his life and enriched by his riches, sustained and preserved by his power. For if the sun, which is an insentient creature, warms the earth and causes it to bear fruit and we are nourished and sustained by God through its means, what will Jesus Christ do by comparison, he who is not an insentient creature, who is not even a creature but who is God manifested in the flesh, who is our Mediator (cf. *Gal.* 3:19-20; *Heb.* 9:15; 12:24), on whom the Father wanted to place everything required for our felicity? That, in short, is what we have to remember.

Now because the papists and all those who call themselves Christians must be taught by this passage of Moses that Jesus Christ alone is king and priest and has united us with God and his Father and also causes the Father to keep us under his protection—they have turned everything said here topsy-turvy. And that error did not start with the papists, for they do not have to say more than is there, for they have enough blasphemies to condemn them a hundred times over. But it is a pity that the devil ruled with such influence that for fourteen hundred years he so blinded those so-called Christians that they invented the sorcerer's fantasy that Jesus Christ was foreshadowed in the person of Melchizedek and that his body is celestial bread and that his blood is the wine to nourish our souls and that he offered up one and the other.

On the surface, that allegory will please those who have willing ears: how Jesus Christ calls his body bread and his blood wine. It seems appropriate that Melchizedek offered up bread and wine because the body of Jesus Christ was to possess that virtue in itself to nourish us and the wine to give life to our souls. But it is not here a question of making some offering to God. Moses says that Melchizedek king of Salem offered up bread and wine. That is to say, he presented it to Abraham. In that case Abraham would have had to be God because the offering was directed toward his person. Moreover, it was not for him alone but for all his company. This is royal largesse granted to Abraham when Melchizedek received him. To relate that to God is to pervert everything, as we observe.

Moreover, our Lord Jesus Christ offered up his body and his blood not because they had previously been bread and wine; but because of the offering he had made of them, they are called bread and wine, that is, they have the property and nature of bread and wine for us. Why are we, with respect of our souls, sustained by the body and blood of our Lord Jesus Christ and why do we have all our life from that? Because the sacrifice which was offered up once is the sum and perfection of every good. So if Jesus Christ had not been offered earlier, his body would not be food for us today, and his blood would not be drink for us. That is why Paul says in First Corinthians that Jesus Christ our Paschal Lamb was sacrificed: 'Therefore, let us eat' (*1 Cor.* 5:7-8). This is the order we must follow: the offering comes first, and afterwards, by its virtue, we are nourished and sustained by our Lord Jesus Christ's body and blood. Thus, in every way, we see that these poor lunatics who have corrupted this passage by Moses knew nothing about our Lord Jesus Christ.

Now since the papists were possessed by Satan and given a reprobate understanding so they could not distinguish between black and white (and that was an act of God), they made themselves so ridiculous that little children would be justified in spitting in their faces. They were content with that error and even added more to that rubbish. And following that, they said one has to offer bread and wine daily because the sacrifice of Jesus Christ corresponds to that of Melchizedek. On that point, they are, in the first place, convicted of a very gross stupidity, even for them. They say there is in their mass no bread or wine after they work their magic on the host, as they call it, and *voilà* a god! And even though we see the bread and even though the wine has a taste, they say that those are species, that is, manifest images where there is no substance. So they want to have you believe that there is no bread or wine, that your eyes, your sense of taste, and all your senses are confounded. They would have you believe that everything was nullified when they pronounced the words they call 'sacramental'. If they had to offer bread and wine, where are those elements? They say, do they not, that there are none, and yet they cite this passage and say bread and wine must be offered. So we see that their nonsense is so stupid that little children can make fun of them and be their judges.

Moreover, if they want to find a correspondence between Melchizedek and our Lord Jesus Christ, what we quoted from the psalm has to remain inviolate (cf. *Psa.* 110:4): there is only one priest because he has been instituted by a particular oath. Consequently, he must always retain his office. But they create priests in our Lord Jesus Christ's stead. As a result, the similarity is obliterated. We do not need additional replies or arguments to reject their stupidity. We need only to take the text as it is, their own confession right out of their mouths, and that will cut their throats. Even so, we see that, insofar as that provides a singular teaching, the devil has tried hard to obscure it, confuse it, falsify it, and even destroy it completely. All the more then must we be ever alert to impress on our minds what is contained in it, and we must be stirred to do that by the solemn oath God intended to make. As we have seen, it is not without cause that he swore that way by his name. He did so to give our faith infallible confirmation so we would not doubt that we have in his only Son everything we need to lead us to our righteousness, our peace, even to the heavenly kingdom. That, then, is what we have to remember.

At the same time it is said that Melchizedek blessed Abraham because he was a priest of the sovereign God. That blessing indicates superiority, as the apostle well informs us when he says that the person who is pre-eminent blesses his inferiors (cf. *Heb.* 7:7). Consequently, in his role as priest, Abraham is necessarily inferior to Melchizedek. Even so, Abraham was father and head of the church. So we must conclude that Melchizedek represented a greater than any mortal man could be. That is why some ancients imagine that he was an angel, but that is just so much folly and nonsense. For when he is called a priest of the living God, it is certain he was a man well known in the land and as king of Salem. That is a lot of hooey. But if he had been an angel, he still would not have been greater than Abraham in the general paternity of the entire church. So we have to come back to that point: although Melchizedek was a mortal creature, he still surpassed the angels of paradise in dignity because of the priesthood, not because of himself, but because of the one whose figure he was. Since David was greater than all the angels, it is said to him: 'You are my son. Today I have begotten you' (cf. *Psa.* 2:7). That is said to no angel, as the apostle says (cf. *Heb.* 2:5). Yet David was a poor sinner, a son of Adam just like the others. So how is it that he is here elevated so high that the angels are put under him? It is because that figure represents the majesty of the Son of God and not just David. Therefore, we must deduce that Melchizedek cannot be pre-eminent over Abraham except in respect of the truth that he was the figure of. So we must conclude that Jesus Christ has been manifestly signified since that time so that the faith of believers might be completely founded on him because, from the beginning, no other salvation has been given under heaven except the one revealed to us in the gospel.

Now it is true there is a common blessing. 'To bless', in holy Scripture, is often taken for 'to pray'. As we will see later, an everyday person blesses another when saying, 'God bless you' (cf. *Gen.* 28:3), as when we greet one another. That kind of blessing is the ordinary style of holy Scripture. But there is a special blessing reserved for priests. That is why it is often said in the law that priests, that is, those who have the authority, bless the people in the name of God (cf. *Deut.* 10:8; 21:5; *1 Chron.* 23:13). The same form has been given to us in the sixth chapter of Numbers, where it says: 'This is how the priests will bless my people: The Lord bless you and keep you. The Lord make his face shine upon you and be gracious unto you and give you peace' (cf. *Num.* 6:23-26). That is the formula that God has given his church. That is also why it is said that when Jesus ascended into heaven, he raised his hands over his apostles as the priests did in order to fulfil the figures of the law by blessing his disciples (cf. *Luke* 24:50). That is the benediction which is spoken of here. That is why the apostle does not argue to no avail that Melchizedek, as priest, was more excellent than Abraham because he blessed him (cf. *Heb.* 7:7). Now Abraham is the father of the whole church. So let us conclude that our Lord Jesus Christ possesses a more than human majesty and that every sovereignty must bow before him who is the Mediator and realize that great and small must acknowledge the sovereign authority given to him in his human nature by God his Father and that every knee must bow before him (cf. *Phil.* 2:9-10). That is how this passage from Paul in the second chapter of Philippians is to be understood. And that is what we have to remember.

It now remains for us to apply this passage to our use, which is that we not doubt how our father Abraham was blessed in a figure by Melchizedek and that today our Lord Jesus Christ, who is the eternal Priest, blesses us in the name of God his Father. That prayer is not in vain. It must produce its effect, for we know it cannot but be answered. So let us conclude that as we put our trust in Jesus Christ, he is our Advocate before God his Father (cf. *1 John* 2:1). If we are cursed in Adam (cf. *1 Cor.* 15:22) and still receive new condemnations daily for our sins and transgressions, yet they will be effaced and repaired because our Lord Jesus Christ condescends to take the office of blessing us. And we also remember the prayer he made once, in the seventeenth chapter of John: 'Holy Father, I pray for all these (that is, the eleven apostles and disciples whom he had already received to himself), and I pray for all those who will believe in my name through their word so that they may be one in me as I am one in you so that we may all be one' (cf. *John* 17:20-21). Just as our Lord Jesus Christ declared those words with his mouth once, so it is that he prays not only for his disciples who already belonged to his flock but also for all those who believe in him through their word.

Therefore, let us understand that when we embrace the teaching of the gospel with true obedience, we will be persuaded that the Son of God is given to us for our sovereign and only good. That is how his prayer will always be effective. There is no need for him to repeat it morning and evening and every day. It is enough that he sealed it with his blood, this one and only and eternal sacrifice which he made one time. We are assured that our prayers are answered when we pray to God in the name of our Saviour. Our prayers would be only contamination and would even contaminate the air if we ever had to look at God to realize afterward what kind of people we are. But our prayers are blessed by the priestly benediction of our Lord Jesus Christ, to whom we must look in order to be participants in all his good things. That, in short, is how we must apply to our advantage and the edification of our faith this passage, where it is said that Abraham, father of the faithful, was blessed. In that, we see Abraham was cursed in himself inasmuch as he borrows a priestly benediction. And Melchizedek also knew that there is in us real poverty and that God must bless us and that we must embrace that fact with all humility if we wish to enjoy the good which our Lord Jesus Christ brings us and offers us daily through the preaching of the gospel.

At that point Moses recounts Melchizedek's benediction: 'Blessed be Abraham of the most high God, who possesses heaven and earth, and blessed be the sovereign God who delivered your enemies into your hand.' He blesses Abraham in the name of God, as we have already cited from the law. We must not understand that when priests possess the office of blessing, they have it by their own authority and that God turned his office over to them and that his praise for it is lessened. When God works through his ministers, it is not so that he will be diminished or that his power will be obscured. What he gives deprives him of nothing. But he is pleased to use such means on condition that people always return to him and draw good from no other fountain. That is particularly why it is said: 'Blessed be Abraham of the sovereign God,' as if Melchizedek were saying that he is nothing of himself and can do nothing, but because God calls him into his service, Melchizedek also calls upon him and invokes his name upon Abraham.

So we see that Jesus Christ has the office of providing blessing, that is, of making us acceptable to God, of effacing all the evil that is in us. But that ought to lead us higher, to the inestimable love of God the Father, who did not spare his only Son but delivered him over to death for our sakes (cf. *Rom.* 8:32). When the principal cause of our salvation is shown to us, Scripture informs us of God's love: 'For God so loved the world that he did not spare his only Son' (cf. *John* 3:16). That is how we are blessed by the priestly authority of the Son of God. But the Father is calling us to himself so that we will pay him homage and give thanks for that great good shared with us through the Son.

In short, we see here that all the good we are to desire and hope for proceeds from God alone and that it is in him that we must seek him. Each person will want to be at ease and possess all that he thinks belongs to him. That is a desire the good and the wicked share in common. But very few seek their good in God. They all want to be very happy, but they scorn the one from whom all good proceeds. It is the same as if a man is very thirsty, is even languishing and is at the end of his tether and someone says to him: 'There is the fountain,' but he does not deign to drink. There is both water and wine, but he refuses to approach and drink. That is the way it is with those who desire and seek to know everything that strikes their fancy and to have everything they realize they need but still scorn God and refuse to approach him. So every time we seek what is desirable for our souls or for our bodies, let us begin by acknowledging that God wills our good and that he so receives us in his mercy that we can approach him and come into his presence and fill ourselves with his blessings inasmuch as it is useful for our salvation. That then is what we have to observe about what is said: 'May the sovereign God bless Abraham.'

After that, Melchizedek adds a benediction for God's giving victory to our father Abraham, saying, 'And blessed be the living God who delivered your enemies into your hand.' With those words we are admonished always to join praises for God with the prayers and supplications we make to him, as Paul also declares in Philippians when he tells us to let our desires be made known to God (cf. *Phil.* 4:6). In other words, we are not to hold in our resentment as unbelievers do when they see something that would be just the thing for them, but they do not receive it. They complain. But what do you expect? Their hearts are closed and they do not appear before God to ask for what they need. That is why the apostle says to let your requests, your thoughts and desires be placed before God. In other words, when you realize you are destitute of one thing or another, look for the good where it is, and there you will find it, namely, in God. Let your prayers, supplications, and thanksgiving show that you dwell in God's presence, and when you have prayed to him, as I said, let your praises be joined with your petitions. For if we pray to him and grumble with discontentment, we blaspheme his holy name. Prayer is to be a sweet smelling sacrifice (cf. *Psa.* 51:19; *Heb.* 13:15). And we offend and outrage him when, dissatisfied with his grace, we want to subject him to our desires. Therefore, every time we pray to God, we must be admonished to give him thanks, to yield ourselves completely to his will, and to acknowledge his benefits. As it is also said in Psalm 50: 'Call upon me in the day of trouble. I will hear you, and you will glorify me' (cf. *Psa.* 50:15). That is how Melchizedek responds concerning Abraham.

In order to understand this better and more clearly, let us note that our prayers are to look to the past and to the future: to the past to express gratitude to God for the good things we have already received from him; to the future to ask him to continue and to persevere until the end as he began. Now that is well worth noting, for here we see Abraham who was raised up high, established as the father of the faithful. He had been blessed by God in respect of all virtues and possessed an excellent spirit within himself, but Melchizedek still shows him that he must be increased graciously until the end and have daily recourse to God. For when he blesses him, he simultaneously gives him a lesson which he must remember and practise all the days of his life. If Abraham needed to call upon God forever, whatever blessings he had received and whatever dignity was his, he still had to practice prayer. What is required of us who are very remote from him? So we see why I said our prayers must look to the future because we always need God's help, and why I said he must have pity on us, hasten to our aid, and increase his blessings in us. And then our prayers must look to the past for occasion of praise and thanksgiving. That is so we can declare that we possess every good thing from him and that we are so content that even if we know perplexity in our troubles, we will continue to rejoice because we have known and experienced him as our Father and because he has also shown himself to be trustworthy by the kindnesses he has already shared with us. That is what we have to observe here.

When Melchizedek says, 'Blessed be the living God who delivered your enemies into your hand,' we understand that every victory proceeds from God and especially that Abraham, by his industry, by his prowess and bravery, did not put to flight the kings spoken of, but that God had given him guidance. It is true Abraham took his enemies by surprise at night, as we have seen, and did so because he was not trained in the art of war. How could that have happened except that God had made him prosper? We see how David had a large army of valiant and renowned soldiers and was himself expert in war from the time God made him king, but he says God gave him feet like deer's and set him on high places and strengthened him to break the bars and bolts of doors[2] and rout his enemies (cf. *Psa.* 18:33-34). So David proclaims that nothing of all the victories he has acquired belongs to him. Even though David, in the eyes of men, had the means to overcome his enemies, he nonetheless confesses without hypocrisy that everything must be attributed to God so that his name will be glorified by it.

How could that apply to Abraham, who had never engaged in war or known what it was to draw a sword, in a manner of speaking? Nevertheless, he conquered a multitude of people who were

[2] French: *'courreaux et verrous'*

swollen with presumption because they had put their enemies to rout, and he pillaged and sacked five cities. God did indeed have to have a hand in that. Even so, we have to gather from this passage that if we should only have to lift a finger, it is God's place to guide us so that we will not undertake anything with overweening pride as if we were capable of doing something. So let those who either have to wage war or do something difficult place themselves in God's hands, knowing there is good reason he is called the God of armies. So much for that point.

In addition, we must apply this to a second usage, which has to do with a spiritual power that is given to us to overcome Satan and everything that is against our salvation. Our battle, says Paul, is not against flesh and blood, but against powers in high places, against the devils and their fiery darts (cf. *Eph.* 6:12). It is there that we must engage ourselves.

Therefore, because our chief enemy is the devil and the darts and the swords and all the means he has to harm us are spiritual, let us learn to call upon God. For what strength do we possess? What agility? So God must engage the battle and we must stand by silent, like people whose hands are tied. It is not that we must not put forth great effort. Believers must fight valiantly against the desires of their flesh, but their power must come from on high to destroy every imagination of their free will and their authority, which is the Papacy's intoxication when they rise up against God in their pride. We have to know that we are powerless in both body and soul. But since God has taken charge of guiding us, let us be aware of that and completely persuaded that he has enough power for us and we can do nothing without him and we can do everything through him (cf. *Phil.* 4:13).

Now let us bow before the majesty of our gracious God in acknowledgment of our faults, praying that he will touch us more and more with such repentance that we will groan to receive the forgiveness of our iniquities, which make us debtors before him. And let us seek for him through the one he has established, our Lord Jesus Christ, knowing that since we are reconciled by his suffering and death, God does not fail to receive us as his well-beloved children, even though we are poor creatures filled with pollution. And may he also strengthen us by his Holy Spirit so that we can be aware that sovereign authority was not given to our Lord Jesus Christ in vain inasmuch as he has enriched us with spiritual blessings, of which we have none in our spiritual nature. May he grant that grace not only to us, but to all peoples and nations on earth.

65

Third Sermon on Melchizedek Wherein Are Treated the Use and Right of Tithes and Also the Oath

Saturday, 24 February 1560

And blessed be the most high God, which hath delivered thine enemies into thy hand. And he gave him tithes of all. And the king of Sodom said unto Abram, Give me the persons, and take the goods to thyself. And Abram said to the king of Sodom, I have lift up mine hand unto the LORD, the most high God, the possessor of heaven and earth, That I will not take from a thread even to a shoelatchet, and that I will not take any thing that is thine, lest thou shouldest say, I have made Abram rich: Save only that which the young men have eaten, and the portion of the men which went with me, Aner, Eshcol, and Mamre; let them take their portion (Gen. 14:20-24).

YESTERDAY WE DISCUSSED at length that Melchizedek, who is spoken of here, was a figure and image of our Lord Jesus Christ because he was superior to Abraham, who was father of the church (cf. *Psa.* 110:4). And just as it is said in the psalm that the redeemer who was to come would be not only a king but also a priest after the order of Melchizedek, we also indicated why all of that is said, how it serves us and what advantage we receive from it. Finally, we also pointed out that it was by virtue of Melchizedek's office that Abraham was blessed to show that all our prayers would be defiled before God and we would receive nothing unless Jesus Christ interceded for us, as that office is also attributed to him in holy Scripture (cf. *John* 14:13; *Rom.* 8:34).

It is now said that Abraham offered tithes of everything to Melchizedek. This indicates again the sacerdotal dignity that was in Melchizedek, as the apostle remembered (cf. *Heb.* 7:1-3). We cannot take it for certain that the word tithe is to refer to the spoils or to what Abraham possessed. Inasmuch as he received nothing that profited him, it does not seem he intended to offer Melchizedek what is not considered to be his. But there was another reason for expressing gratitude to God and applying the good to enrich himself. Even so, we do well to remain with what is certain, namely, that Abraham acknowledged Melchizedek as a priest of God, for if Melchizedek had served idols or usurped a dignity that did not belong to him, Abraham would have been wrong to offer him tithes because we know that making offerings to idols is to honour them and renounce God (cf. *Judg.* 3:7; *2 Kings* 17:12; *Psa.* 97:7). Consequently, Abraham's offering was a witness to and approval of Melchizedek's priesthood.

That is also why the apostle says, when making a comparison between the ancient priesthood which was not under the law and the priesthood of our Lord Jesus Christ, that Levi, who was still in Abraham's loins, because he is descended from his line, paid the tithe, that is, he was subjected to that duty (cf. *Heb.* 7:9). It is true that the same could be said of Judah, from whom our Lord Jesus Christ descended, but the solution is easily found in the fact that Melchizedek cannot be separated from our Lord Jesus Christ because he represents him and all the excellence that is in him derives from the fact that he is the figure of Jesus Christ. So it is for good reason that the apostle shows that he to whom the right of tithes belongs was also subjected to Melchizedek. From that we must conclude that our Lord Jesus Christ is much more excellent than Aaron was, or all his successors, although they were like people separated from the ranks of men. And when he was clothed as priest, it was to show that he was like an angel of God, able to approach his majesty, being the mediator to remove the people's iniquities and transgressions (cf. *Exod.* 28:25; *Lev.* 16:32). So even though all of that was the situation at the time, the apostle still shows that our Lord Jesus Christ far surpassed him in honour and must be exalted above all the images of the law, and we see in that fact that he was the truth and substance of it (cf. *Heb.* 8-10). And if we took all the figures that were in use for a time, it would serve no purpose and everything would be meaningless apart from the true Pattern. So let us note particularly that when Abraham offered all the tithes to Melchizedek, it was to show that although God would have had to establish a priesthood among his people later, it was not to diminish our Lord Jesus Christ's priesthood, which was already imaged in the person of Melchizedek, as it was already established for that time.

Moreover, in the matter of offering tithes to priests, we see Abraham did so before there was a written law, and there is no doubt the Spirit of God induced him to do so. Moses is not recounting here a thing done on a whim or without reason; he is rather declaring how God ratified Melchizedek's office because he wanted to establish him as his priest, and Abraham acknowledged him as such. But we cannot assume from that that there was a general law or that believers were obligated to pay tithes unless God established it in his law (cf. *Lev.* 27:30; *Num.* 18:26, 29; *Deut.* 14:22). What he did—not only so that people would pay him homage with the produce of the earth while declaring it was from his generous liberality—was not simply so that the ministers at the altar, that is, those who served in the temple, would be fed, but because they belonged to Abraham's race. Thus a part of the land belonged to them and they were to enter into possession of it, as it was said to Abraham: 'Your seed will possess the land' (cf. *Gen.* 12:7). Levi was supposed to be a chief in the house of Abraham, but he is excluded, and the house of Joseph is constituted of two chiefs instead, that is, Ephraim and Manasseh. Levi then is deprived of his inheritance, but God had already assigned him his place. That is why his successors are compensated with tithes (cf. *Num.* 18:24). Now God set it up that way for two reasons. The first was so that they would not be distracted from the service which they were charged with or from the teaching. God did not elect the priests under the law just to perform ceremonies, but they served another function, which Malachi the prophet spoke of, which was that they were ordained as his ambassadors so people could seek from them a true knowledge and correct explanation of the law. Consequently, tithes were assigned to them so that the priests would be able to dedicate themselves to the temple service and the instruction of the people (cf. *Mal.* 2:7). That is also why they were scattered throughout the entire land. They did not have their own share of the land to indicate that they had to do in a certain locale as the others did, but they were scattered here and there so there would be no corner of the earth where God would not have his messengers and legal representatives to keep people restrained. That, I say, is why God wanted them to have the tithes and not be occupied with tilling the soil.

The second reason is that if they had possessed the land, God would not have been acknowledged as Lord and Master, as he was when the Levitical priests were his collectors, so to speak, when he placed them in that position in his name to demand the right of superiority and homage that he had over the earth; also, although the children of Israel received what was their due from succession and inheritance from their father Abraham, he would nonetheless have manifested himself to them to show that the earth was his and that he retained proprietorship and that they possessed it on condition that they hold their possession from him and acknowledge it by their actions (cf. *Deut.* 14:28-29). Joined to that also was that offerings would be made to the poor from those tithes, for it is not said that the priests were to lavish them upon themselves, but that they would themselves pay tithes to show that they are not exempt from the general law, but that they are indebted to God for the bread they eat and that everything proceeds from his pure goodness. That, then, is how the tithes contained in the law were special for the people of Israel.

However, the tithe was rather common among the pagans, even for kings, princes, and lords. We see in profane histories that it was required,[1] even with greater rigor in some lands, depending on the fertility of the soil, for certain lands are so fat and produce so much that those who cultivate the land will not be so burdened by paying an eighth as those who pay a tithe.[2] Even so, the word tithe was very widely used and commonplace in all nations. Princes and lords, as I said, since the church began, have applied a part of the tithes to supporting the ministers of the word, as is only right, for as Paul says, if those who ministered at the altar in the Old Testament were provided for, those who offer sacrifices to God today in a more excellent way, that is, those who gain souls to sacrifice to him, are to be likewise supported (cf. *1 Cor.* 9:13-14). And even though God did not define how or with how much they are to be provided for, the law is still in place. So ever since God has been known by the preaching of the gospel and ever since some Christian order and policy have been in effect, tithes have been in use.

[1] Titus-Livius, *Historia romana* XXXVII, 2, 50; XLIII, 2; Cicero, *Actio in Verrem secunda*, lib. III, in particular XLII, 99–XLVI, 109; etc.—*M.E.*
[2] Cf. *Codex justinianus* IV, 61, 8 (*Corpus juris civilis* II, ed. Paul Krüger, p. 186f.); *Codex Theodosianus* IV, 14, 6. On the other hand, during republican Rome, the tax rose only to a twentieth of the harvests in certain poor regions.—*M.E.*

We see in that how the Pope and those who follow him represent tithing falsely, for when they deal with the right of tithes in their canons,[3] they understand it as if it were transferred to them after Jesus Christ brought to an end the priesthood of Levi. All that is only falsehood and misrepresentation, and they falsify and corrupt holy Scripture wickedly. We understand the tithe differently, as has been pointed out, inasmuch as it was not practiced for a long time and people did not know what paying tithes was on the authority of the law of Moses; but tithes were always being paid either to the emperor or to some particular lords.[4]

But now that the matter of tithing has been thus ordered—provided that there is no abuse and no effort to induce belief against all truth that the practice is continued by holy Scripture, but that it is taken as policy—let us hold to the rule that Paul establishes, namely, not to deprive the ox when it works to provide for our upkeep (cf. *1 Cor.* 9:9-13). Greater then is the reason that those who proclaim salvation, who are ordained to that excellent charge, should not be deprived of their food and drink, but that they should be well provided for. Now, as I said, when tithes and similar contributions are applied to good use, we must not inquire into the details of why that is the practice. There are extreme people who want to turn everything inside out. They say: 'Oh, now is not the time to pay the tithes, and because such and such a thing has been abused, that practice must not continue.' You would have to eradicate everything if you listened to them, for they think

---

[3] Cf. *Decretum Gratiani*: 2nda pars, causa 16, q. 1, c. 56; *ibid.* q. 2, c. 3; but especially *Decretales*: lib. III, tit. 30, 'De decimis, primitis et oblationibus,' particularly c. 2 and 26 (passage of the tithes due to the Levites to those due to the priests), c. 14 (instituted by God), etc. Cf. also Pierre Lombard, *Sentenciae*: lib. III, dist. 3, cap. 3.—*M.E.*

[4] Calvin has just said, to the contrary, that 'the tithe was common among the pagans.' See the previous paragraph. What he means is that the payment of the tithe among the non-Christian ancients was obviously not referring to the Bible and was not conferred on the Church.—*M.E.*

Christianity consists in changing the colour of the sun and the moon. But, as I said, if something needs to be corrected, if there is some false opinion introduced by the papists, let that be eradicated! Let us support things that have been well instituted. In other words, let us support the tithes and similar contributions to feed the poor and maintain those who serve the church. Let those good things be restored to their legitimate use, and do not allow the insatiable chasms consume everything. Let us not waste our goods on useless things, on show, in drunken revelries, and other dissolute activities, but let us realize that our goods are sacred and must be preserved for the use of the church, as much to sustain the poor, as I said, as to provide for those who serve God and his people.

That is what needed to be mentioned in passing concerning the right of tithes. We come now to what follows. Moses returns to the king of Sodom, of whom he had spoken (cf. *Gen.* 14:17), but he interrupted his comments in order to deal with Melchizedek. He now adds that the king of Sodom wanted to keep only the persons and leave the spoils to Abraham, as if he were saying that he is asking for nothing of all that had been taken from him by his enemies and that he knows Abraham had acquired it by means of his victory. He is only asking for the return of the persons and the place where he was living. We do not know whether he was feigning, seeing that he was already in Abraham's hand and power, or whether he truly recognized that Abraham deserved to have everything and that much would be required for him and his family to be redeemed from the hand of his enemies. Whatever the case, it is said that Abraham rejects his offer and says he will take nothing from him, not even a thread or a sandal thong, not even a pin, as we say in our language except, he says, what his companions had eaten, for they had not come there to pay their own way, and they would at least have been fed while exposing their lives in order to deliver the people of Sodom. Well, what they have eaten, he says, will remain with them. 'And then I have the men who are with me, Aner, Eshcol, and Mamre. They must have their share of the spoils, for I do not wish to diminish their profit in the least, and it is not my place to lay upon them a right or an obligation. I am being openhanded. I must not hold them to the same standard. Therefore, they will take their portion, I nothing.'

In order to confirm his statement, he lifted up his hand to the most high God, Possessor of heaven and earth, as if to say he swore an oath and that is the way things will be because he is no longer permitted to retract his oath, so that the other will no longer haggle. We see here how Abraham wanted to avoid all obstacles by refusing to profit in any way from what belonged to him. For if the war was just, he could, by common accord, keep what he had taken, but in order to show he was not influenced by avarice or desire for gain when he took up arms, he says he will not keep a single thread; and even this phrase: 'so that you can say you enriched Abraham,' indicates definitely that he was not motivated by ambition. Often magnanimity can be seen in those who want to attract to themselves other people's possessions, but fearing the world's shame and reproaches, they wish to show they can be trusted. Abraham did not proceed that way so that God's name would not be blasphemed because of him. People could have said, 'How is that? That man demonstrated great sincerity up until now, and we see that he worships a personal and private God, and with surprising devotion. He says he left his country because God called him; yet he wages war; he takes spoils, and now we find out he is a highway robber.' That, then, is how Abraham could have exposed God's name to many false charges. That is also why he restrains himself.

Now that is written for our sakes, and we must seek first to follow this principle: it is not enough to possess a pure conscience before God, but we must also seek, according to the example Paul sets before us, to maintain honour and a good reputation in the eyes of our neighbours (cf. *2 Cor.* 8:21). Why so? So that they will not condemn us when they think something bad has been done by our hands, but so that we would encourage them to do well. It is true we will not be able to escape the biting and barking of many dogs, and even when we are without spot or blemish, they will not refrain from disparaging and reviling us. For the Son of God did indeed pass that way (cf. *Matt.* 27:23; *Luke* 23:34); all the prophets and apostles were falsely charged (cf. *Jer.* 20:2; *1 Pet.* 2:12; *2 Pet.* 2:2). So we must be ready for every good work, as Paul says in another passage, and we must avoid speaking evil and uttering cutting remarks, insults, and false imputations (cf. *Titus* 3:2; *1 Cor.* 4:12-13). And insofar as we can, we must not give that opportunity to those who seek it, but we must silence them so that God's name will not be blasphemed because of us.

Here, then, is how we must follow Abraham. We must keep in mind that we are watched from every side, and even when we are not, we still owe it to our neighbours not to give the weak any occasion for stumbling, for they could take us as a bad example. There are always wicked people who ask for nothing better than to accuse us of something, some quarrel, something disgraceful. But other than that, as I have said, our lives are an open book. For God wants us to be exposed as on a stage, bearing his name and his mark, as Paul says to the Philippians (cf. *Phil.* 2:14-15); and he wants us to be light for the wicked despite the fact they are twisted and perverse people, and to show them the right way so that they will be confused by it and not be able to find something to reproach us for and yet be made more inexcusable when they see we serve God with integrity while they give themselves to cheating, deceiving, and the like.

That, then, is how we have to practise that teaching. As for Abraham, we see his good conscience here, for if war is provoked, it seems that no holds are barred, according to an ancient proverb 'Laws cease in times of war,'[5] even though government is more required at that time than in time of peace, but there will be some superior authority so that a captain will be obeyed, so that soldiers will stand firm under their flag, and so that the people will look to their safety and ward off the enemy. So the matters dealing with warfare will have rules, laws, and decrees, but it is impossible for war to be engaged without many grave wrongs. That is why all those who think about drawing the sword should sense horror every time they think about the repercussions. Many innocent people will be killed in such a melee; many houses will be sacked; many will be left orphans and widows; the possessions of those who cannot be blamed for the war will be seized from every source, taken as necessity requires, especially when munitions run short and empty stomachs think about famine and extreme want. That is how war itself always throws everything into confusion.

Moreover, those who go to war, even if they have legitimate reasons and can show the cause that leads them to it and even urges them to it out of necessity, they still allow themselves a great deal of latitude, for they say, 'If my enemy had defeated me, what would he have done? Would he have spared either me or mine? It is certain that if he had had the victory, he would have sacked everything and levelled it to the ground. And since he would have done that, why would I not do the same?' That is how those who make war excuse themselves and take such liberty that they think that even while pillaging and laying waste, they are doing no wrong.

Nevertheless, we see how Abraham conducted himself. It is true that when the children of Israel entered the land of Canaan, they pillaged everything (cf. *Josh.* 6-13). Why? God commanded them to do so, and they could not do otherwise (cf. *Num.* 33:55). And

5 Cf. Cicero, *Oratio pro T. Annio Milone*, IV, 11: *'silent enim leges inter arma'* ['For laws cease in war']; or Lucanus, *Pharsalia*, lib. I, v. 277: *'Leges bello siluere coacte'* ['Laws ceased when the war began.']—*M.E.*

they were even punished very rigorously because they spared the inhabitants of the land (cf. *Judg.* 2:14-15). And God also threatened them, saying that if they let some of them remain, they would be like thorns pricking their sides and even destroying their eyes (cf. *Josh.* 23:13). But there is here a special reason, for Abraham was not armed by God to purge the city of Sodom and the neighbouring cities of their inhabitants or to rule over them. He only recovered his nephew Lot, even though God took pity on the people of Sodom and their neighbours that way because he wanted to postpone for a while the vengeance which was prepared for them. Therefore, Abraham, knowing the reason he had taken arms, does not exercise his freedom or look for subtle rationales the way those who are greedy for gain do, but he declares he will take nothing.

Nevertheless, he cannot keep Aner, Eschol, and Mamre from having their portion, for they were not under him or subject to his authority. They had come there free of charge, so to speak, since they were his friends and allies. They helped him so he could deliver his nephew Lot; so he left for them what they had a right to. Thus we see, on the one hand, the extent of Abraham's self-control; on the other, we see that he took nothing of the value of a straight pin, but the fact remains that he could not prevent loss and damage and that those who belonged to his company did not have their portion of the spoils. And that is to show even better that if the one who perpetrates war happened to be an angel of paradise, he would scorn gold and silver and prefer to die than to profit a copper cent under the pretext that he had exposed his life. Although war in itself always brings many evils and excesses with it, although people say that that is permissible, there will always be much violence, and many people will have to bewail their losses. Some will have their houses burned, some will be pillaged; some will be cleaned out right down to the straw of their beds; others will be plundered of their last stick of wood. There will necessarily be many tears and much wailing in times of open warfare. Thus, one must always be admonished to stand aside with hands tied, so to speak, and refrain from entering into such conflicts, for which there is no remedy, although one would like to behave like angels, as I have said.

Now, in brief, those who defend themselves justly and are forced to do so must still be very vigilant to conduct themselves in such a way that they at least imitate our father Abraham. And if they cannot avoid excesses, losses, and destruction, they are at least resolved that the war will not be engaged randomly in order to have spoils, but for the just defence of the country when it is invaded by wicked violence.[6] They will defend themselves against a king or a prince if the king or prince wishes to attack those who are peaceable and ask only to live in friendship. Therefore, the consideration is not to be to gain prestige and possess other people's substance. But when one takes up arms, let him consider what is recounted here about Abraham with the view to following suit. For the Holy Spirit did not want only to praise him for not being greedy and for disregarding gold and silver, but also to propose him as a living example from which to learn what pattern we must follow to be like him. We could have frivolous excuses to justify ourselves if we pillaged and ravaged on all sides, but that will serve no purpose if we do not follow our father Abraham's example. That, then, is what we have to remember about this passage.

Now Abraham is not content to give a simple response to the king of Sodom. He even swears an oath and says he has already sworn an oath so that there will be no more haggling and

[6] Calvin justifies only a 'just defence of a country', the 'just war' that is defensive, as do Ambrose of Milan (*Expositio in Lucam* X, 53, on Luke 22:36, in *PL* 15, col. 1909), Erasmus (*Utilissima consultatio de bello Turcis inferendo* (1530), Erasmus, *Opera-Amsterdam:* V/3, p. 1-82), and many others (cf. for Erasmus, José A. Fernandez, 'Erasmus on the Just War', in *Journal of the History of Ideas,* 34 (1973), pp. 209-26).—M.E.

negotiators will no longer have occasions to say, 'If you will do thus and so, it will go better this way.' He says, 'I have lifted my hand before the living God.' That way of speaking, of lifting one's hand, is used because men, according as they are obtuse and earthly, need to certify by some sign when they swear an oath that they are calling God as their witness and judge. It is true the expression is equivalent to what we say: 'I declare before God,' or 'God be my witness,' or 'May God strike me.' When we use those expressions, the hair of our head should stand on end if we lie or employ deceitful tactics. God will not renounce himself in order to go along with our lies, and his majesty would have to be annihilated. For his truth is as much a part of him as his unchangeable essence. So the words carry their own weight, but we are very remiss and need to have something or someone to remind us and at the same time cause us to tremble before God's majesty when we swear an oath; and that is why from all time the custom has been for men to lift their hands, and God led them to do that. Therefore, we have lifted our hands in solemn oath, as when saying our prayers. When we lift our hands,[7] it is as if we are calling on God to be pleased to descend from heaven to help us; not that he changes locale or place, but that he extends his power in such a way that we feel it is present with us in time of need. That, then, is how we show by ceremony and outward gesture that prayers join us with God and cause us to enter heaven by faith and God to come down to us to show us he is near.

The same is said concerning the oath. When we lift our hands, it is as if we were saying: 'I call God as my witness and I am here before him as I speak. If I deceive, it is the same as if I had defaced and violated his majesty.' That is how we understand the meaning

[7] The Geneva practice of lifting the hands during prayer. Calvin is going to explain that this outward gesture is a picture of our union with God, a picture of the lifting of the spirit toward God. In two passages added in the last edition of the *Institutes* (III, xx, 5 and 16), Calvin explains the lifting of hands…—M.E.

of that manner of speaking. And let us note well that the oath of believers must be carefully considered two or three times,[8] for those who employ it and take God's name on every occasion show they hold it in contempt. If we reverence God's name the way it deserves (cf. *Exod.* 20:7; *Lev.* 19:12; *Deut.* 5:11), it is certain we will not use it carelessly and toss it around like a plaything. Thus, since oaths fall easily from the mouths of many people, we recognize their godlessness, that they are profane people and do not know God. It is true they will not be afraid to admit it, for when they are heard to swear repeatedly and endlessly in the markets and on the streets, they will respond if they are reproached for doing so: 'Oh, but I still fear God.' Indeed, but they wish to do the contrary, for it is certain that we show our fear of God when we use his name soberly and do not profane him.

And in fact, when you consider what occasions the oath, it is certain we will always provoke God against us if there is any abuse or falsification. Mortal men, as the apostle says, swear by one greater than themselves, and God swears by himself because there is none greater (cf. *Heb.* 6:13, 16). It is necessary, therefore, that in every oath the name of God be injected. It is quite true that when we say 'By God,' we do not spell out that God punish and take vengeance; we do not say that, but it is enough that his name be put forward as judge. Whatever language is used, God does not mince words, and we gain nothing when we try to be clever with him, and it is certain any confusion will always fall on our heads.

Moreover, still when one wishes to swear an oath, it is certain God will be named and called to witness. Now he cannot be a witness unless he is Judge. And then at the same time imprecations are invoked, that is, a man offers to be punished according to his deserts if he abuses God's name. That is also why it is said so

---

[8] Calvin's hearers understood the use of the oath perfectly inasmuch as they had to swear, for example, when making a deposition before the Consistory.—*M.E.*

often in Scripture: 'May God do thus and so to me,' that is, may he punish me in body and soul (cf. *2 Chron.* 15:14-15; *Psa.* 132:2; *Zech.* 5:3). That is not expressed in other passages, but there is only an 'if', and the thought is broken, as in this passage: 'I have lifted my hand to the living God if I take an oath' (cf. *Gen.* 31:53; 44:32; *Neh.* 13:25). And what does that mean? We must understand that God is Judge and will punish me if I lie or equivocate when I speak. That abbreviated and broken style of speech indicates that when we swear, we must be bridled in, so to speak, to avoid provoking God's wrath by our inconsistency and inattentiveness. For it is certain that those who swear so often and on a whim are oathbreakers every time. Those things are inseparable, such that when we see a man who swears at table and in the street, we can say to him boldly: 'My friend, not only do you abuse the name of God, but you also break your oath when God's name is thus profaned in your mouth.' So we must maintain sober speech when it comes to taking the name of God.

But at this point we could ask whether it was permissible for Abraham to swear for such an insignificant thing, for it is said: 'You will not take the name of the Lord your God in vain' (cf. *Exod.* 20:7; *Deut.* 5:11). Could Abraham not be content with simply saying: 'No, I will do nothing of the kind. Receive from my hand what was taken from you, for I do not wish to be enriched by your possessions'? It seems that would have been enough; but we know how dissembling men are, for one will promise wondrous things by honesty, but those who speak that way will intend in their hearts to do the opposite. That is why people do not think they are obligated when they promise something. They say more than they need to say and in flowery terms, as we say, for when there is thus some adroitness, it does not seem there has to be trustworthiness and earnestness because men are given to that. For that reason Abraham had to swear. Moreover, he also needed to remove himself from every temptation and keep to his duty so that even though he was permitted to enrich himself with the possessions of others, he nevertheless refrained from that freedom and removed himself from it by the oath he added. So we see that Abraham had a reason for swearing so that the king of Sodom could no longer reply and also that he himself had a law which constrained him to abstain from what could be construed as an offence and by which God could be defamed among unbelievers.

In addition, we still need to note that he says he raised his hand to the sovereign God, possessor of heaven and earth, as Melchizedek had also used a similar form in his benediction. Abraham was not content to mention God's name, for he wanted to make known the God he worshipped. We know that the world was already filled with many kinds of idolatry and superstition. Everyone had the name of God in his mouth just as today unbelievers boast of worshipping God. The Turks, the Jews, the papists misuse this holy name and only defile it. The Turks worship what they created in their heads and so blaspheme against the living God. For he who does not have the Son does not have the Father, as is said in John (cf. *John* 5:23), and when the Son is not honoured, the Father receives that as a dishonour to himself. For his living image cannot be held in contempt without injury to his majesty. Thus the Turks worship only the devil under God's name.

When the papists are told Jesus Christ is our Advocate (cf. *1 John* 2:1), they say that is unacceptable to them. If they do not dare deny holy Scripture totally, the fact remains that that is an heretical and scandalous position because people will use that as an opportunity to say that the saints do not intercede for us. If we then speak of the free forgiveness of our sins and say it is no longer necessary to waste our time with their idolatrous mass, which is an abomination beyond infernal, they become so enraged that if someone blasphemed a hundred times against the living God, it would not be equal to uttering a single word against that idol. Consequently, we see nothing but the work of the devil in the papists' religion.

As for the Jews, they renounced our Lord Jesus Christ. Now we have already shown that the Son cannot be separated from the Father, and when they rejected him, they closed the door and abandoned the primary feature of the covenant God had made with them because they refused to participate in the salvation which our Lord Jesus Christ brought them. That, then, is how God's name is abused everywhere.

That was the situation in Abraham's time. So that is why Abraham calls him 'Lord' and then 'the most high God'. He does that to distinguish him from idols. The pagans knew well that there was some sovereign divinity,[9] but they always wanted to have a cupboard full of petty gods to their liking. Abraham withdraws from them and says that there is only the Lord who is sovereign. And then he adds 'the possessor of heaven and earth' to indicate that God is not in heaven, as lunatics imagine that he is seated up there observing what is happening in the world and content to have once created all things and to allow us to jump around down here like frogs.[10] So Abraham shows he does not share such an obtuse opinion about God, but he attributes to him an infinite power which extends everywhere. That is to cause us to walk in the fear of God[11] and advise us that we are in the presence of his eyes, that there are no words or thoughts that he does not judge. For God is not the possessor in order to do prodigious things, for he is content with his majesty alone, which is infinite, and he possesses all good within himself. And even if he had created nothing,

---

[9] Cf. Cicero, *De natura Deorum* II, xxxi, 79; *De legibus* II, viii, 19.—*M.E.*
[10] Calvin regularly attacks the concept of God's idleness.—*M.E.*
[11] The fear of God is essential in Calvin's thought (cf. *Institutes* III, iii, 15, 21). Every moment of a man's life takes place under the gaze of God, of a God who is Judge, to be sure, but of a God who is equally merciful and saving (cf. *Institutes* III, ii, 24; and xii, 4).—*M.E.*

he would not be diminished or increased. So when he is called the possessor, it is to show that all things are in subjection to him and that we must answer to him, and it also shows that he so governs the world that nothing is hidden from him and that his office is to lay the foundation for thoughts and to examine all our words and all our deeds so that, as the possessor of heaven and earth, he is at the same time our Judge.

That, then, is what the term 'possessor' means: it is that we walk before God in this life. In vain do we look for places to hide; the fact is that everything will come to light (cf. *Psa.* 139:7-12) and that his office is to lay the foundation for thoughts and, if we think we deceive him today with our clever devices, it will all have to fall back on our heads. Likewise, when God calls himself the possessor of heaven and earth, we are advised to love him as our fostering Father and fear him as our Judge. He is the possessor of heaven and earth because he has sovereign authority over us, and we must appear before his judgment seat to receive the consequences of what we do in our bodies, either good or evil. That is what he possesses in heaven and on earth. Now that possession is not so much for himself, for he pours out upon us all that we need because of his infinite goodness inasmuch as created all things for our use. Consequently, when our God's power and infinite goodness are spoken of, we are wicked ingrates if we do not experience them and are not at the same time moved to love him and give ourselves to him.

This word 'heaven' refers both to the benefits he offers us in the sun and the moon and to the company of angels so that we can learn to conform ourselves to them. If such noble creatures are concerned only with applying themselves to God's service, what are we to do, we who are poor worms of the earth, rebels, poor animals gone astray, each one addicted to his desires and lusts? Is that situation not more confounded than we can handle inasmuch as the angels possess that humility I mentioned and we, for our part, are so filled with pride and rebellion? That is basically what we have to remember, and when we speak of God, may we always associate his power with his essence. And may the name of God not pass our lips as it does for many people, but let us know that as Lord, the Creator of all things, he has reserved for himself dominion and authority over our persons, over all our possessions, and over all creatures and that we must realize we have to give an accounting before him, the kind of accounting that requires us to love him truly and yield in obedience to him. For he does not want to win us over by force and violence because of his majesty but because of the gracious benefits he bestows upon us so that we will be enticed to come to him and always have concern for glorifying his holy name in all we say, in all we think, and in all we do.

> Now let us bow before the majesty of our gracious God in acknowledgment of our faults, praying that he will touch us with them so that we will be humbled before him and displeased with ourselves and in complete confusion so that we may put all our hope in his mercy, which he has shown us in his only Son, and so that we may find our complete refuge in him. And since he has redeemed us at such a high price, let us dedicate ourselves completely to him in purity of body and soul, and let us pay him such homage that we will show him that we sincerely do not desire to belong to ourselves but that we want to give ourselves completely to his service inasmuch as he has been pleased to receive us unto himself. May he grant that grace not only to us but to all the peoples and nations on earth.

66

God Shields and Leads His People
with His Strong Hand

Monday, 4 March 1560

After these things the word of the LORD came unto Abram in a vision, saying, Fear not, Abram: I am thy shield, and thy exceeding great reward. And Abram said, Lord GOD, what wilt thou give me, seeing I go childless, and the steward of my house is this Eliezer of Damascus? And Abram said, Behold, to me thou hast given no seed: and, lo, one born in my house is mine heir. And, behold, the word of the LORD came unto him, saying, This shall not be thine heir; but he that shall come forth out of thine own bowels shall be thine heir (Gen. 15:1-4).

*A*LTHOUGH GOD TRIES to draw us to himself by all the blessings and mercies he pours out upon us, the fact remains that we cannot enter into that effort, but what is worse, we use the occasion to distance ourselves from God in proportion as he draws us and offers us his goodness in such a way that we ought to taste it and yield ourselves to it completely. And we distance ourselves from him more than we should. For when we enjoy times of prosperity and things come to us the way we like, we should, to be sure, rejoice, and all our senses should be caught up to God at the same time. If the weather turns beautiful and serene, our view will extend high and low, and we will discover mountains and valleys far and wide. The same is true of prosperity, for it enlightens us on all sides so that nothing keeps us from seeing the face of God, who is showing us great kindness. Even so, our sight is dazzled when God deals with us gently that way, and while we should be drawn to him, the very good that comes to us distances us from him. Consequently, he has to pursue us and show us that this deeply rooted vice of ours is like an aimless wanderer and is not to be trusted as our goal.

We saw earlier the victory which had been given to Abraham (cf. *Gen.* 14:15-16). That was a testimony of the special love which God had for him. It is now said to him: 'Fear not,' as if Abraham were afraid, perplexed, and anguished. Yet it seems he had some need, and his awareness of need was very useful to him because he could otherwise have been carried away with arrogance or he could have become so free of concern that he would have become indifferent and not been at all free to look simply to God.

It is true there could have been another reason God appeared to him. We know the jealousies which exists throughout the world, and if God blesses someone, there are always enemies and malicious people who will disparage him and snipe at and rail against him. Abraham was not exempted from such calumnies, for some could reproach him for starting a war in the land, and his enemies could avenge themselves one day; others could always be suspicious of him: 'If he always increases his possessions that way, he will rise up against us and chase us out,' for those kinds of suspicions long endure in the hearts of men. Consequently, on the one hand, Abraham could have been distrustful and apprehensive; on the other, he could have been greatly elated because of the victory he had won. That is why God said to him: 'Abraham, I am your shield and your exceeding great reward,' as if he wanted to keep him under his protection, saying: 'If you see that men are against you and threaten you, provoke and rile you, return to me, for I will be your shield. In addition, even though I have let you experience my goodness, have led you and kept you with a strong hand, the fact is that the blessings which you have received from my hand must sustain you and provide for you here below, and your mind must be open and free to rest completely in me and be completely satisfied. For I alone must be your exceeding great reward, which is sufficient for you without hesitation on your part.'

Now the main thing for us is to know how to profit from this teaching, for it is certain God did not speak just one time to our father Abraham, but he wanted to instruct us in his person. Let us first note that God spoke in a vision, that is, by adding some sign by which Abraham might be certain that he was definitely not imagining something, but that what is offered to him is proceeding from God's mouth. For we must be assured and confident of it; otherwise, what consequence would it have for our faith? If our faith should be left hanging that way, it would be tossed about by every wind; it would not be stable. In short, if the promises on which we stand are not dependable and we do not know that it is God who has committed himself voluntarily to us, it is certain we would always be perplexed. For we see that credulity is, by nature, so well rooted in our senses and in our minds that we cannot remain steadfast. There will be those who at times are very stubborn and will continue to trust in things meaningless and false, but when it comes to having confidence in God, unless he draws us to himself forcefully, we cannot come to him. Consequently, we need to be well persuaded that we do not have the promises of our salvation from men, but from God himself, who is their Author.

That is why in ancient times visions as well as dreams were presented, for there is a similar reason, which is that God always imprinted some indication in his word so that it might be authentic and believers could trust it without doubt. Now we do not have such visions today, but those given to the fathers have to serve us now. For we do not have a newly created teaching. Today God does not project a voice into the air so that we have to debate where it came from: 'Who is speaking?' But we have the fullness of the teaching in the law, the prophets, and the gospel. Now, we know how the law was confirmed. We know how the prophets had something like God's weapons to show that they were his heralds and that he ratified everything he wanted to teach through them. As for the gospel, we know the confirmation he gave it by many miracles. Must we, then, look for more than the Son of God, who came down from heaven (cf. *John* 3:13; 6:38, 42; *1 Thess.* 4:16), who was received in his sovereign glory (cf. *John* 13:31; *Acts* 3:13), so that we might know that he proclaims from heaven today the things which are declared in his name and with his authority and that the teaching of the gospel is not something created by men but something we have from him? Since it is true that God has nothing new to offer us today, wanting us to be taught by the law, the prophets, and the gospel, visions would be superfluous. And if someone should ask why we have less privilege than the ancient fathers, he would demonstrate his ingratitude, for everything the ancient fathers had was not just for them alone but for the confirmation of our faith.

Consequently, let us note first that God spoke to our father Abraham in such a way that, by assuring him he was to cling to him and have faith in him, he taught us the same things. So much for that point.

Consequently, the vision Moses is talking about must be today a seal to validate the teaching we have already mentioned and will hear about more fully. In summary, God is speaking here to all believers in the person of Abraham, and he is speaking authentically so that we might be completely persuaded that we will not be disappointed when we rely on what is contained here. Now these words are very succinct: 'Fear not, I am your shield and your exceeding great reward,' but they contain much when we give them close attention.

In addition, we must consider what is said here as if God were providing the reason that Abraham is not to fear. So this is the substance of this teaching: 'Abraham, because I am your shield and your exceeding great reward, you must be completely assured and not a reed waving in the wind, and you must not be driven away, but you must always remain steadfast. In other words, having me as your defender and knowing I have taken you under my protection, you must be content.' So we see here that we can never be delivered from fears and doubts unless we are convinced of God's good favour, namely, that he receives us mercifully and acknowledges us as his children. If we are not confident of that, it is certain we will always be assailed by doubts, frustrations, dissensions, and cares. Unbelievers, to be sure, are self-assured and confident, but stupidly so. Why is it that the great of this world, when they trust in their renown, in their might, in their munitions, in all the means they have to defend themselves with, act like they despise God, as the psalm says (cf. *Psa.* 10) and say that no storm can touch them and that they are exempted from the rank and file of common men? What is the reason for that except they are like blind men, deprived of common sense and ignorant of their weakness? They do not realize that everything here below is only wind and smoke.

So unbelievers have to be as dense as dumb animals if they presume in that way to have power, to have no fear, and to be without worry. Some of them do not even think about God or themselves. They are like profane people we have seen who are intoxicated in the morning on the wine they drank in the evening and sense no apprehension. That is a brutish kind of certainty, one that it is not worth taking into account, but I have said we must always be naturally doubtful and filled with concern until God gives us a remedy for it. Why so? On the one hand, we see how many dangers surround us: we are threatened every hour by a hundred deaths. What is our resistance? What do we have within us? We are only grass, as Scripture says (cf. *Psa.* 103:15-16; 37:2), and experience confirms it. We need only a gust of wind to cause us to wither. And when God shows us the power of his Spirit, we are soon reduced to nothing. We are obliged to sense that whether we like it or not.

Therefore, it is impossible for us not to be always in doubt. And what can happen? We see that between evening and morning many things can happen and bring about many changes. In a word, it will seem that the earth is determined to fail us. And when we have amassed all the things that could be put to good use to protect us, we realize it is not enough, for we understand that there are many pits and crevices to fall into and that, whatever the situation, we will be exposed to death until God stretches forth his hand and shows he wishes to be our Defence. This, then, is a point that must be imprinted in our hearts, namely, that we will be in fear and in doubt until God gives us assurance. In that fact we see how wretched our condition is as long as we are unaware of whose hand guards us. For until we have everything we could possibly wish for, it is certain our chief good will be peace and tranquillity. We will have it, as I have already said, and we will not be able to enjoy it without the assurance of his watchful care.

Therefore, let us learn to withdraw unto God and find in him our refuge so that this world's goods do not defile us. For a while, the devil will be able to entice us and intoxicate us, indeed to the extent that each of us will make ourselves believe that we are out of danger, but in a split second we can be awakened and shown the pettiness within us and how our presumptuousness was overweening pride. Therefore, before God punishes us for such audacity, let us learn to take our full refuge in him and realize that if he gives us the means for maintaining our lives, those means will serve us as long as he is pleased to apply them to our use, and we will know how to use them for our advantage, but in every circumstance, may our confidence not be limited to that.

Now just as we are taught not to waste our time with anything that has to do with being at leisure, likewise, on the other hand, when God is favourable toward us, we must conclude that we will lack nothing. Why not? He makes two things known here, namely, that he will be the shield for the faithful and their exceeding great reward. When he calls himself a shield, he shows he can protect them, even though they are assailed on all sides and the hardships directed against them are severe, but let us also note that a shield would be useless if we were not at war. For in the absence of fear or dread, we will not take a shield with us. It would be a hindrance. A shield, then, is a symbol of war. Now it is not that God is called a shield for a day or a month. So we must conclude that as long as we are in this world, we will experience either one or the other. It is true there will be times of respite according as God supports our weakness and we are not at the end of our tether. He will indeed give us breathing room, but we will never be beyond danger. For if we do not have physical enemies to trouble us, if we do not see swords brandished before us, the devil can still raise them against us overnight, and we have to be ready for that. But there is even more, as Paul reminds us: our war and our battles are not with flesh and blood (cf. *2 Cor.* 10:3-4). In other words, it is not a matter of simply maintaining ourselves in this bodily life and struggling against the outrageous and violent acts that men might visit on us, but a matter of Satan's cunning stratagems, which never cease. Now that is the most dangerous war there is. And what would happen to us if God were not our shield? When we consider what evil and perversity exist in most places in the world and that our enemies are not guided by the Spirit of God, it is an undoubted miracle that we do not perish every day. And if the wicked were not held back by God's secret providence, we would always have a knife at our throats. So then, let us keep in mind what the devil can do, the rage that drives him, and the power he has to harm God's children and take everything from them. It is certain that they will find occasions to skirmish at every moment unless God keeps our enemies in check.

Consequently, we must first realize how necessary it is for us to have God as our shield, for otherwise the life that we have, which is nothing, would be immediately taken from us and we would always be besieged by a hundred deaths, even a million, for we do not have the slightest idea about a hundredth part of the dangers we are exposed to. But since God is our defence and we are sustained by his hand and his power, we can then defy Satan and all the wicked. Even though many hardships stack up against us, we can always move forward. Not that we are completely without feeling, for when it is said that, having God as our protector, we must not fear (cf. *Gen.* 15:1; *Deut.* 33:29; *Psa.* 31:3), that does not mean we are to be without feeling or concern, for our faith would then have to be dead within us and we would not be practised in praying to God. For when it is a matter of praying to God from the heart, we have to be moved by necessity and persuaded that we are very wretched people if God does not have pity on us and stretch forth his hand and sustain us with his help. Now if we did not experience fear and doubt, it is certain all our prayers would be ineffective and the effort would be a cold and empty ceremony.

Therefore, we are told not to fear inasmuch as our trust overcomes all the fears and concerns which might otherwise torment us, overcomes them all even as God's power is greater than all the dangers that threaten us. Using the simile of a balance, we see that the side with the heaviest weight wins. Thus, on the one hand, we must ponder what I have already discussed, namely, that the devil has an infinite number of devices for destroying us and that we live in the midst of wicked people who are like wolves out to devour us or savage beasts intent on tearing us to pieces. Well, we have to know that and, knowing it, we must also realize what God's power is, for it is certain it will overcome all that the demons and wicked people can devise. Just as the help God promises us overcomes all the assaults directed at us, so must our faith overcome every fear and—fearing naturally as we must because we cannot avoid that emotion—we will remain resolved to glorify God. And let us honour him by continuing steadfast within the unconquerable fortress that he is, provided he has his hand extended to help us in time of need.

So much, then, for that defence which is spoken of here. For God, by calling himself a shield, does not leave us without a sword, a helmet, and all the armour we need. He is using a figure of speech to represent the whole. It is like saying we will be so well shielded that our enemies will not be able to wound us in any way, provided God's protection is there. That is why Scripture sometimes says that God is our defence, our strong tower (cf. *Prov.* 18:10), our rock and our fortress (cf. *Psa.* 71:3). Scripture says he is a man of arms and calls him that because of his prowess and great power (cf. *Psa.* 48:8), with which he fortifies us to resist all Satan's assaults. And we need to assemble all these ways of speaking in order to conclude that since he maintains and protects us, we will lack nothing. When we are under his care, there is where the rest of both body and soul lies, and there it is to find its support, as Psalm 91 says. It is there that the prophet says the one who fears God has a protector and a very secure place (cf. *Psa.* 91:2), and it is there that he mocks all the empty things that men trust in and waste their time on, and shows that they do nothing but cheat and deceive. So we have only one protector: God, who watches over us.

It is added that God is a reward, a word which signifies we must not be distracted from him no matter what happens lest we not draw all our felicity from him. Now that is very difficult, for given the fact that we are sensual creatures, it takes a little bit of nothing to divert our attention, as little children will run and bounce around all over the place, and if they are shown a straight pin or given a small coin to polish, they are delighted. The same is true of us. The devil soon wins the day when he presents some distraction or other to get our attention, for that makes us forget God. And if we do not forget him completely, our focus is nonetheless scattered, and he retains little of our attention. Now all our wants, all our affections, and all our desires must be so absorbed in him that we have what is spoken of in Psalm 16 well imprinted in our hearts, namely, that he is our portion and our inheritance and it turns out that our portion is in him (cf. *Psa.* 16:5).

Here we have David, who was a king who could have pleasures and delights. He was honoured by everyone. Yet he shows that that does not restrain him. When he calls God his inheritance, his portion, and his cup, it is as if he were saying, 'The only thing I desire is to have my God's favour. And since I can hope in him and have security in him, then I have all my good.' Besides, that is more than he needs in this world, and it will not even have to be separated from what is essential, for all the good things God does for us in this world are in truth just that many aids to draw us to him and keep us close to him after we have come to him. So we must follow David's example, and if God blesses us and bestows his bounty on us, let us not fail to say that he alone is our inheritance. And if we are deprived of the good things of this world and endure many miseries and hardships, let us not fail to be at peace because God alone is sufficient for us, he alone. That is the meaning of the word 'reward.'

And in addition, it is not without cause that the attribute 'exceeding great' or 'very great' is added. For although we confess that we must adhere to God and that he is our sovereign and only good, we always create a situation in which God does not share the honour. So we must learn to adhere to this exceeding great reward. How? There is no one who does not realize that without God's favour and mercy we would be miserable while having everything we could wish for. But when God stands apart as if hidden and, while we languish, allows us to suffer poverty and need and to be afflicted by the world, and when he allows men to persecute us and be our enemies, when we see that our situation is like that, there is no one who is not grieved. And what is the cause of that? We do not realize that God is our exceeding great reward. We will confess simply that he is our reward, that we must come to him, and that his grace is our chief joy, but we would like for everything else to be added immediately. So let us learn to consider him as our reward so that he will be our exceeding great reward. That is, when we read that response, let us not take a step beyond it since we see that our God is favourable toward us. If we are beaten down on the one hand, as I have said, by poverty, by diseases, or other afflictions, we have God who suffices for us, for he has taken us under his care and will never forget us. Let us be content with being his, for it is certain all the evil we endure now will be changed into good and our salvation. But God must have the honour of being the sole source of our total welfare. So we now see the sum of what is said here.

Now it remains for us to apply that to our use and, as I have said, because we cannot exist here below without engaging in warfare because the devil is our mortal enemy and many wicked people seek only to destroy us, let us make our God's protection our shield and defence. And because we are subjected to so many unfortunate situations, let us also put our afflictions in his hands, knowing he will help us with them. Contrarily, when we are at peace and no one is trying to wrong us insofar as we can tell, let us continue to keep in mind that we need to be sustained and protected from on high. We do not see all the blows the devil might bring to bear on us.

He has many clever tricks up his sleeve. So let us always call upon our God even when things are going well. Thus, even though we are prospering by his kindness and he deals with us so gently that we have the time and means to relax and enjoy ourselves, let us not squander our time on these corruptible good things he does for us, but let us always remain steadfast in him and come to the fountain which never goes dry. That, then, is what we have to remember.

It now follows that Abraham replied to that promise, saying, 'Indeed, Lord God, you promise that you will be my exceeding great reward; yet here I am barren. I have no heir and a foreigner is to be my successor, a man who is a slave and a Syrian, born in Damascus, and that is a testimony of abandonment.' For that reason it is said that he is a 'replacement son,' as if Abraham were forgotten. One could find it strange that Abraham now replies against God's promise since he was to have profited from it and to be strengthened in his faith more than ever. For previously we saw his promptness when he had to leave his father's house and abandon the land of his birth (cf. *Gen.* 12:1-7). He did not have to be begged. He did not spend a lot of time debating with God, but when God but beckons, he sets out without knowing where he is to go, for God only says to him, 'I will show you the land where you are to dwell.' Has he arrived there? He has to be trotted from place to place, tossed about like a ball. He is pursued by famine and persecuted in many ways, but he always remains at peace. And whatever trials he has to endure, he remains invincible and leans confidently on what he was told, namely, that God has taken him under his protection. And now it seems that he is disgusted with it all and finds what he is told insufficient; yet his salvation consists in these words: God is his shield and his exceeding great reward. That is the same as if he had been told that God would never fail him and would sustain him against all his enemies. And what more do we ask? So why does Abraham begin to argue now? Moreover, one might also think that he was too worldly minded when he desired a lineage. Despite the fact that that is a natural desire, it is nonetheless a mark of vanity when men are unduly displeased by not having a lineage. If God gives it to them, they have a reason to thank him, but if he is pleased to humble them that way, they have to remain silent.

So we could say that Abraham was much aggravated since he did not rest on God's word as he should have and as he was accustomed to doing. But we have to note in the first place that although Abraham embraced God's promise and depended on it, he still had strong feelings. He was a mortal man. And we also know that God gives us leave to expose all our displeasures before him and enjoy familiarity with him as a child who presents all his complaints to his father and his father supports him in his infirmities. If a child comes and says that he has a hurt finger, his father will calm him by saying, 'It will soon be well. Tomorrow you will see that it is all right.' In just that way, God is so kind to us that when we come to him as little children and tell him of our griefs and sorrows, he will sustain us. So much for that point.

There will always be some unknown quantity mixed in with faith, and those who are most perfect will continue to have trouble and sorrow, the purpose of which is not to remove every taste they have for God's grace or to destroy the power of his promises, but to encourage their struggle to make every effort to give God the honour due him, which is to trust in what he has promised. Now there is another thing to consider in Abraham. We must not think he forgot what he had already been told: 'All nations will be blessed in your seed' (cf. *Gen.* 12:3). And again: 'I will multiply your seed like the sand of the sea, like the dust of the earth' (cf. *Gen.* 13:16). Abraham, I say, was not so dense that he did not understand the testimony he had already received. Now let us consider the importance of those words, for when God said to him, 'All nations will be blessed in your seed,' that was not in the ordinary way of wishing good fortune for his posterity as a pattern for others to follow: 'May God bless you as he caused Abraham's seed to prosper,' but the promise had to do with our Lord Jesus Christ (cf. *Matt.* 1:2).

Let us now consider how the promise that God is our exceeding great reward can have its effect and be fulfilled. It is certain that without Jesus Christ it is impossible, for our distance from God is so great that there is never a way to approach him. These two points are inseparable: our Lord Jesus Christ binds us to God his Father; we enjoy all the blessings God presents us. In a word, he is our inheritance. That is why Abraham replies here, as if he were informing God: 'And that promise cannot be fulfilled unless there are seed, and you have not given them to me. How will this finally end?' In brief, we see that Abraham was not influenced by ambition. He did not look to having an heir who was his son and bore his name. He was not, I say, driven by such feelings or desires, but he considered how he would be able to enjoy God's promise to be his exceeding great reward. That could not happen without the Redeemer who had been promised to him. So the discussion was about that promise by God. It is as if he were saying, 'Lord, what is going on here? You promise to be my exceeding great reward, so I must adhere to you. You promise to be my reward; so I must assure myself of your protection. But who am I? And who are you? Your majesty is incomprehensible, and I am a poor worm of the earth, and how will I attain unto you? You must come down here.' And in what way? That cannot happen, as I said, except in the person of our Lord Jesus Christ.

Therefore, Abraham, in order to receive the fruit of that promise, makes known the Redeemer, since it is in him that all the promises of God are yes and amen, as Paul says in the first chapter of Second Corinthians (verse 20). So we now see that Abraham was not travelling from one place to another as if seeking his felicity in the goods of this world, but we see that he placed his confidence fully in God and did not consider the promise as lacking in any way. He knew that the fullness of his felicity and his well-being consisted in this: that the Redeemer would be sent because it was impossible for that to be verified without the eventual manifestation of Jesus Christ. To that end, therefore, he wanted to have the ratification of that promise of God, a ratification that was absolutely required.

Consequently, we are obliged to conclude that Abraham's reply did not run counter to faith and that Abraham did not turn his back on it, but he follows the order that God also proposes for us today. In fact, if we do not focus our eyes on Jesus Christ, then every time we want to be strengthened by God's promises, those promises will become clear to us, but we will not be able to enjoy them and apply them to our use and advantage. For example, God indeed promises to be our shield (cf. *Deut.* 23:29; *Psa.* 3:3), but we are unworthy. Moreover, we see in ourselves so many vices that are contrary to faith that we are to be pitied. God promises to be our Father, but we are filled with rebellion and evil intentions. How will the promises be fulfilled in us? That, then, is how all of God's promises, even though they are boldly and plainly expounded, will not have the power to keep us faithful unless we have the Lord Jesus Christ, who receives us unto himself.

When we accept him as our head (cf. *Eph.* 1:22; 4:15), it is certain that, being members of his body (cf. *Eph.* 5:30), we are made sharers in all his riches, that is, in what belongs to our salvation, both of body and soul. When we have our Lord Jesus Christ, God's promises are made sure for us; for if we are unworthy, Jesus Christ possesses enough worthiness within himself to make us honourable before God his Father. Since we are all poor sinners, his righteousness is sufficient to cover all our iniquities and blot them out. If we are filled with stains and blemishes, we will be washed and cleansed by his blood. If we are banished from the

SERMONS ON GENESIS 11-20

kingdom of heaven, the door is opened for us by the one who is its true heir, who was sent to receive us as his brothers and companions. In summary, when we have Jesus Christ, we have God's promises, which are completely secured for us. But without him, there is nothing.

So let us not think it strange that Abraham replied the way he did. It is true he was supposed to trust in what had already been announced one time, but, as I have already said, faith does not at all destroy our natural feelings, our concerns and our desires. Some human characteristics must be mixed with faith. It is very true that faith corrects everything excessive in us, for when we desire something, we have a skewed and twisted purpose which turns us away from God. And then there are our strong feelings, which carry us away. Faith corrects those vices, leads us to God, and makes him our only goal. And then it keeps us from being overly anxious to subject God to our wishes. Even so, some desire always remains. And that is expressed in Abraham's statement: 'Lord,' he says, 'I am walking alone.' When he says, 'I am walking,' it is as if he were comparing his life to a path: 'I shall soon finish my course. A long time ago you promised to give me seed. When will that be? It will be after my death, for I already have one foot at the edge of the grave. I am about to leave the world. And, Lord, it seems you want to let the time pass without keeping your promise. Here I am shut away from my hope if you do not provide for it.' So we see now what Abraham's desire was. It was a holy affection approved by God. And when he asks for seed, his mind is not preoccupied with ambition or vanity or the like, but he desires that seed which encompasses his salvation and the salvation of the whole world.

Moreover, when he says, 'I am walking alone,' it shows he is asking to be sustained since God knew that he was a weak creature and that he was pleased with respect of that weakness so he can help it. So let us learn from the example of our father Abraham to address ourselves to our Lord Jesus Christ, as I have already pointed out that all the promises would otherwise be of no use to us. Moreover, when we sense some infirmity in ourselves, let us run to him so that he will be pleased to sustain us and so strengthen us by the power of his Holy Spirit that we will overcome all the temptations that will confront us, for it is certain that we will find in him all we could possibly wish for and that he will accomplish his will so that we will sense by experience that he did not speak in vain.

Now let us fall before the majesty of our gracious God in acknowledgment of our faults, praying that he will use his infinite mercy on our behalf not only by forgiving our faults but also by leading us by his Holy Spirit and granting us the grace so to walk in obedience to him that our lives will be in conformity with his righteousness, such as he shows it to us. And may he increase his gifts in us more and more until we are renewed and until our old Adam is completely put down and destroyed. May he grant that grace not only to us but to all the peoples and nations on earth.

67

First Sermon on Justification, Wherein Are Discussed the Meaning of Faith (or Believing), Imputing and Righteousness[1]

Tuesday, 5 March 1560

And, behold, the word of the LORD came unto him, saying, This shall not be thine heir; but he that shall come forth out of thine own bowels shall be thine heir. And he brought him forth abroad, and said, Look now toward heaven, and tell the stars, if thou be able to number them: and he said unto him, So shall thy seed be. And he believed in the LORD; and he counted it to him for righteousness (Gen.15:4-6).

YESTERDAY WE SAW that Abraham, lamenting to God that he did not have a child who could be his heir, did not wander from the promise, whereas many people would like to subject God to their desire and will grumble unless he yields to their pleasure in all things and in every respect. Now Abraham did not abandon the bridle, which was enough to make him aware that God was favourable to him and was watching over him in life and in death. He wished nothing more than to know how the promise would be fulfilled. Now he had to have the

[1] The titles of this and the following three sermons are provided in the French text.—*Translator.*

promised Redeemer. And that is why he so ardently desired to have a lineage, not, as we have said, because he was worldly minded, but because, having one, he would be persuaded and confident of God's paternal favour.

And that is better confirmed by the promise God gives him, for the first thing he does is grant his request and rebuke him for doubting, seeing that the promise had already been given to him. 'No', he says, 'that one will not be your heir, but the one who will come from your own body.' It is true that God sometimes grants the things men unadvisedly request of him, but here we see that God approves his servant Abraham's wish. And not without reason, for Abraham was only asking to have the promise ratified by the means required; but because he was in too much of a hurry, God said to him: 'No.' He rejects Abraham's excessive ardour and anxiousness. It is not that he was not permitted to require having the Redeemer shown to him, but there is such a thing as moderation, and we must wait for God's providence in all circumstances, for he knows the best time to do what is good for us. So it is up to us to be quiet and peaceable, and that is also the character of faith, as Scripture says (cf. *Eph.* 3:12). To sum up, we see that God has here shown that Abraham's request was acceptable to him in respect of his desire for lineage, for he knew its purpose.

Because there is some weakness in Abraham, God adds confirmation, for he brings him outside his tent and says: 'Look at the stars. If you can count them, so will your seed be numbered. And since there is an infinite number of stars, such that you are amazed whenever you look at them, so will your seed multiply in an unusual way, and men will be astonished because the increase will exceed their comprehension and imagination.' This passage, which we dealt with in chapter twelve, cannot be explained unless Jesus Christ is established as the head of and link to Abraham's seed. We will see later that Ishmael was born (cf. *Gen.* 16:15), but the promise was not fulfilled. He was, to be sure, Abraham's legitimate son, but he was not the legitimate son of the promise, as Paul says (cf. *Gal.* 4:23).

We must not, therefore, understand that particular begetting to be of the flesh, but we must think higher and distinguish between Abraham's children who remain in their order and their status and are, in this way, God's recognized and avowed children, as opposed to the children who are rejected, although they descended from him. As we see later, Isaac begat Esau and Jacob. Even though Esau was the firstborn, he is nonetheless rejected, though of the same birth. We will not be able to find a distinction between these two children that gives preference to Jacob, for they were conceived together and born together. What is more, Esau is the firstborn. So why is he later considered a stranger without right or place in the spiritual inheritance which God had promised Abraham's lineage? The blessing is taken from him and, as a consequence, his younger brother must receive it, for he now has the right of primogeniture.

We see in brief, then, that if we take Abraham's seed as being those who descended from him according to the flesh, there would be nothing to talk about or to build on. Moreover, although God adopted all of Jacob's line, the majority of them broke away from him. And that is also why God renounced them so often through his prophets (cf. *Isa.* 57:3-4; *Jer.* 2:20). Therefore, that seed must have a head or we will not have the truth of that promise. It is true that they spoke not only of Jesus Christ, as some have understood him too inadequately,[2] but we must hold to this course: that Jesus Christ is set forth before us and we are gathered into him, and that

[2] Calvin attacks those who have completely christologized the writings of the prophets, the Old Testament speaking only of Jesus Christ and having no value for the Jewish people. In two chapters of the *Institutes* (II, x-xi), which he consecrates to the relationship between the Old and New Testaments, Calvin has in mind 'as much this monster Servetus as some Anabaptists who have no more esteem for the children of Israel than for a herd of swine...' (*Institutes* II, x, 1).—M.E.

union will cause us to be esteemed and reckoned as Abraham's children. Consequently, there would be no seed of the kind spoken of here if Jesus Christ did not hold the sovereign position and we had not been united in him as members of his body to be gathered into God's house and, consequently, into Abraham's.

Now, we see that God diminishes that seed in order to increase it. That is his method, which seems strange to the world, but all of us are to be trained in it and accustomed to it. According to the general way of thinking, the firstborn is to attract the second, and then everything is to fit together. But God proceeds in another way. When there is seed, there is a large number, an astonishing multitude, but God cuts it back, God reduces it, diminishes it, so that it sometimes seems that it is almost all consumed, as the prophet Isaiah speaks of it in the tenth chapter, and almost nothing is left to be seen (cf. *Isa.* 10:16-22). But he does that to multiply it later above human imagination so that his power will be all the more acknowledged, as it is wondrous, and so that everyone will be constrained to worship him. For even though many peoples descended from Abraham, the twelve lines in the first case, and then the Ishmaelites and Idumeans, the fact is that there was never a multitude so great in his house as it has been through our Lord Jesus Christ. Those who have no attachment to Abraham according to the flesh were made his servants, for he was, as we will see later, the father of all believers in general (cf. *Gen.* 17:4). So in this way, Abraham's lineage was much greater when God diminished what had descended from Abraham according to the flesh than if he had left the entire number untouched. Now that fact admonishes us not to measure God's works by our thoughts and imagination but to give place to his incomparable power and be satisfied that when he proclaims his word, he is powerful to fulfil it, as will be more amply treated later.

On the point that God drew Abraham from his lodging place and his tent and had him look at the stars of heaven, there is absolutely no need to waste time with that infantile subtlety that God compared the church to the stars because we are citizens of the kingdom of heaven, that we live on earth like pilgrims who are only passing through. That is not the meaning of the passage. When mention of the dust was made earlier, some speculated that the church was included in the image and figure of the dust and will be scorned by the world. All of that is pure bunk. But we understand why God brought his servant Abraham's attention to the stars of heaven and had him look at them. It was to have him contemplate his power so that he would not apply his ponderings and his own knowledge to judge the truth of the promise, which was incredible to him compared to the natural order. Faith will never become a part of us until that vice is subdued and corrected. In other words, we must set aside our natural judgment and empty ourselves of all our wisdom so that we can attribute to God the honour which belongs to him.

Now, let us consider whether that infinite multitude of stars we see in the sky is not an excellent mirror of God's infinite power, for everything was created in a moment (cf. *Gen.* 1:16). That is also why this miracle is magnified in the psalm, for it is he who counts the multitude of the stars and gives them their names (cf. *Psa.* 147:4), that is, he subjects them to himself and his authority. So when we open our eyes to contemplate the stars, we must consider the creation, for in a moment of time, as soon as God uttered the word, the heavens appeared filled with their hosts, as Scripture also speaks of it (cf. *Psa.* 33:6), and behold the heavenly armies which were created in a moment of time and always remain there to obey God. We see that all stars move with exactitude, and although they make a very great revolution in that expanse, the planets, for their part, could stir the firmament and it could all be mixed together. Yet we see it is all so well governed that we are compelled to marvel at it.

Since that is true, it is not without cause that this mirror is placed before Abraham's eyes, for he can then conclude: 'If God can in a moment fill the entire sky, which was previously empty, with stars, could he not also fill not only my house but an entire country, even many countries, when he is ready to give me lineage?' God's power has not diminished. He is not only the Creator of the world, but after creating it, he continues to preserve it miraculously everyday. So Abraham had a definite sign, a pledge that was given to him. And in that we see that God recognized some weakness in him, not that Abraham had no confidence in what God had said, but because he, being a man, could not control himself well enough that he would not ask how it would be possible for all the nations of earth to be blessed in his seed. Indeed, as we said yesterday, he had some weakness mixed with his faith. That is why God added that sign to help him.

Thus we have to note in this passage, as in all others, that God sustains us in our frailty. It is not that he does not deal with us gently, for we have to struggle against all our feelings, against our thoughts and evil actions in order to give place to God's truth and hold that truth as certain and unfailing. But whatever we do, let us continue to be weak in some way, and if we do not know our failing, God knows it. What would happen, then, if his infinite goodness had not spared us? That, then, is what we have to consider in this passage, which says that our father Abraham was confirmed in God's word and in his promise, just as we experience the same thing everyday in ourselves unless we have been blinded by our wickedness, for we do not consider the works of God as closely and as diligently as we should. But if we knew how to profit from all the means God presents to us to assure us of his promises, we would know that if he spared his servant Abraham, since he knows we are a hundred times more fragile, he forgets nothing that can serve to strengthen our faith.

Now Moses adds that Abraham believed in God and it was counted to him as righteousness. This passage is rather simple, and at first glance one would not linger over it very long. The Jews also are so blind and stupid that they do not know what this means. And among Christians, we scarcely find one in a hundred who even appreciates the content of those words. For if these three or four words were well understood, that 'Abraham believed and it was counted to him as righteousness,' it is certain the entire Papacy would be abolished. All of the superstitions in vogue today would cease; all the debates that we have to endure would be put to rest. For this passage holds the key that opens all that is required for our salvation. This passage shows the way to bring to an end all differing opinions. It provides the foundation of true religion. In brief, here the heavens are opened to us when we understand what Moses states here in a few words. And we ought to detest even more those scoundrels who are so impudent as to obscure such great clarity, as do those who say that Abraham was reckoned to be a 'sincere man' and that it was a virtue for him to believe in God. Those dogs must indeed be abominable in our sight, for those are the most egregious blasphemies that Satan can spew out.

Now as for the Jews, we must not be astonished by them yet, for they do not have an interpreter. It is true God's light shines in Moses' face, but they have a veil before them, as Paul says (cf. *2 Cor.* 3:14-15). So they pass over these words without thinking about their importance.

But those who confess being Christian and have Paul's authority to show what this means (cf. *Rom.* 4:3), when they still openly despise God and fight like dogs with the vehemence that is seen in them, where is the intelligence in that? I am not talking about the papists, but there are diabolical minds which claim to be Christian and even profess it openly but will continue to be much worse than the papists. But even in the whole of the Papacy they have concluded that men, since they are damned before God and cursed, can obtain salvation only through faith. The papists will confess that. And those dogs abolish and level everything as if nothing was said here except that Abraham is a sincere man and it is a virtue for him to believe in God. Yet those scoundrels would like to be esteemed and called by the titles master and doctor, but they are so witless and moved with such madness that they would overthrow everything if they could.

All the more must we be attentive to what this passage contains. On the one hand, Moses says Abraham believed in God and, on the other, adds that that belief, or faith, was for righteousness for him. Now the first thing we have to do is define the word 'believe', for without it, everything would easily collapse. That is why the papists are entangled in their errors, for even though they confess in part that we are justified by faith, they still cannot receive or accept what this is completely. The reason? It is because they do not understand this word 'faith'. In order to have a good understanding of it, we must place a conjunction between faith and the promise. People can sing with one voice, but we will not have a perfect melody unless there are many voices and good harmony. The same is true for faith, for if God's word does not come first and faith does not agree with it, there will be no melody. The word of God and faith are inseparable.

Now you could talk from now until doomsday about 'believe', and it would be like Greek, as we say. It would be unintelligible commentary, as it is among the papists, until we understand that God must speak and our ears must be open and attentive if we are to acquiesce in what he says and obey. So what does it mean 'to believe'?[3] It means to accept with such reverence what is proposed by God that we are restrained by it and do not doubt it.

[3] Calvin consecrates an entire chapter of the *IRC* to answering that question, chapter ii of book III.—*M.E.*

We must now move beyond that, for God will sometimes speak in such a way that we will scarcely profit from listening to him. We saw earlier, when he spoke to Cain and asked him where his brother Abel was, that Cain did indeed feel, like it or not, that he had to answer before his judge, and he nonetheless grumbled and was defiant: 'Who made me my brother's keeper?' (Cf. *Gen.* 4:9.) Adam himself heard that voice: 'Where are you?' (cf. *Gen.* 3:9), but he was seized with fear and apprehension, hid himself, and would have liked to find a pit to flee from God's presence. So it will not be enough that we receive the word which God gives us with the authority it deserves, but that word must be qualified, that is, it must be a sure word to cause us to approach God and be sharers in his goodness lest we doubt that he will be our Father and Saviour. And on that point let us be bold to call upon him, consider ourselves his children, and take refuge in him.

So we see, then, how Abraham believed. It is not that he conceived a fantastic notion in his head, for faith comes by hearing, Paul says, and hearing by the word of God (cf. *Rom.* 10:17). So Abraham heard and was instructed before believing. And that was not by a mortal man or some creature, but he knew it was God who called him to be one of his children. Now that would not be sufficient, as we have said, but Abraham heard these words: 'I am your exceeding great reward, I am your shield, I am your defence. Do not fear, for I am the all-powerful God who took you from Chaldea and from Ur of the Chaldees.' And as we will see later and as I have already said in chapter twelve, Abraham did not believe in God in order to hear I know not what that does not relate to him or to hear some private opinion, but he believed in God when he believed that he was preserved and reserved to be heir of the kingdom of heaven. That was his belief.

In order to understand it all better, let us note that there is an individual faith and a faith which comprises all that is required for our salvation.[4] Now whenever God might threaten us, those very people who are hypocrites and contemptuous of his word would be moved and touched in their hearts. And that faith is particular, individual. How many people do we see who, when God's judgment is presented to them, react with astonishment and have a searing iron burning deep inside and wonder what can happen to them from every side? They have to know and they have to learn that whatever they do, they cannot escape the hand of the heavenly Judge. So they do have some kind of faith, but it is only partial and can in no way serve them.[5] There are some who find assurance in a particular promise when they see themselves in danger. If someone happens to console them by telling them that God will have pity on them, they will be able to appreciate that word, but it is only an expectation, a hope. Then there is the man who is gravely ill or reduced to poverty and can present himself before God. Another will find himself in such a great extremity that he will be confounded and yet will continue to breathe easily, knowing that God will help him. Now all of those ways of believing are particular, individual, and are not sufficient for our salvation and cannot justify us.

[4] Calvin develops these two acceptations of the word 'faith', objective (sum of the teaching to be believed) and subjective (what a particular Christian believes) and of others in a passage of the *Institutes*, III, ii, 13. That double notion of faith is explicit in Luther and is very soon perceived as Lutheran by the Faculté de théologie de Paris (I thank Francis Higman for that detail). Cf. *Le Pater noster et le credo en françoys* by Guillaume Farel, edited by Francis Higman (*Textes Littéraires Français* 306), (Genève, 1982), p. 15f. That concept was in fact a break with the development of one Thomas d'Aquin (cf. perhaps *Summa theologiae* 2a 2ae, q. 2, art. 2, and the triple distinction: '*Credere Deo; credere Deum; credere in Deum*').
[5] The idea behind this passage is clearly understood to be double predestination (cf. *Institutes* III, xxi, 7; and even the *Instruction et confession de foy dont on use en l'Eglise de Genève de 1538*, éd. P. Barth, in: *Joannis Calvini opera selecta* I (Munich, 1926), p. 390; éd. latine de 1538, in CO 5, col. 332f), but Calvin does not go so far as to use the expression from the pulpit. R. Stauffer, following others, had picked up on the fact that the theme of predestination scarcely appeared in Calvin's preaching, and the theme of double predestination, not at all. Cf. Stauffer, *Dieu*, pp. 261, 311-14; cf. Higman, *Peuple élu*. Cf. also, in the following sermons on Genesis, sermon 74... and sermon 88..., and related notes.—M.E.

But when we are assured of adoption, wherein lies all our well-being, we are confident that God will be our Father until the end, as he promised that we, being his children, will not perish, but we will be able to call upon him as our God for our certain salvation (cf. *John* 3:16; *1 Pet.* 1:17; *1 John* 3:2-3). So when we have that promise by which God unites us with himself and allies himself with us so that we do not doubt he will ever forget us, that is a faith which encompasses all of his promises. For, as Paul says, the fear of God which precedes faith holds all the promises not only of the life to come but also of this present life (cf. *1 Tim.* 4:8).[6] We can conclude that everything will go well for us, provided God receives us into his grace and accepts us. In summary, that is what we now have to remember concerning the word 'believe'.

So Abraham believed in God, that is, Abraham received the promise which both assured him that God was his Saviour and embraced our Lord Jesus Christ, who was offered to him, through whom he knew we are reconciled to God, even though we deserve to be his enemies and caused him to wage mortal warfare against us because we are filled with sin and corruption. So Abraham laid hold on our Lord Jesus Christ and was fully persuaded that he was the true link that joins us to and unites us with God in such a way that we participate in his life and all that belongs to him. That is Abraham's belief, so we do not take it as lightly as the papists do.

Now, we see in summary that we will never know the worth of the words 'faith' and 'believe' unless we come to the relationship between the promise and acceptance. And what does God say so often through the prophets: 'I will call you my people, and you will say, "You are our God"' (cf. *Hos.* 2:23; *Zech.* 13:9). There we have God speaking first, and that is his prerogative, for what gall I

[6]The French text cited by Engammare as Calvin's reference contains, as the English version does not, the word 'fear', as follows: '*Car l'exercice corporel est peu prouffitable, mais la crainte* [fear] *de Dieu est prouffitable à toutes choses, ayant promesse de la vie presente et de celle qui est à venir.*' —*Translator.*

would have to have to intrude myself and go to God and call him 'my Father', I who am nothing but a worm of the earth, I who am but sin and contagion to be damned forever, whom Satan possesses by nature, for we are all under his servitude! And yet I call him 'my Father,' and the very angels in themselves are not worthy to do that, and yet I arrogate that honour? But when *he* uses the words 'I am your Father,' it is then no longer audacity and wicked presumption for us to consider ourselves among the number of his children, but a sacred trusting in him by which we ratify his truth. Since it is he who makes the statement, it is the highest honour that we are able to consider ourselves such and acquiesce completely. That, I say, is true belief, such as it is shown to us here through the instruction to and example of Abraham.

Now it is said that faith was accounted to him as righteousness, and it is God who accounted it to him. We must now explain this word 'to account', and then the word 'righteousness', while also encompassing the name of God. This word 'to account' means 'to allocate or put down to someone's account' or 'to attribute or ascribe to someone's account.' It is as when a man is in debt, if he has paid, that is allocated to him; or, if he proves he has reduced his debts by doing this and that, then everything is allocated in such a way that he is paid up. Now in our French language, 'to impute' always carries a bad connotation.[7] We will not say that a virtue is imputed to a man, for the word 'impute' conveys some reproach and some guilt. We will say, 'That will be imputed to him as sin.' Now Scripture has a general word referring both to good and evil. That is, God imputes righteousness and does not impute sins. So

---

[7] Cf. Robert Estienne, *Dictionaire Françoislatin, autrement dict les mots françois avec les manieres d'user d'iceulx, tournez en latin, corrigé and augmenté*, Paris, 1549, reprint Genève, 1972, p. 322: '*imputer, imputare. Imputer quelque chose à aucun à folie et à blasme. Vertere stultitiae aut vitio aliquid alicui.*'—M.E. ['to impute, *imputare*. To impute/attribute (turn) something to someone as foolishness/ stupidity or blame' = to blame someone for something.—*Translator.*]

when it is said that faith was imputed or attributed to Abraham, it means faith thoroughly overwhelmed everything that comes from him. But we still would not know the value of this word and how weighty it is without its opposite. When it is said that sins are imputed to us, it means that the court records remain, that the cases against us are over, and all that remains is the passing of the sentence and its implementation. Woe to us when God imputes our sins to us. For it is said: 'Blessed are those to whom God does not impute iniquities' (cf. *Psa.* 32:2). As a result, let everyone be cursed when God wants to proceed as a judge and make inquests into our lives. What does it mean, then, that faith is imputed as righteousness? It means that it is allocated to us because our sins are not imputed, for one cannot be understood without the other. Therefore, the imputation of righteousness results in there being no imputation of guilt for our judgment and condemnation, for the imputation of righteousness is the same as absolution when all is said and done. That, then, explains that word.

Now let us look at the meaning of 'righteousness'. This word does not refer to a virtue, as in 'he is a righteous man,' if he conducts himself without reproach. But this righteousness is a grace that God bestows upon us because he receives us in mercy and wishes to be reconciled to us by his pure liberality. So the righteousness Moses speaks of here is not a quality that we are to seek in men. It is rather that favour God bears us when it pleases him to bury our sins and to pass over them and even to consider us as having fulfilled the law. And why does he do that? Because Jesus Christ is righteous, and the righteousness which he perfected within himself is imputed and allocated to us. And just as he is ours according as he is given to us by God his Father and according as he offers himself to us in the gospel, so he communicates to us his righteousness when we possess him. And God accepts it as if it had come out of our very selves and out of our persons. There you also have the word 'righteousness' defined, and I have now explained things little by little so that we have a correct summary of it all.

We have to come to God's name, for men will indeed impute to us a just or righteous deed because of the appearance of holiness and virtue in us. People will be able to applaud us. There will be many imputations, that is, there will be both testimonials of righteousness and imputations. We will be absolved; we will even be highly praised and esteemed when it is seen that we have lived virtuously, but all that is meaningless. So we must come to the heavenly Judge, as said he is called. And that is notably why Moses says that God accounted as righteousness the fact that Abraham believed. And if everybody had thus admired and approved Abraham's faith and had canonized him, so to speak, as if he had been an angel, all of that would still have been only smoke; but God declares the facts as they stand, he who is the competent Judge and who has the authority to pronounce a sentence of absolution or condemnation. So when God absolves Abraham in this way and acknowledges him and considers him as righteous, that is the main thing.

Thus, we see now how Abraham was justified by faith. Paul says that it follows that he could not merit righteousness by his works and brought nothing of his own to be approved by God, but that God received him freely, which made him one of his children. In fact, Paul follows that path when he undertakes to discuss free justification (cf. *Rom.* 4:2-4). He wants to point out that there is no other hope of salvation but in God's pure goodness because he forgives us of our sins so that we will be acceptable to him. So when Paul enters into that argument, he takes up the theme of Abraham, for he presupposes what is true, namely, that there are not different means by which to be justified before God. There is, in fact, only one. Therefore, if Abraham was justified by faith, so must we all be, without exception. Moreover, if there could be found in mortal man virtue worthy of merit, it is certain Abraham surpassed all others. We have seen how he left the land of his birth, how he renounced himself and all human affections, how he obeyed God in all things. We have seen how long-suffering he was and how steadfast and constant he remained in the midst of trials, and how persistent he was to the end in God's calling. In a word, he failed in no respect. Now we are very far from that kind of perfection. Who, then, will dare boast of being able to obtain righteousness before God by his own merits, seeing that Abraham was excluded from doing so? But what I have mentioned must suffice for us, namely, that there is only a single way to become acceptable to God, and that is the way which is shown in the person of Abraham.

Therefore, we must add the conclusion that if Abraham was justi-fied by believing in God, our works can do nothing to cause God to approve of us and establish the hope that we are to have for eternal salvation: that God must give us everything and we must not pre-sume to bring him anything from ourselves. That will be dealt with at length, but we must follow the easiest procedure we know. Now as I have already said, here are our ABCs, and that is the completion of all our wisdom. Will we not have accomplished a great deal when we have learned the foundations of our faith, when we know what access we must have in order to profit from God's school and what the principal key of every Gospel is and, so that we may be led to it, to know the real goal, so that we may know how we must enter upon the straight path, and how we will reach the inheritance God has placed before us? So when we consider that this passage leads us to that point, it is certain we will give it close attention, or we ought to, or we will be despicable ingrates.

Now, so far, things have been explained so clearly that there is not a small child who cannot understand them. Let us take the point I made about Abraham. He brought nothing that would make him acceptable to God, but he totally depended on the pure grace and liberality which were contained in the promise. Let us look now at the period of time spoken of. Abraham had already served God for such a long time that we would be justified in thinking he ought to be at quits inasmuch as men would always like to have their freedom. So it follows that Abraham was justified all his life by faith and only faith. That would be obscure if it were not explained quite well. And it will be explained better by contrasting the truth with the Papacy's lies and the errors with which those infernal schools are infected.

I have already said the papists will make a sufficient confession, namely, that without faith we cannot be approved by God and will never enjoy any part of his favour. Afterwards, they will confess this principle: we are cursed in Adam. Consequently, Jesus Christ must, they say, confer on us the first grace. That is, because we are plunged into perdition by original sin, Jesus Christ must remove us from it. Now, from that they deduce a false and pernicious teaching by which they corrupt everything that Moses had a clear understanding of and that Paul explained very well. They say that the righteousness they call initial is indeed from faith, from pure and simple faith, but then they say that we must be partly justified by our works. Now that is not clear, but I will explain it in such a way that everyone will understand it. This word 'initial' means 'beginning', for it sounds like they were saying that righteousness is, from the beginning, from pure faith. So the papists confess that God considers us as his enemies and that we are execrable in his sight because all kinds of corruption are in us. So because of our blemishes and pollution, we are necessarily rejected by him. They confess that, and it seems at first glance that they do so to bring men to humility. For they also point out that Jesus Christ must heal all our deficiencies, extend his hand and reconcile us to God his

Father. Now once they have set us on the road, they then say that we must in part earn merit in order to achieve righteousness and that we do that by the merits of our works. As a result, they make free righteousness a one-time act when we are received into the church by baptism. That suffices. There we have Jesus Christ, who has done his share. It is true they add that we cannot be completely righteous at any time, and they have to be aware of that whether they like it or not, and experience also keeps them convinced they are indebted to God in many ways.

But after that, they have their satisfactions and say they compensate God in other ways by doing things which they are not commanded to do, like fasting on a certain day, refraining from eating meat on another, trotting off on pilgrimages, having some mass or other sung, and all those other empty rituals, which are a conglomeration of tactics they have devised to requite God. That is how they occupy the entire course of their lives justifying themselves by their works and their merits after being justified once by faith, that is, after being set on the road. Jesus Christ opens the door for them, but it is up to them to enter, they say, and complete the trip.

They also make another mistake, for they think that when they do some good, if a lot of evil is mixed in with it, that good does not fail to enter into reckoning and they call that partial righteousness. So they work to no purpose by cobbling righteousness together with bits and pieces gathered here and there and heaped into an indistinguishable jumble. They say we are justified at the outset by the pure grace of Jesus Christ, and then by faith. And then again they say we are justified by our works, in part by our satisfactions, which serve to appease God and acquit us of all of the offenses we are guilty of. That is the papists' opinion.

Now let us consider at what moment Abraham was justified. As we have said, he already had the advantages of all virtues; he had renounced himself in order to yield fully to God. So it seems he could have had some righteousness, if such existed in a living creature. And yet his faith was accounted to him as righteousness. From that Paul concludes there were no works to justify him. And when did he not have any works? After working enough to be able to serve as a pattern for all angelic virtues, in chastity, in long-suffering, in obedience to God, in piety. In short, he stripped himself of all affections to be fully in conformity with God's righteousness. After doing all that, he still had nothing to boast of, as Paul says (cf. *Rom.* 4:2). He had to remain silent until he was justified by faith (cf. *Rom.* 3:19).

So we see that, insofar as time is concerned, the righteousness by faith we are speaking of is not such as the papists imagine it, but it is as if Scripture were saying, 'Although we are poor sinners indebted to God and under condemnation of eternal death, he must receive us in a different way, that is, by not examining us to determine what kind of people we are, by not looking for something he can approve in us, but by considering us as righteous because it pleases him to do so, or because we are standing on the promises by which he has intervened on our behalf.' That, then, is the righteousness which endures, which encompasses both life and death.

We must now explain things in greater detail. In the first place, we need to remember what I said recently, namely, that we must look for our righteousness somewhere other than in ourselves because all of us are destitute of it. That is why Paul insists so much on the curse of the human race when he tries to bring us to the teaching that God justifies us freely. For he even points out that pagans are damned, although they have no law, no Scriptures, no prophets. They are already condemned in themselves, and there is no need to say more after that, he says (cf. *Gal.* 3:10-13). For God shows himself to every one in general since he has given us eyes to contemplate his powers in the creation of the world. Now we see that men stifle and suppress that glory, which should be quite evident to them. Consequently, we must conclude that they are all ingrates, even robbers, because they steal from God the honour that is his. As for those who are under the law, they are doubly condemned, for they sin willingly, since they know the will of God, who is clearly manifested to them. There, then, we see the entire human race under the curse (cf. *Rom.* 3:19). Every mouth is stopped, he says, and can make no reply. On that point, he has in mind many passages of Scripture to show that God considered all men, and he found none that was good, and that in them was only corruption (cf. *Rom.* 3:10; *Psa.* 14:1).[8] In other words, they are so fixed in their iniquities that they must be thought of as detestable. That, then, is what we have to note first, namely, that we must recognize our condition until God comes to us and receives us by his mercy and seeks us out while we are still engulfed in the pit of hell. That, I say, is where we must begin if we wish to know how and why we are justified by faith. But that cannot be explained now. So we will save that for tomorrow.

> Now let us bow before the majesty of our gracious God and Father in acknowledgment of so many faults and offences, by which we are more than indebted to him and by which we ought to be completely confounded within ourselves. Yet, let us, being in such a pit of despair, continue to lift our heads always to him since he has granted us the grace of seeking for us to gather us to himself and since Jesus Christ descended into hell to lift us out of it and lead us to the heavenly kingdom. So may that be so imprinted in our hearts that we will be truly lifted by faith so that we will call upon this gracious God who has adopted us as his children and depend completely on him. And may he grant us the grace so to walk that

---

[8] In Romans 3:10-18, Paul refers, in addition to these two verses, to Psalm 5:10; 140:4; 10:7; Isaiah 59:7; Proverbs 1:16; Psalm 14:1; Psalm 36:1.—*M.E.*

we will be governed by our Lord Jesus Christ according as he has incorporated us into him. May he grant that grace not only to us but to all the peoples and nations on earth.

68

Second Sermon on Justification

Wednesday, 6 March 1560

And he believed in the LORD; *and he counted it to him for righteousness* (Gen. 15:6).

YESTERDAY WE BEGAN to talk about the right way to understand how we are acceptable to God through faith. We have come to our first condition and consider what kind of people we are as born in Adam. Now we find that we are all cursed, damned and lost. Until we are well aware of that, we will never appreciate what it means to obtain grace and mercy from God. So knowing that is the true foundation for building well. In other words, after determining what sort of people we are and finding that there exists in us nothing but confusion, we then seek the remedy for our condition somewhere else. In order to make such an examination, we need to go to Scripture. It is true that if everyone thought about himself without flattering himself, he would be his own judge. We do not have to look far before finding something in ourselves that needs examining, for each individual has something like a searing iron burning deep down that reminds him of God's curse. But because we are disposed to conceal our faults and bury them, God offers us a mirror in his word to teach us to judge ourselves in accordance with his standards and not in accordance with our preferences.

So even though men do not perceive at first the poor pitiable condition they are in, yet when they are enlightened and guided by God's word, that instruction ought to suffice to keep them in complete confusion, for if we were of a mind to follow our own way of thinking, each of us would be righteous. As Solomon also says: men are so blinded by love of self that everyone attributes to himself and believes wondrous things about his virtues, but God weighs the hearts (cf. *Prov.* 21:2). But we need to go to a set of scales different from our own, for we are only lying to ourselves when we think we have a lot of meritorious qualities. And if men also consider us from our perspective, it is because they are only looking at appearance. Now what is esteemed and excellent in the sight of men is only abomination before God (cf. *Luke* 16:15). Why is that? Because our works must be judged according to the heart and the hidden intention. Also, there is no purity, and without that it is impossible for men to be pure and clean until God cleanses them through faith, as is pointed out in the fifteenth chapter of Acts (verse 9). On the other hand, we will never serve God with a free affection unless we know he wants to be kind and gentle toward us, as we read in Psalm 130: 'Lord, there is always mercy with you' (verse 4), for, just as you are, so will we always find you near. Now the poor unbelievers who question God's will and are disquieted and fearful, it is certain they will never serve him with willing and glad hearts. And God will accept nothing they are willing to do, for he wants our voluntary sacrifices (cf. *Psa.* 51:19; 54:6). And Paul also says that he loves those who bring to him freely and cheerfully (cf. *2 Cor.* 9:7-8).

So that is what our works are worth, however fine they seem to be, whether they are ours or everybody's, and they are only filth and contagion before God until he cleanses us of our blemishes

and stains and shows us what goal we must aim for and the purpose we must set for our entire lives, namely, that we must honour
him and, being dedicated to his service, make an effort to conform fully to the righteousness he shows us. That will be explained
shortly at length when we talk about the law. During this hour, it
is enough to learn that, because the love of self transports us and
not only is like a blindfold but also beguiles us completely, we are
stupid and do not think about our wretchedness or have the slightest idea of what that entails. That is why I said we need God's word
to condemn us, and that is why Paul collected so many examples to
show that we are all damned (cf. *Rom.* 3:10-18). As I have said, we
should, each one of us, sense that in ourselves apart from any other
judge. But because we are so filled with contagion that we are two-
faced and have so many ways to hide and mask our true selves to
avoid the unadulterated and clear knowledge of our sins, we have
to have the word of God to mirror our true selves.

If men are perverse by nature and there is rebellion and malice
in them and all their affections and thoughts are just that many
inimical attitudes toward God, as Paul speaks of them in the
eighth chapter of Romans (cf. verses 7–8), how could we present or
offer anything to God that he would find good? It is true we could
present him with some foolish pride, but that would only redouble
the evil, for pride is more displeasing to God than all the other
vices. So we must acknowledge that we are such natural enemies
of God that everything we imagine is contrary to him, and we
cannot, throughout our lives, think or say or do anything that does
not heap more grievous condemnation on our heads than that.
And that is also why Scripture compares us to death when we are
abandoned by God (cf. *Eph.* 2:1), and until our Lord declares he is
our life, we are dead. And what can a dead man do?

In addition, we must have a good grasp of this fact, for we would
never open ourselves to God's goodness such as it is shown to us

in our Lord Jesus Christ. We have to be reduced to despair before we put our trust in him. We are inclined to the over-bold notion which is deeply rooted in us that we always want to exalt ourselves. Consequently, God has to bring us down completely so he can lift us up with his hand and sustain us by his power. Even more, we are puffed up with hot air and futile arrogance!

Now before we can receive anything real from God, we must be empty, like poor starving people. That is notably why it is said that God satisfies the poor and afflicted (cf. *Psa.* 132:15). That is why his goodness extends to those who are worthy of it, but when it is a matter of gathering together his church, he must prepare it through suffering, and that is notably why it is said that the Spirit of God had to rest on our Lord Jesus Christ so that he could announce deliverance to the captives, so that he could give light to the blind and bring healing to the sick and strengthen the weak (cf. *Isa.* 61:1; *Luke* 4:18). He fulfils that when he says, 'Come unto me, all you who have laboured and are heavy laden, and I will lighten your load and you will find rest for your souls' (cf. *Matt.* 11:28-29). That is how humility leads us to our Lord Jesus Christ so that we can be made participants in the righteousness he has brought us.

Now humility is not, as many think, presenting an innocent and pleasant face before God, but it is being so empty of any good that the only thing left for us is to cast ourselves at God's feet and acknowledge that there is in us only poverty and wretchedness and no hope of salvation. It is by our knowledge and feeling of wretchedness that we come to his mercy. And those two things cannot be separated. Why does God have pity on us in this way and help us? Because he considers our wretchedness, which inclines him and incites him to be merciful. That too is why Paul, when speaking of our salvation, says, 'It is not of you; it is a gift of God through faith, for you are his creation because he has created you in Jesus Christ for good works, which he prepared for you to do' (cf. *Eph.* 2:8-10).

In that passage Paul excludes any thought that men could conceive that they had any virtues. He is saying in effect that if you attribute any portion of the praise for your salvation to yourself and if you still think that even though you did not earn praise for yourself, you nonetheless aided in the process and need to think about how that could have happened. You were created mortal human beings! In other words, you were created sinners; there was in you nothing but a curse; you were banished and alienated from God, in whom dwells every good thing. So you have to conclude that you were like a dead man. Thus, a new and fruitful correction had to be made to give you some standing in God's sight. Consequently, when you were regenerated in Jesus Christ, you became a new creation. You are, then, a creation of God, each of you, since he formed you and called you to himself without any disposition on your part, but God prepared good works by his Holy Spirit. Since that is the situation, we must conclude that our salvation in no way derives from us, not a smidgen of it, but that it is a pure gift of God which proceeds from his liberality.

So for the first point, what we need to remember is that in order to obtain mercy and grace before God, we must have an awareness of the kind of people we are, how wretched our condition is, and how totally broken we are. Now when I speak that way, it is not to say that we must have an awareness that spins around in our heads, but we must be mortally wounded in our hearts and sense God's judgment, which terrifies us and reduces us to a state of complete despair.[1] For what do we know about having food unless hunger

---

[1] Calvin pushes to its extreme man's awareness of his own wretchedness, to the point of metaphysical despair, which leads the human being to abandon himself totally to God. That experience never appears as intense in the Reformer's dogmatic and exegetical writings. To the contrary, he condemns everything that can cast souls into despair: penitence (*Institutes* III, iv, 3, 17); auricular confession (*Institutes* III, iv, 24); stoicism (*Institutes* III, viii, 10); the preaching of perfect holiness (*Institutes* III, xx, 45); the absence of Christian freedom (*Institutes* III,

is pressing in on us? If we were sated with food and drink, everyone would remain content; we would not look for bread or other sustenance, but hunger forces us to look for nourishment. When we are sick, we look for a remedy, and if a man did not experience sensations or pains, he would die a hundred times without asking for help or wanting it. So, as I have already said, awareness of our wretchedness must affect us in such a way that we are truly at the point of death and become aware of the death Scripture speaks of so that we will aspire to the life that our Lord Jesus Christ presents in his gospel. That is why Scripture rebukes us so often for our sins. God would not take pleasure in dealing with us that way, had he not known the need to. Consequently, as many threats, sentences of condemnation, reproaches, and the like as are found in holy Scripture, God gives us just that many raps on the head to lead us to the humility which is far from being ours, and he does so until he redeems us, even with violence! So much, then, for that point.

Moreover, we need to come to a more ample elaboration of what has been said, and that is because we will be content in our hypocrisy and worry free until we have given some thought to our wretched state as exposed in God's word. And that carefree attitude will cause us to disdain God's grace and be excluded from it. Now God has placed our condemnation before us primarily in the law (cf. *Exod.* 4:21; *Isa.* 6:9-12; *Ezek.* 2:3; 12:2; *Jer.* 1:10). It is true that all of Scripture is filled with it, and when it is said that Scripture is useful, among other things, he cites censures. And then we know what the gospel brings forth: 'Repent; the kingdom of God is near' (cf. *Matt.* 3:2; 4:17). That is how God prepares his elect to receive the free righteousness which is given to them by means of

---

xix, 7). On the other hand, souls are saved from despair by free justification (*Institutes* III, xiii, 3), by the thought that God takes care of them (*Institutes* III, xx, 52), by remembering one's baptism (*Institutes* IV, xv, 3), etc. Cf. also Bouwsma, *Portrait*, chapt. 2, pp. 32-48.—*M.E.*

his Son. That is, he brings us to repentance. And what does that mean? It means we experience a sadness that afflicts us and grieves us so that we condemn ourselves for our evil and punish ourselves, as Paul speaks of it (cf. *2 Cor.* 7:9–11); for he not only uses the words 'sadness' and 'fear', but he says we must have such zeal that we punish ourselves, so to speak, because we are God's enemies.

Now although that teaching is encountered in all of holy Scripture, God has especially established his law for that purpose, and that is why Paul says it produces only wrath (cf. *Rom.* 4:15). When we pay close attention to what is said there, we will find that God is against us and that we cannot approach him without his being armed to strike out against us and cast us into the bottomless pit. It is true the law shows us what it is to live righteously and to acquire righteousness if we were capable of doing so, which we will deal with later at length. It is written in the eighteenth chapter of Leviticus: 'Whoever does these things will live in them' (cf. *Lev.* 18:5). But let us consider whether we ourselves come close to what God commands. But it is true men are still so overweeningly proud that the law, until it is well understood, is not enough to overcome them and to strip them of their foolish presumption. For that was Paul, who was taught the law from his youth up (cf. *Acts* 26:4; *2 Cor.* 11:22; *Phil.* 3:5); he was ranked among the learned; he says he continued to be proud of his virtues, and he thought he was righteous, for he had the law, on which he rested (cf. *Phil.* 3:6) as he disregarded our Lord Jesus Christ. Why? He was looking only on appearance. If, for example, the law says, 'You shall not murder' (*Exod.* 20:13; *Deut.* 5:17), well, he was not a murderer. If it says, 'You shall not commit adultery' (*Exod.* 20:14; *Deut.* 5:18), he is also not seen to be either a whoremonger or an adulterer. 'You shall not steal' (*Exod.* 20:15; *Deut.* 5:19); so he was not a thief. So he thought he and God were completely even. That is how he was at peace in the midst of his vain self-adulations. But then

God awakened him and led him to the depths of his thinking. And when it says, 'You shall not covet' (*Exod.* 20:17; *Deut.* 5:21), at that point he understands that he is convicted and condemned and that there is no longer any absolution. He feels that there are within him many vain things which delight him, that his weakness causes him to conceive many temptations, and that he is aware he did not repay a hundredth part of God's love, which ought to be in all believers. Paul knows that. He sees himself as a poor sinner. He forgets his life, by which he had been deceived, and he knows that he is exactly like a poor rotting carcass before God. The law kills him and he no longer has within himself anything to be confident of (cf. *Rom.* 7:10). That is why I have said there is a special judgment contained in the law that shows us there is only condemnation within us.

For we must now lay stress on each commandment. We are to have only one God. And what kind of God is he? How will we serve and honour him? We will magnify his name as it deserves to be magnified only when we are completely attached to him, when we seek no other good, no other felicity, no other joy than in glorifying him, when people hear only praises and thanksgiving from our mouths, when they see that our aspirations are all fixed completely on him and that we have denounced the world. That, then, covers the four commandments of the first table. And after we have closely examined everything they have to teach us, let us consider ourselves, and we will find that instead of having attached ourselves to him, we are vagabonds, and our thoughts and imaginations influence us and cause us to wander in many directions. What happens when it comes to praying? That action should draw men and lift them to heaven because it is as if we were in the presence of our God. And yet when we pray, how many frivolous imaginations will continue to pass through our heads and keep us captive? Since that is the case, what will the rest of our lives be like? It will be the same with all the commandments of the law when we measure our lives against them. And yet we will not find one single death, but a hundred thousand.

And, in addition, we also see how God in his law wanted to touch us to the quick, for it is said that we must be aware that our hearts are broken (cf. *Psa.* 15:19; 109:22; *Lam.* 3:33; *Jer.* 22:3). For after pronouncing this sentence: 'Cursed will be he who does not do all the things which are written here' (cf. *Deut.* 27:26), he is not content to be the Judge and to have condemned men, but he wants the people to respond, 'Amen.' In other words, he wants everyone to pass through condemnation of his own accord and consider himself thoroughly condemned after having accepted the sentence which he consented to as being just and equitable. Thus the law must cause us to examine our entire lives so that we will experience only despair and, in this way, be deeply concerned to seek our Lord Jesus Christ to be the beginning of our righteousness.[2]

We now understand that these are two things as different as fire and water: that we are considered righteous before God by our works and that we are accepted by him by virtue of faith. As Paul says, if we brought something of our own, it is certain God would be obligated to us even though we are not completely righteous or perfect (cf. *Rom.* 4:4-5). In any case, pay would still be due us for whatever share we might have. Now it is said that faith can in no way be granted along with works (cf. *Rom.* 3:28; *Gal.* 2:16). So we must conclude that since we are justified by faith, works cease and are rendered completely useless.

Now on the surface we would appear to be inflexible if we said that faith and good works cannot be reconciled, for it would appear that faith justifies us in order to give us greater freedom in every iniquity. That is because Paul is speaking in accordance with a certain condition and consideration. He also speaks of the law and faith in the same way (cf. *Gal.* 3:12): the law, he says, shares

[2] This is a reference to the first use of the law. Cf. *Institutes* III, vii, 6-8.—*M.E.*

337

nothing in common with faith. They are incompatible. In what way? Is God not the author of the law as well as of the gospel? Is there contradiction or difference in him? Certainly not, for he is immutable (cf. *James* 1:17). So why does Paul find a distinction between the law and the gospel? It has to do with our justification. The same distinction exists between faith and works. There is a distinction because works are merits. And what is more, we can do no good work apart from faith, as we have already said and will explain further at length. For cause and effect work together, but when we want to set up some merit or other in our works, that is, when we want our works to be good for acquiring grace for us in God's sight and to be satisfaction for our sins, that is, when we want them to be useful for our salvation, they completely subvert faith and thus become useless. So we see that Paul has good reason to conclude that if we are justified by faith, works have no role to play and must disappear (cf. *Rom.* 3:28; 3:20-24; 5:1) because someone could attribute a supposition of merits or virtues to causing God to consider us as acceptable.

At the same time let us note that God justifies us by his pure liberality and only seeks in us our adversities to help us with them so that he alone may be known to be righteous and so that the praise for our salvation will be given to him, just as Paul also comments on it very well both in the first chapter of Ephesians and in the third chapter of Romans (cf. *Eph.* 1:7; *Rom.* 3:22-25). Therefore, he says God included everything under sin so that he alone would be acknowledged as righteous and every mouth would be closed (cf. *Rom.* 3:19) because it is he alone who justifies sinners by the grace of our Lord Jesus Christ and places us on the path of his righteousness. Likewise, in the third chapter of Galatians, Paul proposes this question: How was it possible for God to give his law after the promise? It seems he changed his drift, changed his mind, because he freely justifies Abraham and much later publishes his law (cf. *Gal.* 3:19-21). In it he says, 'Whoever does these things will live in them' (cf. *Lev.* 18:5; *Gal.* 3:12). Paul responds to that, saying that the law was not given to destroy the free promise, but so that we have to be included under sin and under condemnation, as I have already explained; otherwise we will never be able to value God's mercy and seek it, and it will also seem to us that we do not need it.

In fact there are two kinds of people who despise our Lord Jesus Christ and deprive themselves both of all the blessings he has brought us and of the salvation we have through his death and resurrection. One kind is persuaded of their own worth and for that reason have contempt for God in their pride. Like people who have some fine appearance of righteousness, like angels, these devout people who counterfeit great holiness close the door on themselves and have no way to approach Jesus Christ, for they push him far away from themselves. There are others who are apathetic and do not think they are righteous. Why not? Some are whoremongers, others are thieves, and others drunkards, rakes, and so evidently despisers of God that even little children can judge them. The last group is not deceived by pride and arrogance, but they are so intoxicated with Satan that they do not think about eternal life. They have become exactly like animals. That is why Solomon says, 'Blessed is the man who is concerned for his heart and is mindful of fear and who awakens to acknowledge his transgressions and failures' (*Prov.* 28:14).

So in this way we see that the law was given after the promise for a reason other than to condemn us so that we might seek all our righteousness in God and so that all the praise for our salvation might be offered up to him, for it belongs to him. So let us note that last reason, for that is also why Paul discusses that matter at length in the first chapter of Ephesians (cf. *Eph.* 1:3-14). He does not pass quickly over that, but he draws out the same subject as if he wanted it to resound in our ears so that the glory of God would be known and that he alone might be glorified and acknowledged as righteous so that we might know that it is from him alone that we possess all things. We must, he says, acknowledge that we would all perish without God's pure grace. That, in brief, is what God has in mind when he cleanses us of every presumption about our virtues. In other words, he wants to be the only one acknowledged as righteous, and he wants us to be lost and damned within ourselves (cf. *Exod.* 9:27; *Psa.* 7:11, 13; *2 Tim.* 4:8).

Thus, those who attribute to themselves ever so little righteousness, as if they had helped God—since papists call themselves 'co-workers'—commit, it is certain, a more despicable crime than all the thieves in the world. Which is worse? To take from a man his gold and silver and all his possessions or to take from God his honour and the main thing he is seeking and intends to reserve for himself, namely, to be known as righteous? And when poor mortal creatures or vermin of the earth, where there is only contagion and stench, want to put themselves in God's place and say, 'You are not the be-all and end-all when it comes to the work of our salvation, for we have helped in the process,' is that not a damnable blasphemy when men presume to bring a fragment of their righteousness before God? Now we need to remember what was discussed yesterday, namely, that the word 'justify' does not mean we are angels, but it does means he accepts us and approves of us through his pure goodness, even though we are poor sinners.

That is also why Moses used the word 'impute' in this passage as if he were saying that it depends on God's free favour and that we must not inquire into whether the righteousness belongs to the man or whether he was worthy of being accepted. It has nothing to do with all that, but let us be content that God accepts us as just despite the fact we are not. That too is why the righteousness of faith excludes works, for we take from Jesus what we lack. I am not

talking about a part of what we need, as the papists stirred themselves into the mix, but we borrow Jesus Christ's righteousness
because there is not a grain or a speck of it in us. Consequently,
works must be forsaken as we seek our righteousness elsewhere.
For if part of the righteousness were in Jesus Christ and a part in
us, that still would not constitute the whole. And how would it be
fulfilled that all the fullness of grace was in him, which was given
to him by the Holy Spirit so that he might distribute it to each
according to his measure (cf. *John* 1:16; *Col.* 2:9; *1 Cor.* 12:11)?
For it is one thing to acquire and another to receive from God.
When God justifies us, he does so by adoption (cf. *Eph.* 1:5; *Rom.*
8:15-16). Because we are by nature children of wrath, he adopts us
and keeps us as his children (cf. *Eph.* 2:3). And what does he find
in us? Nothing that could compel him to do something good for
us. Consequently, the inheritance we hoped for from our salvation
and which is promised us in the gospel comes from our adoption
by God, and there is in it nothing that belongs to us, for if we
can acquire something, it is certain we would at that time enter
into partnership with God, just as the papists manage to do. But
because God works in such a way that nothing of ours is involved,
that is why he alone is to be glorified.

We now see, in summary, that the righteousness spoken of here
refers only to the forgiveness of sins and the declaration we have
in the name of the Lord Jesus Christ that we are righteous by the
merit of his obedience. But again when Paul wishes to teach us
plainly on our level, he mentions only the forgiveness of sins and
argues this way: 'We cannot be justified by our works' (cf. *Gal.*
2:16). Why not? It is written: 'Blessed is the man whose sins God
forgives, whose iniquities are remitted, to whom his transgressions
are not imputed' (cf. *Psa.* 32:1-2; *Rom.* 4:7-8). All our felicity, he
says, lies in the fact that God receives us in mercy and forgiveness
and buries all our offenses, which make us guilty before him. If

such is the case, it follows that we are wretched until God pardons us, and if we are wicked, where is our righteousness? For God cannot hate what corresponds to his nature; he is the fountain of all righteousness; if he found some good in us, small as it might be, it is certain he would accept it. Therefore, we must conclude that, because we are evil, only unrighteousness and iniquity and every misfortune dwells in us and that we cannot be blessed unless God loves us. Now if he loves us, he must at the same time approve us; if he approves us, we must be righteous.

All those things are principles that must be sufficiently understood. But still we must realize that we cannot be blessed unless God loves us, for while we are enemies, alas, what is our condition? What, then, does our felicity depend on? It depends on God's receiving us into his love.

Let us consider now how he loves us. He must approve us, as I have said, for he cannot renounce himself. If we are detestable to him and he rejects us, how will he be reconciled to us? Let us come to the means, for God cannot change, and if we try to change him, the effort will be futile, as Paul says (cf. *Rom.* 3:20-28; 4:14-16), for God will always remain the same and will be able to separate us and all our lies from his dwelling place. How, then, will we be approved by God? We have to be righteous. Now just what is that righteousness? It is not in our works so that we can pay off our indebtedness to him or fulfil our duty. It is nothing like that. So what is it? God must forgive us of our sins, forget our iniquities, and not impute our offences to us. It is with good reason that David used those three expressions, for one would otherwise think this passage was repetitious, but it is noteworthy that he reiterates the thought because the condition in which man is born is an abyss and he remains deep in it until God draws him out, but it is indeed the abyss of abysses. In short, it is the very bottom of hell. As a consequence, God is obliged to work here in a singular way.

And that is why he adds straightway: 'And in whose spirit there is no deceit' (cf. *Psa.* 32:2), for we need to sense how necessary God's mercy is for us inasmuch as the greatness of our sins is enough to stink up heaven and earth and provoke not only our God, but the angels, the sun and the moon, and all the creatures around us. That, then, is why David magnifies the forgiveness of sins so much. And for that reason Paul also concludes that all our righteousness lies in the fact that our sins are forgiven (cf. *Rom.* 4:23-25).

And let us also take careful note, as I have already mentioned, that David says 'in whose spirit there is no deceit,' for he shows we cannot receive forgiveness of our sins—although God offers it to us—until we are completely confounded within ourselves, until we are awakened, until there is no hypocrisy or pretence to cause us to believe one thing or another, until there is no dissembling, until we are not double-minded or asleep in our indifference; but, to receive that forgiveness, we must be like poor condemned, lost people whom God's judgment pursues until we do not know what to do and are already viewing death as present, so to speak, as if beholding God's hand armed to carry out the sentence of curse which he pronounces against us. That is what we have to note concerning that righteousness if we are to have a good definition of it.

Now that is also why it is said in the fifteenth chapter of Acts, when Paul is dealing with ceremonies, that we must be justified by our Lord Jesus Christ of all the things of which the law of Moses has been unable to justify us. That statement has a rather far-reaching significance, for we must know why Paul speaks of the ceremonies of the law, notably when he says that works can do nothing, can serve no purpose, in making us acceptable to God (cf. *Rom.* 3-4; *Gal.* 2). The papists and even many of the ancient writers who were not practised in Scripture and were something like semi-philosophers focused on that comment about the law and do not think that Paul is not fighting for what are called *moral works*—that is, they think he does not intend to deny we are not righteous before God when we live chastely without wronging anyone, when we live temperately and soberly in all the other virtues. In other words, they think Paul is not talking about that and means that all those works partially merit salvation; *but* they *still* understand that the ceremonies of the law were of no value for justification. Now that is absurdity compounded. In the first place, Paul does not always talk about the ceremonies of the law; and in that respect they were grossly mistaken. And so it is in the passage of the psalm I have just quoted: David placed man's blessedness in the forgiveness of sins alone without any works (cf. *Psa.* 2:1). And the word 'works' includes all virtues in general, those which men can attribute to themselves and in which they find some glory. Now that unfortunate situation, Paul says, shows that we must all present ourselves naked before God, and empty, so that we may be enriched by his pure, free goodness (cf. *Rom.* 4:9-12; *Heb.* 11:6).

Moreover, when he speaks of the works of the law, it is because there was some merit in them because of the covenant we have already cited: 'Whoever does these things will live in them' (cf. *Lev.* 18:5). Let us conjecture a situation in which there was never a public law. Even then men would not be more acceptable to God (cf. *Rom.* 2:12). From that standpoint, he can owe us nothing, for it is said that when we have done all that is commanded of us, we would have to confess that we are useless servants (cf. *Luke* 17:11). Why are we useless? Are we free agents? Is there anything in us which belongs to us and is characteristic of us? Consequently, we still cannot claim any merit if we fulfil the law perfectly. So what does the confidence that men have in their works depend on? On this promise: 'Whoever does these things will live in them.' For God committed himself to that willingly, even though he was not bound to legally. So when Paul speaks of the works of the law, he shows that, despite the fact God made the promise to those whom he promised, those who do everything commanded in the righteousness of law will be considered righteous and will have everlasting life. Yet the works of the law can do nothing. Why not? Because they always leave us under condemnation and we do not cease to offend him, and even the most righteous will still not be able to pay a hundredth part of the debt. And who then can do that, if not all those of us who bow our heads and throw ourselves at the feet of our Judge and beg him for forgiveness, as we will discuss in greater detail later?

Now let us return to the passage that relates to what I have already discussed, namely, that Jesus Christ is presented to us to justify us of all the things which the law of Moses was not able to justify us of. It would indeed seem that, with respect of the ceremonies and all the rest of the law, men had some help in making themselves worthy before God and acceptable to him. For if they fell short, the sacrifices were appropriate remedies, for they had sprinklings of blood for cleansing themselves, and they also had washings which served as satisfaction toward God, along with many other promises. So it seemed that all that was to gain God's approval. Not at all. On the other hand, Jesus Christ had to come to justify us of the things the law could not justify us of. What does it mean 'to justify us of things'? It means to absolve us of them. That passage clarifies what I said before, namely, that the righteousness Moses speaks of here is not a thing that resides in individuals but is God's free forgiveness when he is propitious and favourable toward us and loves us, even though we do not deserve it. What Moses declares here will not be found in all men, but in Jesus Christ we will find what will justify us. How? If the devil accuses us and God is ready to judge and condemn us, our Lord Jesus Christ answers for us as our surety. His obedience acts as a cloak to cover all our rebellion and iniquity. He has made satisfaction for us and has acquitted us of all our debts by the merit of his death. So then he has poured out his blood for our cleansing. In a word, we find in the person of the Son of God everything we need to make us acceptable because our sins are not imputed to us. That, in short, is what we have to remember about this passage.

What we have to do now is move beyond that and talk about how God, having thus received us in mercy once, continues to keep us and consider us righteous all the time of our lives and even in death, for that is the principal goal we must reach. But we cannot deal with that now. Therefore, so that we may remember these things, it will be enough for us to know the way we must become sharers in the eternal salvation which has been brought to us by the Son of God. We must realize how wretched our condition is—not to confess it with our mouths and have some uncertain concept of it—so that we will be broken with such sadness that we will be confounded before God to the point of hating and despising ourselves. When we are thus our own judges, then we have been absolved by God. When we are thus dead within ourselves, then we will find our lives within Jesus Christ. It is not enough that we know we are pitiable sick people, poor and indigent, but we must be completely dead so that we may be made alive by nothing but the grace of our Lord Jesus Christ (cf. *1 Cor.* 15:22). And to gain that, let us achieve the humility that Scripture requires of us, which is to give God the honour which belongs to him (cf. *Psa.* 29:1). It is for good reason that David says the sacrifice that God demands is a humble and contrite heart (cf. *Psa.* 51:17), for otherwise we cannot have access to him until we are fully brought to naught. Thus there must be within us a deep sense of anguish and distress, and at that time we will willingly confess that we are not righteous. And also at that time we will seek all our well-being and salvation in the person of his only Son so that, knowing that he has lifted us from the darkness of death, we will be disposed to open our mouths and preach his unspeakable praises, as Peter says when dealing with the purpose of our salvation in the first chapter of his first letter (cf. *1 Pet.* 1).

Now let us bow before the majesty of our gracious God in acknowledgment of our faults, praying that he will make us feel them more and more and so guide us by his Holy Spirit that we will seek only to glorify him and bless his holy name and realize in how many ways we are bound to him, indeed possessing from him every hope of life that we have, and let us not be lax in serving him, but let us put great effort into bringing ourselves into line with his holy will until we have so stripped ourselves of all the corruptions of our flesh that we are fully reclothed in his righteousness. Now let us all say together, Almighty God, heavenly Father...

69

Third Sermon on Justification

Thursday, 7 March 1560

And he believed in the LORD; *and he counted it to him for righteousness* (Gen. 15:6).

YESTERDAY, WE SAW that we must in no way be sharers with God in our salvation and that all the praise for it must be reserved for him. When we seek out everything that can be found in man, we will conclude that he is so destitute of integrity that there is in him only total corruption and that, consequently, there is only death. It is enough to know that God alone is to be glorified and that we are to be annihilated, so to speak, for we must be given assurance, or otherwise the door of salvation is closed to us. When it is said that we live by faith (cf. *Rom.* 1:17; *Gal.* 3:11), as Paul says, quoting from the prophet Habakkuk (cf. *Hab.* 2:4), he shows that faith is like a key to open the kingdom of paradise for us.

And if that is our inheritance, we must be children of God to attain it. We can be children of God only by believing, as we are told in the first chapter of John (verse 12). Now this believing, as we have said, brings certainty. That is also why it is said we can cry aloud that God is our Father and that that is the only way we can be considered his children. And where does that cry come

349

from? From the Spirit of adoption, Paul says in the eighth chapter of Romans and the fourth of Galatians (cf. *Rom.* 8:15; *Gal.* 4:6). So the Spirit of God must certify that he has adopted us so that we can call upon him as our Father without doubt and without anxiety. That is also why in another passage, in the first chapter of Ephesians (cf. *Eph.* 1:11-13) and then in First Corinthians, first chapter, he is called the seal of the inheritance of salvation that we await (cf. *1 Cor.* 1:7-9). Now since the certainty of faith means that God has adopted us and that our salvation is founded on that, there must be a seal, as it were, of something unfailing. We see now that it is not enough that men confess God as the author of their salvation, which must be attributed to him; they must, for their part, have access to him and call upon him as their Father and be fully convinced that he will never fail them.

Now that certainty has never been understood in the Papacy. They even fight strongly and firmly against it and say we cannot declare confidently that God approves us and that we are in his grace, but only that we can make some probable conjecture about it. Now that destroys all the foundations of our Christian faith. And in fact when Paul deals with the subject, he reasons this way: if we depend on the law and our trust is in it, faith is thereby abolished and all the promises destroyed. Why is that? It is not because God is not faithful, but because we will never live up to what is required for our salvation. For God promises to reward us when we serve him and keep all his commandments from one end to the other. God promises that! Now that condition is currently impossible, for man has never fulfilled the law and no one ever will. Consequently, that promise will never do us any good. So we will always of necessity be in a state of uncertainty and agitation and disquietude, and as a result we will flounder around in despair when we try to bring our works and settle accounts with God. Psalm 143 says, 'Lord, do not enter into judgment with your servant, for no living man will be justified in your sight' (verse 2). So we have to conclude that we will always be distraught and our minds perplexed unless our salvation proceeds from some source other than our merits.

And to understand that better, let us take a good look at what has been said, namely, that we will not please God with empty rhetoric. It is a terrible thing to have him as our opponent. Now that is what he will always be as long as we try to take liberties with his works. We disparage him and want to deprive him of his right, as I have already pointed out that whoever attributes glory to himself and does not confess that God alone is righteous will certainly be fighting against him. Now we will not win our case, and condemnation will always hang over our heads, and, as a result, it will not occur to us that we are willingly provoking his wrath against us.

Moreover, men have to be out of their minds to think that they can put confidence in their merits. That is a double error which invites a third. For it is an error for men, in their confusion, to think they can settle accounts with God the way the papists do. And even though they fall short in many respects, they nonetheless convince themselves to believe he still accepts them. Now God promised nothing except to those who fulfil the whole law. Let us note well this verse where it is said, 'Whoever does all the things written in the law, he will live in them' (cf. *Lev.* 18:5). The text does not say 'just a part of the law.' Similarly, James says that the one who forbade committing adultery also forbade stealing (cf. *James* 2:11). So if a man lives chastely throughout his life and is guilty in some point, he will be condemned (cf. *James* 2:10). Why? What God has joined together, we cannot separate (cf. *Matt.* 19:6). The righteousness of the law is joined together and is a single unit. Consequently, we must not try to cut it into pieces or carve out a particular portion of it.

Let us now consider whether we can acquit ourselves thoroughly in every respect in our lives so that nothing is lacking: 'Alas, who
are we?' As Solomon says, 'Who can say, "I have made my heart
clean?"' (Cf. *Prov.* 20:9.) It is true many think they can, for there
are many hypocrites in the world. But a man must be out of his
mind, as I have said, if he reaches that point in his thinking, for
if he considers the Judge he has to deal with...[1] In any case, if we
take everything into consideration, it is certain that if we bring an
ounce or even half an ounce to God, there will be a ton, so to speak,
to offset it. And what good will that do? So let us learn what kind
of people we are so we will know we are nothing at all. And as I
have said, let us keep in mind that we cannot come to salvation
unless we are assured by God that we can call upon him as our
Father.

Other than the first error, there is the second, namely, those who
think they justify themselves by their merits do not consider the
fact that there is not a single work that is good if God wishes to
judge rigorously. I have already said that even if we did half of the
law or a third of it, that would be nothing, for we will not avoid
condemnation if we fail in a single point (cf. *James* 2:10). But here
is another reason: we do not in any way come close to fulfilling the
law, either completely or in part. And how is that? We said yesterday that God does not judge our works in accordance with our
preferences. He has his standard and his scales. And how does he
judge them? By whether the heart is completely pure and cleansed
of all fleshly stains. And where can such a heart be found? We are
always enveloped in many wicked emotions, and although they do
not dominate us, yet we cannot completely rid ourselves of them.
Add to that the fact that we will never have the required zeal to
glorify God. There will always be some weakness. We will indeed

---

[1] It seems that the composer (or the original scribe) omitted one or several lines
of the text of the sermon.—*M.E.*

try to overcome it, but there is no perfection such as can suffice before his face. For here it is not a matter of saying: 'I think' or 'In my opinion.' We must say: 'God has declared it thus,' and 'God approves it.' So we will be very far from meriting anything in his sight or having consciences that are at peace, for beyond the fact that we, all of us, fall short in many respects and feel remorse everyday, even though we think we do the best we can, we still hobble along. There is always some weakness that defiles the good works themselves.

Has there ever been a better work than Abraham's, when he was ready to kill his son? And yet it is certain he harboured many regrets, which betray his weakness. So even that work is soiled in God's eyes and cannot be imputed as merit. What is the situation now concerning what we do since all of us find ourselves hindered when it comes to setting out on our walk? Even though we may want to be used in serving God faithfully, the fact remains that we do not do so with the integrity and uprightness the task requires, not even a hundredth part of it. As a consequence, we always have to be troubled and perturbed, and if we are not totally blind, each of us knows that.

Now I have already said that we have to be assured that God loves us, that he receives us, and that we are acceptable to him as if we were righteous. And how do we obtain such a privilege? We have to take note of what Paul says in the tenth chapter of Romans, that we cast our eyes upon our Lord Jesus Christ. For when someone talks to us about our salvation, heaven daunts us, for we are not worthy of approaching it. And then we see hell before us, open to swallow us up, because we are poor sinners. So we will ask who will show us heaven, for we cannot reach it. Where are our wings that we could rise so high? The pit of hell, as I have said, is ready to receive us if God wishes to judge us. So we will say: 'Do we know whether our account is clear and we are absolved so that God will not cast us into the pit?' Now on that point Paul answers and indicates the remedy: we must not doubt heaven. Why not? In the person of our Lord Jesus Christ, we know that it is open. We take Jesus Christ, he says, out of the equation when we ask with doubt: 'Who will ascend?' We know that the Son of God declared that there are many rooms in his Father's house and that he was not received there for his particular advantage but so that he might receive us to himself as his coheirs (cf. *John* 14:2). As for hell, he descended into it, for he suffered the torments which were prepared for us (cf. *Rom.* 10:7). He suffered the horrible torments of God's curse, crying out, 'My God, my God, why have you forsaken me?' (Cf. *Matt.* 27:46.) Therein are we assured of the certainty of our salvation.

And that is also what Paul understands in the eighth chapter of Romans. 'Who will bring a charge against God's elect?' he asks (cf. *Rom.* 8:33). In that passage, he contradicts Satan and everything which is against us, as if he were saying: 'Provided we renounce all arrogance and do not imagine we can do anything as we come to God knowing that, inasmuch as he has elected us out of his own free kindness, as he also called us to himself through the gospel, they can bring as many charges against us as they please and we will still be justified and absolved by him.' And how can that be? Our Lord Jesus Christ intercedes for us, he says (cf. *Rom.* 8:34), and by virtue of that intercession, because he is our advocate to appease the wrath of God his Father, that is how we are absolved. And that is the certainty of which Paul speaks in the fourth chapter of Romans, as we have already said.

And the same truth is declared in the person of the poor publican—the receiver of taxes who was rejected by everybody—when he presents himself to God (cf. *Luke* 18:13-14). He does not come to him with his head raised. It is true that he had complete confidence that God would receive him in mercy, and with that confidence he is bold, as we must also be, as we read in the third chapter of Ephesians (cf. *Eph.* 3:12). But when he looks at himself, he lowers his head, he is distraught and only asks for forgiveness, and Jesus Christ says that because of that single statement he was justified. On the other hand, the Pharisee was rejected because he offered the foolish presumption of his works. The publican, who confesses purely and simply that he is a poor condemned sinner, is justified before God (cf. *Luke* 18:11-12). And yet the Pharisee did not attribute to himself the praise for his merits. He did not say, 'I have done this and that, and God is obligated to me for it,' but only, 'Lord, I thank you that I am not a thief or a robber or a dissolute man or like this man' (cf. *Luke* 18:11). That is a fine introduction, it seems, for he entrusts himself completely to God when he declares that all that he is, along with his virtues, comes from the pure gift of his Holy Spirit. But look at that. He allows himself to be inflated by the overweening pride that he is approved because of his merits. That is why God condemns him. For he certainly has to be stupid and then some to think that he holds God obligated because of his works.

We have nothing to fall back on but God's pure mercy, and then we will be assured that he loves us when, I say, we seek all our merits in Jesus Christ and do not fail to call upon God, no matter our unworthiness, since it is not because of our persons or our works that he has adopted us, but because of his pure and free mercy (cf. *Gal.* 4:5-6). That is how we are assured of our salvation.

It is quite true we will always have some doubts since our faith is never perfect, but faith always overcomes when we struggle valiantly and embrace God's promises and use them as a shield against all temptations and all the challenges the devil places before us. So when we speak of the certainty of faith, we do not mean that nothing will shake us and that we will not experience great perplexity and distress sometimes, but we understand that in the end we will conclude that, whatever happens, God will pity us and, with that assurance, we will call on his name.[2] That, then, is what we have to remember now.

With that in mind, we easily understand that those who took the word 'justify' to mean that God changes us and governs us by his Holy Spirit so that we can serve him have made a very serious error. There are indeed those who confess that we are not righteous by our merits, that we do not have a single drop of worthiness in us, and that all the good we can bring is a free gift of God because we, left on our own, can do nothing but sin. They will confess all that and, in summary, say that we are justified by pure grace, that we are justified without our works, that we make no contribution, and that God gives us everything. Have they confessed that? They still continue to destroy both themselves and others. How? They think they have already reached a perfection that lacks nothing.[3], [4]

---

[2] In his accent on the certainty of faith, as on that of the certainty of salvation…, Calvin specifies that certainty never excludes doubt. Cf. *Institutes* III, ii, 15; *In epistolam ad Ephesios commentarius* (on *Eph.* 3:12), in Calvin, *Epistolae I*, p. 210f., passages in which Calvin once again opposes both the decree on justification of the sixth session of the Council of Trent and the Parisian Catholic theologians.—M.E.

[3] Cf. once again the decree on justification of the sixth session of the Council of Trent, in particular chapter 16, but also chapters 8 and 10 and canons 1-3. Cf. the same attacks in *Institutes* III, xv, 7, which are not addressed to the ideas of Thomas Aquinas or Peter Lombard. More must be sought in the works of Clichtove or other 'sophists of the 'Sorbonnique' [pedantic] schools'; thus Clichtove, *Compendium*: f° 142r°-v°.—M.E.

[4] This comment has to do with the expression of Catholic theologians, or 'mediators,' who have taken a step toward the Reformed. Thus we can find here the statement of one Claude d'Espence in his commentary on Paul's Second Epistle to Timothy, of 1563: *'arbitramur ergo justificari hominem per fidem, gratis, per gratiam Dei, per redemptionem Christi, in sanguine ipsius, sine operibus legis, Rom. 3… Gratia enim salvati estis per fidem, et hoc non ex vobis; Dei donum est, non ex operibus, ne quis glorietur…'* Espence, *Opera omnia*: p. 399, col. 1 C-D. Cf. again *Institutes* III, xi, 14f., with a long addition in 1559-1560; and the *Confessio Gallicana* of 1559, in CO 9, col. 731-52. The confession of Claude de Saintes, at the Poissy colloquim, also illustrates Calvin's statement, since he takes it up almost word

For who will find fault in a man when he is utterly cast down in himself, when he is completely undone, when he confesses that he deserves only condemnation and that any good thing in him comes from God's pure liberality so that God alone is exalted and magnified and the man is nothing in himself so that he acknowledges his faith in and pays homage to God—all of which he has from God's pure bounty? Indeed, but we have already declared that if we doubt, the door of heaven is closed to us. Now we are obliged to doubt or be totally enraged when we evaluate ourselves on the basis of our works.

Let us consider the case in which God regenerates a man by his Holy Spirit and the man only gives thanks to God the way

---

for word (cf. art. 13, col. 745): 'We believe that the sacrifice offered by our Lord Jesus Christ on the cross is the price of our reconciliation with God in order to be judged and accounted as righteous before him because we cannot be acceptable to him or sharers in his adoption unless he pardons us of our faults and buries them in the blood and death of our Saviour to demonstrate his righteousness. We likewise declare that Jesus is our full and perfect washing; we declare that his death constitutes our full satisfaction for the payment for the sins and iniquities of which we are guilty, and we cannot be delivered except by that remedy.' Cf. *La confession de la foy catholique contenant en brief la reformation de celle que les ministres de Calvin presenterent au roy en l'assemblée de Poissy,* Paris, Claude Fremy, 1561, f° 12v°-13r°. (I thank Francis Higman for pointing out that last reference). Calvin's theological intransigence still shows through in the development of the sermon. Making large strides toward his thought is not enough; full adherence is required. The least amount of merit must especially not be attributed to man. This brief passage, two years before its presentation, sheds light on the discussions at the Poissy colloquium and their heralded near failure. Cf. Richard Stauffer, 'Autour du Colloque de Poissy: Calvin et le *De officio pii ac publicae tranquillitatis vere amantis viri,*' in *Interprètes de la Bible* (Théologie historique 57), (Paris: 1980), pp. 249-267; and Alain Dufour, 'Le Colloque de Poissy,' in *Mélanges d'histoire du XVIe siècle offerts à Henri Meylan* (Travaux d'Humanisme et Renaissance 110), (Genève: 1970), p. 127-137.—*M.E.* [*"Therefore we conclude that a man is justified by faith, freely, by the grace of God, through the redemption of Christ, by his blood, without the works of the law (*Rom.* 3)... For by grace you are saved through faith, and that not of yourselves; it is the gift of God, not because of works, lest any man should boast...'—*Translator.*]

we mentioned when speaking of the Pharisee and says, 'No. Everything I have is from God'; yet it is necessary, when he prays, to come with assurance. How does he come? Because he is imperfect and weak, he would have many vices mixed among the virtues God placed within him; and those virtues themselves are filled with vice because he has not been completely cleansed of the stains of the flesh. When a man finds himself thus in mid-journey and is still far from his destination, what can he do but doubt? So let us conclude that it does no good to confess that our salvation proceeds from God's pure grace because he governs us by his Spirit; our refuge must be in the forgiveness of our sins. Those who quibble about that are sophists, saying that we are not justified by our works because the good works are not ours but are gifts of the Holy Spirit. They forget the point we have only just touched upon, namely, that our faith must possess a certainty and that that certainty cannot exist unless Jesus Christ is our Advocate and his death is the satisfaction for our sins with the result that we can do nothing unless we confess our debt in the way we indicated in the example of the publican. Now we see clearly that that righteousness is not just for a day, but that it must continue throughout our lives. For although we have profited from God's service, imperfections still remain. So faith and only faith must justify us.

And here we must defeat that foolish and perverse concept of the papists, who think they are partly justified by their works and partly by the forgiveness which they obtained from God's grace, for God must in every respect receive us in mercy, as has been demonstrated. Why? Part of our works merit nothing. And then there is not a single work which is not filled with a vice when it comes to being judged according to the worth God finds in it. So we are shut out in every respect. Therefore, we must come to the conclusion that the most righteous, should they seem like angels, have to be received freely by God.

Now one might object here, for the fact is that those whom God has already called are very different from those who are completely alienated from him, and there is even a great distance and difference in the believer between the time God placed him on the right road and the time he had abandoned him because of the corruption of his nature. There you have a man who has lived for some time like a stray sheep and a lost creature. Well, God comes and illuminates him by his gospel, touches him and remakes him so that he is like a new creature, as Scripture says (cf. *2 Cor.* 5:17). And in fact we cannot be Christians unless we are renewed in that way and are God's workmanship, created in our Lord Jesus Christ to do the works God has prepared. That, I say, is the way it has to be.

It now seems that we have reached the point of absurdity. God justifies the hanged highway robber because he acknowledges his salvation in Jesus Christ. And when he is justified, does he not have a different quality in himself than the one he had before? Yes indeed! So why do we say that free righteousness has its course and its effect throughout a man's life? Now a man of faith will at least have a healthy desire to live in obedience to God; he will be displeased with his vices and will indeed grieve over them, and his principal desire will always be to live in conformity with the law. So when a man of faith is doing that, it must not be said that he is justified as he was from the outset, because he was corrupt at the time and completely alienated from God. Now this is the way to respond to that. When God justifies us at the beginning, that is, when he receives us in mercy, removing us from the condemnation in which we were, he employs a general pardon. And then when he justifies us afterwards, it is not that he does not recognize the good things he placed within us and that he does not acknowledge and approve them, for he cannot deny himself. And since he governs us by his Holy Spirit, even though sin dwells within us, it nevertheless does not reign in us (cf. *Rom.* 6:12),[5] as we read in the sixth chapter of Romans, even though we do not do the good that we desire (cf. *Rom.* 7:18), we still try to. Therefore, God approves that because it is from him, but let us note that he justifies us in our persons and even justifies us in our works by pure faith.

When he receives us initially, he can justify none of the works which are in us. Why not? They are all bad. For, as we have said, what can a corrupt tree bear? (Cf. *Matt.* 7:17.) So God, when drawing to himself poor sinners who are rejected and banished from his kingdom and his church, does not justify their works but, seeing their wretchedness and having pity on them as being lost, justifies them. Now after receiving them, he justifies them in their persons, that is, they are acceptable to him as his children, and then he justifies their works. How so? Not by calling them to account or judging them severely, for there will always be, as I have said, some vice mixed in, or some barriers and similar things which will spoil everything. If a wine is the best in the world and it is put in a foul-smelling cask or in a dirty bottle, the wine is ruined. That is the way it is with all our works. For to the extent God guides and directs us in them by his Holy Spirit, they are good and holy and praiseworthy. But let us consider the kind of vessels we are, filled with infection and stench. Consequently, our works are corrupt and God is obliged to purge and cleanse them. How? By his pure grace in us as it pardons our faults and imperfections. For that reason, just as there is a difference between a man of faith and a man whom God calls at the beginning of the gospel, so justification is a little different, but it does not change in this particular, namely, that God always justifies his own freely, that is, he

---

[5] Calvin's comment on this verse: 'Although sin resides in us, it is nonetheless not right that it have the strength to exercise its reign because the power of sanctification must be imminent and be seen to be superior to it.'—*M.E.*

considers them acceptable, not because of virtues which are in them, for there are none, or because of those which he has placed in them, for they are to be condemned because of the weakness that is in them, but because he justifies those whom he has chosen, as Paul says in the eighth chapter of Romans (cf. *Rom.* 8:30). That, then, is in brief what we have to remember in connection with the question that could be raised here.

Now let us note that other than what the papists think about men's being able to obtain a part of their justification and absolution from God, they are sorely mistaken about their satisfactions. They are blind, I say, because they think they have some virtues God is obliged to approve. It is true they again have the shame of saying their works are worthy, but they mean something very similar. Despite the fact that there is no perfect worthiness, they say, it is nonetheless fitting that God, who is righteous, accept what they find good. Indeed! But their righteousness blinds them so much that they do not recognize their vices, as we have already pointed out.

Their second mistake is that they think they have the ability to pay their debts with their satisfactions. I am not going to list the satisfactions they bring with them, for they are all idle talk and only provoke God more when they want to pay with rubbish and filth, that is, with superstitions they have fabricated in their heads. But what satisfaction can be found that can deliver from God's judgment? But what does an offence entail? We have violated God's righteousness, and then we will use that in partial payment. Indeed, that seems to be going a bit far! Does a man not have to be Satan possessed to stand with that kind of blatant pride? And that is the major part of the Papacy's teaching: that we must pay God off after we fail. It follows, so they think, that we must be justified by their works. That is why they say there is only conjecture, for they are compelled to understand that if a man examines himself, he will find himself short in the end and will be unable to have what is required to close his accounts with God and say, 'I am paid up in full.'

And again, in addition to that conjecture, they have another foolish notion in their heads. If we were certain that God keeps us in his grace for today, we do not know that it is for tomorrow. Now they do not think that faith brings hope with it at the same time and that hope extends both into life and into death. And we even see later that there is still a more serious error, namely, that they are not considering death's last combat, which will be dealt with at God's pleasure.

Let us now continue what we began, namely, that they think they satisfy God and appease him when they bring him some compensation for the offenses and iniquities they have committed. By doing that, they strip Jesus Christ of his honour, and if that should be the case, he alone would not suffice for what is required to reconcile us to God his Father. Now it is for good reason that he is called our ransom, for he has set himself up as a pledge for us with the condition that he has taken our debts upon himself and made full and complete payment for them. So whoever now wishes to pay God usurps Jesus Christ's office, and that is a very damnable error. Nonetheless, the papists base their salvation on that. And yet they reason that although our Lord Jesus Christ has obtained forgiveness for both guilt and penalty, that is nonetheless laid aside in store, even though they are clearly contradicting themselves. On the other hand, they say that our Lord Jesus Christ merited for us only the opportunity for merit. Now, as we have dealt with this earlier, they will say that we are by nature so profoundly wicked that we can do nothing good that God will accept; but they say that when Jesus Christ goes before, he gives us the opportunity to merit, and that is the first merit, they say, so that they give him only some little snippet, some tiny portion, but we give the principal part. Now if it is true that Jesus Christ has only earned for us the opportunity for merit, that is, through him we must obtain paradise, it follows that we will always be indebted to God because of our guilt and the penalty. Therefore, it is a gross abomination for the papists to presume to pay their debts to God by means of their satisfactions.

And then since one evil attracts another, they descend in a deeper labyrinth, for they understand clearly that if men tried a hundred times harder, they still would not be able to satisfy God for all their offences. Why not? We fail miserably in a number of ways. 'And who knows his faults?' asks David (cf. *Psa.* 19:13). Consequently, if we work hard for our satisfactions, the papists are forced to say that we cannot reach the end of them.

But there is a third error, that of indulgences, graces, pardons of plenary forgiveness, which are designed to remove the offenses of those who obtained them. And it is not enough for them to have such indulgences, but they have purgatory, which is like the end and accomplishment of everything, so that we understand they are so tangled in error that they cannot get untangled. Since they have wandered once from the pure simplicity of holy Scripture, the devil has possessed them and given them so many snares and traps that they cannot possibly escape them. All the more then must we be very attentive to this teaching which excludes all satisfactions and sends us to our Lord Jesus Christ to find in him everything that is lacking in us.

In addition, let us note that if we are to understand what it means to be saved by God's pure grace and to have faith imputed to us as righteousness, we must look at death. For when the papists discuss their merits, their satisfactions and indulgences, they invent ideas and speak gibberish to their hearts' content, but since those hypocrites have got their fill of God and have even become hardened against him and have come to believe wondrous things about their entire lives, the devil makes them squirm when they have to appear knowingly before their Judge. For we see how obtuse men are, and while God gives them a time limit, they manipulate it such as they want it to be and mould it to their liking. But when they have to depart this world and are obliged to stand before the judgment seat, which is terrible and feared by angels, alas, what can a mortal creature do in that situation?

Consequently, when we speak of the certainty of faith, we are not talking just about some entrance into God's church, but we have to have an invincible hope of battling against all of Satan's trials, and especially when it is a matter of answering before God that we can remain steadfast against all fears and not be distraught by them. Now that matter is not one of theory but of reality. It is true we must be taught by holy Scripture, but only until God sets the actual date for our court appearance and our consciences are bound and have to appear to hear the sentence of the celestial Judge. Now it is certain that we are only playing games with that difference of opinion. But reality will teach us what I have already said, namely, that we will have to find our full refuge in the grace of our Lord Jesus Christ, acknowledging that, because he is our Advocate (cf. *1 John* 2:1), God will not enter into judgment with us. Why not? We are absolved, not in accordance with our legal case, but in accordance with the absolute eradication of all our faults and iniquities. That, then, is what we have to remember about this point.

It would now seem that we could not have full righteousness if it consisted in faith; for faith, as we have said, will always be weak in us as long as we live. So how will we obtain full righteousness from God? For the effect cannot overcome the cause. If we had only half a sun, we would not have as much light as we have; the sun must be whole so the rays will spread in all directions. So when faith is weak in us, it would seem that we would not be acceptable to God except partially and that he would reprove us. But let us note that faith does not justify us by its power. And that is also why we must not look at the perfection of faith and say that our salvation is perfect. Properly speaking, only God justifies us, as we cited from Paul's eighth chapter of Romans. And that justification is what is spoken of in the third chapter of John, that God so loved the world that he did not spare his only Son so that whoever believes in him will not perish but will pass from death to life (cf. *John* 3:16). That, then, is how God alone justifies us, properly speaking. And that is what Paul says in the fifth chapter of 2 Corinthians, that God appeared in Jesus Christ, reconciling the world to himself, and not imputing sins; for Jesus Christ, who did not know sin was made sin for us so that we might be made the righteousness of God in him (cf. *2 Cor.* 5:18-21). There Paul shows us clearly in the first place how God justifies us, that is, by not imputing our faults to us. So much for that point in the definition of the word.

He also teaches that it is God's own responsibility to justify us. Now he is in Jesus Christ, he says, clearly reconciling the world to himself, and then he is our righteousness, that is to say, we are approved by him. Now how is it that faith justifies? Here is the way, for if we look for the main cause, if we seek the author of our salvation, the only thing we will say is that God justifies us by his pure goodness because he receives us in mercy and does not impute our sins to us, but pardons us of them. Now Jesus Christ justifies us also in his role, for he is the true substance of our righteousness. So where do we look for it? In the washing of his blood, which he shed for us, in the sacrifice which he offered as payment for our sins by rendering full obedience, which resulted in the burying and eradication of all of our sins because he sanctified himself for us, as is said in the seventeenth chapter of John (cf. *John* 17:19). That, then, is the work of Jesus Christ, who justifies us by virtue of his office.

Now the fact that faith justifies us is not because of the power it has or because of some worthiness it brings. And in that the papists are wrong because they make a comparison between faith and works and ask how it is that faith justifies rather than love. And that love, as Paul says, is greater than faith (cf. *1 Cor.* 13:13). It is true they are wrong about this passage; but let us consider how love is more worthy than faith. It is not a matter of all these trivial details, for if a king happened to be the greatest in the world, the question is whether he can dig the earth as well as a ploughman or a vine dresser. Such is the case with faith. It does not justify us, as I said, for some excellence that it has within itself, but because it borrows from Jesus Christ what we lack. And that is why Paul says that the righteousness of faith inverts and abolishes all the righteousness of works and human glory. Therefore, on this point the papists are very dense. And for our part, we must spend all the more time on what we have said, namely, that we are justified by faith. In other words, the way to make ourselves acceptable to God is for us to open ourselves to our Lord Jesus Christ and for him to apply his righteousness to us. That, then, is how faith is the only means and instrument, in a manner of speaking, but God is its cause and author. And the praise also belongs to our Lord Jesus Christ, who is the true substance of it. That, then, is something else we need to remember.

Consequently, we also understand that the papists are engaged in very stupid quibbling when they say that faith itself is a work[6] and that if we are justified by faith, it follows that works are not excluded. They cite what is said in the sixth chapter of John: 'This is the work of God, that you believe in his only Son' (cf. *John* 6:29). There Jesus Christ calls faith a work, as if he were saying, 'That is what you must work at; that is what you must apply your attention

[6] Cf. Eck, *Enchiridion,* ch. 5, 'De fide et operibus,' proposition 4, 'fides est opus,' p. 94.—*M.E.*

to; that is not a matter of works for merit.' Besides, if we confess that faith is a work, which it is not, it nonetheless does not justify because it is a work that we do. If I give alms and claim to gain merit before God in that way, in that way I would be justified by my works. If I help my neighbour and work to support one or another in whatever way he needs, that is how I would be justified in my works. Now there is a different logic in faith, for by confessing that there is only curse in us and that by faith we are going to receive what God offers us, we are not bringing anything from ourselves, but we are all coming to him empty. So faith justifies, not by our bringing something of worth or merit to God, but because God receives from Jesus Christ what is presented to him in our name. That confession—that there is nothing at all in those who come and ask God for righteousness, of which we have absolutely none—must take precedence. Thus we see again in that particular how the papists are quibbling stupidly when they advance the concept that we would be justified by some work if we were justified by faith. Now faith is indeed a sacrifice acceptable to God because he is honoured by it, because we praise him, because he alone is righteous and good; but it is not because of that that we are justified.

Now, in summary, let us note that when God justifies us by means of faith, the grace which he bestows upon us is included in that righteousness because he closes his eyes to the weakness which is in our faith. So faith, in conclusion, justifies because it is lacking. What? Because it is lacking? Yes indeed, for as I have said, it is not a matter of faith's doing something, of its having some vigour of its own, but of its simply receiving what is given by God. Therefore, if there should be only some small spark of faith in us, provided we conclude that we have no life except in Jesus Christ and that he possesses the fullness of life within himself, from which we can draw and be completely satisfied, it is certain he is sufficient.

Therefore, let us learn to believe in our Lord Jesus Christ to the extent that when we have doubts, we will continue to rely on his mercy, which cannot fail us, and always find our refuge in him, convinced that there is perfection of righteousness in him and that we will be made sharers in it. Indeed, if we have but a small drop of faith (cf. *Matt.* 17:20), as Paul says in the eighth chapter of Romans, despite the fact we are surrounded and weighted down by the massive corruption and sin which are in us, which lead only to death (cf. *Rom.* 8:4-11); that small drop of faith is life, provided Jesus Christ is in us. In other words, everything that remains of weakness and corruption in our flesh and other things that could hinder our salvation would all be destroyed by the Spirit of our Lord Jesus Christ. If we possess only some small portion of his Spirit, he will continue to be our full life.

Let us now bow before the majesty of our gracious God in acknowledgment of our faults, praying that he will be pleased to make us feel the power he has placed in his only Son, and may that so draw us to himself that we will cling only to him. And let us learn to gain strength from the trust in him that he gives to us; let us struggle against every weakness, and may every presumption and every hint of pride in us be abolished, and may nothing remain for us to do but confess how righteous he is; and if we do those things, it is his place to pour out his righteousness on us to allow us to enjoy the fruit which flows from it, in other words, to enjoy the inheritance of the heavenly life. May he grant that grace not only to us but to all the peoples and nations on earth.

70

Fourth Sermon on Justification

Friday, 8 March 1560

And he believed in the LORD; and he counted it to him for righteousness. And he said unto him, I am the LORD that brought thee out of Ur of the Chaldees, to give thee this land to inherit it (Gen. 15:6-7).

ESTERDAY WE SAID that God, after receiving believers into his grace, also recognizes in them what he placed in them. For we receive the Holy Spirit by faith because Jesus Christ cannot be separated from him. Consequently, we have to be renewed by believing in God, for we receive his power, which he offers us for communicating with us in his Son. Now God cannot scorn or reject his gifts; so he is obliged to accept the works which he has given us, not that they are worthy of it, as I have already explained; there is always some vice to corrupt them, and they would not be worthy to be applied to accounts receivable or payable. And if God condemned all the good things we thought we were doing or wanted to do, we could not accuse him of cruelty. Why not? There is always something to reproach, but he still continues to accept what is not worthy of him, indeed, because he acknowledges us as his children and supports us, as is said by his prophet (cf. *Isa.* 48:9). So if we ask why God approves our desire to serve him, weak as it is, it is because he spares us and does not want us to be attached to him as mercenaries, as hirelings, but he is content to see that we have a sincere and freehearted desire, just as a father requires no more than that of his child. For even if the child spoils the task, the father will still rejoice when he sees that the child wanted to do well. Thus our Lord, having a paternal love for us, forgets all the evil that is in our works and does not wish to bring it to account. That, I say, is a summary account of how we, along with our persons, are justified in what we do. In other words, God considers us righteous, and our works likewise.

And that is what occasions the word 'reward,' which is so often spoken of in Scripture (cf. *2 Chron.* 15:7; *Matt.* 10:41; *1 Cor.* 3:8), for both in the law (cf. *Exod.* 23:25) and in the gospel God declares that those who serve him faithfully will not lose their labour and will not be disappointed in their expectation (cf. *Luke* 6:23; *John* 4:36; *Luke* 6:35). Why not? They have their certain compensation reserved for them in heaven. Now how does that accord with what we have discussed? That is, if we were considered righteous because of our works, faith would be void and the promises nullified, as Paul says (cf. *Rom.* 4:14). Now they will be in harmony if one depends on the other. And if we want to balance our works against God's grace, it is certain there will be disparity. But when it is said that God receives us in mercy because we are sinners and then regenerates us by his Holy Spirit, he approves the good which he has placed within us, even though that is practically nothing in comparison with the evil which remains. So when we speak this way, it is the same as saying that, in the first place, God has pity on us by not imputing our faults and sins to us and by adopting us as his children, us who were lost and damned!

Then, in the second place, he also justifies our works because he applies his mercy, forgoes judging severely, and does not examine the quality of our works to evaluate their merits or worth, but he looks upon them as Father. There is, I say, no contradiction in that.

Thus, despite the fact that our Lord Jesus Christ declares that he came to call sinners and not the righteous (cf. *Matt.* 9:13), and despite the fact that Paul says he came to call sinners to salvation (cf. *1 Tim.* 1:13-15; *2 Tim.* 1:9; *Titus* 3:5), it is not because of the works we have done that the inheritance of heaven is prepared for us, but because God is gentle with us, because he wanted to show his infinite kindness toward us, and the fact remains that we still receive reward. In other words, when we serve God, we will be compensated, as Scripture so often says.

Now, looked at that way, these two passages, which seem to be inconsistent, are not contradictory. That is because righteousness is imputed to us by faith, and righteousness was imputed to Phinehas for his zeal to uphold God's honour and cleanse the sanctuary of its pollution. Phinehas the priest sees an egregiously infamous and detestable act when a prostitute is introduced into the sanctuary to commit a villainous act which was not to be heard in Israel (cf. *Num.* 25:7-8, 12). Now God arms him and he executes both (cf. *Num.* 25:6; *Psa.* 106:30). And that is said to be imputed to him as righteousness (cf. *Psa.* 106:31). It was a virtuous work. So it would seem he is not justified by faith, but, as I said, the two situations are comparable. For Phinehas was Abraham's son; consequently, God had to receive him in mercy as he did the others. But because God had helped him and because he had been reconciled to God by the same grace he was granting to all his elect, even in the Old Testament. That is how that work is considered as righteous before God. Why so? Because there still remained imperfection and weakness, God had to support him.

Let us return to the first chapter of Colossians where Paul says that we work sincerely to serve God because of the hope which is reserved for us in heaven, the hope which is witnessed to us in the gospel (cf. *Col.* 1:4-5). There Paul shows that when believers take courage and move forward with fervour and desire to serve and honour God, they work with love because they are assured that their labour is not in vain, as we read in the Epistle to the Hebrews (cf. *Heb.* 10:35-36). Now how do they know that? By the witness of the gospel. And what is said in the gospel? That God will favour us because we will believe in his only Son (cf. *John* 3:16). For the righteousness which is offered to us in him, Paul says, has a witness in the law, but it is not helped by the law (cf. *Rom.* 3:21), that is, it is not helped by all the works that we can do. That is because we are founded on the grace of our Lord Jesus Christ. So that passage shows how believers can be much better and more fervently disposed to serve God because they know that their labour will be prized. And yet they continue to find rest in that free goodness which is promised them because their refuge is in our Lord Jesus Christ.

And that is how the papists are grievously wrong. For from the word 'reward' they derive the word 'merit,' as if they were intending to perform alchemy. Now there is a great difference between those words. For what does the word 'merit' mean? It means that God has obligated himself to us and we say, 'I have indeed merited this or that, and I deserve it.' And the one who does not acknowledge the merit is an ingrate if he does not settle accounts with the one he is indebted to. So if we were able to deserve something from God, it would follow that he would be indebted to us and would wrong us if he refused to pay what he owes us. Now it is true he does indeed make himself our debtor, but a voluntary debtor, for he will find nothing in us that would obligate him to us, but he obligates himself to us by his promises. Therefore, there is reward from him, which he gives us freely without our meriting it. It is a huge leap to move from one word to another and conclude that both words mean the same thing when there is such a difference in meaning.

Consequently, we must not be astonished that the papists conclude their arguments this way at all times and become agitated when someone tells them that works cannot justify us. For they presuppose something false, namely, that if God remunerates his own, he has to be obligated to them, there has to be some worthiness in them, and their works have to carry some merit. That means nothing at all. The reason, as I have pointed out, is that when God promised us a reward, it was not because we deserve it, but because it pleases him to add grace upon grace that way, and all as a result of his pure liberality. We must always remember that. And as a matter of fact, what would be the consequence if we expected something from him depending on our worthiness? We would have to return to that anxiety we spoke of previously, namely, that we would always be in doubt and perplexed. Now our confidence must be certain. That, then, is a summary of what we have to remember here.

We must now deal with James' statement which seems to fight against Paul's teaching and that of all holy Scripture, as we have already spoken of it. For James says we are not justified by faith but by works. It does seem we could find no two statements more contradictory of each other than to say that we are justified without works by faith alone and that we are justified by works and not by faith. Yet it is certain that James, who spoke by the Spirit of God, does not contravene the teaching which has been preached and publicized since the church began and ratified by the prophets and finally even better confirmed in our Lord Jesus Christ and by his apostles. But the solution is very simple if we consider James' intention, for he is not discussing what true faith can be and is not at all speaking of true faith, but of a seeming faith, one which is only an image which deceives, an illusion. For he is fighting against those who, under the name of Christianity, take every licence to do evil—since there are many like that today and the devil has tried to blind men so that they would pardon themselves and, under the name 'Christian,' become like animals and to be totally perverted.

And the purpose was also to defame the teaching of the gospel so that people might think it was intended to obliterate good works and to keep people from devoting themselves to God's service, even as the papists are reproaching us for doing today.

So James, having in mind many dissolute and profane people who were seriously misrepresenting the gospel and who were laying claim to faith, says, 'Show me your faith without your works, and I will show you my faith by my works' (cf. *James* 2:18). With that, he declares that he does not intend to deal with faith as we have defined it, that is, as our assurance of God's goodness through his word and our knowing that he is our Father through our Lord Jesus Christ. James is not talking about that kind of faith, and that being the case, it cannot imply works. We have already said that it is by faith that we receive the Spirit of our Lord Jesus Christ. Now he cannot be separated from his Spirit, and we know it is said that he is not only given to us for righteousness but also for sanctification (cf. *Rom.* 6:22). In other words, he is given so that we may be cleansed of all the evil deeds and desires of our flesh and be brought into conformity with God's righteousness. Consequently, if James had been speaking of true faith, it would have been very foolish for him to say, 'Show me your faith without your works, and I will show you my faith by my works.' It is as if he were saying that true faith is so closely joined with good works that without them it is dead (cf. *James* 2:17). In other words, it is invalid, as he says later. Therefore, James points out quite well that he is not talking about the faith that embraces God's promises and makes us certain of our salvation.

On that point, the papists have again made the serious error of creating for themselves a faith which they call 'unformed,'[1] that is,

[1] Cf. Pierre Lombard, *Sentenciae*: lib. III, dist. xxiii, cap. 4, 2, 5; Thomas d'Aquin, *Summa theologiae*: 2a 2ae, q. 4, art. 3s; Eck, *Enchiridion*: chap. 5, p. 100; etc. Same attack by Calvin in his *Commentarius in Jacobi apostoli epistolam*, in: CO 55, col.

without a shape, and say that the law of itself is only a mass like something that would be taken from the earth or from mortar and then roughcast. There you have faith, according to them, and then they say that when love is added to it, it is like someone making a pot out of that lump of earth which previously had no shape. That is an example of the papists' imagination, and that is how they show they have no idea about faith. For it is clearly a singular gift of God. And then it is said that we receive the spiritual adoption by which God renews us (cf. *Rom.* 8:15) just the way he incorporates us into our Lord Jesus Christ in such a way that we are made members of his body and new creatures. So we see that the papists do not know about these things and do not grasp the principles or rudiments of Christianity anymore than animals or dogs. And it is deplorable that in all their schools they harp on these things like baying dogs. They imagine that they are the greatest theologians in the world when they make a distinction between unformed faith and formed faith.[2] It is as if they were saying: there is a God who is neither good nor powerful and a God who shows himself righteous and powerful. That is like creating a twofold faith.

So why does James use the word 'faith' here? And why do we use the word 'church'? Or the word 'bishop,' 'worship of God,' 'devotion,' or 'zeal'? When we speak of the papists, we do not agree

---

403, 406; Calvin, *Epistres*, t. 2, p. 117, 119; and in the *Institutes* III, ii, 8s, in a passage of 1559; in the argumentation of 1539, Calvin refers to another passage of his *Institutio* (III, xvii, 11), where he explains the James passage, but in a different way. —*M.E.*

[2] The distinction between unformed faith and faith formed with love was fought by, among others, Luther. Cf. Luther, *In epistolam S. Pauli ad Galatas commentarius ex praelectione D. Martini Lutheri collectus* (1531, published in 1535), in *WA* 40/1, p. 424, on the subject of Galatians 3:12 (to be noted also in the commentary of 1519, such a critique was not found; cf. *WA* 2, p. 515-519). Michael Screech has given evidence of the expression *'foy formée de charité'* ['faith formed with love'] in Rabelais. Cf. M. Screech, *L'évangélisme de Rabelais. Aspects de la satire religiieuse au XVIe siècle* (Etudes rabelaisiennes 2), (Genève: 1949), pp. 31-34. Cf. also above.—*M.E.*

with them that there is truly a church among them which must be obeyed. There are only some rulings of the church and some traces of the service which was instituted for the worship of God; but the church is where God lives by means of his word. Afterwards, when speaking of the papists, we use words which are honourable, and yet it is not because we understand that they use these expressions advisedly. But we do not always linger over the words. Thus James did not linger over the word, but he took that frivolous boasting which was in the mouths of his mockers, who wanted to be thought of as good Christians, and says, 'Your faith, that is, the faith you mouth about, is nothing.' As we would say today: 'What is the Catholic Church the papists boast of today? It is a whore.' For we know that the true church is the bride of our Lord Jesus Christ (cf. *Eph.* 5:23-25),[3] who must be cleansed and washed by his blood in order to be without stain or wrinkle, as Paul says (cf. *Eph.* 5:26-27); afterwards, she is to be the pillar of truth (cf. *1 Tim.* 3:15). And instead of all that, we have a den of thieves, a whore which has corrupted the worship of God and begets only bastards. We will talk that way. That is James' style, which we are not to find strange, seeing that this is commonplace language for us. Therefore, when it is said that faith justifies us, we will not speak of faith except in the accustomed way. But when James says that faith without works is dead (cf. *James* 2:20), it is to ward off those who misused this word and vainly boasted and congratulated themselves, but it was only falsehood.

Now let us deal with the second part, where James says that we are justified by our works (cf. *James* 2:24). Again it appears that he contradicts Paul. For works must not be joined with faith so that the two share, as we have said; otherwise, we will find no rest if that is to be the case. We must exclude every consideration of our works for calling upon God with true confidence so we can consider

---

[3] Cf. also *Institutes* IV, i, 10.—*M.E.*

ourselves his children; and if we are to hope for the inheritance of
the heavenly life which is promised us, works must be omitted. For
if they justify, what will be the result?

Now this word 'justify' is not to be understood in James as being
approved before God, as being reconciled to him and causing him
to receive us as his children. How then? As he himself declares
in another explanation. For he adds that Abraham was justified
when he sacrificed his son Isaac (cf. *James* 4:21). Now we have not
yet read that he sacrificed him, that is, that he wanted to make a
sacrifice of his son to God. How then? That obedience which we
will speak of shortly was Abraham's righteousness, if it was a question of approving what he did at the time, seeing that it was not
yet done.

Consequently, we must conclude that in that passage James is
not saying that we are acceptable to God, but righteous by decree.
For if I say that the son begat the father, what kind of stupidity
would that be? Now we know that faith is the mother of righteousness (cf. *Rom.* 10:10), that is to say, it is the means and the
instrument by which we are reconciled to God and declared to
be his children (cf. *2 Cor.* 5:17-19). Therefore, faith must precede
righteousness, for it is the mean cause, the cause which is called
instrumental or formal.[4]

Let us look at Abraham's obedience when he was ready to sacrifice his son. If that is the cause of Abraham's righteousness, it
had to be a precedent. What kind of stupidity would it be to say
that the wheat that will grow for a year nourishes me today and
all year long? Even a small child would see that. A long period of
time passed before God ordered Abraham to sacrifice his son, and
yet he was already previously justified. So we see in summary that
we must not try to interpret beyond James' text. But he speaks of

[4] French: *'Il faut donc que la foy precede la justice, car elle est la cause moyenne, la cause
qu'on appelle instrumentale ou formelle.'*

being justified, that is, of being declared righteous. Those jokers he was combating would say, 'We are justified by faith. Why should we bother with getting involved in God's service and being greatly concerned since our works have no value and will not enter into any future account?' First, they pervert everything when they say that works do not enter into the equation, for works will come when God's grace comes. But when they mockingly say that giving oneself to good works serves no purpose, it is like saying they were tearing Jesus Christ into pieces. For we receive him by faith; we are one with him because we are reconciled to God his Father and he abolishes our faults and regenerates and guides us by his Holy Spirit. Those things are inseparable, as Paul says (cf. *2 Tim.* 1:9).

That being the case, James rightly asks, 'How will you be righteous without works?' Faith, he says, without works is dead (cf. *James* 2:20–21). Then he says you can in no way be justified except the way your father Abraham was, if you are believers. Now Abraham was justified because good works were joined with faith. So you must demonstrate the same thing or you are mockers of God who profane a thing so holy and sacred as the words 'faith' and 'righteousness.' That, then, is what James understood in this passage.

But those papist dogs appreciate none of that. Why not? They have contempt for God; they will speak freely of good works. If you listen to them talk, they seem like angels, and we see what kind they are. And would to God they were not so given to their excesses. But you will find no monk or teacher who is not a whoremonger, a mocker of God, dissolute, a drunk, or a blasphemer. In short, it seems they have conspired with the devil to put the entire world in confusion. And yet they will make a show of their good works and speak of nothing else. Consequently, we must not be surprised at their blindness.

But to repeat briefly what we have explained about James, let us note that we are justified and not without works, and yet we are justified. When we say we are justified and not without works, we separate the two. How? The person who is called righteous before God through faith is called righteous because God pardons him of his sins; he puts his trust in the suffering and death of the Lord Jesus Christ, and he knows that he acquires his life through the Lord's resurrection. Therefore, the one who believes in God that way is not justified without works. Why not? God gives him his Holy Spirit; he remakes him in such a way that good works have to be joined with faith. And yet the other statement is true, namely, that we are justified without works, that is, without the help of any good work, so that we always remain indebted to God. So we have two statements where the words are not changed; it will now seem that the statements, we are justified without works and we are justified not without works, are quite different. But that means there are works which are nonetheless not the cause of our salvation by causing us to merit something before God and causing him to accept us because of our worthiness, but it is because our Lord Jesus Christ, as I said, does not bring us a single, simple grace, but one that is double, that is, on the one hand, he covers all our iniquities and offences by the purity of his obedience; he appeases the wrath of God his Father by the sacrifice he offered once for the satisfaction he made for all our debts, and yet he guides us so well by his Holy Spirit, who rests upon him, whose complete fullness he received, that we, provided we do not abuse the grace which he has granted us, are freed from Satan's bonds so that we do not follow the passions and desires of our flesh, which, as Peter says, we must guard against (cf. *1 Pet.* 2:11). That, then, is enough for the explanation of this passage.

Now Moses adds subsequently that God said again to Abraham, 'I am the God who brought you out of Ur of the Chaldees to give you the land as an inheritance.' Here we see that God repeats his promises in order to strengthen Abraham's faith, to nourish

379

and increase it until it reaches its perfection. From that we conclude to what extent Abraham was a living image and pattern for
believers, how he was also an image of righteousness, even though
his righteousness was imperfect; otherwise the promise which is
embedded here would be superfluous. If Abraham's faith had been
so well strengthened that nothing was lacking, God would have
no longer had to speak. Why not? Promises have their purpose
and usefulness in drawing us to faith to lead us to the right road,
to encourage us, to incite us to walk more valiantly, to refresh us
when we are weary, to increase our strength if it should fail us and
become weak in any way. That, I say, is why our Lord gives us testimony of his goodness and declares himself to be our God; it is to
initiate faith in us or to bring it to perfection.

Consequently, we must conclude that Abraham still needed to
be advanced in his faith. So we understand that our faith is not
perfect, that even so God does not cease justifying us. How does
he not? He does not impute the weakness that is in us. In any
case, this passage admonishes us not to be preoccupied with the
foolish notion of many who think they are so learned that they do
not condescend to go to God's school. Consequently, let us realize
that even though we had a faith incomparably greater and stronger
than it now is, we still have to be schoolchildren all of our lives,
that God's word still needs to resound in our ears, and that we
must be reminded of what we have forgotten so that what was not
well founded in our hearts will be imprinted there better, so that
after God has planted his seed in us, he will water it daily, using
the image Paul also used (cf. *1 Cor.* 3:7). It would not be enough
for the seed to be cast upon the earth if God did not send rain
from heaven and water it. If the labourer does his job of cultivating
the earth, his work is vain unless God gives it its increase from on
high. Such it is when we receive the seed of incorruptible life and
God sends rain from heaven, that is, causes our faith to bear fruit

continually, which cannot happen unless he teaches us daily by his mouth.

Let us now consider the content of the first statement: 'I am the Lord who brought you out of Ur of the Chaldees.' That declaration serves Abraham to distance him from every idolatry and the superstitions on which he had been brought up formerly. For, as we are often shown in holy Scripture, we must not worship an unknown God or create one to our liking, but we must know the kind of God in whom we have our refuge (cf. *Psa.* 97:7; 119:69; *2 Thess.* 2:3-4), and he must be set apart and distinguished in all the concepts that men can come up with and deceive themselves with and by which Satan also deceives them. That is why the apostle says in the eleventh chapter of Hebrews: when we approach God, that is, when we wish to have access to him, we must believe that he is and that he is a rewarder of those who seek him (cf. *Heb.* 11:6). So we cannot approach God without believing that he exists, that is, we cannot approach him if we have any doubts or questions, but we must be definitely certain that the God who created the heavens and the earth is the one who presents himself to us and whose will is so well known to us through the law and the gospel that we do not question that it is from God, as the poor pagans have done, agonizing and creating a maze from which they have never escaped.[5] But we know that God has shown himself to us to the extent that we need him, indeed for our salvation. That, then, is point number one.

The second is that we also believe he is the rewarder of those who seek him. Now this word 'rewarder' does not mean God pays us what

[5] One of the fundamental questions of ancient philosophy. We can think of Aristotle's *Métaphysique* (particularly XI, 7, 1072a), the three books of Cicero's *De natura deorum*, etc. Cf. also *Institutes* I, iii, 3, with a long passage of 1559, in which Calvin approaches this question, citing, among others, Plato, Cicero and Plutarch, and another passage in I, xiv, 1 (likewise of 1559) on the same question about God among the pagans.—*M.E.*

he owes us, but that we will not be disappointed when resting in him, for we have to consider the way we seek him. Thus, if we bring our works, this works against him, so far are we from wanting to be united with him. For Paul says that the Jews themselves stumbled when they thought to take pride in their merits and placed the hope of their salvation in them (cf. *Rom.* 9:31-32). And that was reason enough to cause them to fall rather than to advance. So when we want to seek God, it is certain we must be stripped of every vain presumption concerning our virtues, for it is certain that inasmuch as he has adopted us by his pure grace, we will not be acceptable to him except insofar as he pardons us of our sins. That is how we are to be assured, the apostle says, that when we seek God in that way, we will not be disappointed (cf. *Heb.* 11:6).

And that is what is said: 'I am the Lord who took you from Ur of the Chaldees to bring you to this land to possess it as an inheritance.' It is as if God were obligating himself once again to his servant Abraham and that he declared to him that he must not fear that what he heard previously will not be fulfilled. And even though the outcome is deferred and prolonged for a long time, he must always walk patiently, knowing that God never speaks in vain, that he has the times and the seasons to fulfil his will in accordance with his counsel, and that he himself must not yield to the preferences of men. But let us note again that by his former kindnesses God strengthens Abraham's faith, for he says, 'I have brought you out of Ur of the Chaldees.' That helped Abraham greatly to hope more strongly in God after experiencing that God was his Father and Saviour. And even as we have known God's goodness and his support and help, we must even more have confidence in him in the time to come. That is how the experience of times past is always to give us greater certainty.

And that is what God intends when he says, 'I have brought you out of Ur of the Chaldees. It is not for today only that I have shown myself to be your God, but you have been aware that I have sustained you with my strong hand. You were deep in perdition, you were a poor damned soul, and I drew you to myself to cause you to come to salvation. That being true, I have lifted you from the depths of hell, so to speak; now my grace, which you have experienced, is an invincible defence for you; and, for my part, I will always continue it.' Now it is certain that God also offers us this general principle, that one grace which he grants attracts another. He never wearies and is a fountain which can never dry up (cf. *Psa.* 36:9), from which we can draw boldly, and we will always find enough to satisfy us more and more. That, then, is the meaning of 'I am the Lord who brought you out of Ur of the Chaldees.' After displaying his majesty and showing that he is Creator of heaven and earth, God makes a special point of that: Abraham sensed him and knew him as such when he lifted him from the abyss where he was.

Then he adds that it is so he could possess the land as an inheritance. Here, as we have already discussed, God renews all the promises he had given his servant Abraham so that he could have a collection of them, for faith must have the privilege of collecting everything that is to fortify it against Satan's trials and assaults. Negligence is the reason for the destruction of many people, for, as I have said, they think that when they have learned a sentence about holy Scripture, they are great teachers and know enough about it. But what happens? When they find themselves under pressure, they show they are empty, for there is in them no hole so tiny that the devil cannot enter and poison them with his deadly venom. It is like a broken tile on a roof; the rain which enters through it will in time cause the house to rot. The same is true of those who think they have great understanding but remain stupid. The devil then finds holes through which to enter and the result is that the building is on its way to collapsing. We must not be lax in finding ways to succeed, but we must make a collection of all of God's promises and always be aware of how they can help us. And not only that, but let us also try to increase our faith as we need to do because it will always be weak. In short, let us always move beyond where we are.

It is said that God gave Abraham the land of Canaan. It had already been given to him, as we saw in the twelfth chapter (cf. *Gen.* 12:1-3). And that was repeated to him several times (cf. *Gen.* 12:7; 13:15; 15:18; 17:8); his ears are now battered by it. So it would seem that this language was useless and superfluous, but, as I have said, for Abraham it was a very inestimable blessing since he is able to be refreshed and encouraged by it so that he will not fail but always pursue God's holy calling.

In addition, let us note well that God supports him only with words; and we see in that the honour we are to give him and the confidence we are to have in him despite the fact that the outcome he promises us does not appear before our eyes, and in that situation, let us be kept in suspense. He says, 'I have brought you into this land which I am giving you.' 'Well, Lord, you promised in fact to give it to me; but here I am, old and decrepit; when will the time come?' 'Oh, do not worry. I will bless you.' 'Yes, but where is the proof of what I have waited for until now? I am going to die, and I am still a poor foreigner; I do not even have any offspring (as he said previously), and what then will be the outcome, Lord?' 'My word must continue to be enough for you' (cf. *Gen.* 15:2). So the nature of faith is to have our eyes closed and all our senses in waiting to be submissive to God's will and to yield to his truth. Our eyes must be open and attentive to receive what God says to us, and when he gives us the word, let us resolve that that is the way it will be. How? Oh, that is not for us to deliberate about; it is not open to our disposition, but we must leave it to the counsel and will of God, as we have already said. That, then, is how we must honour God, by adding confidence in his holy word.

In addition, we still have to take note of what was declared above, namely, that God simply gave his servant the land of Canaan as a pledge and that he did not want to play games with him. For if Abraham had had only that land, it would have been a very meagre and indifferent compensation for him. For it is certain he was influenced by another outlook. In other words, he saw the very day of our Lord Jesus Christ, as is said in the eighth chapter of John (cf. *John* 8:56). And then he said he was a pilgrim in this world (cf. *Gen.* 23:4); so he had an inheritance elsewhere. And yet when God tells him that the land is given to him as an inheritance, it is not his last goal; his affection is not fixed on it or wrapped up in it, but he is looking beyond (cf. *Gen.* 12:4). For, as we have already seen, since he renounced the land of his birth and left it to live in a foreign and unknown country, he had to be aiming for heaven.

So let us note that even though the land of Canaan is called his inheritance, as it is also called God's place of rest and his dwelling place (cf. *Psa.* 132:14), it is nonetheless an earnest, or a security, more properly speaking. For a security bears a value corresponding to what is to be assured, but an earnest will be nothing. Pennies will be pledged for a deal worth a thousand crowns or a hundred times more. It is a token pledge, of what value? None. Will a bottle of wine be worth a piece of land or a great possession which will enrich three or four men? Even so, that token is destined for such usage. Therefore, the land of Canaan was the heritage of all Abraham's children and of those who descended from his lineage, so that it was for them something like a token of heaven. The fact is that true believers did not depend on that and were not attached to it, as I have already said, but have always had higher aspirations.

So we see, in brief, where God intended to call Abraham, as if he were saying that he did not wrong him by making him wait patiently. For the promises he received previously will be fulfilled, and he must not build on his own expectations. Why not? Let him consider the one who spoke. It is the Lord, who is unchangeable (cf. *James* 1:17)! We change every minute of the day, and that is why we are annoyed and irritated when God does not accomplish what he said at first; or when we consider the brevity of our lives and the time that we have to live is like a moving shadow, we think that God will never come in time. Therefore, we must learn to correct that vice because we hear in this passage what is said to Abraham: 'I am the Lord, who does not change.' And then we hear the saying that a thousand years are as a day in his sight, as is said in the Song of Moses[6] and also similarly applied by Peter (cf. *2 Pet.* 3:3-7). For mockers of God, he says, seeing that time is fleeting, scoff as if God's threats and promises are deceptive. 'No, no,' he says. 'Do not be deceived. He will accomplish what he says even if he delays, for a thousand years are as a day in his sight.' So we must lift our eyes on high and realize that since its is the Lord who is speaking to us, who never changes or varies, he will do what he says, not as we would like, but as he knows to be good. And as for us, we must not be impetuous or impatient, but we must escape from ourselves, so to speak, if we are to come to him, in whom there is no inconstancy or wavering, for he is the Lord. And then let us learn that when he speaks, that must be enough, for his word is infallible truth.

In addition, let us realize his goodness and that he, being so, supports our weakness because he does not speak just once but renews our memory of his promises and wants us to take advantage of them all the days of our lives and be strengthened by them, not so that we will believe in him for a day only, but so that we will be led and governed by his power, not only all during our lives, but also beyond death, until we reach his kingdom, where we will no

---

[6] This idea is not found in the Song of Moses (*Deut.* 32), but we do find, in the context which denounces the iniquitous, the play between one and a thousand: 'How could one pursue a thousand' (*Deut.* 30:32).—*M.E.*

longer need his word and where faith and things like it will have no place. For at that time we will experience the full joy of what we now see obscurely and, as in a mirror, we will see him face to face (cf. *1 Cor.* 13:12).

> Now let us bow before the majesty of our gracious God in acknowledgment of our faults, praying that he will make us so aware of them that we will be humbled before him and always groan under the burden of our iniquities until he has delivered us from the cursed servitude of our sin. And may our only desire be to be in conformity with his holy will and not to live unto ourselves but unto our Lord Jesus Christ, who purchased us at a high price, giving himself over to death for our sins and rising again for our justification (cf. *Rom.* 4:12). May he grant that grace not only to us but to all the peoples and nations on earth.

71

Willing Self-Sacrifice Is Required to Achieve God's Promises

Monday, 18 March 1560

*And he said, Lord G*OD*, whereby shall I know that I shall inherit it? And he said unto him, Take me an heifer of three years old, and a she goat of three years old, and a ram of three years old, and a turtledove, and a young pigeon. And he took unto him all these, and divided them in the midst, and laid each piece one against another: but the birds divided he not* (Gen. 15:8-10).

W HEN IT WAS SAID earlier that Abraham believed God, it was not understood as a special promise but as something related to the salvation of the world, as has been stated. Therefore, it is the same as Moses' proclaiming that in everything and everywhere Abraham had rested in God's word, had placed in it his foundation and support and had put his trust in it so that his faith never wavered, although there were many reasons which could have hindered or shaken or completely overwhelmed his confidence. That, then, is Abraham's simple faith: when he receives without doubt everything which proceeded from God's mouth, without exception.

It now seems he does not continue in the certainty that he had about God's truth, for he says, 'How will I know?' after God spoke to him about the land of Canaan and promised him he would possess it. There is no question there is nothing of such great consequence as the salvation of souls, but he nonetheless doubts. That would seem to be apparent from the outset. In fact, the answer could be given in a word. 'How will you know? Is it not enough for you to know that I have spoken, I who cannot lie, and when a person waits upon me, he will never be ashamed?' (Cf. *Psa.* 25:3.) God had assured Abraham and he asks how he would know! It is as if the word which is given to him offered no witness and he had retreated.

But we have to note that believers, upon receiving God's word, will grant it the authority it deserves, and yet they will grumble inwardly because they do not have the requisite perfection of faith, and they will always experience some qualm and remorse, for in truth those who have profited most from God's word still have not stripped themselves of their natural propensities. It is true faith will dominate their hearts; and that is the source of the peace Paul speaks of in Philippians (cf. *Phil.* 4:7), the faith which receives the palm branch, that is, the victory. But even that is not beyond struggle. Faith will always win in the hearts of believers, but it will often experience severe assaults and seem to be shaken to the point of collapsing. Sometimes it will be suffocated, as in the sea. There will be horrendous waves and gigantic waterspouts, such as would swallow up ships and drag them to the depths of the sea.[1] So through such ordeals the faith of God's children will indeed always be certain and assured, but not without many alarms, as we have said. And still, even if there are no great temptations, believers always share human nature, with its weaknesses, its carelessness and negligence. And what Paul says is true: we see dimly as in a dark mirror (cf. *1 Cor.* 13:12). In other words, we still do not have a

[1] On the combat between faith and the assaults it undergoes, see several passages in the second chapter of the third book of the *Institutes* (15, 17-22, 37).—M.E.

clear and penetrating view into the things which are hidden from us, and we walk as in the night. And that is why it is also said in another passage that our salvation is hidden under hope (cf. *Rom.* 8:24). We know, John says in his letter, that we are children of God (cf. *1 John* 3:2). That establishes our confidence. But the Lord Jesus has not appeared, he says. Why not? We are not yet like God so that we can contemplate his glory.

Thus, as I have already mentioned, the saints, even as they believe, become angry and fret and fume about themselves when they see that their faith is unenthusiastic and burdensome and that there is some weakness and always some residue of their nature in them which keeps them from fully adhering to God. At that point, after recognizing what is wrong with them, they look for the cure. And in that cure, nothing is lacking. It is true that the believers' imperfection is always a vice. And that too is how God humbles his people when they realize they are justified and saved by faith, a faith that is not complete, that is only partial, a spark of which they feel occasionally, and that with great effort. Now God gives them no occasion for pride and presumption and keeps them on a tight leash, and that is because of vice. Yet it is not vice when, after being displeased, they look for a way to be helped so that they will not fail totally. And then they look for some ways to be encouraged so that their faces are not bowed to the ground but lifted on high to that incomprehensible power of God so they can look with contempt on the world and Satan and all the obstacles they see around them. That is what we must learn from what is recounted here about our father Abraham.

It is certain God declared to him that he would possess the land, not only once, as we have seen previously how he repeated the promise (cf. *Gen.* 12:7; 13:15; 15:7). Even so, he had already waited patiently for long years, and we know that God moved him from one place to another. However, his faith was not diminished, and that is demonstrated by the outcome. As the apostle says, he was able to return to the land of his birth to live at ease and in peace, the way he did before (cf. *Heb.* 11:15). Who would have prevented him from doing so? But he abandoned all that and renounced it willingly and preferred to be a stranger in the land of Canaan and live there as a poor famished person, even to be persecuted, than to return to the land of his birth, where he had relatives and friends. And even though he is pursued into all corners of that land to which he had come, he nonetheless prefers that situation, wretched as it is, to the one in which he had previously lived. From that we can clearly conclude that he never repented of obeying God, never become angry or weary of treading the path set before him. The land of Canaan bears good witness to his faith, for without the promise of that inheritance, he would have fallen a hundred and a thousand times.

So when he now says, 'How will I know?' it is not that he is not still waiting for the promise and that he is not steadfast in his determination, but he knows that, with the certainty God has engraved in his heart by the Holy Spirit, with the confidence he has in him, that he is nonetheless not insensitive and that he has profound feelings which afflict him, which stir him and trouble him, as had always been his experience. For the purpose of faith is not to transport us completely out of this world. It does do that in a way, for all our senses must be raised above everything we see that is contrary to God. For there will be a combat within us, like two men, in a manner of speaking, just as Scripture says.[2] Therefore, it was Abraham's frequent experience that God had a reason for keeping him in suspense. During that time, many thoughts passed through his mind. 'And when will this take place? Why

---

[2] We think of the combat between flesh and spirit that Paul describes in Romans 7:5–6, but no Bible passage mentions two men struggling within man such as Calvin describes them 'in a manner of speaking...'— *M.E.*

is God postponing it for such a long time?' That is how we too will often feel in times of such perplexity. When God promises us something, that is how we think: 'And what is preventing him from fulfilling his word immediately? Why is he keeping us here in anticipation?' It is the devil who is presenting us with all those fantasies, and we are also inclined to think that way, and more so.

So Abraham, who had had many battles within himself, speaks familiarly to God: 'Lord, how will I know?' It is as if he were saying, 'I believe, but help my unbelief' (cf. *Mark* 9:24). We also see that this passage from Mark's Gospel indicates that those who desire to lean on God's word and have this gift realize that it is not complete and that there is still some residue of unbelief in themselves. That was Abraham's situation: 'Lord God, how will I know?' he says, as if he were saying, 'It is true your word ought to be enough for me of itself.' And in fact he gives it that reverence: 'I know that you cannot fail me in what you have promised; however, because I know my weakness, well, Lord, grant me even more help so that your word may possess me completely and there will be no flaw in my feelings to hold me back so that I may always walk as you have commanded and be lifted above everything that might attach me to this world. So, Lord, again give me more help so that my faith will be strengthened even more.' Therefore, let us note that Abraham is not asking how he will know, as if he had no idea, but he knew what we have quoted from Paul previously, but he is asking that the promise be fulfilled. In other words, he is asking that what he is certain of will be brought to such completion that nothing will be lacking.

And again, in order to understand this better, we will make a comparison between unbelievers and believers. When two things are contrasted this way, one will shed light on the other. If God promises something to an unbeliever, the unbeliever will say, 'How would I be convinced of that?' We see that type every day. If someone quotes a passage from the gospel to those who do not wish to believe, they say, 'And how will I know this? How will I recognize that?' When they speak that way, it is because they reject the teaching which was the foundation of their faith, which is the first way to approach God. Now they reject all that. Why? Because they want that word to have their approval, because they will prefer to accept and receive some frivolous speculation, and because they will not act when God speaks. That is how hypocrites and unbelievers, when they ask how they will know, dishonour God, scorn his word, trample on it and, as I have said, even though the whole world were there to witness to what is made known to them, they will not believe the first word unless it accords with their liking.

Believers, on the other hand, receive the word in fear and humility with confidence that God cannot fail them, that there is nothing better than to wait upon him and depend especially on his word. They possess that characteristic! Subsequently, they enjoy his promises and have such love for them that they prefer them to everything they can see with their eyes and touch with their hands, and there is nothing in this world that has such power and value for them as the truth which proceeds from God. Yet they understand that a work begun is not finished and that they have only begun. They know that they are only hobbling along, that they are being buffeted about, that they have many heavy winds and storms to confront, and that they do not possess the kind of steadfastness that would be required. So when they ask, 'How will I know?' is God's word firm in them and are they really certain of it? In no way! But they want that word to be confirmed better, their faith increased and strengthened, and they want it to be not only victorious but comforting, without internal combats and uncertainties, with all their senses giving glory to God and saying he is true.

We now see how this passage of Moses is to be understood, and we see at the same time how we must follow our father

Abraham's example. For what does it mean for us if the one who is proposed to us as a living example and pattern of a faith more excellent and perfect than everything else still acknowledges his weakness and comes to the doctor for healing, since he knows he is sick? Have we reached the same level of faith as Abraham? Alas, how far we fall short! Therefore, let us learn not to presume on the fact that our Lord has brought us this far to embrace his promises and consider them as certain and cause us to honour him in this particular, which is due him; let us nonetheless realize that we are not yet walking as fast as we should, not by a long shot. Let us realize that even by thinking we are advancing, we are moving backward; sometimes, by thinking we are moving straight ahead, we are deviating from the path here and there; by thinking we are making strides, we are stumbling. Let us realize that. Let us ask God to help us and support us in our weakness; and may we be able to declare in truth that we already believe. That, I say, is how the children of God are to seek to increase and strengthen their faith throughout their lives. And we must ask God for that, for if we want to possess it through reason and debate, it is certain we will only entangle ourselves in many perverse ideas. And Satan will also have his nets stretched out to entangle us further and we will not be able to escape his distorted confines. So we must pray that God will continue the work he has begun in us until he brings it to perfection.

It is true that what is special in Abraham is that he asks for a sign and a miracle. We are not permitted to do the same thing. But let us note that this proceeded from a special internal stirring, as we find in Gideon (cf. *Judg.* 6:17, 36-40) and in the good king Hezekiah (cf. *2 Kings* 20:8-11). It is certain Hezekiah trusted in God, and after hearing the message brought to him by the mouth of Isaiah, he abided by it because ability and moderation were influencing him. He nonetheless required some miracle, not, as

I have said, because he thinks the word is likely to fail or because he does not feel it sincerely in his heart, but because he is not sufficiently fortified and armed to fight against the weakness and remnant of unbelief that are still in him. As a result, he asks for a sign. But what came to him from a special internal stirring must not set as a precedent or pattern.

The same is true for Gideon. God calls him to be an instrument to deliver his people. Gideon does not resist and he does not consider God's word to be either a fable or a dream, but we know he consented to it. He understands he is not yet as clearly and frankly committed to it as the situation would require in order for him to carry out the charge which was entrusted to him. Consequently, seeing that he does not have enough zeal to overcome the difficulties he anticipates, he says, 'Lord, give me a sign.' Moreover, he is not content with one miracle but turns to a second. When God performed one miracle for him, that the ground be wet and the fleece of the sheep he had sacrificed be dry, he asks for an opposite miracle, that the fleece be wet and the ground dry. And God grants that. Yet Gideon is not rebuked for a lack of faith. And it is certain that if his faith had not been weak, he would not have needed the miracles. The angels will not require signs because they have a full, clear view of what we see but dimly. In any case, this desire is good in Gideon, and he, realizing his shortcomings, wanted to be supported and helped in fulfilling God's word.

The same must be said about what is recounted here concerning Abraham. He is asking God for a miracle. Yes, but the Holy Spirit moved him to ask because God wanted to invest him with a charge for our sakes, as I have already said. We can and we must beseech God to keep us steadfast and resolute in his truth. We must be so displeased with the remnant of unbelief in us that we ask him to cleanse us of it, even to the point of insisting. But it is not our place to choose. We do not have the liberty to ask God for some miracle every day. But let us ask him to make up for what we lack, and may he grant the help and healing he knows we need. So it is not our place to summon him or impose upon him a law or regulation or say to him, 'You will do thus and so,' but 'Lord, you know how weak I am. You also know that my weakness could oppress my faith in the end if you do not help me. So, Lord, help me.' And when this happens, we must close our eyes and our mouths and wait for what is pleasing to God and leave everything in his hand so that in his infinite wisdom he will be pleased to preserve us from the evil we see. That, then, is what we have to remember about this passage.

Moreover, we must not find it strange that Abraham, after languishing a long time, asks God for some relief so that his cares might not overwhelm him and he might have support in order to persist against the great hardships confronting him. That is also why God grants his request and tells him immediately to take a heifer, a goat, and a ram and offer them in sacrifice. We see in God's response that he did not reject Abraham's prayer, for it was a sign of approval: 'I am giving him what he requests, and that for his salvation.' For sometimes God will allow unbelievers, rebels, and hypocrites to have everything they desire, but it costs them dearly. Here we see that God was inclined to answer his servant Abraham because he favoured him and approved his request. So much for that point.

What we have to gather from this passage is that when we admit our infirmity before God and ask him to be pleased to help us in our need, he will never fail us and will be more ready to help than we are to ask. But in any case, let us, as a matter of principle, examine our weaknesses and our shortcomings. And when we realize we are indeed needy, let us ask God more ardently not only to consider our wretched condition but also to provide for it since he has the means at his disposal and has also promised to.

Therefore, when we become anxious to seek God's grace, there we have true repentance. It is also certain he will be faithful and will always be near to answer all our requests, for it is said that he will hear all those who pray to him in truth and without pretence (cf. *Prov.* 15:29).

Likewise, we must note the confirmation of the promise given to Abraham here, for it does not respond to the desires of our flesh, but to our reason and understanding of the situation, but it seems rather that God wanted to confound Abraham. It is here a question of living and inheriting the land. On that point, Abraham could reply, as he did, that the confirmation is not to the purpose: 'And how will I know that I am to possess this land?' He sees himself as a decrepit old man. He already has one foot in the grave. He has no lineage. His wife is sterile. They are already broken with age and half dead. So he asks God how he will know that he is to possess the land. He has no seed of his own, not that he is seeking an heir different from the one God will give him, as we have seen. But that involves life and it implies that God will resurrect him, so to speak, and make him a father and give him a lineage. So when Abraham asks for confirmation of the promise, he already had to be fully persuaded of his hope that God was powerful to restore his vigour, even though he was physically beyond it.

But to the contrary. There is only death in that anticipation and everything our father Abraham has done. For God is not only content with the death that was already in Abraham's body, but he also wants him to be completely surrounded by death. He commands him to kill three animals of different species, namely, a heifer, a goat, and a ram, along with birds: a pigeon and a turtledove. And then he commands him saying, 'You will be in the midst of carcasses, for you must divide them and be in the midst of them, not only to be like the carcass of carcasses, but to be surrounded on all sides by the carcasses of brute beasts.' Alas, he is given poor consolation, but that is also how God strengthens his people.

For if he wanted to accommodate himself to our feelings and our desires, what good would that do? We know how inconstant we are; and he would never yield in every respect to our wishes, whatever and whenever. We are sensual and earthly; we would want God to change and counterfeit his nature and conform to our desires. And if he conducted himself according to our good pleasure, what would happen? He would have to renounce himself and become like us. So let us learn that if we ask to be confirmed in the teaching about salvation and all God's promises, we must not subject him to our thoughts and feelings, but we must be humble and accept what he gives us, even though it seems foreign to us and contrary to our logic, for there is no more agreement between our reason and way of thinking and God's word than there is between fire and water.

So when we read here that God, in order to confirm the promise he had given Abraham, commands him to kill animals and sacrifice them, let us realize God is so ready to help his children that he does not yield to their sensual nature, for, as I said, he would have to renounce himself and assume human nature, which is the complete opposite of his. But he maintains the authority and honour proper to himself. He nonetheless increases the value of the aids he gives, even though they seem to serve no purpose, if we judge them by our standards, for at that time we would say God mocked the things he said to us, since we see none of them realized. But when we move forward with the sobriety and modesty of faith, it is certain God will always value what he has given in the way of aid, as he does for his servant Abraham.

In addition, we have to conclude in general that God always begins the life of his children with death. Why? We must, if we are to reach the heavenly kingdom, be stripped of our old Adam (cf. *Eph.* 4:22; *Col.* 3:9), and the condition we bear from our mother's womb must be annihilated because it is wretched and cursed. For

that to happen, it is now a matter of the first order that we learn to
put to death everything we think of as wisdom, virtue, righteousness, and power and be fully aware that none of it is worth a hill
of beans, as is said in the fourth chapter of Romans: in the person
of Abraham God showed that he calls the things which are not as
if they were (cf. *Rom.* 4:17). And that is also the true figure of the
church. In a word, we must be annihilated in our nature if we are to
possess some quality of being that is approved by God. And that is
also why our lives must be hidden. In other words, our introduction
to the kingdom of God must begin with death. In that we must
be resolute. That death has a long reach, for it presupposes that we
possess not a speck of confidence, wisdom, power, righteousness,
or anything else. Let us realize that by nature we are so cursed that
we cannot aspire to the good or even have a single good thought
that God does not hold in abomination along with everything we
can do and undertake, even though we presumptuously boast of
it. We must realize that. It is a very difficult lesson. Consequently,
God must take a rod to us and be ready to tame us, for his word
alone will never be sufficient.[3]

That is also why Paul places two kinds of mortification in us, but
that is also the ordinary teaching of holy Scripture (cf. *Rom.* 12:1-
2; *2 Cor.* 4:10). We must be modified in our minds so that they will
be subdued and know that we are poor animals who cannot take
a single step without being governed by God's Spirit. And that is
where he begins the twelfth chapter of Romans. When he really
wants to humble believers, he says they must offer themselves as
a sacrifice to God (cf. *Rom.* 12:1-2). How? It is your reason, he
says, which is considered so highly and which the philosophers

---

[3] The word of God alone is not sufficient, to which Calvin joins the rod; a
pedagogical principle dominant in his work and in the sixteenth century: the
loving father chastises his children. Cf. *Institutes* III, iii, 7; iv, 35.—*M.E.*

themselves[4] have magnified so greatly, that must die. The same is true of the will.

Now that we have heard of one kind of death, Paul proposes a second. We must, he says, bear within ourselves the mortification of Jesus Christ so that his life is also declared in the end. And what is that mortification? We must renounce our reason, ourselves, and our desires (cf. *2 Cor.* 4:10). Paul elaborates and speaks of the emotions through which God brings us under control, correcting our presumptuousness and overweening pride. In addition, he teaches us to feel, even forcibly, our weaknesses.

Consequently, there is a death which is inward, as it is called, and another which is outward, which is the second. That would still be hard to understand if it were not spoken of more familiarly. So the death of Christians—I am not speaking of natural death, as when God removes us from this world, but as we must die and live to God—is understood as our having to die to self and to the world in order to acquire entrance into the kingdom of heaven. So we have the death I called 'inward.' And what is it? That is when we are empty of all presumption and do not give rein to our wisdom and say, 'Oh, this will be good,' and we must be willing to govern ourselves, and we must be poor blind people who acknowledge we are stupid to the core until God makes us wise, which is shown in our obeying him. That death, as I said, is the main one.

Then there is the second death, which is outward. That is when God keeps us in sickness and poverty to keep us humble and gives us a sense of being rebuked and treats us that way all the time, so that it seems we do nothing but languish and die every day.[5] For

---

[4] Cf. Plato, *Protagoras* 352 C-D; Plutarch, *Opinion of the Philosophers,* Book IV, chapt. 4-5 (898 E-899 B); Cicero, *On Duties* I, iv, 11; I, xxviii, 101; *Tusculan Disputations,* IV, xv, 34; V, xiii, 39; etc..—*M.E.*

[5] It is the regularly sick Calvin who is talking this way. In the *Institutes,* the Reformer presents the same reasoning and the same examples (III, viii, 2) but equally insists on the believer's patience.—*M.E.*

if some were not filled with reproach and ignominy, they would immediately be filled with pride and presumption. So God has to subdue them, not so they will only feel their fragility and be apprehensive of the ache they have in their arms and hands and stomachs, but so that, because of that, they will understand there is much poverty in their bodies and even more in their souls, so that they will renounce every hint of that pride they are steeped in and which Satan soaks them in. The same is true of those whom God keeps down with rebukes and ignominy and whom men hold in contempt and value in no way. Why is that? So they will learn on their own to look down upon themselves and humble themselves of their own free will. Afterwards, if God sends us some other afflictions, let all of that serve the purpose of mortifying us in our Lord Jesus Christ. That, then, is what we have to remember from this passage in which Abraham is told to kill a heifer, a goat, and a ram.

It is true that some take this to mean three heifers, three goats, and three rams, but the word is ambiguous, and we need not linger over others' musings about these words. They can be translated as triplicates, but some take it to mean the age of three years inasmuch as it is said, 'You will take a heifer of three years, a goat of three years, and a ram of three years.' Others, to show their cleverness, have said it was to represent the three kinds of sacrifice of the law, but such speculations are more to be rejected than argued over, for that would keep us from our true purpose. So it is enough that God commanded Abraham to sacrifice these animals.

Now three kinds of earthbound animals and two kinds of birds are specified. These have been turned into allegories, but we must leave it at that, for I do not want to get involved in that, and, because men are so changeable and our curiosity always leads us astray, I want to exhort you in God's name not to waste your time with such things when you come into contact with them. Since there are many who bring up those kinds of things in their commentaries and worthless talks, ignore all of that and go to something solid where you can plant your feet.

Now in that diversity of animals and birds there is no doubt that Abraham's lineage is imaged, for Abraham offers himself with the animals, and all that would have been acceptable to God in accordance with his nature. We must consider God's intention and purpose. It is as if he had said, 'Kill yourself, yourself and all your lineage.' So we see that the state and condition of the church is here represented by the sacrifices Abraham makes. That is why there is such a variety, for the church, as Paul says, is like the human body. The eye is not the foot, and the arm is not the leg, the tongue is not the ear (cf. *1 Cor.* 12:14-22). Each member of the body has its ability and its appropriate place so that the whole functions very well in harmony. For what would happen if the eye were the leg, and the tongue were the ear, or if the whole human body were an eye or a leg or a head? But since there is a good proportion in the entire body, everything is so well placed that each member has its companions, and we must realize that God wishes to keep us under control so that we will not be satisfied with ourselves individually and thus separated from one another. But he wants us to assemble our various parts, as the saying goes, that is, he wants us to acknowledge our mutual need to serve one another and act appropriately toward our neighbours.

It is the same as if he had declared to Abraham that every church had to be offered in sacrifice to God, no matter the quality or calling of each church. There are some that are like birds, others like rams. We must not at this point look cleverly for any similarity, but let us be satisfied with simple differences, as if we were told that those who wish to live according to God's commands and reach the heavenly kingdom must begin with death. What kind? With sacrificial death. Death would not be enough. And that is the point we must reach. Unbelievers die not only once, but usually, whatever they do, they have to languish just as God's children, suffer much bitterness, distress, and oppression. In a word, as I said, they have to languish in this world, but death does not bring them life. There is only unhappiness when God afflicts them. And that is very far from turning to their advantage. It contributes to their greater disorder and confusion. It is in that way that God makes them even more inexcusable. That is also why they gnash their teeth, storm about, chafe at the bit, grumble, and fume against God. Now, as I have said, afflictions are to tame us and humble us more. But reprobates[6] become even more hardened and, forever stiff-necked, will never yield, even though God strikes them with great blows. Therefore, death for them is mortal, that is, it leaves them as they are to cast them into the pit.

And why does the death of believers bring life? It is because they are sacrificed as a holy offering to God and do not simply die, that is, they do not only undergo the afflictions but also willingly humble themselves even to the point of completely abasing themselves. They yield themselves to God and ask to be his, and they deny themselves so that he may possess them in peace. That is a living death. It is not only living, but it gives life. That is why Paul, in the passage I quoted from the twelfth of Romans, says, 'Brethren, offer yourselves to God as a living sacrifice' (cf. *Rom.* 12:1). If he had said, 'Offer yourselves as a sacrifice,' the matter would have been a bit severe if we understand here what is said about Abraham. But Paul tempers what might seem harsh and austere. There is nothing that can cause us to rejoice more in all our sorrows and troubles than the encouragement Paul joins to it, namely, that not only do we die, but we are offered to God as living sacrifices. In other words, that kind of death brings life.

---

[6] Reprobates have no chance of being redeemed. This is an affirmation related to the principle of double predestination. Cf. *Institutes* III, xxi, 1, 5, 7; xxiii, 3; etc.—*M.E.*

Therefore, we still need to remember that this would be a very insignificant matter, indeed totally useless, which would completely confuse us if we were being afflicted by God's hand and if our hearts had not been humble enough to confess that we are nothing and that we must so yield in obedience to God that we are stripped of all our foolish wisdom, of all our desires and affections, as has already been discussed; but the sacrifice must accompany it at the same time and God must dedicate our death so that it will be blessed and work for our salvation.

Let each person be ready to be sacrificed that way. And if some are of small and low condition, let them not say, 'Alas, God is pressing me too hard,' but let them realize they are called to that, and let them be content to be members of the church. Let us realize that God did not establish such a diversity among people without reason. Then, let those who are great and excellent in the eyes of the world not seek to be privileged and say, 'I am not of the common man. So why will God not at least respect the condition in which he placed me and the many gifts he has bestowed upon me? Why does he not consider them so that I will be spared above the others?' No, there will be no such pleading to be excused from the common condition. But let us know that, from the greatest to the smallest, we are all called without exception to be sacrificed to God and, consequently, to die, indeed until he enlivens us by his power and we fully belong to him and claim as ours only what he has given us. That, then, for that item.

And in the same way, Abraham makes the sacrifice as father of believers, but we must each learn to offer ourselves out of a willing love. And particularly let those whose assigned task it is to bear witness to the teaching realize that it is a sacred sword (cf. *Eph.* 6:17) that has been put in their hands to make known everything that pertains to human nature so that God's children will be renewed and made like new creatures. Therefore, each of us must be sacrificed by the one who teaches God's word, as Paul also teaches at the end of Romans (cf. *Rom.* 15:16). He calls himself a priest, not like the papists, who intend to sacrifice our Lord Jesus Christ, but Paul says that ministers of God's word have the duty to sacrifice souls to God. How? The teaching is like a sword to annihilate every glory and instruct men to confess they are nothing. Therefore, all those who desire to be known and acknowledged as God's children must allow themselves to be sacrificed by his word.

And what does that mean? It means that when we come to preaching, we are not to seek to be soothed or stroked or have our ears tickled with quaint speculations, but let us allow the preacher to get under our skin so we will be pierced, cut to the quick, and deeply wounded, and have to take the bitter medicine and sometimes pass through fire and searing reproaches so that everything will be shut off from the corruption in us; otherwise, there would be no Christianity in us. Now many will come to preaching every day. A lot of good it does! They do not want anyone to get under their skin. And even if someone rebukes the vices they are guilty of, they will be far from applying it to themselves, and they will focus it on their neighbours. 'Oh! They were talking about my neighbour and not about me.' People like that could live at the foot of the pulpit for a hundred years after they die and still grow only farther from God. But let us come to preaching in order to be holy sacrifices there so that everything that belongs to us may be subdued and so refashioned by God through his Holy Spirit that he alone will live and reign in us. So much for that point.

Now at the same time each person must make progress by his own free will, and God's word must teach us how to be priests and that God has established us in that position, as we learn in Revelation (cf. *Rev.* 1:6) and as Peter explains more clearly (cf. *1 Pet.* 2:5). So let us apply that grace which is given to us, that is, let each of us dedicate himself to God. How? When we hear some good teaching and rebuke, let each of us enter into himself and apply it to himself, and let us learn to rebuke ourselves in our hearts: 'Cursed creature, what are you thinking about when you dare raise your defences against God?' Consequently, let us learn to be ashamed of ourselves, and let that reduce us to near despair until God gathers us to himself. And then, when our carnal affections entice us and avarice influences some of us to lay up for ourselves and have no compunction about oppressing our neighbours, and when others of us are given to sensuality, gluttony, and the like, let our thought be: 'Alas, cursed creature, must you now live for yourself and your desires, seeing that you have been redeemed at such a high price by the Son of God? Did Jesus Christ have to pour out his blood, which he shed for you? Does his redemption mean nothing to you, seeing that you forget him this way?' That is how we must willingly sacrifice ourselves and perform for ourselves the duties of minister and priest by examining all our thoughts and emotions and putting to death everything which belongs to Adam and our first nature. That, then, is why the responsibility of sacrificing those animals was entrusted to Abraham.

Moreover, when it is said that he divided the animals into two pieces, we see in all the profane histories that if there were sacrifices, it was the custom to divide them into two pieces and pass between them. That was done to show reverence for the sacrifice better, as if it were said, 'You will pass between these two pieces to acknowledge that what I declare to you is true and that I am not going to betray you.' And that was commonly done among the pagans. It was even the custom among the Jews that when they sacrificed, they divided the sacrifice into two pieces, as is seen in Jeremiah (cf. *Jer.* 34:18) where the prophet reproaches all the kings of Israel and Judah for passing between the pieces of the sacrifice without knowing what that meant. But God wanted to signify to Abraham that it is not enough that we be sacrificed for one moment, but that we must be torn in pieces, as it were, dismembered so that there is no longer any hope of life in us. And not without reason. God brings us to that point, for we are like little worms when they are cut in half. Both ends continue to wiggle, the head on one end and the tail on the other, still wanting to get back together. That is the way it is with us. Even though God has cut and divided us by his Holy Spirit and we are as dead, there is not a part of us that does not wiggle. For we would always like to remain as we are, in our old skin, in that part of us which we bring from our mother's womb. Consequently, God must mortify us in many ways, but we cannot say more about that now, so we will save it for tomorrow.

Now let us bow before the majesty of our gracious God in acknowledgment of our faults, praying that he will cause us to sense them in such a way that we will be properly displeased with them and groan before him and ask him to receive us in mercy as we still continue to aspire sincerely to be renewed. And to accomplish that, may he not allow us to be totally beaten down within ourselves, and may he keep us aware that we are poor wretched creatures until he has devoted us to himself and we are fully mortified within ourselves so that we may lead a better life, which he already causes us to enjoy in this world and of which he has placed within us some seed that will finally produce full enjoyment and perfection. May he grant that grace not only to us but to all the peoples and nations on earth.

72

Waiting for God to Act:
The Practice of Patience

Tuesday, 19 March 1560

And when the fowls came down upon the carcases, Abram drove them away. And when the sun was going down, a deep sleep fell upon Abram; and, lo, an horror of great darkness fell upon him. And he said unto Abram, Know of a surety that thy seed shall be a stranger in a land that is not theirs, and shall serve them; and they shall afflict them four hundred years; And also that nation, whom they shall serve, will I judge: and afterward shall they come out with great substance (Gen. 15:11-14).

E SAW YESTERDAY that it is not enough to sacrifice ourselves to God but that it is a process that must continue. And that is also why Paul, speaking on this subject, sets before us not only the death of our Lord Jesus Christ, to which ours must be likened, but also his burial, in the sixth chapter of Romans (cf. *Rom.* 6:3-11), as if he were saying it is not enough for a Christian to die once and be stripped of all his thoughts and affections in order to be kept captive to God's obedience, but that we must work at it and there must be an uninterrupted order of procedure and true perseverance. The sacrifices cut into pieces that way by Abraham (cf. *Gen.* 15:10) were indeed a grievous sight, seeing that they were an image of God's church. It is as if Abraham had been told that his seed, which God had elected and blessed, would not only have to die but would also have to be dismembered and torn to pieces. At first sight, that is harsh, but we must still come to this point. Yet when God grants us the grace to be nothing in the eyes of the world, let us learn to be steadfast in that condition and persevere as long as we live, knowing that there will always be something of ourselves within us which will keep us from being fully devoted to God and that that something must be eradicated little by little.

Moreover, when we are dismembered piecemeal that way, let us not fear that God will not bless us and restore us. And even that dispersion which we see in the church serves even better to maintain the unity of our faith. For if God's children are scattered here and there indiscriminately, that wretched situation motivates us even more to come together peacefully in God's hands and be united and concerned for one another's salvation. But on the contrary, if the church prospers and flourishes, there are many who spread their wings and take flight. And what is the upshot of that? They break the unity of the faith. So we see that it is for our advantage that God, having mortified us simultaneously, disperses us in the world so that we may be even better held together by the inner power of the Holy Spirit.

Moreover, that is even better confirmed by what Moses adds, namely, that birds were coming down to feed and were seeking so avidly to prey on Abraham's sacrifice that he was unable to frighten them away. Now, as mentioned yesterday, it is neither good nor useful to look for great subtlety of interpretation here, but, in brief, Moses intended to say that when we are devoted to God, our devotion is not enough, for there are always enemies who will try to spoil and corrupt the offering we make. There are some who understand the birds to be devils because they are called the principalities in high places and the rulers of the air (cf. *Eph.* 6:12), but that is too far-fetched and forced. So let us be content that God has instructed us here in the person of our father Abraham that when we are offered to him and all of our wicked nature has been put to death, as it were, by the sword of his word and the power of his Holy Spirit (cf. *Eph.* 6:17; *Heb.* 4:12), we will be assailed on all sides and that there will never be a lack of enemies to torment us and especially to corrupt the sacred offering we make. Now the sacrifices had to be kept intact until they were burned. That is why the birds come to eat and devour them, which was a corruption, as we see.

Now the teaching means that we are to be on guard, for we are much affected by lack of enthusiasm. When we begin our Christian walk, we think it is a *fait accompli*. And that is the reason we are often surprised by Satan. And when we think we belong completely to God, we are very far from the fact. So in order not to be deceived, let us understand that when we have taken pains to mortify ourselves and God reigns in us and we are guided by his Holy Spirit, we are nonetheless not without conflict and trouble. Why not? Because Satan is always on the job, along with the wicked. That is why we cannot interpret this simply as the devils' birds. For do not the wicked and despisers of God try to keep us from serving him and to prevent his name from being glorified in us? Also, how many temptations are we aware of that arise from our flesh and our own natures? So it is not reasonable to interpret all that as being represented by the birds. But, in summary, we are admonished to be on guard and always to resist all the many assaults directed at us, be they infinite, so that we may remain steadfast and unpolluted and God can have his sacred offering, as he must. That, then, is what we have to remember.

And experience shows us as much. Who among us, when we examine ourselves and try hard to be in subjection to God, does not find many contradictions of all kinds? And when we succeed in making peace with that situation, it is then that the devil makes his greatest effort to divert us and thwart us. So when we understand that, what is evident in our father Abraham is also accomplished in us today, and we are thereby even more confident that God is maintaining us in his church. So that is what we have to remember.

Now it follows that at sunset a terror seized Abraham with great darkness and he went to sleep and received a vision. This circumstance shows we cannot serve God without going through times of great anguish, and inasmuch as we approach him, we must be ready to be harassed and tormented to our limits, not that he cannot exempt us from all that if it seems good to him, but it pleases him to test our patience this way and humble us at the same time. And when we learn that lesson, it is difficult to be nothing in our own eyes so that God alone will be esteemed and we will realize our lives depend on his power and his pure grace. That is why, when he brings us to himself, we need to be trained by many hardships and troubles.

Moreover, in order to be an example for us, Abraham had to be struck with fear, as if he were in the pit of hell, so to speak, like a man lost, not knowing what would become of him. Depending on how tender and delicate we are, we run from afflictions. And when it is a question of our being completely reduced to nothing, every fibre of our being resists mightily, which makes it difficult for us to submit to what God demands of us, namely, that we renounce our wisdom and judgment, all our thoughts and desires and all our passions, and die in order to allow him to live in us (cf. *Rom.* 6:8; *Col.* 3:3; *2 Tim.* 2:11). That, I say, can be done only with great difficultly. Why? We always want to remain as we are, and God even has to hold us back by force, as was said yesterday, to keep us in subjection. Consequently, Abraham was gripped with terror so that we will not be discouraged when we are terrified by death and all our instinctive fears urge us to avoid it. If Abraham, a figure of the state of the church, had an angel-like virtue, was frightened that much, what does that mean for us, who are a hundred times weaker than he was? Moreover, we are not dealing just with the figure of the church here; God is causing us to experience that time ceremonially in our father Abraham.

So let us not be surprised when we naturally resist what God requires, but even though we initially resisted strongly, let us continue to gather strength and vigour and pray that God through the Holy Spirit will help us overcome all the discouraging apprehensions we can possibly face. The devil is crafty. When he wishes to gain access to us through our presumption, he makes us believe we can do wonderful things. But when he cannot get to us that way, he uses our weakness to make us despair: 'Do you not see that you are a long way from being able to serve God? You have no natural impulse to serve him. You have as many wicked thoughts and rebellious impulses as you have hairs on your head. So what do you gain by trying to dedicate yourself to God when you see you cannot?' In order not to be influenced by Satan's craftiness, let us remember the terror which befell our father Abraham. And let us realize that God wishes to afflict us in such a way that we do not become insensitive to him, and let us also realize that what afflicts us causes us to back away. We will have to experience much agitation within ourselves, such that we are driven to our wits' end, but let us get beyond that, whatever happens, and let us take courage and never give up, knowing that God will perfect his power in our weakness (cf. *2 Cor.* 12:9). That, then, is what we have to remember about the terror that seized our father Abraham. We will say more about this tomorrow as we follow the text.

We come now to what Moses adds. He says that a great sleep fell upon Abraham with the darkness. Here we see that God did not put him in such darkness that he could not enlighten him immediately. And that is the main point we have to remember, for if our light is the world's light, which is the light of unbelievers, who think they are wise and see clearly and accurately but have wandered into such darkness that they cannot find the right path, we see despisers of God awash in all their appetites. It is true it seems like all the light is for them, for they want to control the world. They want to rule states. They present their discourses in various places, and it even seems that the sun is enclosed in their brains, so bright is their light. And then they are filled with arrogance, and they think they are wise enough to look down upon God and the world. That, then, is the sort they are. They are carried away by their lusts, their ambition, their greed, and the like. But they are only running wild and resisting violently. On the other hand, God's children are seemingly in darkness, as we are shown here, and they are struck with terror, but at the same time God enlightens them enough to know the right way of salvation. They know that God protects them, that he is their Redeemer, and that they cannot fall as long as they follow his word and the guidance of his Spirit.

Thus we see that the darkness that was upon Abraham was much more useful than the ordinary, clear sight of profane people would have been. Why so? God adds vision to it, for this sleep was not natural to Abraham; it was not a sleep to rest the body but to prepare him to receive the vision which Moses recounts. And in fact it is specifically stated that God makes himself known to his prophets through visions and dreams (cf. *Job* 33:14-15). When comparison is made with Moses in the twelfth chapter of Numbers, the text says Moses enjoyed the privilege of seeing God face to face and, because of that, was superior to the prophets to whom God revealed his will in dreams and visions (cf. *Num.* 12:5-8). Thus Abraham had to be put to sleep to be withdrawn from the world, so to speak, for God to appear to him, as we also see in this light which shines in darkness. In other words, when we are in distress, God deals bountifully with us, as the psalm says (cf. *Psa.* 118:5). When we are without counsel, he guides us and directs us; when we are downcast, he lifts us up; and when we are as dead, he revives us.

Something else we need to remember is that it does us no harm to experience horrors and anguish, provided God makes himself known to us and makes us aware that he has not forgotten us and that we have always had his word as a light to show us the way (cf. *Psa.* 119:105). And may we also have the wisdom of his Holy Spirit to cause us to turn away from our rationales and fantasies, by which we are regularly led into temptation. That much for that point.

Now we are told that God speaks to Abraham. The vision, of itself, would have been cold. It would have been only a dead image, but the word explains it all. And that point is important to note, for to the extent that we are subject to our senses, we are carried away by what appears to us. And in the meantime, the main thing, our being taught by God's truth, is left behind. So let us note that this vision which Abraham had was not speechless, so to speak, but God added his word to it so it would bear its fruit and exercise its power. And that word was that Abraham's seed was to be captive for four hundred years. And that was a word very different from what Abraham could have wished for, for, as we have said, he had one foot in the grave. He had to have a lineage or God's promise would have been negated or void. Now he is told, 'Abraham, for four hundred years your seed will be afflicted and oppressed. It will be trampled upon; it will be oppressed by a tyranny more cruel than any other.' What kind of consolation is that? It looks as though God is not content to have oppressed his servant in various ways but wants to shame and confound him even more, for that was like breaking rocks, iron, and steel. And even though Abraham had been wondrously constant until this moment when he hears there will be no end and that things will go from bad to worse for four hundred years, what could he have thought? Now the fact remains that this served him as an inestimable consolation. Why so? The promise is added that God will be the judge and defend the cause of those who are unjustly afflicted.

So when our Lord enlightens us in the midst of darkness, let us learn that he makes us glad in our sorrows, that his intention is not to deliver us at the outset or set us free, but he maintains us in patience so we will not grow weary while we wait for our redemption to come. Even though the approach is difficult and contrary to our feelings, we must yield, for God must not be changed for our pleasure and convenience, but we must do everything within our power to bring ourselves under his control and accept patiently everything he ordained for us. Thus when we hear that God says, 'Your seed will be afflicted,' let us realize, as stated above, that inasmuch as our lives begin with death, the rest we are to hope for from him also begins with wars, struggles, afflictions, and sorrows. So that is how God wants to console and gladden us, namely, by showing us that a man's life is a battleground and that it is there that we must wage our war in one way or another, some of us more so, others of us less so, but the condition for waging the war is general for the entire church (cf. *1 Tim.* 1:18; 6:12; *2 Tim.* 4:7). God puts us to the test depending on what we can bear and, if he wishes to prove us, he gives us the strength at the same time. And he often permits us to be beat down so that he is glorified by lifting us up again. And let us consider it a test of humility to call upon him even more ardently and to acknowledge that the fact we persist comes from him alone. That is a teaching which could be drawn out at length, but the main thing each of us has to do is ponder it and apply our minds to it.

In addition, let us now compare ourselves with Abraham's seed and with one another. Here is the father common to us all, and in him we see God's church battered and tormented by the wicked, but if we have to suffer long, ten years seems like a hundred thousand. And we scarcely find a single person who can remain calm. And experience shows that frequently. For if we say that there are this or that many in prison on the one hand, that one or another of them has been burned, there is good reason for us to feel compassion, and we are obliged to experience it, for, if our brothers are in that kind of distress, we would be brutally cruel to be glad. So it is right that we be moved with pity and groan before God and pray that he not abandon his own; but to be in turmoil at the same time as we are is a sign that we have profited very badly from God's school. And when we think we are filled with faith, we have in fact only two or three specks of it, for here is what we say: 'Will this never end? We see that the wicked are becoming more wicked. Must it always be this way? But must it not be put to an end?' And when boiling pots begin to overflow, the fat immediately runs out at the same time and the meat is burned. That is what will happen today to those who say they are believers.

For most of them are not very circumspect, and they almost all rush ahead without counsel and advice, and that is just what we would always like to prevent, and we do not take into consideration the fact that we often resist God's will instead of yielding peaceably to it. For some will think, 'Oh, now is the right time to do what God commanded.' Indeed, but who told you that? It is more likely it was someone you created in your head. 'Oh, we have to hurry.' Indeed, but here the text says that Abraham's lineage will be afflicted for four hundred years. And indeed, but have we seen the afflictions of the church last for a period of four hundred years? So we see we are very far from being like our father Abraham. Yet he was the pattern of the church. And if we cannot reach such a

417

standard of faith, which he at least had, we must still move forward and aspire to getting closer to it according as God grants it by his Holy Spirit. Yet we find ourselves still being overly impatient. And when we have languished for some short period of time and do not receive some sign that God remembers us and wants to help us, we are immediately displeased because we want him to hurry along in accordance with our will and pleasure. And then, when we have waited for a long time, as it seems to us, and our faith has been disappointed, we grumble against him as if he were doing us great wrong. 'Yes, but who gave you such hope? The fact is that you have some passing apprehensions that you were deceived by.' We must not be surprised if we are often disappointed in everything we expect, for we were supposed to listen to God and his promises, to adhere to them and avoid imagining anything contrary to his word and will. Now we do everything backward. We ignore God's word, which exhorts us to patience and peace, for it is by yielding with patience and peace that we show we are rendering him the honour he is due. Yes, and if we should ever suffer death at his hand, even three or four hundred times, let us remain calm and at peace when it pleases him to test us that way. And if we do not remain calm and at peace, God has to mock us when he sees such rashness.

Therefore, we must study even more closely this teaching which tells us that the church which preceded us was afflicted for four hundred years. Abraham knew it, and he told Isaac, Jacob, and their families about it. They were all aware of it, but they did not become angry with God. They did not throw off the yoke and say, 'What is this all about? Does God intend to let us languish here? Has he not already tested our patience long enough? Will this never end?' They were not so impetuous that they rebelled that way, but they obediently accepted that condition since God wanted to subject them to it. Thus they were willing to be patient.

As for the four hundred years, let us understand that the people were captive in Egypt a very long time, but God has in mind the day of which he spoke, until the people's departure, when they were led out by the hand of Moses. All together, that makes four hundred years. Now there were about two hundred years that Abraham and his successors were still in the land of Canaan, but they moved about, as the psalm says (cf. *Psa.* 105:13), and there was no resting place for them. In the end, famine forced them to leave the country which God intended for them and go into Egypt (cf. *Gen.* 41:57; 43:1; 47: 4), which was a profane and polluted land. And when they are thus deprived of and banished from the land God had given them as an inheritance, they are dead and exterminated from the world, so to speak. And that is what God signified by this four hundred years, as if he were saying, 'You will be the heir of this land, but not personally. Moreover, your children will not immediately take possession of it, but, to the contrary, instead of being masters and lords of it, they will be subjects; they will be held as slaves; they will be tormented when subjected to such tyranny that they will find no help from the world. They will not dare to take a deep breath for fear the enemy will think they want to avenge themselves. They will be under such oppression that you had good reason to be stricken with terror just imagining what is going to happen.'

We now have the natural meaning of the words, and we must apply them to our context so as not to be so hasty or precipitous in wanting to call upon God to do right now what he said, just when we are learning to put distance between the promises and their fulfilment. As for God's promises, we must keep them hedged in, and we must receive them in simplicity of heart and in good conscience, for that is the abiding place of this inestimable treasure. In other words, God's seat and dwelling must be the sincere and pure desire of our souls. As for their fulfilment, we must not expect it right away, as we have said, but let our desires incite us to patience, and let us accept the fact that the fulfilment, the accomplishment, the execution of the promises will be remote, and let us always wait for the occasion to come. And when will that be? God alone knows. It is not for us to know. And let us remain within that limitation so we will know that God will bring it to pass in accordance with his will and not ours, for it is not our place to impose restrictions on him. So that is what we have to remember about this passage.

In order to engage in the practice of patience better, when our Lord promises us eternal life, we have to walk at the same time in this world among an infinite number of deaths which Satan threatens us with (cf. *John* 3:15-16; 5:24; 6:40, 47; *Matt.* 19:29). So life is very far from us; it does not appear to us, but yet the promises satisfy us, and while the manifestation is hidden, as Paul says, and because we cannot perceive it with our eyes, we now consider it as assured and certain when he speaks (cf. *Rom.* 4:16-25). For he also says that he will always be near us (cf. *Psa.* 34:19) and that his help will never leave us (cf. *Psa.* 9:11). Yes, but at the same time he often keeps us in suspense, and we languish in our needs and unworthiness, some in one kind, some in another. And then the evils join together. From the perspective of the flesh, we are the most wretched of creatures. And where is God? He does not show himself immediately unless we are somewhat enlightened by his promises. And he says, 'I will come. And if my promises delay, wait for them.' That is the way the prophet Habakkuk speaks of them (cf. *Hab.* 2:3). He says he will come, but he immediately adds, "'If my promises delay." In other words, if you do not see them fulfilled right away and you think I have only spoken pleasing words, if you not grow weary, for I control the times and the seasons that I know are right (cf. *Dan.* 2:21). So you must not be in a hurry, but you must exercise restraint. Yes, and you must make yourselves captives.'

That, in brief, is the teaching we have to remember about this passage, namely, that we are not to put a time limit on God, but we are to submit ourselves afresh to his counsel and good will. And if he permits us to be troubled all our lives and see nothing better than those who have gone before, let us not grow weary, and since his truth is everlasting and his power never fails, may our faith follow his truth and power and yield to them. Thus, if he wants us to walk farther than we would like, we must nonetheless do so. For if a servant said to his master, 'I have already walked a dozen steps; that is enough; I am leaving; I no longer wish to follow you,' what kind of reasoning would that be? The master must proceed as he pleases and the servant must follow wherever the master chooses to lead him. God wants us to follow him that way so we will be completely his subjects. It is not that he wants us to follow him by force and under constraint or that we cannot endure the work, for at the same time he gives us legs, for it is said: 'I will not leave you in mid-journey. Only follow, and I will give you strength.'[1] But at the same time let us not give ourselves too much credit in our weaknesses; rather, let us always seek the appropriate help, and we will always find him ready and able.

We also need to weigh what is added: that God will judge the people who afflict his church. That, then, is the outcome that is to make Abraham glad when he is told that all the afflictions he will have to endure—he and all those following his death—will turn to their advantage and salvation. Why? Because God will take up their cause. Now it is true someone could reply: 'Why is God not helping us now? Why does he not give us some sign that he wants to help us? Why does he leave us here like poor lost and desperate people?' As I have already said, our salvation

---

[1] This verse does not exist as such, but elements of it are found in Psalm 18:32; in Isaiah 58:11; 66:14; etc. In Isaiah 58:11: '…the Lord will continually guide you…' Cf. also in Psalm 9:11.—*M.E.*

has to be hidden; otherwise, faith and hope would no longer have any meaning.

But when God promises that he will judge us (cf. *Psa.* 7:11; 50:6) in order to sustain us, let us note that that promise is to be applied to the present time, although it is not fulfilled for us to see. Why not? We know that God is unchangeable and does not have whims and moments the way men do (cf. *James* 1:17). It is true he knows the right time to work, but that does not mean he will be kept from doing it tomorrow if he does not put his hand to the task today. The most powerful king in the world, desire it as he may, will not be able to control the situation that way. He must make preparations, look for ways, consider how to provision and fortify himself in every respect. God is not limited that way, for his power is always the same, and he works in accordance with his goodness. So when he speaks to us this way: 'After a couple of hundred years, you will recognize the effect of what I am promising you,' it is as if he were saying, 'The thing is now already done before me, but you cannot understand it. So keep up your courage, and I will show you what I have done in secret but which you cannot see now.' Therefore, when God says to Abraham that he will be the Judge and punish those who have troubled his seed, he does not mean that in the meantime he will forsake maintaining the church, abandon it and leave it as open prey. Not at all! But it is as if he were saying, 'My duty is to help my people and hold them to being perfect like me. Yes, and consequently whatever outrage and offence that is done to them will not go unpunished. And because such is my duty, I will demonstrate it with deeds in the future. But if I delay, it is not because I no longer have the opportunity to act.' Now, as I said, this promise, which extends into a distant future, shows us that God is already with us, that we cannot perish when we place our lives in his hand, and that we will be very well protected. So that, in summary, is what we have to remember.

Now it is true this teaching will seem obscure to some. But why should it? Lack of practice. If we are the cleverest people in the world and know everything taught in schools, it is certain we will never have the slightest idea of what that means if we do not have a personal experience with it. So we must experience it or we will forever be taking baby steps and never profit from it. But once we have consciously realized what it means to give God the honour which is his, when we are persuaded that his nature and purpose do not change and that his power is everlasting (cf. *James* 1:17), when we realize that, it is certain we will finally conclude that he helps us. To come to such a conclusion, we must be certain God will not abandon us, although he does not show he will not do so, but he works in such a way that we will not see his presence. In any case, he will not be idle. That, in brief, is what we have to remember when it is said that God will judge. He is speaking of the future when he says, 'I will judge.'

Moreover, his being the everlasting Judge is like an incomparable fortress for us (cf. *Psa.* 18:2; 62:6; 91:2) when we are attacked from all sides, but not attacked and overcome. So if it is God's responsibility to judge, it is certain we will endure patiently being condemned by the world, being persecuted and harassed, insulted and trampled underfoot, so to speak. Why? God is still and will forever be in control. But why? As soon as someone gives us a slight tap on the head, we are annoyed and angry and would like for God to come down immediately from heaven and act. And if he does not and our enemies remain unpunished, we think we have been unfairly compensated while waiting for him. Now when we react that way, we deprive him of his honour as Judge. And what kind of honour is that, that God is no longer Judge of the world, but idle and asleep! That is a damnable blasphemy. And yet, even though we do not utter it with our mouths, we express it in our hearts every time we are so impatient that we cannot bear with God's postponing his help. For, as I have said, he cannot be Judge of the world unless we are sustained when we rest in him and his protection.

What is the significance of the office of judge? We must not think only of its general providence, but we must think of it in terms of what Paul says in 2 Thessalonians, chapter 1, namely, that God is righteous (cf. *2 Thess.* 1:5-6). And yet if we suffer today, he says, it is like a mirror in which we contemplate what is hidden from us. Why? The wicked are predominant. They have their times of triumph, and then they become insolent and very self-indulgent. They grant themselves every licence to do evil. They are ravening wolves and rabid animals. They only strike violently, murder, devour, and consume. There you have the wicked with their unrestrained licence. Either there is a God in heaven or there is not. If there is a God, we have to conclude that there is a judgment we do not yet know; otherwise we would have to deny God and any divine being completely. So it is not without reason that Paul says that when the wicked act that way, the afflictions of the church and the unjust torments of God's poor children are for us a living picture that represents the out-of-control conditions of our day and the judgment to come. We can then confidently conclude that since God's righteousness does not break forth in its perfection today, we must wait for it at another time and we will then behold the righteousness which is now hidden from our normal perception, but we have to observe it in the midst of darkness through the enlightenment of God's word. Faith, then, will give us eyes to contemplate things not seen (cf. *2 Cor.* 4:18; *Heb.* 11:1). So much for that.

Now on that point let us also note the lesson given here, which is that God cannot deny himself. Consequently, his eye has to be on us when he takes us into his safekeeping; at the same time, he inscribes in his book all the wrongs done to us and all the troubles and hardships we endure, and all those things necessarily come under judgment. In the meantime, may he not allow the wicked to attack us with troubles and hardships; let them scorn him and do violence to righteousness and oppress it, and let them rise up with such pride that he is obliged to show it is his responsibility to destroy them; but let us wait patiently for the time. In a word, we must pay particular attention to what is said in the psalm, namely, that God puts our tears in bottles (cf. *Psa.* 56:8), but we have to weep before him. And that weeping means humility, for there are many who endure. They are like people who are at their wits' end, and we will see great diversity among the sick. Some will be so overwhelmed that they will be unable to breathe; they will complain to God and lament, but they will yield and be governed by him. And then there are the sick who manifest their weakness, acknowledge it, and humble themselves. But there are others who do not sense their evil because their confused and disoriented thinking influences them. They storm about, they gnash their teeth, deluding themselves with the thought that they are kings and princes and that a banquet is prepared for them.

Consequently, some, afflicted by God's hand, are beset with such rage and impatience that they do not groan and weep. Others realize that God rightly chastises them, begin to examine their lives, and condemn themselves and magnify God's righteousness after sensing their weaknesses. On the other hand, they realize that it is a good thing for God to curtail their profuse appetites and that if he did not subdue them that way, they would be immediately corrupted by many vain impulses. They also realize that inasmuch as faith is more precious than gold and silver (cf. *1 Pet.* 1:7), it is rightly examined in many ways and God thus cleanses them of all their vices. Moreover, they will groan because evil makes itself felt. Now it is said of those whose tears God keeps that there is no fragrance or thing so precious that God protects with such care as the tears of his people. Is there any way he could better express how highly he prizes his people, show how much he loves them and cares for their salvation than by speaking of them this way? So let us apply all our attention to this teaching, for without it our faith will soon die, and all obedience will vanish if we are not founded on the assurance that God is Judge and in charge of maintaining his church, of supporting the cause of his people and receiving them with the promise that he will protect them as the apple of his eye (cf. *Deut.* 32:10; *Psa.* 17:8; *Zech.* 2:8). That, then, is how this passage is to be understood and practised.

Now that means that at the same time we are exhorted not to usurp for ourselves what belongs to God alone and what he reserves for himself. We want to avenge ourselves of the wrongs done to us. And what is the upshot of that? God ties our hands with his word when he says, 'I will be the judge, and vengeance is mine' (cf. *Deut.* 32:35). Paul applies that statement in Deuteronomy to our instruction, namely, that since God reserves for himself the authority to punish our enemies, if we usurp that authority, we become idols; we pull God from his seat and install ourselves in it. Will he tolerate that? So let us note that we are not able to sense the outcome and power of God's promises unless we attribute to him what is his, namely, the authority to punish our enemies at a time he knows to be right. In the meantime, if he wishes to relax their bridle, let us be patient and have a humble spirit as we bear persecutions, for humility and persecutions go hand in glove. That, then, is how we must bring the two together: the expectation we have with God's help in accordance with his promises, and suffering, when it pleases him to subject us to times of hardship, harassment, and anguish.

What follows shows us that what is permitted has a purpose: that he will bring to pass, one by one, everything he said to Abraham. 'They shall come out,' he says. At this point the promise ends. If God had simply said, 'I shall be the judge,' it would have been a thing only half said; but when he says, 'Your seed shall be foreigners in a land that is not theirs, and they shall be afflicted for a long period of time, but then they shall come out,' we see the adoption of Abraham's children, which is depicted in the land of Canaan. And if they had remained in the land of Egypt, what would have happened? There would have been no certainty. That statement, then, shows that even though God chased them to the four winds, so to speak, and they were deprived of the land where they were to enjoy their perpetual rest, that promise will still have its power and full effect. 'They shall come out,' he says, 'with many possessions.' That, then, is the conclusion of the promise as they wait for what remains to be done, which is that our Lord, though he delays, does not forget his people under any circumstance and that their condition will not be the worse for it, for their salvation is to depend on waiting. Now, that waiting requires them to languish. In other words, they must willingly put their faith to the test and be patient. Yet, even though we are surrounded on all sides by difficulties and cares and it seems God does not have the means to bring to completion what he said, let us allow God to work, and let us be like poor blind people unless we must be enlightened by his word in the midst of the hardships and torments we have to bear, and let us be prepared for that until he brings us to that heavenly enlightenment, where we will enjoy the good things he has promised us.

Now let us bow before the majesty of our gracious God in acknowledgment of our faults, praying that he will make us feel them more and more so that we will be drawn to him. And when we realize there is nothing in us but a kind of death (when we are abandoned by him), let us be even more urged on to seek the grace which he promised us. And let us so love that grace that it alone will satisfy us and strengthen us to resist all trials, which could otherwise lead us astray. And let us always be engaged in this battle

as we await the fruit of our victory, which is prepared for us in
heaven by our Lord Jesus Christ.

73

The Value of a Good Conscience
and
The Promise Postponed: Waiting Patiently
for the Patient God

Wednesday, 20 March 1560

And thou shalt go to thy fathers in peace; thou shalt be buried in a good old age. But in the fourth generation they shall come hither again: for the iniquity of the Amorites is not yet full (Gen. 15:15-16).

WE SAW YESTERDAY that God is not always pleased with our eagerness for him to carry out what he promised us, for he sometimes delays and postpones longer than we would like because it is useful for us, even though we do not understand. In the meantime, however, he always lets us sense his grace to keep us close to himself. For since we are weak, it is certain we would fall away if we had only the word and could in no way experience God's benevolence toward us. Consequently, although God does not yield to our wishes and desires whenever and wherever, he still gives us some small taste of his goodness and power, and that prevents us from being unduly angered or vexed.

And that is why Abraham is now told he will die in peace and be buried at a good old age. Earlier he had been informed that his lineage would be captive for a period of four hundred years. That was very difficult and painful for Abraham to hear, for instead of God's putting him in possession of the land he had promised him as an inheritance, his seed has to wander, and those to whom the lordship of the land of Canaan had been given are obliged to be foreigners, kept underfoot, and submissive to the extreme. Yet the fact remains that Abraham acquiesced to that word because it was God's good pleasure, and our desires must yield to it, though God has taken into consideration our weakness. For whatever perfection his faith may have had, such as it can exist in man, he did not completely lose its nature; he was not made of iron or steel. Consequently, he has to be given some comfort, and God provides it when he says, 'As for you, I will yet grant you the grace of dying in peace and at a good old age' (cf. *Gen.* 25:8). It is quite true that he is far from obtaining what he had requested, but he nonetheless had to be satisfied with it since God was giving him a sign of his goodness and had not forgotten him. For with that, Abraham can conclude that at the appropriate time God will accomplish what he has now begun. We cannot have the slightest awareness of the witness of God's love without being strengthened in our future hope and in our walk until God knows it is useful and necessary to do what he said and promised.

Now it would still seem cold of God to say to Abraham that he would die at a good old age, for he was already old and decrepit, as we have seen. Moreover, even though God gives him some vigour, it does not give him much joy. And then, since he is to die in the end, what consolation does he have when he hears, 'Your life will yet be extended ten or twenty years; even so, you are a broken and finished old man. Oh, God will strengthen you. But what will the result be? You must still die.' That is a very meagre promise, we would say. But when we understand he will die in peace, we will see he has been promised an inestimably good thing. We will place a great deal of value upon the goods and riches of this world and equally upon the delights and honours and easy circumstances in accordance with each person's natural inclination to be great or rich. He is transported by his covetousness to such heights that he thinks he is like an angel of paradise if he can accumulate many things, if he can acquire great possessions, and if he can gain much by much trafficking. In delights and worldly pleasures, in respectability and honour, that is where men find their blessedness.

Let us now consider those who are the rich and the great of this world and those who revel in their pleasures. The fact is that in the end they begin to decline and will not be able to enjoy their situation to its fullest. For with the approach of old age, we have the beginning of anxiety and apprehension. When a man who wants to devote himself to his pleasures and delights discovers that his energies are waning, God is already cutting back on his dainty morsels, as we say, and if he was at ease, whether he was addicted to this or that thing, one taking pleasure in debauchery, another in gluttony, another in the dalliance of his choosing, God is bringing them down in such a way that they realize every day that their pleasures are withering away. And when they see death approaching, the rich realize they must leave behind their wealth, and death is all the more bitter to them. So we see that what men consider to be their complete felicity is only vanishing smoke, which is the mistress of fools.

There is even worse, for those who have relaxed the restraints all during their lifetimes and given themselves free licence to do evil experience dreadful regrets and anxiety. They remember a lifetime of deeds. A lecher will remember his many wicked and shameful acts as well as the wrongs he has done to the people around him, debauching their households and betraying them. A drunkard will remember he has been useless and that his intemperance led him to excesses of one sort or another. The person who has been willing to enrich himself at the expense of others by fraud, robbery, and extortion will have to condemn himself. That is the kind of torture and hell awaiting all old people when they feel themselves growing weak with age.

For young people, seeing they are in death even before leaving their mother's womb—since we see little children are often born dead—clearly understand that when we enter into this present life, death already has dominion over us. Then they see later that many people are snatched away in the prime of life and that there is no tomorrow, as we say. Even though young people know that, they still become elated when they feel some power within themselves. They are deceived by that and straightway act like animals gone wild that no one can restrain, and they do not think about death. It is true that if someone asks them if they are mortal, they will admit they are. And their hair will even stand on end when death is spoken of. But that is immediately forgotten. But old age puts the brakes on people in spite of themselves when they feel their arms and their legs are feeble and find that their eyes are dim and their hearing impaired, and that every part of their body indicates that death is already near and that they have to leave this world. That, then, is how old people cannot escape the causes of anxiety I have just mentioned.

Even the pagans understood that, for one of them commented that it is impossible for an old man to be at peace, be content, and spend his years waiting patiently for death unless he has a good conscience.[1] They adopted these principles: that those who lived evil and disordered lives are summoned just as if God were sitting on the bench and said to them, 'You must now give an account.' That is always how the wicked, even when not being prosecuted, suffer affliction and gnawing anxiety. So what is left? A man, that pagan says, must always have a good conscience.[2] And he adds that

[1] This reference is to a passage in Plato's *Republic* (I, v, 330e-331a)—*M.E.*
[2] Cf. Plato, *Republic* I, v, 331a.—*M.E.*

a good conscience engenders hope and looks toward immortal life. Even though he did not possess a certain testimony of that, he did have some understanding of it. So he is saying that if a man has lived a life of integrity, that fact gives him good hope that when he comes before God, he will be able to present himself boldly. That hope, he says, sustains hearts and is like a delicious, refreshing drink that satisfies a man. And then he especially calls that hope, as I have explained it, the nurse of old age.[3] Therefore, the nurse of old age is hope. Those are good principles.

But since we must not be ashamed to learn from those poor blind pagans who did not know God, so must we consider in what respect they failed. They started out on the right path, but then they went astray, for they took the figure for the body and the substance. That is what happens if we seek a dependable hope in what we have lived in a saintly way in all purity. Alas, who of us can testify that he has satisfied his duty in every respect? We are far from doing so. For whatever affection and desire we may have to walk in obedience to God, we are always faltering and taking many false steps. Consequently, if we declare one thing in favour of God, there will be a thousand to the contrary, so that we do not know what to think. So we must look for a better foundation for our hope. We must walk in integrity so that we can declare before God and his angels that there is no pretence in us and that we have tried to walk in accordance with the rule set before us. Beyond that, we must rest in his mercy so that he will supply what we lack and not impute to us the many vices that remain in us. For those who have trusted in their virtues in this way have shown that that could not accompany them to the grave.

One of them, who was greatly renowned for his prowess and magnanimity, when faced with death and driven by despair to kill

[3] Cf. Plato, *Republic* I, v, 331a.—*M.E.*

himself, said, 'And what is virtue? It is a lot of empty talk.'[4] Why did he say that? They were steeped in the foolish presumption that they could do much on their own but did not realize that if they pursued virtue, they were still very far from achieving it and that God had to draw near with his mercy to supply what that virtue lacked. That is how arrogance brought them down. That is what happens to all those who have confidence in their own persons. As for us, let us realize that our hope can have no virtue or strength except in God's grace. And that grace of God manifests itself in two ways. On the one hand, it appears when he receives us in mercy and, on the other, when he at the same time governs us in such a way by his Holy Spirit that we desire to do right and do it, although we do it only partially. In any case, that point is continued by God in the statement that hope is the nurse of old age. Therefore, provided we realize what we must hope in, from whom our hope must come, and what it must consist of, we know hope will be a good nurse for our old age and serve us until we die.

It is not, then, without cause that God promises Abraham he will die in peace and full of years. Now when God promises, we must conclude that the matter is in his hand. God does not promise what each of us can do for himself, what we can acquire by our own industriousness, what we have the natural capacity for. It is true that everything would still come from him, for we are nothing but his creatures, but when God promises us one thing or another,

[4] Calvin is here recalling a certain tradition about the figure of Brutus, as he had already done when commenting on the Psalms (1557): 'Brutus…, being of the sect of the Stoic Philosophers, spoke excellently of the virtue and providence of God and magnified it; yet seeing himself finally conquered by Anthony, he exclaimed that everything he had believed about virtue was only words in the air and true foolishness and that all the trouble a person went to to live uprightly and virtuously was only lost because fortune dominates in human affairs' (cf. Calvin, *Psalms*: 2, p. 35, on Psalm 73; CO 31, col. 674.)—*M.E.*

it is understood that we are destitute of it and that we could not obtain it except as a gift or by grace.

Therefore, when Abraham is told he would die in peace, it means that man could not be sustained by hope or have an unimpeded desire to present himself to God if it were not given to him from on high. That is a special blessing and privilege that God gives his children when they die full of years. Why so? For, as I have already said, we cannot hope unless God favours us. And does that emanate from us? Can we acquire his favour by our merits? It is absolutely certain that we acquire it through his free and abounding liberality. So we must realize that this gift comes from him. For who will walk on his own in such a way that his conscience bears witness that he has wanted to serve God? It is true that among pagans there were many who enjoyed an enviable reputation and were held in high regard by men. But it is certain they never would have possessed wholeness or purity if God had not chosen them for himself; they already had to be under the guidance of his Holy Spirit and had to have faith. Now what does faith mean if not that we have been regenerated by God's Spirit? And that Spirit is called the Spirit of justice (cf. *Isa.* 28:6), the Spirit of equity and everything good (cf. *Neh.* 9:20). We must, therefore, conclude that in every way God is doing us a great good when we are able to die in peace and be buried full of years.

On that point, let us acknowledge that men's condition is cursed until God draws his people, his elect, apart from the general population and so adopts them by his Holy Spirit and by the faith of our Lord Jesus Christ that they are able to live in peace among themselves. Now, as I have already said, although men are like wild animals and forget who they are and are so stupid because of the many things they covet that they are blind to reason, judgment, knowledge of God and their salvation Yet when men are thus given over to excesses, they do not enjoy what is their good, properly speaking. If you give little children what they desire, they will not know whether it is good or bad. They will eat food, even stuffing themselves until they pop, if they get what they want. Then they will sleep and run and play, but their minds are still so blunted that they do not have the good sense to say, 'I have a very happy life; I am enjoying a great blessing.' So let us not think that a man is enjoying the good things God bestows upon him until he guides him by his Spirit and causes him to taste his goodness.

Now we see that fault in a small child, but it is even greater in us. Let us take the case of a thirty-year-old man who is highly esteemed, very well off and well spoken of, in good health, and enjoys life. If he is so comfortable with that that he has no fear of God, does not think about the life of heaven, and is always concerned about the things he wants, the desires of the flesh now entice him to abandon himself to them without shame or fear, and then if he still burns with greed and wants to possess even more, how will he, I ask you, enjoy the good things he already has? That is a picture of the young people who still have some time before them, who are at the height of well-being, such as they think of it. And even though God deals with them for fifteen or twenty years in such a way that it can be said their lives are happy, decline is obliged to come, bringing with it regrets, sorrows, groanings, and apprehensions.

As a result, we see there is no felicity, only unhappiness, until one's conscience is at peace. And again we must mention the pagans at this point, for God has spoken through their mouths to make us doubly ashamed if we do not recognize the principles they have taught us, poor blind people living in darkness that they are.[5] It is true they have much debated what man's principal good is and

---

[5] Like Facin, Erasmus or Bucer, Calvin recognizes a quasi-divine wisdom in some ancient philosophers: God has spoken through Plato, Cicero, Seneca, and some others...—*M.E.*

how it might be attained, and the result was—and they are resolute in it—that a person must have a heart at peace, composed and
temperate; otherwise the person is unhappy, and, as I have said, we
are all aware of that unless our minds are occupied with erroneous
and false ideas. In any case, even though we all make mistakes,
there remains some glimmer by which we catch sight of what fades
away and escapes us. If we possess such peace, we have a treasure,
as I have said, which we cannot possibly appreciate enough.

We must now remember what has already been discussed,
namely, that this peace cannot come from a good conscience, in the
sense Peter himself uses this word (cf. *1 Pet.* 3:21). When he points
out the fruit of baptism, when he points out the assurance we have
of our salvation, he is saying, 'If we have a good answer, let our
consciences answer before God and absolve us.' But here we must
part ways with the poor pagans and profane peoples, who have
not been instructed in God's school. From their perspective, what
does a good conscience consist in? In their virtues and deeds of
prowess, in their merits, in their goodness, and in everything that
men prize. That being the case, God allows them to fall into ruin.
We must always return to what Scripture says: that peace comes
from faith.[6] So when we realize that God wanted to be reconciled
to us in the person of our Lord Jesus Christ and that he exhorts
us daily to receive and accept that blessing, it is so that we will be
at peace with him, that he will be a father to us, and that we will
be reckoned as his children. He then by his Holy Spirit engraves
that testimony in our hearts, seals it, and shows us that we are truly
under his guidance, that he has given us the power to be displeased
with our vices and withdraw from this world so we can aspire after
him. When we have that testimony, we then have the peace Paul
speaks of, that peace which guides us in such a way that we have

[6] There is no biblical text that states specifically that 'peace comes from faith,' but
Luke 7:50 comes to mind.—*M.E.*

something to boast about even in the midst of the afflictions and miseries which could otherwise overwhelm us (cf. *Phil.* 4:7). It is also then that we know God's presence in such a way that we do not lose courage, but he governs our sorrows in such a way that he gives them some purpose. So when we have that kind of affirmation of God's goodness and when he keeps his promise to us, even though he does so only partially, we know that we will never be in doubt until we come to the full enjoyment of what we are waiting for.

Now we must note that this peace is chiefly known in death. But we can still be at peace while we have yet some bit of road to travel. But when we have been reduced to silence, we must go to God and be removed from this world. That is how God reveals whether we possess a true, well-grounded faith. For not only does that faith resist at that time, but it also troubles us, and there is even worse for unbelievers, for they have to wage war on two fronts when it comes to death. One is that it is hard for them to leave this world, like having their entrails torn out. For they cannot say with confidence, 'We are waiting for a better life.' So the more they are attached to this life, the harder and bitterer death is for them, and they even have a horror of it. For it is only a matter of existing, as they say. And that is true, but they are mistaken because they do not know what true existence is, that it is only a shadow of the existence here below[7] and that we must be restored so we will no longer be subjected to the corruption which is in us. Now, be that as it may, the poor unbelievers are so attached to this world that they can only leave it with great anguish, as if they were being dismembered, drawn and quartered by horses, as the saying goes.

And there is this other point: at this time they are gladly and keenly aware that they must appear before the Judge. It is true that

---

[7] Calvin still has Plato in mind, to whom he has just alluded. Cf. the myth of the cave, *Republic*, liv. VII, in particular § i-iii, 514a-518b.—*M.E.*

throughout their lives they have indeed attributed to God some authority and pre-eminence, but the fact remains that they have convinced themselves to believe that they will give a good account and God will spare them. And then they shut him out of their minds and bury every recollection of his majesty and righteousness, so far as they can. But in death they are obliged to be confined and realize: 'Here is God, who is calling me, and I cannot escape his hand, for he is righteous. But who am I?' That is how unbelievers are struck with double horror when they face death.

Now the faithful are advised to be strangers in this world (cf. *Heb.* 11:13; *1 Pet.* 2:11). And that is why we must practise this teaching early on if we are not to be caught by surprise. For when we want our dwelling to be in this world, when we are deeply plunged into its ways, it is certain that death will come at our great regret. Thus, let us remember this lesson to move on and keep on going as men who have a journey to make, not as those who have a fixed residence here. So much for that point.

Now about coming before our Judge. We can come before him with our heads raised, for this privilege is granted to believers while they await the day of the Lord (cf. *Titus* 2:13). Why? Because God has adopted us as his children (cf. *Rom.* 8:15; *Eph.* 1:5). If we did not have that certainty, it is certain we would be trembling and languishing, indeed we would be experiencing only dread and trepidation. But when we know God has chosen us to be his children, we come boldly to him, as to our father (cf. *Deut.* 32:6; *John* 14:6; *Rom.* 1:7). And how do we know that? By the witness of the gospel. And since he engraves that testimony on us by his Holy Spirit, and even though we are weak and there is a great residue of our vices within us, nonetheless, when he gives us a desire to walk in fear of him and approach him, even haltingly, that is how faith or unbelief shows itself principally in the presence of death. But in the meantime, believers always receive the fruit of what they have received and embraced of God's promises and because they have held him as their Father and have been open to the grace he was offering them. That, then, is what we have to remember about this passage.

So we see that God did indeed defer his promise in order not to bring it to conclusion as soon as Abraham would have liked. He even put it off for four hundred years. That was a long time, and it could weary a man who had already been tested by diverse hardships and even suffered much. During that time, God does not abandon him at all, for he gives him what cannot be prized enough, namely, a good old age. In other words, he will have the witness within himself: that by wanting to serve God, he is consoled and rejoices because he is persuaded that he will never be disappointed by persevering until the end, since he will die in peace. That, then, is how God gives Abraham an earnest of what he has promised him despite the fact he does not immediately come into full possession of it.

Now what is said about our father is pertinent for us, and we must use it. So let us learn to yield to God's good will when it comes to the fulfilment and execution of all his promises, as we said at some length yesterday. But when receiving this way the blessings God provides, let us not be stupid, for that is often the reason for our fits of anger, our grumblings, our impatience and rebellion. In short, we often give up everything because we do not take advantage of the helps God gives us. Like poor animals, we trample on the good things he does for us, those things which should make known to us the grace which is still partially hidden. So let us learn to savour the blessings God bestows upon us so that we will not be rebuked for putting them out of mind and for senselessly abusing them, but as often as our Lord confirms in us what we hope for and what he promised, let us say this: 'This is God giving me a partial indication that I have not hoped in him in vain and that I am depending on his word, for this is confirmation.' So let us gather together all of God's exhortations and all the helps and training he gives us, since he knows that we gravely need them for languishing in this world and that if we are to do that, we must be armed and fortified to resist all trials and temptations. That, in summary, is what we have to remember.

Now, Abraham is told that he will depart to be with his fathers. That is a common expression in holy Scripture (cf. *1 Chron.* 17:11; *Gen.* 47:30; *Deut.* 31:16; *2 Sam.* 7:12), but let us note that that did not give him much consolation unless he was separated from the rank and file. He had had fathers who were of little worth, for we have seen that all his house was corrupt, that idols were worshipped, and that true religion had been expelled and banished. If Abraham had been gathered unto his fathers who had been alienated from God, what good would that have served? But, as I have said, God used that common expression for death and distinguished Abraham from unbelievers, as if saying, 'You must die, as is inevitable for men, but peace is a singular privilege not given to all. But be content with the death which I am reserving for you and, being founded on the hope you have in me, you will depart this world and come with uplifted face, knowing that I will accept you, not rigorously, but with grace and paternal favour.' Moreover, we must always remember that death is a frightful thing for us, from a natural perspective, as it should be.

And that is when we also see how lost we are, as it is said in Ecclesiastes, but the writer is rebuking men's vanity: 'Who knows whether the breath of man is immortal or whether the breath of each person is mortal?' (Cf. *Eccles.* 3:21.) In other words, do we know whether our spirits are immortal or whether they are like those of animals, which we judge to be mortal, which we believe will perish and pass away with the body? Those words point out the vanity and falseness that exist in us when we are frightened by death, which we will always be unless we have assurance when coming before God with accurate knowledge.

And even the wicked knew that. Take Balaam. He was a deceiver who would sell his tongue or put it out for hire (cf. *Num.* 22-23), if he could. God constrains him to bless his people at a time he wanted to curse them for the reward he was being offered (cf. *Num.* 22:12). In any case, God still has to force out of him this plea: 'Let me die the death of the upright' (cf. *Num.* 23:10). There you have a liar, a henchman of the devil who is forced to confess that all the felicity that God keeps hidden like a treasure for his children is that they can die in peace and with a good conscience. Here we have this wretch who wants to be able to die the death of the upright, and the wicked man is excluded from it because he is filled only with betrayal. We even see that he destroyed, so far as he could, God's people with his evil counsel to have pagan women mixed among the children of Israel. Now even though he showed contempt for God that way in an effort to falsify God's infallible truth, he must nonetheless confess that the only important thing is to die the death of the upright and have an end that is like theirs. So because this is of such significance, let us be more attentive to it.

Everyone will indeed say, 'We have to think about the end'; but when we say that aloud, it then seems we have conspired to distance ourselves from that knowledge that God had engraved, as it were, on our nature so that no one wishes to think about death. It is a very disturbing subject. As a result, we cannot be happy about it unless we forget our vulnerability and the heavenly inheritance which God has promised us. Consequently, that is what we should consider principally. If we do not realize our vulnerability and humble ourselves and condemn ourselves for our vices, we will be attached to this world and subsequently will not think of God as our Judge; we will not walk in fear of him and submit to the teaching he gives us. As a result, the promise of eternal salvation, which we must know is certain for us in heaven, will be meaningless. So let us take note of the difference between the children of God and the wicked.

Moreover, so that we will be able to be present in peace on the Day of the Lord, let us realize that at that time our Lord Jesus Christ will be our Judge. Otherwise, we would not be able to find the rest which would satisfy us, for God's majesty will always terrify us. Consequently, our Lord Jesus Christ must come before. That is why he was ordained Judge of the world (cf. *Acts* 10:42), and our Judge himself will be our Advocate (cf. *1 John* 2:1). So we know the Father has established him as his lieutenant and intended for the office of Judge to belong to him so that we may know we cannot be disowned or rejected inasmuch as he has gained the forgiveness of our sins and given it value by interceding for us before his Father (cf. *Rom.* 8:24, 34). That is how we can be numbered among those who Paul says are waiting for the coming of the Redeemer, knowing that he will not be their Judge to condemn them, but that they are already absolved by grace and that he will not call them to account (cf. *Titus* 2:13), for their sins are already buried by his obedience, and all their blemishes are washed away by the blood he shed.

Now because Abraham was still able to find it strange that God prolonged for such a long time the execution of what he had promised him, he nonetheless adds a reason for not giving him the land immediately and postponing it for four hundred years: 'for the iniquity of the Amorites is not yet full,' he says. On the surface it would seem that that was not to the point. Does it follow, if the iniquity of the peoples among whom Abraham lived was not completed in his time, that Abraham has to be deprived of his inheritance? But God shows him that he wants him to continue to trust him for what he has promised, namely, that he will enjoy his inheritance in the knowledge that it has come to him rightly and worthily and without any wrong or injustice. That, then, is what God had in mind when saying that the iniquity of the Amorites was not yet full. But in a more general way he also wanted to advise Abraham that we must not measure God's works by our own understanding. Why not? We know how small our minds are, and when we get one idea in mind, there are ten others that we are incapable of understanding that do not find their way in. That is because God has his own counsel, which is infinitely incomprehensible. That, then, is an infinite perfection of God's counsel as concerns the government and dominion he maintains over the world. And will our minds be able to contain that? We see what is said in Job and by the prophet Isaiah, that God will not deign to relax his hand (cf. *Job* 12:9-10) when he intends to encompass heaven and earth (cf. *Isa.* 41:20; 66:1-2). That is not to say that God has a hand to take hold of something the way men do; it is Scripture's way of showing us that God will be able to keep his hand closed and the whole world, both heaven and earth, will be enclosed in it like a small speck of dust that we might hold in our hand.

Now at this point how presumptuous would we be if we wanted to be equal to him or have him fit our standard of measurement? That is what Abraham is shown as if God were saying to him: 'You could find it strange that I am not establishing you in the land so that you are its lord and master from the first day. My way of working is different from that of men and they cannot understand it. Why not? You do not know the extent of my patience. Even though you see that the Amorites, among whom you are living, are wicked and perverse, I still intend to support them for four hundred years. That would never enter your mind or your comprehension.' For how would we patiently endure those we would be seeing living lives of unbounded excess for four hundred years? We could never do it. Consequently, God is here showing us the difference between his way of governing and the imaginative ways which come out of our heads and natures. In that way he exhorts Abraham to remain patient and not to come to rash conclusions. That is what we have to remember about this passage, namely, that when we want to reduce God to our desires and have him conform to our way of thinking, we are intolerably rash. For what harm do we do him? As I have said, let us take into consideration the nature of these judgments, which are abysses that exceed the capacity of the angels of heaven to understand. And how will we, who have with difficultly a miniscule understanding, rise above the world, both heaven and earth? How will we comprehend God's incomprehensible wisdom? His ways, as is said in another passage, are unsearchable (cf. *Rom.* 11:33-34). What is his counsel? Who was his counsellor and so highly placed he could understand his secrets? So let us humble ourselves before such wisdom as God's and be content that he is a just Judge, and let us find very good everything he does, since he is also the Truth. That, I say, is the first thing we have to remember about this passage.

It is true there are other teachings dealing with God's patience, which is strange on the face of it. And in fact, if we had to judge whether God had to support the Amorites the way he did, we would immediately say: 'Must we put up with that? Have we not had enough? Since they are so wicked the air stinks with their iniquities, does God have to delay so long? Does his name have to be blasphemed, and do people have to think that he is asleep in heaven?' That, then, is how we would like for God to make haste if it were up to us to judge.

We now read what is said to Moses: 'You will kill men and women, little children, women and old people, so that nothing will be spared and thats that entire lineage will perish there' (cf. *Num.* 31:17).[8] What? Must God be so barbarous? Why are they

[8] Cf. also 2 Chronicles 36:17, which is closer to Calvin's formulation, but it is no

not made to serve as pitiable slaves? But what is the reason for putting them all to death? That is another way we could blame God if we were his judges. We are like little children. When they are told to do something, they will do it. And then, if they are immediately told to do the contrary, they will say, 'Oh, that is rightly said.' That is the way we are. And that should show us our folly, indeed our madness, when we presume to forge ahead and control God's judgments or to talk back or to question how and why he does whatever he does. Consequently, let us first learn to submit to his wisdom, and then in respect of his patience, let us not find it strange if he delays a long time. On the other hand, if he wishes to thunder from heaven and come with a weapon in hand to reduce all to confusion, let us not blame him for that and think he suddenly grows hot with anger and acts too hastily. Why not? Because he has exercised greater patience than we can judge and understand. Let us be content with that. And in the meantime, let us be careful not to abuse his patience and in any way envy the wicked as God spares them.

That, then, is for the end, the time when God will not strike us with heavy blows, and it is to avoid that that we are not encouraged to be easily familiar with him, as Paul informs us that the wicked are heaping upon themselves a store of wrath (cf. *Rom.* 2:5) and daily adding to an already heavy burden when they treat God's patience lightly. For it is certain that because he shows he is good and withholds his hand in order not to chastise us according to our deserts, he gives us time to come to him as he calls us, even enticing us with his gentleness and graciousness. If we then use that time to become even more wicked, if we become bold enough to kick against him, alas, must such ingratitude not be punished doubly? So while God spares us, let us be wise to recognize our sins and not be like the Amorites, who are spoken of here. And

longer Moses who is speaking.—*M.E.*

while we watch the wicked act out their triumphs, let us wait with our father Abraham, though it be for four hundred years. For they will always come to give an account when wickedness reaches its height and they provoke God's wrath, as we have said; and for our part, let us not be so restless and impatient, but let us wait for God to work, indeed in his way and according to his purpose, and not to our liking, which could be for immediate action.

Now let us bow before the majesty of our gracious God in acknowledgment of our faults, praying that we will be so touched to the quick by them that we will weep and groan before his majesty, and while we examine the kind of lives we live, let us be ashamed, but in such a way that we are encouraged by the sure hope by which he has promised to receive us in mercy and has even shown us that he had already received us into his immortality inasmuch as he was pleased to give us some portion of his Spirit. And whatever weakness we have, let us continue to overcome all the trials that might shake us since we have Jesus Christ as our pledge, who will not fail us when we fully lean on him. So let us all say, God almighty, heavenly Father...

74

A Smoking Furnace and a Burning Lamp: Tests of Faith in God's Covenant

Thursday, 21 March 1560

And it came to pass, that, when the sun went down, and it was dark, behold a smoking furnace, and a burning lamp that passed between those pieces. In the same day the Lord made a covenant with Abram, saying, Unto thy seed have I given this land, from the river of Egypt unto the great river, the river Euphrates: The Kenites, and the Kenizzites, and the Kadmonites, And the Hittites, and the Perizzites, and the Rephaims, And the Amorites, and the Canaanites, and the Girgashites, and the Jebusites (Gen.15:17-21).

WE SAW YESTERDAY that when God does not punish the wicked and those who are completely reprobate as soon as we would like, we must not think that he has forgotten to act as Judge, but we must realize he is very patient, as he says in holy Scripture (cf. *Isa.* 34:6). And that is why he says through the prophet Isaiah that his thoughts are not our thoughts and are as far apart as heaven and earth (cf. *Isa.* 55:8-9). The people of Israel were disconsolate because they received no promise that eases their troubles and perplexities. Now God rebukes them, saying, 'Are you measuring me by your standard? I am far from being like you. You are vengeful and seething with your passions.

A little bit of nothing riles you and you immediately raise your hand to strike your enemies. But I want my clemency and goodness to be known inasmuch as I bear with sinners and wait to see if they will return to the right path.' So we see on the one hand that the wicked and despisers of God exceed all limits of propriety and yet are at peace and at ease. Let us not think God is asleep in heaven, but the times and the seasons belong to him. Consequently, we must honour him by being completely persuaded that he will know how to punish them and bring them back in line at the appropriate time. As for us, when he delays his judgments of us, let us not abuse his patience, for that would heap upon our heads a wealth of wrath, for we make our sins worse when we deal triflingly with God, assuming he will have pity on us and is waiting to see if there will be some change or repentance in us.

Moreover, we still have to note about this passage that God did not intend to exterminate the Amorites from the land which was assigned to them until they had corrupted it to the point that they were unbearable. We must keep in mind the psalm's principle, namely, that God has established the boundaries of all nations (cf. *Psa.* 74:17). It is true that if the human race had persisted in maintaining such union, as it should have, the division we see would not exist. But because confusion came about by human error, God immediately set limits for countries so that everyone might live in his own region as if he had been placed there.

Now if we can live in the fear of God where he has placed us, it is certain he will always preserve the order he has established. So whenever peoples are exterminated, it is because God cannot tolerate the iniquities they have committed. It is because of their ingratitude that they are deprived of the blessings he bestowed upon them. In the same way, a vassal is thrown off the land he held as a fief if he rebels against his superior or commits some act worthy of being stripped of his possessions. God gave them consideration. That is why God did not immediately expel the Amorites and their ilk from the world or the land of Canaan. In this way he threatens his people that the land will spew them out if they ever live wickedly in it. That comparison is very appropriate, for it indicates that the land receives us and rejoices, so to speak, to support us and nourish us and provide for all our other needs while we inhabit it as we pay homage to the one who created it for our use. But if we are evil and perverse creatures, our stench has to be unbearable and the earth has to be offended and spew us out. It is like a man who is sick to his stomach and everything has to come up. So God is telling us that the land cannot tolerate our iniquities and must purge itself of them if we do not inhabit it and enjoy it appropriately, that is, in fear of him.

Now we still have to note that God says the iniquity of the Amorites has not yet reached its height. With those words he indicates there will be no repentance. And yet Scripture says that when he delays and does not exercise his rigor at first, he is testing whether those who have fallen short will repent. Those two things might seem to contradict each other, but they belong together when we learn to worship God's deep judgments and not be too curious to inquire into what is beyond all our abilities. God knows quite well what is to happen to us, for everything is present to him. We must not imagine future and past times for him, for everything is before his eyes. Consequently, he knows those who are to convert and those who are incorrigible. He marked them long ago. So why does he wait for them? It is not that he is in suspense or in doubt, but it is to aggravate their guilt and remove every excuse from them. Sometimes he will say that he expects of us good fruit and that we only embitter him (cf. *Hos.* 9:10), not that we can thwart his intention, for he is not like a mortal man, who imagines things that will not happen, for that is characteristic of us to show we are guilty of having cheated and deceived him.

Therefore, let us note that when Scripture says God invites and exhorts to repentance those whom he spares and gives time to return to him and the opportunity to do so as he deals with them gently and with all kindness, it is not because he is trying as if the matter were in doubt, but it is so that men will be silenced and unable to complain that they were prevented from repenting, that God hastened to punish them as soon as they committed a sin so they would be lost and destroyed. Consequently, so that men will not engage in such wailing, God leaves them alone for a while. If they perish in their filth, it is to make their condemnation greater; if they grow worse and become bolder because God spares them, their ingratitude is the more villainous, for they have grossly misused his patience. Moreover, if they submit, it is a singular gift of God, and at that time he makes what he has given them effective, but everything proceeds from him, from the free gift he offers to his elect.[1] That, then, is what we still need to remember about this passage.

On that point, it is said, in addition to the darkness Moses has already mentioned, that there is a smoking oven or a smoking furnace, and the darkness was coming from it in part. Yet there was a burning lamp passing between the pieces of the heifer and the ram and the goat which Abraham had cut into pieces. So there is a lamp in the midst of the furnace, in the midst of the dark smoke, which moves with brightness among the pieces. Moses adds that God then made a covenant with Abraham, promising to give him the land in which he was to be a stranger at the time, and names ten peoples in particular who will be removed from it so that Abraham's lineage may inhabit it.

---

[1] Perceptible here is the system of double predestination, which permits Calvin to explain men's suffering and their feeling of abandonment. Either the former are the elect and these sufferings serve to silence them and teach them patience and trust or the latter are reprobate for all eternity and no repentance is effective. Cf. *Institutes* III, xxi-xxii.—*M.E.*

Now for the first, we have to consider the intention of that figure; for as we pointed out earlier, God does not delight in presenting frivolous matters to feed our eyes, but there is always teaching and instruction in all the visible signs he gives. Now instruction cannot exist without the word, but there must be a similarity between the external figure and what God wants to give testimony to. In the case of baptism, we have water, but we need to know that God did not intend for us to wash in it. So the water has within it some property that indicates the power and purpose of baptism. The same is true of the bread and wine of the Lord's Supper, which show that our lives lie completely in our Lord Jesus Christ, in his body and in his blood, and that same principle must be observed in other signs.

Now when God shows Abraham that oven, or that furnace, it is to inform him of some frightful state with the intention of producing horror in him. From another perspective, when he shows him the burning lamp it is to make him rejoice. For we know that afflictions are commonly signified in Scripture by darkness (cf. *Matt.* 25:30) in the same way the prosperity and grace God causes us to feel are signified by light (cf. *Psa.* 89:15). Now on the surface, we have two very different things so that we have a horrible darkness which frightens Abraham, a furnace which spews smoke that disturbs and troubles him. And yet a lamp casts light, but that continues what we have already observed, namely, that God had to deploy his grace in such a way on the people he had elected that he still used many vexations and troubles and afflictions to ally death with life. So he demonstrated that in the vision we have heard recounted. And in fact, he often calls the servitude of the people in Egypt an iron furnace: 'I have taken you from the servitude of Egypt, as from an iron or brass furnace' (cf. *Deut.* 4:20). He calls it that to show it was to burn and consume a hundred times the people who had been detained there. For we understand that fire, when it is so intense in a furnace, burns and consumes iron, stones, and steel and all other materials, even though the furnace is made only of earth and brick. And what will be the result if it is made of iron? Will its heat not be more intense? So God indicates that the condition of his people will be like that in Egypt (cf. *Gen.* 15:13). But before that happens, Abraham is warned so that he can teach his children and his successors so they will all be prepared to endure these afflictions and find nothing strange about it since God has thus ordained it and their father has borne witness to it.

Now we know it is expedient for us that God prepare us well before hand so we will not be confused when evil assails us, for being unprepared is why we are weak and each of us is caught napping, as we say. But God instructs us that we must experience some such condition or other so as not to end up being novices when confronting evil and then have to struggle against it in earnest, for we will have learned about it in God's school. Even so, God makes it rather clear that we must be like sheep led to the slaughter every day (cf. *Psa.* 44:22; *Rom.* 8:36) and be conformed to the death of our Lord Jesus Christ (cf. *Rom.* 6:5), and that our lives must be hidden because they rest in hope (cf. *Rom.* 8:24), because they rest in various conditions, so that all our wicked desires will be put to death. So although holy Scripture is filled with that teaching, as much as with any other, and although we have it hammered into our ears every day so that we think we have learned it, the fact is that when it comes to putting it into practice, it seems we have never heard mention of it. So we must even more pay attention to this passage, for even though God considered the ancient people, namely, that lineage which was to come from Abraham, he has nonetheless given us a picture of the state of his church. So let us realize that in order to be members of our Lord Jesus Christ, we must be surrounded and pressured by troubles and difficulties. In other words, as we pass through this world, we must be afflicted, in distress and in anguish so that we will fear on the one hand, and be buffeted about on the other. We must be resolved to face that.

In brief, let us learn that for good reason God is here comparing our condition with a smoking furnace, for it is not enough for us to be heated in the furnace, but the smoke is added so that our fleshly senses will be confused and we will not know which way to turn when it comes to being more incited to take refuge in God. That is how the people of Israel were taught by the vision given to Abraham. But that teaching is general among us today because the church will, until the end of time, have to be subjected to many outrages, abuses, extortions, and acts of violence, and it will always have to be in fear, in perplexity and mental anguish. It is true that sometimes we will have times of reprieve and rest, but we will always have to be ready to confront hardship and persecution. And whenever God wishes to test us, our faith must be strong if we are to remain steadfast in the midst of the darkness, no matter how black it is. But the burning lamp has abolished the fear and hardship produced by the smoking darkness. In other words, no matter the situation, God does not allow us to be consumed, even though the smoke is great and violent and it seems that the fire is going to swallow and devour everything. Now God's sparing us is not the result of our nature, for we are less than straw, when all is said and done (cf. *2 Kings* 19:25-26; *Psa.* 35:5). And if we were gold and silver, there would still be so much dross in us that we would be skimmed off. That is why our Lord says through his prophet Isaiah: 'I have not refined you like gold and silver, for from that some good portion of pure metal is drawn' (cf. *Isa.* 48:10). Also, gold and silver would be useless if they had not passed through the furnace. It is true that ore is much reduced, but what is got from it is good and pure and can be put to good use. If we, on the other hand, were tested that way, nothing would remain, for there is only scum and waste in us, and we are so far from being like gold and silver that we are straw, and even less. We are nothing but vanity so that when man is placed on one side of a balance and vanity on the other, as the psalm says, vanity will win, for we are less than nothing, and God declares it (cf. *Psa.* 62:9).

So if we had to be passed through a burning furnace now, what would be the outcome? If the furnace burns very hard and green wood and even burns stones and other materials and reduces them to ashes, what would become of us and our frailty? Consequently, God is obliged to work miraculously when we have to pass through so many hardships while we nonetheless continue to remain in our state. On the other hand, though we have the smoke which painfully blinds our eyes, not only stinging and penetrating them, we still have some light, for we know that God guides us and will bring all our afflictions to a good conclusion and provide life in the midst of death. Since we know that, we still have an inestimable privilege, but it is also a miracle of God, for we cannot say our nature deserves all that.

The vision Moses had is completely related to that. When the people were to be redeemed, he sees God in the midst of a burning bush, yet the bush is not consumed (cf. *Exod.* 3:2). There are thorns that have no endurance when they are set fire to, for the fire is throughout; nonetheless the burning bush remains whole and is not consumed. Why not? God is in the midst of it. Now let us pay close attention to that vision and we will find what I have already pointed out, namely, on the one hand, that when a fire is set and causes such fear and horror that we think we are going to die a hundred deaths and nothing will remain of us, yet in the midst of the fire, God will keep us safe with himself. That is also why he appeared to Moses in the midst of the bush. If the fire had been burning the bush, it is certain it would have been consumed, but because God is in the midst of it and exerts his power, the bush remains and the fire does not harm it, even though it is completely engulfed. That can be our abysmal situation, as seen from the outside, and we will appear to be a lost people. Moreover, when we are condemned that way by the world and even by our own thoughts, we will never fall without landing on our feet, provided God dwells in our midst and lets us sense the power of his presence and help. So let the fire burn. We will remain whole, whatever the circumstance. That, then, in brief, is what we have to remember about this present vision.

Now let us take such advantage of this teaching that, in the midst of all our afflictions, the first thing we will know is that we must pass that way because God has placed us in it. The reason we often grumble and grieve when we have to endure some misfortune is that we do not train our thoughts in this council of God by which he governs his church. For would we dare to rebel against God and enter into a dispute or lawsuit with him? But when we do him the honour of conducting ourselves according to his good pleasure and will, it is certain we will be at peace in the midst of all our afflictions. For he has declared once, and indeed shown us by a visible sign, that he wants us to be tested as if by fire. So let us bow our heads humbly and honour him by being his willing subjects. Now we must take one more step and not only offer our shoulders to receive the burden which God imposes upon us but also to endure being often daunted and dismayed, deprived of counsel, in such perplexity and distress that we do not know what is to become of us. So there must be times when smoke clouds our eyes. And in that way, God wants to put our faith to a better test. So let us not be defeated by the trials which might come upon us both in mind and in body, that is, when God gives no sign of helping us and we see no way of escape. Even so, let us know that he can give us light during those dark times. In fact, provided we keep our eyes open and meditate on his promises, he gives us light, and the outcome will become evident in time, if we trust in him. That, in short, is what we have to remember about that vision.

Now at the same time it is said that God makes his covenant with Abraham and promises him the land of these ten tribes which are named here. We must not separate what is included here. So even though God makes his covenant with Abraham, he does not do so to exempt him from the condition that we have already mentioned. Thus, even though God receives Abraham at such an honourable level, he and his lineage will always be burned, in a manner of speaking, that is, they will be attached to such hardship that they will seem to be surrounded by fire and smoke. It is true that the hope God gives him, namely, that the outcome of their miseries will be blessed, is here made known by that burning lamp which he shows him. And here we have to acknowledge, on the other hand, God's wondrous goodness when he condescends this way to become, as it were, a peer and companion with a mortal man, who was Abraham in himself. Even though he possessed excellent virtues, he was even more obligated to God for them, for he had not acquired them and they were not his by nature. Even so, here we have a poor creature, a worm of the earth. Yet God wishes to ally himself with him. In what way? As if there were two persons who would say: 'Come now, let us deal together.' That ought to astonish and delight us thoroughly when we consider that God is making a covenant between himself in his majesty and us and placing himself in that relationship. And what is more, we have to remember what we talked about yesterday, namely, that when sacrifices were made in ancient times and animals were cut in two, it was a kind of proclamation: 'If I bear false witness and am deceptive, let me be dismembered in this way; let me be punished in such an unnatural way that everyone will learn from the example.' That is what that division of the animals meant when sacrifices were made. Now none of that is compatible with God's majesty, for in the first place everything he promises is infallible truth, and he himself is truth. Moreover, he can subject himself to no punishment, but we understand even better what I have already mentioned, namely, that in order to conform to our smallness, he comes down to us, as if he were forgetting what is proper to his majesty. Now this does not open him up to scorn, for he is far from diminishing his glory when he displays such great kindness that it shines brilliantly, for if he appeared before us in his terrible power, it is certain he would not be as glorified as he is when he is pleased to have pity on us this way and forget and omit nothing needful for us and when he prefers to diminish his exalted state and relate to our senses. Therefore, we can indeed say that God lowers himself when he is pleased to ally himself with us, but his glory is in no way obscured or lessened when he does so.

Now it is true that the word 'covenant' will not occur every time, but what is said of Abraham here extends to the entire body of the church in general. Now there is an infinite number of passages where it is said that God allied himself with the people of Israel (cf. *Gen.* 9:16; 17:7; *Exod.* 31:16; *Jer.* 31:31; *Ezek.* 16:60; etc.). As for us, as the apostle shows in the Epistle to the Hebrews, we have a covenant which is better and more excellent because it is ratified by the blood of Jesus Christ (cf. *Heb.* 7-10). Thus, God not only allied himself once and for all with Abraham, but also with his whole race and his successors at the same time. When he gave us his only Son, he allied himself with us again. In what way? It is not without cause that our Lord Jesus Christ says, 'This is my blood which ratifies the new and permanent covenant forever.' For we call the Old Testament this covenant that God had made under the law because it had to grow old, not in its substance, for what would the covenant be if it were not permanent? It is said that God is the God of Abraham, Isaac, and Jacob (cf. *Exod.* 3:6). So they have to be alive even today. And what is their salvation founded upon if not upon the covenant that God made with them that way? As for substance, that is how we have one and only one covenant.

But in the matter of ceremonies and figures, that covenant was old and was obliged to become outdated. But today the covenant God made with us through our Lord Jesus Christ is so new and different that its power does not diminish and cannot go out of date. It is in that covenant that we must observe our God's inestimable goodness, for that is how he limits himself in order to make an agreement with us, as if he were obligating himself party to party, item by item, as when we have to make a compact. One side will say, 'I pledge to do this and that,' and the other will say, 'And I promise to do this and that.' Ought we not to be totally astonished by the grace God shows us by being willing to make an agreement with us? And yet we scarcely think about it, for every day when we come to the sermon, it is certain the covenant God established in the person of his only Son is renewed, for not only is our memory of it refreshed, but at the same time its effect must also be explained. Consequently, we hear not a single word of promise that does not depend on the fact that God wishes to be reconciled to us. And yet, how moved are we by it?

What is more, God has to re-covenant because we, in our disloyalty, daily break the bond by which he joined himself to us. What obligates God that he does not turn his back on us and denounce and disavow us totally? It is certain we do everything we can to alienate ourselves from him, indeed we resist him. If he had taken into consideration our evil intentions and the many offences which provoked him and with which we wage war against him morning and evening, he would have ample occasion to abandon us. He not only continues his covenant with us but remakes it because he sees we are so perverse that we turn our backs on him and break the compact which he made with us. When we cast off his yoke that way, are we any different from perjurers, since we have turned our oaths into lies? Now, as I have said, he still makes reconciliation and seeks only to forgive and forget all our sins. So it must be said there is a horrid brutishness in us since we do not appreciate that goodness and are not completely captivated by it and forget the enticements of Satan, of this world, and of our flesh. Even so, the point of this passage is to show us how obligated we are to God and how gross the enormity of our ingratitude is if we do not know how to take advantage of the blessing that has been offered to us.

Therefore, let us prize this word 'covenant' more highly than we have before, and let us know that in the person of Abraham God wanted to make himself a party with us in order to work his covenant more intimately and show the love he has for us. Now it is true, as I have already mentioned, that using that as a pretext, we resist; for the closer God draws to us, the humbler we must be. And in fact, we have to remember what is said in the psalm, that he is on high, but he looks upon small things and is near to all those who are crushed in spirit (cf. *Psa.* 34:18). It is true that is a strange situation, but it seems we would have to possess wings to fly above the clouds to approach God; but on the contrary, the smaller we are and the more crushed in spirit we are, the nearer we are to his majesty, which is higher than the clouds and the heavens. Therefore, when we hear that God deals with us intimately, we must not be puffed up, and we must not desire to come to him with our heads lifted up proudly. We can indeed lift our heads in confidence, but in every case we must never forget that humility is the true bond that binds us to him.

And the words of the covenant also carry that meaning, for God always reserves for himself the right of Father and adopts us as his children (cf. *Rom.* 8:15; *Gal.* 4:6; *Eph.* 1:5). And then, in addition to the rank of Father, he also reserves for himself lordship and sovereign authority. Therefore, he wants to be feared on the one hand

and honoured with love on the other. Therefore, the more he deals
with us gently to make us gentle, who are wild animals, let us gain
an appreciation for what he has called us to and for the condition
he has called us to. So when God adopts us as his children, what
an honour and dignity he raises us to! We are not worthy of being
called the most contemptible vermin in the world, for those creatures of God remain in their natural state, and there is only every
corruption in us despite the fact God wants us to be his children.
He gives us the power to call loudly and insistently upon him as
our Father, and he does so, as I have said, so that we may be honoured with a free and abundant love that goes with the honour.

There is also fear because of our indifference. God would be
content to be called Father, provided that would be enough for us,
but because we are so unruly and our natures are so rebellious that
while we claim we honour him, we also kick against him inces-
santly. That is why he must call himself Lord and Master (cf. *Jer.*
3:14; *John* 13:13), for he must create within us not only a reverence
for him but also a fear and dread of provoking him.

The covenant, on the one hand, draws us so gently to God that
we can reveal our hearts and our affections as he reveals his, for he
speaks to us as person to person and condescends like one party
obligating himself to another, although he owes us nothing. However, we must always maintain a fear of him, as Psalm 5 says: 'I will
come into your temple in the multitude of your mercy, and in fear
of you I will worship in your holy temple' (cf. *Psa.* 5:7). With that,
David indicates he would not put a foot into God's temple without knowing that God's hand was extended to receive him. That,
then, is the multitude of the mercy God shows us, and his door
is open to allow us to come boldly to him without doubting that
he will receive us with compassion. But that does not prevent us
from worshipping him in fear, and that does not prevent us from
being so confident, through faith, of his love for us that we will

also be afraid and correct our rebellious acts, for there will always be a jackass in us—and I include those whom God regenerates and renews by his Holy Spirit—that is, there will always be in us a great residue of vices. That, then, is what we have to remember about this passage.

Now it is said that God promises Abraham the whole land, from the river of Egypt, that is, the near bank of the Nile, as far as the river Euphrates, which extended to the other side, that is, in the direction of the area from which Abraham had come. For he had come to Chaldea in Mesopotamia into Haran (cf. *Gen.* 11:31), and that region is designated as the land between two rivers, the Tigris and Euphrates. So God here gives the boundaries of the land he promises Abraham's lineage and specifically names ten peoples in order to confirm what he had said, that Abraham's lineage would be multiplied like the sand of the sea and the stars of heaven. He was alone in his house sterile, as his wife. There they are, closed out of any hope of having a lineage. Still, he has the promise that such a multitude will descend from him that the heavens are not as filled with stars as the earth will be filled with his lineage. It would be easier to count the sand of the sea than the number of his descendants. And God makes that known to him when he declares it is not in vain that he spoke that way. Why? If Abraham was to have children and those who were to descend from his race remained fertile, some country possessing a single people would have been enough for him. Now God is not satisfied with that, but he names ten peoples who will be exterminated. Consequently, the number of Abraham's descendants had to be great inasmuch as there is a country large enough in length and breadth for them to inhabit. That, then, is notably why these ten peoples are mentioned.

It is true Abraham had that land promised to him, but we have to remember what we mentioned earlier, namely, that that promise was only a pledge and that that was not God's goal, but it was his goal to confirm Abraham in his grace because that country was given to him only as a secondary gift. So let us note that Abraham did not consider that land to be the principal gift which his successors were to possess. That information is very useful for us, for if we thought God promised Abraham only that piece of land as his inheritance, what would be the result? For if he were like a father to us, our entire hope would be limited to this terrestrial and feeble life. So we must come to a higher understanding and see Abraham as inheritor of heaven. Even so, he still had a sign in this world that God was his Father. That, then, is what we have to observe.

Now it is true that today we do not have what he had, but we have much better, for Jesus Christ has so dedicated the world that God's rest is wherever we are, provided we pay him homage and adore him purely and in simplicity of heart. Therefore, no land is set apart for God's children, and we do not need it and it would not be useful, seeing that our Lord Jesus Christ fills everything with his power and his Holy Spirit, so much that, wherever we may be, the earth is dedicated to our use. It is God's rest, as I said, and already we are enjoying the fact that he is a father to us and we are children to him. So much for that point.

For the second point, Abraham received the promise when he was told: 'I will give you this land,' even though he received it four hundred years after his death. Consequently, he did not look for a present enjoyment of what was given to him, but he clung to God's simple word and died in peace, as he had been told, although he did not see what had been promised (cf. *Gen.* 15:15). In fact, the contrary occurred. He learned that after he had a lineage, it would be driven from that land and live in some foreign country, one even unknown to him. Even knowing that, he is satisfied to have what God promised, for otherwise the covenant would not have been mutual. When it is said that God made a covenant with Abraham with these few words, Moses understands that Abraham made his response so that the covenant would be accepted and concluded. For if Abraham had disdained what God offered him and had rejected it, what would have happened? The covenant would have been offered, but it would have been broken.

Consequently, two things are to be noted in these words of Moses. One is that God speaks, makes an offer, and articulates it. The other is that Abraham then receives what was given him and in this way, by faith, receives possession of the things that were given to him. Therefore, God's truth is the first truth in the covenant, and the second is Abraham's faith. It is notable that God makes the covenant; it is not Abraham's place to begin it. How arrogant we would be to come and ask God to make a covenant and obligate himself to us! Who are we? Moreover, even without considering our unworthiness, instead of approaching him, we will always withdraw. God must take the first step and draw us to himself of his own accord. He has begun. It is up to us to respond 'amen' and trust his free promises and the goodness which he displays toward us. Consequently, just as God shows himself to be kind and generous when he is pleased to receive us into his love and make himself our Father and adopt us as his children, so let us learn not to be unruly or wild, but let us subject ourselves fully to his word and hold to what he says to us as firm, certain, and unfailing. In that way we will be patient, tranquil, and be at peace until the time comes for God to bring to conclusion what we wait and hope for.

Now let us bow before the majesty of our gracious God in acknowledgment of our faults, praying that he will be increasingly pleased to touch us with true repentance and so guide us by his Holy Spirit that throughout our lives we will seek only to subject ourselves fully to him and honour him as is our duty, and, in this way, may our calling be better confirmed. And because we are so far from doing our duty, may he hide and cast out all our faults until he has cleansed us of all the corruptions of our flesh and clothed us in his righteousness. May he grant that grace not only to us but to all the peoples and nations on earth.

75

Sarah and Hagar: Conflict Following a Bad Decision

Friday, 22 March 1560

Now Sarai Abram's wife bare him no children: and she had an hand-
maid, an Egyptian, whose name was Hagar. And Sarai said unto Abram,
Behold now, the LORD hath restrained me from bearing: I pray thee, go
in unto to my maid; it may be that I may obtain children by her. And
Abram hearkened to the voice of Sarai. And Sarai Abram's wife took
Hagar her maid the Egyptian, after Abram had dwelt ten years in the
land of Canaan, and gave her to her husband Abram to be his wife. And
he went in unto Hagar, and she conceived: and when she saw that she had
conceived, her mistress was despised in her eyes (Gen.16:1-4).

THE QUALITIES OF THE SAINTS which are proposed to us as examples ought to be very useful, for we have the assurance that God strengthens his people, no matter how weak they are by nature, so that their lives correspond to their calling. And that is why we ought to be incited to pray to God that what we do not possess by nature, he will grant by grace. And then, in the same way, we ought also to be more resolved to put forth an effort. And despite the fact we are weak and cannot easily give ourselves to God's service and fulfil our duty, we ought to take heart when we see those who show us the way.

But Scripture shows the vices of those who have faithfully served God and have been like living examples of saintliness; that also ought to be for our advantage, for we have ample occasion to lower our heads when we see those who have been incomparably more excellent than we but have nonetheless sometimes stumbled, even gone astray or completely fallen. Such examples ought to teach us to walk with greater care and be on guard so Satan will not take us by surprise.

Moreover, we are also advised that if we do not satisfy our duty in every respect and on every occasion, God will still support us as he has supported us. That is what makes us overcome all our lack of confidence and why we will continue to move forward despite some failure, and why despair will never get the best of us. And that is also why the shortcomings of the saints are placed before us, so that we will be even more on guard for fear the same thing or worse will happen to us. So seeing our weakness, let us learn to find our strength in God.

As at present, Moses recounts a very serious fault committed by Sarah, the mother of all believers, as well as by our father Abraham. In a single act, many offences were committed against God. For one, they violated sacred marriage and perverted what God had established, a thing that was to be inviolable. For God created a woman for the man. He said, 'I will make a helper for him' (cf. *Gen.* 2:18), and not two or three. And then he declared that they will be two in one body (cf. *Gen.* 2:24). Now we find Sarah attempting to change God's arrangement. That is considerable brashness. That shows a severe lack of seriousness, one that works against faith. As we saw earlier, the characteristic of faith is to remain still. It is in peace and quiet, the prophet shows, that we test our trust in God. It is, he says, by not being in a hurry and not being afraid, but by waiting in silence for the outcome God wishes to provide (cf. *Isa.* 30:15). And here is Sarah, impatient, not waiting for what God intends to do, but she wants to move ahead in accordance with her own thinking. Abraham follows suit. So here in this act is another very serious and reprehensible fault, which is that their faith in God was not perfect, as it should have been.

Moreover, they also presume to interpret God's promise. God's truth must remain pure, and we cannot stir into it our thinking as if it were leaven to act upon the whole loaf. So as many fanciful thoughts as we have in our heads, that many corrupt thoughts are there to infect the pure simplicity of God's word.

Now Sarah and Abraham do that and worse. They choose a means to their liking which God did not approve. Now the least we can do when God guides our steps is not to wiggle a finger, so to speak, without his permission. And what do they do? They make their own decision without asking whether it pleases God or whether he condemns it. So Abraham and Sarah committed a lot of offences in a single act. Why is it that the Holy Spirit wanted that to be known until the end of the world? It was not to make us bolder to commit evil, as if we could use Abraham and Sarah as an excuse, but it was to humble us and cause us to walk in fear and be more watchful, as well as to incite us to pray to God and fight more vigorously against all trials. And finally, even though we feel within ourselves such great evil that resists God's will, let us continue to struggle mightily against all tests of our faith, knowing that God will support us if we experience some lack.

In addition, the father of the faithful, who was so exalted by God, was put to shame. It is as if God had set up a scaffold in the middle of his church and had put Abraham on it to make him acknowledge his sin and serve as a shame until the end of the world because of that act.

Now that teaches us that, if we have offended God, we must not make it an evil to bear the shame of our sin and that God's righteousness must be restored. If he chastises us, we must bear that shame even if everybody has accused us, for we gain nothing by resisting him. Thus God's righteousness is to be more precious to us than our own reputations. So let us not act like those who answer contemptuously after committing some crime: 'What will become of my honour? Must I be defamed this way? Do I have to suffer such shame?' God will not enter their thinking. They will not be thanked because they did not lead a thousand to hell because of the scandal they commit and the bad example they set; that will not contribute to their reputation, and yet they will want others to continue to think highly of them. Now we see that God did not spare his servant Abraham, even though he had already established him as the father of the faithful, as he will make known later and we will see in the following chapter (cf. *Gen.* 17:4).

We now have to be specific about what the story contains. It is said that Sarah had neither conceived nor given birth since Abraham had been promised a lineage (cf. *Gen.* 15:4-5). Consequently, she gives her handmaid to her husband as a wife so he can beget a child by her and thus fulfil God's promise. Now we see here that Sarah's zeal was good. Her intention was good. So it would seem her action was excusable. And in fact God's Spirit intended to show that her fault was not as great as if she had had something bad and devious in mind, for she did not want to make a brothel of her house or be a procuress for her husband. What then? She had no ambition to have a lineage, but she receives God's promise in faith. Her desire was good; she scorns both this world's goods and its ease and everything she has in it to the point of forgetting herself; for we know the power of jealousy in a woman. And yet when a wife wants her husband to take a second wife and have children by him, are we not justified in saying that she is not concerned for herself? Consequently, Sarah must have had a wonderful faith and been on fire, so to speak, to obtain what God had promised him, namely, a blessed seed in which resided the complete salvation of the world. That is a foundation as beautiful as it is wondrous. An angel could not be more perfect in that desire and commitment than Sarah is. Even so, that excellent commitment which causes her to stumble and commit the many mistakes we have mentioned here, that one act, which leads her to commit five or six different sins, nonetheless proceeds from a worthy zeal.

Upon seeing a situation like that, let us each distrust ourselves when we want to follow our own feeling. It is true that was done by a woman despite the special commendable qualities God had given her. We do not see that she ever murmured against her husband. And when he moves her from place to place on occasion, she is as long-suffering as he; she is his companion in all his dispositions; she obeyed God to the utmost, and since she was the mother of all believers, there is no doubt she was appropriately instructed to walk in the ways of God and lean on his promises. And yet we see what happened to her. Why? Because she wanted to give her own interpretation. So what do we have to do? Let us return to the lesson we learned from the prophet Isaiah, which is that our power must be in silence and rest, that is, if we do not wish to be shaken and finally fall, we must use the virtue of patience, just as we are exhorted to do later in the tenth chapter of Hebrews (verse 16), for we are always in such a hurry that if God does not finish what he said, we think everything is lost and that it will not be done on time. 'Oh, God promised this and that, and he does not show us he is willing to bring it to pass. So it is over if I do not step in right now.' We would indeed like to be God's companions. And why? First, because we are not content with his word, we want to stir in some mishmash and some brilliance from our own heads. And that is corruption, as I have said. And then it is as if we only wanted him to be our help and as if we could provide something for him, as if his power were not sufficient. Now that does not occur to us immediately, as someone who might have asked Sarah,

'Do you wish to interpret the matter better than God? Do you presume to help him as if he were not sufficient to bring to pass what he promised without your or any other creature's involvement?' It is certain she would have preferred to be cast into a bottomless pit than to have claimed that. And who would have said to her, 'Are you undertaking to help God as if he did not possess enough of his own power?' Such a diabolical thought would never have occurred to anyone. Nevertheless, we see what happened to her. As soon as she interprets the promise, it is certain she is disappointed because she is adding to God's word and is in that way perverting it and turning it from its true meaning, and then she proceeds by her foolish temerity. How? She is depriving God of his honour because she wishes to use a means he did not establish, but one she chose. So we understand the instruction given to us here when we know how to profit from it.

In addition, let us note that it is not enough to consider a goal which is good and approved but that we must always use the means that God allows. Now we have two ways that guide us in ordering our lives well: one is to aspire to what God calls us to; the other is to know how we must walk. God fails us neither in the one nor in the other, for in his word he puts a target, a bull's-eye, for us to aim at. We can never fail if we keep our eyes and our senses fixed on the purpose God sets before us, and in addition he gives us limits or restrictions that say: 'You will not veer to the left or to the right. That is your path. Walk in it.' Thus does our Lord proclaim that his will is an excellent guide and that if we do not veer from it, we will always walk the right path to reach our goal, which he is leading us to. That, then, is what we have in God's word.

And yet, it is not enough to say, 'My intention is good'; and I am not talking about that good intention the papists fantasize about when they say, 'I do that with good intention, even though it is completely contrary to God's word.' But when our good intention is founded on God's truth and we can say that our desire is to serve God and that he is content with that because I am intending to do what he commands, that is still not enough, but we must concentrate on how we go about it. In other words, fully wishing to obey God, we follow his commands, that is, our steps are led and guided in such a way that we undertake nothing but what he approves and what we know he requires of us.

That is how Sarah offended, and Abraham too, because he so easily believed her. For it is quite certain that Abraham was not motivated by a wicked lust. He was not lecherous or given to excess. He kept faith with his marriage. And it was not his idea to seek a second wife, for it could have been said that he used that hypocritically as a pretext, but that did not occur to him. He is waiting for God to do what he said. So this is Sarah's idea. In fact, she wants to enjoy the blessing she expects from God, which is not for a worldly and corruptible good but for the salvation of her soul and the whole world. The same is true of Abraham. Being influenced by her, he was motivated by no other desire than to have a lineage, and his pursuit was not worldly. They both want to acquire only what they need, that is, they could not be children of God without that lineage they were anticipating. Their fault, then, lies in the means. They want God's word to have its place, but they want to carry it out. It is their fantasy. When they put themselves in charge, it is as if they wanted their powers to be mingled with God's. And since they are following their notion, they indicate that God is not enough for them.

But the fact remains, as I said, that if we are to regulate our lives well, we must move only in the direction we should, but we must always carefully ask whether our means are acceptable and whether God permits them. In fact, experience shows us if we are not circumspect, we will often be carried away by one extreme or another. We see people of great zeal who say, 'How am I to do that? Oh, God has to be served and honoured.' And then they will say, 'This is what will advance the cause of the gospel. And then, are we not obliged to help our brothers?' Wondrous are their undertakings! In fact, they will have good motives, but they will not be better than Abraham's and Sarah's. Yet they do not want to tread heavily, but they will make some very serious mistakes. And what will be the outcome? They will often have some good way to go about it, but they will discover in the end that God does not want men to take a lot of liberties and dismiss him and put him on the sidelines. Such people will be disappointed with their efforts in the end. And it will do them no good to complain, for they will have thrown themselves into the ditch. The path was set out before them, that is, they should not have attempted anything that was not allowed by God's word. Now they wanted to be wise. They wanted to be quick to the task and join hands with God. And then they wanted to insert a part of their own wisdom, but that only spoiled everything. We see that at every turn. So let us avoid undirected zeal.

Many Jews did not crucify our Lord Jesus Christ out of malice or because they hated the teaching he brought, nor did they reject the salvation of the world when they later persecuted the gospel. Paul testifies that they had a zeal for God and that it was intense because they thought everything was lost (cf. *Phil.* 3:5-6) and that their entire religion would be struck down if our Lord Jesus Christ were to be put first. But their zeal was undirected.

Consequently, for our acts to be approved, they must be motivated by zeal and prudence. Now that prudence will not be found in us. We must seek for it in God's word and in his Spirit, as he says in the thirty-third chapter of the prophet Isaiah, for there he rebukes all the counsels that men imagine and fabricate without consulting him or allowing his Spirit to preside at their deliberations.[1] Those, the prophet notes, are the two mistakes men commonly make. In other words, they do not give the Holy Spirit the pre-eminence he ought to have. That is, they act without seeking instruction from God's word. That being the case, let us be advised to cling to the pure simplicity of faith and be careful not to add any of our own notions. Then, since we are tending in the direction God calls us, let us adhere to the acceptable ways he has established so that we will not deviate to the left or to the right. And third, when we are moved by a worthy zeal, let us control it so that we will not be carried away by unguided impetuosity. Let us ask of God, and let us allow his Spirit to preside over us. That, then, is in short what we have to remember.

But let us add what has just been said about being patient, for when it comes to God's promises, it is certain we rip them to pieces every time unless our minds remain calm. The vice of haste is so deeply rooted in men that they will rush ahead unless they are forcibly restrained, so to speak. So we must struggle against our excessive desires and bring ourselves into line with God's will, and once he begins, we must allow him to complete his task and work the way that seems good and expedient to him and not to us. That is what we need to note.

Now as for this second marriage, we have already said that Sarah and Abraham perverted God's order and profaned the marriage he had sanctified and blessed so there would be good and worthy partners among people. It is true that the unfortunate custom which ruled at the time led them to do that. And on that subject we still have to be admonished not to lose the custom of marriage. For what God declared at the creation of Adam seems to have been buried, namely, that two would become one flesh and that the man would have to be satisfied with one helper (cf. *Gen.* 2:18, 24). It is as if that were put underfoot. Why? The custom is against

[1] Cf. rather Isaiah 30:1–2.—*M.E.*

them and they think that what is in vogue among men and what is the prevailing custom is the law and that everything is permitted since everyone is in agreement. As today, the papists are becoming hardened against God's truth, even though it is quite clear to them; for if they can claim: 'If this has already been the practice for such a long time and everybody goes along with us,' they will have established the practice and God will seem to be shut out. Why? Men took over whenever they did what they did, and their kind have continued long.

Now that is how Abraham and Sarah were led astray in that particular. In that country of the East, it was a very commonly corrupt practice for a man to take several wives; for this evil continues even today among the Turks, and the Jews relaxed their practice. God rebuked them for it through the prophets (cf. *Mal.* 2:14-15), but he could not keep them from it, for they always gave in to it. So at the time, there were many women who were going from man to man. For men did not know or serve God, and the sanctity of marriage was violated in that practice. Abraham and Sarah were blinded by that, for they did not inquire as they should have, in keeping with Jesus Christ's admonition, whether that was so from the beginning (cf. *Matt.* 19:8). For with this single statement, our Lord Jesus Christ destroys any argument that can be alleged by men. How so? It was even permitted in the law, and examples of it are as commonplace as anything else. 'Indeed, but what did God institute,' he says, 'if he is the author of marriage? He must be believed and followed. He says that the two will be one flesh.' So Abraham has a veil before his eyes when he does not adhere to God's first institution, as he should have. However, when things are in a state of confusion in the world and people have given themselves great licence and turned from the right path, let us be advised not to have our minds occupied with that, but to push aside all those troubles and indiscretions and ponder God's truth without adding human speculations to it. That, in short, is what we still have to remember.

Nevertheless, we see by the reward meted out to Abraham and Sarah how God chastises his own. Moreover, when men take more liberties than they should by adding all this hodgepodge that they bring with them, they turn everything they hope for upside down and God mocks their folly. What happens when Abraham takes Hagar as his wife? It is true she conceives and that was miraculous in itself, for Abraham was old and decrepit, but he nonetheless begat a lineage. So it appears that Sarah was a prudent woman and her counsel was the best for the world, and even that Abraham was foolish for not thinking he was supposed to assist in God's promise. Now that is how our Lord often permits those who are rash and undertake things that blossom in their own minds to prosper and then become forgetful of him, for it seems that God has blessed them, favours them and in this way approves what they have attempted. When he has thus extended his hand to them, what can one think but that he agrees with them and indicates that their undertaking and counsel are good? So it seems that when men prosper in their enterprises, God folds under their brashness and foolish presumption. Indeed, our Lord permits them to do so for a time only to humble them and bring them to confusion later.

Therefore, even though our counsels have some success and fortunate outcome at first, let us be careful not to applaud ourselves for what we have done against God's word, for if we were to have the best results in the world, we will always be condemned for our folly. Let us not judge from the first results, for our Lord will turn all our hopes on end in a moment of time, and we will remain in confusion. And that is also why we must return to him. But if he occasionally permits things to turn out as we desire, let us not for that reason be hardened and obstinate, but let us realize we have exceeded our limits and confess that we have failed and are guilty in our hearts so that God will pardon us our excesses and not abandon us. That, then, is what we have to observe about what Moses recounts.

In addition, we must note that Abraham had already lived ten years in the land of Canaan, for he had left the land of his birth long before, as we have seen that he had remained in Canaan until after his father's death (cf. *Gen.* 11:32; 12:4-5). Sarah waited for a long time to see whether God wanted to give her a lineage. Was not ten years long enough? He gives no semblance of beginning. She could certainly be excused for being patient so long. And now that Hagar conceives without delay, it could be said that God is making her counsel prosper because he accepts it. But let us learn that it is not enough for us to exercise great patience. We must see it through to the end, for ours is not a journey of three or four days; nor are our struggles for three or four days, but we must continue until we die. So, as Paul says, let us learn not to look back but to look to what lies ahead (cf. *Phil.* 3:13). So much for that point.

After we have endured a long time and demonstrated great constancy and perseverance of faith for a period of ten and twenty years, let us not think we have done our share. And not only that. Let us then be on guard more than ever. Abraham had overcome many and grievous trials. We saw how the famine drove him from the land of Canaan (cf. *Gen.* 12:10), but he did not succumb; he remained firm and constant. It is true he failed once in respect of his wife, and that was indeed a weakness (cf. *Gen.* 12:11-13), but he nonetheless returned to the land of Canaan because God's promise has a grip on him and possesses him (cf. *Gen.* 13:1), and he is concerned about nothing else. In a word, we see in him an invincibly courageous heart and a mortal man. And that trial, what is it? It is but a small puff of wind, a fly passing before his eyes, and without thinking about it, he becomes a corrupter of God's order! He breaks his marriage vow. He turns away from the promise and interprets it badly. Then he goes beyond what is allowed. In a word, he acted very stupidly; and that trial is quite insignificant. Let us see in that our weakness. All the more then must we take refuge in God and cling to him as being hidden under his wings when he brings us the grace to walk uprightly for a long time. That, in summary, is what we have to remember about this.

Moreover, since Hagar's conception, insofar as it concerns Abraham and Sarah, was only a semblance of success, let us learn again that we need to be deprived of everything we might hope for, and let God deprive us of what we might desire so that we will always prefer his holy word to what we might naturally consider to be appropriate, expedient, and useful. That is another thing this passage instructs us about.

The fact remains that in the end God shows them their folly when Sarah is afflicted by her handmaid, and Abraham is also vexed, persecuted, and blamed, even though falsely. And that, I say, is a just compensation for their wanting to move the situation forward on their own. Sarah was saying, 'It is possible I will be built up.' That word signifies she has a house. It is true that in the language this word 'son' comes from 'to build up' by similarity, for the verb 'to build up' is related to the similarity.[2] Now in marriage there appears to be no building except that of children. So when Sarah speaks of a building, it is because there are children, there is a family, and seed will follow. That is what sustains the world and also each house. If a man and a woman live without successors, it is as if they had travelled the whole road of life and that nothing remained after their deaths. But if a house is left behind, the house remains established.

So in that way Sarah wanted to be built up, that is, to have a house established. And God thwarts her plan. She is obliged to be despised by her handmaid, as she deserves to be, for it is the

---

[2] The Hebrew verbal form in Genesis 16:2 is *ibbânéh*, from the root *bnh* (to build, to edify); and 'son' is *bèn*.—*M.E.*

handmaid who built. But on what foundation? On that false notion which she got into her head and even on a bold notion contrary to God's word, one which brought with it a kind of blasphemy, since God had wanted to condemn her severely, even though it had not occurred to her that he would. Now Abraham, who too quickly took his wife's counsel, now has her as his judge. That is what happens when we abandon God and his word and listen to men. Those very people who have corrupted us and led us to perdition have to blind us later and cut our throats, in a manner of speaking. Why? We have preferred them to God. So he has to avenge himself for the contempt we have shown for his majesty inasmuch as we have chosen creatures and worms of the earth over him. Consequently, Abraham, whose authority was greater than the woman's, subjected himself to her over against God. A man can indeed follow his wife's word in a worthy undertaking, but Abraham abandoned God and let himself be influenced by shallow advice. As a result, his wife must now blame him, condemn him, call him despiteful and corrupt and wrong, and insult him greatly, even though he is innocent of it all.

And now we first have to note here the example of man's ingratitude. Hagar had been honoured by her mistress more than she deserved, for she was a handmaid, not like the ones we have today for hire, but she was a servant for life and death, a slave, as we say. Sarah had such authority over her that there was no question of paying wages, for she had to live and die under her mistress's hand. It was not necessary to come to terms back then as now: 'Will I have food? Will I have wine to drink? Will I have this? Will I have that?' For when they wanted to give her oat bread, she had to be content. That was the condition of serfs back then. Now here is Hagar, who is so honoured that she is a wife of her master, Sarah's companion. She forgot the position from which she came to the extent of scorning her mistress. Here we see a notable example of the ingratitude of people who cannot stand the idea of being lifted up by God, especially when they are lifted from a base condition, when they are immediately changed and no longer recognized. If there was any modesty in them before, there is now only pride and haughtiness. And where does that come from? From their ingratitude toward God and their neighbours, who have helped them and extended a hand to them. This example is given to teach us to correct that vice, when we are infected with it, so that we will not follow the example of Hagar, who is here assigned to ignominy. For God gives her a sentence of condemnation, as we will see farther along (cf. *Gen.* 16:9). That, then, for that point.

But Sarah and Abraham deserve to have Hagar as a thorn in their side. Why? As I have already said, Sarah wanted to pick up on God's right and authority and contribute what was not hers to contribute when she came up with a new way of marriage. It was an illegitimate form of marriage which was totally repugnant to God's institution, which is not to be violated by men. So Sarah takes from God when she gives to her servant. Where does she get the authority to make Hagar her husband's wife? Neither she nor even the angels of paradise have it, for God had already provided a contrary way. So it is quite right that she is chastised, as we now see. Thus let us learn that when we offer our hand to someone to help him, we are always to do so in good conscience and not to show contempt for God, and we must not take as our own what he rightly permits us. That is also the meaning of the proverb, that if we take a man from the gallows, he will himself place us there. Why? For let us consider who most often motivates us to give pleasure, to gratify and favour one another, to do a good turn, as we say. We do not consider what God promises us, but what is worse, we appear to have conspired against God, and all the favours, kindnesses, and pleasures that we provide are designed to snatch from God the superiority he reserves for himself and to do more than we are permitted. So let us not be surprised if those whom we gratify beyond all reason later rise up against us, for we first rose up against God. So let us take heed when it is a matter of giving something or other to men that we not give what God reserved for himself, but let us give what he has placed within our hands and intends for us to share with others. Let each consider his ability and the means that are given to him from on high, and thus let each employ his efforts to please his neighbours, to help them in their time of need and nothing more. For if we go beyond that, it is certain God will know how to compensate us. And if Abraham was not spared, even less will we be.

Moreover, when we see that Sarah is so hot with anger that she comes straight and rants against her husband, we are admonished to keep our passions bridled, for we can give them just a little leeway and they will take charge and we will lose all restraint and be a raging fire. Sarah, as we have pointed out, was with good reason called mother of the church, and God gave her what she needed. When he gave her the honour of raising her to such a high position, it is certain he did not do so simply to adorn her with a frivolous title, but he immediately gave her the requisite qualities. Now she comes against her husband, whom she gave such reverence that she called him her lord, not perfunctorily, as Peter points out. He says that faithful women do very well when they conform to her example by yielding to the mastery owed to their husband (cf. *1 Pet.* 3:5-6). Now she pounces like a wild animal without considering that she is subject to her husband by God's command. And what is the reason? Her passion blinds her to the point that she loses all reason, moderation, and modesty. You would say she is no longer herself. All the more then must we work to repress our passions when we see such outrageous and impetuous actions and realize we could not gain control if the long hand of God did not grant us the grace to overcome them. So when we tremble with such anger, let us be prudent and use great effort to calm down. That is what we have to remember.

And even what Sarah adds must strengthen this teaching for us. The first thing she says is that the wrong done to her comes from Abraham. And then she takes the name of God in vain (cf. *Gen.* 16:5b), which will be discussed later. But when she unjustly accuses her husband, that ought to advise us to calm down, even though we have suffered some wrong, and to consider carefully whether we have been wronged out of malice or inadvertently, or who perpetrated it or how the person went about it. So we must inquire carefully when we have been stung with words so we do not go off half-cocked the way Sarah did. For it is certain we will do a hundred times worse than she did because we have learned much less than she did in God's school. So let us be advised to be very calm when we endure wrong so we will not blame our neighbours out of hand and will also remember Paul's admonition that love is not distrustful (cf. *1 Cor.* 13:5), that we must not accuse men before we are sure they are guilty. So that is how we are to take even more advantage of Sarah's example. But the rest will be drawn out tomorrow, at God's pleasure.

Now let us bow before the majesty of our gracious God in acknowledgment of our faults, praying he will touch us increasingly to the quick and bring us to such repentance that we will continually groan before him and also struggle valiantly against all our vices and corruptions until we are cleansed of them. And let us take more and more advantage of his will until we have learned to honour him as we should. In other words, may he govern us, use us, and so direct our steps that our only guide will be his holy word and we will have no other desire or inclination but to conform our ways to his. May he grant that grace not only to us but to all the peoples and nations on earth.

76

Submitting to One's Social Status:
The Order of the Day God's Will:
Obedience in Marriage,
Obedience to Superiors and Parents

Saturday, 23 March 1560

And Sarai said unto Abram, My wrong be upon thee: I have given my maid into thy bosom; and when she saw that she had conceived, I was despised in her eyes: the LORD judge between me and thee. But Abram said unto Sarai, Behold, thy maid is in thy hand; do to her as it pleaseth thee. And when Sarai dealt hardly with her, she fled from her face. And the angel of the LORD found her by a fountain of water in the wilderness, by the fountain in the way to Shur. And he said, Hagar, Sarai's maid, whence camest thou? and whither wilt thou go? And she said, I flee from the face of my mistress Sarai. And the angel of the LORD said unto her, Return to thy mistress, and submit thyself under her hands (Gen.16:5-9).

*W*E BEGAN YESTERDAY by saying that we have our work cut out for us when it comes to suppressing our emotions if someone insults us or when it comes to considering who is right or wrong so we do not accuse out of hand the person who might be innocent. As we experience too often, our strong feelings, our passions, blind us, and these feelings deprive us of all sense of reason, restraint, and fairness. All the more, then, must we be careful not to implicate anyone who has nothing to do with the situation. Sarah must serve as an example for that. For a moment she was so distraught by her anger that she blames her husband, who is innocent in this case and had not intrigued with Hagar. He had not supported her out of pride and audacity, and yet Sarah said he wronged her. It is quite certain she did not intend to condemn her husband indiscriminately, but, as I have already said, the bitterness in her heart caused her to speak irrationally.

What is more, she even adds God's name and asks him to punish her husband and to judge between the two parties. Now it is certain that when she speaks this way, she is abusing God's name and profaning him. How serious is a person to call upon God to act as judge when moved by a frivolous matter and some empty, unfounded opinion? Yet that is what Sarah did. Consequently, we have plenty of opportunities to ponder such examples in ourselves.

In the first place, let us realize where we end up if we relax our restraints when we become angry or impetuous, for God will be blamed endlessly. And when men afflict us, we then have to address God, we will be so incensed and out of control that God will not enter into our thinking, since we are in contact with him every day. And in fact those who have sworn and blasphemed think they have a good excuse at hand when they say: 'Oh, I was angry.' They think God ought to be subjected to their whims of anger. And when they spit in his face, in a manner of speaking, they should be forgiven. All the more then ought we to remain circumspect at those times and be, first, aware of the reverence we owe God's name. And, second, let us also realize that if we are angry and enraged after being offended and vexed, we will lash out uncontrollably against God and any creature. That, I say, is what we need to remember about this story.

However, let us learn what it means to invoke God as judge. When we have some quarrel or altercation with our neighbours, you will hear words like: 'Oh, God knows about this.' 'Let God be the judge.' 'May God punish the one who is wrong.' Most often, even though we have a good case, we are not altogether innocent. For out of a hundred disputes which occur among men, it will be very difficult to find one in which both parties are not at fault. It is true that one will always make a better case than the other as it deals with the main cause, but unfortunately there are many inconsistencies and minor attendant circumstances. And if one begins badly, the other, wishing to put the blame on him, will utter some word without thinking. And fuel is thrown on the fire. In short, somehow or other, it will turn out that some fault will be found in the one who is the most just and would be absolved by men.

Now in such a case, what is it to invoke God except to provoke his wrath willingly and cause him to take the side against us? Is it not enough to have our neighbour against us without also angering God and provoking him against us? Let us keep in mind what is said: God will not leave unpunished those who take his name in vain (cf. *Exod.* 20:7; *Deut.* 5:11). Let us be aware of the majesty his name has so we will not defame or diminish it. And being aware of that, let us always bear in mind that we need his mercy; and in whatever good case we may have, even though our conscience is clear, there can always be some unseen wrong that we did not intend that everybody would absolve us of a hundred times, but for which we would be condemned if God chose to exercise his rigor against us. So let that teach us to be even more circumspect.

In the meantime, we see how the devil finds and penetrates the tiniest of imperceptible openings to gain entrance and stir up discord and disturbance, even between a husband and wife, who are supposed to be joined together and united as a single person. If there has ever been a marriage in which two individuals have walked in the fear of God with one accord, it was certainly Abraham and Sarah. Even so, there they are caught off guard, for it was not their custom to cry out and squabble in the house and make charges against each other, but it nonetheless happened. Here we see Satan cleverly at work. He catches these two individuals off guard, who were like two angels living together on earth. Now what are we to do, we who are so weak and so prone to disobedience? As soon as we have the slightest occasion to be upset and angered, we will be quick to rant and rave. And if we had lightning in our hands, we would destroy everything. So let us learn to pray that God will temper our passions when we see we are under their influence and that he will close all access to Satan so that we will not be caught off guard by the one who is using every means at his disposal to draw us into his traps. That, then, is what we have to pay attention to.

And even if husbands and wives know the duty God has given them, it is God who joined them together in his name and who consecrated that bond by which they are united in such a way that they cannot be rancorous toward one another and show clear contempt for God, which would be an insult directed at God if the marriage is transgressed. Thus, husbands and wives must all the more carefully maintain peace and harmony among themselves. And should it happen that, because of weakness, they fall into some contention, let them realize that that is the fruit of sin. And the unity and harmony I spoke of is implicit in the marriage contract. And if that situation prevails, it is certain that the blessing and grace of God will shine upon it and we will see a harmony such as exists among the angels of paradise. But when there are flaws in the marriage, let those who see themselves distraught by troubles and irritations bear in mind that they are receiving the fruits of their sins. And that will serve to encourage them to greater patience and gentleness, and the husband will not be so quick-tempered against his wife. The wife will also more humbly support her husband's disposition and inclinations. For if we think about our sins and understand that they cause all the miseries we endure, it is certain we will always be humbled. That, then, is what we always have to remember about this passage.

Now it is said that Abraham leaves Hagar under the authority of his wife. He does not make a big case of this, as he could have done. He could have bitterly rebuked Sarah's excessive passion and said: 'What do you want of me? What reason have I given you to come and talk to me that way? You are acting like a stupid woman. You should consider first whether I caused your problem or was an accomplice. And since you are bickering this way without thinking, that is reason enough for me to rebuke you sharply.' So Abraham could have exercised his right of superiority, but he does not and abandons the dispute. He only says: 'I leave your handmaid in your hands to deal with according to your right. If she is insolent with you, if she speaks contemptuously to you, it is up to you to put her in her place! I leave her in your hands.' Here we see great wisdom in the holy patriarch, for what would he have in fact gained by doing otherwise when he sees his wife in this fit of temper? He would have only added to the problem. For we see what follows. When Paul exhorts the faithful not to engage in squabbles and controversies, he rebukes that kind of rankling malice, saying, 'Avoid giving yourselves to insolent behaviour, for everyone wants to win' (cf. *Titus* 3:9), for the word he uses means that everyone of us desires to be top dog, as we say, and come out on top, whatever it takes. And since that is true, troubles and contentions arise because neither side will yield, and a little dispute will often turn into such a great uproar that you would think it was worth taking up arms over. That is what happened to Abraham. But he possessed such praiseworthy wisdom before God and men that he quietly put out the fire which was already big and had grown so large that he would never have been able to put it out. In the same way, let husbands learn to bear with their wives as weaker vessels, just as Peter admonishes them to do (cf. *1 Pet.* 3:7).

Moreover, that is not to say that Abraham did not know what it means to govern and that he did not have a grip on the reins when he needed to. We will discover a lot of harebrained people who will say, 'Must my wife have pre-eminence over me? Is that not the reason I am the master in my house?' They would scarcely know how to control a small child, and they want to have an uncontested kingdom. And without saying more, we will often see that those who speak that way are corrupt people who do not have an ounce of brains, who have no counsel to give, no prudence or even civility. Even so, they will always claim the mastery and the supremacy given to them. True, but they would always have to begin with themselves and reason would have to govern them to the extent they would be capable of making free choices, of being uncontrolled. And then, being free, they would use the right God gives them and they would be superior. But those who talk that way want to be husbands and heads of household with permission to shout and rant and rave and turn everything upside down and strike and batter.[1] That, then, is what they claim they have.

Now Abraham was well aware of what it meant to govern his wife and his household, but at the same time he knew what it meant to let go of his right and humble himself and yield. When we have nothing to gain, if we wanted to go to extremes in the matter, we would only add evil to evil. Abraham was well aware of that. Therefore, let Christian men maintain that restraint and not always act impetuously. And when they see some failures in their

---

[1] This Calvin text is even more modern, an unconditional criticism of the patriarchate. Calvin often had to deal with matrimonial disputes every Thursday during the sessions of the Consistory. Husbands often appeared for having beaten their wives. As is the case with Jehan Chiccand, Jehan Addor, then Jehan Fourby, on 29 February 1560, etc. (cf. *Registres du Consistoire*, t. XVII, f° 14v°; 151r°; 18r°).—M.E.

wives, let them support their wives. And then, in general, let us practise that same teaching, and when we see some angry person, let us have pity on him. Since the devil has already got his hands on him and has already gained too much control over him, let us try to reverse all that so that the fire which is already much advanced will not advance further. The same applies to those who are already on fire with anger. And what will be the outcome if we anger them and light the fire at both ends? The one who is already greatly inflamed in his feelings will become more hardened and will never come to repentance. If at that time we support the one who has popped off his hinges, it is certain that an hour later, not the following day, he will sense his evil and see that he is obliged to his neighbour: 'That man was in a position to put me in my place and I would have become completely enraged and the devil would have owned me. But he let my fault pass as a storm passes. So I am greatly obliged to him, for he gained my salvation.' And in that way we win the poor souls which were on their way to hell, if we know how to use moderation and kindness when necessary in order to rebuke more effectively later those who have made peace with their anger. That, then, in short is what we have to remember.

Now there is even more, for we know that Abraham's household was for the time the true pattern and image of the church. It is true that there was also Melchizedek, as we have seen (cf. *Gen.* 14:18-20), but all the rest of the world was alienated, so to speak, from the true religion, for superstitions and idolatries were in vogue everywhere (cf. *Josh.* 24:2). Even so, God raised up that house to be like a holy place where he wants to reside in this world. And in fact, he preserved that house intimately by his angels as if it had been his own dwelling place. Nevertheless, we see that Abraham, who was its head, was blamed by his wife. We see that his wife forgets her place at this time and is not dutiful toward her husband and that she raves as if everything were lost and has no sense of discernment. When we see that, let us bear in mind that we must not be too surprised that if troubles occasionally befall the church, some will take sides against the others. That is deplorable, true, and we must try hard to keep such an evil from happening. But when God wants to humble us to that extent and there even seems there is no church in this world, we must nonetheless overcome such trials. At the same time, let us find ways to remedy that evil, which is as insidious as any and is like a deadly plague. And let us take great pains to show we are God's children by securing peace and harmony, as we are taught to do by our Lord Jesus Christ (cf. *Matt.* 5:7).

Now it is said: 'When Sarah dealt harshly with her servant,' she fled from her into the desert until the angel met her and asked: 'Hagar, Sarah's maid, where are you coming from? And where you going?' Here we see a great capriciousness and changeability in Sarah. She had been moved by such a great zeal to have a lineage that she forgot everything else, for the greatest desire in a woman is to have her husband joined with her. But for her that is nothing in comparison with the desire of her heart and all her other senses to have that blessed lineage, as God had promised it to her. She now sees Hagar pregnant; and even though she herself is despised, a fact which nettles and irks her, must she forget God's promise, which she had so highly prized? Must she abandon what is for her eternal salvation as the result of some spite and grief she conceived in her heart? For it is not a question, as we have said, of having a child who would possess Abraham's worldly goods, but one of having a lineage destined to bless all the nations of the earth. For this is a very strange situation for Sarah. But that is what it means to be poorly grounded. Sarah commented on God's word, as we saw earlier, and now she loses all zeal and desire for it. And God's truth is so powerful that when we depend on it, our faith is victorious over the entire world. But when we depend on our imaginations, all that is required is a puff of air to knock us down and a tiny mite to throw us into confusion so that we no longer see a slender ray of light where we thought we saw with full clarity. That is what happened to Sarah.

Although Sarah thought God was her benefactor when she married Abraham, she has nonetheless already demonstrated that she was approaching the situation with doubt when she said: 'I may have children' (cf. *Gen.* 16:2). And that comment should have pierced her heart and awakened her to think: 'But what am I saying? "May." If I were certain of God's will, I would not be saying, "I may have." My resolve should be complete and unfailing.' But she takes the promise and proceeds as she does. She now shows clearly that she was thwarted and that, in proportion to her haste, the outcome had to be confounded. When she sees her handmaid pregnant, she could pride herself that it had happened in accordance with her counsel, but that accounted for Hagar's becoming more wilful. Now that things take a different turn, she vacillates and then is completely downcast.

So this is what we need to remember: when we are not well grounded in God's word and have not regulated and measured all our works by it, all that is needed is the slightest trial in the world to frighten us and throw us into disarray and we forget everything, and all our former plans vanish. We see this just and equitable punishment of God in the person of Sarah, and it teaches us to restrain ourselves and not undertake everything that comes to mind and say: 'That seems good to me. I want it to happen this way.' If we do, we will get what is coming to us. Our Lord will frustrate everything we expected and hoped for, and at that moment we will show that we do not know what true steadfastness is.

Meanwhile, let us note that God, when punishing Sarah, showed he was acting as a father toward her and castigated her in a fatherly way for her salvation. As we have said, if things had happened the way she wanted, it is certain she would have become even more insubordinate and would have forgotten what God promised her, for it was not in Ishmael that she was to have that blessed seed, as we will see (cf. *Gen.* 18:10; 21:1-3). So she would have taken Ishmael instead of Isaac and, as compensation for her deception, would have had only a pale representation of what she imagined. And Jesus Christ, who descended from Isaac's line, would no longer have meant anything to her. So there we have Sarah, who would have been on her way to hell if God had left her unpunished. But when he restores her despite her sin and many faults, he shows her pity and she returns to her salvation.

It is true that we see a very great overreaction on her part, and she shows no restraint in what she does and she changes in that way and is inconstant; and since she desired a lineage, she does not consider the consequences. We see as many vices that will condemn her, but God gives that a very different meaning, namely, that he pardoned her faults and even turns them for good. In that, we see that we need God not only to spare us when we offend him, that he draws good out of evil, not that we are innocent, for God makes us so by his incomprehensible counsel; he even works outside the order of nature, as he also draws light out of darkness (cf. *Amos* 5:8). Even so, we still see he even heightens our offences for our advantage, since he humbles us and redirects things in a direction different from the one we had planned. So much, then, for Sarah's being so involved in her tangled emotions that she has no sense of judgment and forgets what she possessed previously.

And in the meantime we also see, if a person pursues his cause, that it is very difficult to apply restraint. It is true the word Moses uses signifies 'to humble,' but it also means 'to afflict.' And it is very certain Moses wanted to show what Hagar's situation was when she returns to her former condition by declaring that she must be submissive in spite of her scorn. But in any case, there is no doubt Sarah wanted vengeance when Hagar was forced to flee in desperation. For she went into the desert to die, and would have if God had not stayed Sarah's hand by an angel. So we must conclude that, this time, Sarah did not show the kindness she should have in support of her handmaid.

And that lets us know that when we are devoted to ourselves and to our interests and to what we think is rightfully ours, we always exceed our limits. Consequently, there will never be equity among men unless each individual yields and we try to get along with one another, either giving up or losing something. For if we always insist on remaining unyielding, we put such tension on the bow that it breaks. If there were only two men in the world and each was self-centred and unrelenting and refused to give in, it is certain the earth would not be big enough to contain just the two of them. And what will happen when we are obliged to live in large groups and deal with a variety of types, all having different personalities and vices that cannot be tolerated and everyone being at the other's throat? So let us note that we will never be able to treat one another equitably unless we very carefully practise that gentleness and humility which cause us to deal fairly with one another so we can live together. So there you have the first and second obstacles when we focus our attention on ourselves at those times when we are wronged by a superior and think we have a good case. We will not be satisfied with having won but will want to walk all over our opponent when we have obtained what was our due. We will have to congratulate ourselves. For when someone says, 'I have been wronged. Well, let that wrong be corrected.' Is it corrected? Oh, that fellow has to get on his high horse and attribute new crimes to his opponent, and by so doing he always begins a quarrel which should have been buried. That is what happens. And let us keep in mind that could be us when someone wrongs us, for if we insist on prosecuting him, it is certain we will always go too far. And yet, let us always support those who have fallen short, and let us be satisfied when they have realized their error and repented of it, and let us not seek more than that if we do not want to step over the line. That, then, is what we have to remember from this passage.[2]

Now we see that God did not excuse Hagar, even though her mistress afflicted her and forced her to leave the house and flee without knowing where to go and that God still condemns her instead of absolving her. Thus we have to remember that in the matter of the right of superiors, if the one who is a subject is wronged in some way, even though he can, in the presence of God, condemn the one who has authority over him, he must nonetheless yield his neck and bear that yoke. And that is a teaching which is indeed demanded of us, for we know by nature that everyone would like to be the greatest and that ambition is so deeply rooted in the heart of man that that vice fills his life until God purges it by his Holy Spirit. And even though he purges it little by little, some small residue remains. And believers feel they have to battle against themselves every day to avoid feeling any superiority as a result and to remain little and humble. When understanding that we become thus haughty when those who have some authority over us abuse us with it, it then seems that we have the licence to kick back. And that is why those under authority revolt against their princes at every turn. That is why children take a stand against their fathers and mothers and leave home and engage in dissolute acts to show they have abandoned all reverence. That is why servants kicked back against their masters. All the more, then, must we give heed to this teaching which Moses gives us here.

Hagar was badly treated by her mistress, and the afflictions forced her to go out among the wild animals because she could not take it any longer. At first sight, it is true, you could say she

[2] This is the attitude of Calvin and the ministers of Geneva toward conciliation at the Thursday meetings of the Consistory.—*M.E.*

was right, and we can dispute this and that point and come to a conclusion; but we make a mistake if we do not listen to God, for he alone is a competent and sufficient judge of the case. And what does he say? 'Hagar, Sarah's maid.' It is with good reason that the angel designated her as such. It is true her mistress would no longer have gone into the desert to seek her; she had so seriously gone against custom that it seems she possessed every freedom, but in the eyes of God she is always under obligation. We have here a decree pronounced by God: 'You are a handmaid, no matter the circumstance.' It is as if he were saying: 'You stole yourself. And even though you bear your theft with you and men do not see it, God does. And do not think you have gained anything, for you are still in the condition you were.' And it is noteworthy he says to her: 'Sarah's maid.' He could have as well said: 'Abraham's maid,' but he uses the name 'Sarah' as if he were saying: 'You can claim that your mistress was too cruel to you, that she was too hard on you, but there is no reason that breaks the relationship between you. You will always be her handmaid. Why so? God has ordained it to be that way. It is not your place to throw off that yoke, but you must bear it patiently.' That, then, is the teaching we have to gather from this passage.

In order to understand this better, let us first note that we are not talking about servitude the way it would be today. As we have said, back then people did not have hired servants, but they held them as slaves for life. Since we are all created from the same lump and are all descended from Adam and have all descended from Noah's ark and consider what we are by contemplating the person of our neighbour, that is a very harsh and odious condition, and it even seems to be inconsistent with our nature that one person should dominate another in such a way that he has complete authority over him, free to do whatever he pleases without law or regulation, so to speak. Nevertheless, even though it is a curse of God which does not correspond to the order God established between men at the beginning, it must nonetheless prevail and be enforced. But we especially see in that servitude the results of original sin and Adam's fall. As a matter of fact, we even see that it has persisted among Christians, for Paul does not command masters to give up their servants, but he says, 'Treat them humanely, knowing that both you and they have a common Master in heaven, before whom you both will have to give account and there will be no partiality. That does not mean that the master argues for his rights. Indeed not! For the master will be punished if he does not grant his servant what belongs to him. Before men, you remain unpunished, but God is your Judge, and he will uphold the quarrel of the small, of those who are despised and treated unjustly' (cf. *Eph.* 6:9; *Col.* 3:22-4:1; *1 Tim.* 6:1-2; *Philem.* 1). Paul gives that same kind of exhortation to those who are slaves under masters, but he allows masters to continue as masters. So we see that even though that condition was very harsh and bitter, it is nonetheless approved by God.

If we now compare that servitude with the obedience of subjects to their princes, their magistrates and judges, children toward fathers and mothers, current servants with their masters and mistresses, it is certain it is a much more pleasing and preferred situation when subjects obey their superiors and magistrates than when the poor people are slaves and are horribly afflicted. And even the obedience that servants owe their masters is more tolerable than that, for a servant will be taken care of. Why so? Will he not obey the one whose bread he eats and from whom he even has his wages? As for children, the situation is monstrous unless they can yield peaceably and obey their fathers and mothers as their principal desire. And that will even lead to the child's praise when a father vexes him and deals with him severely. If a child endures patiently, that will be accorded to him as praise and ought to cost him nothing, in a manner of speaking.

Therefore, since God wanted the slaves in days gone by to remain under the yoke, even if they were treated with the obligatory humaneness, let us be apprised that today there is no excuse if we think we are completely forgiven if we claim we are not receiving what is our due, that we are not being treated as we would like. So when those under authority want to revolt, claiming: 'We are too hard-pressed by taxes and tributes; that imposition is too harsh and burdensome,' it is certain they are kicking back against God, as Paul points out (cf. *Titus* 2:9-10). The same applies to servants when they do not want to put up with their masters' ways of doing things and when maids want to revolt against their mistresses and tolerate nothing. Let such unendurable situations always be addressed to God. The matter is more serious for children. When they cannot remain obedient to father and mother, they are more manifestly waging war against God.

This, then, in summary, is what we have to remember: those who are inferior in status must always honour those whom God has established at higher levels and subject themselves to them voluntarily if they wish to be subservient to God. And even though their superiors abuse their authority and are not as humane as they should be, even so the order that God established must not be violated or broken for that reason.

It is true that we must make a distinction at this point. If we are afflicted in our hearts, we must bear it with long-suffering. But that is not to say we are to disregard God's sovereign authority in order to please those who are pre-eminent over us, as when kings wish to constrain their subjects to follow superstitions and idolatries. When they do that, they are no longer kings, for God did not resign or abandon his right when he established principalities and dominions in this world. And when he granted mortal creatures the honour of being fathers and having paternal authority over their children, he does not relinquish always being the only Father, full and complete, of both bodies and souls. But when kings want to pervert true religion and when fathers also want to train their children variously and to remove them from obedience to God, let the children make distinctions here; let the same be true for servants and handmaids and all the subjects of princes and magistrates in general; let them so humble themselves that they will bear with patience all the wrongs done to them. Yet let them be advised that it would be better for them to die a hundred times than to turn away from the true worship of God. So, let them render to God what is God's, and let them scorn all edicts and all threats, all commandments and traditions, and let them consider all such things as dung and garbage when worms come and take a stand against the one to whom alone obedience is owed. But, in summary, let all those who are subjects remember what Paul says, for it is the true interpretation of everything dealt with both in the seventh chapter of Romans and throughout holy Scripture: 'Obey in the Lord.'[3] With that, Paul includes all human obedience within the obedience which precedes and possesses sovereign rank. Consequently, let us note that God has not elevated the kings and magistrates of this world to such a high status that they are not subjected to him. The same is true for fathers and mothers. So Paul is indicating how and to what extent we are to obey fathers and mothers: namely, we have those limits in God, he says. In other words, we can in no way diminish God's authority in order to please men of any status, quality, or dignity. That, in brief, is what we have to continue to remember.

Now although Hagar claims as an excuse that she fled from the presence of her mistress and wants to use that to make her

[3] Cf. in fact Ephesians 6:1... In his commentary, Calvin explains that that command includes a synecdoche, fathers and mothers including all authorities, and he continues: 'Yet it follows from that that father and mother must be obeyed in such a way that the reverence due God, who holds primary allegiance, is not offended.' Cf. Calvin, *Epistres,* p. 532; Calvin, *Epistolae I*, p. 275. In the Epistle to the Romans, it is rather at the beginning of chapter 13 that Paul deals with the obedience due magistrates. Cf. Romans 13:1.—*M.E.*

case look good, God's angel, nonetheless, continuing the decree he had already pronounced, says to her: 'Return to your mistress.' So when we have not been long-suffering and some brief fit of temper has got the best of us, let us learn that we still must return to the status in which God placed us. For if we continue the way we are going, it is certain God will show us in the end that it is against him that we are battling inasmuch as we are not following the order of rank of which he is the author. Therefore, let those who are subjects learn not only to be long-suffering for a while but also, if they have rebelled, to acknowledge their fault and understand: 'It is true I have resisted a man or woman, but God still takes this case as against himself. And what would I gain by resisting God? So I must return to my status. Why? Because God approves it.' In a word, we have to remember that we could present all the finest excuses we can imagine, that we could even have everybody approve everything we do, and that everyone could pity us and justify us in every respect, but that would serve no good purpose until we return to our duty before God. Therefore, we must always come to our calling knowing what God enjoins, and at that point, let us know we must submit without dispute, for submission is divine and not human. In other words, it comes from God and was not invented by the whimsy of man. That, then, is what we must remember.

Now I said that we must consider our calling. For when the Pope claims the superiority that he says he has over the entire Church, we know that it is the devil's tyranny and that he subverted the Son of God's entire empire when he elevated himself with such infernal pride. There is, therefore, no calling. But when a husband is angry with his wife because of her failings, he will be so angry that he would like to put her away, if that were permitted, and he thinks: 'Now the fact is that God keeps me attached, for marriage is a sacred institution. Therefore, even though I have a faulty wife,

I must reconcile differences with her and try to bring her back the best way I can, but I must bear in mind that God wishes to chastise me in that way.' Thus, let the husband return whatever the circumstance, knowing that it is not his place to separate what God has joined together, as our Lord points out. Let the wife also do the same thing. If she has a coarse husband who torments her, a bad manager who lays waste all her goods, and because of that she has drawn away from her husband, it is true she is not unfeeling, but she will still always think: 'You must nonetheless return to your husband. Why? Since we are joined together by God, if I separate myself from him, it will not only be separated from the man but from the living God.' Let each person, then, consider his status. Let subjects do the same with respect to their princes, and let us realize that we cannot remove ourselves from obedience to those whose subjects we are and thus wage war against God and resist his power. And if we resist him, he will, in the end, have to make us feel our brashness and overweening pride and confound all our undertakings.

Now let us bow before the majesty of our gracious God in acknowledgment of our faults, which are so great that their number is infinite and so enormous that we should be completely abased by them, were it not that this gracious God has been incomparably merciful toward as. So let us pray that by continuing his goodness he will cause us to sense that he supports us all the times of our lives and cleanses us of all our wicked desires and governs us in such a way by his Holy Spirit that we, both great and small, are all his subjects. And at the same time let us live with one another as we try to do our duty and patiently endure our neighbours' shortcomings. And let us so yield that the remnants of our strong feelings will not end in our recklessness and ruin, but let us rather be led by him who is the Father of peace. And since we are to be brothers together, let us be his true children inasmuch as he has declared he is our Father (cf. *Jer.* 31:9; *Mal.* 1:6; *John* 14:6). May he grant that grace not only to us but to all the peoples and nations on earth.

77

The Lesson to Be Learned from Hagar's Obedience: God's Grace Comes First

Monday, 1 April 1560

And the angel of the LORD said unto her, Behold, thou art with child, and shalt bear a son, and shalt call his name Ishmael; because the LORD hath heard thy affliction. And he will be a wild man; his hand will be against every man, and every man's hand against him; and he shall dwell in the presence of all his brethren. And she called the name of the LORD that spake unto her, Thou God seest me: for she said, Have I also here looked after him that seeth me? Wherefore the well was called Beerlahairoi; behold, it is between Kadesh and Bered. And Hagar bare Abram a son: and Abram called his son's name, which Hagar bare, Ishmael. And Abram was fourscore and six years old, when Hagar bare Ishmael to Abram (Gen. 16:11-16).

LTHOUGH GOD, who has total authority over us, deserves to be heard without question and can command with a word, he nonetheless, because he especially demands that we obey him with an open and free affection, often adds promises to his commands, promises by which he tries to win us over. If a king or a prince wishes to show his right, he does not give the reason for what he says, and he is even content to declare precisely what pleases him, and his subjects have to comply with his wishes; but when a father wishes to urge his child in a certain direction and persuade him, he speaks with him frankly and familiarly and condescends to explain to him why he is giving him the order he is, what the reason is and the advantage he will reap. He also influences him with worthy, attractive promises.

That is the way our Lord deals with us every day. For even though he can command us with a simple word, as we have already noted, he continues to draw us with fatherly kindness and gentleness. And we see that here even in the example of Hagar. Despite the fact that she had been a rebel with a spiteful and perverse spirit and would have been so ungrateful that we can judge she did not have any sense of loyalty, the fact remains that God still uses this procedure, after telling her she must return to her mistress, in order to cause her to be submissive (cf. *Gen.* 16:9), even though she was treated harshly, to suffer, and to be long-suffering. Even so, it is said that she will have a child in a situation where previously she had been without hope, there in the middle of the desert, there where no one could help her. Now it is said that she will bear a child, as if the angel were saying to her: 'Do not find that servitude harsh and oppressive, for it is much better to be in the house of Abraham than to die here among wild animals. And thus will God bless you.'

As a consequence, we must remember this: when our Lord, after commanding us to do what he can simply demand of us, shows that he is so kind to us as to add his promises, he shows that we, by doing what we should, act immediately in behalf of our advantage, that that ought to affect us more deeply, and that, if we are not moved by it, our ingratitude will be even more base and inexcusable.

Moreover, when we understand that God is proposing promises of celestial life, let us compare what was said to Hagar: that having a child is here only a matter of a terrestrial benefit. Now our Lord is leading us much higher, for he is calling us to an inheritance of immortal life (cf. *John* 3:16; *Rom.* 6:23). Surely we are cold and thankless, heartless, if we are not moved by such kindness. Here, in a word, is how we must take advantage of God's promises: they must be like goads to prod us along more effectively so we can have a prompt and joyful desire to walk even better in the fear of God and serve him willingly. So much for that point.

Now Hagar is told that the child will be barbarous and like a wild man. Why? Because his hand will be against everyone and the hand of everyone will be against him. It seems that God is here proclaiming a curse rather than a promise. And in fact, there also had to be in Ishmael some small glimmer of God's grace to Abraham, for Abraham would have placed his complete confidence in that, as in fact he could not refrain from doing. Even though God would not have made Ishmael Abraham's heir, Abraham still has confidence in him. And that is how we are accustomed to occupy our time with what pleases us in this world. If we see something which happens to please us, we are completely held back by it, and that fact prevents us from getting to what is the principal thing. Consequently, God had to moderate his grace in the person of Ishmael in such a way that Abraham would not put his confidence in him and would continue to look beyond. And that is why everybody's hand was against Ishmael, as if he had been told: 'It is true that this child will not be for peace, for he has enemies on all sides. No matter what, he will resist his enemies.' Now it would be much better to have peace with all our enemies than to be able to defend ourselves in battle. Therefore, we understand it is as if God were giving Ishmael a small portion of his grace for Abraham's sake.

But as for the rest, he reserved the principal thing for the legitimate heir, for we see that God's mercy generally extends to all creatures, and then he does good to those to whom he has drawn near, even though he does not acknowledge them as his children, but he still wants to show that he has some affection for them. Yet what is written in the psalm remains true: the infinite good things of God—which we can very well comprehend—are reserved for those who fear him (cf. *Psa.* 31:19). So God pours out his liberality as much on all creatures as on those who are in his church and who have the outward reputation of being in it; even so, the inheritance always remains the possession of those for whom it is ordained. That, then, is what we have to remember concerning what is promised for Ishmael.

When the text says he will live in the presence of his brothers, it means he will be a body apart, that is, a body that will not be included among the others, but that he will be a people. For the person of Ishmael is not only spoken of here; the reference is to his entire lineage, since a great people has descended from him. So our Lord is showing that Ishmael will not only have his distinct house, but he will have a region and a country. In other words, the successors of his race will have renown and be called peoples by the name of their fathers. Now it would have been of greater value for them not to have that distinction and to be included in Isaac's lineage, but because God had excluded him from that spiritual good, he leaves him only a remnant of what concerns this frail life. Now, in the world's view, it is desirable to be free and unimpeded, to be subject to no one, and to be accepted as one of the group. That will always be the world's desire. Consequently, it is not without reason that our Lord says that Ishmael will beget children who will be multiplied and become a people. And so it happened, but we must always distinguish between that temporal grace which was given to Ishmael and the adoption which was reserved for Isaac, as we will see in the seventeenth chapter (cf. *Gen.* 17:19-21). In brief, here our Lord shows that, out of regard for Abraham, he will continue to show pity to Ishmael but only during the course of this present life. He also shows that for Ishmael the door of the heavenly kingdom will be closed. That is, the promise of the kingdom will not be given to him. We cannot completely condemn him or those who are his descendants as if all had been damned without exception. That must be left in the secret counsel of God; but we are considering here the promise by which God chose Isaac and his lineage. It appears the door to the heavenly life was open to Isaac's lineage but closed to the others, so far as we can judge from our perspective and understanding.

Now we need to note here that God's goodness deserves to be prized, if only for food and drink, but there is nothing that men prize as much as delights and pleasures, honours and wealth, which snatch them up at the expense of the hope of the eternal salvation of our souls. So when our Lord takes care of us and deals with us kindly on earth, let us learn to prize his goodness in everything and everywhere, and may nothing be too small for the exaltation of his name. But let us not be caught up in these earthly benefits, but let us consider the purpose for which we are created, and let us always ponder what I have already cited from the psalm: that infinite mercy of God's goodness which he preserves and keeps hidden, as the words of the prophet have it, for those who fear him (cf. *Psa.* 31:19). That, in brief, is what we have to remember about this passage.

At that point it is said that Hagar speaks again: 'I have even seen here afterwards the one who sees me.' It is true she begins there. In other words, 'Indeed the Lord has seen me and considered me,' but she adds the reason: that God saw her before she was aware of it. The first thing Moses shows us here is the advantage of this vision: that Hagar, who was like a wild animal gone astray, was thinking that God was asleep or had his eyes closed and that she now knows that his providence extends everywhere, that he controls all things and disposes of them with his hand. That, then, is already a great advantage.

The second thing is that she condemns herself for her stupidity, for not knowing God, even in that place and in her extremity after he had appeared to her. Now this is written for us. So let us weigh carefully all these words, for they are heavy with meaning. When she says: 'You are the Lord who has seen me,' I understand that for a brief time she was much better instructed than she thought, for we know much when we are persuaded that God governs the world and that everything is at the disposal of his counsel and will. It is easy to confess that there is a God while at the same time stripping him of the governing of the world, and it is easy to confess with the mouth that he is all powerful without understanding that power and the content of that word and that attribute which we ascribe to him casually. For what will remain to God if he does not have sovereignty over the world? Now that sovereignty is not idle, for we are sustained by its power, which he displays in his powerful and beneficent word, as the apostle says in the first chapter of Hebrews (cf. *Heb.* 1:3). In short, being in heaven, he does everything he wishes, as Psalm 105 says. If God does not possess that power, it is certain we make of him an idol and a phantom, and it is all only a shadow of his full majesty.

We have here, then, a singular piece of instruction. When we are resolved in our hearts that everything is governed by his hand and that all that happens is by his will, not only according as he has foreseen but ordained—when we have done that, then is God seated on his throne to preside with the pre-eminence he deserves.

Now Hagar did not know that, not that she would have heard it often in Abraham's house and from the mouth of her master and husband.[1] Be that as it may, she continues to go about her daily

---

[1] With the word 'husband,' Calvin gives us to understand that Abraham had married his servant; she had only been a concubine. Neither in the commentary at the beginning of Genesis 16 nor in the preceding sermons did Calvin advance such a conjecture. Quite the contrary: 'Yet Hagar is improperly called "wife" (*uxor*) because she is brought against God's word to lie with another (*in alienum*

duties without knowing what it is to be under God's protection, and when in the desert, she even thinks God has forgotten and abandoned her. That is the way we are, even though we have the teaching drilled into us that God is not closed up in heaven reigning up there apart, but while dwelling on high, as the psalm says, he considers the lowest of the earth and even cares for the smallest and most despised of things (cf. *Psa.* 113:5-6). Although we hear that repeated every day, we give it little thought. All the more, then, must we ponder what it means, namely, that we are aware that nothing is done and nothing happens by chance and that those who imagine any kind of event show that they are worldly people. But God always watches over us, and he watches over us in all our paths, as Jeremiah says: 'Lord, I know that it is not a man's place to direct his own paths; it is your office alone.'[2] If we apply all our efforts to understand that well, we will make great progress. Otherwise, we will possess nothing certain; we will always be flitting around in the air; and as soon as some small breeze blows, we will be shaken and indeed confounded in the end. There is only God's providence in which to find rest and have confidence. That much for that point.

Now it is true God looks upon his creatures in various ways, for we must fulfil what is said in the psalm: that the wild animals themselves know and sense his mercy (cf. *Psa.* 50:10–11), and humankind even more so. No matter what, he still has a special

---

thorum inducitur). However, let us know that this association (*concubitum*) was so illicit that it was midway between lechery and marriage (*ut inter scortationem et conjugium quasi medius fuerit*).' Cf. *Commentaire*, p. 185; *Commentarii*: col. 224f.; sermon 75, f° 484a.—M.E.

[2] Cf. the nearest reference, Jeremiah 11:17... In his lessons published in 1563 (Calvin had begun his lessons on Jeremiah in 1559 and had already preached on the book of Jeremiah between 1548 and 1550), the Reformer comments: *'Scitote igitur vos nihil esse in vobis, sed in Deo et in beneplacito eius.'* Cf. *Praelectiones in Jeremiam*, CO 38, col. 119.—M.E. ['Know, therefore, that you are nothing in yourselves, but in God and in his good will.']

care for his children, whom he holds as intimate acquaintances. So he keeps a closer eye upon them, as a man will observe closely what happens in his neighbourhood while his affection is fixed on his own house at the same time. Thus, although God watches the entire world because he is its Lord, he continues to watch more closely his church, for it is there that he wishes to be known, and it is there too that he wishes to show even more clearly his power and his providence, for it is said that he is the one who watches over Israel (cf. *Jer.* 31:28; 44:27; *Dan.* 9:14). Now he does not abandon watching over the unbelievers in part, but he has nonetheless established his dwelling place in his church, so that it is chiefly there that he wishes to stand watch, and we always maintain that principle as unfailing. In other words, while our minds are wandering abroad and we see everything without discrimination and there is only darkness all around, God watches over us and knows why he places within us such great troubles, knowing that he has the means to remove us from them. And yet nothing can happen that he has not ordained. That, then, is for this first point.

Now, as we have said, Hagar accuses herself of ingratitude and stupidity when she says: 'Have I [not even][3] here looked after him that sees me?' Now this passage has been explained so diversely that if I tried to recount it all, there would only be confusion. And it is a wonder no one has given more attention to the words which are assembled here, for no one did that at first, given the fact that the expositors have not evaluated what this word 'even' means in this statement. So Hagar, when saying: 'Have I [not even] here looked after him that sees me,' understands that she, being at ease and enjoying prosperity, did not know God, that that was still not

---

[3] This word, rather than the English 'also,' follows Calvin's translation of the Hebrew, with the addition of the negative, implying a positive response: *"N'ay je pas icy mesmes veu apres celuy qui me veoid?"* [Heb. 'Have I even here seen after him who sees me?']—*Translator.*

a wonder inasmuch as it is a common vice to forget one's place at times like that. And then, if for a time she was, in her mind, alienated from him, it was a very great evil and vice, but after coming to the desert in such extremity, she was no longer able to bear up and did not know what would become of her. Afterward, even after God appeared to her by his angel and showed her her duty, she remained there like a completely stupid rock until God finally forced her eyes open, so to speak. That, then, is what she means: 'Have I [not even] here looked after him that sees me,' as if she were saying: 'Alas, I should have at least had my eyes directed toward heaven when I was going through such affliction, for nature teaches those who have troubles to turn to God.' Even unbelievers, I say, have that tendency, even though they do not yield to it willingly or from an upright and well-ordered affection; but be that as it may, when they are hard-pressed, they think about seeking God, especially when necessity prods them.

So Hagar thinks: 'Alas, I was incredibly confounded at that point; I had no hope of help. So I was obliged to think about God and raise my cries before him so that he would have pity on me. I did not do it. He appeared to me later by his angel, and I was not touched. I remained dense. What does that mean except that I must have been out of my senses, like a poor animal, no longer a human being?' We now see where that line of thinking leads when Hagar says that she 'saw after the one who sees her,' indeed, in the circumstances she mentions, there in that desert place, uninhabited by men; and since she was in despair, like a cursed and condemned creature, she still did not think about God until he awakened her forcibly, so to speak.

Now at this point we have to note it is not enough to know that God can provide for the governance of the human race and that he even keeps an eye on us to dispose of our entire lives unless we are immediately touched to the quick by that teaching. Many people will babble on about God's providence, but it is all just so much speculation. Some of them even falsify and corrupt the purity of that teaching and will always raise questions about God's providence, questions which have no substance, however. So we have to note that this teaching will never be well understood unless we apply it to our situation in order to have practice with it in case of need. So much for that item.

However, at this point, we have to observe that after God has chastised us, we must return to him if we were far removed for a time, and may that not be only a future time, but may we also, because of our past faults, be moved by a true sorrow so that we will be ashamed of ourselves and condemn ourselves. It is true that shame and self-condemnation belong together, and we need both if we are to be instructed clearly. It is true that repentance finds its source principally in a conversion that changes us so we can return to God and govern our lives in obedience to him. But we can never be inclined in that direction unless we have given close attention to our past lives and unless, after acknowledging the sins we have committed, we are displeased and angry with ourselves. May we be ashamed of having been so badly informed, and may that pierce our hearts, so to speak, so that we will be so grieved in our hearts that we will groan before God. That is particularly why it is said in Ezekiel: 'You will remember your ways' (cf. *Ezek.* 16:61), for the prophet shows how we are drawn to repentance, namely, by being aware that we have provoked God's anger against us, that we are on the way to hell, and that we deserve to have him cast us away without ever showing mercy. So when we have come to that point, it is then certain that we will begin to take courage to go forth and place ourselves again in God's hands and yield to his authority. That is also how Paul speaks of it in the sixth chapter of Romans when he says that believers can judge for themselves what the fruits of sin are: 'For before God called you, what were you? When you thought of your past lives, you are to blush because of them and be ashamed' (cf. *Rom.* 6:21). And then he shows that again more clearly when he says in 2 Corinthians that if there is no sorrow, there will never be true conversion in men (cf. *2 Cor.* 7:9-10). And that means that men accuse themselves and take vengeance on themselves because they were like God's enemies. So that is what we must first remember: that when we have gone astray and the devil has tossed us about for a while and we are like lost people, we must think about our offences and be displeased with them if we are to return to God, and we must not wait to be condemned anywhere but in ourselves, and we must do it without delay.

Now because we are a long way from doing that, we must try even harder. And what do they do, those who boast a bit of being repentant? They never want to hear their offences spoken of, but they continue to hide them as well as they can. In short, hypocrisy so blinds the eyes of most of them that they would like to be praised by God and man the way they praise themselves, deceiving themselves in their vanity and lies. That is the kind of people they are, and we are all naturally inclined to do that. So, as I have already said, we must make a special effort and overcome ourselves in that respect and think hard upon our offences and experience such anguish over them that we have no difficulty condemning ourselves. And let us not wait for God to call us to account or bring a case against us and press his case hard, but let us take the initiative, for, as Solomon says, blessed is the man who fears in his heart (cf. *Prov.* 28:14).

Moreover, let us consider what Hagar accuses herself of and condemns herself for. In the first place, she did not look to God, and then that can only be a mark of ingratitude and a base and inexcusable act of stupidity. In fact, it is not a small or insignificant fault when we do not look to God, for what can we do, wretched creatures that we are, but be addressed by him. It is said he will be near all those who call upon him and truly take refuge in him (cf. *Prov.* 15:29). Since God promises to be near those who seek him, when we are not thinking about him and are even turning our backs on him, do we not deserve to be abandoned by him and then have the devil transport us hither and yon? Now, in every case, not thinking about God is a vice that has reigned at all times in the world and is as commonplace as anything else. And what is worse, we still cannot come to him, even though he watches over us and draws us to himself as if pulling us by the hair; and therein the evil is compounded. And that is what Hagar blames herself for.

For, in the first place, her stupidity consists in the fact that she did not seek God; and in the second place is her ingratitude when she is urged to do her duty, even by an angel. That shows the obstinacy of her rejection of the good he presented to her, as if she were keeping her eyes closed while God is showing he has opened his on her.

Now we find all that within ourselves when we examine ourselves without pretence or flattery, for we not only forget God when we are too comfortable with ourselves, but even if we are prodded on like mules to examine ourselves, who of us tries to come close to doing so? At those times, some contain their resentment with difficultly, others storm about and act like wild men, or else, when asked to examine themselves, they are like mindless animals that have no sense of common reason; and very few will be found who seek God. As for those who seek him, most of them will only cry out and howl, as we have already said, and that will only make them more guilty. For it is for them a natural reaction to say, 'Alas, what am I to do?' and 'May God have pity on me,' while keeping three doors closed to reject God further, and that will serve for their greater condemnation, for they cannot claim ignorance or use it as an excuse since they themselves have declared that their recourse has to be only in God. Nevertheless, when they diligently sought him, it was only a howling of animals without a clear understanding of what it means to come to God and put their trust in him.

So let us pay close attention to what is taught here, namely, that we must consider in Hagar a living example of the fact that we will never be better advised to take refuge in God and realize that he governs everything by his providence in order to keep us within it and allow us to yield to his guidance. Never, I say, will we have that without being forced to. And then, let us always realize that we are needy, that we are unbelievably dense and slow-witted, even like stubborn horses. Instead of moving forward, we back up, we only kick against all the warnings God gives us. Now if we learn that from Hagar and apply it to ourselves, let us at least learn that when God urges us persistently by his word, he adds corrections to awaken us and purge us of her kind of stupidity so we can take advantage of the corrections and not be completely incorrigible. For even though Hagar does not show much evidence of piety and fear of God, she is nonetheless, in the end, overwhelmed by afflictions, and it is then that she received the teaching which the angel gave her. If Hagar had only followed the warning that we heard, that would not have been enough for her, but the vision causes God's instruction to motivate her.

Now that is what we also have to apply to ourselves, as I said, for God works in two ways to get us to himself and lead us to the right path. When we have been turned aside from it, it is by his word that he exhorts us to return to him (cf. *Isa.* 21:12; 65:2). It is as if he had his arms extended to say: 'Come, return,' and: 'I am ready to receive you' (cf. *Isa.* 44:22). And then he uses his rods to quell our rebellion or rouse us from our indolence or cleanse us of our hypocrisy. For everyone has to be drawn to God in those two ways. For, on the one hand, we have that teaching every day and, on the other, there is no one God does not warn to return to him. And when we experience some affliction and trouble, it is always a sign of his wrath and that he does not become angry without cause. Consequently, we have to conclude that he does that to make us acknowledge and examine our sins. Thus, since God uses those two ways, let us be advised that they are not useless for us but that their usefulness is demonstrated for us here. That much we see in what happened to Hagar.

Moreover, it is quite true that God must consider us before we consider him.[4] For if he waited for us to come to him, it is certain we would only further alienate ourselves from him. Consequently, what is said to the prophet Isaiah must be verified in all men, both great and small: 'I appeared to those who did not inquire after me; I approached them when they were far off, and I have said to those who did not know me: Here am I; here am I' (cf. *Isa.* 65:1). That is also why Paul says to the Galatians: 'Now that you have known God, or rather have been known by him' (cf. *Gal.* 4:9). Those words show us that God's grace must come first, for we would never seek him if he did not come to seek us in the depths of hell, for that is the depths to which we have sunk by nature and that is the curse we bear from our mother's womb.

Moreover, God sought us more boldly and plainly when he brought us to knowledge of himself and made himself known to us in the face of our Lord Jesus Christ through his gospel. But after that, the fact is he often considers us when we are not thinking about him. For even though we have been taught that we must call upon him, we are still amazingly cold. And do the most capable see how significantly they fail by not calling on him? And yet, how are we to abandon ourselves to him in the exercise of our faith if not by prayers and petitions? And there is not one who does not know he continues confused when he has to pray. Consequently,

---

[4] A brief statement which once again denies man's free will. It is God who takes the initiative. Cf. *Institutes* I, xv, 8, and especially II, v.—*M.E.*

let us bear in mind that God must often look upon us when our backs are turned on him and we are asleep, and he must watch over us and even open our eyes. Until he does, we close our eyes when we are confused, even totally blinded by our desires and worldly concerns. We must, I say, always have our eyes open if we are to govern ourselves, but we must not allow our spiritual laziness to put us to sleep. So when God supports us in such a way that, after he has called us to himself, he assures us he will be near to all who call upon him, let us not be like that poor Hagar, but let us know the goal to which we are called, namely, that when we find our complete refuge in God, he will never abandon or reject us because his promise cannot fail: 'Knock and it will be opened to you. Ask and it will be given to you. Seek and you will find' (cf. *Matt.* 7:7). That, then, is a practice we must observe.

Yet, if we still cannot completely do our duty and are experiencing hardship and God helps us and we do not think about him, let as bear this in mind: 'Alas, how have I sought my God as I should have? I know I must not pray to him for the sake of appearance, but how am I to pray as I should? Have I the power of God as it has to be imprinted in my heart? Have I tasted his goodness as I should have? Let us think about all these things. And when we find so many faults within ourselves, let us conclude: 'Oh, God saw while I saw nothing.' That, then, is what we have to remember.

In fact, we see what he says through his prophet Isaiah, in chapter thirty. After reproaching the Jews for becoming profoundly corrupt and even for making graves with their impious deeds, for imagining that they could mock everything holy, and, in a word, for abandoning themselves to such evil deeds that they could not be corrected, he adds: 'I will indeed chastise you. But after you have eaten the bread of adversity, I will nonetheless return to you (cf. *Isa.* 30:20). And also, when your minds have become dull, insensitive and unreasoning, the devil will be in such control that you will no longer understand anything, you will still have the voice of the one who will admonish from behind.' This phrase 'from behind' needs to be noted, for God compares himself to a mother who keeps her eye on her child when she takes him for a walk. The child runs about and has a good time, but the eyes of his mother are always on him. She is always near him. Likewise, a young child will always have his teacher, who is behind him and knows how to punish each of his misdeeds. So God follows that procedure and says, even though we were wandering astray and fleeing from him and the devil was keeping our eyes blinded to make us go in many directions, 'I will be behind you. It is true I will not show you my face at first, but I will nonetheless be gracious unto you and from now on you will follow my admonitions and my ordinances so you will not deviate either to the right or to the left.' That, then, is how God ordinarily works with us, and we are to sense it. And when sensing it, let us at least admit his kindness to Hagar and say: 'I saw after one who sees me.' In other words, we have not been wise enough to see God while he sees us; and we have not seen him the way he sees us, but he has always made provisions for our thinking about that. And when we are condemned for this vice and displeased by it, let that motivate us to consider more carefully praying to him and calling upon his name. That, in short, is what we have to remember about this passage.

Now Hagar is not content to confess once that God had his eye on her when she was not thinking about him, but she wants there to be a perpetual memorial to it. And it is certain that, in making the confession, she disgraces herself and is content to bear a reproach forever, but she makes it to glorify God. What are we going to do by comparison to match this poor creature, who in the end was banished and chased from the church, so to speak, as we will see, if she still wanted God's grace to be known and celebrated everywhere forever and was still willing to be subjected to the disgrace of condemning herself and making a perpetual memorial to it? Consequently, if we bury God's benefits after sensing them, woe unto us. But it still is not enough for us to be grateful to him for them for a day; we must, as far as we can, desire that the memory of them will last from age to age and that he will be glorified in us. And let us at the same time be humbled, as we deserve to be.

We see how the holy patriarchs and prophets used that example. Moses did not remain silent about his faults,[5] but even though they could have been considered quite insignificant, he thought them to be more heinous. And then there is David, who not only admits to being an evildoer, but he says that if God does not extend all his mercies to look upon him with pity, he is undone. And that way, he is not concerned for his reputation, as many scoundrels are, who say: 'What? I will be disgraced. Must I bear such shame?' They disgrace the name of God. They expose it to shame as much as possible, and still they want to pass as honourable men. All the more then must we hold to the teaching that we endeavour with all our might to make known all the blessings we have received from God and to confess that we are very far from fulfilling our duty toward him, that we are slack, ingrates, rebels, neglectful, and vile. So let us be content that all those things come to our notice so our Jesus Christ may cover us with his mercy, for men must condemn themselves if they wish him to absolve them. That then is what we have to remember.

It is then said that Hagar bore Ishmael and Abraham gave him that name as the angel had commanded. We must note here Hagar's obedience. We have already seen how she had been better

---

[5] As the nearest reference, one can only think of Exodus 3:11: 'Who am I that I should go to Pharaoh?' Calvin does not consider this as a refusal but as an expression of humility. Moses considers himself weak and inadequate for the task to which God calls him. Cf. Calvin, *Pentateuque*, p. 24; CO 24, col. 41.—*M.E.*

informed of and persuaded about God's providence and how she humbled herself and was corrected in the things in which she had failed and how she magnified the favour he had shown her. That, I say, is how that vision was useful to her. But she immediately adds actions to words. There are many who open their mouths to give indications of repentance, but when it comes to actually repenting, they neglect to do so. So, Hagar shows her confession was not pretence when she returns to Abraham's house. By returning, she could be in fear of her mistress and treated more harshly than ever because, in addition to being hated, she could still be scorned for running away. Now we see the same thing in Abraham. It is true that his obedience deserves more praise than Hagar's, but be that as it may, Hagar's must serve to instruct us.

Abraham, for his part, names the child born to him 'Ishmael.' From that we have to gather that Hagar not only knew God's angel in the desert and that she did not condemn herself there, but when she returned to the house, she gives a full account of what happened to her. Abraham could not have guessed that the child was to be named 'Ishmael,' that is, he could not have known that 'God had heard'[6] if Hagar had not told him. So we see that she was not only moved to be displeased with her rebellion, with her ingratitude and her stupidity while she was hiding, but when she is in the house, she declares both her misery and the mercy of God, who wanted to visit her while she was in such extreme anguish. And that is also how we are to act. We are not to keep hidden away and buried what God has taught us, but we are to try at the same time to build up our neighbours, not for show, as many do who are comfortable with themselves as they pretend to preach God's favours to extend their wings and babble on at length; and instead of giving praise to God, they keep it for themselves. Now that

---

[6] *Ishmâ'ê'l* comes in fact from the root *shm'*, 'to hear, to answer (prayer),' which was always known.—M.E.

is not the way we must be influenced by ambition, but we must acknowledge our faults and spiritual poverty and realize that God alone must be glorified and that we must experience only shame, for all glory belongs to him. Thus we see that Abraham profited from what Hagar said to him and accepts God's command, even though it comes to him through his chambermaid. That shows how we cannot be obedient without humility. When we allow ourselves to be instructed by God, not when he sends us angels, but at those times the poorest creatures in the world might show us that it is God's truth they are bringing us so that we may learn to bring ourselves into line with it by following the example of our father Abraham, father of all believers, if we wish to be considered as his children.

> Now let us bow before the majesty of our gracious God in acknowledgment of our faults, praying that he will be pleased to move us to such repentance that we will groan before him and be fully overwhelmed until we are lifted up by his mercy. And may he not only pardon our offences, but may he also cleanse us of them by his Holy Spirit and teach us to return to him and persevere until the end. And may we not only be taught by the mouth of men and shown what the road to salvation is, but may he also open our eyes and penetrate our ears so that we will receive all the corrections he sends us so that we will devote ourselves even more to him by renouncing ourselves because we cannot obey him except by condemning ourselves. May he grant that grace not only to us but to all the peoples and nations on earth.

78

Confidence in God's Power to Renew and Save, Our Assurance for Obedience

Tuesday, 2 April 1560

And when Abram was ninety years old and nine, the LORD appeared to Abram, and said unto him, I am the Almighty God; walk before me, and be thou perfect. And I will make my covenant between me and thee, and will multiply thee exceedingly. And Abram fell on his face: and God talked with him, saying, As for me, behold, my covenant is with thee... (Gen. 17:1-4a).

MOSES PASSES OVER thirteen years from the time of Hagar's return until God speaks to his servant Abraham again. Now it is likely that during that entire time Abraham was content to have Ishmael and that it seemed to him that that was to be the status quo and that he was already enjoying the promise he had been given. Now we know that he was mistaken on that point, as he will learn later (cf. *Gen.* 17:19), for it was not in Ishmael that the blessed seed was to be given to him. So he corrupted God's promise by following a foolish fantasy, as we have already seen; for when he took his second wife, it is because he interpreted God's word badly, for at the time, he turned his back on the simple message he was to adhere to. God had declared to him that he would give him seed (cf. *Gen.* 12:7;

13:16; 15:4-5). Now that was to be understood according to the order which God established at the creation of the world and was to be inviolable. So God did not want to contravene what he had instituted, namely, that each man have a wife and each woman a husband (cf. *Gen.* 2:24). Yet Sarah, as a result of a foolish intrusion and an immoderate desire, wants Abraham to have seed from another source. So we see how they deviated from the right path. And in doing so, they corrupted the promise.

And there likewise is Abraham, who is asleep, so to speak. And because he sees Ishmael in his house, he thinks he possesses what he had so much desired. And it is even likely that because of such an error, he delayed the fulfilment of the true promise; for God wanted to punish him by not giving him Isaac right away because he had diverted his attention and feelings to Ishmael. And that is how we often prevent God from doing what he promised us inasmuch as we have many distractions which tugged at us. We enthusiastically feed on our foolish vanities and our witless notions when we should be coming forth like starving people with our mouths open to receive what he is ready to give us. Consequently, there is no way for God's grace to enter. That is what happens to us, and it should not surprise us, for this vice was in Abraham, who was a living example of all saintliness, some of which we have seen and will hear more about later.

Therefore, when we read Moses' words that Abraham was eighty-six years old when Ishmael was born (cf. *Gen.* 16:16) and was ninety-nine when Isaac was promised to him, let us realize that God let him wait such a long time because he had deceived himself in his imagination and deserved to be deprived of the true blessing, seeing that he was wasting his time with the one who was born according to the flesh, the one whom he had begotten against God's law and the order of marriage; and in addition, as we have said, he had corrupted the purity of the promise by following his own imagination and by not waiting for what God had proclaimed when he fathered Ishmael. When we realize that, let us apply it to ourselves as we note that if Abraham had not been spared because he veered from the clear understanding of God's word, God must keep us on a shorter tether, and we must not try to add anything to what God says to us, but we must receive it as is. And because our feelings vary and shift easily from one thing to another, let us pray that by the Holy Spirit he will guide us in such a way that we will know what his will is, and knowing it, we will apply it fully to ourselves. That, in short, is the first thing we need to learn.

But there is another thing, namely, that when God gave the promise, it could not be destroyed by Abraham's sin. Consequently, God overcame everything that stood in the way of the fulfilment of his word. And that is how he fights against our vices so that his mercy and his truth will always be victorious. As for us, it seems that we conspire to subvert his mercy and make it ineffective and remove it as far away from ourselves as possible. Now he must correct such grievous sin, for we would otherwise deserve to be totally deprived of what we hoped for, for we know that the result of all promises must be united with faith, as the apostle says: the word the Jews heard was of no advantage to them because faith, he says, was not united with it (cf. *Heb.* 4:2). Therefore, when we are so perverse as to wander off into our fantasies and imaginations, taking one for the other and blinding ourselves, would we not deserve to have our Lord abandon us completely and withdraw his hand and show us, because we have not opened ourselves to his grace, that he must place it elsewhere when it finds no place in us? He does not do that, but nonetheless, having pity on our perversity, he still does what he said, but in due time. And he also corrects us because of our sins. Therefore, let us take note of these two vices. When God sometimes prolongs the time we think has already come, let us know that it is because we have been too hasty, that we have involved our own wills and have been too impatient. Let us acknowledge those reasons. Consequently, we must frequently be made to wait. However, let us learn to blame ourselves for the annoyance and inconvenience when we have to wait a long time, and may we be kept from seeing that God wishes to fulfil what we hope for in him according to his word. Why? As I have already said, we hinder him with our impatience or our unbelief or some other vices which are sometimes hidden from us. And even when we think well of ourselves, every one of us can condemn himself for doing that. For we would like for our Lord to deal with us according to our good pleasure, and we can never be content with what he knows to be in our best interest, but we would like for him to please us in each and every detail. And then when he does not work as we would like, in other words, as we have imagined it, we must help him along and find some means, which we are not allowed to do. So let us not find it strange when our Lord allows us to wait impatiently longer than we would have liked and longer than we thought it would take, for there was a reason for it. And when we undertake some foolish enterprise, let us be humble and groan because we close the door to God, so to speak, who knew the appropriateness of his timing, but we wanted to get ahead of him, and he wants to show us that our impatience only delays his work and that, but for our impatience, we would have already had his mercy and truth.

Moreover, let us not stop hoping in him under any circumstance, and when we have to suffer for our foolish and brazen deeds, let us be convinced that in the end God will continue to work so that we will have reason to bless his name for what was done for Abraham, in accordance with the confirmation given here. It is true that thirteen years was a great deal of time, but even so, after God delayed for a long time, he still did not give up on doing what he said despite the fact Abraham was not worthy. That, then, is what we must remember, namely, that we are displeased. When we stir in our own preferences to avoid God's access to our lives, let us not be discouraged and fall into despair, but let us know that in the end God will fight against our evil tendencies and, after chastising us for a time, will show us that his goodness and truth triumph. That, then, is what we have to remember in sum.

Now the text says that God appeared to Abraham and said to him: 'I am the Almighty God; walk before me and be perfect.' That vision was to assure Abraham of God's word so that he would not doubt that it proceeded from God, as the subject was dealt with above. So there are two things to look at here: one is that God speaks, and that is primary, for faith comes by hearing (cf. *Rom.* 10:17). And if we have all the visions in the world, unless God opens his mouth to instruct us and give witness to his truth concerning us, it is all useless; we would all be seized with fear, and our faith would evaporate and we could have no time for calling upon God and resting in him. Therefore, the primary thing is that God speaks, but we must be certain that it is he whom we hear, indeed the one who is infallible truth (cf. *John* 14:6), who does not vary, who is unchangeable (cf. *James* 1:14), who stretched out his hand (cf. *Isa.* 23:11; *Jer.* 1:9) as soon as he spoke the word to fulfil it (cf. *1 Kings* 8:15; *Rom.* 4:21) and show there is nothing disappointing in anything that proceeds from his mouth. That much must we be assured of. Now both come together here, namely, that God appeared so that Abraham would have a notable sign that indicates God's majesty so he could be certain that there was nothing to fear and that he could lean confidently on the truth which was certain and unfailing.

Now there is also the word, as I said, and for our part we must be content that we have the word, for visions today would be more than we need. It is true we desire them in proportion to the impatience of our minds, which can never be satisfied, but let us consider how God confirms the teaching which we must accept today. For the visions which Abraham had (cf. *Gen.* 17:4; *Rom.* 4:17-18; *Gal.* 3:7) must serve us today, and since he is our father, we must be united and one with him in a true commonality of faith. Consequently, when God appeared to him, it was so we can know that we do not receive from men what is contained in holy Scripture, but that it is the same teaching that was confirmed by all the visions Abraham had. Following that was the law, which was authenticated as much as anything else at the time the earth was set in motion. The mountain was filled with fire and smoke; and then if someone approached it, even an animal, it was a matter of death. God thundered in such a way that if the heavens had opened and his glory had been visible, there would not have been a more certain approval than that. And then many miracles were immediately added, as the psalm says: he spoke to our fathers in the column of fire to show that the law (cf. *Psa.* 99:7), five hundred years after it had been given, was not to be doubted or disputed. Why not? It is not without reason that the prophet reminds the Jews how, when the law was given, God spoke. He spoke from the column of fire. Inasmuch as that is the case, the law must carry its authority for us, for as the prophet spoke concerning his time, the same instruction must also be dominant among us today.

Moreover, we not only have the law, but we have the confirmation of the prophets. And then there is the gospel which not only shook the earth but also the heaven, as the apostle says (cf. *Heb.* 12:26). Since that is true, it is not a matter of looking today for visions like Abraham's, for we are to be confident in them because of the testimonies that God gave to the law and the prophets. Therefore, we have to come back to what Moses adds later. It is true he brings in other propositions, but because this is added, it is better that it be explained together.

Therefore, he says, 'I with my covenant.'[1] That statement is heavy with meaning. When God says 'I,' he puts a distance between himself and all creatures and also all thoughts which could enter our heads. Just as we are disposed to accept Satan's lies, delusions, and illusions, so are we slow to find rest in God and his word. It seems that there is a root of unbelief so deep in all our senses that we are completely turned from believing and adding faith to God's word. And yet our ears are open enough to listen to Satan's impostures and deceptions. All the more, then, must we prize this phrase and the import of the word 'I.' When God speaks in precise and concise terms this way, it is as if he were saying: 'Be content when you know that I am speaking. For how are my glory and my majesty to be valued in your eyes? Who am I? In what kind of esteem am I to be held? How highly is my truth to be prized?' That, then, is how God exalts and magnifies himself to forestall all objections and all disputes so that when we know it is he who is speaking, we will come to this conclusion: that we must be diligent in obeying him always and in every respect and not intrude ourselves and say: 'How is that? Why? When?' Let us wholeheartedly accept everything that we know comes from him. That, then, is what we have to remember about this passage.

Consequently, the vision given Abraham served him well. Why? Because he did not yet have what was required of him and what is given to us to provide us with confidence in the law and the gospel. There was no written teaching. He had to be content with some small taste of the word, and yet his faith surpassed ours by far. There is no wonder our Lord assured him with visions, for the time required it. But now God does not parcel out small pieces of food for our souls, but he satisfies us with them, which we have

---

[1] French: '*moy avec mon aliance.*' '*Moy*' is emphatic: '*I*,' 'as for me.' Here is the French Scripture cited at the beginning of the sermon in Engammare's edition: '*Moy, voicy mon aliance…*' (Gen. 17:4a).—*Translator.*

before our eyes in Scripture, which contains the keys of the kingdom of heaven to open its door for us so that we have easy and
familiar access to our God and the display of his affection and the
revelation of his wondrous secrets. So inasmuch as we possess all
those things, we would show great contempt for God and trample
underfoot the infinite grace he grants us if we do not leave aside
the visions and acknowledge that we are confident in his word
because of the many miracles which were done. Finally, we have
our Lord Jesus Christ, in whom God has fully revealed and manifested himself (cf. *1 Tim.* 3:16). We now lack nothing. We must
value this very highly as being from God.

So that is how that vision served no other purpose than to
inform Abraham that it was God who was speaking. We know it
today, and although we know it by different means, let us remember this word 'I.' And if we should hear all the men in the world
speak, if that were possible, and say that the angels had come to
speak to us, and if everyone should cry out: 'This is the way we
want it to be,' we have no other words. So if we should hear a
hundred million voices, let us disregard them as speaking claptrap
and mere drivel. In a word, let this word 'I,' when God utters it,
satisfy us and delight our whole being, all our desires and all our
emotions, and let us be so convinced by it that we will hold in bold
contempt every word presented by the adverse camp, no matter its
high rank, however glorious, however majestic, however exalted,
however excellent it may be, even if it should be made up of all the
sovereign empires in the world. That, in brief, is what we have to
remember.

Now he tells Abraham forthwith: 'I am the Almighty God.'[2]
There are different names in the Hebrew language for 'God.'[3] This

---

[2] In Genesis 17:1, the name of God is *ĕl shaddai*. In his commentary, Calvin
translates it with 'God Omnipotent' and 'God Almighty.' *Commentaire*, p. 193.
It is the traditional translation that Münster and Pagnini always propose.—*M.E.*
[3] In addition to the tetragrammaton, Elohim, Adonai, El, etc.—*M.E.*

is one of them, but word for word it signifies 'mighty'; and it is attributed to God because not only does all power belong to him, but he is also victorious, although some derive this second title from 'fullness of good things,' as if our Lord were saying that he is bountiful in all largesse and is even the source of all good things that satisfy us, but the term most often refers to God's power to resist his enemies, to put to flight everything that confronts him, and also to maintain his church. In short, there is no doubt that God wanted to give Abraham a definite reason at this time for trusting him and remaining steadfast, as if he were saying: 'All your welfare and all your felicity lie within my protection.' We always have to note that when God attributes to himself these titles, he does not do so for his own advantage—what need does he have to do so?—but it is for our instruction that he does so. When God calls himself 'mighty,' when he calls himself 'all powerful,' we are not to understand a secret and hidden force within himself that is in heaven, but we must realize he is strong and powerful on our behalf. In other words, he wishes to display his power to sustain us because we belong to him, not that we deserve it, but because he has adopted us (cf. *Gal.* 4:5; *Eph.* 1:5). So if God tells us that he is our Father (cf. *Deut.* 32:6; *John* 14:6; *Rom.* 1:7), let us immediately realize he is all powerful so that we can rest in him and not doubt that when he takes our side, we can scorn both Satan and everything he can contrive and all this world's assaults; if we should have a million enemies attacking us, we will always be able to say: 'God is on my side. I shall fear nothing' (cf. *Psa.* 56:4; 118:6). That, then, is the point God wanted to bring his servant Abraham to.

Now we know that what God gave him was placed on deposit at the same time so that it belongs to us, for we are heirs, for we are imitators of his faith (cf. *Rom.* 8:17; *Gal.* 3:29; *Eph.* 1:11). Consequently, there is no doubt that everything promised him will be useful for us. Therefore, the account of what God declared once and for all to his servant Abraham is to resound in our ears over and over without end, namely, that is, we must meditate upon God and realize he is powerful and mighty, that we should not doubt, providing he takes care of us, that all will go well, and that we will always land on our feet, not that we will be without many troubles and afflictions. God would not have to have great power were it not for the fact that we will see many troubles and have to be subdued a hundred times a day, but we must use God's infinite power as a shield, seeing that the devil conspires to do everything he can against us, that the world grows haughty, that we are like ships at sea in the midst of many storms and tempests. So let us keep before us God's power, and let us be so influenced by our confidence that our faith will always be victorious, even though we are shaken in the world of our flesh, and let us nonetheless possess that strength within ourselves so we can say: 'God will suffice for rectifying everything that is against us.' That, in brief, is what we have to remember about this word 'I.'

And in fact, if we do not know God as he is, how will we be able to give ourselves to him? But when we know that he is strong enough to protect us and that his power does not lie idle within him, but that it is for our salvation, it is then that we have to be grossly stupid if we do not come and submit ourselves to him, for he is our sovereign good, our only good, and we would otherwise be exceedingly wretched.

Now on that point he tells him to walk before him and be perfect. Here we see that God is aiming at two things in his desire to instruct us. One is that we not doubt that he is our Father and Saviour, indeed because of his free goodness; and the other is that, because he is pleased to accept us as his children, we honour him and give him the love and reverence he is due, for he does not want us to abuse his goodness. If the only thing we had to do is say, 'Oh, God promised me that he will be my Saviour; so I am content,' while carousing, abusing every teaching, freely giving ourselves over to every vice, we would be tearing God's grace to shreds. So let us note that God adopts us on condition that, since he is our Father, we are also to be his children, that is, we are to give him the obedience he is due. That much he declares to us as in a painting and in a living image in the person of our father Abraham. For we must be like him in order to be members of the household of the church.

But let us learn, however, that our salvation does not depend upon any uprightness of life that we might have. It depends on God's free goodness. If it had been said: 'Abraham, walk before me, and be perfect,' and God had then added: 'I will at that time show that I am the Almighty God,' we would think that Abraham's salvation was based on his uprightness and holy life. But when God tells him that he will be his Saviour, as he has just testified (cf. *Gen.* 15:1) and is now confirming, and then adds that he walk in uprightness, we see in that fact, as I have already said, that our salvation does not proceed from any power we might possess—and I am also speaking of the power God gives us. For even though God commands us to walk in uprightness, that does not mean we can do so, for he must give us the ability by his Holy Spirit. Even when God works in us and remakes us and imprints his law on our hearts, that does not mean that when we serve him, doing the best we can to please him and submit to his righteousness, we do not in that way acquire grace and favour before him. In no way! But, on the contrary, we must always rely only on his free goodness, and we must know that he will continue to deal with us until the end in the same way he began and that he will accept us as righteous despite our many weaknesses and vices.

Now we must add this in passing as a matter of secondary importance, namely, that since he is so kind and bounteous toward us, receives us in mercy who are damned and lost creatures, and since he always sustains us, even though there are so many weaknesses within us and we are always condemned and subject to his judgment, he nonetheless buries all our failings. Since it is true that God deploys the infinite treasures of his bounty upon us, that is good reason for us to try to devote ourselves to him. That, in brief, is what we primarily have to remember.

That is also why Paul says we are not called to filth and pollution so we can abandon ourselves to every iniquity (cf. *Rom.* 6:1), but we are called to devote ourselves to the worship of our God. He deals with that at length in the first chapter of Ephesians. Peter also tells us we have been removed from the darkness of death to glorify our God and proclaim his praises, not only with our mouths, but also with our entire lives (cf. *1 Pet.* 2:9-12). Therefore, let us remember this: that since God adopted us as his children and declares it in his gospel, it is so that we will learn to worship him as our Creator and bear him the honour that is his as our Father, as he also demands through his prophet: 'If I am your Father and your Master, where are the honour and love that you have for me?' (Cf. *Mal.* 1:6.)

And we must still note what he says: 'Walk before me, and be perfect,' for 'walking before God,' as it was expounded when Enoch was discussed, means that we do not consider how the world goes about its business, for we will often only see that everything is in confusion; and if we want to follow the common path, it is certain we will be corrupted a hundred times a day. How many stumbling blocks does Satan place before us every day? So many that if we consider what is done and the extent of the excesses, it is certain we will always be like stray animals. What must we do then? We must learn to collect ourselves in God. People are perverse and malicious, and they will always lead us to evil and to hell if we choose to believe them; and the devil also uses them subtly. That is why I said he places stumbling blocks before us to turn us from the right path. In short, it is difficult to keep order in our lives and walk in the holiness and fear of God if we do not collect ourselves in him and say, 'I do not consider what others do unless they provide me with a good example, but if they yield to every iniquity, I must not follow them. If I walk among thorns, I must guard against being pricked by them. If I walk in filth, I must be resolved not to foul myself with it; rather I must be even more careful to avoid being contaminated and polluted. And how will I do that? I will place God before my eyes and say, "It is to him that I must give an account of my life and before whom I will have to appear in judgment." So I must keep my eyes especially on him and not on another when it comes to ordering my life.'

And that is also why he adds the word 'integrity,' or 'fullness.'[4] It is true that that is taken to mean 'perfection,' but it also means 'fullness, uprightness, purity,' wherein is no pretence. That is why Scripture often will say a 'perfect heart' (cf. *1 Kings* 8:61; *2 Kings* 20:3; *1 Chron.* 12:38; *Psa.* 101:2; *Isa.* 38:3), and its negative, a 'double heart' (cf. *1 Chron.* 13:33; *Psa.* 12:2; *Sir.* 1:36). In a word, God requires of our father Abraham that he serve him in purity of life, as we have already said that that is the goal of our calling. And that is also why Peter exhorts us in his second letter to make our election sure, to make it steadfast and approved (cf. *2 Pet.* 1:10), when we walk in the fear of God. It is now quite certain that if we are to order our lives well, we must keep the Ten Commandments, for it is not our place to construct the laws, as we see men governing themselves mostly by their foolish devotions, so much so that they think God is indeed supported by them and obligated to

---

[4] Genesis 17:1 ends with '*weheyèh tâmîm*,' which Calvin first translated as 'be perfect,' as in his commentary, '*esto perfectus*' in Latin. Cf. *Commentarii*, col. 234; *Commentaire*, p. 193. The common Latin translation was '*perfectus*,' the translation Münster preserves. On the other hand, the Zurich version adopted by Vatable has '*esto integer*' (without annotation). Cf. Münster, *Biblia Hebraica*, p. 35; Vatable, *Biblia*, fᵒ 10rᵒ.—M.E.

them, just as they fantasize in their foolish imaginations. As for us, we must realize that God is our Judge and that, consequently, he is our Legislator and that it is to him that we must be subjected, that his law is to be our rule, but that is not yet everything. Since we have to please God and not men, let us consider what he is. He is spirit. Therefore, we must serve him in spirit and in truth (cf. *John* 4:24). That is the source of that fullness mentioned here. So when we realize what it means to walk before God, we will conclude that we have to be empty of all hypocrisy and insincerity, that it is not a matter of putting on a fine countenance to please him, but that we must be first cleansed of all the dark places in our hearts and of all pretence, and that we must have such fullness and integrity that we can proclaim we worship him from our hearts, as we read: 'Israel, what does your God ask of you but to walk before him in integrity and uprightness?'⁵ If we do that, all the rest is nothing. We see that even among the pagans, for many of them enjoyed great renown for their virtues. Those who were never marked by any hint of infamy, who never did anything wrong, seemed to be angels. So what? The virtues were apparent to men while their hearts were filled with overweening pride. They even took for themselves God's honour and acquired for themselves a reputation, esteem, and goodwill; yet they were filled with villainy and wicked desires. So that is how what is exalted and excellent in men's eyes is only abomination before God.

Let us learn, then, that the uprightness of our hearts must come before all the rest and that we must not apply just our steps and our hands and our feet and our legs and our eyes to the worship of God, but that our hearts must move forward and guide and sustain all the rest. And our hearts must be cleansed because we are by nature always entangled in our hypocrisy, and there must always

⁵ This is a resumé of Ezekiel 36:22-27. Cf. also Psalm 15:2 and Proverbs 2:7.— *M.E.*

be a purging which precedes us. And that purging depends on our examining ourselves diligently. We are all satisfied with ourselves, and we all persuade ourselves that we are top-notch saints. We do not want anyone to find anything reprehensible in us and, as a result, we squat in our filth and heap God's wrath upon our heads (cf. *Isa.* 5:25; 10:4; *Jer.* 4:8; 30:24). And when we have heard the sermons every day, we will all seem to be confused, but some will be filled with hatred and rancour, and others will be filled with avarice, others with evil desires, others with cruelty and malice, as others are given to their vices; there is an abyss of wickedness within us. Consequently, if we always remain that way, alas, what good will it do us if we profit so little from the teaching we hear that we end up with greater and more horrible condemnation? Therefore, since we see that we are so given to hypocrisy and that there are many who hide their pretence under God's name and think they have done all they need to do when they come show their faces at the preaching services, all the more then must we understand from this passage that we are doing nothing if we do not walk with integrity and uprightness. Because the Jews gloried in their elaborate devotions, because they had great pomp in their sacrifices and the temple was magnificently adorned, Jeremiah, because God looks upon faith and truth, turns to God and says: 'Oh Lord, these men are mistaken about the things they foolishly have confidence in, and you will not waste your time with their fine displays, for you always consider the truth of the heart and the pure affection that you especially require.'[6] That, in brief, is what we still have to remember.

Now God adds for greater confirmation that he will establish his covenant between himself and Abraham, not because he had not already done so, but to show him what the result would be.

---

[6] Cf. Jeremiah 7, especially verse 5... Cf. also Isaiah 1:11-17; Jeremiah 6:20; 9:7; 17:10; Hosea 6:6; Amos 5:22-24; etc.—*M.E.*

Abraham does not immediately understand what is made known to him; yet in the meantime the covenant remains confirmed and in effect. And then God corrects Abraham's error and makes him glad so that he will have a better idea about his role and quit wasting his time over the empty hope he had conceived when he interpreted God's word wrongly. We know, within the limits of our infirmity, that we need to have God remind us daily what we have already learned in his school, for if we hear preaching about his mercy a hundred thousand times, it will never be enough. Why not? Our memories must be refreshed. That much for that point.

Moreover, we have learned only half of what we think we have learned. And when we are disposed to be good students, we realize our ignorance the more advanced we are. If we thought we were great students from the first through the tenth, we realize it is nothing and that there was only foolish pride in us, or very little faith. So our Lord always needs to speak to us again and again.

But there was a special reason to speak repeatedly in Abraham's case because he had turned aside from God's promise because of a frivolous opinion which he had accepted too credulously from his wife and because he had been too quick to obey his wife, who had rashly added to God's word. He had to be removed from that situation, for we see that he was asleep, so to speak (cf. *Gen.* 16:2). For thirteen years he finds joy in Ishmael, but in the end he has to chase him from the house and realize that he is cut off from the church. That is why it is now said to him: 'I will make my covenant,' as if our Lord were saying: 'Do not continue in this direction, for you have got off the right path. And if you continue this way, you will find only confusion in the end. So come back to the realization that you must submit to the simple act of looking to me when I said at the beginning that I would be your God (cf. *Gen.* 15:1) and give you seed (cf. *Gen.* 12:2; 13:16; 15:5). You must realize that it is not this lad who has now been born into your house, but you must hope for and wait for another.' So we understand how God both confirms Abraham's faith and corrects the error that had preoccupied him.

So when we come to hear God's word, let us realize that our faith needs to be advanced as we go along; and inasmuch as there are uncertainties mingled with it and we are so wrapped up in many empty expectations, our Lord has to disperse those uncertainties and shine more and more light on them so we can correct our errors, for only with great effort will our faith ever be pure. As long as we are enclosed in this body, there will always be some earthly weight within us that allows us to see only in part (cf. *1 Cor.* 13:9). That, then, is what we need to remember about this text that says God will make his covenant with Abraham.

Now he also adds that he will multiply him greatly. At first Abraham does not know what God means, but God made it clear in time; for we see that if the situation had remained as it was and Abraham had waited for Ishmael, God's promise would have been set aside. But God wants to prepare him, for he does not immediately correct him of the error that was in him, but he removes it from him little by little, wishing to return him to the acknowledgment that he had had only troubles and had been surrounded by uncertainties and darkness. That, in summary, is what we have to remember here, namely, that we are to allow our Lord to remake our minds, for they are subject to many illusions. Satan does not have to create many doubts to take advantage of us; we have, each of us, deceived ourselves, and God must work little by little to teach us to abandon all our personal feelings, all our opinions, and to subdue our reasoning and our wisdom so that we may be his subjects and obedient to him.

Now let us bow before the majesty of our gracious God in acknowledgment of our faults, praying that he will increasingly make us aware of them and draw us to sincere repentance and strengthen us to struggle against our vices all of our lives until we die. And may we be strengthened to that end by the power of his Holy Spirit, and may he give such effectiveness to the suffering and death of our Jesus Christ that we will not only be forgiven of our sins but that our old Adam will be put to death and buried along with all our worldly desires, which are wicked and full of rebellion. May he grant that grace not only to us but to all the peoples and nations on earth.

79

The Covenant: God's Initiation of Eternal Salvation

Wednesday, 3 April 1560

As for me, behold, my covenant is with thee, and thou shalt be a father of many nations. Neither shall thy name any more be called Abram, but thy name shall be Abraham; for a father of many nations have I made thee. And I will make thee exceeding fruitful, and I will make nations of thee, and kings shall come out of thee. And I will establish my covenant between me and thee and thy seed after thee in their generations for an everlasting covenant, to be a God unto thee, and to thy seed after thee. And I will give unto thee, and to thy seed after thee, the land wherein thou art a stranger, all the land of Canaan, for an everlasting possession; and I will be their God (Gen. 17:4-8).*

E SAW YESTERDAY the intention of the opening state-ment when God makes himself known and declares that it is he. He does so to provide us with such a firm confidence that our faith will never be shaken when it is fixed on him and his authority. Since we must be certain that nothing is lacking in anything God has promised us, we must, on the other hand, also close our ears to whatever comes to us from men inas-much as we know that it is only vanity and deceit, for we must not be moved by every wind, as Paul says (cf. *Eph.* 4:14) and mix men's

words with God's. God would no longer have the high rank he
deserves if men were his companions. So our faith must be fixed
firmly in him without being remotely distracted by anything else.

It is now said that Abram will be called father of many peoples,
and for that reason God expands his name and says he will be
called Abraham. With that expansion, he signifies that Abraham
will be the father of many, or of a multitude. And with that, God
declares his intention that many peoples will be counted among his
lineage; even kings will arise from it. That much for that point.

The emphasis is on the fact that he will be as much the God
of Abraham as the God of his seed. And as a pledge he assigns
the land which had been promised him as an inheritance. But he
nonetheless repeats that he will be his God and the God of his
lineage to indicate that that is what Abraham must seek. Now we
have to consider here how that promise was accomplished, that
is, how Abraham becomes the father of many peoples. It is true
that from Ishmael arose many people; and Abraham had children
with Keturah, as we will see later (cf. *Gen.* 25:1-2). Moreover, the
Edomites are descended from Esau, who was of his race. So there
he is twice called the father of many peoples. But because the Ishmaelites and Arabs, that is, the Edomites, were cut off, they were
no longer that blessing of the body of the church, properly speaking. So the blessing God gives him in this passage cannot be related to that. The fulfilment of that word must be found elsewhere.
It is true that the twelve lines represent the twelve peoples,[1] but all
of them must remain together. And when they were separated in
that revolt which ten tribes instigated, that was like a body torn to
pieces, and it was a vengeance of God because the Jews were thus
scattered as a result of their pride and rebellion. Those who left
David's house renounced the Redeemer of the world and all hope

[1] This is a reference to the twelve tribes of Israel. Cf. Genesis 30:35, 22-26;
Genesis 49.—*M.E.*

of salvation. That, then, is a disruption which must not enter into the account here.

But Abraham was made the father of many nations when the dividing wall was broken down and those who were previously estranged from God were brought together. For we cannot enter the church and be considered among the faithful if we are not made one with this ancient people. But that is not done according to the flesh, but by faith. God has created such a union among us that we are made children of Abraham (cf. *Gal.* 3:7). That is also why Paul says God made of the two one (cf. *Eph.* 2:14) and that our Lord Jesus Christ was the stone on which we are all built (cf. *Eph.* 2:20). If there were, by way of comparison, two different cornerstones of one house, there is now one. In other words, if there were many peoples, yet, because we are called inhabitants of Abraham's house, he has been established as the father of many peoples. And that is what the prophets understood when they said the Gentiles will come take on the garment of a Jew and say: 'We will walk together with you, for we must worship only God. Therefore, we must now be your brothers because God has declared himself to be our Father and has adopted us to make us sharers in the eternal inheritance' (cf. *Zech.* 8:23; *Mic.* 2:8; 4:2-5). There is no variation in God (cf. *James* 1:17). It is true that in the beginning he chose Abraham's lineage, and that was done on condition that there would be only one body, as it is said in the tenth chapter of John that if there is one shepherd, there must be only one flock, gathered together so there would not be one group here and another group somewhere else (cf. *John* 10:1-16). It is true there will always be a separation in the church. Be that as it may, the fact is that since we have one head (cf. *Eph.* 1:22; 4:15; 5:23), we are joined together in such a way that that separation in times past no longer exists. So much for that point.

Another question must still be resolved, for it would seem at first sight that there is a contradiction when the text says that Abraham will be the father of many nations, that his seed will be separated from the rest of the world and that God will reign in the midst of his seed. As for the statement about Abraham, we cannot say the text had in mind the Gentiles, who have long since been gathered into the church and who had access to it. In fact, all of Scripture clearly shows that the statement is addressed to Abraham's lineage according to the flesh, for it is said: 'You are the heirs of the promise' (cf. *Acts* 3:25). That is how Peter speaks in Acts. And then Paul notably expresses that Jesus Christ was the servant of that people and that he came to fulfil the promises made to the fathers (cf. *Acts* 13:32-33). So it follows that God wanted to choose Abraham's line according to the flesh so that it might be his church.

In fact, as we will see later (cf. *Gen.* 17:19-23), no others were circumcised. Now circumcision was not a frivolous and empty act. It was a testimony by which God showed that he wanted to have this people dedicated to himself as sacred. And that is also why it is said to Moses that God, intending a direct line, chose his portion in that lineage as if he were omitting the rest of the world. Even though all peoples belong to him, he still wanted to be Lord in Israel. That is also why it is said that he did not act that way toward all nations and had not manifested to them his ordinances (cf. *Psa.* 147:20). To be sure, it was to show that God was the Saviour of his people because he considered them as a heritage which he included in his church to say: 'You belong to me, and I am approaching you so you will be my friends and I will make known to you my goodness and my favours in such a way that you will sense by experience that I am your Father and that you can trust me for salvation and call upon me in complete confidence.' That is the way God worked with his ancient people.

As a result, we must conclude that he was in truth the God of the Jews, that is, the God of the people of Israel. So why has it been said of late that many peoples were to come from Abraham?

Because we have been gathered into his house and he is the father shared with all believers, and we must not take into consideration the race we are descended from according to the flesh, but the faith which is the means that unites us with Abraham (cf. *Gen.* 3:7). The two are in good agreement, but here we must advance step by step. And that is a very necessary teaching which will serve as the key to understanding many passages of Scripture. And then we will also see how useful it is to us. We saw previously the great extent to which the world had given itself to idolatry and superstition. On the one hand, there was Melchizedek (cf. *Gen.* 14:18-20); there was a small handful of people scattered here and there who served the living God, but they were hidden, in a manner of speaking. Uncertainty was everywhere. Abraham himself was deep in that abyss of unbelief when God called him, for he drew him out of the gulf of hell, so to speak. Abraham did not naturally possess this privilege of being chosen by God along with his lineage, but it is wholly because God ordered it that way. And that is why Paul says that because the root is holy, that is, because God chose Abraham, in his person all the branches which come from him are holy (cf. *Rom.* 11:16). That is how the Jews were natural heirs of the heavenly kingdom. I say 'natural,' not, as I have said, that they were not by nature cursed in Adam, as others, and considered children of wrath (cf. *Eph.* 2:3), as we all are without exception, but they were natural heirs because they were adopted. For when God chose and adopted their father, he immediately added that he also chose his seed. That, then, is how the Jews were sanctified, not because of their first nature, if we have Adam in mind—if we consider the general origin of man—but they were heirs by nature because our Lord wanted to show his bounty and continue it in their behalf from generation to generation and from hand to hand, and he offered himself to the Jews as their Father. That is why throughout Scripture they are called God's inheritance (cf. *Exod.* 15:17; *Deut.*

9:29; *1 Sam.* 10:1; *Psa.* 28:9), which follows what I have already stated from the Song of Moses (*Deut.* 32:9). And that is also why they were called a kingdom of priests (cf. *Exod.* 19:6), for God was ruling among them so completely that they were all like small kings, being governed by him in complete freedom, indeed to walk in fear of him and in subjection to him. But that is much more excellent than all the dignities and honours of this world, than all its kingdoms and empires. There was also a sacrificial system and all were removed, so to speak, from the common pollution, for we know that we bear pollution that is rooted in us from our mother's womb, that we are cursed and polluted and despicable before God. There was no other holiness except that which proceeded from the grace which had been given to them. That is how Abraham's children according to the flesh were separated from the rest of the world.

In the meantime, Paul shows that all those who descended from that race according to the flesh are not considered true Israelites (cf. *Rom.* 9:1-18). Why not? There is Ishmael, who was chased from the house forthwith (cf. *Gen.* 21:14). There is Esau, who deprives himself of it and is immediately rejected.[2] There are those who descended from Keturah, who possess nothing of the church and who share nothing in common with it. And then among the Jews, we see how many yielded to excesses.[3] To be noted here is the fact that God presents his grace in a different way and that it is received in a different way, and this will be better understood in

---

[2] In fact, Esau sells only his birthright, not his belonging to the Jewish people. Cf. Genesis 25:32-33. And yet Calvin considers primogeniture as the heavenly blessing Esau deprives himself of. Cf. *Commentarii*, col. 355; *Commentaire*, pp. 295-296.—*M.E.*

[3] Cf. Genesis 25:1-4; but the biblical text says nothing about the people who were born of his children, with the exception of the Midianites (cf. *Gen.* 37:28; *Exod.* 2:15; etc.). In his commentary on this passage, Calvin is not more prolix. In this sermon, he allows himself to be led along by the context.—*M.E.*

us. For today we follow in the place of Abraham's children, having been grafted into their place (cf. *Rom.* 11:19), we who were like wild plants and useless trees. And yet we have the bond and place of honour that belonged to the ancient Jews. For by virtue of the fact that our Lord called us into his church, we are called his children (cf. *John* 1:12; *Rom.* 8:16; *1 John* 3:1). In fact, his grace is offered to us every time the gospel is preached. God has his arms extended to receive us, as his prophet Isaiah says: 'I have extended my hands to this rebellious people evening and morning' (*Isa.* 65:2). So our Lord calls us and invites us so gently that it is possible to come to him; but many are rebellious and wicked, as that passage says of the Jews. How many deaf ears are there when God's word resonates loud and clear and reverberates so that the rocks themselves are moved? How many hearts are filled with pride and venom and evil that reject God's grace? Some are profane and completely defiled and dissolute, and if you speak to them of paradise, it means nothing to them because the promises concerning it are only fables. Others are even aroused against God and attack him to spite him and would like to destroy his name so far as they could. Others are so dense that they cannot distinguish between black and white. Others are fickle, and as soon as they perceive some attraction to God's word, they avoid it like the plague after looking into it a few times out of curiosity.

Therefore, God presents his grace to us in general and to everyone without exception, yet it is not always received in the same manner. It is like well-sown seed that do not always fall on good soil. As our Lord Jesus Christ says, some fall in places where they will not grow. Some will fall on stones and will not be able to take root because the sun burns them. Some will fall on the road, and they will be trampled underfoot. One out of three will fall on good soil (cf. *Mark* 4:3-8). And then the devil tries to sow corruption among the good grain, and the result is that there are many hypocrites in the church, many who despise God, and they must be tolerated. They occupy the place of believers and are counted among the others. And sometimes they are even more advanced, and about all they do is boast openly of being servants and officers of the church. In a word, if you were willing to believe them, only they 'have it right,' as we say.

That is the way it was with Abraham's lineage a long time ago, for God had chosen all of them and borne witness to them that he would be their Father and Saviour. That is how they are dedicated to him by virtue of the promise. Now as for them, they distance themselves from the church and, having thus become dense because of their godlessness and ingratitude, they deserve to have God renounce them and refuse to acknowledge them. Consequently, on the one hand, they are the holy lineage and, on the other, they are wicked and polluted, as Jerusalem was called a holy city and a den of robbers (cf. *Jer.* 7:11), and Sodom and Gomorrah, as it is called in Isaiah: it was a righteous city (cf. *Isa.* 1:9-10, 21). Why? Because what God had ordained could not be eradicated by the wickedness of men because he wanted to be worshiped in the temple that had been built there in accordance with his word. The temple at Jerusalem was not built at the whim and will of men; its foundation was the word of God, which could not be overthrown, try as men might. And we also understand what our Lord Jesus Christ said at a time of very great indulgence: 'We know what we worship' (cf. *John* 4:22). So the temple still remains holy. And that is also why the gospel writers use the term 'the holy city' so often (cf. *Matt.* 4:5; 27:53; *Rev.* 11:2), not out of mockery, but because God had chosen it as his dwelling place (cf. *Psa.* 9:11; 135:21). Yet Jerusalem did not cease to be Sodom, a den of hell. Those who held sway there were princes of Gomorrah and robbers, as they are called by the prophet Isaiah (cf. *Isa.* 1:10).

So we see how these two agree, namely, that when God gives us his word, there is such power that it sanctifies those he called and chose. Yet they do not stop profaning his word, and in that way they destroy God's promise to the extent they can, but it will always remain in force because God cannot lie and will always remain faithful. But their kind are nonetheless deprived of the inheritance. They are shut out and banished (cf. *Jer.* 31:36). That is also why the prophets sometimes call them 'seed of Israel'; and that was the most honourable designation they could give them; but when speaking of them that way, they were speaking with reproach, as if they were saying: 'Go, you wretched people, who are descendants of this holy patriarch who was called Israel by the very mouth of God' (cf. *Gen.* 32:29), because God had made him victorious in his eyes. 'And you have come from him, but what kind of people are you? What likeness is there between you and your father, from whom you have descended?' And when the prophets spoke that way, they added: 'Go, you sons of whores; you have come out of a whorehouse, you seed of Abraham,' which is very appropriate. 'You are sons of Canaan. You have descended from whores and whoremongers.' And when saying that, the prophets do not mean that all the Jews were illegitimate and the marriages had been corrupted among them. So they are not speaking of the flesh, but they are showing how they had been born of legitimate marriages while continuing to be sons of whores because they had been corrupted and depraved by superstition and idolatry and in all other vices and iniquities. Those ways of speaking seem strange at first, but we must get used to them and continue to return to the principle I mentioned.

In a word, that is how Abraham's lineage was chosen and adopted by God and consequently made a holy and sacred lineage, a priestly kingdom, as we have said. Yet little has been gained by those who scorned the great privilege of being called by God, and that was their great condemnation because they were so wicked and perverse as to reject that incomparable privilege and make themselves unworthy of the heavenly inheritance that was offered to them.

Let us now look at ourselves, for we replaced them when they were cut off, Paul says (cf. *Rom.* 11:15-24). But if God did not spare the natural branches, and that was all consumed as by fire, what will happen to us, who are aborted children in comparison with the Jews, from whom we have been drawn out and who were our fathers? We were without God, Paul says. Descending from Gentiles, we had no hope of life because God had not allied himself with us (cf. *Eph.* 2:12); we were people lost and damned, accursed creatures; and God put us in the place of those who were the holy lineage. And do we think we will be spared? But let us walk in fear and concern. And if we are standing today, let us fear falling whenever we want to be proud and arrogant people; not that we have to be in doubt of our salvation, but so we will correct every presumption; so we will, on the one hand, be in a position to be condemned by God in order to be absolved by him when we are humble and insignificant; and so we will not, on the other, desecrate ourselves after he has dedicated us to his service and even cleansed us by the blood of our Lord Jesus Christ so we will be pure and washed of all the pollutions which previously made us detestable in his sight (cf. *1 John* 1:7). That being the case, let us realize today that, since the dividing wall has been broken down (cf. *Eph.* 2:14), we are no different from the Jews, who were descended from Abraham's race according to the flesh, that God has sanctified us, that we belong to his household and are, in a word, his own children.

But let us also note that when that grace is offered to all, it has to be received. And when we have received it, let us persevere until the end with a rigorous constancy of faith. Our curse will be increased in proportion as we do not profit from the blessing God offers us every time the gospel is preached to us, for it is through preaching that he invites us to himself in the gentlest way possible and testifies to our adoption. From day to day he confirms it to us so that we will be made more confident of it. So for our part, inasmuch as we are Abraham's children by virtue of the promise God addresses to us as well, let us not break that covenant and nullify it by our evil disposition, but let us place ourselves in the hands of the one who wants to possess us, just as he also gives himself to us. And what kind of swap is that? God wants us to be his. And what does he gain by that? What are we that is special? It is true that to the extent we are his creatures, there is some excellence in us—indeed, because it has pleased him by his grace to give us authority over the entire world; but even though we are by nature repugnant and detestable in his sight, he is nonetheless pleased to possess us as his own. And then by his Holy Spirit he gives us value as it seems good to him. In any case, we are as dear to him as a man who would have a heritage, and he gives himself to us at the same time; he wants us to possess him, and he wants to be ours. Therefore, so that this may be the case, let us not have an unstable faith, but a steadfast faith until the end so we will cling to our God, who wanted to join himself with us in this way and be one with us.

In addition, in order to understand this better, let us note that this promise brings with it the eternal salvation of souls, for it says: 'I will be your God and the God of your seed after you.' It is true the words are not stated exactly that way, but the points are inseparable just as in the case where our Lord Jesus Christ says: 'For my Father is not the God of the dead. He is the God of the living' (cf. *Matt.* 22:23). That being so, it is certain that by virtue of that promise, Abraham believed he could attain the heavenly life and that his death could not negate it, but he believed that this was a passageway for going through this world as if on a pilgrimage to reach his eternal rest. The same is true for all his seed, those whom

God received to himself, since many excluded themselves from it by their evil deeds. In fact, believers under the law understood it that way, for one could say that our Lord Jesus Christ commented subtly on what was obscure, but we understand that God enlightened those who believed in him so that they understood the power of this passage. The prophet Habakkuk, speaking for everyone, said: 'You are our God; we shall not die' (cf. *Hab.* 1:12). The prophet's conclusion, then, is that this people could not perish or suffer evil. 'And why are you our God?' he asks. Therefore, in order to make his point and show that the natural meaning of this passage was always known by the church, he declares that those who had the intelligence and the ability to make distinctions did indeed know how to profit from that promise, which was not hidden from them. And in fact, that is also why the psalm says: 'Blessed is the nation whose God is the Lord' (cf. *Psa.* 33:12). Consequently, the whole of men's felicity lies in the fact that they realize they have a living God who has presented himself there, wherein lies and consists their complete welfare. It follows, then, that that is the substance of everlasting life. For if we accept men's felicity in this life, it will be very meagre. So we are obliged to move beyond that.

That is why I said that when God informs us he will be the Father of Abraham and his seed, he simultaneously points out that he will be the Saviour of those who are allied with him by faith. True, it is added that he will give to both Abraham and his lineage the land of Canaan as an inheritance, but that is only a seal to confirm the gift. And in fact it is repeated at the end that he is the Lord. It would seem that he had used redundant language at this point, but when we consider the whole, we will see that God had good reason to repeat that promise, that is, he was the Lord inasmuch as the promise carried the same meaning, as if the land of Canaan were understood to be, as I have said, only some visible sign or some pledge of what was contained in the statement: 'I will be your God.'

It is true that when God lodged his people in the land of Canaan, it was called a holy land. Why? Because he was worshipped there; because the true religion was known there. And during that time the other nations were occupied with their idolatries. And God sanctified the land of Canaan when he gathered his people there. Yet if the Jews had idled away their time, as men are much inclined to seek out the trifling things of this world, it is certain they would have shunted aside the heavenly inheritance and, in so doing, would have subverted God's intention. For the land of Canaan was to cause them to move beyond this world and lead them to heaven. In short, if we want an appropriate example, it would be like a boat on a sea or a lake for them. When a man is seated on a boat, it is true that he does not move, but the boat must if he is to get where he is going. So the Jews had to be lodged in God's rest, as it is called, so that they might be borne higher, that is, to the heavenly rest. Therefore, if they were going to enjoy the land of Canaan and be satisfied with owning it, it would be like a man who wanted to leave one side of the lake but would be drawn in the opposite direction and would have gone down the Rhône River to the sea. Such is the case with the Jews, for God says at the outset: 'I will be your God.' And then he adds: 'I will give you the land of Canaan,' as if to say: 'Be careful not to put the cart before the horse. And when you hear that I give myself to you and that you possess me, learn to be content with that. It is true that you will enjoy the land, but remember that I am calling you to a higher purpose, to worshiping me, too trusting in me, in the knowledge that when you are in my safe keeping, you cannot perish. And that will take you farther along!'

So we now see a summary of the content of this passage. It remains for us to apply it to ourselves. Since Abraham was made the father of many nations, let us realize that God wants that promise to serve us today. Although it was written first to instruct the Jews, it is also addressed to us. It is true that God speaks to the person Abraham, but he does so on our behalf, and Abraham also makes a contract there not as a private person, but as the one who was ordained father of all those who were to believe. Consequently, when God spoke to him, he did so for our advantage and usefulness.

So what do we need to remember from this passage? That the Creator of heaven and earth is our God. In other words, he acknowledges us and accepts us as his children, for these are reciprocal facts that cannot be separated, as we see in many other passages of Scripture (cf. *Exod.* 6:7; *Lev.* 26:12; *Deut.* 29:12; *Jer.* 7:23). It is true that as Creator of all things, he is also God, but when he adds that he is our God, he informs us that he brings us such a salvation that we cannot perish, and we are also marked as being members of his household. And when we say that, we are back to the point that we are heirs of the heavenly life. When our Lord makes us that promise, let us realize that he does not want us to yield ourselves to this world or to all the corruptible things in it, even though he gives us now some taste of his goodness. And whether we eat or whether we drink, we already understand that he is our sustaining Father, and that makes us certain that we are his children, that we are, in a manner of speaking, hand fed by him and maintained at his expense. At the same time, he does not want us to be attached to this world because he wants to support us differently in the hope of eternal life. That is why he says to Abraham: 'I will give you this land for your pilgrimage, or for your pilgrimages, in the plural,' as if our Lord were saying: 'You have long been a wanderer and will be until you die, not only in this strange land, but when you think you are well settled, you will have to move from country to country, now in one region then in another; you will have no place to plant your feet; you will be like a bird on a branch, for you will be forced from one place to another, and you will never have a permanent dwelling place' (cf. *1 Cor.* 4:11). So you must become accustomed to that. And even if our Lord allows many believers to remain where they were born, they still have to keep their hearts lifted higher as they pass through this world and enjoy the things they possess as not possessing them. Let those who sell be like buyers, and let those who buy be like those who do not buy, as Paul says (cf. *1 Cor.* 7:30-31). Why? We must always keep in mind that this world is only a figure, indeed a figure which is passing away and vanishing forthwith. That, then, is the main thing we must remember.

On the other hand, we have here a great deal to rejoice about when we see God presenting himself to us this way so we can find in him every perfection of life, of joy, of rest and glory. But meanwhile let us also learn to have such confidence in him that all the rest means nothing and we can say: 'We are well and timely blessed since God has declared that he is our Father and our Saviour.' And let us also note that our lives and our salvation depend on God's grace and his love, for we are always seeking to be saved and achieve the eternity of glory, but we do not have the means. We do not know wherein our lives consist and where they come from, for they are given and communicated to us. Consequently, we have to remember that when God puts himself forward, he speaks neither of paradise nor of his glory, nor of a crown or joy or felicity or anything else, but he offers himself. Why? Because when we have done with talking and uttering all our desires that exclude him, what is left? Only misfortune and misery! So let us learn to honour him this way: when we seek for the things that belong to our felicity, let us come directly to him; and since we have him as our God, let us know that when he gave himself to us, he omitted nothing.

He has now made himself known to us in the person of his only Son so that what the ancient fathers had as a shadow we have in truth, we have its substance doubled. Woe to us, therefore, if we are not caught up in pursuit of such grace and do not forsake this world and say with David, 'Blessed is the people whose God is the Lord' (cf. *Psa.* 33:12). It is true we could well rejoice since God causes us to prosper, for all the blessings that we have here below, which aid us in our passage through this world, are just that many blessings from him. Even so, when we have drunk and eaten, when we are fed and sustained day after day by his grace, and when we realize that by doing that he is already showing he is our Father, we must still return to the fact that if his face is not shining on us (cf. *Psa.* 80:3), it all means nothing if we are not assured of his paternal favour. But on the contrary, when we are hungry and thirsty, when we experience fear and doubt, when we are even persecuted unto death, provided the light of his face is shining on us, and when we realize that since he has received us once, he wants to sustain us until the end—when we have all that, we will always continue to be blessed, even in the midst of all our miseries. That in brief, then, is what we have to remember.

Now it is said that God presents himself as the Father as much for Abraham as for all of his posterity so that we may know he wishes to extend his grace and increase it among us and even continue it from children to children for a thousand generations, as he promised more clearly in his law (cf. *Exod.* 20:6). And that is to be particularly noted because if God declared himself to be the Father and Saviour of those who trust in him and lean on his promise, that would already be a great deal, but when he says that he is already the God of those who have not been born, of those who will come three hundred years and a thousand years later, it is certain that believers are to be much more confident that God receives them with their race.

It is true, as we have already said, that all the children of the flesh are not heirs of the promise, for there is God's unknown election which controls everything, and because we do not comprehend that election, we must make judgments about it depending on its purpose according to each person's adherence to God with purity of heart. That is how the promise is confirmed. But God offers it in general to those who descend from the race of believers, from the smallest to the greatest. And that promise is not empty, for there is, by virtue of that promise, still some remnant of the saved, whom God pulled from the pit, so to speak. The Jews had become so perverted that, in the time of our Lord Jesus Christ, there was almost no longer a trace of that covenant. For what did that covenant have to do with the worship of God and purity? It is true the temple sacrifices were performed. There were also pomp and ceremonies, but all of that provoked God's wrath even more, for if some presented impressive fronts, it was hypocrisy. They were filled to overflowing with vice, and it appeared as if they had plotted against God to cast him far from themselves. Yet God had preserved some seed. Even though they were few, there still remained a remnant. Why? Because God's election, Paul says, is irrevocable (cf. *Rom.* 11:28-29) and must overcome all the obstacles men place before it. And as he says in another place, if we are liars, that does not mean that we can abolish God's truth, that he will not remain faithful, and that he will not always be steadfast in what he has declared (cf. *Rom.* 3:4).

So even though many children alienate themselves from the church that way, let us note that they close the door on themselves and thus close off their entrance into salvation, that God still validates what he once said, that he will be the God and Father of those he sanctified unto himself, and that he will always preserve some few seed. And that is how we must increasingly confirm the testimony he gives us of his paternal favour. Since he extends his grace, his goodness and mercy to the children of the children and from age to age, how could he fail us? Therefore, let fathers who have children and hear that promise bless God doubly and magnify him for not being content to reserve them for himself but for also wanting to include their children in that promise. And let them sing with David: 'Alas, Lord, was it not enough for you to look upon your servant with pity, but even after my trespass, you have to keep your eye on my family, and it has to be governed by you' (cf. *Psa.* 89:4-5, 29-33, 36; 132:11; 147:13). That is how those to whom God gives lineage ought to rejoice more and more and not doubt that God sheds the riches of his bounty on them and that what belongs to him is also dedicated to them because they have already received it. We will reserve the rest for tomorrow.

Now let us bow before the majesty of our gracious God in acknowledgment of our faults, praying that he will make us so aware of them that we may be led more and more to repentance. And let us pursue it all of our lives so that we will make every effort to put to death all our affections and yield to his righteousness. And in that way may his name be glorified throughout the totality of our lives, and may he so strengthen his covenant with us that we will be able to cry unto him and call upon him as our Father, and let us not doubt that we, being under his protection, are safe on all sides and blessed because he will turn all of our affections and adversities to our good and our salvation. May he grant that grace not only to us but to all the peoples and nations on earth.

80

An Explanation of Circumcision and Baptism

Thursday, 4 April 1560

And God said unto Abraham, Thou shalt keep my covenant therefore, thou, and thy seed after thee in their generations. This is my covenant, which ye shall keep, between me and you and thy seed after thee; Every man child among you shall be circumcised. And ye shall circumcise the flesh of your foreskin; and it shall be a token of the covenant betwixt me and you. And he that is eight days old shall be circumcised among you, every man child in your generations, he that is born in the house, or bought with money of any stranger, which is not of thy seed. He that is born in thy house, and he that is bought with thy money, must needs be circumcised: and my covenant shall be in your flesh for an everlasting covenant (Gen. 17:9-13).

E SAW YESTERDAY the promise which was given again to Abraham to make him certain of his salvation. Moses now adds that a sacrament was attached to the word, as if God had wanted to seal the promise he had made so that it might be more authentic.[1] In that statement, as we dealt with it yesterday, God proclaimed that he is our God and that we have all we could desire, for in him lies the perfection of all good things. Yet if we consider the weakness that is in us, we will realize

---

[1] Cf. *Institutes*, IV, xiv, 18, 20; etc.—*M.E.*

that that addition is not superfluous inasmuch as God gives us a visible sacrament in addition to his word. And everything depends on what he says, which is his covenant.

It is true the covenant, properly speaking, is made with words. When both parties are in discussion and some agreement must be arrived at, specifics are listed, and then both parties decide what they are willing to do. Therefore, since God blesses us and honours us by allying himself with us, he has only to declare his will and require of us what our duty to him is. The covenant, then, as we have said, consists in God's love for us and his calling us, not to disappoint us but to accomplish the things that pertain to our eternal salvation, and our role is to consent to his word with true faith. But let us consider whether we have God's promises in accordance with the requirement. Even though we willingly add faith to it, let us consider whether we have the steadfastness and strength not to flinch and waver when a trial comes our way. Steadfastness and strength fail us, for we are, first, so slack that God cannot call us without using many means, and when we do come to him, it only takes a little bit of nothing to lead us astray. Consequently, since God is aware of those two vices of ours, he helps us by giving us his sacraments, which are to serve as visible words so that both our eyes and our ears can be instructed.[2] The word addresses the ears and is received by them, but the sacrament has the advantage that the eyes are influenced and we contemplate what we have previously heard. We can take the example of baptism today, which will be more easily understood, for we more easily understand the things currently in use.[3] Baptism succeeded circumcision, which is

---

[2] It is rare that Calvin treats hearing and seeing on the same level, privileging, as we know, the word over the image… This twofold attention to the senses finds his theological support in a verse of Psalm 34 (verse 15): the ears and eyes of God are turned toward the righteous.—M.E.

[3] Calvin regularly transitions between circumcision and baptism in the *Institutes*. Cf. book IV, xiv, 23-24; xv, 17; xvi, *passim*. He writes that 'the accomplishment

God's covenant, as will be explained more fully. How so? Do we not find in the gospel everything we can desire for our salvation? In it, we possess Jesus Christ. He communicates himself to us, as Paul says in the first chapter of 1 Corinthians. Moreover, do we not have there everything God knew to be necessary and useful for our instruction?

In addition, it is said that we are saved and justified by faith (cf. *Rom.* 3:28). Now faith comes by hearing (cf. *Rom.* 10:17). So it would seem that baptism would serve no purpose and that the term 'the covenant of God' was incorrectly applied; and it would seem upon first consideration that it was used to disparage the teaching which is perfect in every respect. Let us note that there is no contradiction between things that are relevant to one another. If baptism and the word are considered separately, you could attribute to one what is taken from the other, and by exalting one you would abase the other. But when baptism is used as an accessory to the word, there is some equality and what is said about baptism is far from being a contradiction—it relates to the word—and ought to apply to baptism. And how can that be? Because we are so dense and unlearned that we do not understand what we are told. In other words, when we are washed by the blood of our Lord Jesus Christ (cf. *1 John* 1:7) and see the water with our eyes, that is an aid added for our understanding. We know what it is used for: to cleanse us of our filth. We see that and are better instructed than we would be if only the word had been dinned into our ears. Afterwards, we see the water sprinkled on the face of a child as if he had been plunged into it. And what does that mean? A death (cf. *Rom.* 6:4). So we understand by that that we must die to ourselves (cf. *Col.* 3:5; *Rom.* 6:6-11). And then we understand that baptism is not to leave a person under the water, but that he must

of baptism is the same as the accomplishment of circumcision' (*Institutes* IV, xvi, 11).—M.E.

563

be renewed. The entire process is to signify that we must die to the corruptions of our flesh so that newness of life will follow and God will reign in us. Then, we know the water serves to refresh us and is an element we cannot live without. From there we must move to the image that we are dry and that there is no life in us unless it is given by the Holy Spirit. It is not without reason that he is called living water (cf. *Rev.* 22:17). Therefore, that is how the institution of baptism is not superfluous and at the same time is in very good agreement with the institution of the gospel, for they are joined together, and that is required for our justification.

With that we see that circumcision was given with the promise, as we saw above (cf. *Gen.* 17:4-8). As for God, it would be enough that God had spoken, but because he knows how weak men are and that their faith would be soon shaken if he did not strengthen it and add some supports, that is why he ordained and set forth the sacraments. Now we have to note in the word 'covenant' that the sacraments afford a testimony of God's grace to assure us and nourish our faith. And that is a point worth noting, for there are some who have interpreted these matters very badly, thinking that the sacraments were only a couple of signs men use to make known which God we serve, like the white cross and the red cross between enemies when they are at war. They think that by being baptized we proclaim before men that we are Christians, but they have forgotten the main point, namely, that the word 'covenant' means that we need to be assured today of God's goodness, wherein lies our salvation.

Consequently, every time God speaks of the covenant, let us realize that it is reciprocal between him and us. In other words, he contracts with us to adopt us as his children and his people and also declares he receives us under his protection and, in so doing, assures us we will never perish. As for us, we must accept and receive what he offers us. If we do not view this as a mutual agreement between God and us, it is certain the word 'covenant' ceases to have meaning. Moreover, we know that every covenant carries with it obligation. Now God condescends to obligate himself willingly to us, even though it is impossible for him to owe us anything, but he nonetheless submits to that condition. Now the obligation is only through the promise. There will sometimes be an obligation in fact among men, but it must be voluntary on God's part. Why? Because he testifies to us of his will. Now if there is promise, faith in it is required. At the same time, if there is promise, there is substance to cause us to rejoice and be strengthened and simultaneously have the assurance we can call upon God because he invites us to himself and confirms the promise is not empty.

Consequently, we see that all the sacraments bear witness to God's grace and goodness so that men can be fully confident of them and rest in them; and having such a pledge, they can at the same time call upon God as their Father and take refuge in him for their salvation. That, then, is what we have to observe.

Now when God says, 'This is my covenant,' it is true that he is giving a visible sacrament which is appropriate for the word, but, as I have already said, the sacrament is not to be separate from or unrelated to the word, for it is rather a visible word. Beyond what God says, he points as with his finger to what was not visible under the sign that is evident, and he does that because we are dense. Thus, even though that way of speaking could be considered harsh, it is still very useful for building our faith.

God then later declares: 'This will be the sign of my covenant.' So when he uses a single comment to represent his word to us, let us apply it to the sacrament. And then when he says 'sign,' he indicates the distinct relationship between the word, which is the substance, and the sacrament, which is placed before our eyes to give us greater confirmation.

In addition, let us note that circumcision was given at the time God wanted to choose a special people for himself. And even though we could ask at this point why he waited so long, we must nonetheless exercise restraint and not ask to know more than we are allowed. We know God did not want to choose a particular people until he chose and adopted Abraham. What if we asked why? Can we know the answer? Indeed not. That exceeds our capacity. All we can do is have the good sense and modesty to yield to God's counsel, which is both too exalted and too profound for us. So let us simply be content with his will, knowing that he was thus pleased and had good reason for doing what he did. He is not accountable to us. That is not to say he has the responsibility to subject himself to us to tell us his whys and wherefores. So he must exercise and test our humility when he tells us what he ordains without showing us why and designating a certain purpose. Still we must grant him the honour he deserves by confessing that his will is the guide for all wisdom and that it is with good reason that we cannot comprehend his counsel, seeing we are so insignificant and dense.

Now even as God waited until Abraham's time to choose a particular people, so he did not want to give circumcision until then. Yet those who preceded and those who came after were not without a sacrament, for sacraments existed from the creation of the world, as we have said.[4] They were not invented on a whim, for we are told that Abel pleased God with his offerings because of his faith (cf. *Gen.* 4:4).[5] They had to be founded on a definite assurance of God's goodness. Consequently, the fathers always had some sacraments, even before Adam's fall. The tree of life, as we

---

[4] Calvin considers 'the tree of life' in Genesis 2:9 as a sacrament... Calvin likewise considers the rainbow in Genesis 9:13 as a sacrament.—*M.E.*

[5] In sermon 21, however, Calvin does not associate Abel's offering with sacrament, but he treats it as accepted sacrifice and faith.—*M.E.*

have pointed out, was a sacrament which figures our Lord Jesus Christ, not as a redeemer but as indicating he was the life of men even before they were lost and damned. That, then, is how God has given the kinds of helps he knew to be proper and suitable to retain those faithful to him and to strengthen them more. But when he chose Abraham's lineage to the exclusion of all other nations on earth, he wanted to add circumcision as a privilege. So it is not without reason that he gave a special sacrament at the time as if it were a singular benefit which was not known previously. That much for the first point.

Now if we want to spend our time coming to conclusions based on our imaginations, it seems to be stupid and ridiculous that God instituted a sacrament that witnesses to the eternal salvation of our souls by locating it on the shameful part of men. So if we want to rise up in our pride and announce what we would consider good, it is certain we would reprehend God for folly. But what he did is very appropriate. How so? He is dealing with something majestic so that we may be blessed, whereas there is only curse within us; it is so that we may be sanctified, whereas we are profaned and polluted; it is so that we may be righteous, whereas there is only sin and iniquity; it is so that we may be pure and clean, whereas there are only stains and pollutions; it is so that we may be renewed to be, as it were, angels of paradise, whereas we were held under Satan's tyranny and death. God, then, is opening his kingdom to lead us to everlasting life. And what does he do to indicate that? 'Let the end skin be cut from the shameful part of men.' That would be considered so strange that if we wanted to judge this with our own ideas and imaginations, as I have already said, we would reject the whole notion. But that is how God wants to humble us and wants us to know that what seems to us to be folly surpasses all wisdom. What must be done then? It is not a matter of debating this matter rationally, that is, of bringing our opinions to bear, but of realizing it is God who ordained what we think is odd. Consequently, let us be held captive to his authority and reverence him by being satisfied with what pleased him, as I have said. And until we reach that point, it is certain we will never be able to apply faith to the teaching of salvation, for we must become foolish, as Paul says (cf. *1 Cor.* 3:18), if we wish to profit from God's school. All our wisdom consists in becoming nothing under him. But in fact we see how he takes on those who are audacious and filled with pride and say: 'How this? And why that?' As a result, all those who do not yield humbly to God's word must in the end create for themselves labyrinths of thought and rush headlong into them, never able to find their way out. All the more must we remember what was just said, namely, that we not be wise in our own opinion, but so abased that we find good and just and wise and upright everything God has ordained without there being anything to criticize or question. That, in summary, is what we have to remember now.

Yet it is certain we will have wondered to some extent why God ordained this sacrament, which was of such importance and power in that part of the human body. We will surely find some obvious reason. Circumcision deals with two points, as baptism does today. The first is that we are condemned because of our nature, which results in our curse: God's wrath and his horrible judgment are visible in it. And inasmuch as we nonetheless realize he receives us in mercy and has such love for us that he does not consider what we are but as his children since he is pleased for us to be members of his only Son. Those two points now belong to baptism as they did formerly to circumcision. Therefore, God wanted to show in that part of the body that the seed of men was cursed as is everything that proceeds from it, and that all of that must be cut off and removed, as if he wanted to destroy men in themselves and show them that the door of life is closed until they renounce father and mother and themselves. That, then, is how God, not without good reason, instituted that ancient sacrament in that part of the body to show that what proceeds from the generation of men is execrable and must be abolished.

In fact, since God's image was erased in Adam, he has not been able to produce a lineage except in his own image, and the result is that we are all children of wrath (cf. *Eph.* 2:3). That is the inheritance we have from our mother's womb, which is only iniquity. We are corrupt and perverted, and all our thoughts and affections are at enmity with God, for we are rebellious against him in and through everything. It is true that that is not obvious at first glance, but sin is in a child even while in his mother's womb and makes him subject to eternal damnation. Why? At first a child does not produce his fruits, but he is a little serpent descended from the line of the Serpent to show that there is in us only venom and poison. Consequently, we see that, in ancient days, God very aptly pointed out that men's seed had to be declared accursed.

The second point of the sacrament deals with the promise of salvation. If we are ashamed that this spiritual sacrament is established in that part of the body, let us be ashamed at the same time of being saved through Abraham's lineage. If we do not wish to accept the salvation which is presented to us in Abraham's seed, we are all in a state of perdition, for there is no other way to salvation. Therefore, even though the sacrament in itself can always be considered foolish and absurd even if we would like to have confidence in what we think about it, the purpose that we see for it now is to close every mouth and to sustain us in the hope we have in our Lord Jesus Christ.

So God has saved us. How? By the seed of Abraham and consequently of Adam too. But that seed is corrupt. There are only sin and death. That is true, but our Lord Jesus Christ has sanctified us, and then he was conceived in the womb of his mother miraculously, not naturally; yet he descended from Adam's and Abraham's race. Since he was born of a virgin, he is necessarily of human seed. That is the way God wanted to save the world. So we must not be amazed if the visible sign given previously, before the coming of our Lord Jesus Christ, corresponded to that. In other words, since death comes by the seed of men, so also must life proceed from the seed of men. That is what we need to remember about that.

Moreover, even though only males were circumcised, God also included women, for they were dedicated in the person of males, and it is enough that God wanted it and ordained it so. As I have already pointed out, it is our place to remain silent when we know his will, for it must be sufficient for our complete guidance. Therefore, since God sanctified all his people, both male and female, through circumcision, let us realize that this sacrament was common to women as well as men. Women were not circumcised, but they still participated in the grace that was figured and witnessed in that sign. That, then, is what we must remember about circumcision.

Now there is also a particular day assigned. Circumcision is to take place on the eighth day. It is true some have thought this means God spared little children because they were too tender on the first or second day and because he wanted them to wait until they had enough strength not to be injured or hurt. But could God not also protect them on the first and second day as well as the eighth? That kind of thinking is barren and profane.

As for the number of days, given the fact that there is no definite approval of them in holy Scripture, we cannot proclaim one without being able to conclude by an ordinary way of interpreting holy Scripture that God waited for the eighth day. We know he ordained the seventh as the day of rest (cf. *Gen.* 2:2-3) to indicate that men are to rest and refrain from their own works all the days of their lives. Only one day is dedicated as the day of rest, and that day must serve the entire week and, consequently, throughout the course of human life. That is rather well known about the day of rest. Thus, when circumcision was ordered for the eighth day, that also means that men must die within themselves. There is also some similarity between circumcision and the day of rest. So why is one day added? We cannot say, except with probable reason, that even though we must renounce ourselves every day of our lives, God declared that we will not achieve the goal of emptying ourselves of all our affections and thoughts and of everything that is of the malice and corruption in our souls until we depart this life. So we must take as our task the practice of putting to death everything that belongs to our nature. Until we have fought well and valiantly, the principal victory will not take place until God has drawn us and gathered us to himself. That, then, is an acceptable reason in keeping with the common practice of interpreting Scripture.

Consequently, the first thing we have to remember now, since circumcision was given to the Jews as a sign of repentance, is that inasmuch as we know they had to be abolished because they had the heritage of their fathers and mothers, they had to be renewed by the power of God's Spirit. That is why we read so often in Moses that they are to circumcise their hearts. Moses reveals the truth about that outward and visible sign when he says: 'Circumcise your hearts' (cf. *Deut.* 10:16; 30:6; *Lev.* 26:41), as if to say: 'It is true you do indeed bear a mark in your bodies to show that what belongs to man must be cut off in you, but you must go further. In other words, everything that has to do with evil thoughts and emotions must be overcome and excised.'

Moreover, since men's holiness and renewal do not lie in their righteousness but depend on a special grace God grants them, it is worth noting the text says: 'Circumcise your hearts,' in the thirtieth chapter of Deuteronomy (cf. *Deut.* 30:6). When Moses attributes that statement to God, he does so to show that what was figured by circumcision cannot be accomplished by men's efforts. In fact, we have to have instruction in all the sacraments. In other words, we bring nothing that is ours, and we know that we are passive, which means we must accept what God wants to do. It is as if we were saying to him, 'Lord, you alone are the one who works; and let us receive and endure.' In fact, circumcision can be performed on the day of rest, as our Lord Jesus points out in the seventh chapter of John (cf. *John* 7:22-23). Now it had been said that all works were to be refrained from on the day of rest (cf. *Exod.* 20:10; *Deut.* 5:14); God wanted men to have their hands tied and be dead, so to speak, and not to dare lift a finger, but they were nonetheless to perform circumcision on that day. Therefore, it follows that circumcision was not a work of man, but of God. The same applies to all sacraments.

Even more must we make effective use of this instruction because of the blasphemy which has been in the Papacy. Those vile people, when confessing—since they cannot deny the sacraments are means of God's grace and signs of their salvation—add subsequently that men continue to merit it by a performed work. They invented the idea that even though there are no works in the sacraments, they have nonetheless invented this diabolical blasphemy that there is a 'work performed,' that is, a work done by man such that he has merit before God. Now because such an abomination has held sway and the papists still defame the sacraments today and turn them into a lie with that sacrilege, the more must we hold to what we have already dealt with and is stated by Moses, namely, that God represents us as dead within ourselves, so that he can work in us and accomplish what he has declared. As for circumcision, it was a witness to and a figure of repentance.[6]

Then follows the promise given in Jesus Christ, the promise of righteousness. For that reason, Paul calls it the seal of righteousness

---

[6] Cf. *Institutes* IV, xiv, 20.—*M.E.*

by faith. He says that Abraham was circumcised (cf. *Rom.* 4:11). 'Of what use was that sign to him?' Paul is only stating what we have already seen (cf. *Gen.* 15:6). Abraham was not yet circumcised when he was told that his belief was reckoned to him as righteousness. Is it for nothing that God instituted circumcision? Not at all, says Paul, for at the time Abraham was fully justified the moment God accepted his faith (cf. *Rom.* 4:10), and he immediately received a sign as certification. In other words, the promise of life was more authentic when the seal was given. It is noteworthy that Paul uses that comparison (cf. *Rom.* 4:11). As decrees and public instruments have a seal, so God had to seal what Abraham was already assured of in respect to righteousness. And what did that righteousness consists in? In our Lord Jesus Christ. Therefore, circumcision testified that those who were thus marked were members of God's Son.

It is also noteworthy that Paul, in another passage, says in the second of Colossians, for the other was in the fourth of Romans, that we are today circumcised (cf. *Col.* 2:11), not, he says, with a sign like that of the Jews, for it is not with human hands, but we are circumcised spiritually in our Lord Jesus Christ. Indeed, and we are baptized because we are buried with him in baptism (cf. *Col.* 2:12). As a result, we share in the newness of life that he acquired for us in his resurrection. So we see here how baptism followed circumcision, from which fact it follows that circumcision was a temporal sign. And then it follows that today we have in baptism what the ancient fathers had in that sign which was commanded of them, for if the similarity did not exist, the one would not be substituted for the other. In fact, the grace of our Lord Jesus Christ would be obscure, as would be the grace his Father. Consequently, everything that was formerly represented by circumcision is today demonstrated and declared in baptism.

Now the matter we have just touched upon does not contradict the text we have read from Moses when he says that the covenant of circumcision will be everlasting (cf. *Gen.* 17:13). One would conclude otherwise if one were not practised in Scripture, but what is called everlasting relates to Jesus Christ. I am referring to the law. How? We have already spoken of the day of rest. God declares as much through Moses as through his prophets that his sanctification of his people was a sign and a memorial, indeed an everlasting memorial (cf. *Exod.* 31:16; *Num.* 18:19; *Isa.* 24:5; 55:3, 13; *Jer.* 32:40). The fact remains that the day of rest was not just for a while, as Paul also says. He says that that has to be counted and numbered among the shadows of which Jesus Christ is the substance and body (cf. *Col.* 2:16-17), as was also the case with the sacrifices and everything else.

Every time God speaks of the ceremonies of the law, he says: 'Behold what you will observe forever' (cf. *Exod.* 12:24; *Lev.* 22:31; *Deut.* 6:17; 8:6) and 'that you will do over and over' (cf. *Exod.* 12:14). As for the Passover Lamb, it is said that it is an eternal witness that God delivered his people, took them as his inheritance, and wants to sustain them until the end. That, then, is the meaning of all the ceremonies of the law that are called everlasting. Why? Because they had no meaning that would not last forever and be permanent. The ancient fathers had for their time what we have in the sacraments today. The salvation of their souls was incorporated in their ceremonies. So God had his reason for providing such sacraments and signs in perpetuity, seeing that their effect endures forever and can never fail.

Let us also note that the perpetuity of the shadows and figures of the law consists in Jesus Christ, who is their substance. It is true that our Lord Jesus at his coming brought to conclusion the ceremonies as concerns their practical usage, but they were completely confirmed in the power of faith and the usefulness we receive from them. That is why he declares he did not come to destroy the law (cf. *Matt.* 5:17), and the ceremonies are included.

It is true that they have been abrogated, as it is said. That is, the ceremonial law has ceased and no longer exists. So was it to no purpose? Not at all, but the apostle rightly states that all the ceremonies were incorporated in the phrase 'old covenant' because they had to come to an end. What is old must fall into decay and finally come to naught (cf. *Heb.* 8:13).[7] But when the apostle speaks that way, he does not, as I said, include the power of the old covenant, that is, the ceremonies commanded in it. He shows, on the other hand, that our Lord Jesus Christ confirms them all, and their certainty and permanence, which are in Jesus Christ, are in the sacraments, not in the external appearance or the practice and use of them, but in what the ancient fathers were taught about them: that God, having adopted them as his children, will also be their Saviour in this life and the life to come. That, then, is how circumcision was both an everlasting and a temporal sacrament, an everlasting sacrament in its power, in what it signifies, and in the advantage the believers receive from it, and a temporal sacrament in its outward use.

That is also why it is said that, on the one hand, at the coming of the Son of God there is a new world, as it were, a new world in respect of the law and its shadows and figures, but that, on the other hand, he confirmed them in their power because we now know the purpose of it all. Therefore, let us note, since we have baptism today, that the ancient fathers had circumcision and that baptism has taken its place. We must conclude, in keeping with what we have said, that God's grace would be lessened or would not be as clearly witnessed today as it was back then if we had not had what was in circumcision.

In fact, we have already said that we are advised of what kind of people we are and of the burden we bear from our mother's

---

[7] See also chapter 9 of the Epistle to the Hebrews for the development of what follows.—*M.E.*

womb as lost and condemned creatures, namely, God's wrath. The water indicates that we are not worthy of living in the world, that we must be straightway plunged into death, that all our senses, all our thoughts and affections must be destroyed. That, then, is the repentance that comes first. And that is also why it is said that we are baptized unto repentance (cf. *Mark* 1:5). That, then, is the first conformity that exists between baptism and circumcision.

There is another conformity, namely, that we recover in Jesus Christ what we lost in Adam, that is, the purity of righteousness, in order to be able to appear before God as his children, and that he shows himself to be the Father both of our bodies and our souls. In brief, we lack nothing today that was given to the ancient fathers. As for them, they were taught as much as they could understand and what was expedient for them. It is true they were taught less fully because of the absence of our Lord Jesus Christ, but God knew what was appropriate for them and provided it. Consequently, they had what sufficed for their salvation. But today, inasmuch as God provides all the treasures of his goodness at the coming of his only Son, we enjoy a greater clarity in baptism than the Jews did at the time of the law and the prophets. That, in short, is what be have to remember here.

Now as for baptism, no certain day is assigned to it, as is the case for circumcision. People needed that to be led by figures because they did not have the substance and truth given to us in the gospel. We must not be surprised that God kept them as his children. We no longer instruct small children the way we instruct those who have reached maturity. We do not spend a lot of time with those who already have discretion and judgment as we do with those who are still weak. We have not only to chew the words and syllables, but each letter. Consequently, God ordained what was appropriate for the ancient church,[8] as Paul calls it. He gives us in

[8] This expression Calvin is able to draw from Acts 13, Romans 3-4, and

our day what is appropriate for the teaching of the gospel, which is much fuller and clearer than the teaching was in earlier days.

Moreover, because baptism followed circumcision, we must conclude, as I have already said, that the temporal sign had to come to an end at the coming of our Lord Jesus Christ. That is why Paul says there is neither circumcision nor uncircumcision since the appearance of our Lord Jesus (cf. *1 Cor.* 15:57). By speaking that way, he shows that the Jews are no longer to have confidence in that ancient sign. And then it would be an extravagant absurdity if baptism and circumcision were merged, for circumcision says that Jesus Christ will come, and baptism points out and declares that he has come. Therefore, we see that this sign that God gave Abraham served until figures were no longer needed. We must now have new and different instruction according as God has separated us from that people, not that we do not have the same promises, not that we do not have the truth in Jesus Christ concerning everything that was figured in him, but because there is a difference in the manner of instructing and governing ourselves according as it pleased God to teach us.

Now what remains to be said will be reserved for tomorrow.

Now let us bow before the majesty of our gracious God in acknowledgment of our faults, praying that he will cause us to sense them more and more so that we will be so displeased with them that we will groan unceasingly under this wretched burden we bear, and may he draw us so powerfully by his Holy Spirit to be changed and renewed that our corrupt natures will be abolished. And if we do not immediately reach the goal he calls us to, let us nonetheless not lose courage, but may he strengthen us so we will not lose courage, but may he strengthen us so that we will struggle until the end in the assurance that he will bring us to joy in the victory he has promised us (cf. *1 Cor.* 15:57) when he takes us from this world.

Galatians 4.—*M.E.*

577

And may he sustain us so that we will always be considered as his children, and may we enjoy the freedom of claiming his name and having our refuge in him despite all the vices and imperfections which still indwell our flesh. May he grant that grace not only to us but to all the peoples and nations on earth.

81

By God's Will, Not by
Circumcision and Baptism

Friday, 5 April 1560

*This is my covenant, which ye shall keep, between me and you and thy seed
after thee; Every man child among you shall be circumcised. And ye shall
circumcise the flesh of your foreskin; and it shall be a token of the covenant
betwixt me and you. And he that is eight days old shall be circumcised
among you, every man child in your generations, he that is born in the
house, or bought with money of any stranger, which is not of thy seed. He
that is born in thy house, and he that is bought with thy money, must needs
be circumcised: and my covenant shall be in your flesh for an everlasting
covenant. And the uncircumcised man child whose flesh of his foreskin is
not circumcised, that soul shall be cut off from his people; he hath broken
my covenant. And God said unto Abraham, As for Sarai thy wife, thou
shalt not call her name Sarai, but Sarah shall her name be. And I will bless
her, and give thee a son also of her: yea, I will bless her, and she shall be a
mother of nations; kings of people shall be of her* (Gen. 17:10-16).[1]

Y ESTERDAY WE DEALT with why and for what purpose
God in ancient times gave his people circumcision,
which was in effect during the time of the law until the
coming of our Lord Jesus Christ. In brief, we said that from all

---

[1] Calvin also preaches on verse 17 in the sermon.—*M.E.*

time men needed to be strengthened in God's word because of the weakness of their faith and also because of their slowness to believe and great lack of steadfastness, which leads them to turn from the truth unless they are kept in it by many means and much assistance. At that point, it was said that circumcision at that time was to separate the people God had elected and chosen from all foreign peoples, who remained in their first condition. For we know that the entire human race was cursed in Adam. Consequently, God marked as his people the lineage of Abraham's descendants.

He now adds that he will be the God of those who are born of Abraham and bear his mark, and not only of those but also of all those of his house, whether they were born in it or purchased from somewhere else. In short, God declares that he wants all the house of Abraham to be blessed and that he considers it and avows it to be his. With that we understand even better how God's goodness upon Abraham increases, for we see that when blessing him God receives those who were considered with great difficultly to be worthy of being in the number of human beings. For even from that time servants were so despised and rejected that people considered them human only with great difficultly. They were held under such a yoke that they were used like oxen and beasts of burden. Their lives and deaths were subject to a master until the ordinances God provided for the people of Israel through the law (cf. *Deut.* 5:14), as will be pointed out.

Thus we can contemplate how God showed himself to be kind and liberal toward Abraham, seeing that he united with him all those who belonged to him. Yes, even though they had been despised as human beings, we have to remember that circumcision was a sign of God's adoption, so much so that servants are his children and heirs of the heavenly life. And at the same time and with great difficultly they were considered worthy of living in the world, but they were used almost like animals. So let us realize that when God calls us to himself, he wants us to be assured of his goodness in all things at all times, that we can call upon him with great confidence, that he will hear us since we have private access to him. And that still continues in the same vein what we have been saying, that God has neither omitted nor forgotten anything that will confirm the faith of his elect and his children.

In the meantime Abraham was advised that it was his duty to put great effort into making his entire house a temple of God where God would be worshipped by great and small in common accord. Now that same exhortation applies to all believers today. So the person who has both children and family must consider seriously that everything is committed to his charge because he must one day gives account to God. And the person who is master and head of household must always bear in mind that the superior powers of this world are not to diminish God's sovereign authority but to lead us to it. Consequently, it is right that each of them apply himself to instructing not only his children but also his wife, servants, and handmaids so that God will have the mastery he reserves for himself and so that men will always be under him. And what is also said about each individual household applies likewise to all cities and countries, namely, that when God establishes kings, princes, and magistrates, it is with the condition that they be concerned for his honour and realize that their subjects are put into their hands not for the temporal government, which concerns only the frail life of this world, but especially for God's rule to be set up in the midst of those over whom he presides so that God may be worshipped and given homage. That, then, is what we have to remember, namely, that the more clearly God shows how much he loves and prizes us by being pleased to gather together with us those over whom he has given us charge, there is a mutual obligation to exert great effort to maintain this gift pure and entire; and we must also remember that those whom he wanted to bring together with us and with whom he has joined in the hope of salvation may be truly dedicated to him, and that we apply all our efforts to that end.

Now if that were put into practice as it should be, it is certain that those who have a family would not be so negligent when it comes to honouring God, which we see to be the case. In addition, even though he notices that his servant is dissolute, debauched, and a despiser of God and that his maidservant has many vices and that, in a word, God is not honoured in his house, he overlooks all that, provided he can profit from it, provided everything is to his advantage. And let us not doubt that the honour God grants his mortal creatures suffers great loss when they are unconcerned about worshipping him and their households are not like temples, as they should be, as Paul says about believers (cf. *1 Cor.* 3:16). And in fact, as the pagans have said about each household's being a small image and reflection of the kingdom and civil government,[2] so must there be agreement and similarity between these little groups which are assembled this way when God wants to rule over them. That, then, is what we have to remember about this passage.

And let us note what is said about the servants Abraham buys, that even though they are not sanctified by race but are a polluted people, yet, because they are members of his household, they have to come into line and be included in the number and company of God's children. With that we understand all excuses are stopped when masters say: 'And it is not for three days or a year that I am hiring this fellow or that a maidservant is continuing with me.' In any case, we understand that God wants everything to be dedicated to him and that when he chooses individuals, he simultaneously chooses the households so that he may reside in them and so that the households, as I have said, will be like small figures of

---

[2] Cf. Aristotle, *Politics* I, ii, 5; ii, 7 (with a citation from Homer, *Odyssey* IX, 114); x, 1-5; III, vi, 7; Xenophon, *Economics* I, 1-7; etc.—*M.E.*

temples which are offered and consecrated to him. The same is true of countries in which individuals come and go. For even though they do not belong to the body of the people, the magistrates who are in charge must apply their authority to see to it that God's honour is not blasphemed and that scandals and enormities and other dissolute acts that would infect the church and bring shame upon God's name do not occur, and they must apply a firm hand to maintain good government everywhere. That, then, in brief, is what we have to remember about this passage.

Now it is said again that God's covenant will be kept, not that circumcision would be its principal or one of its main features during the time of the law, but God presupposes what was declared yesterday, namely, that the sacraments must not be separated from the word, for they are otherwise perverted and turned from their true and legitimate use. As today, if we should consider ourselves acquitted before God by outward baptism, we would profane what God sanctified, and that is a kind of sacrilege, the sacrilege of paying no attention to the simple figure and not considering the substance. So let us note that when God speaks of keeping the covenant and adding that every male is to be circumcised, it is not that he is content with the visible sign; but he wants every male to be circumcised exactly as he ordered it as a testimony that this entire people is holy in his sight and elected by his grace, and he wants that people to renounce themselves and everything that is characteristic of man to be cut off and abolished. For, as we have stated more fully, there are two aspects of circumcision: Abraham's seed was elected by virtue of our Lord Jesus Christ and was blessed and holy. And men also had to acknowledge at the same time that, from their mother's womb, they could possess no heritage but God's wrath and total damnation and that, consequently, they had to be stripped of their nature.

That, then, is how this passage must be understood concerning the keeping of the covenant, namely, that the word of God is always its foundation and that we consider what God requires in the covenant for the addition of his promises. With that in mind, we see that in the Papacy they have corrupted everything to the extent that everything they call 'sacrament' has been falsified. I am leaving aside the things they have invented to their liking and called 'sacraments.' But in baptism we see many flaws. It is true that there remains a fundamental aspect to it in spite of them and Satan. God had to show it was not in vain that he made his gospel known once and for all throughout the entire world, but in any case the fact remains that in all their incantations they do the best they can to abolish the sacrament. Is there a single bit of substance in it? It is true they mumble incoherently enough when they conjure and practise magic. There is an abundance of words, but there is not a single word of instruction. When we speak of substance, we know it must be understood for the edification of the church because our faith addresses Jesus Christ and we are instructed in the will of God his Father concerning the use and advantage of the sign.

So we see how the Papacy tramples on baptism, which they think they hold from our Lord Jesus Christ. They disregard its intention because they speak an unknown language and only babble. The same is true of the mass, in which they think they are performing a consecration which changes the bread into the body of Jesus Christ. We see them mumbling and breathing on the bread like sorcerers. There is a question as to whether the word sounds loud and clear and whether that word is a word of faith (cf. *Rom.* 10:8), as it was called even by the ancient teachers they dare not reject. Consequently, knowing that the devil cleverly turns men from the regulation given to them relating to receiving the sacraments correctly and duly, let us learn, as I have already pointed out, that, in order to keep God's covenant, we must not dwell on what we see with our eyes, but we must always hold that the sacrament is a visible word and that it is not enough to consider what God shows and signifies unless he declares at the same time the thing he had shown us and certifies that the figure is not vain and frivolous but accomplishes through the power of the Holy Spirit everything he shows us. That, then, is again what we have to remember.

Yet let us consider carefully not having literal baptism today, as Paul calls it.[3] Now he calls it 'literal' when we do not consider God's counsel and do not understand what he wants us to acknowledge through the sacraments. For the sacrament is dead when we put our glory in it without considering that God wanted to inform us that we are completely sterile and that there is only aridity in us until he waters us with his Holy Spirit, who is the living water.[4] We also realize we must die to ourselves in order to share the glory of our Lord Jesus Christ. And then too we realize that we must be washed of filth. Therefore, if we do not realize that, it is certain we completely violate God's covenant. So much for that point.

Now the fact remains that God does not want this visible sign to be abandoned, for, as we have shown, it is useful for us to be strengthened by such means. Consequently, we must accept with complete reverence the help God gives us so that our faith will be fortified on all sides. And yet the person who would prefer to reject the sacrament under the pretence of being satisfied with the word, that person would also destroy the word. Since there are many who have gone off the deep end who will say: 'What do I need with the Lord's Supper since I have Jesus Christ and possess him through the gospel? What more can I ask?' It is true that we have none other than Jesus Christ, but how do we possess him? Through the gospel! Yes, but does the Lord's Supper not help at the same time?

---

[3] Romans 2:29 is the closest reference.—*M.E.*
[4] Cf. Zechariah 14:8, where Calvin interprets the living water as the Holy Spirit. Cf. *Praelectiones in duodecimo prophetas minores,* CO 44, col. 371-72. Cf. also John 4:10-11 and Calvin's interpretation.—*M.E.*

Now if we consider the degree of perfection in our faith, we will clearly see that we do not yet understand and completely possess Jesus Christ. For in proportion to our being born in him, so, in a manner of speaking, is he daily born in us (cf. *John* 3:1-21; *1 John* 2:29) because we do not reach the full measure of man until we depart this earth. Consequently, our Lord Jesus Christ is not completed in us in his power until we no longer need the visible signs, no more so than the angels of paradise, that is, until we become completely spiritual. It is true that Jesus Christ is not separated into two parts, but we do not in any case contain his power fully.

So our faith, being weak, must grow and improve. And because we know only in part, our Lord Jesus Christ always has to guide us; and to guide us, he uses means that he knows are appropriate for us. Therefore, let us learn that God's covenant cannot be maintained unless we join with it the thing that cannot be separated from it. In other words, we must use the external signs to confirm the teaching that should be sufficient if we were such as we should be, and the signs are given because of our vices. We remain ridden with vices. And when God thus has pity on us and sustains us, how thankless of us if we do not peaceably yield to what he has ordained so that we will fulfil everything, knowing surely that everything is needful! And that is also why the threat is added that every male who is not circumcised will be exterminated, that is, cut off from his people, because he has violated God's covenant.

Now, we first see how filled with malice men are and how vile they are. When God gave circumcision to the people of Israel, as we have said, he offered himself as their Father. He adopted them as his children. He made them heirs of the heavenly kingdom. He made them members of his only Son. Those are blessings of inestimable value, and yet he has to threaten the scorners because they reject such a precious gift. What is to be done? If someone offers us food and drink for three days, he will not have to threaten us to make us take it. It is true little children will not always be present at dinner time when they are playing, for they are caught up in their play, but they will come back when they become hungry. And if they miss by an hour, they will know how to come back by the second. Now when it is said that every male who is not circumcised on the eighth day will be cut off, our Lord blames that failure on men's perversity because they are not moved or touched to the quick to receive the gifts he offers them, but they choose to wander astray as if the adoption by which eternal life is promised them were nothing. Now even though that was said formerly to the Jews, let us consider whether we do not need to be prodded the way they were. Therefore, when we hear the command to humble ourselves and be ashamed of our perversity, may God, because we are so insensitive, apply threats to us after giving himself to us so liberally. So much for that point.

In addition, when it is said that every male will be cut off, even though on the surface that would be considered crude, we still have to bow our heads and accept the statement which the sovereign Judge gives us. And in fact we have already stated above that God addresses the fathers and gives them the promise as a deposit for the advantage of their children. So just as the fathers receive the promise of salvation in deposit for their children, likewise, when they reject it, they and their lineage are cursed and viewed as abominable. And then there is no need to argue that the little children can never do anything about it. For what does God owe them? As we have pointed out, all are cursed in Adam. If God receives them as a privilege and they reject that privilege, they are again in their first condition. Consequently, a person cannot plead against God as if he were doing the children some wrong, for the fathers should be like guardians of this treasure that was assigned to their keeping. Inasmuch as the fathers are thus rebellious against God, both they and their whole lineage are going to perdition (and there is a lot of criticism of that teaching). For, as we have said, it was because of the pure and free goodness of God that the children were chosen, supernaturally so. In other words, they were removed from the condition in which they were born. Why would they not be deprived of the promise if they reject this blessing which is offered to them by God's pure liberality?

And we must also pay close attention to this. In other words, they broke God's covenant. For it is the same as if Moses were saying that because the fathers, by not circumcising their children, leave God with his promise, willingly renounce it and throw it off, they and their children will remain the way they were, and God abandons them the way they were, and with good reason, as I have said. Could we find a judgment more equitable than that? There you have men who are lost and damned in Adam; God chooses those whom he is pleased to choose, as if he were drawing them out of the pit of hell. He opens the kingdom of paradise for them and shows them that he is their Father in life and in death. It only remains for men to receive this by faith. Now if instead of doing that, they reject the grace that was communicated to them and spit on the riches placed before them, are they not obliged to remain in their poverty? Consequently, the long and short of it is that since God invites us to himself and we have this word and the sacraments along with it to strengthen us, let us also for our part come with a spirit of humility and receive that word as a good seed so that it will bear fruit in us. If at the same time we do not show we want to confirm God's grace to the extent we can by using the sacraments the way he ordains, it is certain our ingratitude will be the more inexcusable. And in fact we violate God's covenant. In other words, we will show and declare that we are unwilling to share anything in common with him or that we do not wish him to associate with us. And woe to those creatures who separate themselves from the heavenly Father, who divorce him whose they knew they were, in whom are all their felicity and well-being. That, then, is what we have to remember about this passage.

Now God, in brief, shows us in what reverence we must hold the sacraments, which are like pledges of the love he has for us and like guarantees that Jesus Christ is given to us so that we can possess them and share in all his blessings. For what he received was not for himself, since he did not need to be enriched except to support our poverty and penury. Therefore, when we see that God draws near to us by means of the sacraments and opens to us the treasures of his grace, let us with humility and reverence receive what is presented to us in them. That in brief is what we have to remember so that holy baptism and the holy Lord's Supper will not be polluted by our ingratitude today.

Meanwhile, let us note that the need for circumcision was not so rigorous that the children perished if they did not receive this sign; it is certain God's people did not fail to acknowledge a child who might die in four days. Why? Because it was not legal to circumcise before of the eighth day, as we have said. Consequently, the children of Israel could die without receiving the sacrament and still continue to be heirs of the life which belonged to Abraham's lineage. Why? God's word is sufficient for their salvation. When this statement was made: 'I am the God of your seed after you,' the salvation of Abraham's lineage was established. And that truth is immutable and sufficient to save the children to come. And it produces its effect. Now as we argued yesterday from Paul, circumcision is added, not that righteousness from God is included with it, but so that it can aid and strengthen men so that God may in that way show them what he promised them by mouth (cf. *Rom.* 4:10). Therefore, we see that the children of Israel were saved provided there was no scorn or rebellion and God's grace would not be profaned by their rejecting the sign which had not been given to them in vain or without purpose.

Now that ought to be put into practice, for we see that the world always gives itself over excessively and without restraint to ceremonies and the like. In the Papacy, salvation has to be incorporated in those external things, and yet they leave out Jesus Christ, who is their totality. Signs must be cursed and rejected if they do not lead us and direct our attention to our Lord Jesus Christ, who is the goal to which we must always look. Consequently, because that kind of vice is rooted in us, let us note that God did not want to attach the power of his Holy Spirit or his free election to visible signs, but he only wanted men to use them as something good and useful relating to their salvation.

And we must even be all the more attentive to that teaching when we observe the abuse perpetrated by the Papacy. They had to create a limbo for little children who would not have been baptized. Why did they have to? Because they adopted the principle that baptism is necessary for salvation, and then they began to split hairs over this passage of John chapter three: 'He who is not born again of water and spirit will not enter the kingdom of heaven' (cf. *John* 3:5). Indeed, as if that referred to baptism! And even if it had, as if there were a strict and urgent necessity, as we have already said. Now that is a foolish opinion that the papists were preoccupied with, namely, that baptism is absolutely necessary for salvation, and yet they are not aware that they were blaspheming against God. For the children of believers are sanctified from their mother's womb, indeed if only the father or the mother is a believer, by virtue of the promise that God will be the Father of those who are begotten of us. To believe otherwise is to accuse God of falsehood and to detract from his word openly, as if it were only partially useful for the salvation of his people.

Moreover, at the same time they also took from our Lord Jesus Christ what belongs to him in order to attribute it to baptism and consequently make an idol of baptism. For what does it mean that we cannot be saved unless water is placed on our heads? It means that God can do nothing and has resigned his right and that our Lord Jesus Christ does not cleanse us and is not the pledge of our adoption and our inheritance (cf. *Titus* 3:5-7), and it means that all that is to be acquired from the water. Consequently, when we see that those wretches were thus obtuse, we must all the more observe what Moses shows us here, namely, that the children were not cut off unless God's covenant was broken, that is, unless the fathers disregarded baptism, rejected it, and disparaged it as frivolous and of no advantage. So if the fathers are as depraved as that, oh, it is certain they and their children are cut off and banished from the church and, consequently, from all hope of salvation. And then the stupidity of the Papacy attracts still other corruptions. For if a child is in danger of death, a handful of water is immediately required, and let the first person encountered exercise the office of baptizing, and, in the absence of a man, let the women get involved. And that is just one more immense absurdity, for to whom does Jesus Christ say: 'Go, baptize all nations in my name'? Not to everyone in general, but to those whom he established to proclaim his word. That much for that point.

So then, he excludes women. So if they usurp that honour, it is as if they were baptizing in spite of God. For no one, the apostle says, is to take that honour upon himself (cf. *Heb.* 5:4); and let each man step forward and say, 'I will do it,' but God's calling must be in it. So if that office does not even belong to all men indifferently but only to those whom God ordained to it, how is it that women dare move into it? Where is their calling? Consequently, we see how one error leads to another. However, let us learn to find our complete rest in God's pure word and embrace this promise for the salvation of all those who come after us: 'I am your God and the God of your seed after you.'

In addition, let us honour baptism because of its revered role so that it will serve to confirm the word, not that it needs to, for the word is sufficiently authoritative, but let us honour it because of the weakness of our faith and so that it will encourage us to bless God's name for making himself known as our Saviour and the Saviour of all who belong to us. That, then, in a word, is what we have to remember about this passage.

Now at that point it is said that Abraham fell on his face, but in order to testify more emphatically to what he told him, God declares that his wife will no longer be called Sarai, but Sarah. For the letter 'i' indicates a modification, as if one were saying 'my mistress' and indicated that she was the mistress of a private household. And that name had not been given to her randomly, even though the ancient fathers customarily named their children that way; yet we see that names were often given prophetically. Such was the case with Abraham at first. For from Abram, God made Abraham. That is also true for Sarai, for he made Sarah of it. So he extended Abraham's paternity in general because he was to be the father of the entire church. He also extended Sarai's authority and superiority and, in so doing, declared that she had not only the authority of a household but that she would be known as the mother of all believers, no matter their origin. In short, we see how God brought together everything which could help Abraham's faith so that he would have no doubts. Even though the promise was long delayed, God did not want to disappoint him, and he never forgets his truth or fails to bring it to full effect. And that is why he says he will give lineage to Abraham and Sarah.

Now we see here how God tolerated Abraham's fault as well as Sarah's, for she, through her rashness, was excluded from God's blessing. And God, to punish her, was indeed able to raise up blessed seed from another source and thus say to her: 'You came here bringing your excessive pride as if you wanted to impose an obstacle to keep me from raising up lineage from you. That, then, is the unbelief that produced such presumptuousness. Now since that is the case, I will fulfil my promise, but you are not worthy of enjoying that honour because you excluded yourself from it.' God could use her that way. We see that he overcomes Sarah's folly and is no longer concerned that she did not believe or that she was too impulsive or that she attempted more than she was allowed or that she even dishonoured him. For when men get it into their heads that that is the way things are to be, God uses a simile. 'What!' he says. 'Will you close me in as in a circle?' And in fact, all those who wish to measure God's promises by their own understanding are drawing a circle around him as if to say: 'You will not leave that place. Turn this way, turn that way, as you think best, but you will not budge an inch if it does not please us.' That is the kind of madness men fall into when they want to bring God around to their way of thinking when he acts.

That is what Sarah did. Nevertheless, our Lord pardons her for an enormous fault and wants her to be mother of all believers and her name to be changed and for her to be a princess throughout the world, not to wear a golden crown but to have a much nobler dignity. That is so that she will be joined with Abraham and we will all be gathered together in their bosom and be heirs of the kingdom of God. So we see how God's mercy is incomprehensible, as Scripture tells us so often (cf. *Exod.* 20:6; *Deut.* 5:10; *Isa.* 30:18). Now that is not to make us bold to take advantage of God's gracious gifts, for if he worked that way with Sarah, it does not mean that he imposed a law upon himself. Therefore, let us be quick to accept peacefully our Lord's grace each and every time he offers it. Yet when we have done everything we should, let us realize we still have many faults which could remove us far from the enjoyment of the blessings God proposes for us unless he, in his incomprehensible mercy, makes up for what we lack. And even the pardon granted Sarah belongs to us all. For how are we saved? It is because Sarah conceived Isaac. For Jesus Christ came from Isaac (cf. *Matt.* 1:2; *Luke* 3:34). If, then, God had not pardoned Sarah, we would all be lost, for there was no way imaginable for men to be saved by their own efforts or virtues, but God had to work so that all praise would be given to him for our salvation. That, then, in brief, is what we have to remember.

Now at that point Abraham falls on his face as a sign of reverence, and then he says with joy in his heart: 'Alas, will a hundred-year-old man have a son, and will a woman of ninety years bear a child?'⁵ There is no doubt here that Abraham yields in subjection to God as he wanted to do, becoming a servant and totally submitting to what he was told. Now it is true that there is some reply, even though Moses says Abraham fell on his face and then adds nothing, as if he had remained silent; but that silence is worth more than all the cries in the world, for it is the same as our Lord's saying: 'I know those who are faithful to me.' Abraham's silence, then, was a true confession of faith because he honoured God, considered him to be truthful, leaned on the simple word that had been given to him, and rested on it. Now the prophet Isaiah attributes faith to that silence. 'All your strength,' he says, 'is in your quietness' (cf. *Isa.* 30:15). In other words, he makes no sound but listens to God and makes no reply. That is how it was with Abraham.

And yet he seems to weaken when he says: 'Is it possible?' But we need to note that his response does not proceed from unbelief. And that will be expounded at greater length later, and we will also see it in Moses' account. So Abraham did not offer resistance here and did not dispute with God, as if to say: 'That is impossible,' but he experienced a joy and an astonishment which moved him to speak more than was in his heart. That, then, is what we have to remember.

⁵ Calvin begins to explain verse 17, though the text read ended at verse 16.—*M.E.*

Some think it is only a matter of rejoicing, and here they highly praise Abraham's faith as if he had no feeling in his body, and they base their thinking on what Paul says: that he did not consider his feeble body or Sarah's womb, which was completely dead, but he knew that the one who was speaking was powerful to bring to completion what he had said (cf. *Rom.* 4:19-21). Let us note, however, that Abraham, even though he had a strict faith in God, was still a man. And that means there will always be a weakness of faith in us. Let us suppose that faith was completely perfect, that nothing was lacking; that does not mean we do not still have our human emotions. For before Adam was corrupted, he had his feelings, but they were in moderation. Today our feelings are quite excessive, but even so, if they should be regenerated by the Spirit of God, we are still not without feelings. So Abraham, receiving in pure faith what was permitted to him, does not abandon his human reason. He does not abandon the common order. 'What? I am a hundred years old. My wife is ninety. So how will it be possible?' That is how he thinks about his remark. He is filled with joy. But it is affected by astonishment. In other words, he is standing there confused, given his previous experience. He is thinking: 'How can this be?'

Moreover, he struggles against all that, and that is what Paul understood when he said that Abraham did not consider his body dead and incapable—not that he did not have some understanding of his old age and did not regard his body as half broken—that he did not have the power in himself to bring about what had been promised, for if he had thought otherwise, it would not have been virtue for him. If he had stood there completely stupid, it would have been easy for him to believe in God. Who would have kept him from adding faith to God's promises if he had not been tested time and again? We can see the quality of his faith by the many obstacles he had to face: his old age and his wife's sterility, which he could not understand all during his life, his wife's reaching the age of ninety, and the many other difficulties he overcame. He entrusted himself totally to God, assured that he would provide for everything that seemed impossible and that might prevent him from believing that God would bring to completion what he had declared. Thus, when we read this story and hear that Abraham added such faith to God's word that he did not consider his body, which was half dead, or his wife's womb, which was closed and dead, but that he gave God due honour by assuring himself that he would complete what he had told him, let us also know that he is powerful today to bring to fruition what proceeded from his mouth.

Now let us bow before the majesty of our gracious God in acknowledgment of our faults, praying that he will be pleased to cause us to sense that we are poor and wretched creatures and that there is in us only damnation and death. Yet may he let us taste his goodness and hope in it and so establish ourselves in it that we will always be kept firm and constant until he removes us from this earthly pilgrimage and receives us into the eternal inheritance, which he has promised us and which we await, not of ourselves, but through our Lord Jesus Christ. And may he have pity on our many weaknesses, both to cleanse us of them and to forgive us of them, until he brings us to the full perfection of glory, from which we are still so far. May he grant that grace not only to us but to all the peoples and nations on earth.

82

Ishmael's Primogeniture Is Superseded by Isaac's Election

Saturday, 6 April 1560

Then Abraham fell upon his face, and laughed, and said in his heart, Shall a child be born unto him that is an hundred years old? and shall Sarah, that is ninety years old, bear? And Abraham said unto God, O that Ishmael might live before thee! And God said, Sarah thy wife shall bear thee a son indeed; and thou shalt call his name Isaac: and I will establish my covenant with him for an everlasting covenant, and with his seed after him. And as for Ishmael, I have heard thee: Behold, I have blessed him, and will make him fruitful, and will multiply him exceedingly; twelve princes shall he beget, and I will make him a great nation. But my covenant will I establish with Isaac, which Sarah shall bear unto thee at this set time in the next year. And he left off talking with him, and God went up from Abraham (Gen. 17:17-22).

YESTERDAY WE BEGAN by pointing out that Abraham did not doubt so as not to disparage God's promise, but the difficulty of believing had to come into play so that he might learn the better to exalt God's power in order to attribute power to him. Not only can his power accomplish all things without the use of lesser means, or intermediaries, but as for intermediaries, he works against them, for, as we have said, if we do not keep in mind our deficiencies, we will never value God's grace the way it deserves, and, moreover, our faith will never be tested. For example, if a man is so arrogant that he thinks he has everything he desires, he will seek for nothing in God, for he is already so puffed up that he will explode. And as a result he has contempt for what God could offer him. He is blind to the extent that he does not know what it means to believe. For this word 'believe' means that God promises us what we do not see (cf. *1 Cor.* 13:12; *Heb.* 11:1) and even what we do not understand. And yet we conclude that he cannot fail us when he has spoken. That is how we believe. In other words, we honour God when we say that he will bring to pass what he has said, even though we do not perceive how, even if everything should seem to be impossible.

This is the way Abraham doubted. He was not caught up in such a way that he did not think about how it would be and that it was difficult and that it was unbelievable that he could become a father at a hundred since he had never begotten a child in the flower of his life. It is true he had had Ishmael about thirteen years earlier. But what did that mean? He had only that child and no others, as we can easily gather from the course of the story. So it seems very strange to him that he can beget a lineage. As for Sarah, she was passed the age of conceiving. It is impossible that Abraham did not consider all that, but we see even better how he glorified God by not spending his time reasoning things out and coming to conclusions, if he had followed his own disposition, but he is caught up in astonishment and yet accepts what God presents to him. For what we have already cited from Paul must come to pass, namely, that Abraham did not consider his body, which was already dead, as a door that shut out God's promise, nor did he make a judgment based on what he knew about his wife, but he believed simply that God is all powerful. Now that power entails the execution of what he says, for we must never separate God's power from his word.

So when Abraham confesses that God is all powerful, he means God will apply his hand to the task and produce a definite and unfailing effect in fulfilling his promise. Consequently, we must look upon it as brought to conclusion inasmuch as Paul testifies to it. Yet Abraham continued to be like a man lost and, on the surface, deeply disturbed by these perplexities. What? A hundred-year-old man is going to beget another child and a ninety-year-old woman is going to conceive! From that let us learn to lean so firmly on God's promises that we reject all conjectures that might come to mind and that we are always able to say: 'God has spoken!' Thus, what he has said must come to pass. It is not that we have lost touch with reality and the things we understand are not affected, but when we pass on and even when our faith lifts us above everybody, that is how we believe and also how we reserve for God what belongs to him.

Now Moses adds that in the end Abraham could not refrain from speaking. He had thought in his heart and was caught up by his thought. For he does not say what is in his heart, but God wanted Moses to tell us.

He then says: 'Oh that Ishmael might live before you.' Here it seems that Abraham, satisfied with Ishmael, disregards what had been said to him about Isaac, about that child which was to be born of Sarah, even though he had not yet been named. In fact, we cannot offer the excuse that when he said, 'Oh that Ishmael might live before you,' Ishmael did not suffer from some infirmity. For that means that that is enough for him, provided God leaves him with what he gave him. Some have thought that Abraham was afraid for Ishmael, as if God wanted to take him from him. And thus, because of the paternal care he had for his firstborn son, he preferred to be excluded from the second promise rather than to lose the son he already had before his eyes. But that is too forced, as is very clear. So there was no doubt that Abraham was under such tension, as it were, that he did all he could to abandon that grace which had been given to him more fully at that time.

As for Ishmael, he was already a blessing from God, but there was somewhat of the great fault mixed with it: Abraham had provoked God's wrath, indeed as fully as he could. He is satisfied with Ishmael, and that is because God did not enlarge his heart, as he would have to do. For we always have to note what is said in the psalm: 'Open your mouth and I will fill it' (cf. *Psa.* 81:10). With the word 'mouth,' our Lord shows by a figure of speech that we must have our senses open to receive his liberality, which is infinite, for we are like slender vessels. There are no containers as narrow as our affections when it comes to receiving God's grace when it flows down upon us. Our Lord reproaches us for being obstacles to his being more liberal and bestowing the blessings we could wish for so that we would be greatly satisfied with them, but our unbelief withers our senses and we are so small and so limited in faith that we can scarcely receive driblets of what would otherwise flow from a large fountain.

So Abraham did not open his mouth like a man whose faith is perfect, for he has Ishmael alive, and that already seems to him to be quite a lot. In order to understand that better, we can conclude from experience that we are like sick people who ask for only some small alleviation when pain becomes intense. They do not seek healing so much as some relief. If a man has a high fever, his head splits with pain. He feels weak throughout his body. He complains of his kidneys or of his legs; all his members feel beaten and broken, and he cannot stand it anymore. Now if the doctor comes and says: 'Patience, for tomorrow you will be given such and such a remedy; then you will go on such and such a diet; during the night you have to do this and during the day you have to do that; and then everything will be taken care of, and the prognosis is good.' At that point the poor patient will ask, 'Can I just get some relief?' He is not thinking about the healing. That is what happens, and everyone knows that only too well. And that is what prevents us from fully enjoying God's blessings, which we would have because they are near us.

So, in summary, we need to note that vice of Abraham's, for when saying: 'Oh that Ishmael might live,' he shows he does not have a lot of enthusiasm for Isaac, not that he has disregard for that blessing of God, but he speaks without thinking. And we see in that that we are often imprudent because we do not make the connection between two things, but we are like little children who are wavering and easily influenced one way or another. If you offer a child something he likes, he will take it with great pleasure; but if you present him with something else, he will let everything escape. Because he does not have the judgment to use both hands but thinks he can take everything with just one, he will let it all slip away. Afterwards, if he has something else, he forgets everything he had previously and runs to it and is caught up in it. That is what Abraham did, for he cannot put those two situations together and handle them as one. He must have thought: 'God has given me Ishmael. It is true I am not to be satisfied with that. To the contrary, every time I look at him, I must be admonished for being in too much of a hurry when I rashly believed my wife when she commented on God's word (cf. *Gen.* 16:2). We should have looked at things more simply. I even broke the marriage bond.' Abraham should have thought: 'In any case, I have Ishmael, and God has pardoned the many sins I committed. In addition, he promises me more. Consequently, I must embrace both at the same time and use restraint until it pleases him to make me rejoice in what he promises me.' That is what Abraham would have done if he had judged soberly.

How is that? He forgets almost everything. He did not have the presence of mind to think about all of those things, but he speaks his mind freely, and he did not first consider in his heart what he means. Seeing that the father of believers sinned this way out of ignorance, let us realize that God wanted to advise us in the person of Abraham how useful it is to think ahead and judge maturely and not act precipitously, for every time we do, it is certain we think we are taking the bull by the horns, as the saying goes, but we will lay hold of nothing, our emotions will be seeking after an illusion, and we will think we have gained everything when we have achieved our illusion, but there will be no substance in it. Consequently, seeing that we are so badly guided that we do not apply our senses to determining modestly that we do not know what it means to make distinctions, let us learn to use restraint and not to be so caught up in our own thoughts that we are held back and prevented from receiving all the blessings God is ready to bestow upon us. That, then, is what we have to remember.

But especially let us put into practice that teaching we cited from the psalm, that the more God blesses us (cf. *Psa.* 81:10), may those blessings always suffice to increase and deepen our faith. For we will in fact find that God rightly accuses and condemns us when we do not open ourselves to him as he demands and when ingratitude is joined with disbelief. It is certain that if we knew how to take advantage of all the good things we have already received from God's hand, our faith would grow daily and we would be better able to enjoy his blessings at the end of the year, ten times more than before. Likewise, throughout the rest of our lives we would understand much more about our God's goodness and be sharers in all his largesse, were we not ingrates. It even seems that the more God shows us his liberality, the more we find occasions to push him aside as if he were a mortal man who wearied of doing good or who thought that by using up his largesse he would no longer have anything. That is how we dishonour God.

And we must more closely note that if God does something good for us, he does it to encourage us to hope even more in him and to hold on to what he has given us, praying that he will continue to bless us. But in any case, let that good not be the end, as if to say that is enough, for we must always be hungry and thirsty for more while being satisfied at the same time. We are always to be satisfied to a degree with God's blessings. That is a way we thank him and praise him and experience such contentment that we are at peace. But in any case, we must always be hungering, realizing our emptiness, and we must always ask for more until we leave this world. For as long as we live here below, it is certain we are in a desert, hungry and thirsty. In this way, God wants us to learn to direct our earnest requests to him daily and take refuge in him. That, then, is what we have to remember about this passage.

Now the text says: 'Sarah will indeed bear you a son, and I will establish my covenant with him.' Our Lord is now working against Abraham's lack of faith and says to him: 'What is more,' for this statement is like saying: 'You would be satisfied if I chose to believe you. But I am not looking upon your vice, for I will still add what you are not hoping for and what you cannot understand, which is that your wife Sarah will bear for you the son that I spoke of.' In the first place, when God confirms his word, we see that there was some uncertainty in Abraham and that what had been said to him once was not enough. That, then, is a vice worthy of condemnation. For if his faith had been perfect, would it not have been enough that God had declared his will in one statement? Must we provoke him and put him to the test to the extent that he is constrained to give us assurance, as if he could fail us? Let us conclude then that Abraham is being reproved for his disbelief when God says: 'What is more, Sarah will bear you a son.' He is repeating what he had said to him. Why? It is with good reason. Abraham must be told that he was still uncertain and that he did not know what to think, not, as I said, because he had considered the difficulties and was prevented from believing, but because he could not immediately conquer the apprehensions that confronted him. But to conquer them, he must be helped and supported and God must confirm what he said to him. For the true help that God gives us comes when we are tempted by Satan and the things we see in this world after God gives us one promise and then makes two or three more. When we are troubled and beset by some distrust, we too will certainly come to that point. What must we do? Let this be our thought: 'God has promised me his mercy; it cannot fail.' Now if a promise seems to be too meagre because some great distress is pressing us hard, we must then add, as I said, the second and third; we must remain steadfast and read and listen more. And when we see our Lord assuring us many times, let us come to this conclusion: 'We must take courage and struggle the harder and overcome all trials.'

So what we have to remember about what Moses recounted is that God said to Abraham: 'Sarah will bear you a son.' In brief, we have to note how, if we are to approach God better, we must rise, little by little, so high that we will overcome our present lives and lay hold of the hope of the eternal inheritance which is ours. In short, God's promises, as they are laid together, must provide for us a ladder so high that we will always move up step by step until we reach the place he has invited us to. That is so we will not waste our time with this world, but so that, knowing that our inheritance is up in heaven, we will aspire to it and find there our complete rest.

Now, we see at the same time how God discerns between Isaac and Ishmael. He says he will establish his covenant with Isaac, and in that way Ishmael is excluded, not completely, but to show that he must not glory in his primogeniture and that he must be under his brother and submit to him or be banished from the house, as it finally happened (cf. *Gen.* 21:14). As a result, we see how this difference occurred between Abraham's two children, that the firstborn does not have the honour of being the heir of the promise, but the second does. If we ask why, it is true we could claim that Ishmael is from Hagar, who was a servant, but he is still Abraham's firstborn. Even Sarah acknowledged him as her son. He is Abraham's legitimate son, indeed by marriage. He was Sarah's adoptive son. Isaac comes next, and before he is born, God already establishes him as heir of the heavenly life. If we ask how that happens, we must talk about God's free election. We will not find in Ishmael the reason he was rejected until he showed himself to be a mocker, as we will see later (cf. *Gen.* 21:9),[1] but he had already been rejected. If we ask what Isaac had done by way of merit to explain why God established his covenant with him, we can only answer that it was by God's pure goodness. For those who claim God foresaw that Ishmael would be perverse and evil only rattle on without any reason or foundation, for it is certain Ishmael and Isaac would have been equal if God had not guided one by the Holy Spirit and abandoned the other. So we must always come back to the point that there was no good in Isaac by which he was to be preferred over Ishmael, but it pleased God that Isaac would be a mirror of his goodness and that in him we might learn to realize that our salvation comes only from God's good pleasure to elect us, not only before we were conceived in our mother's womb, but before the creation of the world.

If there is any blessing in that and if it is the fruit of God's free election, when we honour him as our Father, let us taste his goodness and place our confidence in him, and let us beseech him earnestly and make every effort to walk according to his righteousness. How can we do that? We did not acquire it by our own

[1] Calvin will preach on this text at the end of May, but the sermon is lost.—*M.E.*

power or industry; we do not have it by inheritance. So God must be at work in the process. How? By confirming his free election. That, then, is what we have to remember about this passage when it says particularly that God will establish his pact with Isaac. Now that discussion will be drawn out more fully elsewhere (cf. *Gen.* 25:11),[2] but to understand Moses' point here, we must understand that principle. But let us move along.

The text says that God answered Abraham concerning Ishmael, that he will bless him and make great nations come from him, but that the covenant will be with Isaac. The first thing we could ask here is whether Abraham had any other concern for Ishmael than the earthly life, for it seems that we could gather that from the words 'As for Ishmael, I have heard you.' How so? He will be rich and powerful; he will have a great lineage. If Abraham's prayer was answered in that God gives Ishmael only earthly and corruptible goods, it would seem that Abraham dealt with Ishmael as an animal and asked for him only that he would be at ease in this world and have no concern for the eternal inheritance. At first glance we could think that, but at this point God did not intend to answer Abraham in every respect, for if he had already answered him, woe to him, for he was satisfied with Ishmael. When he says: 'Oh that Ishmael might live,' it was equivalent to abandoning Isaac, not that he thought about doing so. We always have to remember that.

Yet Abraham's mind is so confused and in such a jumble that he is no longer able to make distinctions. So if God had answered him as he requested, the situation would have been going badly, but he answers him only in part, that is, to the extent it was expedient, for that is often the way God answers us. And yet he does not do what we ask him to. He does not grant us all our wants and wishes, especially in the way we thought he might. Consequently,

---

[2] But the sermons on Genesis for the summer of 1560 are lost.—*M.E.*

he does not reject us, and our prayers are not empty or useless; yet he does not have to conform completely to our liking, but he must judge according to his infinite wisdom what is good. That is how he answers us every day. The same was true for Abraham. In brief, that is how our Lord understood that Ishmael would be blessed in Abraham his father's favour, as if to say: 'Yet will I remember that he is your son. It is true you did not beget him in a legitimate way, but I am forgetting that fault. And to show that I love you, yet will I extend my blessing to him, but only in part. So I will give him lineage. It will be great. It will be rich. He will lack none of those things, but my covenant will be with Isaac.' Here again we see that what was given to Ishmael is nothing in comparison with what is reserved for Isaac. That much for one point.

For the second, we can conclude that God's covenant was not to be understood for this present life, but for the immortality of heaven. Those are two things we have to note here. As for the first, it would seem strange that God gave the name Ishmael to the first, who was so important, and the name Isaac to the second. For Ishmael means 'God has answered.' That is an excellent name that bears much meaning. Now what does the name Isaac mean? 'Laughter.' It does not seem then that there is as much value in expressing God's grace in Isaac's name as in Ishmael's, but when the text says that God had answered him, it was in particular; it was not that the fulfilment of grace would be in Ishmael. So we must restrict that only to an individual and a circumstance. And what is said about Isaac was to show that there was a full joy and that Abraham had rejoiced over false signs in Ishmael. Not that he would not have some occasion to bless God, but lingering long over the situation was a great vice. So his joy had been excessive, and yet it vanished away, for there was no durability in it. But in Isaac there is reason to laugh, that is, there is full rejoicing.

Let us come now to what we have discussed. We are shown here that what God reserves for Isaac is without comparison to be valued more than what he gave Ishmael. And yet Ishmael is ennobled. Princes will descend from his race. He will be head and father of a great people and is to be renowned afterward. When he receives that and God nonetheless says: 'That is nothing,' it is nothing by comparison with Isaac. Let us learn to look with contempt on all that belongs to this world in comparison with the heavenly life. That is what this passage teaches us. And we will be much profited if we remember this lesson and practise it well. For we see in fact how easily we are distracted and that all our senses and appetites pull us down. And our Lord, what does he ask? Every time we read his word in private and come to hear it preached, it is the same as if he were saying to us: 'Do not be like animals, whose heads are always lowered, but look on high. Be pilgrims in the world and aspire after me since that is where all your felicity lies.' That is all God wants of us every time we are instructed in his word.

Now it takes little to distract us. For the person who is urged on by avarice asks only to accumulate piece by piece. And the person who is led by ambition to acquire honours and make himself look good will always be in pursuit of that obsession. Because that is so, let each of us try to use restraint here. All the more must we observe what is shown to us here. We will never aim for where God is calling us, never be able to devote ourselves to the heavenly calling unless we scorn base and transient things, scorning them by using them in moderation, as God will permit, and by being ready to let go of what we possess, by not being excessive in our appetites; and may all that cause us to live soberly and temperately. That much then for the first point.

Now the second is to show that from all time God has allied himself with the elect, not to nourish us on the fat of the land here below but to draw us higher. And that serves us very well. For if we thought Abraham was blessed by God only for this terrestrial life, what would it mean? What would be the meaning of the hope of the eternal salvation that we are to have at the coming of our Lord Jesus Christ? Where would we be if that were the case? It would be like having diabolical spirits who wanted to obscure God's grace in this place. And even that dog Servetus always had that to say about Abraham, that he did not know who God was, but that he worshipped an angel in a picture, that he never knew what the heavenly kingdom was, and that all the promises of the Old Testament belonged only to the flesh. Now the devil raised up that instrument to falsify the gospel teaching and make it suspect. Now what hope can we have in eternal life unless we know that since Abraham has gone before us and only had very obscure figures, he nonetheless saw the day of our Lord Jesus Christ, as Jesus Christ himself proclaims in the eighth chapter of John? (Cf. *John* 8:56.) Otherwise, we would think today that the gospel only declares something new. And we would soon be shaken by that something new, and our faith would evaporate. Consequently, we must remember this point as a necessary principle of our faith, namely, that from all time God has shown that he did not create his elect just to show that he was their Father in this world to nourish their bodies, to give them ease, conveniences and pleasures, but that he created them to lead them higher, to establish his covenant with them. That, then, is what we have to remember.

Now it is said that the covenant will be with his seed after him to show that all those who succeed to the promise given Abraham must place themselves under the sign of Isaac. From those words we can judge that Ishmael, first, was not banished from the hope of salvation until he cut himself off by his godlessness, as we will see (cf. *Gen.* 21:9). So let us understand that God's covenant was established with Isaac, not to reject Ishmael completely, but Ishmael, the firstborn, had to come join himself to his brother, who was lesser than he, and be of his lineage, as it were. In a word, Ishmael had to renounce his primogeniture in order to share the salvation which was promised Isaac and his seed. Abraham had been told previously: 'I will establish my covenant with you and with your seed' (cf. *Gen.* 17:7). But was not Ishmael his seed? No. That is, God, by accepting him as the firstborn son, grants him the honour of being considered Abraham's child, for, in order for him to be Abraham's child, he would have to be the child of his brother Isaac, so to speak, his younger brother. So we see how God intended to subdue all Ishmael's pride and give lustre to his own goodness so that we might realize men have nothing to offer and that we must receive everything from him and that he was totally free to dispense his grace as he pleases, without men's bringing anything to it.

Thus we now understand this passage, and we need to note it well, for we will see later that Ishmael was circumcised (cf. *Gen.* 17:23), which would have been a very great absurdity if he had had no hope of salvation. We have seen that circumcision was a spiritual sacrament. God intended for Ishmael to be circumcised. It is quite obvious that that sacrament would have been profaned if Ishmael had had no place in God's church. We must harmonize these two things, that is, how it is that Isaac is the only heir but that Ishmael is nonetheless circumcised as a sign that he belongs to the number and rank of the children. Now, as I have said, the harmonization is very easy. Ishmael, as for his name, is not to be a head in God's house and is not to be considered a patriarch, but he must be considered as one of Abraham's servants. So Ishmael must come into the house and submit to the sign of Isaac, his brother. Why? For two reasons. One is that he, God, wanted to show his election in a living image so to speak; the second is that our Lord Jesus Christ was to issue from Isaac and not from Ishmael (cf. *Matt.* 1:2; *Luke* 3:34). Now Isaac was cursed in himself as were the others. And, as we have already pointed out, it would be an error to try to find in his person some difference that would make him distinct from his brother Ishmael. So Ishmael would, on the whole, be of the same value as Isaac if God did not distinguish one from the other. But free election is, on the one hand, seen here; on the other, God wants our faith to be directed to our Lord Jesus Christ. Consequently, he ordained Isaac to be the father of Jesus Christ so that the promise would have to be fulfilled in him.

We now see how God gave Ishmael what is mentioned here in Abraham's favour so he could sense God's blessing, and yet he reserved for Isaac what belonged to the inheritance to show that he was the only heir, not that he would not have companions, but that it was like withdrawing them, for we know that nothing is diminished for us when we attract many brothers who are sharers in everlasting life with us. If a man who succeeds his father, however rich he may be, called thirty or so heirs with him, it is certain that in the end scarcely anything would remain for him. But the situation is different concerning the heavenly life, for, as I said, our portion will not be lessened if we have a hundred thousand brothers and are all joined together to succeed to the salvation God proposes for us. That is how Isaac's situation would not have worsened if he had had many brothers with him. And if Ishmael had remained in the house, there would have been as many riches without reduction. But if he is cut off from them, God's promise still remains intact and in force, and it is Isaac's seed that succeeds, not that the effect appears immediately, but it is always apparent that his seed was chosen.

That is not mentioned here, but we must remember what was said earlier. God had said: 'I will multiply your seed like the sand of the sea and the stars of heaven' (cf. *Gen.* 15:5). That is what he told Abraham. And what is that seed? Isaac. It is in him alone. It is not said that God will multiply Ishmael's seed, as we will soon see (cf.

Gen. 17:20). It is true it seems God promises more to Ishmael, for he says he will multiply him mightily (cf. *Gen.* 17:20).

So God seems to give Ishmael more, but the reason is so that we will recognize God's infinite power better in the smallness of the church. For if the church immediately flourished and had great splendour, God's grace would be obscured, and we would not perceive it so well or so clearly. For that reason, the children of this world increase. They spread far and wide. They rise up so high that it seems they are to rise above the clouds. They fill all things. And we see how their sudden prosperity intoxicates them and how in a moment they reach their ultimate height. However, the poor church will creep around on the land. It will be hidden in its small numbers. There will be nothing by which it can be much esteemed. But when we see those small beginnings and God working beyond our ordinary imagination and what we could have expected, he shows us he is governing his church miraculously, and as a result his power is even better recognized. That is what has been happening since Isaac and Ishmael.

It is worthy of note that it is again repeated that Isaac will be born of Sarah the following year. And that is always a rebuke to Abraham for trying to introduce an illegitimate seed in the place of the one that had been promised, which was to be legitimate. He has nonetheless shown that God will not fail to accomplish his work, even though he had delayed. So Abraham is well advised of the evil he committed when our Lord proposed Sarah to him. It is as if he were saying: 'When I promised at the beginning to give you seed, you should have expected it in accordance with the way I established when I joined husband and wife. You took a second wife and in so doing violated the law I intended to be forever permanent. Thus I acknowledge here your fault.' That is one thing he shows him. But another is that God consoles him and informs him he will not fail to give him a child by Sarah. And that must we always remember when our Lord confirms us in his promises and then supports us in our weaknesses and in our vices. Then let us learn to condemn ourselves as we taste his goodness so that our faith will not be held back but always moving forward at a good pace. That is how we are to put that passage into practice.

At that point, it is said that God went up from Abraham. In other words, the vision ceased. It is not that God ever distanced himself from Abraham, for we know his being is infinite. He fills all things, and we must not imagine that he moves from one place to another, that when he is here, he is not there, that when he is in heaven, he is not on earth. To believe that God is limited to one spot in space would be an unbelievably stupid superstition. So his being is infinite. And yet we know that his power is present in all who believe in him and that at that time he dwelled in Abraham's house, not the way men do, but his domicile and sanctuary were there, as his altar was set up there. So how did he go up from Abraham? The vision went away. Scripture customarily speaks of God's presence by the external signs he gives (cf. *Exod.* 29:45; *Psa.* 132:14; 135:21; *1 Tim.* 6:16), as we will see later when Jacob says: 'What is this place if not the gate of heaven? This is the house of God' (cf. *Gen.* 28:17). That is the ordinary way holy Scripture speaks.

After that we also have to note another reason, not that it can be elaborated now when it is said that God went up in order to teach us to raise our attention above the entire world. When we wish to call upon him, when we think about him and give him the reverence he deserves, let us not be so dense as to place him down here, but let us know that he rises above the entire world. As it is also so often said in Scripture, he inhabits heaven, not because he is enclosed by it, for the heavens do not hold him, as Solomon says (cf. *1 Kings* 8:27), but because we are to learn to correct all our earthly affections when we think about the infinite and incomprehensible majesty of our God.

Now let us bow before the majesty of our gracious God in acknowledgment of our faults, praying that he will be pleased to make us so aware of them that we will be displeased by them. And because we are so filled with hidden vices, with which we are even accustomed to flattering ourselves overmuch, may he enlighten us sufficiently both by his word and by his Holy Spirit so that we will be ashamed of ourselves. And after realizing the infinite number of evils within us, let us be more enthusiastic about having recourse to his mercy and praying that he will not fail us, but that we will always walk in accordance with his holy calling. And if we take many false steps, may he stand us up again and continue to strengthen us, as he knows he needs to. May he grant that grace not only to us but to all the peoples and nations on earth.

83

Confidence in God and the Place of Instruction

Monday, 15 April 1560

And he left off talking with him, and God went up from Abraham. And Abraham took Ishmael his son, and all that were born in his house, and all that were bought with his money, every male among the men of Abraham's house; and circumcised the flesh of their fore-skin in the selfsame day, as God had said unto him. And Abraham was ninety years old and nine, when he was circumcised in the flesh of his foreskin. And Ishmael his son was thirteen years old, when he was circumcised in the flesh of his foreskin. In the selfsame day was Abraham circumcised, and Ishmael his son (Gen. 17:22-26).

*W*E STARTED OFF by saying that when it says that God went up, that statement does not refer to him or his essence, but rather to Abraham, for since God is infinite, he fills heaven and earth. Now if he is everywhere, he cannot change place by going up or down, but Scripture speaks like that, saying that God descends when he gives some indication to men that he is near them and wishes to make himself known to them more familiarly. That, then, is how that teaching is related to our senses. For if we do not have some visible sign and testimony that God wishes to draw near to us, it is certain we are wandering and scattered, so to speak. But the opposite is also true. When God shows himself to us manifestly this way, he must take such measures that we feel we are called to contemplate his exalted state, not to attach him here below or to think of him in fleshly or earthly ways, as we said when he appeared to the ancient fathers when he would come down, in a manner of speaking, not that he moved from any place, for that is impossible, but so that men can understand him when he comes to earth, as it were.

For if such a view of God had been permanent, what would have happened? The fathers, who were to worship God in spirit and in truth (cf. *John* 4:24), would have become so sottish that, given the fact that men are always inclined to think only about this earth, that would have detracted greatly from God's majesty and glory. So the visions had to serve to move them and awaken them and at the same time draw them on high so they could worship God spiritually and not succumb to some witless imagination concerning him, as we are much accustomed to do. In a word, we see how God had pity on men's ignorance and weakness every time he appeared, for that was like coming down to them because they could not rise to the heavens. But he also realized the possible danger that men would not think that they had to have their faces looking down here below and would create in their heads fanciful concepts, as is their custom. So that is why God, after showing himself by visible signs, also withdrew his majesty on high so that believers might learn to worship him in all humility and realize that they are superior to all creatures and that they must not confuse him with the visible elements or anything created or anything subject to corruption, but that they must lift him above everything they can see and everything they can understand and that they must rise above all of that when it comes to speaking of him. That is why it is said so often in Scripture that he inhabits the high places and that his dwelling and his pavilion are above the clouds (cf. *Psa.* 113:4; *Isa.* 57:15), and even in the prayer we say 'who art in heaven' (cf. *Matt.* 6:9).

Even so, he does not fail to say in his law that he lives in the midst of the cherubim (cf. *2 Sam.* 6:2) because at that point he wanted to assure the believers they could not be disappointed by calling upon him because he was near them and they had familiar access to him inasmuch as he had chosen the holy place in which he was making his residence, not to be shut up in it, as we said, but to show his grace and power. Now because people could take advantage of that and men would have been able to make a superstition of the fact that God was showing himself to them so familiarly, they were informed that he lived on high so that they might seek him in faith beyond all things visible and not confuse him with the things of this world. That, in brief, is what we have to remember when it is said that God went up from Abraham.

It is also noteworthy that Abraham did not obey God because he had some vision before his eyes that could astonish him, but that he obeyed when that vision disappeared, that is, when God withdrew into heaven, so to speak, and he could with his natural sense imagine that he was distanced from him. That tells us that God was still unchanged in his purpose, that his will was not changeable, and that he always sustained the one who had once testified to his will by fearing and revering him. That was reason enough for Abraham to have that vision. That is a very useful point for those of us who can apply it wisely. If God makes himself known in any way, we must certainly be moved with fear and astonished. For whatever resistance we may feel or however dense or stupid or obstinate we may be, we are nonetheless compelled, in spite of our hardness, to be moved when mention is made of God's majesty, to which we are subject. For inasmuch as he holds all things in his hand and guides them, we have to conclude that we cannot thwart his dominance. So when it seems God is present and we have to seek his face and appear before him, we must not be surprised if we are moved at those times and yield to him. But since our minds are fickle, we seek only to distance ourselves further, and when we achieve that, we think God no longer sees us and we are thus hidden and removed from his presence. That is what makes us bold to loose all restraints and have greater contempt for God's word. As a result, our former zeal and affection vanish.

And that is our situation, and experience shows it only too clearly. We see those who have some devotion standing here in the congregation. They will hear the teaching offered to them. They will be moved by it. It will pierce their hearts. It will sound out their thoughts and their desires. They will even think they are caught up in the fear of God. They will make themselves believe that. But what happens when they return home? They will get busy with their daily affairs and business dealings, and some will give themselves over to their amusements and loose behaviour, and others will abandon themselves to their vices and gross iniquities. In short, everyone will follow his natural bent and persist in his old ways, burning the candle at both ends until it goes out.

So it is quite certain that Moses rightly expressed that situation concerning Abraham, that when he was circumcised and had the same done to Ishmael and all his house, God was not there, that is, the vision had already departed and disappeared. Nevertheless, Abraham continues to conform, for he has a firm and steadfast purpose. In fact, when Paul himself exhorts slaves to obey their masters and fulfil their responsibilities, he makes it a point to tell them not to do so to be seen, as men-pleasers (cf. *Col.* 3:22). That is how hypocrisy shows itself—when we are watched and have some witness, we are capable people and are afraid of failing so as not to be criticized and so no one will be able to rebuke us. But if we fail and the sin is pardoned, we do not then experience much remorse or many scruples. For that reason Paul says that if everyone tries to do his duty, he must look to God; at that time, he says, you will not seek to please the eyes because God sounds the hearts and thoughts (cf. *1 Chron.* 28:9; *Jer.* 11:20; 17:10) and nothing is hidden before him (cf. *Job* 28:11; *Ezek.* 28:3), and he does not have to show himself to say that he judges all our acts and examines them (cf. *Rom.* 2:6; *1 Pet.* 1:17), for even though we are hidden from our own view and senses, oh, he still sees and contemplates everything. It is said he inhabits the high places (cf. *Psa.* 113:4; *Isa.* 57:15), but that is to observe what is done among men. He also takes care of the small, who are afflicted and trampled underfoot (cf. *Matt.* 18:4-14), and yet he diminishes the haughty pride of those who rise too high (cf. *Psa.* 31:23).

So in order to find our worship of God good, we need to remember that we not only must be moved when we hear the sermon, receive the sacraments and receive other instruction about God's majesty, but we must already be resolved to walk before him, aware that he knows all our thoughts, which are hidden away from men, and aware that he knows our hearts a hundred times better than we do, for a man will deceive himself at every turn, and we hide things from ourselves that even we do not know about or have the slightest inkling of. That is not true of God. Let us make up our minds to worship God, even though no one sees us, and may no one be able to accuse us when we do the contrary: Nonetheless, let us worship God, who knows all things. That, in a word, is what we have to remember about this point.

Now it is said at the same time that Abraham acted the very same day, which shows the promptness of Abraham's faith. And we still have to gather worthwhile instruction from that, for we see how hesitant and cold we are. Each of us ought to realize that from our own experience. But God wants to be served promptly without question or delay. As soon as he speaks, we must have our hands ready to carry out his commands, our feet poised to go where he calls and guides. Since we are so lazy and dilatory, we would always like to have a work assignment beyond the following day or month or year. That is why we need to remember especially what is shown us here, namely, that we set to work without delay. What Moses praises Abraham for is not to pat him on the back but to give us a mirror image of how God is to be obeyed. That, in brief, is how we are to act if we are to be children of the one who was called father of all believers and of God's church. In other words, as soon as God speaks, we are to bring ourselves into line with what he says.

Now many things hinder us. It is true we will not say that God may wait for one year or ten, but no matter, that is what we are hoping from him with our delaying tactics. We will always say 'tomorrow,' for there is still something holding us back; we will take on responsibilities so we will be delayed, and our final intention is to delay and push the time forward. Quite like bad managers when they are badgered and pressured to pay what they owe, they will ask for an extension. It is not that they are thinking about fulfilling or are intending to fulfil their responsibility the next day or in a week rather than at the present time, but they think they are ahead of the game. And then, at that point, they are still planning some other way to escape their responsibility. That is what we try to do with respect of God. So let us learn to conform so God will not have to wait for us. What would happen if a man had a servant and said to him: 'Come with me. Go there,' and the servant said: 'Wait a bit. I do not have time now. I have something else pressing. I cannot do that now, but I will do it later when it is convenient'? If a child answered his father that way, would that be tolerated among men? Certainly not, for the one who has superiority expects to be served when it pleases him. Would it not be the height of absurdity to take more liberty with God than with mortal creatures? Consequently, we are to be even more incited to subject ourselves to our God as soon as he utters his word and be ready to execute it, struggling against all hindrances. Let us each urge ourselves, goad ourselves, seeing that we are like mules that only move if they are beaten, and let us put a lot of effort into trying harder. And Paul also gives us the Philippians as an example when he says that as soon as the teaching of the gospel was preached to them, they yielded to it so quickly that there was no question of postponing till the next day, but they received what had been declared to them in God's name (cf. *Phil.* 1:5). In saying that, his purpose is not just to praise a people but to give a pattern for what we are to do, which is in line with a general teaching in Isaiah: 'This is the acceptable time. This is the day of salvation. Call upon the Lord when he is near. Seek him when he can be found' (cf. *Isa.* 49:8; 55:6). Now we do that when we seek God at an opportune time, when he can be found; and that carries with it an oblique threat, that we could encounter trouble later and the door would be closed to us because we must call upon God when he presents himself to us.

It is noteworthy that the text says: 'on the same day.' It points as with a finger at the time and even at the minutes as if to tell us that we must not haggle about the time, saying: 'And when will this be? I can do that tomorrow. I can do that in a week.' That rules out all personal activities and tells us that if we are not ready and prepared on the spot, it is a sign of rebellion, and let us not try to deceive him or mock him unless we do so with a pleasant face, the way we see all hypocrites do. So that is what we have to remember about what Moses says concerning the day Abraham was circumcised, and that he did not delay, but that he conformed to God's simple will and was satisfied with it and carried it out.

We also read that Abraham was ninety-nine years old. But for one year he would have been a hundred. We are told his age for a reason, for we know how slow old people are; they are even melancholic and not easily managed, and are even recalcitrant. It is true that at whatever age we are God can only with great difficultly gain some control of us, for young people are like horses unaccustomed to bridle or saddle and cannot be made to yield, or they are like young bulls which do not know what it is to wear a yoke or pull a plough. Even so, that shortcoming is found principally in old age, where those who have lived a long time in the world think they are excused from learning more. And what do they say? 'Have I not learned enough? Does someone have to teach me my lessons like a child?' They think that with age they have acquired the privilege of not being directed or instructed. That is base ingratitude. For what are men especially to learn in this world if they should live a thousand years? Is it not to subject themselves to the one who created and formed them and has authority over them? They should think about that and ponder it every day of their lives. But no, they think that since God has provided for them a long time, they no longer owe him subjection, which is now like leisure time, like perpetual time off to do as they please in their stubbornness. That is why John addresses them in his epistle, saying: 'Listen, old people, for he who has been from the beginning is speaking to you' (cf. *1 John* 2:13-14), as if to say: 'You poor fools who have been making arguments for sixty or eighty or a hundred years, thinking you are privileged not to be governed any longer by God's instruction, what will you present for all the time you have lived in the world that compares with that incomprehensible eternity which is in God? If you compare yourself with him, what do you have? So do not make arguments from your old age.' Now, as I have said, John gives exhortations to correct the foolish, excessive pride which is in old people because they think they are so wise they no longer need to be instructed and are also embarrassed to correct themselves when they are shown their faults.

It is noteworthy that Abraham had almost reached a hundred years of age when he was circumcised. Consequently, we see another and better approval of his faith and humility when he is completely restored at such an age to what had been promised him by the mouth of God. Now we must consider here the act in itself.

According to appearance, we could say it was a great folly that Abraham, a very decrepit old man, should cut his flesh and cut it in such a place. It was a shameful thing. Even so, although that seems folly to the world, Abraham does not refuse, but completely abases himself and abandons his reason and all the arguments and debates that could be presented. He looks only to God and says: 'This must be done.' We see in that how men will never be ready and well disposed to serve God until they are emptied of all their prudence and are no longer governed by their own minds, saying: 'That seems good to me. This is my opinion,' or asking: 'What will be the result? What will that entail? What sense does that make? What is the purpose of that?' Until men stop asking questions like that, it is certain they will turn their backs on God rather than show him their faces and comply with his commands. But if Abraham had wanted to make a reply and had not had the humility to give God the honour he was due, could he not have said: 'What is going on here? God took me from the land of my birth; he made me abandon my kin; he made me give up what was most desirable; he brought me into a strange land where he has uprooted me and made me move from one place to another since I have been here. Famine even drove me out of it; I returned; he tested me in many ways. And if he wanted to have me serve him, why did he not demand circumcision of me in the beginning?' For Abraham knew that this was a sign that testified to him that God had dedicated him to his service.

Now Abraham could have thought: 'Until now I have served God to no avail. He has mocked me, for up until now I have not had this sign, and he is giving it to me quite late, now that I have one foot in the grave.' That is a case Abraham could have made. All the more must we learn to resolve to follow God's word simply without coming up with elaborate reasons, for once we begin to pay attention to our own opinions, it is certain we will always be so entangled and preoccupied that a fly could distract us from obedience to God. It is with good reason that we are shown that man's mind is like a labyrinth so deep that it is impossible to get out of. So let us learn, as I have said, to have only these principles before us: God has authority over us; all wisdom is in him; and what he ordained is good and righteous and equitable, even though we do not know why. Let us follow that path. We must resolve to let God govern us. Why? He possesses an infinite wisdom with which to work. Then there is his goodness. Then there are his righteousness and integrity, which are perfect.

That, then, is what moved Abraham to abandon all his fantasies so he might accomplish what he had been shown and taught. Let us not think he was stupid or without any understanding, for all these things had happened to him previously, and he did not serve God without the devil's working to corrupt him as much as he could. God's children have always had to engage in battle when they had to fulfil their duty. Thus Abraham, as I have said, was not unaware, but he overcame what his native intelligence showed him because he made a shield of the power and authority and incomprehensible righteousness God had over him. Thus when our minds anxiously search for reasons not to obey God, let us learn to say: 'And who are you, wretched creature, that you want to be wise beyond your God?' So let us admit that our intelligence is only folly when it comes to contemplating God's wisdom and also when it comes to experiencing his righteousness, his integrity and equity, and may that work to reverse all the fine reasons we might imagine to say that things must not happen that way, but especially let us learn to humble ourselves and say: 'It is not your place to determine outcomes, but your God must rule and be the Master.' That, then, is what we have to remember.

Then we are immediately admonished to prepare to do what God orders, even if it is when we are broken with age and completely powerless. If God presses us at that time and requires more than it seems we can do, nothing must turn us from obeying him. For it is certain that what was said to Peter will be fulfilled in all believers. Our Lord said to him: 'When you were young, you girded yourself to your liking, you bound yourself, and you walked where you pleased, but when you grow old, someone will gird you differently. You will have to be tied and bound and led to your death, and you will have to endure what you would not choose of your own accord' (cf. *John* 21:18-19). Thus will our Lord sometimes give us pleasant days in our youth; at least he will maintain us in a way that we will be able to judge that he spares us because he knows what we can bear and sees that we are weak. That is why he deals with us more gently. But when we become old and it seems to be time for us to rest, it is then that he causes us to enter into combat and sends us what we had not foreseen because we did not think about that teaching well beforehand. Thus, in the example of our father Abraham, let us accept that principle. Even though we have reached the age of fifty and it seems, in proportion as our strength diminishes, that we should be treated more delicately, and even though we do not know what God is reserving for us, we must be ready to suffer what we did not expect. That is how we must profit from this passage when it speaks particularly of Abraham's age.

And there is more, for we heard earlier that he had more than four hundred servants[1] in his house whom he could equip and send into the battle (cf. *Gen.* 14:14) when he helped his nephew Lot. How was it possible for the man to have control of such a multitude of people? For if we have only a dozen men, there will always be conflict because of the diversity of opinions. Here Abraham had to convince over four hundred men to allow themselves to be circumcised, to receive a wound, even dangerous and very

[1] In fact 'three hundred and eighteen.'—*M.E.*

painful. And then the same was done to small children, for there were many in his house who were born of the servants themselves. That would have been a difficult task to get men of thirty or forty years of age or older to let themselves be governed by a single word from Abraham, for the vision had been given to him alone. He commands his servants and says: 'Cut! You must receive a wound, one which will give you great pain and could be deadly, for all that is needed with such a wound is a small fever followed by immediate death.' He could have imagined that. Then again, one who was circumcised might have had children and thought: 'Alas, must a poor little creature so tender be wounded this way?' Abraham could have been greatly perplexed, but he executes God's command.

So let us learn that we must overcome all obstacles that could move us and keep us from obeying God. The devil will always have many tricks to put before us so that when God speaks, we will say: 'Alas, I am not foolish enough or strong enough to do that. The thing is beyond my capability. It is too difficult.' The devil will always have such devices. And yet we must always come to the conclusion that we cannot judge what is possible since we only see situations with our eyes, but let us conclude: 'God must have all authority in heaven and on earth, even if everything has to be reversed.' And then let us know and be persuaded that what we lack is in God, and he will give us the means to overcome everything even if we should have to jump over mountains, as the saying goes; even if we should have to rise above the clouds, our Lord will provide everything, provided our trust is in him.

Those are the two points that we have to note: one is to raise the seat of God's majesty so high that the only subjection is to pay him homage and be at his feet to conform to what he says, for it is not our place to construct a seat for God. But when he speaks, it is so that he will be exalted and magnified in all our thoughts and all our affections, as if his seat were set up on high for us to listen to him with all reverence and to find all our help in him. That, then, is what we have to do.

And the other is that when we get some notion or other into our heads and say: 'Just what must I do now? And how will we bring that off?' let our conclusion be: God will provide. And even if there is no clear outcome and we should be left completely uncertain, God still rules over everything we could place before him, for our requests cannot interfere with or diminish in any way the special right he has over us. That, then, is how we must be confident when it comes to serving God. There are many who are motivated by their arrogance and inconstancy and close their eyes and throw reality to the winds. They are unmindful of anything that might get in their way. Why? They are so preoccupied with their burning passion that nothing is impossible for them. Now we must not be bold to wiggle a finger in favour of our preference, but when it is a matter of walking where God calls us, we cannot be overly confident. Let us move forward with confidence, and if it comes to scorning every creature high and low and if everybody should try to thwart us, God must nonetheless have his right, which cannot be taken from him. So much, then, for that point.

Because putting that teaching into practice is difficult, we must remind ourselves of it very diligently morning and evening and practise it every day of our lives as we need it and as necessity demands. There is nothing so easy that we cannot find some bump or hurdle that will keep us from acting. When God commands us to walk, it takes only a straw in our path to stop us like a large mountain. That is the way God sometimes wishes to test our constancy and power when he commands things we think are completely impossible. As today in the preaching of the gospel, does there not seem to be haughty arrogance, as the papists in fact mock us and especially as those princes do in their courts, where ambition, bravado, and pride shine. They will say: 'And what do those opinionated fools think they are doing? They want to convert the world, and where has it got them? They are withdrawn into their little corner, where they bluster as if they had already won. All that is necessary is a puff of wind to bring it all down. All you have to do is blow on it and, poof, it vanishes. When we want it to go away, it will be as easy as getting rid of a fly.' That is how the people of the world make fun of our boldness and confidence when they see us preaching and working.

And there are others who think they are cleverer and wittier. They will say: 'That is very apropos. No matter how hard they try, people will always remain the way they are. They think they are going to convert the world, but they are wasting their time and effort. They will not bring it off.' Yes, but those who think that way are not considering the power of the Spirit of God. That power, when it works to that end, will overcome all the difficulties that battle presents. So it would indeed seem impossible to do what we intend to accomplish, that is, serve and honour God. Impossible? He commanded the gospel to be preached. So that point must not be disputed, but the outcome must be understood as concluded as soon as he has spoken, as we have said; and then magistrates will often be tempted not to do their duty because they fear sedition and insurrection.

Now Abraham had the occasion to fear that his house would be very disturbed and dismayed. He ruled over it peaceably. He was obeyed. It is a singular blessing to live in peace in one's country as well as in one's house. So Abraham could think: 'What are you doing, coming here to sow disorder where there was previously peace and everyone was doing his duty? Every one was fulfilling his responsibility in my house. Everyone was pulling his own weight. Must everything now be thrown into confusion?' Thus magistrates will often fear, thinking: 'Oh if we do our duty, there will be great

danger and we will be threatened from all sides. What means do
we have for resisting our enemies? They are like rabid dogs. And if
they open their mouths, nothing will be left of us, for they are like
gulfs that swallow everything. Alas, it would be better to remain
quiet. It is true God must be honoured, and we would do wrong
to turn tail and run instead of advancing, but we must nonetheless
strike sails. There is no way out.' Fears like that can come up every
day. Consequently, even more must we have the teaching imprinted in our memory that God will provide for each one of us where
we are as we fulfil our calling in the battle against everything that
seems impossible. And that is the second point.

And that is how we understand that there can be no obedience
without faith. For even though we are to honour God by placing
ourselves completely in his hands and subjecting ourselves to him
simply, even though only misfortune must follow, in a manner of
speaking, he nonetheless still has mercy and compassion on our
weaknesses and, in order to stir us on better, adds that he will
provide for all the difficulties which hinder and perplex and even
dismay us. So he adds the promise, as it is said that the angels will
watch over us in all our ways (cf. *Psa.* 91:11). In other words, when
we have made up our minds to follow our God, he will always
give us direction and provide a way and have his angels themselves
guide us. So let us remember that by serving God sincerely, we
will incite everybody's rage against us, and when troubles of many
kinds arise, let us conclude: 'Yes, but is God not in control? Is his
providence asleep? And when he commands us to do what seems
good to him, does he not also have the means to cause us to prosper as well as to bless our labour so that everything will turn out
well? Therefore, as I have said, let us bring God's goodness and
grace together with his authority. We spoke earlier of his integrity
and his wisdom, but it is still not enough to say: 'God has superiority over us; God is the fountain of all wisdom; he is the fountain

of all righteousness.' That is not enough for us to say unless we add that it is by his providence that he disposes of all things so well that what we think is in absolute disorder will be brought to absolute order. Although we see only shadows, he will cause his brightness to shine. When we think we cannot make it through, he will hold our hand and give us passage, and what we think is difficult, he will make easy when it pleases him to do so. But we must always come back to this point: we must allow him to act and govern while we wait patiently for him to show us what he can do and what we cannot even begin to imagine. That, then, is what we have to remember.

Yet we also see how Abraham did not waste his time when he taught his family. There is no doubt, as we will also see in the following chapter (cf. *Gen.* 18:19), that God bore witness that Abraham was concerned to direct his whole house and have him worshipped sincerely and with simplicity of heart. That will be discussed in its place, but it must now be considered as a fact. Did he in that way do his duty? We see how his servants submit easily and that there is no resistance when this difficult thing is required of them. We have already shown that that could not be done without serious pain. Would anyone ever have thought that there would be such agreement that all of them, from first to last, would say: 'Here is my body for you to cut, to trim, even at the risk of my life. Here is my child. Do with him as you please.' How does it happen at this time, seeing that Abraham is in easy control, that no one resists him? God causes him to experience the fruit and reward of the good affection he enjoyed for instructing his family.

It often happens that men will leave God behind and forget him, provided they can profit from it and be served to their liking and contentment. That is what everyone looks for. When a great prince wants to govern his states, will he think: 'Here is a man who fears God. I must choose him'? Indeed not. And when he wants to give orders to his servants, will he be much concerned whether they are God-fearing people? Not at all. But he will consider this: 'That fellow is able to handle my affairs; that fellow is right for the job; that fellow has skills I can use.' And God takes a back seat. And that is also why there is no fidelity in those great courts. Even though princes want to make idols of themselves, they will have as many traitors as they have servants, and they will always have to be suspicious and uncertain. And even among the little people, when a man thinks he has a servant or a maid, provided he can profit from them, it is all the same to him. God will still be scorned. That is why many occasions of disorder arise, for we deserve such recompense, but in Abraham we see the result of his work to instruct his family and guide it in such a way that God might be served and glorified. That is also why his servants obey him contrary to men's opinions, and the result is that nothing is impossible for him. So if we want our Lord to favour us with overcoming all hindrances and obstacles, let us learn to apply ourselves diligently to that undertaking, keeping in mind that each one is to govern his house in such a way that honouring God is its main business.

Moreover, one could ask at this point how Abraham circumcised Ishmael since he had been cut off from the church, so to speak, but that problem has been resolved in part. It will be enough to say a word or two about it now. Ishmael is cut off if he does not join together with his brother Isaac, who had not yet been born or even conceived. God still did not exclude him from all hope of belonging to his church or of not being banished from it, provided he seek his blessing elsewhere, that is, in the one who had received him as a deposit through promise, although he had not yet been born (cf. *Gen.* 12:2; 13:16; 15:4-5).[2] Now

---

[2] With these few words: 'God still did not exclude him from all hope of belonging to his church,' Calvin lets us understand that Ishmael was not predestined to reprobation, a significant difference in regard to double predestination.—*M.E.*

when Ishmael was thirteen years old, he soon shows that he is disrespectful of God, for when his brother Isaac is born and later weaned, he reveals his godlessness[3] and is then completely cut off from that blessing which had been promised to Abraham's seed; but even now he still retains some right. And if he had walked in the fear of God and in the way we said, if he had considered his primogeniture as nothing, if he had humbled himself and had asked only to be under his brother Isaac, to be born later, as under his head because God had wanted to honour Isaac that way, he would have retained that blessing. And that is how he was circumcised, and not with false signs, for the promise belonged to him until he completely deprived himself of it.[4] Thus we see that our Lord presents his grace generally, as much to a house as to a people, for little children will be baptized in a country and in a city indiscriminately. Why? Because God's grace is common to them all. Afterward, many of them cut themselves off, but they are doubly guilty. However, the sacrament is not profaned, for it must be joined with the promise. Now the promise is general to all those who honour God and to their children. Consequently, that is how Ishmael was circumcised and how all of Abraham's family was circumcised, for there is no doubt that there were some hypocrites mixed among them, that there were mockers of God who offered only temporal obedience out of pretence, as it is said in the psalm that the enemies of our Lord Jesus Christ will lie to him and pretend to be his subjects (cf. *Psa.* 78:36-37). Even so, the sacrament belonged to them since God had dedicated Abraham's house and had made it like an earthly heaven, so to speak, because he wanted to build there a temple, as it were,

---

[3] Cf. Genesis 21:9, in Calvin's interpretation.—*M.E.*
[4] The responsibility of separating oneself from God's grace is always incumbent upon the individual, even if, as in this passage, we might think Calvin allows Ishmael to use his free will to reject God. Cf. *Institutes* II, ii, 17; III, ii, 11.—*M.E.*

and because he wanted to show himself to Abraham as good and useful for his salvation. That, then, is what we have to remember.

And to conclude, we are shown again that Abraham wanted his whole house to be made holy unto God when he circumcised not only those who were born in his house but also those he had bought. Even though they had been brought up in the midst of idolatries and superstitions, he nonetheless tried to bring and gather them all to God, just as everyone must do in accordance with his position and the ability God gives him.

Now let us bow before the majesty of our gracious God in acknowledgment of our faults, praying that he will make us increasingly aware of them and that we will learn to be displeased with them and ask for forgiveness and be corrected so we can fight against all our wicked desires and the many corrupt things that live within us and are deeply rooted there. And though the struggles are difficult, let us not fail to try our hardest, not seeking the power within ourselves but within the one who promised to strengthen us. And when we experience his grace, may he draw us to himself by his Holy Spirit, and may we persist increasingly in our obedience, declaring that we do not bear his mark in vain but that we surely show we desire to commit ourselves completely to him and be fully his. And in order to do that, let us renounce ourselves so he can use us in peace. May he grant that grace not only to us but to all the peoples and nations on earth.

84

Generosity after the Example of Abraham: A Demonstration of Self-Denial

Tuesday, 16 April 1560

*And the L*ORD *appeared unto him in the plains of Mamre: and he sat in the tent door in the heat of the day; And he lift up his eyes and looked, and, lo, three men stood by him: and when he saw them, he ran to meet them from the tent door, and bowed himself toward the ground, And said, My Lord, if now I have found favour in thy sight, pass not away, I pray thee, from thy servant: Let a little water, I pray you, be fetched, and wash your feet, and rest yourselves under the tree: And I will fetch a morsel of bread, and comfort ye your hearts; after that ye shall pass on: for therefore are ye come to your servant. And they said, So do, as thou hast said. And Abraham hastened into the tent unto Sarah, and said, Make ready quickly three measures of fine meal, knead it, and make cakes upon the hearth. And Abraham ran unto the herd, and fetcht a calf tender and good, and gave it unto a young man; and he hasted to dress it. And he took butter, and milk, and the calf which he had dressed, and set it before them; and he stood by them under the tree, and they did eat* (Gen. 18:1-8).

MOSES' MAIN PURPOSE is to tell us that God is not content to promise his servant Abraham just once that he would give him lineage by Sarah, but he confirmed the promise even better. For we know that people, being weak, need to be told often what is useful for their salvation, for what we hear slips our minds or we think ambiguous thoughts, and as a result our confidence is overworked and would even be in danger of going extinct if God did not help it and give it points of support. And that is why he must speak a second and third time so we will be more convinced of his truth. So that is why Abraham had to have a second vision and hear that God wanted to raise up a lineage for him from which he could hope for blessing and salvation. And he did it also to ratify what we have already seen, although God answered Abraham in part with Ishmael, while the promise was established in another (cf. *Gen.* 17:19).

Moses now mixes together many circumstances. For before explaining that the angels made themselves known, he says they appeared as human figures and walked in the heat of the day as if they were worn and broken. So he says clearly that Abraham saw three men coming toward him in the heat of the day. He then rose and asked them to rest under the tree which was near the tent and have their meal and be refreshed to finish their voyage. To receive them hospitably, he went so far as to kill a calf and bring good things from his house. When Moses recounted all that, he concluded by adding that God would accomplish what he had already heard concerning Isaac's being born to his wife Sarah (cf. *Gen.* 17:16, 19). Now that example is given so we will learn to be more hospitable toward those in poverty and need. That is the way the apostle applies it to faith when he says that the patriarchs received angels thinking they were men (cf. *Heb.* 13:2) and did not know that God had sent angels from heaven and honoured them by making them hosts to his angels. Why? Because they were humane to receive strangers. It is as if the apostle were saying that God, in the person of our father Abraham, wanted to show that it was an acceptable service to him, like a sweet smelling sacrifice (cf. *Lev.* 2:2), to see people, even unknown people, in some need and help them. For even though we do not receive angels every day, God nonetheless accepts that as if he were being received in person. And in fact he demonstrates it, the apostle says, in what we read about Abraham.

But first let us look at what is recounted here. We could ask whether it was Abraham's custom to rise and go meet those who approached his tent. Although he was opulently rich and possessed a large quantity of livestock, he did not enjoy all the world's conveniences. He did not have a house. He lived only in his tent, and the most beautiful room he could offer his guests was the shade of a tree, for he was a stranger in that land and continued to move from one place to another. God was testing him in that way and exercising his patience. So if Abraham had entertained all passers-by with such great liberality, he would not have been able to provide for them, for we know that many people would take advantage of that kind of largesse if someone so easily gave of his goods without considering why or to whom. Abraham would have been drained of everything very quickly. But we can see from what followed that he knew them to be people of quality and worthy of honour and that they should be treated with greater courtesy than most. For there could have come to him some man who would have been satisfied with a piece of bread and a glass of water, and Abraham would have shown his good will that way. If he had given refreshment in the shade to a man tired and weary from the heat of the day and had given him a piece of bread charitably, it is certain God would have valued all that, but Abraham recognized some dignity in these angels and bowed reverently before them.

He says: 'My Lord, may it please you to grant this favour to your servant.' Those words show that Abraham was moved when he saw that those to whom he was speaking were honourable people, but he sees they are in need. For in those days cities and villages were not as frequent as they are today. Inns and taverns could not be found as easily as today. We must note that difference in the times, for otherwise it would seem strange that Abraham ran to meet them, but he knows they will not find lodgings, and he sees that the heat is oppressive, that the poor men, even though they are of status and quality, could grow faint. He has pity on them, not out of courtesy, not as some extend a hearty welcome to a man because he is rich. Those who react that way show they do not care for those to whom they are subservient, but they do so for their own advantage. For if they did not expect some compensation for it, they would not expend their substance. That or ambition goads them on. For when one is expansive and liberal toward the rich, that is most often done out of ambition or sincere humaneness; but when we are concerned to help in times of need, that is when charity and goodwill show themselves, not that it is a vice to practice humaneness toward the rich and mighty—God did not forbid that as if it were something unlawful—but it is a question here of whether we have a test to determine if we do good to our neighbours out of charity or not, for it is, as I have said, the true touchstone to tell whether the act is free, that is, whether we expect no return or thanks from man or are moved by compassion to say: 'That person is suffering from need and privation. I can help him. God has given me the ability. I must do so.' So that is what the true feeling of charity is like. In other words, there is no consideration of compensation, but compassion guides us and urges us to help those from whom we expect no reward. That was Abraham's feeling.

Now because he bows and says: 'My Lord, if I have found favour before you,' and addresses his remarks to only one person, some have understood this passage too subtly. Not that the teaching they draw from it is not good and holy, but we must be concerned not to pull Scripture in too many directions, for splitting hairs over it deprives it of its majesty in the eyes of mockers. An effort has been made to prove with this passage the three persons who make up the essence of God, and it was so commonplace that many thought it ought to be accepted without contradiction, for Abraham sees three and worships only one and bows before him and says: 'My Lord, if I have found favour before you.' On the surface, one might judge that is the case. In other words, God was revealing to Abraham the secret of his majesty when he came to him this way in three persons. But when we consider the whole passage more fully, it is certain that interpretation is not consistent. Why not? In the first place, Abraham would not have requested God to come lodge with him or entreated him to have his feet washed and take bread. For if he had not thought he was a mortal man, there is no doubt he would have simply worshipped God and offered sacrifices to him, as we saw Noah and those like him do (cf. *Gen.* 8:20; 15:17). Moreover, when Abraham speaks to one, he does not straightaway continue using the singular, but he says immediately afterward: 'Rest yourselves,' and thus we must not linger over a syllable as if some mystery were locked up in it.

And then Moses also says that now one spoke, now the other, and then all three together, not that all three spoke at the same time, but when one had spoken, the other was able to speak in his rank. Moreover, we will see that only two angels were sent to Lot (cf. *Gen.* 19:1). And what would become of the principle of our faith, that the Father cannot be separated from the Son or the Son from the Spirit? Thus we see how what seems firm on the surface soon vanishes and that there is no true substance to it. That is why we must be satisfied with the simplicity of holy Scripture, and we must also note what we have stated about the apostle, that Abraham did not know who his guests were (cf. *Heb.* 13:2) and thought they were mortal men, and God nevertheless grants him the honour of lodging his angels. So that resolves that question.

Now the text says that Abraham humbled himself greatly before them, and it was a matter of showing them kindness. He, on the contrary, should have been entreated and sought after; yet it seems he is here asking for a great benefit, which we see him doing with a free and open expression, and what is recounted here about him is to show us how our charitable gifts can be approved by God. Paul, when exhorting the Corinthians to help the poor during a great famine in Judea at the time, tells them to do nothing under compulsion, but with simple devotion and a cheerful heart (cf. 2 *Cor.* 9:7). Why? God, he says, loves those who give joyfully. That is a principle Paul gives us when we have pity on our brothers to help them in their poverty and be bountiful with what God gives us. We are to do it freely, not, he says, out of sorrow and importunity, and not even of necessity. For if we do good and talk about it, we cannot avoid always experiencing regret. And when one hand gives, the other will be withdrawn, and we would like to refrain from it if we could. So when Paul says: 'Do nothing under compulsion,' it is as if he were saying: 'Do not help your neighbours because God is compelling you to and you cannot escape doing it, but do so with a free heart.' And how can we do that? It is always very difficult for a man to take from his pocketbook and rejoice and find pleasure in doing so because he thinks he is diminishing himself. It is true that worldly people, when they give liberally, will find pleasure in expending their wealth and even wasting it. But why is that? It is because one passion overrules another. That is an aspect of avarice, which is rooted in everyone until God roots it out of those he chooses.

Now ambition, on the other hand, will be predominant in others, and avarice and ambition are not incompatible. And the person who is filled with vainglory and insists on making a big show before men in order to gain renown, honour, and praise, will continue to be a miser. And he will not be able to restrain himself. Why not? Ambition controls him, but he is still obliged to spend. He will pilfer and plunder where he can, for if he is liberal and prodigal, he must also have the wherewithal and not care where he gets it. It does not make any difference to him as long as he has it. So we see how apparently contrary passions, as contrary as they can be, work together. And that is how it is with all those who spend a lot and give liberally when it comes to making oneself look good before men. Like a drunkard who is a miser and would like to stop drinking to save money, he is driven by that passion to get drunk. Is he drunk? He is useless; everything is a waste; all his goods precede him to hell. And he still does not care. But as I said, it is because men are like dumb animals (cf. *Psa.* 49:12, 20) and their passions and desires drive them in one direction, then in another.

That was not the case with Abraham. When Paul exhorts us to give joyfully, he points out that that joy is to arise from the fact that we are glad to be able to fulfil our duty toward God and to use well and charitably what he has placed in our hands so that we will be able to give a good accounting of it. And let humaneness impel us. Let us consider it the best reward we could wish for, that for God's honour we have helped a brother who would have been in danger without us and that we had the means to do so when God brought him to our attention. That is the joy Paul speaks of, and that is how we are to understand it. We see here that Abraham was led by such an affection, for he entreats and makes requests and asks his guests to be good enough to grant him the honour of submitting to them, as if they were giving him a great gift. So let us note that God accepts our gifts when they are made with an open and liberal heart that is not under the compulsion of necessity.

As for the saying 'Wash your feet; I will bring a piece of bread for your refreshment,' it was the custom at the time to wash a guest's feet, for people did not have the kinds of shoes we have today. And that country was very hot, as it is now. It was so hot and dry that the best one could do for someone going along on the road was to give him some water to refresh him; otherwise, his strength would wane overnight. That is also why Paul says, when speaking of widows, that those are to be chosen to serve the church who have customarily done good to all of God's servants. It is noteworthy that he says they washed their feet (cf. *1 Tim.* 5:10)—using a part to refer to the whole—for many who read that passage are astonished how Paul speaks of the feet and think that it is a part of some ritual,[1] but we must consider the nature of the locale and then the customs of the time.

In addition, when it is said that Abraham hastened and killed a calf and that Sarah prepared a meal and that everyone got involved in it, we have two things to note. One is the conduct of Abraham's house and the abundance he provided for the angels, even though he did not recognize them as such. As for the first, it would seem useless to talk about it, for what reason would one have to preach about knowing how to manage a kitchen and how each person is able either to skin a calf or put water on the fire to boil it? This does not seem to be an appropriate argument to present in sermons, seeing that the pulpit is the place for teaching about faith and the fear of God. We are to be instructed in the teaching of our Lord Jesus Christ and in the trust we are to have in him, wherein lies our salvation. We must be exhorted to long-suffering and all the rest. But when all is said and done, this deserves to be noted for our instruction.

When it is said that Abraham hastily killed a calf and the entire household did what was required, Sarah was not spared and the servants were quick to obey their master, for the world does not think God is being served when it is a matter of domestic duties. And that is why all the work of men is wrongly considered. For if

---

[1] Calvin is certainly attacking the monastic practice of washing the feet of brothers and guests or the papal practice of Maundy Thursday, which depends more on John 13:14 than on 1 Timothy.—*M.E.*

we put into practice Paul's lesson when he says: 'Whether we drink or eat, or whatever we do, let it all be done to the glory of God' (cf. *1 Cor.* 10:31), it is certain that when a mechanic entered his shop, his mind would be made up: 'I offer myself to God here. He calls me to do my work, and although I work to earn my living and provide for my home, it is an offering sacred to God, and he accepts it as a sweet smelling sacrifice.' The same is to be said for the wife, whether she is spinning or lighting the fire or sweeping or doing something else, the simplest thing in the world, as long as it serves the home. Servants too and maids, while making the bed, sweeping the house, washing the dishes, are to think: 'God is calling me to himself and he is the Master of us all. Since he has given me this calling, I must hold to it, for it is he that we all serve. And even though the world looks down on these things, these things are precious to him, and he does not reject them.' That, I say, is what we should have impressed on our minds. Yes, but the person who is getting ready for his dinner thinks of nothing but his stomach; there is no thought of God. The man who is trying to get ahead is not aware that God has called him to his vocation so that he is obliged to earn his living honestly by serving his neighbours. In short, everyone turns his back on God when it is a matter of seeking praise. And that is why time is so badly employed. All the more then must we observe this conduct Moses recounts about Abraham's household so that we may know what is called 'economy,' that is, managing the home. We need to know that that regulation is a service God demands of us. Consequently, in all these small things, we must have our eyes directed on him, the same as when we do what is excellent and much esteemed by men.

That, then, is what we have to remember when the text says everything was made ready without debate, just at Abraham's simple command, and Sarah offers no objection either. And that is said so that men will learn to govern their families in such a way that they are each ready to fulfil their responsibilities as head of household. The same is true for women. They are not to be surly or peevish when their husbands display liberality. What we see most often is that if the husband has some good intention, the wife insolently resists, there is always disagreement, and there will never be harmony. Consequently, both must learn their lesson here, and we must realize, as I have already said, that God is honoured when households are governed in peace and each individual plays the role in which he is cast, that is, his calling.

And there is also the liberality we need to take note of in the second place, while not forgetting what we have just touched upon, namely, that Abraham was not imprudent or foolhardy when he threw everything to the wind, so to speak, for it is certain he did not always receive his guests in such a way. But he does what he does because he sees they are people who deserve to be treated honourably. That is to serve as advice and exhortation to be bounteous at the appropriate time and place, for there are some who will follow the practice of giving everything without knowing how or why. We see that folly in the Papacy. On solemn days, one person will give five dollars, another twenty. How will they give it? In nickels in order to make a big show and draw it out. And then to whom? Oh, no need to consider to whom; it does not matter! However, our Lord wants us to know clearly and to consider those who are in need. It is true we need not be too diligent in inquiring, for many poor people would die of hunger if we tried to probe everyone's need, how he is getting along, and we would never begin to give a single charitable gift if we tried to know everyone's situation in detail. It is a matter of considering the need insofar as we can judge when we see people in need, and then we must help. Yet we must also pay attention to what Paul says, that we are principally to be tender-hearted and quick to give to those who are of the household of faith (cf. *2 Cor.* 8-9; 8:7; *Rom.* 12:8).

On that subject, our Lord binds us more closely with his children, who share brotherhood with us, just as a man will be more bound to help his wife than a woman with whom he has no connection. Therefore, as our Lord brings us closer together, he immediately encourages us to do good according as we have the means and opportunity. In any case, we must exercise moderation during those times when people give on a whim without knowing why and others give with excessive restraint, wanting to give nothing without knowing exactly where their gift will be used, and we must have the prudence to judge well: 'There is a man who needs our help. We need to look into that.' And on the other hand, there is this approach: 'There is a man who serves God faithfully. I must consider him more carefully, as if God had pointed him out to me. I must give even more liberally and try hard to help him when I see him oppressed by need.' That, in brief, is what we have to remember from this example of Abraham.

Now it is true a rule cannot be imposed when it comes to giving, for if everyone gave everything he owned away, it is certain he still would not acquit himself before God. We know we have received from him everything we have, and yet he says he receives from us the good things we do for our neighbours who are in need (cf. *Matt.* 25:35-40). We must remember that, for when we help a poor person, it is like lending to God, indeed at great interest (cf. *Prov.* 19:17). But even though we cannot do perfectly what would be required, nonetheless, if each of us, to the best of our ability, does good when the occasion presents itself and we see there is need, God accepts it and even receives it as a loan. And how can we lend him anything, seeing that all things are his? For after using up all that belongs to us, if we put our own lives into it, we would still not pay him what he is due. That is true, and we see his mercy when he accepts the good we offer him even though it is not a hundredth part of what we owe him. Consequently, we are even colder and stingier if we do not put ourselves out to help our neighbours inasmuch as we see that our Lord spares us, for he can require and demand everything we have; it is his. He can abandon us in our poverty. Now he does not want to do that, but he wants everyone to do good with what he has at his disposal, and he wants him and his household to live joyously as a result and, if there is an overabundance, to realize and say: 'Well, God has given me this so that I may have more opportunities to thank him.' But when God is that generous with us, we must not be devoted to him so that we will be open pits and consume everything, but so that we can live in such a way with what he gives us that we will turn our eyes toward our neighbours. And if we should realize there is need among many people who suffer, let us be moved; let us have bowels of mercy, as Scripture puts it (cf. *Col.* 3:12), and let us be kind to them. Consequently, since our Lord exercises such liberality and also shows he requires of us his portion of what he has placed in our hands and wants us, because of our love of him, to do good with it for our brothers, must we not say, if we are not moved by that, that we are harder than iron or stone?

In addition, in order to have that free good will to fulfil our duty to be charitable, let us put ourselves in the place of those who suffer, for otherwise it is certain we will never be able to lay out our goods for the needs of those who lack. That is also why the apostle, when speaking of prisoners, tells you to remember them as if you were with them in person (cf. *Heb.* 13:3). For we will never be affected or moved unless we put ourselves in their place because we are preoccupied with the love we have for ourselves. Consequently, that love must be changed into the affection we are to have for our neighbours and into the concern that we are to have for their needs and sufferings. The same is true as concerns all the poor in general. When we would like to do good without pretence, without regret or compulsion, let us have this thought: 'Alas, if at this moment

I lacked food and drink and did not have a piece of bread, what would I want? I would want everyone to go to the trouble to help me in my need. So now that I have not only something to eat and drink but something with which to help those who are in poverty, what am I to do? Must I restrain myself? Must I have a compassion of iron and steel at those times when God wishes that I let it loose to do as nature itself teaches me? It is to do for others what I want them to do for me[2] if I happened to be in the kind of condition they are in who suffer today in poverty.' That, in brief, is what we have to continue to remember about Abraham's liberality.

Now when he says, 'Wash your feet, pass the heat of the day, and eat to strengthen your heart,' it is to confirm what I said a moment ago, namely, that we must consider seriously those who are in poverty and help them as opportunities arise. It is true that we must be more inclined and more moved and affected in favour of the household of faith because God particularly recommends them, but the fact is that when God points to them as with his finger, this must suffice for us: 'That person needs your help.' That is better confirmed by what Abraham adds: 'that is why you have come to your servant.' He does not mean that the angels had purposely come to his tent in order to say: 'Here is a place to stay,' but he relates it to God's providence, as if to say: 'God led you here by the hand when he saw that you laboured thus and could be tired and weary from the road and could be perspiring because of the heat of the day. That is why he brought you to me, for he knew you could be helped here.' Now we have to derive good instruction from those words, that is, in proportion as the needs are great, God calls us to exercise our responsibility and also gives us a reason to

[2] Cf. Matthew 7:12; Luke 6:31, but also Tobias 4:16. This is what is called Christianity's 'golden rule.' Cf. also Thomas Aquinas, *Summa theologiae*, 2a 2ae, q. 37, art. 1, or *Institutes* II, viii, 40. Compare that with Seneca's comment in *Letters to Lucilius*, XV, 94:43: '*Ab alio expectes alteri quod feceris.*'—*M.E.* ['May you expect/ Expect from another what you do to/for another.']

practise our charity. This will be better understood by a particular example.

If we did not see great indigence, it would be a foolish desire for honour to speak about charity and say: 'I want to give'; and yet we see many who are like that and would propose to give. Give how? For show, to say: 'People must think of me as a man who gives liberally.' We, on the other hand, must think, because of the many poverty-stricken people in our midst, that it is God who summons us and calls upon us to demonstrate and give true approval of what our charity is. Even if a time of famine comes, when the papists are accustomed to saying that the door of heaven is open for the purchasing, we must understand that God is waking us up so we will be the more diligent to do good. For God could cause grain and wine to increase so that there would never be poverty or famine. He could also make it so that there would be no poor people in the world, but he wishes there to be and, as Solomon says, the poor and the rich meet together and God created them all (cf. *Prov.* 22:2). In other words, God made it that way so that the rich will mingle among the poor so that those who have means will think: 'God wants me to have something to do good with.'

In time of famine, generally speaking, we see that God has removed his blessing from us. Why? It is true he wants to chastise the sins of both the poor and the rich, for famine is a flail of his wrath, but at the same time we must take into consideration that God sends famine so that those at the time who have abundance will display their largesse even more and make a great effort to do good, for it is said that the blessing of the people will be upon the person who opens his storage barns in times of need (cf. *Prov.* 11:26). On the other hand, the poverty of the poor cries vengeance against those who keep their barns closed, for that is a sign they have neither pity nor compassion. So let us note that when Abraham our father is proposed to us here so that we may know from his example that if our neighbours experience some need, one because of hunger, another thirst, another nakedness and another sickness, God is directing them to our attention—and it is not by chance that these encounters occur and we see now one man who is hungry, now another who is weak, now one who is thirsty. Let us realize that our Lord is inciting us that way to do what we should. And when we consider well such providence from God, it is certain we will be more inclined to apply our efforts, each of us, where we live. And at the same time we know we have to give an accounting to God. And if men themselves do not say: 'Alas, I have cried out,' God will nonetheless, for our condemnation, be satisfied that he has drawn our attention to them himself as if to say: 'If you have a single speck of human feeling in you, show it, for I am here asking for what is my right, and I want you to offer me the sacrifice which is mine; otherwise, it is certain you are defrauding me and you will have to answer to me because you have kept for yourself what I placed within your hands, within your limits and ability, to help those who needed it.' That, according to this passage, is what God had drawn their attention to.

Thereupon, Moses adds the main point, for what we have explained up until now are particular circumstances, as we said at the beginning. So he comes to the main thing, which is the promise God made to Abraham through the angels. But a question related to their eating remains to be asked. If they were angels, they had no need of physical nourishment. Angels are spirits, and even though they were clothed in human bodies, they were exempted from that need.[3] Why do we eat and drink? That is how God shows us our frailty and declares that our lives depend upon non-living things. Then bread, wine, and water and all the other foods give us what they do not have. God, with food and drink, gives us vigour and

[3] Cf. particularly *Institutes* I, xiv, 5. Calvin developed an angelology throughout his life.—*M.E.*

substance, and yet none of that is in them; there is no feeling in bread and wine. We see that in this way our Lord shows us our frailty and wants us to walk in this world with one foot always raised, knowing that our lives are only a shadow, since we know we are sustained by such means. Now angels, as I said, are not to be placed on that level. And that is why some people have thought that these angels only gave some semblance of eating, that they in truth did not, that Abraham thought they did, and that it was some kind of vision. But those people did not consider that these angels did not have phantom bodies, that they had real human bodies. How? What did they become shortly afterward? Indeed, he who made all things of nothing, can he not create bodies just as he did at the first creation, and then return them to nothing after using them? We do not have to be great philosophers when it is said that the angels appeared in human form, but let us realize that God gave them bodies for the moment. And yet we are not to think that they were made men, for it is certain Jesus Christ often appeared under the law as a human figure while not yet taking on human flesh. We must remember that Paul says that in the fullness of time, God sent his son, made of woman, that is, born of woman. So our Lord Jesus Christ was not made God manifested in the flesh (cf. *Gal.* 4:4), as Paul also speaks of him in another place (cf. *1 Tim.* 3:16), as it is said in the first chapter of John (cf. *John* 1:14), until he was actually sent as the Redeemer, lived in the world, endured suffering and death, and was raised again. Therefore, it is certain the angels were never men, even though they had human bodies, but God clothed them that way when he wanted to use them for a temporal act. Thus, when it is said they ate, it was not because of necessity, as Jesus Christ, no longer possessing a mortal body, ate after his resurrection (cf. *Luke* 24:46; *John* 21:13-14; *Acts* 10:41), for he was raised to the heavenly life and to his divine glory. Why did he eat? It was to prove that it was he and not a spirit and to

strengthen his disciples' faith. So Jesus Christ's eating after the resurrection has to do with the disciples' instruction and not with any
need he might have had. So we conclude that the angels ate not
because they might have had to but because they were living with
Abraham under ordinary circumstances until they gave him the
promise that we have spoken of and will deal with more at length.

Now let us bow before the majesty of our gracious God in
acknowledgment of our faults, praying that he will be pleased to
touch us to the quick with them so that we will hasten to his mercy
and daily pray that he will receive us in mercy and not permit our
carnal flaws to have control over us, but that he will beat them back,
cut them off and put them to death until he has completely cleansed
us of them and brought us to the perfection to which we aspire.
And may he especially be pleased to touch us with such a feeling of
charity that we will ask only to do good for our neighbours and to
know we are not to be devoted to ourselves or our advantage, but to
live together as brothers with those whom God has joined us with.
And may all the abilities he has given us in deposit be so common
among us that we will be able to give a good accounting of them.
And because we are still very far from doing what we should, may
he be pleased to tolerate us until he removes us from self-love and
corrects that vice in us so that we will not think of anything but
the union he has placed between us and consecrated by the blood
of our Lord Jesus Christ. And let us think about the inheritance of
the heavenly glory that is ours together so that, while we live in this
world, we may also learn to live with one another as we ought and
as he commands. May he grant that grace not only to us but to all
the peoples and nations on earth.

85

Sarah and the Virtues of Truth, Fear, and Humility

Wednesday, 17 April 1560

And they said unto him, Where is Sarah thy wife? And he said, Behold, in the tent. And he said, I will certainly return unto thee according to the time of life; and, lo, Sarah thy wife shall have a son. And Sarah heard it in the tent door, which was behind him. Now Abraham and Sarah were old and well stricken in age; and it ceased to be with Sarah after the manner of women. Therefore Sarah laughed within herself, saying, After I am waxed old shall I have pleasure, my lord being old also? And the LORD said unto Abraham, Wherefore did Sarah laugh, saying, Shall I of a surety bear a child, which am old? Is any thing too hard for the LORD? At the time appointed I will return unto thee, according to the time of life, and Sarah shall have a son. Then Sarah denied, saying, I laughed not; for she was afraid. And he said, Nay; but thou didst laugh (Gen.18:9-15).

HERE MOSES TELLS US more clearly how Abraham was confirmed in the promise he had already received, for it was not enough that God had declared to him once that he wanted to give him a son, for it is a difficult thing to believe and it was of the greatest importance because the salvation of the world was based on it and contained in it. Consequently, that promise had to be confirmed many times. If Abraham, being a man, could be partially weak and have to be taught repeatedly, then we, having a far less perfect faith than he had, must profit from God's school from day to day. We do not have visions the way he did, but it must be enough for us that God wants his word to possess its majesty in itself. As soon as we know his will in it, let us conclude certainly and unfailingly that it will be just as he proclaimed it.

Now because God had spoken in Sarah's absence, he now asks where she is, not that he does not know, as we will soon see (cf. *Gen.* 18:13), but to show that he wants her to share in the joy which is given to them both. 'Where is Sarah your wife?' Abraham says she is in the tent. Doubtless that was the way women at the time kept to the house, for it would not have been thought appropriate for her to come out to receive unknown men. It was enough that she had prepared the meal and had done her duty without being seen. That is why she was remaining in the tent. For the greatest and most proper virtue women have is that of modestly remaining quiet in their households and not appearing without purpose.

At that point, the angel announces he will return at the time of life,[1] that is, at the end of the term when Sarah, after conceiving, has given birth. He calls the 'time of life' the ten imperfect months[2] that children are carried in the womb of their mother, that is, when the child has had its full term and Sarah has a son. At that she laughs. Abraham accepts what he is told because it is not new to him. He understands that God is confirming what he had already heard. So he is not moved as he was before, except that his faith is strengthened and he in no way doubts that God will bring to pass what he says. Now Sarah, although it is possible she heard from her husband what it was about, nonetheless laughs as

---

[1] In Hebrew *kâ'eth Sayâh.*—M.E.
[2] The 'ten imperfect months' signify the ten lunar months, the time of gestation picked up from Antiquity.—M.E.

if the thing were completely impossible and says: 'How can this be? We are already old and broken down, and will we still enjoy the companionship of marriage? That time of life has passed. And then there is the question of having pleasure. How can that be? Now that my husband is already a hundred years old and I am scarcely little younger, we have to forget what that aspect of marriage was. I am to conceive, give birth, and be a mother at such an age? That is against nature.' That made Sarah laugh. Now she is speaking within herself, Moses says. She is not going to tattle here and there as if she were questioning God's promise. Her mouth is closed, but she is debating within herself and having her reasons for concluding that her having a child is not a settled matter.

Now the angel, who is finally called God because he began to reveal his heavenly majesty after eating and drinking in a human figure, makes himself known there in the person of God and with a glory which is neither earthly nor human when promising a child against the natural order. So because the angel had begun to manifest the majesty given to him by God is called God at this point, and since he exercises his divine office by rebuking Sarah for something only she knew ('Why did Sarah laugh?'), she denies it because she is afraid. He points out that it is not without reason that he rebuked her, for that laugh proceeded from unbelief, and he says: 'Nothing is difficult or impossible for God.' The word Moses uses means 'hidden and incomprehensible view,' that is, 'Is there anything God does not know and is not under his hand?' That indicates that Sarah, by her disbelief, disparaged God's infinite power when she evaluated what was said to her about her being able to conceive. Even though she compounds her offence by lying and makes her sin more grievous, that nonetheless proceeds from a holy feeling because she is afraid, for she sees that she is not dealing with a mortal man, but with the living God. Even so, she employs lying and hypocrisy.

That shows how corrupt we are, that the good draws us to evil, and a good principle for us to follow is to avoid vice, as we will soon see at length.

Now God does not engage in long inquiries and says: 'You did; you laughed,' as if to say: 'No need to plead further. What do you mean by lying in my presence? What wrong you do me when you contradict me in this matter, after offending me so grievously!' Thus he condemns her without further ado. That, in brief, is what is recounted here. Now we see how God continued his talk with Abraham, not that he began to do immediately what he had said. That teaches us to wait, and waiting is the substance of faith, as has already been pointed out at length. Let us remain peaceable and allow God to work on his own schedule, and let us not think we can summon him on the spur of the moment, since we are always in a hurry, but let us be patient and allow him every liberty in bringing his work to perfection in accordance with his will, for everything depends on his authority. In the meantime, inasmuch as our faith is weak and we are not steadfast enough to persevere in resting in God from day to day and month to month, let us learn to fortify ourselves anew again and again, to renew our memories again and again, and to amass a treasury of promises that cannot sustain us to the extent that we will never falter, even as the end seems far away.

Moreover, here are repeated the very words that we saw earlier. Thus we would think we have needless repetition: 'I will return at the time of life. Sarah will have a son.' And yet he is speaking to Abraham. He had not forgotten what had been announced to him before. So let us note that although Scripture does not always vary in language and have a refined rhetoric to please us with novelty, that is not to vex us, for there are many who are hard to please and want someone to provide them with something new. So let us not yield to that kind of frivolous desire, but even though God repeats what we have already heard and batters our ears daily with the same thing, let us realize that we need it. For if the father of the church, Abraham, who preceded us by many generations, was strengthened that way, what does that mean for us in our day?

However, as for Sarah's laugh, we have to compare it with what was recounted above. For when this message first came to Abraham, he laughed the way his wife did (cf. *Gen.* 17:17), and yet he was not corrected so severely; that laugh was even tolerated as if there had been no wrong. The same is not true now for Sarah, and yet the exterior act is similar in both. So we see how God does not judge by appearance, as is said in another passage of Scripture (cf. *1 Chron.* 28:9), but he probes the hearts and thoughts; our works and our words are evaluated before him according to the heart's feeling. That should be closely noted, for although we confess as much with the mouth, we still cannot put it into practice, for we think, provided we put on a good front, that God has to be satisfied. And that is the currency the majority want to be paid in. So we cannot come to the truth and say we walk before him without pretence and that we are not two-faced; and even more must we pay close attention to what is shown here in a living picture, so to speak. Abraham laughs because God promises him that he will have a lineage by Sarah. Sarah also laughs. Abraham is not condemned and it appears that he committed no fault, for God does not impute it to him. Sarah is rebuked very harshly and very severely. And why does God find such a difference in two similar situations, absolving Abraham and blaming Sarah and reproaching her for laughing? Now as we have said, the reason is quite evident. It is the intention that was different. For when Abraham laughed, it was not to reject God's promise; it did not diminish his power, but he was deeply pleased within himself. It is true that some human emotion was involved, but the truth is that he opened the door to that truth, which he knew to be incomprehensible in God, as Paul also testifies, noting that he did not consider his body, which was already quite feeble, or Sarah's womb, which was effectively dead (cf. *Rom.* 4:19). He did not consider any of that, but he closed his eyes to everything that might prevent him from adhering to the promise. In that way he glorified God. In other words, he gave God the honour he was due, confessing that it was enough that he had spoken, for he was powerful to fulfil it, and nothing was impossible for him. That, then, is how Abraham did not shut out God by laughing that he might not carry out what he had promised.

That is not the case with Sarah when she laughs, for she is spending her time thinking about what her thoughts might be, based on her understanding. 'How is that? I was a sterile woman in the flower of my youth; I was married for a long time; I was not able to conceive. My time has now passed. Since I am ninety years old, how is it possible I could produce a lineage, seeing that I have not been able to during the time God gave me?' So what is said about her is like a fairy tale, like a dream, not that she wishes to call God a liar, for she was taught otherwise, and it is certain she sensed such a fear of God in herself that she never would have dared to imagine such blasphemy in her heart, but even so, she is caught by the thought that the thing cannot happen because she cannot imagine it. That is how she is influenced by the limitations of nature. Now as for her, we must not be amazed by her, for at the same time, because of her surprise and imprudence, she wants to bring God into her sphere, as if he could only be what she understood him to be. Now that is a bad standard for measuring, for it is said that God does not have to open his hand in order to hold the world; when his hand is closed, he holds the heaven and the earth like a speck of dust (cf. *Psa.* 95:4; *Isa.* 40:15). So with God's infinite power in mind, are we to judge him by our understanding? Could we outrage him more egregiously than that? That, then, is Sarah's sin. She thinks that what God proclaimed as she understood it applies to him and that she can understand him as she imagines him. Thus we see there is good reason for God to condemn her so severely for laughing.

In order to take advantage of this teaching, let us first look at what Moses recounts. Sarah did not open her mouth but only conceived in her heart some doubt which proceeded from distrust. If such a secret thought is rebuked so harshly, what will be the lot of those who abandon restraints and boldly grumble against God and challenge his word? If Sarah's sin, though hidden from men, is so great, as we see by her present condemnation, alas, what will happen when we are so bold and foolhardy as to wag our tongues after God speaks and try to make a case against him? If we attempt to oppose him, will we not have to be more severely condemned than Sarah was? In addition, let us learn that our sins do not have to be uncovered and made manifest in order to enter into an accounting before God. Whenever we think everything is buried, he will be obliged to show us that nothing is unknown to him (cf. *Psa.* 139:2), as all Scripture says, and frequently, and that is why we are stupid and why we change him, for when we hide our faults, we think that he must see nothing, that we have blindfolded him, and that there is darkness between him and us and we imagine we deceive him every time, not that that is our direct intention, as we say, but the state of things shows that we will be bolder to play games with God than if he were a mortal creature. All the more then must we pay attention to what Moses tells us, namely, that even though Sarah laughed only in her heart, that became known and she is summoned before God because of that laugh which she thought was unknown.

Moreover, if such a laugh as Sarah's was condemned that way, what will happen to those who openly mock God and are so possessed by Satan that they would want to change the truth into a lie? For never did Sarah want to reproach God or even think about doing so for not being faithful in everything he said, but she failed at that point because of her imprudence, which resulted from her limited notions of God. Now as I said, hers was not a fault which stems from malice or deliberate intent to be so stupid and wicked before God. And what will happen when men become venomous toward God and would like to make a liar of him so that everything he says is fable, at which point they demonstrate that they do not take him into account and that they dare to disgorge their blasphemies like howling dogs? How horribly will God punish those sins, seeing that he did not pardon Sarah for a laugh that resulted from simplicity and imprudence? We will speak more of that when we talk about Ishmael's laugh (cf. *Gen.* 21:9),[3] for his surpassed Sarah's, because he was not only caught up in and preoccupied with some idle thought, but that was when he was scorning God's grace and despising his brother Isaac, who was to be a father to him, though younger than he, because he had the promise of everlasting salvation and because the inheritance was deposited in him. Now that laugh, as we will see, was a capital crime before God.

So let us learn to humble ourselves so that when the word is preached to us, we will receive it, as James says, with a spirit of humility (cf. *James* 1:21), that is, with a spirit of meekness, so that we will not be arrogant and enter into disputes, so that we will not engage in hairsplitting and be rebellious, but let it be enough for us that God has spoken, and let us receive seriously and meekly what is brought to us in his name. And, moreover, let us not only avoid as a deadly plague the laughs characteristic of the wicked but also those which might come at unguarded moments. And when Scripture wishes to declare that men have reached a state of such egregious sin that they are completely hopeless and there is no longer a remedy, it calls them scoffers (cf. *Prov.* 14:6). Now we

[3] This sermon has been lost.—*M.E.*

must not only guard against such scoffing, which is associated with manifest blasphemy, but we must also guard against all doubt. For if we want to judge by the censure of Sarah's act, none of us would make an effort to excuse her: 'Alas, that poor woman was preoccupied and she laughed, but not because she diminished God's word and even less because she scoffed at it, as do the wicked and reprobate, but she found the situation strange and laughed because of that.' That is how we should judge Sarah's sin, and if we do, we can forgive her. But yet we have to note that she disparaged God's infinite power because she proceeded to judge in accordance with her own understanding.

So in order to avoid tripping up the way Sarah did, let us come to the remedy Paul notes for us in the person of Abraham, namely, that we give God the glory he deserves (cf. *Rom.* 4:20). And how do we do that? We are delighted with astonishment when we think about his power, knowing that we cannot reach it or attain to it or even approach it; and so, realizing that all our abilities flow from and are rooted in that power of God, let us be satisfied that he does what he says and as he knows it; for that surpasses us. But still let us not be so filled with pride that we want to measure out his portion to him and say: 'How does he do it?' Is our judgment to enter into it? Not at all. But let us have our eyes closed and our ears open. That is, let all our senses be submissive, and let us be open to receive what is proposed to us in his name, knowing that what proceeds from him carries such authority that we must not question whether or not we are to accept it, for that would be to subvert his truth and lessen his power in our minds. So let us take care not to be caught up in our conjectures and wild and fanciful imaginings, for that is the same as shutting God out. When we give our understanding precedence and want it to rule and when we take the liberty of judging with the knowledge in our heads, it is the same as taking

God's place and wanting to snatch from him the right which is his to do whatever he pleases.

Now when it is said that the angel adds: 'Is there anything impossible?' it is to confirm better what we have just touched upon, namely, that never will we trust God until we have learned to rise above everybody and not to spend our time pondering what seems to us difficult and impossible, but to realize, since God is all powerful, that that is good enough reason to permit him to accomplish everything he wishes without having men control him or say to him: 'What are you doing, or how will you go about it?' So men must not go that far, for that would be totally contrary to the nature of faith, for it is not without reason that we say faith is based on humility. Now humility means that men not only abase themselves but also exalt God, not that we can diminish or advance him in any way, but we exalt him when we leave him as he is. So what he requires of us is that we take nothing from his right by our evil disposition and ingratitude, but that we leave him as he is. In other words, we must truly confess what we say with our mouths, namely, that he is God Almighty, for with that confession we will come to know that nothing is impossible for him. And we will then conclude that inasmuch as that is true, everything he says must be carried out and completed. And how will he do it? It is not our place to think about that; it is not our place to come to any conclusions; but we must adore what is kept secret and hidden from us.

Moreover, when this statement is read and declared to us: 'Nothing is impossible for God, or difficult,' it is not to make us wander from the purpose, as many extremists do when they want to discuss questions such as: 'Is it possible for God to make a mountain without a valley, or can he make a stick without two ends?' That is how the devil gave the audacity to men to launch forth like bulls or wild animals to mock God's power. Now when Scripture speaks that way, it is because nothing is difficult for God. Scripture does not keep us in suspense or leave that statement indistinct or vague, for its purpose is to keep us from doubting anything he proposes. So do we wish to profit from this teaching? Let us be so locked up in the confines of God's word that we recognize his will in it. For if we understood that statement ('nothing is impossible for God') in a general sense, we would wander in many directions endlessly and without limitation and would find many obstacles that would break us at every turn. So in order not to abuse that teaching and profane it with our foolish and outlandish speculations, let us know that God wants to apply his power to put in play and accomplish everything he says to us. So if we wish to know what God's power is to the extent we can conceive it, we must inquire into his will. How? Through his word. For in it we have a definite witness. In it, we know what God promises us, and that is what he wants us to lean upon. And when we are taught by him, we must conclude that since God has spoken, he is powerful to bring to pass what is said. That, I say, is the honour we are to give him.

But those who speak of God's will apart from his word and his promises put the cart before the horse and ruin everything. That is how the papists themselves entered into many profane disputes, for they debate about God's power in their diabolical synagogues and ask whether God could, within his power, condemn the virgin Mary, and they conclude that he could in his absolute power but not in his ordinary power. That is how they make God contradict himself. For we know that his election and his eternal counsel are unchangeable, and yet they want God to be divided into parts, so to speak, for if God cannot condemn his elect, they say, he has limited power by which he must govern himself. And if they say he can condemn them, he is therefore changeable, for he promised that they would never perish. We see what kind of labyrinth those wretches have entered into because of their insane curiosity when wanting to inquire into matters which should remain unknown to them, and yet they disregarded what should be quite obvious to them.

And in fact we see something similar in a matter common to all. For when the papists fight to maintain that stupid and brutish notion that when they breathe on a piece of bread and, behold, God, and the bread is changed into the body of Jesus Christ, what do they claim in order to maintain such a dim-witted and even terrifying idea? 'What? Is not God all power-ful? Did he not create the whole world from nothing? So why is he not able to change the body of his Son into bread?' That is how those devils abuse God's power. But when they have suf-ficiently debated their nonsense, we always have to come back to the question of whether God wants the body of his Son to be in the form of this bread, that is, whether Jesus Christ wants his divine essence and his body and blood to be encapsulated under that kind of whiteness, that is, whether he said that the bread and the wine would lose their substance and that noth-ing would remain except his body and even his divine essence. Those ideas are so egregious that we must consider them as execrable blasphemies disgorged against God's majesty and the majesty of the Lord Jesus Christ. For we must not abuse God's infinite power that way and apply it erratically and fancifully, but let us always be immersed in the word, and from it let us learn what his will is, and let it teach us to be resolute in what it proposes for our instruction in the law, the prophets, and the gospel, and let us be content with it all. And then when he seals in our hearts by his Holy Spirit all the teaching contained therein and all the promises which are ours, let this be our con-clusion: God is all powerful. And that is also how Paul, in that passage I quoted (cf. *Rom.* 4:20), joined the two together, that is, that Abraham gave glory to God when he believed God was powerful to do what he had promised. Paul does not say that

God is powerful to do what Abraham had imagined, but what God had said, and Abraham knew that it would be done.

And we also need to note what is said about Sarah, that she denied it because she was afraid. It is certain that that denial was a much greater sin than we might think at first, for that is the same as saying to God: 'That is not so.' And there you have God saying: 'You laughed,' and hearing in return: 'I did not,' does that not give the lie to God? And if we were to answer: 'Oh, but that was not Sarah's intention,' that would be true, but let us realize how rash we have to be when we go against God like enraged beasts without thinking. And it is indeed noteworthy that we are told Sarah was afraid. And that fear means she realized this was a serious matter. She understood and appreciated God's majesty. That is a good point, as I have said. For when we hear God speak, we must be moved with fear and humble ourselves before his majesty if we are to give him the homage and honour he deserves. Sarah experienced that, but that point, which is so good and praiseworthy in itself, what does it cause her to do? It causes her to give God the lie, it puts her in opposition to him and makes her so impudent that she says: 'No, I did not laugh.'

Now let us contemplate in this mirror what kind of people we are. If Sarah, being governed first by a good intention neverthe-less stumbled so severely that she completely destroyed herself and placed herself at the bottom of hell, what, alas, will become of us? So let us learn to empty ourselves of every presumption and not be pleased with or compliment ourselves on what we think moral excellence is. For often when men justify themselves, God con-demns them, even doubly and triply. So when we think we have a good motive, let us know that we will soon deviate to the left or the right unless God miraculously holds us back and that we will be capable of making missteps and blunders or of stumbling even though we are on the right road. In fact, if we examine our works closely, we will often continue to fall short despite our laudable zeal. If I persist in a good cause, I will nonetheless fall short in one way or another, and God will always find occasion to rebuke me for a single deed, even ten or twenty times. True, my intention will be good, but we are so corrupt that when we think we do good, vice remains present in us, should God wish to judge us rigorously.

In addition, let us note that reverence for God always carries with it hypocrisy until the Holy Spirit works in us. It is a good and praiseworthy thing that we are touched by reverence when someone talks to us about God and we experience some horror, knowing that he is our Judge. That is good because it is like a door to lead us to humility and obedience, but that fear, as a result of our natural disposition, will bring in its wake only hypocrisy and lying. Why do men practise such empty piety unless they want to acquit themselves before God? Even the most wicked and debauched cannot flee from such a fear, for they realize that one day they will have to give an accounting to God. So finding themselves between a rock and a hard place, they seek some means by which to acquit themselves, but what is that means? Deceit and illusion, and as a result all hypocrites are but liars who mock God and play games with him, as if they were dealing with a small child. That, in short, is what we have to remember.

And let us also note that it does not matter if we have a servile fear which causes us to tremble before God's majesty, but his Holy Spirit must cleanse us of all pretence and insincerity so that we will desire to live in conformity with his will and make such an effort to yield ourselves to him that we will experience fear and think only of attributing to him the honour and reverence that belong to him.

But there is one more thing to note, for Sarah was not only afraid because she saw it was God who was speaking, who had sounded the secrets of her heart. This she knows well: 'If this were a man, he would not rebuke me for that laugh, for I did not laugh with my mouth. So since he probes to the depths of my heart, it is God.' Sarah was well aware of that, but that is not all. Something else touches her more deeply, namely, that God rebukes her for her fault. We will often feel that it is God, but the fact is that we will not be brought to our knees at his feet to humble ourselves as we should. Why not? If we do not examine our consciences, if we do not sense how guilty we are before God, we are apathetic and only wag our heads. But when our God summons us and shows us that the office of being our Judge cannot be removed or taken from him, we must appear before his seat like pitiable malefactors. When we know that, we are brought to humility and fear.

We see the reaction of the Samaritan woman when our Lord Jesus Christ speaks to her about living water, that is, about the Spirit he would give and his offering to give himself as Saviour of the world. She only mocks and plays around, for she was a dissembling person who had been accustomed to jesting and bantering. 'And how could you draw water? If you had something to draw with, you could spare us all a lot of trouble. That would be very welcome!' She is full of sass and impertinence. It is not simply a matter of playing around or even mocking our Lord Jesus Christ, who was nonetheless opening for her the door of paradise. She is not moved by that, but when he asks her: 'Where is your husband?' and she answers she does not have one, he responds: 'True, you have had five, and the one you have now is not your husband, but you are a prostitute' (cf. *John* 4:16-19), for she had often been repudiated. Now when our Lord Jesus Christ speaks thus and reveals how vile she is, then she says: 'Oh, Lord, I know you are a prophet.' So much for her glib tongue, for she is cut to the heart when she is shown her sin. So let us note that until our Lord teaches us to sense our faults and be displeased with them and reveals himself as Judge so that we will be aware that subterfuge cannot help us escape the condemnation we deserve, we will never be humbled. So all pride must be corrected in us, and we must no longer remain in our hypocrisy but sigh and groan after God touches us to the quick with the knowledge of our sins. That, then, is what we still have to remember about this passage.

As for what is added, we also have to conclude that after pleading many excuses, we gain nothing, for it takes only a simple word to confound us: 'Yes, you did. You laughed.' God does not give her an involved explanation, but he silences her with a word, and he does it to show us that when we are dealing with God, it is not a matter of using subtleties, for after we have looked for places to hide and have dug very deep, he will still penetrate every crack and crevice. And yet if God does not appear to us in person today, let us not forget that his duty is to probe the thoughts of the heart. In fact, that is the nature of his word, its purpose and its power. As the apostle says in the Epistle to the Hebrews: 'The word of God, more powerful than a two-edged sword, probes the thoughts and intents of the heart, cutting even to the marrow of the bones' (cf. *Heb.* 4:12). Why? It has that absolute and just authority and the duty to exercise it. Therefore, every time God admonishes us for our vices, let us endure his rebukes so that we will learn to submit to his goodwill. So as often as we hear God's word preached, we must realize that we must examine ourselves, that no one is to console himself, but that we are already condemned in ourselves and need to be absolved by God's mouth.

Moreover, after being shown the vices which are in Sarah, we see her virtue, for what she says is a sign of continence: 'We are old, and there is no longer a question of my living with my husband.' And it is another virtue that she calls him her master, even her lord. Peter rightly quotes this passage when he exhorts women to submit to their husbands. He tells them to follow their mother Sarah, who called Abraham her lord (cf. *1 Pet.* 3:5-6). It is not enough simply to utter the word, and Peter does not spend time over language, but he demonstrates that Sarah attributed to Abraham what belonged to him. Now in our day, in the great courts, it is certain that when the great ladies say 'Milord,' they will continue to be venomous and have as much respect for their husbands as for their valets. And when the husbands say 'Milady,' they would like to gnaw out the hearts of their wives, whom they should love as their own bodies. So it is not a matter of fine language, but let each person acknowledge his position with all simplicity, and let us learn to humble ourselves so that when we associate with people humbly, we will also be pure and free of pretence before God so we will please him, him who loves truth alone.

Now let us bow before the majesty of our gracious God in acknowledgment of our faults, praying that he will touch us with them more and more so that we will groan before him and ask him to pardon them and magnify his mercy in our Lord Jesus Christ. And realizing that we are completely damned and lost until he receives us in mercy, let us pray that he will so work in us by his Holy Spirit that we will renounce ourselves, and may he so guide our faith that we will learn to glorify him as he deserves, and may we be so withdrawn from this world that we will be founded in his enduring and eternal truth. And may we fight so forcefully against all our wicked affections that we will aspire to his heavenly kingdom, to which he calls us and which he wants us to possess even now by hope. So let us now all say: Almighty God, heavenly Father...

86

The Coming Judgment on Sodom and Gomorrah

Thursday, 18 April 1560

And the men rose up from thence, and looked toward Sodom: and Abraham went with them to bring them on the way. And the LORD said, Shall I hide from Abraham that thing which I do; Seeing that Abraham shall surely become a great and mighty nation, and all the nations of the earth shall be blessed in him? For I know him, that he will command his children and his household after him, and they shall keep the way of the LORD, to do justice and judgment; that the LORD may bring upon Abraham that which he hath spoken of him. And the LORD said, Because the cry of Sodom and Gomorrah is great, and because their sin is very grievous; I will go down now, and see whether they have done altogether according to the cry of it, which is come unto me; and if not, I will know (Gen. 18:16-21).

E HAVE TO CONSIDER here a story which is memorable among others for teaching us to hold to the fear of God and to walk in such a way that we do not provoke his wrath against us the way the people of Sodom did, who are spoken of here. Now we can see by Moses' account that God declares his goodness toward his elect when he exercises his judgments toward those who have contempt for his majesty. And those are also the two things he attributes to himself when he wishes to be known by us, for he says in Jeremiah that whoever wishes to boast, 'let him boast that he knows that I am the God who exercises righteousness, judgment, and mercy' (cf. *Jer.* 9:23-24). So on the one hand we have to note that God, being Judge of the world, cannot allow iniquities to go unpunished. He will delay for a while, but he must still show that he did not sleep while he waited for sinners, but he exercised his patience to invite them to return to the right path. And then when we learn he is our Judge to humble us before himself and to hold us restrained and bridled according to his will, there is also his mercy, which he makes known to all those who seek him and take refuge in him (cf. *Ezra* 8:22; *Psa.* 34:8-10; *Isa.* 65:1). We also see that when it is said he visited Abraham's house to gladden his heart with the promise he had given him before and also to make Sarah a participant in such a blessing. Moses now adds that God goes to Sodom and Gomorrah to execute vengeance on the people who deserved it.

Now it is noteworthy that he says God does not want to hide from his servant Abraham that deed and says: 'Shall I hide from my servant Abraham what I intend to do?' In that, we see that God, having received his elect in his grace and love, gives them such instruction as is appropriate and useful for their salvation (cf. *Acts* 20:20). And he also adds two noteworthy reasons: 'He will grow into a great nation,' and 'I know he will instruct his family to walk in my path.' With those statements, Moses declares that God continues his favours toward those whom he chose for himself and whose cause he takes up because of his pure goodness and gratitude when he wishes to do good for them. But since instruction is spoken of here, let us note this point we have touched upon: that it is a privilege and special benefit that God bestows upon his church when he makes known his judgments so that it will be taught about its salvation.

It is true that the wicked and those who belong in no way to God will indeed feel his hand sometimes, and that will be to remove from them every excuse, but God nonetheless, from the beginning of the world and in all ages, wanted to reserve as special for his people the knowledge of his judgments, as Amos says: 'Will God do anything that he does not reveal to his prophets?' (Cf. *Amos* 3:7.) We understand by that, not that God obliges himself to do nothing he has not revealed, but that it was to show that the people of Israel were very ungrateful if they did not know how to profit from what was announced to them daily, for God's hand extended everywhere. Profane people were often chastised, and yet there was no prophet in Egypt, Assyria, Chaldea or even in the nearest neighbouring countries, as Moab, Idumea, and others like them. They did not have prophets or teachers to make known to them the hand of God. But the judgments of God which befell Judea here and there are declared. For Isaiah and Jeremiah and prophets like them not only predicted to the Jews what was to happen to them, but they also made known why God exercised his judgment on foreign peoples (cf. *Isa.* 42:9; 44:26; 48:1-6; *Jer.* 33:3; *Ezek.* 24:24), which was, as I have said, that God from all time wanted to demonstrate the love he had for his church and the concern he had for the salvation of his elect when he instructed them concerning all the punishments and corrections that he was sending upon the world.

Now from that we must also conclude, in general, that since God began to do good for us, he continues, even though he may have no other reason than considering what he began in us. And that is a very noteworthy point, for men always try to discover in themselves and in their persons why God has to instruct them, why he has to pour out his blessings upon them. They think they will be able to obligate him. But we see God does not go beyond himself, so to speak, when it comes to doing good for those faithful to him, but he wishes to add grace upon grace to show his riches are infinite. And that is why he says first: 'Shall I hide from my servant Abraham what I intend to do, seeing that he will become a great people and that in him all nations of the earth will be blessed?' Who raised Abraham to such a position of dignity and honour? Did he attain that by his own industry and power? Certainly not. It is a free gift of God. We must also consider these words seriously, as if our Lord were saying: 'I have chosen Abraham to bless him so that he may be a mirror of my goodness and of my honouring him by making him the father of all believers, for from him and his race will come the Redeemer of the world. Because I have thus begun to do good for him, I wish to move forward until I bring to perfection what has now begun.' So we see how God does not seek a reason beyond himself to do good; but he draws it from himself because he is the fountain of all goodness, and even the blessings that he poured out upon us (cf. *Psa.* 33:5; 103:10) motivate him to continue until the end, as Paul says: 'He who has begun a good work in you will perfect it until the day of our Lord Jesus Christ' (cf. *Phil.* 1:6). That, then, is what we have to remember.

Now that teaching ought to serve us in two ways: to confirm us in good hope for the time to come, and to motivate us to glorify God and praise him for being pleased to add his blessings in this way, the second to the first, forever and without end. I have said that we have the opportunity to hope that God will never fail us when we understand the gifts of grace we have already received from him, and that of itself is to give us boldness to call upon him after becoming aware that from hour to hour we could fail if God had not provided for everything we need. And how can we be persuaded that we must never fear that he will fail us? By the fact that he has begun. Let us be satisfied with that reason. So since God has shown that he is our Father, he wants us to be convinced that we will feel that he is our Father until the end and that he will not stop doing good things for us inasmuch as that will be necessary. And then we are persuaded at the same time that we can open our mouths and pray when we lack something: 'Oh gracious God, you know what I need; may you grant it.' Consequently, we will always be able to call upon God with full confidence when we are aware of the good things we have received from him, for he is not like a mortal man who wearies of doing good things for us. For the most generous person will be drained dry in the long run; and because he diminishes himself, he will not always be able to provide. But as for God, his riches are far from diminishing when he pours out his bounty upon us so that we may sense even better that the more we come and draw from his bounty, the more we will always find. For depending on our familiar access to him, we know that he has the means to provide for us all that is needed for our salvation. That, then, is what we need to observe about hope.

And then someone has to stay after us to get us to praise him as he deserves when we see that he increasingly shows himself to be kind to us and does one good thing for us and then begins again with another and does not forget any kind of good thing to do for us. In brief, without number and without count, we see we are filled to satisfaction with his bounty. So woe to us if we remain silent and do not thank him for so many good things, in which he wishes to be glorified, and rightly so.

In addition, it is said, in the second place, that God knows Abraham will be diligent to instruct his family. In so saying, he shows it is not only to refresh Abraham's ears that he tells him what is to happen to Sodom and Gomorrah, but to give him useful information. For God does not want his word to be idle in us (cf. *1 Thess.* 2:13) and he does not want us to make a showpiece out of it and say: 'God revealed this to me; I know it and others do not.' It profanes the teaching God communicates to us when we do not use it in a way that profits us. So is God here proclaiming that he does not wish to tell Abraham about the ruin and destruction of Sodom and Gomorrah so that he will be satisfied and that in this way his curiosity will also be satisfied? No, it is so that he will receive instruction not only for himself and his private usage, but for all his house. So we now see why the examples of God's judgment are placed before our eyes. It is so that they will serve us as restraints so we will not provoke his vengeance against us. And that is what Paul says: 'My friends, let no one deceive you with vain words, for because of them, God's wrath falls upon rebels' (cf. *Eph.* 5:6; *1 Thess.* 4:6). After speaking of the sins which the world thinks of as nothing, he says: 'Be careful not to have fellowship with the wicked and despisers of God who say: "That is only a small venial sin. There is nothing especially bad in that. It is a natural sin," but think about all the admonitions God has directed at his church.'[1] And what are they? They are all the punishments that God administered to correct sinners, as discussed more fully in the tenth chapter of 1 Corinthians, when he says that what we read about God's punishments visited upon Israel belongs to us and that they are living images to show that God will not spare those who provoke him that way. He says: 'There is, on the one hand, whoredom, which was horribly punished. God shows us that that is a sin he detests. On the other hand, wicked desires are punished. So let us learn to abstain from them. God thunders against any rebellion. Let us learn, therefore, to be obedient and restrain ourselves peaceably under his hand. That is the unbelief that God condemns with such grievous punishments. So let us learn to conform simply to his word.'

Such is the case with Sodom and Gomorrah. So let us note, as I have already said, that every time it pleases God to reveal his judgments on the wicked, he wants to instruct us at someone

---

[1] In that sentence Calvin is not citing Paul but picking up his interpretation of Ephesians 5:6-7.—*M.E.*

else's expense. Moreover, there is a reason behind his predicting to Abraham what was to take place. It is true that if Abraham had seen the city of Sodom and the four others destroyed there where previously an almost earthly paradise existed and he had witnessed such a terrifying and hideous sight, it would have made the hair stand up on the heads of those who heard about it, and he would have had enough instruction. And when God predicts before the event what is still hidden, the instruction is much more trustworthy. And that is so unbelievers will be even more deeply touched and convinced that God's hand had passed that way. Example: If God sends some calamity on a country that has greatly sinned, we are well taught by the law that adversities are God's flails to punish sins and are curses coming from him, and that is not by chance (cf. *Deut.* 29:21-27; *Ezek.* 5:11-16). Even so, inasmuch as we cannot be sufficiently persuaded that that would be appreciated since we are inclined to attribute things to bad luck, happenstance, and mishap, or I do not know what, all those misunderstandings befuddle us and keep us from contemplating God's judgments. But when God says: 'I shall do such and such a thing,' even though we do not think about it and it is even something we do not ordinarily see, oh, it is then no longer a matter of arguing about or imagining luck or chance occurrence. Why not? God shows us it is he whom we must consider. And that is why the prophets doubly served the ancient people, as God threatened the Jews for a long time when they fell into sin and he declared they would have to be brought to account in the end. He even told them the source of the evil (cf. *Jer.* 7:20; 14:12; *Ezek.* 6:11). When they learned from experience that the prophets had not spoken in vain, they were even more convinced, and when the faithful heard the prophets' threats, they profited from them. And when they heard the threats, they did not wait for God to perform them; they were moved by fear and concern and prayed that God would receive them in mercy.

677

Some prepared before such calamities occurred, others became stronger in long-suffering, and God caused all the afflictions he sent them to work for their salvation. That, then, was the purpose of the prophecies.

Now it is true that today God will not send angels from heaven and will not raise up men to predict things that will take place in ten years, twenty years or thirty, but it must be enough for us that, because of the many times it was demonstrated under the law, it is he who sent the wars, plagues, and famines (cf. *Jer.* 27:8). Since we have ample testimony of that, what more can we ask for? So let us learn to walk in fear and not be so ungrateful as to complain that we do not have the revelations that were given before, for we have also come to the fullness of time. What do we have in comparison with the ancient fathers? They were considered as small children. So we must not be surprised that God implemented the lack of teaching which existed in those days when he predicted the hidden things that were to come. But since God has spoken fully today in the person of his only Son and we have in the gospel such teachings as we could wish for, there is no longer a need for prophecies. So let us note that even though we do not have prophecies, our situation is not worse than that of the fathers, for the prophecies came to an end at the coming of our Lord Jesus Christ, and he testified sufficiently well to what we needed. In any case, let us always remember this point, that God had a reason to declare his judgments before he carried them out and that he wanted to use them to teach us that we must look to him and not be carried in every direction by our foolish imaginations when some noteworthy calamity happens, but let us know that God has called us to himself and wishes to be known as Judge so we will walk in fear of him. That, then, is what we have to remember.

Now it is quite certain that when Abraham was advised before the destruction which was at hand for Sodom and Gomorrah and the three other cities, the information was not only for him and his household, but for all ages. And it must be accommodated to our time. Consequently, when we hear that story, there is no reason for us to doubt and say, 'How did that happen?' For there are those introductory remarks God made to his servant Abraham. Therefore, we must not imagine that lightning was unleashed by some natural causes or by some kind of turbulence of the air or the earth, but God stretched forth his hand in such a way that the blind themselves can understand that he wanted to put forth an example worth remembering so that we will tremble every time we hear how those cities were totally destroyed.

Let us also note that we are told here that God knows Abraham will instruct his children to walk in his way after him. First, there is instruction, and then what kind it is is noted. In other words, we are told the nature of that instruction and then how it extends beyond death. So in the person of Abraham we see what the responsibility of all believers is, principally the responsibility of the fathers of family whom God set up as heads of household and to whom he gave life, children, and servants so they would be diligent in teaching them. For when a father has children, his responsibility is not only to feed and clothe them, but his principal responsibility is to guide them so that their lives will be well regulated, and he will dedicate his full attention to that. He will also do that for his menservants and maidservants. That has already been discussed, and that is why I am touching on it more lightly now, but we must not forget or pass over negligently what is expressed here, namely, that God values his servant Abraham's piety, which is shown in the effort he will make to serve and honour him and to guide his family and those entrusted to his charge, for it is particularly stated that he will teach them to walk in the way of the Lord. Consequently, we see the nature of the right kind of instruction. For someone could be rather careful to give many rules and many laws without providing stability. There can be no foundation to build on unless God dominates and people obey him and conform to his word. That, then, is what we have to remember.

When fathers of family and those of some pre-eminence get ready to teach, they must not be presumptuous and say: 'This seems good to me,' and then try to subject everybody to their opinion and their concepts. 'What? Shall I teach what I learned from God in his school?' What we have to remember from this passage is, briefly, that no one will ever be a good teacher unless he is God's pupil. So let there be no teaching authority that advances what we invent and what our minds come up with, but let us learn from God so that he will dominate and alone have all pre-eminence, and may great and small bring themselves into conformity with him and obey him. That much for that instruction.

At that time there was no written law, and even less gospel, but Abraham still knew God's will to the extent necessary. So Abraham is without Scripture, but even so, he does not presume to or attempt to set up laws to his own liking, but he asks God alone to govern and show the way to everybody else and lead them, for he does not wish to say: 'Let us go the way I say,' but, 'I am teaching you what I have learned from God. And may he alone have all mastery, and may I be a teacher only if I speak as by his mouth.' That is the second point we have to remember here.

So what is to be noted here is that heads of family must go to the trouble of being instructed in God's word if they are to do their duty, for if they are stupid, if they do not know the basic principles of religion or of their faith and do not know God's commandments or how prayer is to be offered to him or what the road to salvation is, how will they instruct their families? All the more then must those who are husbands and have a family, a household to govern, think: 'I must establish my lesson in his word so that I will not only try to govern myself in accordance with his will, but that I will also bring to it at the same time those who are under my authority and guidance.'

Now in the third place, Abraham will teach his family to walk in the fear of the Lord after his death, just as if it were said that the faithful man is not only to get honour for God and live tomorrow, but that he leaves good seed after his death. For God's word is the incorruptible seed of life; it endures forever. And even though heaven and earth tend to corruption and will pass away, the word of God must always retain its power (cf. *Isa.* 40:8; 55:11). Therefore, it is not without reason that it dies with us and is extinguished when God withdraws us from this world and we carry everything off with us, but let us work, though we are weak and mortal and must depart this world, to leave the word of God with a root here. And when we are dead and have turned to dust, may God be honoured and may his memory endure forever. That, then, is what we have to remember.

If each individual in the privacy of his home is bound and obliged to do that, what will be required of those who have a public charge, who are to proclaim God's word, who are constituted as teachers? What will be the responsibility of princes, of magistrates and all judicial officers? It is quite certain that they have a stricter obligation. Consequently, in brief, since it is a matter of sustaining God's truth and ensuring that it is received and obeyed, may that not be for three days or for as long as we live, but beyond our death.

Now since God spoke that way, he is saying that Abraham's children, whom he will teach, will do justice and judgment. With those two words, Scripture comprises what concerns the second table of the law. Moses says they will do justice and judgment. That shows us what the way of God is and how we will show we are obeying him. For those two words, as I have said, involve uprightness and equity so that we may be kind and give ourselves to charity and help one another and protect everyone's right and not defraud and to abstain from doing wrong and violence to one another and even help those who need our help.

Now it is certain that in God's law there is nothing but justice and judgment, for in the first table we see how we are to worship God, how we are to revere his name, and how we are to practise calling upon him and trusting in him so that we will devote ourselves this way to his service and dedicate ourselves to it. All of that is properly called justice and judgment. Now as I said, that commonly involves our neighbours and the rule of living right with men in uprightness and equity; but that is an ordinary way of speaking in Scripture, and the prophets are filled with it (cf. *Isa.* 1:27; 5:16; 28:17). When they deal with God's law, they sometimes depart from the first table and speak of uprightness and equity. They cry out against fraud, violence, robbery, and such like. Those things, in brief, mention a part while signifying the whole. In this way, although there is here only a type and a portion of God's way, God, in general, nonetheless wanted to declare that Abraham would teach his family to govern itself in all equity and uprightness so that no one would rise up against his neighbour, that no one would commit fraud or do any wrong. That is what we have to remember.

Now why does God separate the first table of the law from the second? Because it is impossible to walk in love with one another unless the fear of God comes first. Thus, when each person does his duty toward his neighbours, that is a direct confirmation that we honour God. We are devoted to ourselves. Until God conforms us to himself, we would each like to exalt ourselves, but after becoming aware that God is our Father, we then practise fraternity together in a mutual, harmonious union. That is why it is said that God requires fidelity, judgment, and mercy, and that that is the sum and substance of the law; not that God forgets his role, not that he wants his service and his honour to be scorned, but he declares in summary that when we walk in integrity of life, there will be no fraud or malice in us, that we will try to maintain everyone's right, help our neighbours and walk in brotherly love and in that way demonstrate and confirm that we adhere to God as our Father. For the faith that we have in God is hidden like the root of a tree, but the fruit tells what kind of tree it is, and the fruit is uprightness, equity, humility, and the like.

So what we have to remember is that, in brief, in order to live right, we must not consider what the world approves and how we can acquire a good reputation, but let us learn to conform to God's simple will and what he attests to us. Let us hold to that so that it will be our bridle and our full wisdom to guide us.

Now after speaking that way, God adds: 'The cry of Sodom and Gomorrah is great and I have now come down to see if it is true. If not, I will know.' Previously he had said: 'Shall I hide from my servant Abraham what I must do?' God was not deliberating as if in doubt. He wanted to prepare Abraham better so that he would be attentive to what he would be told. When God speaks, we are rather cold and remember only with great difficulty one word of a dozen, and we immediately miss a matter of instruction. And although Abraham was zealous to obey God and accustomed to receiving his word with all reverence, he was nonetheless a man and needed to be sharpened. Now if he needed sharpening, much more do we who have not yet come close to his piety.

God now says that the cry of Sodom is great. What was that cry? People were living high in Sodom and Gomorrah. They did a lot of banqueting because the land was fat and fertile, as Ezekiel says (cf. *Ezek.* 16:49), but we will talk about that more fully later. Then there were the people of Sodom and Gomorrah, and of Zeboiim and neighbouring cities, who are having a merry time in their pleasures and lusts. Consequently, there was no cry, but their sins were so detestable that the air was resounding with them, so to speak, and their sins were demanding vengeance. And this is a good and useful lesson that we must draw from it: that while sinners are drunk with their pleasures and think all is right with the world, the outcries are flying and rending the sky asunder and in God's ears. And the more men make merry and the more asleep they are in their iniquities, the more God's judgment is alert and everything is registered before him. That, then, is what is proposed for us here.

Now it is certain that God wanted to compare the condition of Sodom and Gomorrah with his heavenly judgment, as if to say: 'These people are like animals in their great iniquities and they are having such a good time that they think everything is asleep. And yet the cry has risen on high while all is at peace down there.' Now what is said about Sodom and Gomorrah pertains to us. In other words, our Lord wants this to wake us up. So let us learn that if sinners deceive themselves with a feeling of confidence, they increase God's wrath toward them; and if we are not rebuked here below and are even encouraged by others, that only increases the outcry as if we were being called before the judgment seat of God at the sound of the trumpet while we try to exempt ourselves from it. So we see how people take advantage of stopping their ears so they hear nothing, even those who can endure no correction when they fall short. And the world is filled with that kind of sin, for we would all like for God to give us a free pass, even if he had completely abandoned us. And if we have offended both God and the world, we still cannot tolerate a negative word or being rebuked in any way whatsoever. Consequently, we want people to give all our sins the silent treatment, and we put them behind us; we do not want to think about them, for they are the cause of melancholy,[2] we like to think. What do we gain by doing that? For our sins still

---

[2] Calvin speaks regularly of melancholy…, a major theme of the Renaissance.— M.E.

cry out. They will indeed be able to pass in silence here below. We do not think about them; we forget them, but when the cry rises on high, heaven resounds with it, and God hears it and says that the cry is great, whereas we want to be left in peace down here. What have we gained by going to sleep and stopping our ears? Alas, let us entreat ourselves to fear him, and let us be docile and listen to the admonitions we hear when we fail. And even though no one steps forward to say something, let us, on our own, begin. In other words, may our consciences be awakened, and may God's law resound in our ears and in our hearts, and let us think carefully about our iniquities and transgressions. That, then, is what we have to remember when God says that the cry of Sodom and Gomorrah is great.

Now when God adds that he went down to see whether things were going as reported, it does not mean that he is unaware of anything. As we said above, God does not have to go down. He cannot move from one place to another; he is not limited to a single place so that it can be said that he is enclosed within it and that he is at one time on high and at another down below, but that descent of God is a declaration that he acts in accordance with his judgment. For while he tolerates sinners and withholds his hand, it will be thought that he is absent or far removed. In fact, that is why he says he will remain in his tent and watch how the people govern themselves in the future. So God keeps himself hidden, so to speak (cf. *Isa.* 45:15), and while he is hiding, he does not punish the sins that are committed. On the contrary, when he extends his hand and lets it be experienced that he is Judge, it is then said at that time that he descends. So much for that manner of speaking.

But we must understand why God says this. It is to inform us that he does not unexpectedly deal rigorously and severely with men and that he does not send lightning without purpose, but he waits, he is long-suffering (cf. *Rom.* 2:4; *2 Pet.* 3:9), and he never chastises those who have offended him unless he knows the cause. We must always remember that God is not like mortal man. He does not need to make inquiries or have witnesses in order to know what is going on, for everything is present to him; but those are examples drawn from men's experience to clarify what I said. For we see how we are inclined to grumble. If God punishes us until we are thoroughly convinced, it is certain we are seeking to justify ourselves, and that is when grumblings and accusations against God arise, as if he had acted too hastily: 'We have scarcely tripped up and there God's hand is immediately stretched out against us. Alas, should he not help us since we are so weak? And then, what did we do? What have we deserved in his sight?' We will hear those blasphemous remarks. And it is certain that those who dare not say them aloud think them in their hearts. Consequently, because we are disposed to justify ourselves in our hypocrisy and acknowledge nothing about the offences we have committed, and because from there we give ourselves leave to grumble against God, saying he acts too hastily and is too severe. Even more then must we note what is shown here, namely, that he is patient and does not punish right away and that the outcry resounds in heaven before he ever chastises the guilty. For he is not content for the cry to reach him in heaven, but he wants to show that he is fully aware, that he never reaches for the rod except when men are so incorrigible and sense that they are so guilty that they have no more tricks left, and that, like it or not, they must remain defenceless before their Judge and their hearts, which condemn them. So until a person reaches that point, God says he gives counsel to men and does not want to deal rigorously with them. That, then, is what we have to remember.

Now to sum up, we must return to the point we touched on earlier, that although God could punish Sodom and Gomorrah without having denounced anything, he nonetheless wanted to predict it to his servant Abraham so that we will consider what is seen later as a faultless judgment. God wanted to show that he was at work at that time because he wanted us to be aware of it all today so that we will not only tremble every time we hear that such a judgment has been carried out, but so that it will also keep us in the fear of the one who has shown that he is a severe judge and so that we will not doubt that he is the same today. For he does not vary or change in his nature (cf. *James* 1:17). So let us learn to walk in all humility under him, and let us not doubt that although he was very rigorous and the punishments themselves which we still see today are as frightful as those which have been recorded, we will still always find him full of mercy and pity and that he will be ready to receive us in mercy, provided we are our own judges. Let us not abuse his patience, but let us anticipate his judgment, and let us think about our sins morning and evening, sigh and groan, for it is certain that our groanings over our sins will appease the cries which reach God's ears. And when we are displeased with our iniquities, even though we do not speak of them, it is certain the cries which rise to God will cease. But if we, in our stupidity, think we have won, the cries will increase to our confusion and destruction. May we not come to that, but may we know how to profit from this story as it is elaborated more fully.

Now let us bow before the majesty of our gracious God in acknowledgment of our faults, praying that he will bestow his infinite bounty upon us, and inasmuch as it once pleased him to adopt us as his children and give testimony of his grace in the Lord Jesus Christ through the teaching of the gospel, may he increasingly confirm us in it so that we will persevere in calling upon his holy name until the end. And may we rest completely in him and try to serve him in such a way that his holy name will be glorified in us, and may we have the assurance that he truly lives in us by his Holy Spirit (cf. *Eph.* 2:22) and leads and guides us, and may he support us in our infirmities because we can never completely discharge our duty, and may he accept the service that we render him, even though we are still very far from the perfection and goal toward which we must aspire. May he grant that grace not only to us but to all the peoples and nations on earth.

87

The Expediency of Sobriety and Humility When Questioning God's Actions

Friday, 19 April 1560

And the men turned their faces from thence, and went toward Sodom: but Abraham stood yet before the LORD. And Abraham drew near, and said, Wilt thou also destroy the righteous with the wicked? Peradventure there be fifty righteous within the city: wilt thou also destroy and not spare the place for the fifty righteous that are therein? That be far from thee to do after this manner, to slay the righteous with the wicked: and that the righteous should be as the wicked, that be far from thee: Shall not the Judge of all the earth do right? And the LORD said, If I find in Sodom fifty righteous within the city, then I will spare all the place for their sakes (Gen. 18:22-26).

E SAW YESTERDAY that God is in no hurry to punish the transgressions and iniquities of men, but as for what is said about long-suffering (cf. *2 Pet.* 3:15), he also demonstrates it by the fact that he does not wish to exercise rigour until sins have reached their fullness, as has already been discussed in the case of the people of Sodom. So, in brief, we see how God tolerates sinners and deals with them kindly to see whether he will be able to win them. For it is certain that God's goodness and clemency are to serve us by inviting us to repent. God seeks to win us

689

in a gentle and loving way, but when we have reached the extreme, it is then that we must pay what remains unpaid, and the punishment doubles, and rightly, because we have abused God's mercy and amassed a treasury of wrath, as Paul says in the second chapter of Romans (cf. *Rom.* 2:5). That is seen even better in what Moses adds, namely, that God would spare Sodom if only ten righteous men should be found there. So, in that, we see the quality of God's mercy and pity. He waits until men have reached such excesses that they are beyond correction and their evil is beyond hope. On the other hand, Moses also shows us Abraham's concern for those poor wretches who were already condemned by the mouth of God and for whom he has compassion when he hears of their approaching destruction and for whom he tried, insofar as he could, to appease God's wrath.

So these are the two points we must note in this story: one is that God is always a just and severe Judge who spares men insofar as possible, deals with them patiently until there is no longer a remedy and then must add the final touch. The second is to learn in the person of our father Abraham that when we see men on the way to perdition, we are to have some compassion for them as creatures without substance in the image of God and as people who concern us and are joined with us.

First, it is said that the men departed and went toward Sodom and that Abraham remained before the Lord. It is possible that two angels went away and that the main figure remained and that Abraham stayed with him. Whatever the case, even though Abraham has permission to return home, he cannot do so because of his anguish over the terrifying message he heard, namely, that God had come to perform the final execution of his wrath on Sodom and the neighbouring cities. After hearing that, Abraham experiences such fear that he cannot yet leave God without asking whether there is a way for that severe condemnation to be held back or at least moderated in part. That is Abraham's intention.

And that is why he says: 'And if there are fifty righteous, would that not be enough to spare the city?' God grants it. And from fifty he goes to forty-five. From forty-five to forty. From forty to thirty. From thirty to twenty. And from twenty to ten. At that point he must say no more. For it was a very strange thing that in five cities, as we will see later (cf. *Gen.* 19:25), there would not be ten men who feared God. For when the righteous are spoken of, it does not yet mean there is a faultless perfection as if they were like angels of paradise, but Scripture calls 'righteous' those who have a disposition to walk uprightly, even though there are weaknesses and vices in them (cf. *Hos.* 14:9). For it is incredible that there are not ten righteous people in five cities, as I said, who possess some uprightness and integrity. And when Abraham hears it, he must be silent and turn away from them.

In addition, let us note the introductory words Abraham uses here, for he does not interrogate God without due respect, but he asks his pardon for undertaking to inquire into what he has announced. Then he confesses that he is dust and ashes. And then again, twice, he excuses himself for asking God to be patient with him if he is overly insistent. Now when we are dealing with God's judgments, we need to note that we are not permitted to discuss or imagine randomly or to open our mouths to speak against or make any inquiry unless it is with all reverence and humility. For we must remember what Scripture says, that his judgments are like a great deep (cf. *Psa.* 36:6), and if we wanted to enter it rashly, we would be swallowed up a hundred times over. So when God's judgments are spoken of, let us learn to suppress our pride and presumption and not give rein to our curiosity to know more than is allowed and not seek to be crafty; but if we bring up some question or doubt, let us always control ourselves and be content with what it pleases God to reveal.

In addition, if everything must be hidden from us, let us be ignorant, for we must learn from God's mouth what he wants to give us to know and what he knows is expedient for us to know; and we are mad if we want to know what God knows is not useful to us. So there is a kind of ignorance which surpasses all the kinds of wisdom in the world, which is that we do not presume to know anything except what God is pleased to tell us, for he does not spare when he teaches us what he knows to be profitable for our salvation, but he also wants to test our humility in that he does not always show us the reason for the things he does. That, then, is the rule we must hold to in this.

It is true that sometimes the faithful do stand up to God, in a manner of speaking. Even Jeremiah is moved to the point of saying: 'Lord, what is this? How do you permit such greatly confusing things that are happening?' (Cf. *Jer.* 12:1.) Habakkuk also says: 'How long, Lord, will you permit iniquities to flow like a flood?' (Cf. *Hab.* 1:2; 3:8.) Now it is true that the Lord could find some vice in that, for our true wisdom would be to agree with God by receiving what he is pleased to teach us and by being captive to it with all our senses. So when the saints happen to raise such questions, it is certain they are overstepping their bounds and are not at all excusable, but they still have not gone overboard, as do the wicked, who are more like dogs barking at God when they cannot bite. For we hear Jeremiah's opening remark. He affirms that what God does is right and well ordered. So before assuming the boldness to inquire why God tolerates the wicked and does not punish them immediately, he says: 'Lord, I know that you are righteous,' which is as much as to say: 'Although it comes to mind that I should be greatly tormented because I find it strange, I will still impose this bar between us in order to avoid being tempted to blaspheme against you or doubt your righteousness, for, Lord, I am completely convinced that you are righteous and that you do

nothing that is not good and right.' Habakkuk is also passionate about God's righteousness, but, as I said, there is still a bit of
excess in the fact that they are disturbed and cannot completely
and simply accept what God was pleased to do.

Now there is here a special consideration in Abraham, for he
does not intend to dispute with God or oversee his judgments to
determine whether they are equitable or not; he is only moved
with pity. We must note both this concern which moves Abraham
and its goal. For when we pray to God, sometimes there will be
such intensity that we will not think about everything. We will
be engulfed in our desires, and yet the requests we make will be
good, as when Samuel prays for Saul (cf. *1 Sam.* 15:11, 35). He
had already heard that Saul was rebuked and had to forfeit the
kingdom (cf. *1 Sam.* 15:26). So it seems that he wants to contend
with God and prevent him from carrying out what he promised.
For since he continues to pray after the condemnation was already
declared, we could say there is some disagreement he brings before
God and openly takes a stand in favour of Saul. Now Samuel con-
cedes to what he is told and acknowledges that God must have
full and complete freedom to punish those who fall short. So he
does not pretend to diminish in any way God's sovereign authority,
but, as I said, it is out of the compassion he has for the one who
was anointed king, for he had been God's minister in that anointing. That passion, I say, prevents him from taking everything into
consideration and assessing it, and he hastens as one who is completely caught up in his perplexities and unable to bring the matter
to a quick conclusion.

That is how the faithful can be confused in their praying while
still pleasing God. And there is not anyone who does not experience it. Sometimes, like little children, we avoid praying. It is true
that we must always hold to the principle of so conforming to
God's will that we ask nothing of him except faith, that is, we ask

nothing of him except to be grounded in his word.[1] But if we have this general foundation, many perplexities will also arise and we will often be astonished and dazzled. The example of Paul is even stranger than that of Samuel, and even that of Moses, for both are similar in this respect: Moses and Paul ask to be cursed. And what is the significance of that? Paul says: 'I ask to be cursed and cut off from Jesus Christ and his kingdom for the salvation of my brothers' (cf. *Rom.* 9:3). And Moses says: 'Lord, erase my name from the book of life rather than not saving this people that you have put me in charge of' (cf. *Exod.* 32:32). That is a very harsh and strange way of speaking, and it would seem these two holy persons were out of their minds. In fact, that is not a sober judgment. They did not analyze their thoughts or they would not have come up with the decision to say: 'We have to go that far,' but they forget themselves. Moses well knows that it is impossible to be erased from the book of life. Why? Because God must bring his elect to salvation. So how can he ask that his name be erased from the book of life? How is it that Paul asked to be cut off from our Lord Jesus Christ, seeing that he well knew that whoever is engrafted cannot be removed (cf. *Rom.* 11:11-32). And those whom the Father has given the Son will not perish but have everlasting life, as is also stated in the tenth chapter of John (cf. *John* 10:28). Paul was well aware of that and even taught it to others. So how were they transported the way they were? We must consider their goal. Moses is so moved for the salvation of the people that he does not consider himself and forgets himself. He is not speaking randomly or at cross purposes. His prayer would have been very bad if God examined it closely, but he pardons him for his great vehemence because that is not the direct intention of his prayer. The same is true of Paul. He is urged on by such ardour that he has no regard for himself, but for that people who had been chosen by God. Both are concerned for the

---

[1] Cf. *Institutes* III, xx (great chapter on prayer), particularly §11-13 and 27.—M.E.

salvation of God's people because he had elected and chosen and adopted Abraham's lineage. That, then, is what transported them.

Now as for Abraham, inasmuch as he is aroused to pity when he hears that Sodom and the neighbouring cities are to perish, he speaks, he pleads, not that he wishes to be a party adverse to God, but that he wishes to join hands with him to delay what he has decreed. He comes in all humility as a suppliant. We must note these initial words, as we have already said, for he presupposes as clear and settled that God, being the Judge of the world, can only be equitable. Now since Abraham is convinced of that, he forgets himself for the sake of God's glory. He does not abound with hostile questions; he only asks that God be pleased to answer him.

So let us note this first. If it befalls us to inquire into God's judgments, let us have the sobriety and humility to be convinced that he is righteous, as we have already noted in the Jeremiah passage (cf. *Jer.* 12:1). And being thus humble, let us note second that we are to ask him to teach us what he knows to be good for us. And let us remain at peace when we see that he is not pleased for us to know more. These two things are required when it comes to inquiring into God's works: one is to proceed in all humility. And what is that humility? It is confessing without knowing whether one thing or another is righteous, for we are to understand God's righteousness by faith, even though it might be incomprehensible to us. I am not speaking just of his hidden righteousness, but of when he punishes sinners or spares them, when he chastises the good and those who desire to obey him or he deals with them in some way which may seem strange to us. That, I say, is how we must be convinced in our hearts in every case that God does nothing which is not righteous or equitable.

Yet we must be content, as I said, that he is pleased to teach us how holy Scripture sometimes informs us, to the extent we can understand it (cf. *Gen.* 22:18; *Exod.* 32:35; *Isa.* 3:16–17), why God works in one way and another. Well, there is nothing to complain about there, but when things are unknown to us and we do not see that God wants to lead us further, we must remain steadfast at that point and not try to know more than he shows us, for we will only wander astray and, in the long run, remain confused in all our thinking. That, then, is what we have to remember. The more that teaching is a part of our regular practice, the more we must rehearse it and heed it, for there is no more common vice than that of taking a stand against God. It is true that we will not summon him before our judgment seat as if he were obliged to give an account to us, but since we are impatient when he does not work as we wish, it is certain we attempt to make a case against him. And when making this case, we will certainly fall into blasphemies, and it will happen every day unless that sobriety I spoke of holds us back.

So we must be all the more attentive to the example presented for us here in the person of Abraham, for even though he takes the liberty to question God, it is not with any haughtiness or presumption he may have, as if God were obliged to submit and give a response, but he comes to entreat him. But how? It is not that he wishes to reply against God or grumble about his righteousness and equity, but it is out of the compassion he has for the poor people of Sodom and their wretched condition. And in fact, we see it in the words that he uses: 'May you never come to that. Could the one who is Judge of the world include the righteous with the wicked?' When Abraham speaks this way, he follows the principle that it would be repugnant to nature to practise any iniquity. When he says 'the one who is Judge of the world,' he is speaking not only of God's power and majesty, but also of his nature. Judges on earth will indeed be able to say they will often be wrong and condemn the righteous and approve the wicked. And why? Oh, they are human beings, subject to much depravity. And then they are elected or else they have bought their offices and assume them because of ambition and enhancement of self. But there is none of that in God, for he is Judge. His very essence cannot be separated from his office as Judge. That being the case, it follows that he is perfect righteousness and the standard and pattern for all good, for all uprightness and equity. So since Abraham has it imprinted in his heart that God is Judge of the world, he concludes that it is impossible for God not to be equitable in every respect. 'Far be that from you,' Abraham says, and he says that first in order to avoid overstepping his bounds or complaining in any way about God or obscuring his glory. That, then, is what we have to remember.

While speaking with God, he also listens to the answers he is given. Thus, when we want to ask why God works in one way or another, let us go to Scripture and ask there and accept what we find. But when Scripture keeps us in suspense and does not close the door to us, let us realize that we must be ignorant and in that state we will be much wiser than if we seek more than is allowed us. Therefore, in order to interrogate the mouth of God, we must, as I said, yield simply to what he tells us. Also, when we doubt, let us try to profit from what he is pleased to teach us by his word. But let us not flit about in the air and say: 'We will rise above the seas; we will delve into the deep places.' The word is in our hearts and in our mouths (cf. *James* 4:13-14); let us be satisfied with it.

Moreover, one could raise a question about Abraham's argument, for he says: 'Would you destroy the righteous with the wicked?' It seems he is imposing a limitation on God: because God is righteous, he must not punish the good with the wicked. We see the opposite here, for it will often happen that our Lord, when chastising the wicked, will mix the good with them and make them suffer and endure (cf. *Matt.* 5:45). We have the people of Israel who were punished for their misdeeds: God chased and banished them from the land he had promised them as an inheritance (cf. *2 Kings* 24-25).

Yes, but was not Daniel, one of the three outstanding righteous, carried away with his companions? (Cf. Ezek. 14:14.) And then there is Jeremiah, who is chased into Egypt (cf. *Jer.* 43:6-7). And then there is Ezekiel, who was carried off into Babylon (cf. *Ezek.* 1:1-3; 24:15-27). And there are others: Ezra (cf. *Ezra* 7:6), Nehemiah (cf. *Ezra* 2:2; *Neh.* 1), Joshua, the high priest who returned (*Ezra* 2:1-2; 3:2). We see Zerubbabel and his father, Shealtiel (cf. *Ezra* 2:2; 3:2). All those were children of God and walked in fear of him. They possessed some integrity of life. How is it then that they are punished impartially with the wicked? It seems that God cut them off from his people and cursed them because that condemnation also falls on their heads. 'The land will spew out its inhabitants because you have polluted it with your contagion and the corruption that rages there. I had dedicated it and consecrated it to my service, and you have completely corrupted it with your iniquities. Therefore will it spew you out like filth' (cf. *Lev.* 18:25, 28; 20:22). Now that, as I said, will be Daniel's lot. Thus it would not seem that the argument Abraham advances would be appropriate: 'Lord would you destroy the righteous with the wicked?'

Now let us note that God has diverse ways to perform his judgments, for sometimes he will spare the wicked because of the good, even though the good are small in number among them, and we will see it in this text, as it will be dealt with later in its place, for everything cannot be said at once inasmuch as God delays exacting vengeance on those who despise his majesty when there are good people among them. At another time, he will punish the good along with the bad, but that does not mean he does not make a distinction between them in the privacy of his counsel. It is true that to the eye they endure as the others do and their condition will not seem to be better, and sometimes even the best will be dealt with more severely than the wicked who are totally reprobate. He will give them good times and they will take advantage of his patience. And that is why it is said that judgment begins with the house of the Lord (cf. *1 Pet.* 4:17). So unbelievers enjoy life and clearly mock God and scorn his majesty under the false impression that he does not touch them even with his little finger; but they convince themselves that they are on good terms with him and promise themselves peace and assurance, as it is said in Isaiah, as if they had plotted with death, having an understanding with the grave to say: 'Even though the flails and storms pass over the whole earth, they will be exempted from them' (cf. *Isa.* 28:15). Yet there is God's poor church, which will be afflicted and persecuted until the end, and it will seem that God wants to pour out all his wrath on it.

Therefore, not only will the good be mingled among the wicked, but what is more, he will take the good and chastise them to show them that he does not intend to allow them to be lost. Yet he will allow the sins of unbelievers to remain asleep, as it were. So we see how God's judgments are diverse, but the good are always under God's protection whatever the circumstances. It is true on the one hand that when he punishes them among the wicked, he finds a reason within them to punish them. Daniel, as I said, is praised by the prophet Ezekiel (cf. *Ezek.* 14:14). And it is even from the Holy Spirit that the witness comes that he is among the three most righteous whom God names. Even so, he confesses that he was banished notably from the land of Judea. It is not only said that he confessed his sins in a disordered way, as do many out of hypocrisy, but he says that he confessed his sins and those of the people. So God will always find something to reproach in the best and most saintly. Even so, he does not wish to punish them for their faults, but he punishes them because they are mixed among the whole. And on that point it is said that God makes them profit from his punishments because he converts it all into medicine.

About that, we must note two passages from the Psalms, where it is said in one: 'Lord, remember me with the good pleasure that you have toward your people and in the free favour you bear them' (cf. *Psa.* 106:4); and then the other passage: 'Lord, do not punish me in the day of the wicked' (cf. *Psa.* 6:1). Now the prophet, on the one hand, beseeches God to remember him so that, as he says, 'Let me participate in the favour you bear your people out of love for them' (cf. *Psa.* 106:4). For even though God shows himself severe toward the church, he still declares that his mercy will never depart from them, as he also says in this passage: 'I will punish their transgressions with the rod, but my mercy will never depart from them' (cf. *Psa.* 89:33-34). And, to the contrary, in another passage the prophet requests: 'Lord, do not punish me among the wicked' (cf. *Psa.* 28:3), as if he were saying: 'Let not the chastisements that you send upon me be mortal.' So we see the distinction God knows how to make when things appear to be confusing. For, as we have already said, he will deal more severely with his church than with the unbelievers. Why? Because they are his children (cf. *Prov.* 3:12), and he chastises them first. Sometimes we will see such desolation that it will seem he has rejected his elect, but he always knows his own and preserves them. And if he deals with them harshly, he gives them the strength to bear their afflictions patiently (cf. *Rom.* 5:3; *2 Cor.* 1:4). He consoles them by his Holy Spirit (cf. *John* 14:26), and that is worth much more than if they were at ease. So whatever afflictions the good endure, our Lord gladdens their hearts and gives them but a small taste of his paternal love, as if to say: 'Still will I not fail to be your Saviour.' When they have that, they have an inestimable good.

In fact, it is like threshing grain in the barn. The flail passes over the straw and over the grain. Both grain and straw are struck, but afterwards the wheat is gathered up and the straw is thrown on the dunghill. And then the wheat is winnowed. It is thrown into the air to remove the useless straw, but the grain is preserved. Thus our Lord will cause the flails to pass over the good, who are like the good grain; and he will also cause the wicked to undergo the same, like the straw, and on the face of it everything will be confused, but the outcome will show he has not forgotten his own. So that comparison is true when it is well understood. God would have to renounce himself if he destroyed the good along with the wicked. Why? He chose them and poured out his favours upon them to show he considers them to be his children. And then he has to love righteousness. So he will always keep the good and will be obliged to condemn the wicked, for he hates iniquity. And that is natural to him, as we have said. But we must understand this word 'destroy' in the sense that we stated.

This, then, is the instruction we have to glean from this passage: when everything seems to us to be upside down and heaven and earth are confused, we must nonetheless remain steadfast in our conviction that God will always protect his own (cf. *1 Sam.* 2:9; *Psa.* 12:7; *John* 17:11). He knows them and will never forget them. Then we have to apply that, each of us to the extent we can. We must not only glorify God, confessing that he is righteous and equitable, but we must also be patient and humble ourselves under his mighty hand so we will be helped to bear our burden when the time comes. How then can we be patient and bear with all humility the corrections he sends us? And whenever we trust him to be our guarantee (cf. *Heb.* 7:22), he has the means to pull us from the pits whenever we fall into them. Why? Because he forgives us of all of our faults and accepts us as righteous. We must not imagine any righteousness in ourselves which would obligate God to us, but we must find our righteousness in our Lord Jesus Christ and make him our shield and guarantee (cf. *Psa.* 3:3; 18:2; *Prov.* 30:5).

So when the Holy Spirit seals in our hearts the witness that God has adopted us as his children (cf. *Eph.* 1:5) and given us a sense of fearing him and of serving him, let us know that we have the guarantee of our adoption (cf. *1 Cor.* 1:22) and know that he wants to be our Father and Saviour and that the inheritance of eternal life cannot be taken from us (cf. *Col.* 3:24; *1 Pet.* 1:4). And this is how we must hope. When it appears to us that things are lost, that only death is before us, let us continue to wait for God to make a distinction between us and the unbelievers and reprobate. Why? Because it is otherwise impossible. For he would have to renounce himself, as I said. And that is how our salvation is based on God's eternal essence. And even though it sometimes seems our salvation is shaken, he will not let it fall all the way, but he will lead us to his goal and demonstrate that he can finish the work he has begun. That, then, is what we have to remember about this point.

Now when Abraham says: 'Lord, fifty righteous will be found,' he does not mean that there exists an angelic perfection in those fifty so that God might have no occasion to punish them, but he means that they are not people who are given to excessive vices. Why? He had heard this comment: 'to see whether they have reached the height of sin; if not, I will know it' (cf. *Gen.* 18:21). So he calls those 'righteous' who are not possessed by Satan, who have not abandoned themselves to despising God and rejecting his yoke, but who still have some good seed in them and desire to do good and live their lives in obedience. Now he says: 'Is it possible fifty will be found?' There is no doubt that he advances that number to induce God to exercise pity. Now one could ask a question here since Abraham presumes to be more humane and more piteous than God, who is the fountain of all goodness and mercy (cf. *Psa.* 33:5; 103:11). So it appears that Abraham is here attributing more to himself than is permissible, for when God declares what kind of God he is, he says: 'I am the patient God, long-suffering, gentle, kind, and merciful' (cf. *Exod.* 34:6-7; 20:6; *Jer.* 3:12). Will that be found among men? It is true that if we are sons of God, we must partially resemble him, but the resemblance is like a drop of water in the sea. And we are still much less so in comparison with God, for it is impossible to minimize ourselves too much when we compare ourselves to the infinite fullness of his goodness.

So it would seem that Abraham had elevated himself by foolish pride when he usurped God's office, for he wishes to show mercy to the people of Sodom and Gomorrah. How? Will he surpass God in goodness, as we said? He takes nothing unto himself. He leaves everything in God's hand. He only shows that he has pity on and compassion for those who are perishing. For when we ask God every day to have pity on his church and even when we pray for the wicked, it is not that we presume to surpass God in goodness and pity; but it is rather to testify that we are in accord with him as his children, for he offers himself also as an example when he says: 'I cause my sun to shine upon the good and the wicked; you must be like me in that respect, loving not only the good but also the wicked, who are not worthy of it, and seeking to gain their salvation (cf. *Matt.* 5:44-45). So that is the kind of person Abraham was. He did not think he was kinder than God or more piteous, but he wanted to declare his disposition, that he was kind, as if to say: 'Lord, behold, you have imprinted in my heart that feeling of love that I must have for my neighbours. They are your creatures, created in your image. They are my brothers. They are of the same flesh and the same lump of clay. Since that is true, Lord, I will now take the liberty to pray for them.' That, in summary, is what we have to remember.

So how are we to follow our father Abraham's example? We must have compassion on all those who are perishing and try to intercede for them and be their advocates before God—not, as I have said, that we have more pity than he who is its fountain—and try to make known that we are his children when we endeavour to conform to him and his will.

Now Abraham had several special reasons for being moved to such pity to intercede in favour of the people of Sodom. In the first place, he was sorely tested because he had delivered them not long ago and could himself judge that the war he had undertaken was cursed by God: 'What? For whom did I go to that trouble? For devils. It looks like I took the sword in hand and armed my people and neighbours to battle against God.' So Abraham could have been tested by that. Now he preferred to be inclined in the other direction. In other words, he did not think that God wanted to deliver them by his hand, that he still had not realized some good. So his thought was: 'By using me, God helped the people of Sodom. He gave me the victory. Could it be that God granted me such a favour and now no longer sees in them anything but iniquity, as in hell?' So because of that victory God gave him, he thinks the people of Sodom are not so completely hopeless.

That is how he practises what was later written by Paul, namely, that love is not suspicious (cf. *1 Cor.* 13:4-5). For even though we hear that the world is given to excess, we still must not judge by comparison, but we must rather hope that those who are like ferocious animals today can be returned to the right path and that if we do not see a single good one, there may be a hundred who are hidden from us. And in fact, Elijah thought he was alone in his time and thought that everyone had abandoned God's service. And yet the answer given to him was that there were still seven thousand who had not bowed the knee to Baal, although he did not know who they were (cf. *1 Kings* 19:10, 18). Consequently, we are always to remember that God keeps some seed which are hidden from us and that he will still be able to put his hand on those who are like lost people and remake them. That is how God judges with love those who were half devils, so to speak. Therefore, let us learn from his example to have hope for those who are still alive, and let us avoid preventing God from showing mercy on those on whom he is pleased to show mercy, and let us pray for the worst and the most depraved until God shows they are totally cut off without any hope.

Now let us bow before the majesty of our gracious God in acknowledgment of our faults, praying that he will not only grant us the grace to examine ourselves without any pretence but also to profit from the examples he gives us. And let us learn, because he is a righteous judge, not to provoke his wrath and to serve him in such a way that he accepts our obedience, even though it is imperfect, and may he show us such kindness and clemency that he will always keep us as his children. And when it pleases him to afflict us, let us bow our necks, subjecting ourselves to him in all humility and praying that he will cause us to profit from his corrections to cleanse us of all of our wicked affections until he has fully removed them from us. May he grant that grace not only to us but to all the peoples and nations on earth.

88

God Reveals Only What We Need to Know

Saturday, 20 April 1560

Peradventure there be fifty righteous within the city: wilt thou also destroy and not spare the place for the fifty righteous that are therein? That be far from thee to do after this manner, to slay the righteous with the wicked: and that the righteous should be as the wicked, that be far from thee: Shall not the Judge of all the earth do right? And the LORD *said, If I find in Sodom fifty righteous within the city, then I will spare all the place for their sakes. And Abraham answered and said, Behold now, I have taken upon me to speak unto the Lord, which am but dust and ashes: Peradventure there shall lack five of the fifty righteous: wilt thou destroy all the city for lack of five? And he said, If I find there forty and five, I will not destroy it. And he spake unto him yet again, and said, Peradventure there shall be forty found there. And he said, I will not do it for forty's sake. And he said unto him, Oh let not the Lord be angry, and I will speak: Peradventure there shall thirty be found there. And he said, I will not do it, if I find thirty there. And he said, Behold now, I have taken upon me to speak unto the Lord: Peradventure there shall be twenty found there. And he said, I will not destroy it for twenty's sake. And he said, Oh let not the Lord be angry, and I will speak yet but this once: Peradventure ten shall be found there. And he said, I will not destroy it for ten's sake. And the* LORD *went his way, as soon as he had left communing with Abraham: and Abraham returned unto his place* (Gen.18:24-33).

*W*E SAW YESTERDAY that although we have many troubling thoughts and cannot get rid of them, we must be firmly resolved that God is righteous and that we cannot be shaken from that truth, for otherwise the devil will always have tricks to pull us in every direction and we will be fighting against God at every turn without being aware of it. And in order to be assured of God's righteousness, let us think about what is said here, namely, that God's essence is not without effectiveness but that, as God, he is also the standard of all equity and uprightness, of all wisdom. All power belongs to him because he is worthy and his majesty conveys it. Consequently, when we think about God, we must not deprive him of what is proper to him. Since many people will confess rather easily that there is a God, they do not know him because they only imagine him as a phantom. So when someone speaks to us about God, let us think of him as inseparable from his essence, that is, from his righteousness, his wisdom, and power, and all that coheres in him in his fullness. With that in mind, even though our minds are confused because we are ignorant and weak, we will always conclude that our ignorance is no reason to diminish God's perfection in any way.

That is also why David, even though he felt he was lost, declares that whatever happens to him, God will be justified in what he says and be victorious when he judges (cf. *Psa.* 51:4). It is not a matter of speaking about others here. David is not chatting leisurely or babbling on in the shade, but speaking after being summoned to receive a sentence of condemnation for the egregious crime he had committed in murdering Uriah after taking his wife in adultery and exposing him as prey to God's army (cf. *2 Sam.* 11). After realizing that, he finds himself very frightened, but no matter, God must, he says, be justified in everything he says and be victorious when he judges.

Now, that victory of God which David speaks of occurs not only because he is the most powerful but also because it is acknowledged that everything he does is good and well governed; not that God borrows his governance from somewhere else, but that he cannot fail in any of his works. These two things are joined together. In other words, God is justified, that is, declared righteous and known to be so, and he is victorious when men condemn him, that is, when men are so filled with pride, indeed so enraged, that they wish to bring a case against him with the intent to condemn him, as Paul also concludes from that passage (cf. *Rom.* 3:4). And in fact we see the audacity of mortal men, for at every turn they want God to be inferior to them. They experience that madness and temerity, or rather that rage, and in spite of themselves God will maintain his righteousness and make it known and cause those who try to work against it to confess it when they are convicted of it.

Let us not expect our Lord to constrain us in spite of ourselves to confess that he is righteous, but we attribute to him the praise he deserves. And, as I have said, when we have many divergent thoughts, may our faith still adhere to the principle that everything in God is perfect.

Now this has greater impact when God is called Judge of the world (cf. *Psa.* 94:2), for it shows that to him alone belongs all authority so that we will not presume to make ourselves judges. And Paul also exhorts the faithful not to go beyond their authority by judging one another. We must, he says, all find ourselves before the judgment seat of our Lord Jesus Christ (cf. *Rom.* 14:10). So you, who are you to judge your brother? It is as if he were saying: 'If we wish to judge by our understanding and imagination, thinking, "That seems good to me," that is bad, and if we have no word of God on which to stand, we, by that very fact, usurp God's authority and make ourselves idols.' Such will not be our intention, but the deed demonstrates it. Why? God preserves for himself alone the pre-eminence to judge us. And we must pass that way and appear before his seat and keep our mouths shut in order to hear what he is pleased to proclaim. So now when we forget our humility and would like our opinion to be believed, is that not the same as putting ourselves in God's place? So let us note that when it is said that God is Judge of the world and that we are to walk according to our station in life and not take into our own hands the authority to judge which resides in the one who possesses all majesty in himself. That, then, is what we have to remember about this passage.

Now that teaching is even better confirmed by the comparison Abraham makes here when he says: 'Alas, I am but dust and ashes, and yet I presume to speak with my Lord.' It is not enough to know that God is to judge us and that he is so good and just and wise that nothing can be found to criticize him for, but at the same time we must consider who he is and what our status and condition are; for until we do, there will be within us some pride and foolishness that will exalt us more than is permitted. So what Abraham does is consider who he is. And that is why he calls himself dust and ashes.

Paul also brings us to that point and he wishes to repress that diabolical haughtiness which is characteristic of men when they do not wish to subject themselves to God and receive all that Scripture teaches about his wondrous and incomprehensible secret councils. For if we wish to speak about election, which surpasses all human understanding inasmuch as it is a thing which seems strange to us because God, before the creation of the world, predestined to salvation those whom he was pleased to choose and also condemned and dismissed to internal condemnation those whom he did not wish to choose. If we follow our own imaginations, it is certain we will never stop making a case against God. Now Paul, to put an end to that, says: 'You, O man, who are you?' (Cf. *Rom.* 9:20.) When he says 'O man,' in that word he includes all that anyone could say to humble us, as if he were saying: 'Put on one side of the scales your condition and, on the other, the majesty and incomprehensible glory of your God. What do you find there except God? You are obliged to be completely delighted. The angels of paradise are constrained to lower their eyes when they worship their Creator (cf. *Rev.* 7:11). What then does that mean for you? Can you understand that wisdom, you who are man? And if you cannot understand it, must you intrude your insolent back talk to keep God from judging the way he knows is expedient and to oppose his sovereign power to say that must not be so because your mind cannot tolerate it? Is that not an enraged fury?' That, then, is the instruction you have to gather from this passage where Abraham says he is but dust and ashes.

Now it is true that Abraham knew his soul was immortal and that man is comprised of two parts, that is, his body, which is only dust and decay, and spirit, which is immortal because God imprinted upon it his image. But he takes what is in himself contemptible, as Scripture teaches us, and gives us that precept as if he were saying: 'Alas, it is true God made me a rational creature and placed me in a position higher than the animals, but, in brief, I nonetheless inhabit this mortal body, which is only dust and mire, and hence I am only rot and decay' (cf. *Gen.* 2:7; 3:19; *Eccles.* 3:20). That, then, is Abraham's state of mind.

In addition, let us note that Scripture, with good cause, humbles us by showing us the frailty in our bodies so that we have good reason to glory in our souls. Why? So we can contemplate in our bodies the condition of our souls, which would otherwise be hidden and unknown, for we are so devoted to our earthly affections that, even though there is some reason to distinguish between good and evil, we are nonetheless more given to excess than brute beasts until God governs us by his Holy Spirit, just as he rightly said above: 'I will no longer strive with men, for they are flesh' (cf. *Gen.*

6:3). That is also the same as comparing them with donkeys and oxen (cf. *Isa.* 1:3), as if he were saying: 'There is only flesh, and if they have some rationality and some ability to distinguish between right and wrong, it is to make them even more inexcusable. Even animals restrained their desires to some extent, but human desires are insatiable gulfs and are like the Furies, who pervert every order of nature.' So because we cannot see the poverty in our souls right away, we must begin with our bodies and know that we are taken from the earth and that a little bit of nothing can annihilate us. And from that point let us realize that indeed our souls inhabit these bodies and, although they have a heavenly origin, they now nonetheless are so corrupt with our perverse desires that what we think is clear to us is only pure stupidity. And then what we think we have related to judgment and discrimination is only enmity with God and rebellion against his righteousness. That is what we have to realize.

When it is said in Scripture that every man is flesh and is called dust and ashes (cf. *Gen.* 3:19; *Job* 30:19; *Psa.* 78:39; 103:14), let us not understand that as referring to man simply as body, but that we are greatly blinded by pride and arrogance and that God wishes to advance our understanding by the body, which is visible to us. For example, we have Isaiah saying that man is only grass and that even though he seems to have vigour in himself for a time, he is like a green herb or a flower which will soon wither (cf. *Isa.* 40:6-8). If the wind but blow upon the grass, it turns to fodder, or if the grass is cut, it immediately dries. Thus man has nothing to do with it, and yet it must all disappear. On the surface it would seem that only bodies were spoken of, but what is added shows that anything excellent and worthy in men is included. Why? The word of God, as the prophet says, lasts eternally (cf. *Isa.* 40:8). If the prophet had only wanted to crush the pride which is in us by showing that our bodies are subject to corruption and decay, he would not have brought in God's word. There is immortality in the soul, but he shows that everything is weak, and even if the soul had no immortality of itself, it has it from God.[1] Furthermore, what it has will be for its greatest condemnation when God wishes to blow upon it.

So what is shown here is that all our certainty and vigour consist in God and that God communicates to us through his word what is required for our salvation, as Peter, a faithful expositor of this passage, points out: the word of God is the incorruptible seed which we possess (cf. *1 Pet.* 1:23). Such is true for other passages, as when the life of man is compared to a shadow, as when it is said that man is but flesh, a wind that passes away, not to return (cf. *Psa.* 78:39). It is certain that the Holy Spirit includes in that comparison all the faculties and all the virtues which we are accustomed to boast of. So let us note that when Abraham calls himself 'dust and ashes,' it is the same as confessing that he is nothing. Thus when we consider the frailty that is in our bodies, we will understand that we are subject to many illnesses, and then inasmuch as we are indolent in this world and death awaits us and swallows us up, let us realize that if there are great deficiencies that we perceive with our eyes, those which we do not see are even greater, and let us give that close attention so that not a single speck of pride or presumption will remain in us. That, in brief, is how we must use that teaching.

We also need to observe the situation because the more Abraham approaches God, the more he is led to humble himself. Why do men, making themselves believe they are wonderful, take pride in their worth or their godly lives, or you name it? And there are even many, even a majority, so foolish and mindless that they find grounds for boasting of their wealth, their heritage, their good

---

[1] If the soul is immortal, it is nonetheless created. Cf. *Institutes* I, xv , 2, 5. Calvin here opposes those who affirmed that the soul was immortal by means of its own power, particularly the neo-Platonists.—*M.E.*

reputation and dignity. What is the reason for all that? It is because they do not draw near to God and give him any consideration. For as long as we remain here below in this life and have our affections attached to things created, those things dazzle us because we find in ourselves something to esteem and we always have some foolish notion of ourselves. But when we come to God, at that moment everything vanishes. That, then, is good and useful information if we know how to use it to our advantage: for it is when we are tempted by vainglory and ambition to boost our reputation that, in order to erase everything, to correct it and destroy it, we say: 'Alas, and when I appear before my God, how will I be able to stand there? His majesty causes the mountains to flow as if they were only snow or butter; it splits the rocks asunder (cf. *Nahum* 1:6). And how can it cast me into the abyss a hundred thousand times when I am there before him? What constancy is there within me? What worth?' That, I say, is what can reduce a man to strict humility to bring him to obedience to God so he does not deceive himself by arrogance. And that is when he will know that God is at work within him. For, as I have said, it is at that time they will be stripped of everything they might conjure up to exalt and magnify themselves. That, then, is what happened to Abraham.

In fact, that is also why Isaiah says the angels of paradise hide their faces when they are in God's presence because they cannot bear his majesty, which would dazzle them (cf. *Isa.* 6:2). If the angels of paradise are brought to that understanding, what must that mean for us by comparison? For we must always return to the realization that we are but dust and ashes (cf. *Gen.* 18:27). All the more must we practise that teaching, for it is the main point of our wisdom. We are to ponder the kind of people we are so we will scorn ourselves.[2]

[2] It is characteristic of Calvinist theology to exalt man's scorn for himself (to love oneself is denounced as a 'deadly plague'; cf. *Institutes* III, vii, 1, 4), until the moment he is, for the *n*th time, lifted up and enlightened by God's wisdom and goodness.—*M.E.*

It is true that we are to hold in high regard the gifts of God which are conferred on us so we will give him the praise he deserves; but it is not a matter of our keeping back a smidgen of it to say that we are to be esteemed. For the very good things that God bestows upon us will make us more confused because we abuse them. But after we are reduced to nothing, after we attribute to him everything without depriving him of his right, and after we confess his power, it is certain that power will support and sustain us. For God abases us, not to abandon us, but to lift us up to himself so that we will know that he alone is all powerful. For when we confess God's power and righteousness, they will be like intellectual concepts for us unless we are first stripped of any righteousness we think we have in ourselves. The same is true of our reason and wisdom as long as we choose to give too much liberty to our own competencies and usurp for ourselves a part of God's honour. So we must rid ourselves of that and be enlightened by God's wisdom. And being blind, we will see much more clearly than when we think we understand what surpasses our understanding. That much for this passage.

Now here it might seem at first that Abraham used too much subtlety and even cavilled with God when he reduced the number from few to small to arrive at ten. It is as if he wanted to prove something false by a clever trick by saying: 'There is a man who is ten thousand crowns rich. Will he be impoverished if ten are taken from him, for he would still possess a large sum?' And then later when we say: 'If ten are taken from him, what is that?' And after that, we say little by little that he will not be impoverished if we take from him some amount or other. In the end, by gradual reduction, he who was ten thousand crowns rich has lost everything.

It seems Abraham proceeds that way and says: 'If five men were taken from fifty, would the city perish?' And when the answer is no, he moves to forty. And then he reduces the number by ten and says: 'And if thirty were found?' He reduces the number even more and arrives at twenty and finally at ten. When he bargains that way, it seems, as I said, he wanted, with subtlety, to catch God off guard. But we have already seen both the reverence he had for God and his humility. So what he proposes to God here with forty and thirty and twenty proceeds unquestionably from his earnestness. He did not wish to use eloquence and disguise his cause with fine words, but he was moved, and almost astonished he speaks and proposes what seemingly comes to him out of nowhere. That, then, is the primary thing we have to remember.

We have to learn this, as we touched upon yesterday, that Abraham possessed an amazing love because he had such concern for those who were already condemned by God's mouth, not that he wanted to dispute what he had heard, but because he realized they were human beings. And then he knew about the grace God had shown them recently. Afterwards, he remembered that they were created by God in his image and likeness (cf. *Gen.* 1:26). That, then, is why he is deeply moved with compassion and does not stop trying to gain their salvation until he sees there is no longer a remedy, for at that moment he stopped asking (cf. *Gen.* 18:32-33), as we will soon see.

In addition, if Abraham had such a concern upon seeing the threat which was made against Sodom, must we not in our day be moved when we realize that everything is so perverted that iniquity is taking over everywhere like a flood? For we must not wait for God to reveal from heaven that he will lash out against the iniquities which have grown so enormous. We have his law, which thoroughly threatens those who are contemptuous of his righteousness. We see that the whole earth is filled to overflowing with them. That ought to move us to groan and pray unceasingly that God will be pleased to have pity on our poor world despite its corruption and that he will show his customary mercy by removing from perdition the definitively lost so that they may be exempted from the final vengeance, from which they will not otherwise be able to escape. That is what we have to remember.

Let us all the more be moved to pray to God since Abraham's prayer was answered up to six times and God supported him when he wanted to intercede for Sodom and Gomorrah that way, and let us know that our sighs and groanings will also be acceptable to God when we have pity on the poor sinners we see on the way to destruction. If in any and all respects we do not obtain all our requests, that act of worship will still be approved by God. And we have even greater reason to pray if it was said that Sodom and the neighbouring cities would be spared if God should find in them ten righteous men. When we pray for the poor church in which God has his seed and the trees he planted with his own hand, that is, the elect, whom he protects, let us realize that we do not pray in vain when we pray for the church, that our love will not be disappointed, and that our Lord will stay his hand and show pity and mercy,[3] although he is close to displaying horrible vengeance according as the great majority give themselves over to excess and provoke him.

Yet let us note what is said when God stopped speaking to Abraham and withdrew and Abraham returned to the tent in which he lived, for in these words Moses signifies that Abraham finally acquiesced, not wishing to strive further, seeing that God had supported him with an inestimable favour and permitted him to unburden his heart with such familiarity. So Abraham remains there silent. The reason? Because God stopped speaking. And the conclusion is that if God found ten in Sodom, the city would still not be destroyed. Not that God obligated himself by that concession to a perpetual law; for it is said of Jerusalem that if there were three righteous men, each of them would save his own

[3] The other pole of Calvin's preaching is God's mercy, patience, and pity toward the elect.—*M.E.*

life, but the wicked would not fail to perish (cf. *Ezek.* 14:12–23). So we see that God did not bind himself forever to do what he had done to Sodom and Gomorrah, but he wanted to show one time how much he prized Abraham's requests. There is no doubt that in doing that he wanted to testify how much he loved him so that Abraham would lean more confidently on his goodness. So it was very necessary, on the one hand, that God be constant, for it is not without reason that God tells him beforehand about the execution of Sodom. For still today and even until the end of the world, we have a mirror of God's vengeance in what was done to those cities. But also, on the other hand, Abraham had to be persuaded that God had taken him under his protection so that he would be assured that if the entire world should be swallowed up and lightning from heaven should strike in all places, God would preserve him because he had taken him under his care.

Now what remains significant here is that God stopped speaking. With that, Moses shows us that it is not our place to cause God to speak at our pleasure, but that he will speak when he pleases and also stop, and then we must restrain ourselves. And that is what we talked about yesterday when we said we need a bridle, seeing that our minds are so curious that when we grant them great liberty, they are insatiable. And we also see what happens to those who want God to satisfy them. You will find lamebrains who do not have the slightest idea about the Lord's Prayer who nonetheless want to raise profound questions. And if you ask them: 'Do you know how to pray to God?' They answer: 'Oh, I do not know.' In any case, there you have some poor dumb animals! Yet they come and propose obscure matters about which they understand nothing. And if you then advise them of their duty and quote for them the witness of Scripture to exhort them to sober judgment and say: 'Wait until the last day, for now we must see in part and dimly (cf. *I Cor.* 13:9-12). And when our Lord makes us participants in his glory (cf. *1 Pet.* 5:1), we will then see him as he is, as John says (cf. *1 John* 3:2); and at that time we will know face to face what is hidden' (cf. *1 Cor.* 13:12). If you answer them that way, they say: 'Oh, I am not satisfied with that'; or else if you give them a solution using holy Scripture, teaching what God says and declaring that we must stop at what he says, they say: 'Oh, that cannot satisfy me.' There you have some agitated brains without an ounce of reason, and yet they want God to satisfy them. How? Their folly, their arrogance, and their curiosity resemble an enraged animal. And how will God be able to satisfy them? And that is where they are. And there is not one of us who would not proceed impetuously if we were not restrained.

Let us remember the lesson Paul gives us not to seek to know more than we are allowed to know, but to think soberly (cf. *Rom.* 12:3). It is notably for that reason that it is said that God stopped speaking. Abraham did not, though not by his choice, but Moses shows that when God stopped, the decision was his and that it was within his pure and free discretion to speak and answer Abraham, but he was not subject to him and there was no need that compelled him to speak. Thus, men must not think too highly of themselves and say to God: 'You must answer me and satisfy me,' for God preserved for himself alone the right to speak and to stop speaking when it pleases him.

Now we have to relate that to holy Scripture, for it is certain that in it God has told us everything that is necessary for our salvation. It is with good reason that Moses says about the law: 'This is your wisdom and understanding' (cf. *Deut.* 4:6), and the way to teach at that time was very obscure. Even more so ought the law to be our wisdom and understanding today since we have all perfection of wisdom in the gospel, as Paul also says in Colossians.[4] Thus there is no doubt that our Lord displayed his treasures in Scripture

[4] Cf. Colossians 3:14-16, which Calvin compresses greatly.—*M.E.*

because they were useful for us. But that is not to say we will find in Scripture everything that fits our fanciful imagination, and it is not to say that all our doubts will be resolved. For if we were to collect the questions that men raise, it is certain we would have an endless stream, but God considered what was profitable for us. That is also why Paul calls Scripture profitable (cf. *2 Tim.* 3:16), namely, it is to show us that God did not want to satisfy our ears and that he did not want to reveal in detail everything we want to know, but he considered what was good and advantageous for us. But what are we to do for our advantage? Heed what edifies, says Paul, when he speaks of prophecy and shows why Christians are to assemble, not to show off, not to be admired for being clever and having a deep understanding, but to consider what edifies, for we must adhere to that simple fact (cf. *1 Cor.* 14). And that is how we have to practise this teaching in which it is said that when God stopped speaking to Abraham, he departed, as if to say that ought to be enough for us. And if we do not find in Scripture some revelation about all the things we would like to know about, those questions must be suppressed when God stops speaking.

Now it is not only said that God stopped speaking, but that he departed. And when God leaves, it is no longer a matter of proceeding or of engaging in a dispute, for when we are in an unknown country and there is neither sun nor moon and we are in deep darkness and cannot see a single road or distinguish between water and land, if we walk in that place, we will no doubt stumble and break our necks or drown in rivers or ditches. Thus, when God leaves, it is certain we are deprived of all light. Do we want to run in the darkness? We will, as I said, break our necks in our arrogance. Therefore, let us note this word that God departed.

And that is also why Moses adds that Abraham returned to his tent. So we must learn to remain in our status and do nothing more than bear the measure of our faith (cf. *Rom.* 12:3; *Eph.* 4:7), and we must remember it is God who will distribute to us what pleases him. In any case, while we are in the world, we must be instructed by him and be increasingly conformed to what he knows to be our good. In addition, let us wait for the day of full revelation, that is, for the time we are remade and are no longer of the earth. That is something else we have to remember.

Now let us return to what Moses recounts about God. Up until this point, generally speaking, we have shown that we must be such school children of God that his teaching is sufficient for us. It now remains for us to know what teaching is contained in this place, that is, on the one hand, God shows that he is righteous and will not allow the iniquities of those who are completely incorrigible to remain unpunished; and on the other he shows he is nonetheless full of pity, kind, meek, and long-suffering (cf. *Exod.* 34:6-7; *1 Pet.* 3:15). And that is principally what we are shown, as we see even in this vision Moses had. For that vision must serve us as a pattern when it comes to inquiring what is to be known about God, for it is certain he showed himself in a singular fashion at that time, wanting this to be a pattern to guide to such knowledge and understanding as we can have in this world. So when Moses asked him to appear to him, he says: 'You will see my back, but you cannot yet look upon me face to face' (cf. *Exod.* 33:22), for it is said that we must be remade and completely changed if we are to recognize the glory of God, which is still hidden from us (*1 John* 3:2). Now Moses was privileged above all others, but he still only saw God from behind (cf. *Exod.* 33:22), that is, only in part and not in his fullness. Yet he is told that God will show him his glory. How? By passing by. He says: 'I am your God, the everlasting God, who shows mercy to a thousand generations and am long-suffering, kind, and endure the poor sinners who convert to me. And yet none will remain innocent before me. Iniquities must be accounted for' (cf. *Exod.* 34:6-7). That much God declared to Abraham at this time.

721

So we must remember that teaching and take it with us everywhere we go, and let us so cling to our God's goodness that we will not put him to the test when we persist in our crimes and evil deeds, for he does not want us to abuse his patience in any case. And let us note that when it is said he is inclined to mercy, he exhorts us to repent immediately, for he did not forget who he is when he destroyed Sodom and Gomorrah. He had not yet told Moses what we have just recounted, but he was already such as he was. Yet that did not keep him from destroying those cities, for he was strongly resolved to do so. And they are given to us as examples, the apostle says, so that the fire of Sodom and Gomorrah is for us like a mirror of everlasting fire which is prepared for all those who despise God (cf. *2 Pet.* 2:6). So every time mention is made of that horrible execution, let us be repentant and confess our sins before God so that we will be able to sense the mercy which he presents before us. That, then, is in brief what we have to remember.

And as we go about our daily lives, let us always be submissive to the teaching which holy Scripture shows us so that we may trust in God, and, trusting in him, let us always hope to receive remission of our sins, and he will not fail to receive us, even though we are not worthy. But especially let us learn to fear him so we will not provoke his wrath against us. But, notwithstanding the grace and kindness he presents to us, let us not think that he has abandoned his office as Judge, but may that teach us to walk in greater fear before him. And when we hear him speak, let us remember what he has told us, and may that be locked in our memory so that it will serve as a guide for our entire lives until we reach the enjoyment of his infinite goodness, of which he only gives us a taste today.

Now let us bow before the majesty of our gracious God in acknowledgment of our faults, praying that he will be pleased to touch us more and more with true repentance and tolerate us in our infirmities and vices, not to encourage them but to cleanse us of them by his Holy Spirit until he has brought us in every respect into conformity with his holiness; and may he so withdraw us from the corruptions of this world that we will be truly joined and united with his angels, for he has been pleased to call us into one and the same salvation. May he grant that grace not only to us but to all the peoples and nations on earth.

89

Responsibility in Preventing the Prevalence of Evil

Monday, 29 April 1560

And there came two angels to Sodom at even; and Lot sat in the gate of Sodom: and Lot seeing them rose up to meet them; and he bowed himself with his face toward the ground; And he said, Behold now, my lords, turn in, I pray you, into your servant's house, and tarry all night, and wash your feet, and ye shall rise up early, and go on your ways. And they said, Nay; but we will abide in the street all night. And he pressed upon them greatly; and they turned in unto him, and entered into his house; and he made them a feast, and did bake unleavened bread, and they did eat. But before they lay down, the men of the city, even the men of Sodom, compassed the house round, both old and young, all the people from every quarter: And they called unto Lot, and said unto him, Where are the men which came in to thee this night? bring them out unto us, that we may know them (Gen. 19:1-5).

SINCE WE NEED to have God's grace preached to us daily so that we will learn to trust him and have our refuge in him, we also need to have his judgments placed before us so we will be kept restrained. For we see how inclined we are to evil unless the fear of God holds us back. Now inasmuch as we ourselves would be ready at every moment to fight against God, the first thing we need to know is that his power is fearful against those who scorn him (cf. *Ezra* 8:22). Let us also know that his office is to punish the faults and iniquities of men (cf. *Lev.* 26:41; *Psa.* 39:11; 89:32) and to call all things into account. Therefore, since we received a very useful instruction previously when Moses declared to us how God took care of his servant Abraham and afterward chose them, he continued to show his grace and goodness toward him; he now places the city of Sodom before us as a mirror so that we will have a horror of giving ourselves over to such evil deeds and to such great enormities (cf. *Gen.* 19:5), as we will see later that those cities were filled with them.

Moreover, even though the city of Sodom had reached such an extreme in all evils that we must loathe it, it can still serve us as an example, for it is not without cause that the prophets even compared the people of Jerusalem to those of Sodom (cf. *Isa.* 1:9; 13:19; *Jer.* 23:14; *Amos* 4:11). It is true that at first glance we would find that harsh, and there is no doubt that those to whom such harsh language was spoken were angry and that the prophets had undergone great abuse. For that severity cannot be endured by such a rebellious people without many denials and arguments. But in any case, the Spirit of God did not overstate the case when he cried out that way against the king and counsellors of Judea, against the most honourable people, against the priests, even against the governors of the people, and called them 'princes of Sodom and peoples of Gomorrah' (cf. *Isa.* 1:10). That is how the prophets spoke to the Jews.

Today we are no better than they were, for if we compare city with city, Jerusalem, which was the royal seat, which was even the holy place of God, the place where he had established his palace, which was like an earthly paradise, was it not much more than the noblest and most excellent cities in the world today? No city deserves to be as prized as Jerusalem was, not Rome, not any city in Europe or Asia. Yet we see how God speaks of it by the mouths of the prophets.

Ezekiel gives the reason. It is because the Jews could claim that they had not gone so far as to forget all natural uprightness and do worse than animals. 'True, true,' he says, speaking to the people as if to a woman, 'the iniquity of your sister Sodom, did she begin with that very vile and despicable crime? (Cf. *Ezek.* 16.) No, but their country was fat and fertile. They took to eating lavishly and indulging in every intemperance. And when they were quite drunk, their hand was tightly closed and they felt no pity or humaneness. The princes offered no help, but there was only cruelty and feeding on the poor, even gnawing out the marrow of their bones. They burned with greed; the ravaging thefts remained unpunished; and that is what pushed them beyond all wickedness. Therefore, look to yourself.'

So that is what we have to observe, namely, that in every case, God considers what is appropriate and useful for our instruction and is mindful of everything we need to draw us to himself. On the one hand, he invites us with all gentleness and kindness; he declares that he is the Father of all those who conform themselves to him (cf. *Deut.* 32:6; *Isa.* 22:21; *Jer.* 31:9). And of all that we have rather ample testimony above in the person of Abraham and in all his household and will have more even later. Now God has invited us gently because he sees we have a tendency to shake off the yoke and would go astray at every turn. Therefore, he proposes something for us to fear so that that will repress our unrighteous desires and so that we will not be rash and confront him and give ourselves a licence for every evil. He tells us we have good reason to tremble every time we think about the kind of vengeance he visited upon Sodom and the neighbouring cities. And as I have already said, let us not think that that is far removed from us, but let us realize that since God wanted that story to be left in writing for us, as the apostle also points out (cf. *Jude* 7), the city is to be like a general pattern that the Lord uses to show us his judgment, which is prepared for all the wicked and all those who despise his majesty, so that we will learn not to abuse his patience. That, then, is a warning we must heed if we are to take advantage of the story which is contained in the current chapter.

Now Moses begins with Lot's kind treatment of the angels. He says that the two angels came to Sodom while Lot was seated at the gate and, upon seeing them, went to meet them and bowed before them, which means that he lowered and inclined his head to the earth according to the custom of the country, and besought them to come lodge in his house. If you ask why two angels came to Sodom and three came to Abraham, we have already given a brief reason and what we can gather from it, for Scripture does not tell why three angels came to Abraham and only two to Lot. Those who say that two were sent to Sodom, one to deliver Lot and the other to destroy all of the cities there and rain fire upon them, make a grave mistake. For we will see how the two angels accompanied Lot when they made him leave the city (cf. *Gen.* 19:16). But there is nothing new in that, for God bestows his favours in such measure as it seems good to him. And we know that Abraham was privileged above the others inasmuch as he was father of the faithful (cf. *Rom.* 4:11-12; *Gal.* 3:7-9). So if God manifested himself to him more familiarly, we must not find it strange. What is more, although God sometimes sends his angels throughout the world to help unbelievers, who do not belong to the body of the church, our Lord Jesus Christ still wants to be the particular possession of those who believe in him. For he is also their Head.

We have seen that, of the three angels Abraham saw, one possessed greater dignity than the other two. Therefore, even though God declares the paternal love he has for Lot when he sends him his angels, that is not to say that Abraham was more recommended and even that he does not make himself known to him more privately in the person of our Lord Jesus Christ when he appears as an angel because he was to be like a mediator, not that he had taken on human flesh at the time, but he still had the office of being the Mediator between God and the angels because he is their Head as well as that of the faithful who live on the earth. So that is why Abraham was visited by God in a more singular manner and Lot continued to feel that God was favourable toward him and that he only needed two angels to come to him to remove him from that pit in which he was and also to make him escape that horrible condemnation which was near for all those cities.

Touching Moses' statement that Lot was seated at the gate, that does not mean we have to imagine, as some have done, that Lot came that evening to the gate to welcome the guests who were arriving in the city of Sodom, for there is no good basis for that; but it is possible he was waiting for his shepherds, as we have seen that he had a quantity of animals to feed (cf. *Gen.* 13:5-6). He could have had different occasions for being at the gate. Now when he entreated the angels, that was also possible, seeing some appearance of virtue in them; for we must not think that he bowed before each one of them and that he had entreated them to the point of annoyance, no. 'Sirs, you have before you a servant who will lodge you. Do me the honour of entering my house.' It is certain he would not have employed that language indiscriminately. So we have to note, as mentioned above in the story of Abraham (cf. *Gen.* 18:1-3), that Lot knew that these were uncommon people and that there was some virtue in them for which they deserved to be received and welcomed. That, then, is what moved him to show himself humble before them and cordially disposed to bring them into his house.

We also have to remember what the apostle said, namely, that because Lot dealt kindly with the strangers, God granted him the grace to receive the angels without thinking about it (cf. *Heb.* 13:2), for he did not consider them as angels of God: he would not have prepared food and drink for them, knowing that they had no need of it. Nonetheless, God does him the honour of lodging in his house in the person of his angels.

The same thing will not happen to us today, but the apostle's exhortation, nevertheless, is not useless. If God does not send his angels from heaven for us to lodge, it must be enough for us that Jesus Christ has declared that what we do to the least of the poor who come and ask us for aid and relief in his name, he considers it as done to himself, and that will enter into account as if he himself had received it (cf. *Matt.* 25:40). For it is not without reason that he says that in the last day he will call into the kingdom of God his Father those who have felt pity, those who have had compassion on the poor who were in dire need, indeed those who say: 'I was hungry and you gave me to eat. I was thirsty and you gave me to drink. I was cold and you warmed and clothed me. I was in prison and you visited me, and if one asks: "When, Lord? When did we do that for you?" be satisfied,' he says, 'that I allow into my accounts everything you do for the smallest who come to you in my name. It is as if I were presenting myself to you and cried out, requiring you to help me. So when you are thus kind and compassionate toward your neighbours, it is the same as if you had placed it in my hands' (cf. *Matt.* 25:35-37, 40). Solomon also says that God receives everything we can do that is good and helps those who suffer lack and poverty (cf. *Prov.* 19:17). That, then, is how the apostle leads us to the example of Abraham and Lot, who both received God's angels, even though they had not thought about it.

Now that informs us that when someone is in need, we must not consider whether or not he will be able to render us an equal service, for what return can we receive from a stranger who is passing through. We will never see him again. So it seems that what we do for him is completely lost. And then even though the poor are our neighbours, they do not have the means to compensate us when we have used up our substance and think we are diminished by as much. And that is also the reason many people are stingy, for they do not have God in mind. They are only and always considering men. Since Lot and Abraham had the honour of receiving the angels of paradise as their guests (cf. *Heb.* 12:2), when it is a matter today of being kind and generous toward those who suffer lack and indigence, the apostle tells us that we must not consider the status of this person or that and say: 'This person is not worth troubling with. What compensation can I expect from this poor wretch?' We must not think that way, but let us know that just as Lot and Abraham lodged the angels, God now also receives from us everything good that we can do. When we have that conviction well imprinted on our hearts, we know that what we do for the smallest and most despised of this world, God looks upon it as if we did it to the very person of his Son, to whom we owe everything. So that, in brief, is what we need to remember.

As it was shown above, according as our Lord allows us to know men, we must also note that we are to appreciate the gifts and spiritual qualities he placed in them. For who moved Lot to humble himself this way before those powerful men? He could indeed wag his head or take no notice, but he had high regard for them and honoured them. Why? It is certain that he was led to that reverence because he saw they were men endowed with excellent qualities and that God was dwelling in them. With that, we are admonished that, inasmuch as our Lord placed his qualities in men, we are to honour and respect them. For when we suppress the light by which he wants his glory to shine among men, such ingratitude is directed toward God. Making his glory shine can be practised in many ways. For when a man is lifted up by God's hand, so to speak, we must realize he wants us to use him. And if there are qualities

God placed in this or that person, they must be put to good use and manifested. But if we try to destroy them, as I have said, we do not trespass against mortal creatures but against the living God. Likewise, if God places valour and integrity in someone, we must hold that person in honour. As we read in Psalm 15, as we are to hate those who have contempt for God, although they are people of condition and influence and of the highest stations in the world, we are nonetheless only to be angry upon looking at them because they pollute the earth to the extent they can and obscure God's glory; we must nonetheless honour those through whom God presents himself to us, for that honour is not addressed to creatures but to the one who wishes to be glorified in their persons and who set a few glimmerings of his majesty to shine in them so that he might be recognized in them.

That then is what we have to remember regarding what is said about Lot when he humbled himself before those he had never seen and who he thought were passing through. He did not know they were angels from God, but he is nonetheless content to see people in whom there is some worth. We must not think that Lot was influenced by their riches, as pomp always dazzles us. Lot had a different and simpler consideration, namely, that he did not doubt these people were worthy of being received graciously. Therefore, he wanted to receive them into his house so that they would not be exposed to any shame or harm, for he knew that the city was unbridled and that if the travellers did not have some small shelter where they would be hidden, they could be subjected to many out-rageous and ignominious acts, which indeed happened, as we will see. That, in brief, is what we have to remember.

And there is also this point to note. When we see the wicked have taken such licence and been so bold that we cannot, despite all our efforts, repress them in any way, and since we do not have the ability or authority to punish them, let us at least oppose their evildoing and impede their satisfying their wicked desires. For God has many ways to help the good so that they will not be afflicted or oppressed. It is true he will not always use an armed hand to prevent someone from troubling or wronging us; even so, our Lord gives us the ability to provide refuge and comfort for those who could be tormented and trampled underfoot, whose being wronged we are to oppose if we have the means to help them, even though we may not have, as I said, the personal influence or the power to do so. That is what we are to remember about Lot's example.

Now it is certain he lodged the angels not only to give them something to eat and drink, but he was anticipating what could happen, namely, that they could encounter evil throughout the city because there was moral depravation there because every evil was permitted. For the people of Sodom thought they were free to make no distinction between good and evil. Consequently, Lot wanted to protect the travellers and preserve them from such injustices. And by his example we are instructed to do the same. And even though it is not by an armed hand or by authority, let us do so, but by peaceful means and such means as God orders us.

It is then said that he prepared food for them. So we have to remember what was stated above, namely, that the angels ate, not for any lack they might have had or for their nourishment, but because the time had not yet come for them to reveal they had descended from heaven. And we need not speculate here too cleverly, for inasmuch as God created bodies for these angels and caused them to live in human form here below for a brief period, he was also able to cause them to eat and drink, even though it was not for their sustenance. Their bodies, even though they were real, were not subject to feelings, but they took on and clothed the bodies for the sake of others, not their own. In any case, that did not prevent them from eating and drinking, as we pointed out earlier that Jesus Christ ate and drank after his resurrection despite the fact that he had departed this mortal life and was exempted from all the conditions to which we are now subject (cf. *Luke* 24:43; *John* 21:13-14; *Acts* 10:41). And if Moses, for the space of forty days (cf. *Exod.* 34:28), and also Elijah were without food and drink (cf. *1 Kings* 19:8), and Jesus Christ for a third (cf. *Mark* 1:13), when he began to preach and was raised above all the requirements of this frail life, it is certain that after his resurrection, he had no need to eat or drink, but he did so for the sake of his apostles and disciples so that they would know that he was not a phantom. So that is why the angels ate at this time. And if one asks: 'But for what purpose? And also for what purpose did they appear in human form?' God wanted it that way for the good and instruction of his servants. So we do not find what follows strange. So much, then, for that point.

At that point, Moses declares the condition of Sodom and says that when night came, all gathered together as if the tocsin had been rung, as we say, from every street corner and the ends of the city, great and small, from the old to little children, came together to lay siege to Lot's house. Therein we see that when we begin to live debauched lives, in the end we fall into such confusion that men are worse than brute beasts. There is still among the animals a natural sense that guides them to assemble into herds. When night comes, they lie down to rest or, if they go to search out prey, they still have some retreat and are content with what they are able to have. But when we read this story, we see that the devil so possessed all the inhabitants of that city that they come with a rage and fury to fall upon Lot's house. So they first had to abandon all reason, and then before men they had to abandon integrity and shame, having become hardened in all kinds of depravity.

It is true that God had not been honoured and served in Sodom because the people there did not know what true religion was. Melchizedek was not far away, but we see how the world only wanted to wander from the pure worship of God. The people of

Sodom had already been unbelievers for a long time, like people gone astray, but even so, they were still supposed to have some feelings of remorse, for God never leaves people without some sense of discrimination between good and evil so they will be their own judges, as Paul says (cf. *Rom.* 2:14-15), because just the thoughts they have in this life will serve as witnesses before God when the Last Day comes. Consequently, even though God's law had not yet been given, even though there had been no prophets in Sodom to preach daily, there was only Lot, who had withdrawn into his house without authority or esteem, but it is certain God made them inexcusable, for he was producing in them some mark to prick their consciences and make them feel that the licence they were taking was a villainous and detestable thing. And then we see that the most debased among them will still experience some shame when their vileness becomes known. Despite the fact that they are far removed from any good, God has so imprinted on them such a disposition for it that they cannot shake themselves loose from it. Now if they attribute to mortal creatures the authority to judge their evil deeds, can they strip God of his authority to judge them?

Here you have a wicked man. Although he mocks God and men, nonetheless, when he is shown in the light, he will feel fear; and although he did not fear the gibbet, he still cannot completely abolish the sense of shame and would like to have his depravity hidden. Why? Like it or not, he is obliged to feel that those who see him are his judges. Now, as I said, will he at this time be able to deprive God of his right to judge everybody, both great and small (cf. *Eccles.* 3:17)? Whatever the situation, we see here, when men are thus abandoned by God, even though they experience remorse and scruples, even though they would like to be hidden under the earth to commit all their transgressions without being seen, they nonetheless harden themselves so that their desires are so wild that they no longer have any reverence for God or experience shame from men, which prevents them from exceeding all restraint.

That is why Paul, in the first chapter of Romans, says that when men have not given God the honour he is due and worthy of, he abandons them little by little until they trip and fall into such confusion that they give themselves over to all kinds of depravity (cf. *Rom.* 1:21-32). For as soon as men are guilty of the sin of not honouring God as he deserves, that is when they fall away from him. It is true some are more guilty in this respect than others; nonetheless, when godlessness is in vogue and men try to live like brute beasts, they must finally end up living like animals. In other words, if they are sacrilegious, they will be thieves and robbers, and if they defraud God of his right, they will practise brutish cruelty among men. And then, if they do not sanctify God's name, they will desecrate themselves in their own persons and adopt brutish passions, says Paul, forgetting themselves and dishonouring themselves (cf. *Rom.* 1:26-27). They do indeed want to be honoured by everyone, but they themselves engage in ignominious acts which others would not participate in with them, for they submit their bodies to vile deeds, as happened in Sodom. So let us learn to profit from such lessons.

Although Moses recounts here a story of a small city, let us nonetheless realize that God's judgment excludes no one, especially not those who deviate from the good. And especially now that we are exhorted by the law and the gospel to remember God, it is certain that if we act like unruly and wild animals, a more horrible and more frightful condemnation will await us than the one that befell Sodom and Gomorrah. Our Lord Jesus also teaches the same thing (cf. *Matt.* 10:15), for he declares that those who were taught the gospel and remain obstinate in their rebellion and have not been brought to obedience to God, they will be more harshly treated in the Last Day than the people of Sodom and Gomorrah.

Why? There is less of an excuse because those poor wretches had neither prophets nor Scriptures, from which we always have dinned into our ears the teaching by which God wants to win us to himself to possess us in peace and lead us by his Holy Spirit. That being true, we must not think we gain anything by taking pride in that, but let us walk in earnest concern, in fear, and in humility.

Moreover, let us note that when the bars have been broken down, there will be no longer an end or restraint. It is a very strange thing that Sodom came together for such an egregious act. The text says that both young children and old people were involved. Now the old folks should have had contempt for lecherous and similar dissolute behaviour. For even though they were debauched throughout their lives, their age should have corrected them, not that they would have been better for it in the eyes of God, but, even so, it is a battle against nature when old people are still so entangled in their ungovernable lusts that they pursue them irrationally and indiscriminately. As for the little children, they should have been ignorant of such wickedness. And then shame should have been like a blindfold to keep them from seeing such enormities. So we see that they were all so given to their exorbitant desires that it was like they had plotted with Satan to crush all uprightness and all shame. That should make our hair stand on end. Now Moses is recounting that to inform us that if the devil ever finds a way in and things become corrupt within a city, we will end up in the same abyss as Sodom and forget every law and every regulation and be more wicked in our vile desires than the brute beasts themselves.

Thus those who hold public office must be vigilant to repress wrongs early and make an effort to take preventive actions.[1] For when weeds have taken over, there is no longer time to pull them

---

[1] It is indeed the magistrate's, not the Consistory's, responsibility to supervise good morals and repress wrongs. Cf. *Institutes* IV, xx, 9 (with emphasis on Romans 13:3).—M.E.

out, but if you root them out early and at the right time, you will control them. The same is true of vices and crimes. And those who have oversight and authority serve God so that men will live together in complete uprightness and in good order. It will cost them practically nothing, so to speak, to keep the peace, but if they act like blind men for a time and pretend they do not see, iniquity will gain the upper hand in no time at all, and before long it will be impossible to maintain order. As when a storm is raging and preparations have not been set in place in time and location, it is certain that ships will not be prevented from sinking to the bottom of the sea. Thus it is when the wicked are allowed to become audaciously bold and do evil; that is, no one can prevent them. That makes for hell where there used to be paradise, and the result is that it cannot be corrected subsequently. So when Moses places such a mirror before our eyes, let us learn to restrain ourselves and refrain from things that would cause others to stumble, and let us do what we can to keep them from doing so. If we see some danger, we must alert others insofar as we can. As when we see there is some danger of a plague, we are anxious to exhort and admonish others to take precautions. Now, when we see vices, there is no plague more deadly. Now if we allow them to continue on their way and persist in their lifestyle, everything will be lost and laid waste. So let us all be vigilant, great and small, but principally those to whom our Lord has entrusted the responsibility and whom he has raised to a position of governing and preventing men from going astray and giving themselves over to every kind of gross behaviour. That, in short, is what we have to remember.

Now it is said that the people of Sodom said to Lot: 'Bring out to us those who entered your house so that we may know them.' There are some commentators who have stupidly abused the text, understanding the word 'to know' in the often scriptural sense of getting acquainted. Even though their intention might have been such, yet they were so dense that they would not have spoken so modestly, but since we see that whoremongers are putrid in their filth and delight in speaking the foulest language they can, even inventing words that violate nature, in a manner of speaking, to show how much pleasure they take in their vile deeds, there is, consequently, no doubt that the men of Sodom were dissolute in their speech as well as in their everyday lives. But at this point they give themselves a noble cover for their shame: 'Oh, we need to know what kind of guests you have,' for they were proud of being natives of the place. They were saying to Lot: 'Who are these strangers?' They now approach as if Lot had wronged them greatly. 'What is going on here? You are living in our city with our permission, and yet you are more presumptuous and assume greater liberties than the citizens themselves. For you come here and give lodging to people we do not know. And how do we know they are not spies? Must you receive here people you like without advising us?' That, then, is the cover the people of Sodom give themselves as they desire to commit the detestable act that we will see later.

Now what we have to note here is that the iniquity of the wicked will not always be apparent, and they will even find as many pretexts as possible to conceal their true intentions; but in the end God will show what kind of people they are, and all their efforts to disguise their true selves with subtle and deceitful words will be in vain, but when all is said and done, God will put them to shame by placing them on the scaffold, as it were, so that their infamy and disgrace will be seen from a distance.

It is not enough for us to know that God reveals hidden vices that way, but we must make good use of that knowledge. So let us not think we have profited a great deal from it if we use rhetoric to make ourselves look good while deceiving others, making them think we are reasonable and correct in our evil. Let us not think, I say, that our situation is better than theirs, for what the prophet

Isaiah says must be accomplished: 'Woe to those who call evil good and darkness light' (cf. *Isa.* 5:20). We must particularly apply that teaching to the point that when we think we have escaped detection because we dazzle people with our clever language, our condemnation will be double before God. That is because we heap evil upon evil when we, by our hypocrisies, fictions and lies, try to overturn all order in our desire to make vice into a virtue.

So let us learn, when the people of Sodom use the cover of wanting to know what kind of people entered their city, that if we claim something that is false and people do not immediately catch sight of our evil intentions, we will not be better than the people of Sodom and Gomorrah, and we will not be able to escape God's hand anymore than they did. And if we follow their example and hide our intentions and pass ourselves off as being good citizens when our intentions are only evil, we will indeed have to bear the punishment. So let us be forthright and scrupulous. And when we are tempted to do wrong, let us not look for excuses to cover and hide our intentions and deceive everybody unless of course we want to increase God's wrath as if we were provoking him knowingly. That, then, for that point.

It remains for each one of us to practise that teaching, which could be drawn out further, but it is enough that we be informed how we are to use it profitably. There is Lot's response and what he does, which is to leave his house and close the door behind him, and he offers to hand his daughters over to the people of Sodom so that no harm will come to those he has granted lodging and taken under his care. We see a great virtue in Lot in that he does not spare himself and places himself in the midst of such madness as if he were forfeiting his life. That is a very praiseworthy magnanimity which we see in Lot inasmuch as his life is not as precious to him as the protection of those whom he received and to whom he gave his word to lodge them securely. Now mixed with that virtue is vice, because, being without advice and not knowing what to do, he is ready to abandon his daughters.[2] Now, since time does not allow us to develop that point, we have to note here that we must struggle constantly when faced with a matter of danger to our lives to prevent an evil which will occur and some great harm which might come to our neighbours. That much for that point.

Moreover, when God gives us the desire and zeal to oppose evil and prevent it, we are to pray that God will also give us wisdom and discrimination to know how to govern when the difficulties are so great that we are at our wits' end, but that will be dealt with tomorrow if it please God.

Now let us bow before the majesty of our gracious God in acknowledgment of our faults, praying that he will so touch us to the quick that we will be displeased with them and disturbed by them and kept so humble that we will not only please men and be approved by them, but that we will also have a clear conscience before God and his angels and be so guided that each of us will think about being a good example for his neighbours. And let us avoid all stumbling blocks when we see Satan trying to pervert us and corrupt us, using one against another, and let us be even more on guard and extend our hand to those who have gone astray and bring them back to the right path. And being instructed in the fear of God, let us also try to further one another in it and strengthen ourselves more and more until we reach the goal to which we are called. May he grant that grace not only to us but to all the peoples and nations on earth.

---

[2] In his commentary, Calvin condemned Lot without excuse.—*M.E.*

741

90

Lot Defends His Guests at All Costs

Tuesday 30 April 1560

And Lot went out at the door unto them, and shut the door after him, And said, I pray you, brethren, do not so wickedly. Behold now, I have two daughters which have not known man; let me, I pray you, bring them out unto you, and do ye to them as is good in your eyes: only unto these men do nothing; for therefore came they under the shadow of my roof. And they said, Stand back. And they said again, This one fellow came in to sojourn, and he will needs be a judge: now will we deal worse with thee, than with them. And they pressed sore upon the man, even Lot, and came near to break the door (Gen. 19:6-9).

W E BEGAN YESTERDAY by showing that Lot possessed singular integrity when he was resolute in preventing an outrage against those he had lodged in his house.

Yet there was a vice mixed with it, indeed a great one and worthy of rebuke since he is ready to expose his two daughters to the absolute shame of being common whores. Since Lot reaches that point, there is no excusing him of gross failure. So we see here in one act two different qualities, for Lot is to be praised for defending those entrusted to him by God, but he is to be reprimanded for not sparing his daughters and being ready to expose them to such depravity, as the text relates it. There is no doubt that if he had been able to redeem with his own life that wrong the people of Sodom wanted to do to his guests, he was ready to die. Now he has no one to advise him, for the situation has reached such an extremity that he does not know what to do. He knew no one was expecting him to settle a quarrel, and the people of Sodom would have left him in peace if he had not taken sides with those he had undertaken to help, and there would have been no need for him to put himself up as a pledge or as a hostage. In a word, he was ready to be sacrificed to save those whom he had given lodging. But seeing that he would gain nothing, he has no recourse but to offer his daughters, for he knows that the people of Sodom are inflamed with a vile lust. He sees there something coarse and brutishly unnatural, so he thinks it is better to prostitute his own daughters, shameful as it is. Since Lot was a man who feared God and is known to be 'righteous' (cf. *2 Pet.* 2:7), he was, according to the apostle, afflicted in his heart and tormented upon seeing Sodom's evil deeds (cf. *2 Pet.* 2:8), and it was like being in an endless and relentless Gehenna, and we must not think that he is making light of whoredom or that he had no shame or that it was immaterial to him that his daughters would be prostituted. We must not entertain that opinion about him, for, as I have already said, maintaining his daughters' chastity was dearer to him than his own life, but he is at his wits' end when he sees that he cannot appease the rage of those wild animals. For the people of Sodom were deprived of all sense of humanity, being, as they were, carried away by such a base and brutish passion that they were willing to violate nature.

That is how Lot did not fight with men who still have some reason and judgment and who cannot be pleased by friendly means; and seeing that they are worse than brute beasts and that the devil possesses them completely, he is obliged to come to that decision. And could we think that he had a reasonable excuse in his own mind? And there are also those who would like to justify him in this matter. And some even think that he was astute in saying what he did, thinking that the people of Sodom would not accept his offer because they were not interested in enjoying his daughters, but that is to speculate without any basis. And what a dilemma we would have when judging if Lot had not been distraught and did not know what to do when he offered his daughters rather than see such a brutal and outrageous act committed against those whom he had in his charge and to whom he had given his word!

First off, we see what we touched on briefly yesterday, namely, that when God was magnanimous to allow us to fulfil our duty without peril or threat or anything astonishing, we are not ready to die to do what is commanded; and that is still not all, for our zeal must be allied with reason, good counsel and wisdom if we are to be able to discern what is expedient and entrust ourselves to God, for an ill-advised zeal will always be reprehensible. So we see it is not enough that God gives us a firm courage to fulfil our responsibility boldly, but that we also need him to govern us with his Spirit of wisdom. And that is also why counsel and wisdom are attributed to the Spirit of God, who is to be our guide to everything good. On the one hand, we must be sustained by his power, for we are unimaginably weak. And when it comes to striking hard, those who seem to be the boldest will be found to be the weakest, and experience well shows that those who proclaim their own wonders are real cowards and are so fearful that a little bit of nothing will make them collapse completely. Consequently, the first point, then, is that our Lord places that strength within us so that when we perceive some danger before us and have to endure hatreds and quarrels, we will still move forward without being broken or weakened; and let us not think, since God commands us to obey him, that we are beyond anything that could bring us back to the way of men. So much for that point.

But do we have that power? God still needs to show us what is good and useful to do, for otherwise we will sometimes be perplexed, we will look in all directions, we will find no success in our affairs, a straw will bring us to a standstill and we will not know which road or path to follow. But that is how we have opportunities to place ourselves completely in God's hands so that, on the one hand, he will enlighten us and show us the path we have to follow and will give us counsel in all our deliberations, in all our conclusions and undertakings. And yet he also strengthens us in such a way that we will not be cowardly or afraid, but will valiantly overcome all the obstacles that Satan devises to make us lose our way.

Yet we are warned about giving the bridle to our ill-advised zeal. It is a generally accepted proverb that God approves everything done with a good intention. Now it is true that if we define 'good intention,' if it should be well regulated, it could be accepted. But because men appeal to a 'good intention,' even though they fail and go wrong, even though they wander far astray and want to oblige God to find everything they do good despite any stupid mistakes they make, that is too foolish and outlandish by far. Therefore, let us realize that so-called good intentions cause us to trip up and fall into many disastrous situations. And when we think we are serving God, we only offend him and anger him against us even more.

Even more then must we apply our attention today to knowing what God's will is so that it may instruct us in everything and everywhere. As a matter of fact, we see what happened to the world when it took the liberty to do everything that struck everyone's fancy, for what is called 'God's service' in the Papacy is nothing but a pit of abominations and sacrilege. And yet those who work in the midst of such godlessness think they are doing wonderful things. Even so, God detests the whole bit. So let us cast out all our presumptions and not think our Lord yields to our imaginations and thoughts, but let us learn to bridle our zeal, as I said, so that it always conforms to his will and his word.

Now it is true that we indeed have a certain and infallible rule in God's word to guide us throughout our lives, but that is not enough for a general teaching. The word must be preached for us every day because we need our Lord to provide new counsel, for the person who knows how he is to govern himself will still often be taken by surprise, and things will happen to him that will make him hesitate or put him in danger at one time or another, and he will not know which way to turn. There is no one who does not experience such vexations that trouble his mind, except some adventurous types who fear nothing, whom we also call fools; but for those who are moderate and desire to serve God and walk in their calling, it is certain they will often find themselves uncomfortable or embarrassed, even at every moment of the day in some particular acts. Consequently, we are all the more exhorted to humility so that our Lord will provide counsel as often as need arises and instruct us, guide us and extend his hand to us and, if he allows us to go astray or fall a bit, lift us up and restore us to the right path.

That, in brief, is what we have to remember about this passage when we see what happened to Lot, who, possessing an excellent and praiseworthy virtue, nonetheless failed and committed a detestable sin before God and men. Seeing that, let us know that by his example God calls us to invoke him and learn to conform ourselves to the guidance of his Spirit and seek his counsel, not just for the conduct of our lives in general, but for the particular acts in which our frailty and weakness show themselves. For our Lord, in order to bridle us in better, will, I say to all, show us in the same way that the wisest and most capable will realize they do not have such wisdom that our Lord does not need to work in them. That is what we have to remember.

We have also to note that the virtues of the saints always possess some spot or stain, and so they do not merit approval before God. And that is to suppress this foolish pride with which the world has been intoxicated and continues to be throughout the Papacy. For as soon as there is some small appearance of good, those arrogant fools want to keep God obligated to them and they always have the word 'merit' in their mouths, but if they are examined, it is certain that the most excellent works they can do will not surpass Lot's virtues and what Moses recounts here, let alone saying that the papists, while thinking they serve God, only provoke his wrath because they are given over to their diabolical superstitions and corrupt and pervert everything pure; but still let us take the case of their giving of alms, which are called sacrifices of a sweet smelling fragrance (cf. *Phil.* 4:18). It is certain that that is nothing in comparison with what is recounted here. For the papist considered the most saintly will never give alms so willingly as Lot when he wanted to provide for the angels, and the papist will not possess such a complete zeal or one which deserves to be as highly esteemed as the zeal of Lot, who disregarded himself to the extent of being ready to die rather than permit an outrage against those he had received under his protection. Nonetheless, we see that if God wanted to call Lot to account, he would be condemned in his virtue because of the vice that is associated with it. Therefore, how outrageous and insane it is for the papists to think they can glory in and take comfort in those works by which they think they gain merit before God and acquire paradise.

Thereupon, since it pleases God to give us the desire to obey his word, let us nonetheless be aware that, whatever good disposition we may have, even though we made a considerable effort to do right, there will always be something to fault, there will always be vices which will occasionally be obvious to us and sometimes hidden from us, but that God still sees them. Therefore, let us have this conviction constantly before us: that when we do the best we can, we will still deserve to be condemned and have God upbraid all our virtues and all the works we think are outstanding, all of which he would reject if he had not accepted them out of his pure goodness and mercy. How then will our works be received by God? By our doing what he commands us to do, even though there is much to fault. For if we think we offend God in everything we do, how could we apply ourselves to doing good? We have to know that God accepts what we do to serve him. On the other hand, we have to be aware that there is no worth in us or in our works that obligates God. So let us realize that when God gives us some worthy zeal, it pleases him to do so since he placed it in us; for what belongs to him he never forgets.

However, because there is always weakness in our virtue and many side roads along our path, and because we only hobble along and, instead of running, we stumble along and get off the right path, God pardons us for all that and forgets it. So that is how God accepts our good works, but they are still far from being meritorious, as they are called, and they would be rejected and condemned if God decided to examine them rigorously. That, in brief, is what we have to remember.

Now it is true Lot tries to appease the people of Sodom; he even calls them his brothers. But what brotherhood did he have with them, seeing they were devils, resolute in their evil and contempt for God and nature? But here Lot did not consider the kind of people they were; he only wanted to appease them by calling them brothers inasmuch as he was living in their midst. For according as we are joined together, that in fact must serve us as a bond to hold us closer to one another. So Lot respected that connection that God placed between him and the people of Sodom when he wanted him to live in their city. Yet we know he did not defile himself with their abominations, as we have already pointed out in the apostle's passage, namely, that not only did he hate the evil he saw committed daily in Sodom, but he separated himself and distanced himself from them (cf. *2 Pet.* 2:8), and his heart was grieved, which showed he had a true zeal for serving God, and, as a result, he was in constant torment while seeing things in such profound disorder.

Here we could ask: 'Why does Lot offer his two daughters to the people of the city, and why were the people looking for two men for their villainous cupidity?' But it is not all that rare that when there is some puff of air in the city to ignite the fire because everyone has been corrupted and when one person has set the evil in motion, everyone will fall in line without knowing why. Let us take the case of a people who have become so depraved that there is no fear of God in them and no integrity. The moment an evil person initiates a quarrel against a good man, if there is one among them, an army will immediately rise against him. Why? When the devil takes possession of men, God leaves them with him and abandons them in their depraved state; and without knowing why, they always tend toward evil and are ready to do battle against God and everything just and upright. It is true it is a monstrous thing to see such moral abandonment. But look! We have experienced it here.[1] We do not have to go to Sodom, for since things had been in such disarray and there were no longer laws or fear of God or honesty or integrity that might restrain the wicked, iniquity came like a flood, and they all became so perverted that if a wicked person had but lifted his finger, he would have been supported and no one would have inquired into why he was doing what he was. But if a man who fears God had wanted to maintain a good cause, he would have been completely defeated, for everyone would have taken up arms against him. Why? It is as I said: when great corruption dominates a place and people have made vice into

---

[1] This surely calls to mind the conflicts with Ami Perrin, Philibert Berthelier, Nicot Du Chesne and some others in the 1550s (cf. Grosse, *Berthelier*; Gautier, *Genève*, 3, pp. 557-628; 4, pp. 63-87). Was not Gaspard Favre, Perrin's brother-in-law, reported to have said that 'if he ever became a censor, he would establish houses of debauchery in the four corners of the city'? (Gautier, *Genève*, 4, p. 50, note 2.—M.E.

a virtue, only a small puff of air will start a fire throughout the entire city and everyone will come out as if the battle flag had been brought out! When the wicked become aroused and they seem to be set on moving heaven and earth, and you ask them, 'What has been done to you? Who has driven you to this?' they do not know. But the devil has blindfolded them and put them in such a state of mind that they are like madmen and do not know what they are doing. All the more must we keep ourselves bridled in and pray that God will not let iniquity gain such a foothold in our midst and allow us to imitate the wicked and ally ourselves with them in such a way that equity is perverted by common accord. That, then, is what we have to remember about this passage.

Now let us come to the people of Sodom's response: 'Come out. Stand back,' as if they wanted to put him on trial as a criminal. There you have despisers of God, wicked people who have forgotten their nature, like dumb animals, worse than donkeys and dogs. And yet they have the audacity to call Lot and summon him there as if they were supposed to interrogate him about who permitted him to intervene and prevent them from carrying out their wicked design. For the wicked and God's enemies not only pardon themselves for every evil and take pride in their vices and despise God, but they also want to make all decent people believe that they have not done wrong and that, as the proverb says, it is the lamb that is troubling the water.[2] Now that was a difficult trial for Lot. But we learn from it that we are to be content God has tested us—even though we are falsely accused by men and the good we have done has been turned into evil—and that those who offend and harm us do not fail to rise up against us as if we were grievously wrong. Let us bear that patiently, and let it be enough for us to have God as our Defender. For we are not better than the apostle Paul, who

[2] The proverb is from Aesop, *Fables*, 221, 'The Wolf and the Lamb' (before La Fontaine, *Fables*, Book 1, fable x).—M.E.

says he walked in honour and in ignominy, and exhorts the faithful by his example, by doing good, to shut their ears to hearing evil,[3] as if he were saying: 'My friends, let us not wait to be praised by men since we will have a good testimony before God and know that we have made an effort to do our duty, for there will be such ingratitude on the part of men that we will be wrongly offended. But we must be hardened to that and not seek our reward in this world. Rather, let us be humble so that we will be able to present ourselves before God in such a way that we are always witnessing to the fact that he knows our integrity.' That, then, is what we have to note in this testing of Lot. He wanted to serve God and possessed a solid and praiseworthy zeal, but he still stumbled badly, as we have said.

And here you have devils who want to trample Lot underfoot and summon him as if they were sitting in a judge's seat and had something to bring against this man who had walked so faithfully. So, seeing that he underwent such a combat, let us also be ready for the same, and let us not find it strange if, after serving God and our neighbours, we are discredited and the wicked spew their venom against us, which is their way of saying: 'Here is a foreigner. He has not been here long, and yet he wants to be a judge.' In the first place, Lot was not setting himself up as a judge over them. And we see that he does not dare open his mouth to rebuke them, although he is justified in doing so, and more than justified, so far is he from daring to speak as vehemently and severely as he should; he is ready to consent to the evil rather than provoke them, for they are already enraged and he finds no way to appease them except by consenting to their depravity and yielding his own daughters to them. And you call that being a judge? So we see that Lot was like a deaf mute in that situation and did not try to do anything but

---

[3] This verse, in the terms given by Calvin, is not found in the Pauline epistles. Elements are found in Acts 20:17-38; 1 Corinthians 4:3-13; 9:19-23; Philippians 3; 2 Timothy 3:11-4:5; etc.—*M.E.*

please these wicked and perverted people, not that he approved their iniquity, but he was, as we have said, so caught off guard and bewildered that he did not know what to do, and yet he is called 'a judge'!

By that we are put on notice that whenever we but want to do a part of our duty, we will receive venomous jibes from those who have contempt for God, and they will proudly resist us and be obliged to condemn us, and we will have to endure reproaches and false accusations. So let it be common knowledge among us that God will test our consciences on those occasions. We encounter that daily, for those who do not want anyone to approach them or reprove them in any way, when they hear some hint of a correction, they will get on their high horse: 'What have I to do with you? Are you my judge and superior? Do I not have someone who oversees me?'[4] If some private individual wants to rebuke a very obvious vice and if God is offended and the person opposes a stumbling block, here is the common response which is directed against him: 'And who are you? Is it your place to reprove me?' And with that the wicked, in order to have some excuse, will say: 'What? Do I not have my overseers? Is there not an authority to set things straight when things are not going right?' Indeed, as if an authority prevented God from being honoured and his word from running its course and brotherly admonitions from being given, as God commanded (*Matt.* 18:15-17). And what is God's authority? Is it not that he be served and honoured and that equity and uprightness be maintained among men? But that pack of dogs has no shame of hiding behind the noble words of 'justice' and 'lordship,' for when they want to be excused from all correction, they mention those

---

[4]Geneva was divided into twenty-five 'dizaines' [groups of ten], with two 'dizeniers' delegated to the Council of Sixty. The 'dizeniers' could denounce matters of morals to the Consistory, which would summon the people and give censures and admonitions.—*M.E.*

over them. And they will also mention their preachers. 'What? Do we not have our ministers to teach us? Oh, if Preacher So and So reproved me, I would tolerate it, but you, who are you?' But if the preachers were to do so, they would complain about that too, for this is their common reply: 'Oh, you are not my prince.' Indeed, as if someone had to be a prince to rebuke those who do wrong. Now that is great theology![5] But we see these dogs talking that way all the time, and we do not have to go to Sodom to find that kind of example, for it can be found over a hundred thousand times in Geneva!

Therefore, let us learn to do what we are supposed to in such a way that if the wicked speak viciously of us and vent their accusations and have their reasons to charge us with calumnies and some pretexts which the world will find fitting, let us overlook it and remain so steadfast that we will in no way yield to their audacity, but let it fly in their face despite anything they can do when they see that we will remain steadfast, and let them babble on incoherently and howl like dogs, knowing that they will have to stop with the passing of time, after God has tested us thoroughly, as we have already said.

Now we need to note also that the people of Sodom claim: 'You are one person, and you are a foreigner.' They take confidence in their numbers and glory in the fact that they are citizens and the others are nothing by comparison. Now it is true that in every state there have to be some definite standards for distinguishing one group from another, but that does not mean a foreigner can say nothing, that he cannot receive fair treatment, that he cannot condemn evil, that he cannot, in a word, serve God. We must know whether a foreigner is obliged to approve and submit to what the civil government and order permit when scandals occur that

[5] It is rare that Calvin uses the word 'theology' in a sermon, here in an ironic sense.—M.E.

blaspheme God's name and crimes are committed and evil deeds are done. Does the government require that? It is certain it does not. The government requires that natives have their privileges, that they have what belongs to them, and that those who live among them consider their condition and be satisfied with their status.[6] That will always be something God approves. But the wicked abuse all the good things God does for them and pervert their right use, and they do the same thing with civil government. It is a mark of God's grace that man can live in the country of his birth, but when he cannot, the person who is not forced to leave his hole in the wall, as we say, is he not even more obligated to walk in the fear of God? For that blessing does indeed deserve to be acknowledged.

Moreover, if a man has a drop of common sense and humanity within him, it is certain that if he has this privilege, as I said, of staying in his house in the place of his birth, he will have pity on foreigners, for God tests them more rigorously and does not treat them so gently. That is how the good and faithful know how to employ God's graces. But what will an evil man and a despiser of all justice do? He will say: 'I am a citizen; you are a foreigner.' That is, he will have contempt for God and want to be left as he is and not want anyone to mention his vices. He will want to fight one and torment another; he will want to pillage another person's possessions; he will want to indulge himself in intemperance and drunkenness, venery, and every other kind of moral degradation,

[6] A distinction was made in Geneva between foreigners, inhabitants, natives, bourgeois and citizens. An inhabitant is a foreigner who comes to settle in the city, wishes to live according to 'the holy evangelical religion' and receive the authorization to live in the city; he has no political rights but pays taxes, and his children are called 'natives.' It is the city Council which grants the bourgeoisie, relatively easy to obtain during Calvin's time, but often burdensome (the Reformer obtained it 'gratis' in 1559). The bourgeois enjoys full political rights. The citizen is a male and legitimate descendent of a bourgeois. Cf. *Livre des habitants de Genève*, t. 1, 1549-1560 (Travaux d'Humanisme et Renaissance 26), ed. by Paul-F. Geisendorf, Genève, 1957, pp. vii-ix.—*M.E.*

and he will want it kept silent. Now that is to abuse God's blessings vilely, and that is a very ordinary practice. So let us note that when our Lord gives us some advantage from our worldly standpoint, we must use it with all sobriety and humility, and we must not become prideful when we do. For what will happen in the end? If someone looks into who our fathers are and those who follow us, we will in the end be found to be like the people of Sodom, that is, as Isaiah speaks to the people of Israel about them (cf. *Isa.* 1:9-20). We will be as depraved as the people of Sodom and Gomorrah.

So what we need to remember about this passage is Sodom's reproach of Lot for being a foreigner. We have to consider what their intention is for reproaching him. It is because they want their pit of hell to be maintained and devoid of God, and they do not want his word to be heard, and they do not want to be informed or warned that they are sinking into every wickedness, and they do not want to be criticized. Now, as we have already said, those who live in the place of their birth must treat foreigners humanely. And since they have the advantage of a God-given rest, we are to use it in such a way that God will be served by everyone in common accord and that what the civil government requires does not prevent God from being honoured and his word from being received by great and small.

Moreover, when the people of Sodom say that Lot is alone, they are, as I said, taking pride in their number. And that is what those who have contempt for God do. They think that whatever they are accustomed to doing among themselves is permitted and they make of custom a law for themselves. We have a rather notorious example of that practice in the Papacy. And of both practices, as a matter of fact. For what do the papists use as a shield today when we point out their infamous teachings, which we show to be sacrilegious and apostate statements that have corrupted the entire worship of God, among which there is no purity of religion and everything is filled with errors, blasphemy and idolatry? Their most common defence is to say: 'And we have here a handful of people who want to guide us. Do we not have Italy and France and this place and that? Does the Catholic Church not reach out in all directions? And here we have a scurvy crew who would like to reform us and be everybody's judges?' That is their first defence. 'What?' they say. 'They were born three days ago, and we have longevity on our side. The way we live was not established today or yesterday, but five hundred years ago, a thousand years ago! And the devotions, have they not always been such as they are? And the Mass, was it not established long ago? And then there are the other ceremonies, everything we call the worship of God, the administration of the church and the authority of the prelates.' So that is how the papists today followed the people of Sodom. For all their claims you need only a few words: 'Well, you are princes of Sodom and people of Gomorrah,' for it is certain that if they spoke with the mouth of the people of Sodom, they could not better approve their religion. There you have the people of Sodom saying to Lot: 'You are only one person.' And with that the papists say: 'We are an infinite multitude.' Now will that protect them against God? They protect themselves with their claims, but their claims are only leaves, for in the long run they will be aware that they gain nothing by such vauntings.

So, for our part, let us be strengthened when we see that the enemies of the truth, fighting openly today against God, arm themselves with the same defence that the people of Sodom used against Lot. And then when they say that they have their customs and that they have long practised everything we rebuke today, they are, in that matter, still mistaken, for they are so impudent that, while being prevailed over, they want to have everybody believe that longevity is on their side. Now it is certain that true longevity is not to be found in four or five hundred years, or in a thousand, for the devil has been the seducer from all time and has held most of the world in his tyranny and subjugation, but we must remember God, who is eternal; we must remember the law; we must remember the prophets; and we must finally remember the gospel, Jesus Christ and his apostles. That is what true longevity is, and it is in those places that it must be sought. Now the papists want to hear nothing about that. In them is only impudence, for they are like brothel prostitutes who have no shame or sense of disgrace in all of their vileness. And they are not only like whores, but they need to be sent off to Sodom, where we see they are already headed.

At the same time, the people of Sodom make a threat when they say they will deal worse with Lot than with the ones he is defending. We see in that that they had so forgotten their humanity that when they encountered resistance to their wickedness, they were incensed with such rage and violence that they are ready to kill in the same way their lechery incites them. Although Lot tries to appease them, although he is subservient and although he flatters them, in a manner of speaking, by calling them brothers, and he grants them his own daughters to abuse, they are nonetheless so enraged that they threaten to kill him. Let this teach us that when we rebuke the wicked and despisers of God, we must prepare to go to war, a war that often imperils both our lives and our possessions. For a wicked man has only to be prejudiced to persecute God's children to the limit when they anger him and say something he does not like. For since the devil, who is a murderer from the beginning (cf. *John* 8:44), governs them, they have no choice but to be given over to that kind of malice and inhumanity, as is obvious (cf. *Isa.* 1:10). So if you prick an evil person and one who has contempt for God, venom must spew forth. So let us realize that when we make an effort to resist evil and bring about God's service and honour, we will be rewarded with evil people as our enemies. And what will they do? Some will disdain us and withdraw from us; others will contrive in every way to bring us to ruin and try, whenever an occasion arises, to harm us and do us ill. Let us be ready for it and be strengthened by what happened to Lot later.

Moses adds that when Lot was assailed furiously, the angels, although they were still in the form of men and had not revealed themselves, reached out, laid hold of him, and pulled him back into his house (cf. *Gen.* 19:10). Here we have something to strengthen ourselves with when we have to withstand many conflicts with the wicked in order to fulfil our duty toward God. Here is what Lot says: 'They have come under the roof of my house, and so I must protect them.' That shows Lot demonstrating to the people of Sodom what he is proposing for himself as the thing he is obliged to do before God. He holds to that path with constancy and acts valiantly in behalf of the angels, who were remaining hidden and seemed to need Lot to protect and help them for a while, but in the end when Lot can no longer endure, the angels extend their hand and blind the people of Sodom (cf. *Gen.* 19:11). So let us learn to walk sincerely, as God teaches us to do in his word, and let nothing sway us to the right or to the left, but let us be determined to follow this line of thinking: Does God will it thus? Did he order it? It must be done. So much for that point.

Now we must especially remember what we are shown here, namely, that when God entrusts someone to our keeping, we must spare nothing in providing for him to the extent we can. And as much as we also see that nature provides us with this rule: that when people come into contact with one another, even though two of them have never seen each other, if one of them is experiencing some misfortune, let the other have pity. And if another wishes to do him some harm, he will say, 'No. He is my companion.' What? They had never seen each other except for a day! It is true, but it is a natural impulse which makes us inexcusable when we fail to help those who are joined with us. So when we live together, we have to look at it as if God were bringing us together and recommending that we take care of one another naturally. So that is the rule Lot gives us here when he says: 'They have come under the shadow of my roof; they have taken harbour in my house. Consequently, I must defend them.' Now if we are all obliged in our own homes to help those who share some familiarity and commonality with us and some proximity to us, even more must those who possess a public office, who have the sword of justice and God's authority to maintain each person's right, give account before God if they oppress the innocent who are unjustly downtrodden. Why so? Because he wants them to be protectors of the people, as is said in the person of Hezekiah through the prophet Isaiah (cf. *Isa.* 32:1-2). It is this way for all those who are instructed. We must all, from the greatest to the smallest, help those whom God places before us and with whom we have some association, knowing that God has come near to us in this way so that some may have help and alleviation from the others.

Now let us bow before the majesty of our gracious God in acknowledgment of our faults, praying that he will make us sense them more and more so we will be displeased with them and humble ourselves and even thank him for bringing us into the right road and advancing us along it, and let us know, since there are so many weaknesses in us that merit our being rejected, that we have a serious need of his infinite goodness. And since we are aware of his meeting our needs every day, let that teach us to humble ourselves so that we will have nothing to boast of except his pure mercy, which he shows us every day and has shown us in his Son, our Lord Jesus Christ. May he grant that grace not only to us but to all the peoples and nations on earth.

91

Sodom's Fate: A Reason to Fear God Righteously and Be Ministers of Salvation

Wednesday, 1 May 1560

But the men put forth their hand, and pulled Lot into the house to them, and shut to the door. And they smote the men that were at the door of the house with blindness, both small and great: so that they wearied themselves to find the door. And the men said unto Lot, Hast thou here any besides? son in law, and thy sons, and thy daughters, and whatsoever thou hast in the city, bring them out of this place: For we will destroy this place, because the cry of them is waxen great before the face of the LORD; and the LORD hath sent us to destroy it. And Lot went out, and spake unto his sons in law, which married his daughters, and said, Up, get you out of this place; for the LORD will destroy this city. But he seemed as one that mocked unto his sons in law (Gen. 19:10-14).

*W*E SAW PREVIOUSLY how Lot, not knowing he had given lodging to God's angels to protect them from the harm the people of Sodom wanted to do to them, did not spare his own life while the angels remained as if hidden in the house. That shows us God does not always make his power known at the outset, and that is to test our zeal and the enthusiasm we have for fulfilling our duty and vigorously carrying out what he commands us to do. God could indeed make it so that we would incur no difficulty in serving him and it would be only a game, so to speak, and men would offer no resistance or opposition, each person even being for us, and that people would even lend a helping hand; he could even deliver us from all trials and give us such power that we would sense no struggle when doing our duty. Now, he allows us to face hardships, to be abandoned by everybody, to find frequently no resolution of our affairs, to be thwarted from all sides, to be in fear, perplexity, and anguish. He wants us, I say, to serve him under such circumstances. Why? As I have said, because in this way he tests our constancy and steadfastness to know whether we are serving him from the heart. Otherwise, you could not distinguish between hypocrites and those who have a pure and sincere affection for following what God commands if it was a question only of having a merry old time, as they say. But when we face such obstacles that we have to force ourselves and even if we see death's threatening hand, let us not fear exposing ourselves to it and enduring much hatred and many reproaches. Under those circumstances, our sincerity is confirmed and we know ourselves. And others also know by experience that we are not serving God out of pretence, but that we are completely devoted to him to overcome everything that would be contrary to the obedience we owe him.

So that is why the angels remained hidden for a while, as if they had no power and needed Lot's help, which they could have done without and do finally demonstrate they could have done without, for they reach out when Lot can do no more and is in the jaws of wolves. The people of Sodom are so enraged against him that there is no longer hope that he can stand his ground. At that point, it seems the angels had not stayed in the house for any fear they might have had, but the sincerity of Lot's faith had to be proved in this way. So when our Lord no longer conceals his intentions for a time and no longer pretends to want to help us and be our shield and defence, he will, when the time is right, make us aware that he never abandons us and is at hand to lift from death those who are already dead. For we must reach this conclusion for the reason I have already given, which is so that the help we receive from God will be all the more glorious and we will have cause and reason to magnify him when he works for us in an extraordinary way. And when we realize he has truly taken us out of the tomb, so to speak, let us give him all the praise.

So, in summary, what we have to remember about this passage is that our Lord does not immediately display his power when he sends us into the fray, but that he is there as one who is standing back and allowing us to be so strongly impeded that it seems we are supposed to fail. And yet it seems that we, trying to make sense of the situation, think that he has abandoned us and sees nothing, or else that he is unwilling to put out his hand to help us. That is how our weakness shows itself. Now, have we been thus humbled and willingly examined with the result that we know we desire to remain steadfast in his service and struggle valiantly against Satan, against all the world's assaults, and against all temptations? When our Lord has left us in that condition for a while, he then makes himself known to us in our time of need and sustains us in order to give us victory after we have been like conquered peoples who, nonetheless, did not yield in the battle but show the truth of our faith and of the uprightness he has placed within us. Consequently, let us not be astonished that since we are weak, we will still have to undergo great and bitter confrontations. Let that not discourage us, but let us wait for the time God knows is right, and then we will see clearly that he is able to extend his hand very far (cf. *Psa.* 119:173; *Isa.* 26:11; 59:1). And even though he is in heaven and we do not perceive him with our eyes, his power will nonetheless reach us.

Now when it is said that the angels struck the men of Sodom with blindness, it does not mean that they plucked their eyes out, but that the men of Sodom were so blind with rage that they groped for the door with obstinate persistence. Feeling that God had put a blindfold over their eyes, they were so hardened in their fury that they tried to force their way violently into Lot's house as if they wanted to spite God.

Now we have to note here that God has many ways to ward off the blows when he sees that the enemy is persecuting us without pity and are completely given over to evil, that it seems they are wild animals which have their mouths open to swallow us up or their claws extended to tear us to pieces. So when God sees we are oppressed to the limit that way and when he is pleased to show he is our Saviour, he has many ways to show it. For although he permits our enemies to have understanding and judgment, to be subtle and crafty, and then to be armed in such a way that it seems nothing keeps them from destroying us, we will nonetheless be amazed that he will deliver us without our knowing how. But sometimes, when our enemies have subtle and deceitful ways to entrap us, God will frustrate their efforts, for they will be deprived of the power to execute their attempts. But here Moses shows us another way that God acted when delivering his servant Lot: he stupefied the people of Sodom to the point that they saw nothing. It is true it was at night, but earlier they had found Lot's house and had made their way there. So when this change occurred, why do they not think it was God who blinded them? But with that example he strengthened our hope that God will indeed provide for all our needs. If he does not assure us in one way, he will assure us in another, for everything is in his hand, as we have said. If it sometimes seems that our enemies have many devices to cast us into their nets, let us know that God knows how to surprise the wise in their cleverness, as it is said (cf. *Job* 5:13), and that he even confuses and stupefies them when it pleases him.

So that is a way he has of helping us, if it pleases him to use it or if he is pleased to permit our enemies to take counsel together, plot, deliberate, and make decrees, and then in the end he will say to them, as he speaks through his prophet Isaiah: 'Have you taken counsel together? Have you deliberated and made decrees? Nothing will happen, for every force and power that rises up against God must be struck down' (cf. *Isa.* 45:20-24). Therefore, let us be aware that God, when he so wills, will remove from our adversaries their spirit; or if he does not, he will break their arms and legs, their feet and hands, so that after taking counsel together, they will be overthrown. That is because they do not understand God's power, which is infinite. But as for us, we must be as pitiable blind people until he makes his brightness shine. And when our minds are darkened, that is, when we are weighed down with uncertainty, let us never fail to contemplate by faith the grace God promised us, although it does not appear in deed and experience.

We also have here a very useful admonition not to be obstinate concerning God. For although the people of Sodom continued to grope for the door, what good did it do them, except to show they were struggling with a definite evil disposition against God? For, as we said, did they think they were stupefied by chance? If there had been an iota of reason in them, they should have sensed that God had given a sign of his wrath and vengeance on them. So when they fly off their hinges that way, is it not obvious that they are taking up war against God? And will they finish it? So what is in their minds? But that is how Satan urges the reprobate along.

That example is to give us a sense of such horror that we will learn to walk humbly before God so that we will not be hardened to the point that we will be deliberate rebels. And when we see the wicked behaving irrationally when they sense that God is opposing their audacity and working against them, but that they do not leave well enough alone, let us realize Satan has them in his grip. And when God preserves us, let us know he has bestowed a wondrous grace on us. So let us use that teaching to our advantage.

And when we see those who despise God being poisoned with evil this way, although they see clearly that God is against them and they continue to pursue their evil, let us realize that that would be our natural tendency and we would imitate them, but that we, for our part, must guard against becoming hardened to evil, as the psalm exhorts (cf. *Psa.* 34:14). For there would be no end or limit to our being possessed by a diabolical rage that would pit us against God, and, were we to be broken and crushed a hundred times, we would not give up if he did not restrain us. And we have that kind of experience before our eyes every day. For are not the enemies of truth sufficiently convinced that they are fighting against God? And although they sense his strong hand, which ought to frighten them, do they not persist with such furious obstinacy that they appear to want to rise above the clouds to joust with God as if they were lifting up great mountains? That is a much too common vice. All the more must we be admonished, as I said, to walk in the light God gives us and not dim it or extinguished it by our ingratitude.

Moreover, if we fear being blinded that way by God, let us examine ourselves, and if sometimes he withdraws his light and we are like lost and irrational people, it is then that we must sense that he is punishing us for not following the right path (cf. *Psa.* 39:11; *Isa.* 13:11; *2 Pet.* 2:9) while we were enlightened by his word and his Holy Spirit. Let us realize that, return to him, and pray he will not allow us to be stubborn until the end. That, briefly, is what we have to remember about this passage.

At that point, Moses recounts that the angels told Lot that they had come to destroy the city of Sodom and that the outcry had been increased before God. Then they promise him he will depart in safety, not only he but also those who belong to him, his wife and children, even his sons-in-law, who are to marry his daughters. First, we see again what was dealt with earlier, namely, that God does not display his vengeance until the iniquities of

Sodom are full and he can no longer tolerate them. And that is to confirm what was said: that God is patient in the use of severity and rigor against those who have fallen short and offended him, but that for a time he pretends not to see. Because of his goodness, he is patient to invite them to repentance and to win them over, if it were possible, because he sustains them (cf. *Rom.* 2:4). But when he has waited for a long time and men grow worse instead of mending their ways and when it seems they want to mock his goodness fully and abuse his patience, it is then that they must come to account without mercy. Why? They have laid up that treasure of wrath Paul speaks of (cf. *Rom.* 2:5), and their perdition sweeps over them like a terrifying flood. And because they had no fear of God and became as confident as murderers and mocked his judgment, everybody has to fear them, and the people have to know how God showed himself to be their frightful Judge and each person has to be transfixed. So the angels say they are sent to destroy Sodom because the outcry was very great. If God had used such a punishment immediately, we could think he had gone too far. It is true we would still have to avoid comment, for we will gain nothing by blaming him. He will not need to go to a lot of trouble to justify himself; his justice will make itself known without any help. And if we growl threateningly, we will have to remain confounded. But still, since we see that Sodom's sins were known before God and recorded, as it were, and since he was not provoked by them but always provided for them abundantly and with gentleness, as our Lord Jesus speaks of them (cf. *Matt.* 10:15), and since they continued to enjoy the many blessings he bestowed upon them, we see that, since God delayed for a long time what Scripture witnesses to as true, namely, that he is compassionate (cf. *Exod.* 34:6-7; *1 Pet.* 3:15) and sustains men because of their frailty (cf. *Psa.* 39:5, 11; 62:9), seeing they are like a wind or like leaves that immediately wither (cf. *Job* 13:25; *Psa.* 1:4), and we see also that he does not wish to display his power against them, but in the end he shows himself and declares himself to be the Judge (cf. *Psa.* 7:11; *Isa.* 2:4; *Jer.* 11:20), indeed, after waiting long and being disappointed because men were so obstinate that their malice was totally incorrigible.

Now from that we have to learn, if our Lord deals with us gently, not to be deceived by self-congratulation as if God had some occasion to be satisfied with us. For often, when we provoke his wrath, he will nonetheless continue to show himself as a father full of gentleness and kindness (cf. *Isa.* 9:6; 22:21; *James* 1:17). But that is not to say we have to take time off and rest in our filth, but let us always examine our lives. And after we take a good look at our ingratitude toward God and become aware that we are not walking in such purity as is required, that he does not enjoy the fruit from us as would be reasonable inasmuch as we belong completely to him, that we are not as devoted to his service as is required, let us be displeased with that kind of vice, and let that call us to repentance, knowing also that God invites us in that way as if he were saying: 'Come now, you have angered me beyond measure, but I remain ready to pardon all offences, provided you return to me; and you have already experienced that, for you see that I continue to be as a father to you. Therefore, do not continue in your evil deeds, but knowing that I am ready to show mercy, return to me.' That, I say, is what we have to remember—if we are to avoid reaching the extreme of Sodom and Gomorrah—every time our Lord grants us rest and ease, every time we enjoy prosperity, even though we deserve to be severely chastised by him, and even though we are diligent to deserve it. That, in brief, is what we have to remember about this passage, which says that the cry of Sodom is increased before God.

Moreover, even though our sins are covered on earth and no one makes a stir over them and no one takes us to court over them or complains about them to take vengeance, let us also remember that the outcry still continues to resound in heaven. That is how iniquities are hidden among men. For we see that the most wicked will sometimes have no accuser to take them to court, and they will even be applauded, and they will be feared. And then they will think they are safe and will remain unpunished because, from men's perspective, they will be spared, but we must think the way Moses shows it here, that if our sins do not speak here below and men also cover up for them and we are also spoken well of on all sides, the outcry still resounds on high. So let us not waste our time thinking we have gotten off scot-free because no one has taken us to court or challenged us to a duel, but let us learn rather to appear daily before God's judgment seat and review our entire lives and condemn ourselves in order to be absolved by him, as it is said that man is blessed if he frightens himself with self-condemnation and does not wait for someone to come and read him the riot act and confront him with his evil deeds to confound him and show him that his punishment is near.[1] So the man who is not expecting that is blessed if he urgently encourages himself to fear.

Now we also have to note the promise given to Lot here, for what he is told here about Sodom's destruction is to get him to embrace more ardently the salvation he is offered and also to get his complete attention so he will obey God promptly, use the means the angels provide, and be bold. So there are two reasons why it was necessary for Lot to hear this. On the one hand, he had to accept more ardently God's grace and say: 'Alas, even though this place is to be completely destroyed, God does not fail to extend his hand and show he has pity on me. So I must depend confidently on him.' But Lot had to be urged, for he was very slow to understand, as we will see more fully (cf. *Gen.* 19:16). For God had to visit him with such fear that he hastened to withdraw from the confusion

---

[1] The nearest reference is to Calvin's commentary on a verse of the Psalms, Psalm 112:1 or 128:1.—*M.E.*

in which he found himself and in which he would have remained and perished with the wicked, as we saw in the case of Noah (cf. *Gen.* 6:3).[2] For when God predicted to his servant the flood which was to occur six score years later, he had the same two reasons we have just touched upon; for, on the one hand, Noah's attention had to be got forcibly so he would let God guide him, and he remained steadfastly assured despite the fact the world was to be a hundred times changed. Nevertheless, since God had looked upon him with pity, Noah could not perish and God's salvation was unfailing because God had seen to it. So Noah had to be assured so that he would not hesitate to call upon God in the midst of all the approaching difficulties and to remain resolute throughout, and he could not be disappointed in his expectation, provided his faith did not fail and provided he honour God by being confident that he was faithful to keep his promise. Noah had to have such a confidence or he would have perished. Moreover, he had to be urged to be frightened and afraid, as the apostle says in the eleventh chapter of Hebrews (cf. *Heb.* 11:7). For if he had not pictured God's vengeance on the world, it is certain he would not have burdened himself for six score years with building that ark which God had spoken of, for people thought he was totally stupid and addled for cutting down the forests and spending a lifetime doing so, and I am not talking about how men lived at that time, but about immediately after the days are lessened. It is certain Noah would never have had the constancy to stick with the task like a galley-slave, in a manner of speaking, and bury himself in his work day and night, eating little, giving up tilling the soil and similar activities because the ark held him captive, but since he knows it was not in vain that God declared to him the punishment he intended to deal out, he became active and took on an unconquerable courage. Thus it was with Lot, for he first had to be assured of God's will as it was

---

[2] According to Calvin's interpretation.—*M.E.*

proposed to him; otherwise, if he had not been seized with fear, it is certain he would never have budged. For it is certain that it is faith alone that gives us legs for walking and makes us active; otherwise, we would be like dead men. In a word, faith is the soul of souls. Just as our soul gives life to our body, which would otherwise be like a pitiable carcass, so our soul will be as dead and will remain without any power unless faith gives it life. That is why I said faith is the soul of our souls if we possess God's word.

Now that is how Noah was raised above all trials and also the way it happened to Lot. For the second point, they had to obey God. Now that could not be done if they had not feared the vengeance they had been told about. As a result, we observe the usefulness of that teaching. We have now to apply it to ourselves. On the one hand, every time God presents his mercy to us, let us receive it in such a way that we do not doubt that, in the midst of all the dead people that surround us, our salvation is very certain and unfailing. Why? Let us be satisfied that our Lord has cast the eye of his goodness upon us and that we have testimony that he loves us and is kindly disposed toward us. So since God has declared his will to us in this way, we see what our salvation consists of. And that is how we must look with contempt upon all the dead who could rise up against us.

Now it is not enough that we have tasted God's grace and can rejoice in it, but we must also use it as God commands. Therefore, let us learn to withdraw from all the world's pollutions. Since we see that the wicked are totally blind, let us know that we possess a time of enlightenment and not of darkness; since we see that they have contempt for God, let us be moved and gripped by fear, and let us learn how to restrain ourselves, whereas they are totally unrestrained. That, then, is how, after finding our support and rest in the promises God gives us of our salvation, we must at the same time be encouraged by them to devote ourselves to his service with such promptness, determination and constancy that we will never be turned away from serving him. That again is what we have to remember about this passage.

Now when Lot is told to take with him those who belong to him, even his sons-in-law, he is all the more certain that God does not want him to perish. For if God had spoken only about him personally, he could have doubted: 'Why is it that God does not withdraw my wife? Why does he want my daughters to perish? I am already old and decrepit; my daughters are young; when I am left desolate, what good will my life be to me?' So Lot could doubt whether God sincerely wanted to withdraw him from death. But when he sees that God gives him much more than his own life, he is even more confident, knowing that God has good reason to speak to him in those terms by his angels. But we see, as previously, that in Sodom ten righteous people had not been found. As for the sons-in-law God had chosen, it is likely he had taken the least corrupt; they scoff when he exhorts them to save their lives and brings them the message of salvation he had heard from the angels' mouths. So when those two, the cream of the crop, scorn God's goodness and even reject the admonition of their father-in-law, they not only have no reverence for him, but they also have contempt for the angels sent from heaven. It is as if they wanted to make a liar of God. When that kind of brutish godlessness exists, what shall we say about the rest? So we see here, as I have already said, God had good reason to declare that in the city of Sodom there had not been found ten people with enough understanding of the good to follow it.

Now we could ask at this point why God, knowing that Lot's sons-in-law would reject his grace, nonetheless invited them to depart to save their lives. It would seem that such an invitation would be useless, but we must not find it strange that God invites to the hope of salvation those who are unworthy, the very ones he knows to be hardened. As we see that the gospel is preached to all without distinction, I say that when it pleases God, the gospel will be preached in a city, and where the seed is sown, as our Lord Jesus Christ says, a part will fall among thorns, another on the rocks, another on the path (cf. *Matt.* 13:4-8). Only a small amount will bear fruit. And yet the teaching, although it is to serve for the salvation of men, is a door of death unto death (cf. 2 *Cor.* 2:15-16). We often see that in our own experience. Now if anyone wanted to dispute why it is that God scatters his word broadly, it seems that person is profaning it because it is despised, trodden underfoot, and the wicked rant against it, and that is the reason his name is blasphemed. Now we do not know the reason hidden in God's counsel, but let us be content that he wants to make the wicked inexcusable when he places his salvation before them, shows them the way to salvation, and opens to them the door of his kingdom, as if to say: 'Enter,' urging them to come to him. That is to make them even guiltier. Let us be content with that.

And there is still another reason. God wanted to show the kind of malice and perversity that are in us when we change life into death and medicine into poison unless he works in us by his Holy Spirit. For when we see unbelievers continuing in their condition and held there under Satan's tyranny, that gives God's grace all the more glory, for we in no wise differ from them except that we have been prepared by the one who had pity on us and elected us before the creation of the world and except that he testifies of his grace to us today when he calls us to himself, not only by his word, which issues from men's mouths, but also by the power of his Holy Spirit. For God must speak to us in two ways or he will never gain anything, and we will never be teachable and never will our ears be open to hear him unless he speaks both inside and outside of us. Outside, I say, by his ministers, for he wanted the gospel to be the instrument of his power for the salvation of all who believe, but also he must speak by his Holy Spirit in here, in our hearts.[3]

So that is why God wanted Lot to exhort his sons-in-law to leave Sodom—so they would be saved. And yet they did not accept that grace. That was, I say, so they would be guiltier and so Lot would no longer have any regret concerning them, seeing that they had contempt for God's goodness and would not profit from it. So, seeing such base ingratitude, Lot had a reason to make up his mind and say: 'Alas, since God had pity on those men, who nonetheless rejected his grace with definite malice, I must no longer contend for them, for they no longer deserve my recommendation and my pity since Satan possesses them and I see they seek only their own destruction. Let them have their way then.' That is how Lot had the opportunity to become more content.

He also had to think about the fact that our Lord had been singularly good to him because he had kept him in fear of him and had not permitted him ever to be abandoned and sink to the level of saying that he did not know what it meant to have God's promises. For that, in a word, is what Moses condemns in Lot's two sons-in-law, namely, that they had no regard for God to reverence him or tremble at his threats or lean on his promises. That is the height of all perdition. For at the outset, men do not think they are struggling in that way against God, but they are overlooking their many faults, and they think that that is of little consequence. They still retain a type and form of religion, which makes them think they are not willingly scorning God. And then the devil later gains greater possession of them and bewitches them so that they no longer have any sense of discrimination between good and evil, and they become completely like animals. That is the picture that is proposed for us in these two men, a picture we see every day if we are attentive to considering God's judgments such as he

[3] Once again a gesture must have accompanied the word.—M.E.

shows them to us for our instruction. For how many people do we see today who think of the word of God as something other than fable? How many think about eternal life? How many are so stupid, indeed raving mad, that they say the death of a man and the death of a dog are the same, and have no idea of what the grace of God is when he lifts them out of death? But then they have been asleep so long that they think they need not think about the second life and that everything that is said about it is only wishful thinking. For who has come back from the other world? Who has ever seen paradise or hell? That is the way the wicked think. And when we try to reclaim them by showing that God is a just Judge, oh, it is all and only fable, and they snap their fingers at it. By doing that, they show they have entered that madness of mocking God absolutely.

Consequently, what is recounted here about Lot's two sons-in-law gives us a mirror image of how those who become accustomed to evil stumble. They forget God and turn their backs on him, for in the end there is no remedy for healing them of their spiritual maladies. For, as we have said, they even change medicine into poison, and mocking God's promises and threats that way is to redouble God's wrath.

Now, in order to profit better from this passage, let us note what is said by the prophet Isaiah, namely, that we learn to tremble every time God speaks (cf. *Isa.* 66:5), for the mark he gives all believers is that we tremble at the sound of his word every time it enters into our ears. That, then, is the true foundation of all godliness and religion, namely, that God's word has such majesty for us that we are struck with humility and reverence and submit ourselves totally to it as soon as it is presented to us. Now, that trembling is not to make God's word hateful to us or make us flee in terror, but we are to be motivated by his threats not to put him to the test and not to use fear of him wrongly so that we will know that as soon as he indicates some sign of his wrath, we must not shield ourselves from immediately returning to him, but let us tremble to receive the salvation which he offers, seeing that we are completely lost. That, in brief, is what we have to remember.

Moreover, to that end and disposition, let us learn so to accept the salvation God proposes for us through the gospel that we make an effort to attract our neighbours to it, and may each one of us not be so devoted to our own persons that we forget the others who are to be recommended to him. So let us think about being accompanied by those who are on the way to perdition, not to follow them, but to lead them back to the right path, and let us win them since God grants us the grace of being ministers of the salvation he communicates to them.

Moreover, as often as we try to lead to salvation those who are far removed from it, if we do not do everything that would be effective and only beat the air, so to speak, and even if we are mocked and rejected, let us nonetheless know that it is a service acceptable to God (cf. *Psa.* 69:30-31) when we are concerned to save from perdition those who have devoted themselves to it. Now if we are to be concerned for those who scorn God, reject his grace and are completely infested with the devil, if we are still to have pity on them and extend a hand to lead them back to God, what concern are we obligated to have for our poor brothers when God has joined them with us in such a way that we know they are members of our body (cf. *Rom.* 12:4-5; *1 Cor.* 12:12-27; *Eph.* 4:5; 5:30), what concern, I ask, are we obligated to have for them when we see them in some trouble or difficulty? As we see today that the wicked have conspired to obliterate every memory of our Lord Jesus Christ, so also we see the efforts they are making against the poor church. Alas, are we not more than animals if that does not move us to pity and we do not groan for God to consider helping those he has elected and who suffer for his name's sake and for the testimony of our Lord Jesus Christ? That, then, is how we have to put that teaching into practice when we see that Lot immediately rose up and was concerned even at night to entreat his sons-in-law to leave that hell they were sunk in.

Therefore, on the one hand, let us try to do the same thing for those who are poor lost souls; and then, as I said, let us realize, on the other hand, that we must all the more consider our poor brothers first and cover them with our prayers when we cannot do better, and may God show that he has not only taken them under his protection but that he has the means to repel the enemy's vehemence. And however great their fury may be, he will be able to beat it back so that they will be completely confounded and we will, in the end, have the means to glorify his holy name.

Now let us bow before the majesty of our gracious God in acknowledgment of our faults, praying that he will cause us to feel them increasingly so that we will try to rid ourselves of them until he has remade us completely, and may he cleanse us of all the corruptions of our flesh, which are still too great and which we do not resist as we should. Also, may he support us increasingly until he has made us completely like himself and his righteousness, to which he calls us every day by his word. So let us all say: Almighty God, heavenly Father...

92

Abandoning the Past without Looking Back: No Small Feat

Thursday, 2 May 1560

And when the morning arose, then the angels hastened Lot, saying, Arise, take thy wife, and thy two daughters, which are here; lest thou be consumed in the iniquity of the city. And while he lingered, the men laid hold upon his hand, and upon the hand of his wife, and upon the hand of his two daughters; the LORD being merciful unto him: and they brought him forth, and set him without the city. And it came to pass, when they had brought them forth abroad, that he said, Escape for thy life; look not behind thee, neither stay thou in all the plain; escape to the mountain, lest thou be consumed (Gen. 19:15-17).

*P*REVIOUSLY MOSES PRAISED Lot's faith because he simply obeyed God and even tried to save his sons-in-law along with himself. On the other hand, we are told his sons-in-law made light of the threat and thought that it was made up. Now here is the third point. Lot, even though he had received God's promise and was moved by the threat, was nonetheless weak in faith. There was no perfection in him such that from the outset he walked as he should have and as he was commanded. He showed himself to be cowardly. Thus we are taught that, although the children of God desire to conform themselves to him and revere his word, they nonetheless will not walk as boldly as required, and sometimes they will even be so cowardly that they will not know whether they ought to advance or retreat. That is what we now see in the person of Lot.

Now we are informed that there is a great difference between the scorn characteristic of unbelievers when one speaks to them as God commanded either about his promises or his threats (cf. *Jon.* 1:2; 3:1; *Matt.* 28:19-20; *Acts* 16:9-10; 17:30) and between the weakness that is in those who possess some goodwill and who are inclined to come into line with God. Consequently, on the one hand, we are obliged to know that there is no excuse if we are not moved when God's threats or promises are mentioned. We must certainly be overwhelmed with stupidity and Satan has to be in charge of us if we have no disposition to depend on God's promises or be daunted by his threats.[1]

But when we possess some goodwill and yet are only able with great difficulty to generate any enthusiasm, we must indeed be aware of our fault if we are to condemn ourselves for it and groan before God. But still we must not lose courage, but we must work hard against this vice that we perceive. And we have to remember our Lord Jesus Christ's comment that the spirit is willing, but the flesh is weak (cf. *Matt.* 26:41). With those words he wanted to let us know that even though we are disposed to follow God wherever he calls us and to be prompt in acting according to the grace that he grants through his Holy Spirit, we will always be cold and slothful. Why? We are partly held back. If we were fully renewed and God's Spirit were in charge of all our senses and desires and affections, it would cost us nothing to run, even very fast; as soon as God gives a sign, and we would be on our way to go where he calls

---

[1] We have here what amounts to a pastoral discourse on fear. If the hearers are not moved by the discourse, this would be a near proof for them that they are inspired by Satan, not by God. Cf. *Institutes* I, xiv, 18; III, ii, 11; and iii, 9.—*M.E.*

us, but because there is still a lot of our earthly and slothful nature within us, we have to watch and pray as our Lord Jesus Christ exhorts us to do (cf. *Matt.* 26:41a).

And we are in fact no better than Lot. It is true we have a fuller teaching than he did. For having left the house of Abraham, his uncle, he did not have the continual experiences of being confirmed in the fear of God, as he would have had if he had always remained with Abraham. But in that particular he surpassed us, for even though he had plunged into this gulf called Sodom, he still bore the distinction of being 'just,' which was attributed to him by God's Spirit (cf. *2 Pet.* 2:7). Moreover, we observe the integrity in which he walked. And God also honours him by sending him his angels. Still, what was his faith like? It was so weak that he immediately forgot what he was told, or he was at least so astonished that he could not obey God simply, that he had no objections, that he did not back away, and that he did not have strong feelings that turned him aside and moved him away from the right path. So since we see what happened to the one who has such an excellent witness, do we not have an occasion to lower our heads and be humble? In addition, let us use the remedy proposed by the Son of God, namely, that we be watchful (cf. *Matt.* 26:41), that is, that we not think so highly of ourselves that we become hardened in our indolence, which we are very inclined to do, indeed, devoted to doing. And because God has to work within us, let us pray that he will supply what we lack.

Moreover, we must note what is said here: that the angels urged him insistently. In other words, they rebuked him for delaying. From that we have to draw a lesson. When we have been taught what we must do, if we do not have the perseverance to obey God at the outset, we have to be urged and he has exhorted us to correct our tendency to delay. He does not have to do that just once, but repeatedly. That shows us it is not enough to have the simple teaching to recognize what is good and what God approves, but we have to have goads to urge us on further. That is why Paul says that Scripture is useful (cf. *2 Tim.* 3:16), not just to show us the will of God, for when we know it, we will remain the same without being aware of any change within ourselves. There will be no zeal, no enthusiasm, no desire. So what is necessary since we have the teaching? God must add other helps to make it effective and enter into our hearts. It must have a living root. Its fruit must be evident and break forth. That is why we have to be prodded, Paul says.

Now additional exhortations would not be useful, but God must rebuke us, must make us ashamed, confound us, or everything we might have heard would be useless and remain inert, so to speak, because we are so dull-witted and worldly that we will never follow where God calls us unless we are forcibly dragged along. So if Lot needed the angels to urge him insistently, let us not be surprised today if our Lord comes and commands us to hear his word every day so that we will be disciples all of our lives. There are some who think that they are wise enough when they have heard thirty sermons; but let us realize that our Lord has subjected us to that perpetual order, which he knows is useful for us. Also, let us not find it strange or vexing when we are told what God has commanded, when emphatic and harsh words are used, and when we hear rebukes that are a bit sharp at the beginning, for our sensitivities are very delicate. So if our Lord prods us and sometimes raises our hackles and even lashes us with a whip, so to speak, or strikes us like mules, let us yield to it, knowing that it is profitable for us. For when we examine closely what is in us, we will then find that God's teaching will be, so to speak, disregarded, and we deprive it of all its power unless God empowers it in the way I said.

Moreover, continuing what we have mentioned, since our Lord pursues us earnestly this way, let us profit from his exhortations and threats so we will not be confounded or discouraged by the weakness of our faith, just as Lot was not completely rejected. Although the vice of being cold that Moses speaks of was certainly to be condemned, God always continues to draw him. Consequently, let us not lose courage despite the fact that our faith is weak and we sense many hindrances which hold us back and sometimes even cause us to step back instead of approaching as we should. And it is just in this way that we must hope that God will uphold the weakness of our faith, provided we do not give ourselves credit for it, and we must also have compassion on our brothers when we see them weak, as Paul exhorts us to do in the eleventh chapter of Romans so that if we are stronger than they and God has fortified us better (cf. *Rom.* 11:16-24), we will be resolute and walk with a sincere courage to conform ourselves to his will and accept forthwith those who lag behind, come after us, follow us at a distance, even stumbling occasionally without showing they have profited from God's word, as would be required.

Today we see a lot of people like Lot's two sons-in-law, for they are filled with such pride that the word of God means nothing to them, and no matter how much you explain to them, they are never convinced by reason. Why not? They are so blind they do not acknowledge God in any way, they willingly become like dumb animals, and they would like to deaden their consciences and become so mindless that they can make no distinction between good and evil. We will also see many dogs in the world that openly make fun of God's word. Sometimes they will pretend to listen to it, but it is not because they have a true understanding of it. They are like many profane people, and today the world is full of that kind of contagion and pollution. But there are others who have some worthy disposition; God has placed some seed of fear in their hearts, but they will be held back, some by greed, some by ambition, others by hesitancy to commit. So people in that situation will have a good opening, but you will not see God's word touch them; it will move them and change them, and stir them to devote themselves completely to God's service, but when it comes to admitting their spiritual poverty, they will not be able to lift themselves out of the mire into which they have sunk. We will see many people like that today.

Now to reject them as if they no longer had hope would be much too severe. It is true we must not encourage them in their vices, but let us employ a remedy which we have already mentioned in God's word, namely, when the teaching does not have enough power to move them, let us rebuke them, let us place before them God's approaching judgment, which is against them. And let us continue to expect that our Lord will extend to them more grace, for we will see many who are held in that muddle of the Papacy. Now it is certain we will always be right to condemn them because they remain there as in Sodom and Gomorrah. For even though God threatens the wicked who rule there, they are nonetheless unable to get out of that situation, but our Lord can work over time. And if he does not do so today, it will be tomorrow, and he will show that he had reserved them for himself. So that is what we have to remember about this passage where it is said that the angels urged Lot insistently when dawn broke.

Now that is not all, for Lot delays after being urged that way and the angels prodded him, even with threats: 'Take heed, or you will perish in this vengeance which has been prepared.' Despite the angels' vehement insistence, this poor man still delays deciding whether he will go. He had resolved that it was necessary to obey God, and he not only believes that he must obey, but he has the desire and will to, but he has not done so. So we see it is not enough for our Lord to put in our hearts a zeal to follow him, but he must also at the same time give the power to carry through, as Paul says in the second chapter of Philippians when he says we must walk in fear and heaviness of mind, like people who are trembling, for it is God, he says, who gives both the willing and the doing of his good pleasure (cf. *Phil.* 2:12-13). When he tells us we must walk humbly, he adds the reason, for, he says, we can do nothing. That being true, God must give us the will, for it is not natural for us to have a single good thought unless he inspires it in us. And when he does, we will still be only halfway down the road to having one, and our legs will fail us, and whatever good intention we may think we have, the power must still accompany it, that is, our Lord must guide us in such a way that we will fulfil what we know to be his will. That, then, is what we have to remember here when it is said that the angels urged Lot insistently but that he continues to delay until they take hold of his hand.

Now that informs us at the same time that if God's word does not have the power in us that it should have, our Lord must constrain us as if by force. And in fact he uses it in us as we experience it enough that when a man has some fear of God, he will sufficiently condemn his own vices, indeed even though he does not sense them in himself. One person will be influenced by some ambition or other, or he will be displeased with it and groan before God because he cannot rid himself completely of it. Another will experience a different kind of greed and have such little confidence in himself that he will wholeheartedly devote himself to acquiring the goods of this world. Another will sense in himself a different evil, but he would like to be completely healed of it. In any case, the one will hold on to his ambition and the other to his greed; even though they try to succeed every day. The fact is that they will remain captives until our Lord provides a way out. That is why he brings them down when he sees them given over too much to vainglory, and when they seek to be esteemed and rise in the eyes of the world, he will take from them their opportunity. That is like a bloodletting he gives them to purge all those bad humours. That is the case when he removes one good from another, seeing that one is too much influenced by the other, and he removes a part of its substance. Now it is true that that is harsh on the face of it. But look! Our Lord has to use such remedies against diseases. For if you give only good food to a sick person, it will do him no good if there is something in his stomach that hinders digestion. Purgings are necessary when something bad is present. And sometimes it is even good to give antidotes. And God does that for his children. So let us learn that when God does not treat us as we would like, he will send loss of goods to one, he will give afflictions to another to keep him humble and unpretentious. When he uses such harsh tactics as that, it is as if he were seizing us by the hand and saying: 'Come.' When a father sees that his son does not want to come at first when he beckons and that the child is unruly, he will reach out and give him a good shaking. So it is that God must work with us because our ears are deaf. And when we hear what he wants to command us, we will agree and say: 'That must be done. It is only right for us to be subjected to his will.' But if we do not budge, that is why he must shake us and make us come forcibly, as it were, in spite of ourselves. That, then, is what we have to remember about this passage.

And in fact, how many are there who would have remained lost if our Lord had not drawn them out by the hand without their knowing it? For even though many, actually the majority, would have understanding of God's word, they would nonetheless still be bogged down in those curses of the Papacy if God had not pushed them out by force, so to speak. Many are satisfied when they realize that even though they are trying to serve God, there is much to reproach in them, and they think they are thereby forgiven because they have thought there is. Now our Lord, seeing them in that situation, kindles some persecution or other for them. They become frightened, and they have to find new lodging. There is no longer a question of halting between decisions. Although the wicked do not intend that outcome, our Lord nonetheless uses that means to provide for the salvation of those he has elected and does not wish to remain in that abyss, and he pulls them out. So it is God's hand that urges those people along, and we must realize that fact if we are to profit from it and mollify all the bitter thoughts we might entertain when our Lord cuts us off from much of what he had given us, provided he leaves us with the main thing we are to desire, even though he drove us away with a slight breeze or a great whirlwind and impoverished us and crushed us, from the world's viewpoint. In short, let us be as people half dead; let us realize that in that way he gains our advantage and advances our salvation, as if he had seized us by the hand. And in order to be more assured of that, let us consider how slothful we are, and we will find that we are more slothful than Lot was. That, then, is in brief what we have to remember.

As for the threat he made, let us note that our Lord needs to get our attention because we are not willingly quick or disposed to come to him. It is true that it was a hard thing for Lot to hear: 'You will perish in the vengeance visited on the wicked and the reprobate if you do not protect yourself from it.' Even so, Lot had to be prodded, given his disposition to delay. It is true our Lord will always watch over his own, for none of his elect can perish because our Lord Jesus Christ preserves them all, just as he says in the tenth chapter of John (cf. *John* 10:28). Yet, as we have said, we are weak and wilful, which means our Lord must guide us so that we will not come into his austere counsel (cf. *Jer.* 23:18), but so that we will use means that are appropriate and suitable for us. Example: There are libertines who think that if God has elected them, they cannot fail to be saved, and as a result they will put God to the test and devote themselves to complete perdition. Now that is a sign that they are totally reprobate, for God's election is always accompanied by faith, and faith is allied with humility. And humility, what does it mean except a renunciation of ourselves and the laying hold of God's judgment with an ardent zeal to invoke his holy name and to find all our refuge in him? Therefore, those who claim that God has elected them and that they cannot perish nonetheless yield themselves to every evil; they, I say, show clearly that God has abandoned them and that the devil possesses them. So our Lord is in possession of a way which he knows to be good and useful for us, which is that he threatens us and warns us to take heed to ourselves lest we perish with the reprobate. Now that is not possible. It is true that it is not possible according to his austere counsel, but neither must we enter it. Each of us must enter it for himself, and at that time we will humble ourselves and be afraid of perishing with the wicked, and, being afraid, we will take heed to ourselves and separate ourselves from them when we see they are lighting the fire of God's wrath. Let us not be participants in their corruptions for fear that they will draw us into the perdition they are headed for and are rushing into.

So that is why it is said to Lot: 'Make haste so that you will not perish in the destruction of the city.' Therefore, we must be warned daily about such a thing, as Paul so indicates when he says: 'My friends, let no one deceive you with vain words, for because of these offences God's wrath comes upon unbelieving children and rebels' (cf. *Eph.* 5:6). He speaks that way to create concern in the faithful so they will straighten up and not give themselves over to the corruptions that the despisers of all righteousness abandon themselves to. We must consider the fact that God's wrath could destroy us the moment we offend him, not, as I have said, that God changes or varies in his eternal counsel (cf. *James* 1:17), but he is always concerned for our condition so that he can remove from us all presumption and any false sense of security, for nothing works more against us than that. For what is the negative effect of presumption and a false sense of security? In the first place, we give no glory to God, and then we can in no way experience the need we have for his help. And then we have no desire to pray, for all the practices of faith are dead in us. Consequently, we always need to consider what kind of people we are and how fragile our condition is and that we could fall away from one day to the next, indeed at any moment. So let us be concerned to pray to God diligently that he will grant us the grace to be so displeased with our vices and ourselves that we will place all our trust in him. That, in brief, is what we have to remember here.

Likewise, Paul, speaking to the Gentiles after giving them the example of the Jews, says that those who stand should take heed for fear of falling (cf. *1 Cor.* 10:12). Not that he wants to put us in doubt, for we must always be certain and assured that God will sustain us until the end, and since he has begun his work in us, he will bring it to conclusion (cf. *Phil.* 1:6), but that is because we have double assurance. One we lay hold of because we are becoming hardened when we are puffed up with presumption and think we do wonders; the other we lay hold of when we depend on the promises God made us that we will never fall away. Now that assurance does not mean we will not tremble when we consider our sins, which we must consider morning and evening. That, then, is how, in brief, we must profit from this passage.

Now we are told particularly that God wanted to spare Lot when he took him by the hand. Moses advises us that when God removed Lot this way by force, he was declaring a singular mercy toward him. Did he not deserve to perish since the angels had delivered to him the message that the city of Sodom was to perish and, in so doing, they had promised that God intended to save him? So when Lot heard that and still did not hurry, even after some insistence, did he not indeed deserve to be abandoned by the angels, as if to say: 'Well, since you want to perish, remain and be destroyed'? But when they seize him by the hand, we see how God showed him his kindness and goodness by fighting against the vice of procrastination, which signalled great ingratitude. Following the statement that God wanted to spare him, that word carries a lot of weight. And in fact our Lord must do the same for his elect every day, or even though he has refashioned them by his Holy Spirit in such a way that they seek to be his subjects, they will still commit very serious sins, yes, and without thinking about it, sins which would deserve their being cut off from the church; and they would in fact fall into horrible confusion if God did not have pity on them. In fact, if God displayed the kind of rigour we deserve, alas, how many times in our lives we would give him an occasion to leave us and abandon us completely! So there is no other help for us if, after seeing we are so badly informed that we almost reject the blessing and salvation he offers us, he does not support us and still spare us, disregarding our unworthiness but always continuing his mercy toward us, which we are more than unworthy of. So let us learn that this is not written just for Lot, but that we must apply it to our use so that we will magnify God's grace and goodness such as they are declared to us.

Moreover, in any case, let us not congratulate ourselves, for if God spared his servant Lot once, that does not mean he is always obligated to do the same. Therefore, having been helped, let us think about ourselves more carefully and be on greater guard in the future so we will not be called into account for rejecting his grace and putting a distance between it and ourselves.

It is then said that the angels, after taking Lot out of the city, said to him: 'Escape for your soul's sake—that is, to the extent your life is dear to you, consider saving yourself—and do not look behind you and do not stop in the plain, but flee quickly into the mountain so you will have refuge there.' Since Lot was told to save his life after the angels took him from the city, let us mark better what has been said, namely, that mixed with his faith there were still many earthly interests which could corrupt him to the extent that he would not know whether he was coming or going, that he would not know whether he was to follow God or to turn his back and go the other way.

Now everything that is written about Lot is for our common instruction. Since our Lord has placed us on the right path, let us be advised not to let go of the reins and wander hither and yon, for we will not be able to turn away ever so little without being like wayward people, and we will no longer find any direction. Let us also be advised that Lot was previously zealous. He was not satisfied to accept what he heard concerning himself in this message from God, but he had concern for his sons-in-law. He ran through the city at night, even after that tumult which was like a message of death (cf. *Gen.* 19:14). He had been attacked at his house, and it seemed he might have perished there.

And at that point he exposes himself to every danger. And immediately afterward, we see that he acts as if he is asleep. So even though we have walked for a time and have even been very zealous, let us realize that in a moment we would be changed and, instead of being fervent, we would be dead and all of the praiseworthy desire we had for serving God would immediately evaporate if our Lord did not continue and we did not make an effort and stir the fire. Paul uses that comparison when speaking to Timothy when he tells him to kindle God's gifts: 'You must stir them up' (cf. *2 Tim.* 1:6). It is like having a good fire. If the burning embers are separated little by little, the fire will die out. They must be brought close together. They must be moved about and stirred. That is how we need to be truly awakened, for otherwise we would be quickly brought to ruin. As I said, even if we had begun well and had possessed angelic perfection, it is certain we would degenerate very soon and immediately become like lost people. So that is what we have to remember when it is said that the angels, in a manner of speaking, almost renounced Lot when they prodded him a second time: 'You have been advised that if your life is dear to you, you must consider escaping soon.'

Yet we see how God persevered in having pity on his poor servant Lot, seeing him thus mentally slow and destitute of counsel, seeing him cowardly and beaten down that way, for the angels were not content to extend a hand to lead him, indeed forcibly, but they dragged him outside of the city, saying: 'You must not go back; you are now outside of that abyss where you would have perished if God had not shown you pity, and you indeed deserved to perish since you delayed so long. You are now outside.' So let us realize that our Lord will sometimes protect us, even in spite of ourselves. And in that fact we also see that he does not do so for a day, that we are not sustained by his power the way we would like, and that we are led by his Holy Spirit, but we see that what he has begun, he is bringing to conclusion, even though we do not see it.

Now that is not all, for Moses adds that the angels ordered Lot not to look behind or to stop on the plain, but to flee quickly to the mountain. Now there is no doubt that Lot, despite the fact that he had lived in great anguish in the midst of such damnable pollutions as those that reigned in Sodom, had nonetheless become somewhat attached to the land's fertility, which had enticed him when he left the company of his uncle Abraham. He had seen the land of Sodom as an earthly paradise, as we have seen (cf. *Gen.* 13:10-11). Lot looks at the land and is immediately drawn to it. That is the beginning of his perdition, for he considers nothing but being at ease in a good and fertile land. Since he lives in it, there is no doubt he is accustomed to living there the way the land supports him. He was a man at ease. He had a lot of livestock. He had servants and maidservants, as we have seen (cf. *Gen.* 13:5). Consequently, there is no question that he enjoyed the fat of the land available to the inhabitants. When we enjoy prosperity that way, when we have more than enough to eat and drink, it is difficult to live soberly and temperately.

In addition to living soberly and temperately, we will be delicate, as we see in those who had been well fed. They have had plenty. They had income from rent and investments. People like that, even though they are not given to gluttony and drunkenness and enjoy a good reputation, they still will not be able to detach themselves from this world. This is what they will say: 'I am not accustomed to dealing with heat and cold, hunger or thirst. It is true I do not require abundance and sumptuousness, but if I did not have bread and wine and my accustomed fare, what would I do? I would be a miserable creature.' That is how those who have had plenty continue to coddle themselves, as we say, and are so soft they cannot willingly deprive themselves.

There is no doubt Lot was resistant for that reason, for the angels had good reason to say to him: 'Be careful not to look back, and do not stop on the plain.' And even after taking him out of the city, they urged him, saying: 'Protect yourself. Save your life.' When the angels speak to him that way, it is an indication that Lot had not completely forgotten the delights of Sodom and was having trouble leaving behind his good life, for he could not take with him his house and furnishings and entire family. So there is no doubt that he had regrets and was displeased and anguished because he feared poverty and that when he saw himself facing such difficulties, he would fall into despair. We need to pray to God concerning such situations and strengthen ourselves. But what happens? When we have to face some fear, we think we are forgiven in God's sight, and we say: 'Alas, if I did not have these problems, I would be resolute,' and it does not occur to us that our Lord is showing us what kind of people we are, how weak and clumsy we are when it comes to doing good, so that we will run to him and ask him to strengthen us. That does not occur to us. So let us pay particular attention to what we learn here.

Moreover, seeing that Lot is hastened to leave and that God gives him no time, let us keep in mind that it is not our choice to procrastinate when our Lord gives us incentive to walk, but that we must immediately set out. And if he sometimes hastens us more than we would like, let us endure it patiently, for he knows the reason behind it. He would have forewarned Lot if he had wanted to and would have sent him that message sooner in order to warn him about the vengeance he intended to visit on Sodom and Gomorrah. And he gives him notice at the present time to test his faith and, while testing it, to show him how weak he is so that he will have a better idea of the mercy he has on him. And our Lord also wants us to be instructed by Lot's example how, in truth, he must have pity on us often, even always, for we would perish at every moment if he did not maintain us and save us miraculously by extending his hand to each of us. So, in brief, on those occasions when our Lord calls us to himself in times of turmoil and very hastily, more often than we would like, let us follow him, knowing that he does it for our welfare and salvation.

As for the expression 'look behind,' we will mention it farther along when Moses tells us what happened to Lot's wife (cf. *Gen.* 19:26). But we have to note here that since our Lord proposes a goal and sets us on the way he wants us to go, he simultaneously wants us to pay very close attention and not look back and be distracted. Now there are many ways to look back, for when we leave behind something desirable, we will often be tempted to stray and turn aside from the path on which the Lord is leading us. How many people we see who are nostalgic for what they left behind and say: 'I should never have done this; I should never have done that,' and end up concluding: 'Oh, I wish I could go back.' That is how many people feel when they do not find what they thought they would in God's church. They say, 'Oh, this is not what I thought it would be. What would I do here? And when I go back, I will still have this and that.'² In a word, many people look back that way and distance themselves from God and rush away from the right path. Others look behind when they think they have done enough if they have walked just three steps, for they think that God has to be satisfied and that they have finished their journey. Let us learn not to look back in any way. How? As I said, let us realize our Lord calls us on condition that we dedicate our lives and deaths to him and never abandon serving him, and that we never give up after trying to do our duty for a month or a year, or ten or twenty years, but let us always persist and keep our minds on that. And let us not say: 'I have already done this. I have endured so much. Why does not God allow me to rest now?' So let us not look back that way as if God ought to think we have done enough, or look back at our pleasures and delights, for the devil will always place enough enticements before us to turn us away from God. That, then, is what we have to remember.

And then we read: 'Do not stop on the plain,' for that plain was an earthly paradise. So when Lot had lingered as long as he could, it is certain that those words could still calm him and he could finally go so far away that he would not have fully known that what had been told him was as much about Sodom's ruin as about the salvation God had mentioned to him, for we see that we release the bridle of our understanding or of our eyes or our ears and we are immediately corrupted and led astray. In short, we could not devote ourselves ever so little to the vanities of this world without having completely turned away from God. And that is also why David teaches us to pray: 'Lord, turn my eyes away so I will not look upon vanity' (cf. *Psa.* 119:37). If Lot needed the admonition not to stop on the plain and cast his sorrowful eyes about, we must even more avoid all such temptations,

---

² Calvin echoes here the regrets of certain French refugees arriving in Geneva.—*M.E.*

for we are not more capable or stronger than he was. That, then, is what we have to remember.

In conclusion, he is told to flee to the mountain, which signifies that when it pleases God to separate us from this world and to remove us from its delights, honours, and riches, and when he wants us to be, as it were, in this desert, if that is the way he wants to save us, let us be ready to receive it and seek only to yield to his will. The remainder will be delivered tomorrow, God willing.

Now let us bow before the majesty of our gracious God in acknowledgment of our faults, praying he will be pleased to bury them and pardon them and not allow us to remain in our corruptions and held back by fragile and transitory things, but may he lift us up by his Spirit to be truly citizens of heaven and pilgrims on this earth. And because we need much help to come to him, may he be pleased to provide it according to our needs, and may he always support us and grant that the help he provides will be useful for us, and may it bear fruit for our salvation, such that even if we limp along or tend to delay, we will not cease to follow until we reach the place of our joy and felicity, namely, that eternal inheritance which is ready for us and was acquired for us by our Lord Jesus Christ. May he grant that grace not only to us but to all the peoples and nations on earth.

93

God Answers Prayer and Brings Judgment

Friday, 3 May 1560

Look not behind thee, neither stay thou in all the plain; escape to the mountain, lest thou be consumed. And Lot said unto them, Oh, not so, my Lord: Behold now, thy servant hath found grace in thy sight, and thou hast magnified thy mercy, which thou hast shewed unto me in saving my life; and I cannot escape to the mountain, lest some evil take me, and I die: Behold now, this city is near to flee unto, and it is a little one: Oh, let me escape thither, (is it not a little one?) and my soul shall live. And he said unto him, See, I have accepted thee concerning this thing also, that I will not overthrow this city, for the which thou hast spoken. Haste thee, escape thither; for I cannot do any thing till thou be come thither. Therefore the name of the city was called Zoar. The sun was risen upon the earth when Lot entered into Zoar (Gen. 19:17b-23).

WE SAW YESTERDAY that God forbade Lot to look behind so that he would not linger over those delights by which he had been nourished much too long, given the corruption which was in the land of Sodom. It is noteworthy that he is commanded to flee into the mountain as if God wanted him kept there like a recluse. Now that condition was harsh, but that is the way our Lord wanted to test Lot's obedience: by getting him to renounce willingly the many pleasures he had enjoyed while living among the people of Sodom and by getting him to be unhappy with possessing his grace, as if he were saying to him: 'Think only about this singular good that I am doing for you by exempting you from the destruction which is to fall upon all the cities. By doing that, I am showing you that I have chosen you, that I will to preserve you as my own. And you must endure as you prepare to live without the comforts and conveniences you were accustomed to in Sodom.' That, then, is why Lot is told to flee into the mountain.

Now he refuses, which is a sign of ingratitude, for he should have been so delighted by the grace granted to him that it should not have occurred to him to speak against God's command. He still asks God to let him go into a small nearby city, and he obtains his request, for he claimed that he could not be safe in the mountain, that the city was small, and that it was insignificant that he withdraw into a little corner of it. So we see that Lot was not completely cleansed of all of his earthly affections, and yet we see God's inestimable goodness in the fact that he supports him and does not condemn him as severely as he deserved, but allows him to withdraw into that city.

What is more, he says he will wait until he has arrived there because he can do nothing until Lot is safe. Now we have to think here that although God does not command each of us to withdraw to the mountain, he is nonetheless showing us how he wants us to live. We must view that as if he were sending us a message from heaven. Example: We will not be able to serve God in a place where we would have greater advantage and profit, for if we want to enjoy what would be desirable for us, we will have such distractions that could necessitate our abandoning God. When our Lord says to us: 'You cannot have both because you cannot be joined to me and at the same time have what the flesh desires' (cf. *Matt.* 6:24). When God shows us that, it is like having an angel descend from heaven to declare that God wants us to live this way, as if we were living in the desert, that is, in a place where we do not have everything at our disposition. So we must submit to that and not follow Lot's example in that he refused the good God was offering him. For if our Lord pardoned him for that fault, it was not to give us such licence but to teach us about the kind of ingratitude that is in man when he is simply to follow God's will, and how to answer: 'That is not the way it is supposed to be, but you must do what I demand,' and that is because man prefers to do his own will rather than God's. Lot was not that presumptuous, but he was carried away by his own inconsiderate appetite.

So that is how we are advised to keep ourselves on a very tight leash when our Lord tells us what pleases him and what he requires of us so that there will be no discussion on our part about it, but so that we will peaceably acquiesce in what he tells us. That practice is very necessary for us even today, for our Lord calls us in that way to knowledge of his good news to test how we value such a treasure while withdrawing from what we could wish for and placing ourselves in his hands to renounce all the desires of this world. And then we do not know what can happen to us, and although our Lord spares us and has spared us until now, we do not know what he has in reserve for us. All the more, then, must we ponder this teaching, which is that whether on a mountain or in a desert or in the grave itself, we are willing to proceed without talking back, wherever our Lord wants us to go.

At this point we could ask, inasmuch as Lot was not founded on God's word when making that request, how he was answered, for we cannot call upon God without faith, as Paul says (cf. *Rom.* 10:14); and we also have this statement from the prophet that when we ask God for what is good according to his will, he will grant it (cf. *Jer.* 29:12-13). It is noteworthy that Paul says we must pray and make our requests in conformity with God's will or they will not be pleasing to him (cf. *Rom.* 12:1-2). Likewise, we hear what James says, that when we pray without faith, we must not think we will obtain anything from God. Now faith brings a certainty which depends on the testimony we have about God's will. Everyone is not to create his own ideas about what seems good to him, but God must speak and we must accept his promise if we are to be certain that we will not be disappointed and can boldly depend on what he says to us.

Lot loses patience, becomes rashly bold, and says: 'No, Lord, let me not go to the mountain.' He clearly takes a position against God, who had said to him, 'I wish to save you in the mountain.' He speaks against that. Now how does that test him? Now we have to note that Lot's prayer is based, in principle, on faith, but it is in part sinful because Lot at least deviated from what God proposed, and that will happen to us sometimes, for we will not pray haphazardly. I am speaking of those who are strictly taught in the word of God. They will not pray capriciously, not knowing whether God wishes to listen, but if they trust him and do not doubt that he wishes to be merciful, then they have the command to pray (cf. *Luke* 21:36; *1 Thess.* 5:17; *James* 5:16). They will learn that and will adhere firmly to the fact that God wishes to be their Father (cf. *Isa.* 9:5; *James* 1:17). Afterwards, they will not turn from the way which they are shown. In other words, they will call upon God in the name of Jesus Christ (cf. *John* 14:13; 16:23). Consequently, they will have a rather strong feeling and would like for God to please them and, in a way, subject himself to them. Not that they utter such a blasphemy, but they will nonetheless be blinded by their desires and go beyond measure and forget their status when they pray.

So there you have a prayer offered in faith.[1] But there is some unbelief mixed with it because men, as I have said, are not so restrained or so well advised that they conform to God's will at all times. So when we happen to go beyond our limits in some

[1] Calvin returns to Lot's prayer.—*M.E.*

respect, we deserve God's rejection, for we profane his name, but he nonetheless has pity on his own, even though they fail and do not adhere to the right path, or they ask amiss in their petitions. That is what happened to Lot. Consequently, let us not find it strange that God answered him, even though he fell short, but let us not use that as an excuse to loosen the bridle and require him to yield to our fancy. Let us not take that liberty, but let us give heed to what God has promised us so that we will be assured that he will hear us in our petitions when they are offered in the certainty that I spoke of and in strict obedience, for it is impossible for us to ask for what is in conformity with God's will unless our wills are submissive, indeed completely beaten down.

In addition, we have to note that Lot spoke prudently when he realized those he had lodged and had previously thought were mortal men were actually God's angels. There we have two angels who say to him: 'Save yourself in the mountain,' and he says: 'No, Sir.' He should have spoken in the plural when addressing them, but knowing there are two angels, he moves a step higher and addresses only God, for he knows angels have neither the authority nor the power to do what pleases them but are only ministers (cf. *Heb.* 1:14), and he knows that God reserves his authority for himself alone and that it is also from him alone that we must hope for all good things, and he knows that it is to him alone that we must offer the sacrifices of prayers and petitions (cf. *Psa.* 50:14; *Heb.* 13:15; *1 Pet.* 2:5). That, then, is a very useful point.

The angels appear to Lot. He does not pray to them or give them the honour which belongs to and is to be reserved for God. In short, he does not make idols of them, but he knows that God alone is the author of all good, that prayer must be addressed to him and that the angels must remain in their order and rank. I say that this point is very useful, for we see how men in all times formed idols for themselves, claiming that God manifested his power by means of angels. And that was even common in some way among the pagans. That is what gave rise to idolatry, for the pagans were somewhat aware there was a sovereign God, but because he manifested himself and the people had understood that from their fathers and believed that angels were sent from on high, indeed with such authority that God's glory shone in them, as they are also called thrones, dominions, principalities, and powers (cf. *Col.* 1:16)—that is what led the poor ignorant people to entrust themselves to angels and hold them as guardians of their salvation and as mediators who could acquire for them grace and favour with the sovereign God. All the more must we pay close attention to what Lot shows us, for, as we have said, he sees the angels with his eyes and yet does not pray to them. He leaves them and says: 'Sir,' when he addresses God alone. He indicates that he adheres only to the oneness of God without tearing him to pieces, as do the poor blind who are devoted to superstitions. We have a virtue in Lot which is placed before us so that we will learn not to diminish or obscure the excellence, the power, the goodness of our God, even though it pleases him to use his angels in his service for our salvation.

Moreover, continuing with what was said, we see in the person of Lot how difficult it is to bring all our affections and desires under control so that God can govern us and rule over us in peace and without conflict. For if Lot had always been restrained by uprightness and integrity while living in Sodom and it had been only a matter of living well and loosely and being utterly dissolute, if Lot had separated himself at that time from the wicked and always restrained himself because of his fear of God, there is all the more reason not to doubt that he, when seeing such vengeance was near, was touched more to the quick than he had been previously. We nonetheless still see that he is unable to strip himself of his earthly desires. Therefore, let us learn to hold ourselves suspect because there is nothing more difficult than to die to self to the extent that we are no longer led and urged on by our wishes and desires. And that is even the first lesson that our Lord Jesus teaches in his school, namely, to renounce ourselves (cf. *Matt.* 16:24). Consequently, all the more do we have to try hard to do that, seeing that we will, both from the first day and with great difficulty all of our lives, be able to reach that goal because we can will nothing of our own accord, but we will wait for God to show us what pleases him when it comes to following him.

Also, as for that vice, everyone would be like Lot if our Lord had not conquered us and so strengthened us that we could use force against and do violence to all our affections. For who is satisfied with his condition? When God shows us that he wants us to serve him in some way or other, who conforms without objection? To the contrary, everyone envies his neighbour: 'And if I had that. And if I had such and such a possession. And if I had this or that means.' That is how we are at war with God without thinking about it, for everyone considers what he does not have and would like to be what he is not. Why? Ambition will drive some; avarice, others. And then we are still so entangled in such a diversity of appetites that, if God should grant what we ask, there would be no steadfastness, as we see in the example of Lot. For he says: 'Lord, I could not be safe in the mountain,' and then he goes there. He forgets the kind of person he is and, having wanted one thing, rejects it, and what he first rejected, he returns to later. When God wants him to do one thing, he does not want to do it, and when God grants it, he no longer cares for it but chooses the opposite. That, then, is the way we are when we think about it. In other words, no one can yield strictly to the condition in which God ordained him, but he has an itch now for this, now for that. All the more must we learn that when our Lord declared we cannot be his disciples until we renounce ourselves (cf. *Matt.* 16:24), that principle is to be our general rule for behaviour. In other words, each of us must live according to the means he gives us and not desire great things, as we are also advised in the psalm (cf. *Psa.* 131:1), and not engage in conversations in our minds the way most people torment themselves with those kinds of concerns. And that is the reason many people make nothing but trouble, now for one reason, now for another. Why? Because they have no appreciation for the meaning of that rule for behaviour, that each individual walk in the calling in which he is called. Indeed. And let him abide by it, as Paul says in the seventh chapter of 1 Corinthians (cf. *1 Cor.* 7:20).

In addition, we see that Lot sought further to be more at his ease when he asks God to permit him to retreat to Zoar, for he says: 'That city is small. It is nothing. Why will I not save my life there?' Whatever the situation, if we examine what drove him to that, we will find that, first, he was not resting in God as he should have been; second, he was still attached to his earthly desires. Now those were two great vices! Then he says: 'I will not be able to be safe,' as if he wanted to give the lie to God. So let us take note that we cannot follow the path our Lord is leading us on when we are rebellious. Protest as we may that that is not our intention, the result is evident. Therefore, without inquiring further, let us learn how to walk in the calling we have from God.

And then, in order to avoid all rebellion, let us learn to bridle ourselves and strive against our appetites so that we will not pay undue attention to our pleasures and benefits. For that is what seduces everybody. Some will want to have their fill of eating and drinking and would even be of such disposition that they will say: 'I have had this or that thing; I was once treated better.' In brief, if we remain attached to our feelings that way, it is certain that wherever we are, we will only be depressed and dispirited. We encounter many who are out of touch with reality, and as a result some will dislike a place and others will not find the air to their liking. They will be in search of one thing or another and will never find anything that will please them. It is true we naturally look favourably upon what fits our own bill, but there are many who conspire, so to speak, to imagine some misfortune and condemn all the factors associated with it to make others believe that our Lord deprives them and defrauds them of what would be appropriate for them. For that reason, let us learn to cut back our unnecessary desires and to be content with what pleases God, knowing that he will bless our entire way of life, provided that we are seeking to serve him and that if we have all the bread and wine we need, God will change into manna what he gives us. And if the water is not safe, he showed on one occasion that he could change the bitterness of the waters and remove other impurities from it in order to make it good and useful for his people (cf. *Exod.* 15:23-25). In brief, we will never be at rest and know what it is to obey God until we can close our eyes and say that we receive joyously and with thanksgiving what God gives us and that we know it is from our Father's hand that we must receive our portion.

Let us note, however, that in the person of Lot, Moses shows us our hypocrisy. For when we ask God for more than he permits and for what is even repugnant to his will, we begin to rationalize and claim we have some justification and that our requests are not bad or deserving of condemnation. Lot says: 'This city is small,' and then he repeats it. 'No, Lord. Is this city not small? What are you granting me?' Here, as we have said, is Lot, who is overly committed to his pleasures and delights. Furthermore, he is rebellious against God and so disguises the situation and proposes such pretexts that it seems he is right to ask God for that and is even done a great injustice if he is refused. And what kind of city is that? An out-of-the-way little corner. 'Do I have to be banished from the world? Must the mountain be like a prison to create horror and fear in me? Must I be removed from the company of men?' It is true God permits us to present to him such reasons as come to mind, not that he needs them, but so we can pray to him with greater confidence inasmuch as he grants such familiarity. Yet we must always be modest and submit all our requests to the will of God.

Consequently, Lot is in no way excused when he reacts against what he was told, no matter how convincing his pretexts, but we see as in a mirror, as I said, how inclined we are to deceive ourselves and dazzle ourselves with our own illusions, but all of that serves no purpose before God. Thus, when we sometimes hear much fine talk that says what we desire is good and praiseworthy and that God must not condemn it, let us not deceive ourselves, for when we justify ourselves, we open ourselves to double condemnation; but following Lot's example, let us realize that everything men imagine in an effort to make excuses for their vices is only insignificant drivel before God. That, then, for one point.

But then he says: 'I cannot be safe in the mountain.' Although Lot has not gone so far as to say he wishes to eradicate God's promise, we still detect a kind of blasphemy. God had said to him: 'Thus will you be safe.' 'I cannot argue to the contrary,' he says. For it is not only a matter of saying he cannot. God does not leave that matter open to doubt, but he confirms Lot will be safe in the mountain. He assigns that refuge to him. So to say he will not be safe where God leads him by the hand, is that not to reject the salvation which is offered by God's goodness? In that, we are warned that every time we do not yield simply to what God shows us and teaches us by his word, the result is in the end that, insofar as we can, we close the door on his grace and wish to exclude ourselves from his help, which is what we deserve. Lot also deserves to have God abandon him when he says: 'I cannot be safe,' after God promised. Yet, let us note that when God speaks, that ought to be so sufficient for us that we will wait patiently for him to do more than anything we can imagine. And when things seem impossible to us, let us know that God has means that are unknown to us. When he made the simple statement 'You will be safe there,' should we be in hell, so to speak, that is, should we be in the depths of death and beyond help, it will still be true because God declared it. 'But that does not seem possible to me.' Yes, but we must not stop at what we think; we must rather understand God's incomprehensible power, not with our mind, but by faith. For faith is to overcome everything that is of the world. That, then, is the teaching this passage gives even now.

Yet, as we have said, Moses puts before us here an example of God's wondrous goodness when he answers Lot's prayer, although his request is irregular and extreme and he does not know what he is asking for, and he will be punished accordingly later. It is, therefore, a singular privilege we are allowed when our requests are not well ordered and yet our Lord often grants us what we ask despite the fact it does not completely conform to his will. He will bear with us in our faults if we implore him even as our desires are immoderate. Why? Because, in general, the faith in which we offer our prayers is cold.

But we have here two points to note, namely, that our Lord will not always act toward us as he did toward Lot, and then that, if he answers us, it will not always be to our advantage. I say that God often refuses us when we ask him to do something that would not be good for us, but our prayers nonetheless do not fail to be agreeable to him (cf. *Psa.* 102:17). For example, if I have some hardship, if I am troubled and in distress or suffer some lack, if I am sick, I would indeed pray to God and pray primarily with humility and then in faith, knowing that all my well-being and welfare depend on him. I will pay him the homage that belongs to him, placing my life and my death in his hands again. Afterwards, I will acknowledge that I am not worthy of being received by him, but that Jesus Christ must be my advocate (cf. *1 John* 2:1). Yet there will be some cries of pain when sickness presses me and I cry out: 'O Lord, when will you give me health?' I would like for God to heal me at that very moment. I will pray for him to moderate my affliction and ease everything immediately. That is a prayer based in faith, yet there are some excesses mixed in, which are as many faults, and God will not grant those prayers. Yet he will not fail to answer me in another way, which he knows to be appropriate. And yet he refuses me because of my excessive desires. That, then, is how we are not to pray the way Lot did when he was permitted to go to the city he was asking for. But even though our Lord answers us, let us note, as I have already said, it will not always be for our advantage, but rather for our chastisement, as it in fact happened to Lot.

We see how he left the city and offended God another time. And because God showed himself so gentle with him, that was the cause of a new sin he committed. His being answered contributed to his confusion. The same will happen to us. But still God granted Lot a singular grace since this corrective action was temporal, but we see how he answered those who abandoned themselves to their extravagant desires. It is true he caused it to rain flesh on those who were not content with the manna (cf. *Num.* 11:31). They were satiated, but the meat was still in their mouths, the psalm says, and God's wrath came upon them (cf. *Psa.* 78:23-31). Those people did indeed receive their requests, but they paid very dearly because God showed himself as dealing with them too easily. Thus, God showed pity on his servant Lot in that place when he limited himself to a light chastisement and eventually led him to the mountain. And yet let us not find it strange that our Lord often refuses what we ask of him, for we do not know what is expedient and useful (cf. *Rom.* 8:26). So let us do him the honour of providing for us as he sees fit. And let us receive peaceably what pleases him, even though we do not have everything that enters our thoughts. That, then, is what we have to remember.

But we see an additional and greater grace when the angels say to Lot: 'I can do nothing in this place until you leave.' It is true the angels could do nothing because they had a twofold commission. One was to protect and save Lot; the other was to destroy the five cities, which we will see later. That, then, is why they say they will be able to do nothing. Yet we see that since God had determined to destroy Sodom and Gomorrah and the other cities, he also wanted, along with the severity of his judgment, his mercy to be associated with saving Lot. Consequently, God obligates himself willingly to us in such a way that when he executes his judgments on the wicked and those who despise his majesty and are totally incorrigible, he nonetheless finds the means to protect us and cannot, that is, he does not wish to do the rest without protecting us.

So what we have to remember about this passage is that when God realized that the iniquity of Sodom and Gomorrah had reached its peak, he sent his angels to carry out the final execution and destroy those cities because there was no longer any remedy. Even so, he did not forget to show mercy on the one he had chosen and elected, namely, Lot. For he says through Moses: 'I will show mercy on whom I will show mercy' (cf. *Exod.* 33:19). With those words, he signifies that even though he destroyed and cast down all the people as he had declared, he would always continue to give place to his goodness. But how? Not according to men's good pleasure. 'I will show mercy,' he says, 'on whom I will show mercy. And how will I do it?' With that he lets us know we cannot place demands on him. Furthermore, when it seems that everything is to be levelled, he still knows who his own are (cf. *Exod.* 33:19). He has marked them. They cannot perish no matter what happens, even if the heavens and earth vanish away a hundred thousand times. So let us now note that in the person of Lot God has given a definite and sure teaching, namely, that even if it seems everybody in the world is in confusion, his judgments will never be so horrible that he will not preserve us, that he will not take care of us, that he will not deliver us of all the uncertain things before our eyes. Why not? We must not look for the reason within ourselves, but in his free mercy. So let us realize that God has, in a manner of speaking, obligated himself not to give full rein to his rigour because we are mixed indiscriminately among the wicked, but that we will nonetheless be preserved. At the same time, that is to cause us to walk in humility and take refuge under the shadow of his wings (cf. *Psa.* 17:8; 36:7); it is also to make us know that our salvation rests in his protection and that we have no defence unless he is pleased to defend us (cf. *Acts* 26:22) because he chose us before we were born.[2] That again is what we have to remember about this passage.

Now when it is finally said that God rained lightning and fire on Sodom and Gomorrah and the neighbouring cities, it seems on the surface that that account is simple and almost cold. But after we take everything into consideration, we see that God places before our eyes what happened so that we will be profoundly moved by a thing so simple that if great spectacle and rhetoric had been desired, Moses would have been up to the task. It is true that elsewhere this is well described more gravely, that is, in a nobler way, as if our Lord wanted to resound from heaven[3] so that we will conceive a horror of this judgment he has executed. But whatever the case, Moses' way of speaking is appropriate to cause us to contemplate, as if it were before our eyes, the judgment which in a moment fell on Sodom and Gomorrah. It is said that God caused fire and lightning to rain from heaven.

Now it is true lightning smells like sulphur, and this is also

---

[2] On the election before the creation of the world, cf. especially *Institutes* II, iii, 8; III, xv, 5; xxi.—*M.E.*

[3] Calvin is certainly alluding to Isaiah 13, Babylon's destruction foreseen and described on the model of Sodom and Gomorrah's (cf. verse 19). Scripture very often mentions Sodom and Gomorrah's destruction (cf. Deuteronomy 29:23; Jeremiah 50:40; Ezekiel 16:49; etc.).—*M.E.*

something associated with sulphur. There is also fire, and those things occur sometimes, but here Moses wanted to point out that when God destroyed these cities, he used an unusual approach, and that this lightning did not have a natural origin. As in fact this was like an earthly paradise, it is the most beautiful and fertile of all lands blessed by God. And it was levelled to the ground in a moment. There are five cities and nothing is preserved. And that was not just on one occasion, as when lightning strikes; even though everything is knocked down and there is great desolation, some trace still remains of what existed there before. But here there is only an abyss, indeed an abyss which still smells of sulphur. And in the order of nature, that explanation should not undergo a change which would be perpetual; but since Moses spoke simply that way, it was to give us an opportunity to have before our eyes what he rather starkly recounts without flashy words so that we would have more leisure to consider the execution which was carried out at the time.

Now let us note particularly that if God destroyed Sodom and Gomorrah, he wants us to realize that he testified at that time that he will be Judge of the wicked until the end of the world and that they will not be able to escape his hand. It is true that God does not always send lightning from heaven, but the lightning here is like a visible sign of all the chastisements and punishments he visits on the world. That is why the psalm says that God will rain lightning, fire, and burning sulphur and suchlike upon the wicked (cf. *Psa.* 11:6). There is no doubt that the prophet had Sodom and Gomorrah in mind, for we find that in many other passages (cf. *Deut.* 29:23; *Isa.* 13:19; *Jer.* 50:40; *Ezek.* 16:49). The prophets use that rather common image, for it is familiar to them. Now everything depends on that reason I mentioned, namely, that God wanted to testify on that occasion that he is armed to execute his vengeance on all the wicked, especially after he waits for them patiently and they remain obstinate in their evil deeds, or when there is no longer a remedy. He is ready to strike against them, strike, I say, in whatever way that seems appropriate to him, for he has the means enclosed in his war chest to show that he can judge in many ways. Also, it would not be right if his wrath could show itself only as lightning. It would seem that his power would be limited to a single element, but God, as I said, demonstrates that all created things are subjected to him; and when he wishes to use them, they are also weapons to wreak his vengeance, such as he has ordained. We saw earlier that he had used water when he wanted to consume the whole world in that deluge (cf. *Gen.* 7:11-24). Now he used another means in Sodom and Gomorrah, for he sends lightning from heaven. And that is how he strikes down those who despise his majesty by punishing them in some way, now by pestilence, now by war, now by famine, now in this way or another. And what we have declared is verified in the psalm, that his eye is fixed upon the wicked (cf. *Psa.* 11:6). And when they think they are well hidden from him, far removed from him, he finds them in his time and finds them to strike them, just as he struck Sodom and Gomorrah. That, then, is what we have to remember when it is said that God caused fire and brimstone to rain down. It is from the Lord, says Moses, and from heaven. When he says 'from the Lord,' it is to make it clearer that it was an extraordinary act and that God emphasized as with his finger that he could not bring greater destruction to those cities.

It is true that lightning never falls from heaven unless God is at work in it, for we know what is said in Psalm 104, namely, that the winds are his couriers and messengers; the fire which flies in the air is also sent by him (cf. *Psa.* 104:4). Such are just that many signs by which God shows us his power, when he thunders and sends lightning, when he sends rain, storms and whirlwinds. But here especially Moses wanted to point out that God did not follow the order of nature when he deployed his arm on this one occasion so we would have a perpetual reminder worth remembering. When we hear Sodom and Gomorrah spoken of in our day, may the hairs of our head stand on end as if God opened the heavens and said: 'I will destroy all those who have resisted me to the end. It is true I am patient, but after I endure much, the wicked will yet have to come to account' (cf. *Nahum* 1:3; *Wis.* 15:1; *Sir.* 5:4; *Rom.* 2:4). Now when we hear that, let us learn to conform ourselves to him in fear, and let us ask his pardon for our sins. Let that teaching be ours, and in future let us always keep ourselves bridled in lest we achieve the height of every iniquity and heap upon ourselves a treasury of wrath (cf. *Rom.* 2:5).

And yet we do not envy these wicked people who boast their triumphs, these despisers of God's word, enemies of true religion, these persecutors of the church, these vermin, these thieves who seek only to shed innocent blood. Since we see that God is tolerating them for a time, let us not think they have a better situation because of that, but let us wait until the time comes, that right time when God will strike them, as he will do, and we will know at that time that it was better to be in distress and trampled under their feet than to be exalted as they are and face God's devastating destruction that befell those who are spoken of here.

Now let us bow before the majesty of our gracious God in acknowledgment of our faults, praying that he will cause us to sense them to the extent they will displease us and cause us to groan until he receives us in mercy. And let us not abuse his fatherly kindness, but let us so subject ourselves to him that our only goal will be to glorify his holy name and struggle against all the wicked desires we are naturally inclined to until we are completely cleansed of them, and let us learn to be satisfied with what he is pleased to give us. And even though we do not have everything we want in this world, let us be so receptive that we will not cease to bless his holy name and bless him with joy and thanksgiving, even though we have to suffer. And to do that, let us learn to appreciate the testimony he gives us of his paternal goodness. When he calls us to the hope of salvation, let all else be to us as nothing, and may we hold in contempt all the things considered precious by these poor blind people who have no other desire than for the things which belong to this fading and corruptible life, but may our eyes always be fixed on the things that concern the heavenly life, to which God calls us and to which we must aspire. May he grant that grace not only to us but to all the peoples and nations on earth.

94

God Watches Over and Protects His Own Despite Their Faults

Saturday, 4 May 1560

Then the LORD *rained upon Sodom and upon Gomorrah brimstone and fire from the* LORD *out of heaven; And he overthrew those cities, and all the plain, and all the inhabitants of the cities, and that which grew upon the ground. But his wife looked back from behind him, and she became a pillar of salt. And Abraham gat up early in the morning to the place where he stood before the* LORD: *And he looked toward Sodom and Gomorrah, and toward all the land of the plain, and beheld, and, lo, the smoke of the country went up as the smoke of a furnace. And it came to pass, when God destroyed the cities of the plain, that God remembered Abraham, and sent Lot out of the midst of the overthrow, when he overthrew the cities in the which Lot dwelt. And Lot went up out of Zoar, and dwelt in the mountain* (Gen.19:24-30a).

WE SAID THAT God wanted the judgment he visited on Sodom and Gomorrah to be so noteworthy that it could not be doubted and that everyone would have to use it as an example and for instruction. And that is the way it had to be, for men have the evil disposition to obscure God's works as much as they can. And that ingratitude is seen everywhere, but especially when it comes to dealing with God's punishing some

815

offences, we choose to see nothing. Each person gladly closes his eyes, for we always look for some excuse or else try to avoid being admonished and leave God aside and have a good time. That, so far as it lies with us, is how hypocrisy neutralizes the corrections that God places before our eyes.

All the more, then, must we observe what is said here about what appears to be the visible hand of God when Sodom and Gomorrah were destroyed. For that was no ordinary rain or storm. Nothing like it had ever happened before. And nothing like it has happened since. It was an act of the Lord. He had to make it felt that at that time he had declared himself to be Judge, indeed forever, so that it might profit us not only in our time, but that it might also be spoken of until the end of the world. And let us tremble at every mention of it inasmuch as God did not spare that land which he had blessed with such fertility.

And when it is said that every sprout from the earth was destroyed, it is to show how despicable the inhabitants of the land were when God had to extend his hand with such rigour. They were not only guilty and deserving of punishment and chastisement, but the land also suffered because of the iniquities committed in Sodom. In any case, the land bears God's marks to witness that the abominations that had reigned there were finally intolerable and that God had to declare that everything was recorded before him and that the cry of it had reached heaven. That, in brief, is what we have to remember. What some have tried to expound cleverly—that the Lord had rained down by the hand of the Lord, that is, that Jesus Christ, by the power of God his Father, had destroyed these cities—will best be left alone, for such comments will serve only to subject our faith to mockery. So Moses' intention is rather clear, namely, to distinguish the fire and lightning that fell on Sodom and Gomorrah from the other lightning and storms that came upon them, as if he were saying that what happened was nothing if it was not a miracle, indeed a manifest miracle in which God displayed his arm as if the heavens had opened for that blow.

Now it is said that Lot's wife looked behind him and turned into a pillar of salt. This chastisement would, on the surface, seem to be excessive. As for Sodom and Gomorrah, we must not be astonished if God punished them in such a frightful way, for, as we have said before, they had been nourished by the grace of God, indeed with all delights, and that had to cost them very dearly because they abused their riches in gluttony and intemperance. After the rise of their fierce inhumanity, they were like insatiable gulfs and felt no pity or mercy for the poor. They never considered helping those who experienced some indigence. That is the intemperance and gluttony, the pride, the inhumanity which had provoked God's wrath, especially when ingratitude was added. And then followed the brutishness that resulted in their loss of shame and their indulging in repulsive infamies that are beyond naming. Now we cannot find it strange that God punished them according to the measure of their iniquities, but we have an opportunity to humble ourselves, as we have shown, and, since God deals with us and nourishes us gently, to remember to bridle and restrain our appetites so as not to yield to intemperance. And then, let us not allow possessions to cause us to grow proud. And let us be aware that if our Lord has given us enough so we can help our neighbours, he has placed in our hands an opportunity and ability which will witness against us if we do not acknowledge all those possessions as coming from him. That is what the example of Sodom is to teach us.

But what do we have in Lot's wife? The poor woman turns around while following her husband, and she had to be walking in front of him, for it is said that she looked behind her husband. And that look, considering the astonishment, did it merit her being turned into a stone? Consequently, one would say that God punished here a very mild fault in a very harsh way and that the severity was excessive. That is how men would judge it according to their understanding, but we need to learn to bow our heads and acknowledge guilt, both for ourselves and for others, permitting God to exercise his sovereign authority, to dispose of us at his pleasure, realizing that what he does is just and equitable. And if we get it into our heads to think otherwise, let us overcome that audacity, knowing that it is very sacrilegious. For we must all appear before the judgment seat of the one and only Judge (cf. *Rom.* 14:10; *2 Cor.* 5:10). It is not our place to usurp, but to accept what he makes known. And as I said, let us know that what proceeds from him is an irrevocable decree. Let us acquiesce in it. That is how we learn from the person of Lot's wife to accept God's judgments as good and just and without fault despite the fact that in our opinion we could condemn them and that, were it not for the honour we hold him in, we would be tempted to do so because we are haughty and much too bold. Still, the fact is that when we consider the situation up close, Lot's wife committed a very serious fault that we must not minimize. For there was God's prohibition: 'You will not look behind, and you will not stop in the plain.' That was said to Lot, but it was also said to all those with him. If we think going against such a small prohibition is an insignificant matter, it is certain we have a false value system and a false standard.

In addition, let us note that God had spoken frighteningly to Lot and his wife, for this threat should have moved them: 'Save yourself and your life, and do not perish.' That is how God commands Lot's wife. At the risk of perishing in Sodom, she is not to look back. But, whatever the reason, she looks back. If we say that it was because things were confused and she did it without thinking, that still does not remove her offence. And it is particularly likely that, in the first place, she did not believe because she wanted to know whether or not that was the way God had foretold it. When the word alone does not satisfy us and we want to see the execution and the outcome, we indicate that the word is questionable. Now that is an intolerable blasphemy. Moreover, we can gather from our Lord Jesus Christ's statement in the seventeenth chapter of Luke that Lot's wife had some regrets about leaving Sodom and would have liked to remain in that comfortable nest (cf. *Luke* 17:29-37). And it is likely she was a native of the place, though we cannot be certain, but the fact remains that our Lord Jesus Christ, when exhorting us to ponder her example, shows that she was still attached because of some worldly affections and was unable to follow where God was calling her.

He proposes that example for us to show how we are to aspire to the heavenly life when we hear the gospel preached when God is presented to us as Father and when he offers us the hope of the salvation he has prepared for us. So when God calls us this way, our Lord Jesus Christ informs us that we must leave this world and not be given over either to riches or to pleasures or to honours or to anything else, for we cannot be ever so slightly enticed by the temptations that Satan leads us into without losing our appetite for what is offered us from the kingdom of heaven. Now because we are always inclined to seek out base, incorruptible things, Jesus says, 'Remember Lot's wife. You know what happened to her and how God punished her for simply looking back.' It is as if he were saying we must exercise tight control over our senses, for as soon as we think about worldly things, we have gone astray. On the one hand, we receive a nudge from Satan and, on the other, an attack of weakness, for we are pitiably weak and so inconstant that we are immediately carried off, and our human nature will cast us in every direction. So we now see that Lot's wife's offence was no small thing.

Now on the other hand, let us consider the wondrous grace God granted her. He pulled her out of the deepest hell, so to speak, and yet she is still wandering in her thoughts without realizing that the God who pulled her out is to possess her completely and that he is to use her and she must fully retain her affection for him; she is still tempted by unbelief, and there are things she misses that hold her in the confusion she had—will we be able to excuse those faults? Even so, let us permit God to have what belongs to him, for neither will we gain anything by wanting to remove him from his judgment seat or having an opinion contrary to his. So even though we open our mouths to say that God was austere and severe with Lot's wife, let us realize he will always be found to be just and that all we will have to do is lower our eyes and yield to everything he says and everything he does.

But let us use the response and exhortation given by our Lord Jesus Christ and realize that God wanted to use Lot's wife to give us useful instruction until the end of the world, namely, that since he was pleased to call us and extend his hand and continue to deal with us kindly and invite us to himself, let us be attentive to receiving his word, and may it incite us in such a way that we will hasten to our goal, which is set before us (cf. *Phil.* 3:14), and let us be careful not to be distracted or turned aside in any way, for it takes little to corrupt us. And just as little children are distracted in many ways depending on whether they are shown a cherry or a toy or who knows what, so are we so given to vanity and wandering that the moment we catch sight of something or other that can cool us to serving God or move us from the right path, we are, as I said, so bewildered that we no longer know the meaning of the teaching we previously heard. That, then, is what we have to remember, for when we have God's word and substantial instruction to edify us, we must abandon all those speculations that attract those who do not seek to be profitably instructed and who do not seek pasture for their souls in that word, but whose ears are open only to satisfy their foolish preoccupations.

Now we could ask here whether Lot's wife was so completely changed into a pillar of salt that her soul also became salt. In fact, there have been irreverent people, eccentric and ill-intentioned, who have been like baying dogs mocking what Moses recounts as if it were a fable. They say: 'What agreement is there between salt and flesh, blood and skin?' Others have found an obstacle in that, thinking there was some kind of absurdity involved. And yet they have said it is a pillar of salt, that is, it was to last forever, as it is called a covenant of salt (cf. *Num.* 18:19), which is to say it is preserved so as to be incorruptible. And that is how our Lord speaks of it in his law, because salt prevents corruption (cf. *Num.* 18:19; *Lev.* 2:13.) So they concluded that Moses, using a figure of speech, called Lot's wife a pillar of salt because God wanted this to be a lasting memorial so that people would know from age to age that she had been punished for her lack of gravity. But I have no doubt that Moses called that rock or that mass into which Lot's wife had been turned 'a pillar of salt' because there was some definite impression by which one could judge that it was not an ordinary stone. For there was something distinct that made this chastisement by God memorable for all those going and coming, so that as soon as their eyes fell upon it, they would perceive some sign that would admonish them.

As for these mockers who ask what agreement exists between salt and the human body, I now ask them what agreement there is between an ox and a donkey, a chicken or a hatchling. You have an egg, which is a dead thing, and yet our Lord brings forth living creatures from one every day. And when we see the birds of the sky, if we did not know how they are produced, who would think they had come from something dead, as we know it? Let us then contemplate the ins and outs of everything our Lord makes in nature. The philosophers themselves can say that that consists in the continual changes that take place, that the elements have such an affinity for one another that they have to borrow to accomplish such changes.[1] That is how the order of nature is maintained.

But for all that, if we find it strange that Lot's wife was changed into a stone or into a heap, how will we believe that our bodies, after decaying and becoming ashes, will be something that can be restored? And today they are subject to decay so that they will share in the glory and immortality of heaven, of the very nature of God, as Peter says (cf. *2 Pet.* 1:4). How would we find that credible? Therefore, let this single principle suffice for us, namely, that God, who created all things from nothing, then disposed of all created things in such a way that he will make changes which surpass all our minds. Whatever the situation, we are obliged to grant him that liberty, namely, to dispose of his creatures according to his will. And if we do not understand his power, are we to be astonished? For in what high esteem will we be able to hold it? It is an infinite thing which surpasses our understanding, indeed the understanding of the angels of paradise. And will a poor worm of the earth want to elevate itself so much that God can do nothing if he is not judging? Consequently, it is only right that God have this privilege over all his creatures, that of disposing of them as he pleases while we are in confusion about it because it is expedient that we humble ourselves because we do not understand why he does what he does.

Now it is not said that the soul of that woman was changed into salt. It is quite certain that Lot's wife will rise in the Last Day. That which became a pillar of salt will be restored to its state at that time, and her soul lives in the meantime. We do not know whether God pardoned her and whether that punishment was temporal or not. It is true we will do no wrong by coming to that conclusion, not to resolve anything, for rashness will otherwise be involved, for we must always prefer to be inclined to hope appropriately than to

[1] Cf. perhaps Aristotle, *Physics* VI, 5; *Of the Sky* III, 1-8, particularly 7, etc.—*M.E.*

conclude wrongly. So it is likely that God punished Lot's wife in her body while intending to save her soul.

In fact, we have to remember that our Lord often uses such corrections for his people, whom he does not spare in their flesh so that that will be to their advantage and serve for their salvation. And yet we still have occasion to tremble every time we hear that story, and it is the main thing we have to adhere to. If we find here material for good instruction, it is certain our minds will no longer itch to engage in useless speculations. But we will be satisfied that our Lord gives us a good lesson for our salvation, namely, that we learn to be watchful and follow steadfastly where he calls and not to be turned aside by this world's desires.

Now Moses then adds that Abraham arose in the morning and looked toward the plain, which was the place he had heard would be destroyed, which was near Sodom and Gomorrah, which God had predicted to him (cf. *Gen.* 18:20-21). It is certain Abraham was very concerned because of his nephew Lot. In fact, we saw earlier how he had exposed himself to death in order to save him from the hand of his enemies (cf. *Gen.* 14:13-16), and his love had not lessened. So we can indeed acknowledge that he was in terrible distress, not knowing what had happened to his nephew. And because he dared not go all the way to Sodom, it is certain he was held back, knowing that it was not God's good pleasure and he did not have permission, for he would not have spared his steps and would have gladly forewarned him. But when he realizes he was not allowed to do so, he has to remain where he was. And yet we still have a clear admonition, for when we encounter some hardship, we are often very perplexed and want to anticipate and set everything straight everywhere. Now it is true that, according to the means God gives us, we must not be like blocks of wood and not remedy evil to the extent we can. But restraint is everywhere the order of the day, as we say. So we must consider what we are allowed to do and the ability God has given us, and we must restrict ourselves to those limits. And if sometimes we think: 'Alas, what might happen? And what will that mean?' let us, under all circumstances, remain content to pray to God, for he does not want us to have hands to reach everywhere in the world and manage this thing or another. That, then, is what we have to remember when it is said that Abraham had to endure great anguish, and he shows it, for very early in the morning, he is already where he had left the angels. And that is said to show that he had scarcely slept, knowing what was to happen. So much for that point.

Now, for the second point, he knew the destruction of Sodom had been foretold to him because he could use it to teach his children. It is noteworthy that Moses relates this: 'Shall I hide from my servant Abraham what I have undertaken, for I know he will be careful to teach his family and show them the righteous deeds and judgments of the Lord?' (Cf. *Gen.* 18:17-19.) So Abraham, for those two reasons, comes to the place where the angels had told him about the fulfilment of what was to happen to Sodom, because he did not know what had happened to his nephew Lot. There is no doubt he was there making supplication before God, as we will soon discuss. That much for that point.

But we see how he was also moved because our Lord showed him that that was to be useful for him. So he wanted to receive the instruction which was given to him. And even though he in no way doubted what had been announced to him, he wants to look at such a spectacle. Why? He will be more deeply moved and touched by it and therefore a more faithful witness to the future. For it is certain that Moses wrote that story as Abraham had taught it and that it was never forgotten among the Jews who had descended from him. It was always declared among them from generation to generation what we have read about their father Abraham, who also taught his son Isaac. And then Isaac declared it to Jacob, so that today we can be assured of it. Now it is a good assurance when it is said that Abraham not only heard from the mouth of the angels that Sodom was to be destroyed along with the wicked people there, but that he also saw the thing, and it gave such a clear and simple picture that he could witness to God's hand as if it had appeared to him from heaven. That, then, is what we have to remember for that point.

Now Moses adds that God, upon destroying Sodom, remembered his servant Abraham in order to save Lot. Here we see even better what we recently touched upon, that is, that Abraham was not so inhuman that he did not pray to God for his nephew. For it is said that God declared his goodwill toward him as if he had given him his nephew's life. That presupposes that Abraham had a special affection for him and prayed to God with an ardent zeal and was consequently answered.

We could now ask how it can be said that Abraham was the reason Lot was saved, seeing that he is called 'just' (cf. *2 Pet.* 2:7). We know that he pleased God and that, living in Sodom, he was in continual torment and that he detested the iniquities being committed there, that he was the enemy of evil and separated himself from it. We know that. We have a subsequent testimony of his humanity when he received the angels, thinking they were men, unknown people to be sure, from whom he expected no reward (cf. *Gen.* 19:1-5). All of that was a sacrifice acceptable to God. And he is proposed to us today as an example to follow. How did God deliver him from Sodom so that he was not destroyed with the rest as a favour to and in consideration of Abraham, as if he were not thinking about him? The answer is easy. It is not shocking that God saves someone, and I am talking as much about eternal salvation as about removing us from some dangers in relationship both to the one and to the others. And yet, when God accepts Moses, we know how he valued him in many ways. And yet it is certain it was only a favour to Abraham. For the promise that God made, saying, 'I will be your God and the God of your lineage after you' (cf. *Gen.* 17:1-2), was not abolished. Although Abraham had died long before Moses' birth, God's promise was still in force and permanent. Therefore, Moses was accepted by God as a benefit to Abraham, and the benefits he receives depend on that and derive from that source, but the fact remains that God does not fail to hold his servant Moses in high regard.

The same is true for all. And when I mention one, I do so to show that God opposes none of his elect inasmuch as he invites them to himself and loves them, indeed with undeserved love. And then because he also values the gifts he placed in them and looks farther into the future, he does good for them because he permitted their fathers to take care of their children and their lineages, indeed for a thousand generations (cf. *Exod.* 20:6; 34:7; *Deut.* 5:10; 7:9). That, then, is what happened to Lot. For even if Abraham had never existed, it is certain God would have shown himself as Lot's father and would have delivered him. And the reason? Because he had chosen him to be one of his. And then he lived in him by his Holy Spirit. And the gifts he had placed in him, he approved. And because Lot was one of his children, he had to receive the worship he gave him, not to be obligated to us in any way, but everything proceeds from his pure liberality. In any case, we have God saving Lot and saving him because of the love he had for him without consideration for Abraham, but he nonetheless did not fail to show his paternal goodness toward Abraham when wanting to save Lot, his nephew. So let us learn that God will often show his kindness in different ways, and each one of us must profit from it. And that is so that we will be better aware of our obligation to him. That much, then, for one point.

And let us also learn that since he continues his mercy toward us, it is because he is pleased to accept us among the number of his children. And then as a benefit to his church in general, he increases and declares his gifts to us as well as to those who are close to us. It is certain that since God joined us to the body of Jesus Christ, the prayers which are offered by the entire church are offered for our salvation. For we commune together as members of a body. And when God has pity on us and displays his mercy, it is toward his children as well as toward the members of his body (cf. *Rom.* 12:4-5; *Eph.* 4:25; *1 Cor.* 6:15). In that are comprised, as I have said, all those he has elected. And then he answers in particular the prayers of those who care for us. So that is how God binds us to himself in many ways. And we need to ponder that well. For Paul, speaking of himself, does not doubt that the Corinthians are concerned to pray for him (cf. *2 Cor.* 1:11). Why? So that, as he says, grace and praise will be given to God by many mouths (cf. *Psa.* 51:15) when many have called upon him that way. That, then, is what we have to remember.

We will pray to God daily, and we must not pray each one just for himself, but we are to extend our love and concern to all believers, even to those we do not know and have never seen (cf. *Eph.* 6:18). Now when we hear that our Lord provides for his own and that he does not deal with them with all-out severity and even that he sometimes helps them miraculously, we have to keep in mind that our prayers have not been in vain (cf. *James* 5:16) and that we are even more bound to thank God for hearing our prayers for those we commended to him. That, then, in brief, is what we have to remember about this passage.

Moreover, this ought also to serve as further instruction, for God shows us that Lot, 'just' as he was, could still have perished in Sodom if God had not remembered Abraham. It is as if Lot had been abandoned because he had chosen to live in Sodom after being influenced by an overwhelming attachment (cf. *Gen.* 13:10-11). As we saw, he beholds a fertile land and seeks there his profit, his comforts and conveniences, and yet he forgets the main thing and comes there and places himself in hell. Why? He is looking for an earthly paradise. In other words, his concern is only for this fragile life, and it does not occur to him that he is plunging into a pit of destruction. Consequently, he deserved to be abandoned by God and to perish with Sodom. So since he is maintained in integrity, there is no doubt it was because of concern for Abraham and the household he had been brought up in. For even though he might not have been circumcised, he nonetheless had to retain some part of that blessing that God had bestowed on Abraham, even though he had not engaged in the solemn covenant with him, as we observed in the seventeenth chapter (cf. *Gen.* 17:2-22). That, in brief, is what we have to remember about this passage.

Finally, it is said that Lot withdrew to Zoar and came to the mountain where he lives. Here Moses declares more clearly what we talked about yesterday, namely, that Lot demonstrated his inconstancy in the fact that he had entreated God to let him live in the city of Zoar and had refused to go to the mountain. And then he goes there, and we see in that fact how there is no resolve or steadfastness in our affections, but that we are like a sick person, that we twist and turn from one side to the other without respite. When a sick person asks to be turned, he does not know why except that he is uncomfortable. And then when he is on his other side, he wants to be turned back to the previous side. He will have himself turned from one side to the other, over and over, endlessly, because discomfort distracts him. The poor person does not know what he is doing when sickness weighs on him. Moreover, those desires cannot be based on reason or controlled. That is true of all our affections which are not subjected to God's will because we will think we are far ahead of the game when we possess one thing and another. We think we have the world by the tail, as we say, and as soon as God grants what our hearts desire, we are dissatisfied and not even sorry we asked for what we have, and we immediately return to the other and would prefer it: 'I did not know what I was asking for.' That is true, but after spending our time on such folly, we will always return to it. That is what we have to remember from this example of Lot, namely, that if we give our desires too much leeway, we will always be perturbed, and we will be tormented and so agitated on all sides that if we acquire one thing today, tomorrow we will want its opposite.

Moreover, let us note that that was a just punishment for Lot since God discouraged him from living in Zoar, where he lived too gladly. He must have thought that Zoar and Zeboiim and the other neighbouring cities had caught some infection from Sodom. And if the inhabitants of that city were not still completely perverse, they were still marked with so many blemishes that they were abominable in God's sight. And that was stated. Since he wants to live in the midst of those people he had previously detested, he is clearly putting God to the test (cf. *Gen.* 13:10). Now God pardons him again for that imperfection, however vice laden, but he still must not remain unpunished. Therefore, God confounds him because of his inconstancy, and because what he found good he soon finds bad, God turns that to his welfare and salvation. Now is Lot discontented in Zoar? He withdraws to the mountain. And now he does wittingly what he had refused to do to obey God. For the place of refuge had been assigned to him in the mountain, as we said. That, then, is how he repents.

But the fact is that in that repentance there is still a vice to be condemned, for it is not enough that Lot did not go to the mountain, but because he did not wait for a completely new commandment from God, he is guilty, even if everyone thought he had done the right thing. As I have already said, it is true God turned that to his advantage. Yet we will see later how God blinded him on the mountain (cf. *Gen.* 19:30-35). He had been sober in Sodom, and he will get drunk on the mountain. He had been chaste in Sodom, and he will commit an act of abomination and incest. We will look at all those things. And that will show it was not an upright and pure virtue that Lot repented of when he did not remain in Zoar but withdrew into the mountain. Why? It is certain our acts must always be governed by God's word; we must obey the one who has all authority over us. And when we do that, we will never fail. When we follow God's commandments, we do something that cannot be challenged. No, for we have his word. Will we not seek to know what pleases God? We could be respected by everybody and applauded from every side, except that everything we do will be only dung. Why? As I have said, we must not waste our time with appearance, as unbelievers do, but God must have, above all things in our lives, the honour of our effort to subject ourselves fully to him. Consequently, obedience is the mother of all virtues.[2] Now was Lot obedient? Not at all. When God sends him to the mountain, he recoils and asks that he be permitted to live in the city of Zoar. And when he is settled there, as by the mouth of God, he was supposed to remain there, but he does not wait for God to have him go to the mountain; he goes there without being commanded to do so. And how? With a troubled and unsteady mind because he does not go with a settled intention and resolved purpose, but because he sees himself there in a state of confusion. That is why we cannot attribute this to a strict repentance and say that this is an act worthy of praise, even though God gives it a good outcome and gains Lot's salvation, but we will see later how he

---

[2] The expression is Augustinian (cf. *The City of God* XIV, xii, 31) and repeated in the *Institutes* (II, viii, 5). Calvin specifies regularly that faith is the root and mother of obedience; cf. sermons 14 and 15. We also call to mind Erasmus's adage from Aeschylus: *'Oboedientia felicitatis mater'* ['Obedience is the mother of felicity'] (Erasmus, *Adages*: no. 4059). Cf. finally 1 Samuel 15:22 and Hosea 6:6. We must also emphasize that in two sermons out of three Calvin mentions the obedience owed to God.—*M.E.*

punishes him (cf. *Gen.* 19:31-35). We also see in that that God has to have pity on us even when it seems our acts are only good, and he will always find something to condemn in them and that would bring us to destruction and perdition, except that he introduced his hand and healed our vices in such a way that what would lead to death he changes to good and salvation (cf. *Deut.* 23:6).

Now let us bow before the majesty of our gracious God in acknowledgment of our faults, praying that he will be pleased to purge us of them day by day and yet support us in such a way in our weaknesses that he will always continue to receive us and confess us as his children, even though we remain far from the perfection we must aspire to. And may it please him to keep us so joined to and united with the body of his church that, as he has dispensed the fullness of good things through Jesus Christ, who is our Head, we will also share in all the gifts he has received for his elect. And may he so dispose of our lives that he will not allow us to be like wandering animals, but that we will follow the path he has shown us, and may we be held fast by his Holy Spirit, and may he repress all the wicked desires which could corrupt us and turn us from the kind of obedience we owe him. May he grant that grace not only to us but to all the peoples and nations on earth.

95

Gluttony, Drunkenness, and Incest

Monday, 13 May 1560

And the firstborn said unto the younger, Our father is old, and there is not a man in the earth to come in unto us after the manner of all the earth: Come, let us make our father drink wine, and we will lie with him, that we may preserve seed of our father. And they made their father drink wine that night: and the firstborn went in, and lay with her father; and he perceived not when she lay down, nor when she arose. And it came to pass on the morrow, that the firstborn said unto the younger, Behold, I lay yesternight with my father: let us make him drink wine this night also; and go thou in, and lie with him, that we may preserve seed of our father. And they made their father drink wine that night also: and the younger arose, and lay with him; and he perceived not when she lay down, nor when she arose. Thus were both the daughters of Lot with child by their father. And the firstborn bare a son, and called his name Moab: the same is the father of the Moabites unto this day. And the younger, she also bare a son, and called his name Benammi: the same is the father of the children of Ammon unto this day (Gen.19:31-38).

THE STORY RECOUNTED for us here ought to give us strong motivation to pray that God will not allow us to fall into such a sin as Lot's and at the same time warn us to maintain sobriety and temperance, for drunkenness was the cause of an act as despicable as can be found among the most wicked people in the world, and if he had persisted in it, he would have been no better than the people of Sodom, from whose midst God had only recently caused him to escape miraculously (cf. *Gen.* 19:16).

Now it is said that Lot's two daughters slept with their father. That is incest, which is against nature. And they realized it when they got their father drunk. That filthy act would bring them shame, but they do it anyway, and they seem to want to show contempt for God. They give birth and each names her son by the name of the father, for Moab means 'of my father' and Benammi means 'son of my people.' They boast that they gave birth to lineages, indeed by a villainous and egregious obscenity, and they seem to want to broadcast their villainy throughout the world. That is how God blinds them. As for Lot, we see that drunkenness got the best of him, and he is so brutish he does not know when his daughters go to bed with him or when they get up. So let us take such advantage of this story that we learn in the first place to place ourselves in God's hands so that he will keep us and not allow us to fall into such gross sins. And then let us be careful not to provoke his wrath by intemperance and gluttony in such a way that we give ourselves free rein and forget everything that is upright and shameful. And before coming to the teaching, we will have to handle some questions briefly that could be asked.

It seems absurd that Lot's daughters can give wine to their father on the mountain. They withdrew into a cave. There they were shut away from the rest of the people. But where do they find wine? There is no doubt, as we mentioned earlier, that Lot, having a large family, would have taken with him some of his servants and saved something from his possessions (cf. *Gen.* 19:1). And even though that was not expressed, it can easily be surmised and concluded. As for what the daughters say about there being no more men on earth, it is because they did not think they should be married to serfs such as they were at that time. Consequently, they conclude that only by their father could they have seed and lineage. That much for the first point.

Now we can also infer that they were not influenced by wantonness, for each one is content with having conceived. Since they do not continue in that base behaviour, we see they are not intentional prostitutes. Moreover, the older daughter spends one night with her father and then makes room for her sister. There would have been some jealousy if they had been motivated by a base affection. So we can easily judge that it was only a foolish desire for a lineage, for they thought their father, being old and decrepit, would soon die, as they claim. So they thought that there would only be desolation, that they would be left alone, and that there would be no one to help them. So that is the kind of destitution that incites them to prostitute themselves with their father.

Let us now look at what Moses recounts here. As for his two daughters, let us note that if people once permit themselves this thing and another, whatever wonderful excuse they offer when they slip from the order God established, it is certain they will commit the most villainous and inexcusable acts in the world. From the outset they think they have a fine and reasoned excuse, as Lot's daughters thought they washed their hands of the matter when they said: 'Our father is old; there are no more men on earth,' and said it without pretence, for they did not try to find some subterfuge to hide their whoredom, as we have already pointed out. Only the zeal of having children motivates them, which they think will give them some consolation. That is what motivates them. But they still pervert the order of nature.

Therefore, let us learn to remain within our limits. And when we have things to consider, let us not do what seems good to us and give ourselves too much licence and latitude, but let us always consider what God approves. And we will be doubly guilty especially in our day if we are compared with Lot's daughters, for they had neither the law nor the prophets; they had only what God had engraved in their hearts, what we call the 'law of nature,'[1] to give them some understanding of good and evil. Even so, we still condemn them because we detest the act they committed. So let us look more closely at ourselves, seeing that we have such a clear teaching of God's will, and let us deviate neither to the left nor to the right, but let us follow only what God shows us and undertake nothing beyond his will. For we can have all the finest intentions imaginable, and it is certain we will always stray beyond our limits and in the end forget all reason if we have the audacity to do more than we are allowed. So the first thing we have to observe is to be careful to follow only what our Lord permits and not to take pride in our own judgment; for it is certain men will always fall into a kind of madness when they think they are wise enough to say: 'That seems good to me, and it will succeed.' When we reach that point, we will necessarily fall into times of terrible confusion. And that is the way God punishes our temerity.

Now we also have to note that although Lot's daughters have a good intention, as it is called, that still does not absolve them of the offence they committed. It is true the enormity of the sin is not such that they had committed whoredom out of wicked lust, but they cannot under any circumstance be excused. Consequently, we must all the more be warned not to yield to our good intentions, as they are called, and turn from God's will, but let us always remain within it, where we are shown the way and which we must always follow without deviating in one direction or another.

As for Lot, it is a grievous thing that a holy man who had the witness of the Holy Spirit was brought so low he committed incest with his daughters two nights in a row. And what Moses recounts would seem to be unbelievable, namely, that he committed incest without being aware of anything, that he did not know when his

[1] About natural law, cf. Romans 2:14-15, *Institutes* II, ii, 22, and sermon 97.—*M.E.*

daughter came to bed with him and when she got up; but there is no doubt God punished him in that way because of his intemperance. For was it not a great weakness in Lot to get drunk so soon after leaving Sodom? It is true that some try to minimize his fault because he was overwhelmed by anguish. They say that it was easy for him to be caught off guard by wine, although he scarcely drank, for we know that sorrow withers the brain of a man and he will be easily troubled and that that was Lot's situation. But it is quite certain he would always have to groan because of the very recent memory of God's horrendous vengeance on that once fertile and fat land where so many souls perished. Should he not have been moved and amazed at such a judgment of God to weep over it even for a year or two or three? Should he not have been in such fear of God that if he had previously had any integrity, if he had lived chastely, all those virtues would have increased? Therefore, when he drinks too much and gets drunk and is not aware of his daughters' trick, but lets wine overcome him, does he not deserve to have our Lord make him totally stupid, and does he not deserve to lie there like a wooden log and have less feeling and reason than an animal? So let us realize that that stupidity Moses is speaking of does not come from simple drunkenness, but that God wanted Lot to be thus deprived of his senses so that we will learn to hold drunkenness in even greater horror.

Moreover, as I said, Lot's example should admonish us to pray that God will not lead us into temptation (cf. *Matt.* 6:13; *Mark* 14:38; *Luke* 11:4; 22:40, 46). When Lot lived in Sodom, it was like living in the midst of devils. It is certain that city was like a kind of hell, and yet he is there like an angel. He worships God and remains unpolluted, even though he has sufficient opportunities to become corrupted, but he always conducts himself in such a way that, as we have already seen, he is called 'just' (cf. *2 Pet.* 2:7). That very honourable designation is attributed to him by the Holy

Spirit. Did he leave Sodom? Did he take refuge there? It seems he is there under God's hand as if in an earthly paradise chosen for him by God to keep him uncorrupted. He commits an act so vile that the hair of those who hear of it ought to stand on end—that a father cohabits with his daughters!

So when we see what happened to Lot, let us consider the time and the place, and let us learn to make no presumptions about our virtues, and when God has granted us the grace to walk in obedience to him and to live without rebuke, let us always be vigilant and also know that we need God's help, for we can stumble at any moment. There is no one, though he were the most saintly and perfect person in the world, who cannot fall into ignoble and shameful acts. And in that way God advises us that our free will and all our strength are powerless. So let us learn throughout our lives to pray morning and evening that God will lead us in such a way that we will be sustained by his hand and that he will not allow us, as the devil is always preparing ambushes for us, to be overcome by temptation. And especially must those who have served God for a long time, who have been living examples of his holiness, be even more instantly urged by that example to walk carefully and bear in mind that it takes but a brief moment to fall and break a neck, in a manner of speaking, if God does not sustain them. So, in the person of Lot, we have to note that our Lord is calling us to himself so that we will call upon him at all times and in all places not to allow us to be overcome by Satan's devices, for his nets are always extended to ensnare us. That, then, is what we have to remember about that point.

Now as for the time, Scripture often shows us that the judgments God displayed three or four thousand years ago are to guide us today. And yet we see that Lot soon forgot what God had shown him. Today the destruction of Sodom and Gomorrah is to give us instruction, and Scripture speaks of it very often (cf. *Isa.* 1:9; 13:19;

Jer. 23:14; *Lam.* 4:6; *Amos* 4:11; *Matt.* 10:15; *Rom.* 9:29; *2 Pet.* 2:6) so that we will tremble when we hear it mentioned. With great difficulty Lot keeps his back turned—it is true he had lived in Zoar for some time—but hidden in a cave, he forgets what he had seen with his eyes; at least he continues to give in to drunkenness and intemperance. So let us examine ourselves more closely, and let us be careful not to follow him in that particular. And if we should be the best regulated people in the world, we could still be deceived by temptation and snared by Satan if God were not guiding us and had not helped us. And we see examples of it every day. Those who have lived in the Papacy with such a fear of God that they are esteemed as virtuous people came into the church where there is better order and much regulation, where they have opportunities to be drawn to God, where his word resounds daily in their ears. They forget who they are and go to sleep. And what causes that? Presumption. So let us think about ourselves. And if we should be, as I said, in the best regulated place in the world, where God's word is preached to us daily, where we encounter no scandals that pervert, there is still enough evil in each of us that we need not draw it from somewhere else. Consequently, the only remedy is to pray to God that if he has begun the work of salvation in us, he will finish it. For we need his help, not once but for the entire course of our lives. That, then, is still what we have to remember concerning the place Moses speaks of.

And experience, as I have already said, ought to confirm for us that that is true, for even though we do not see bad examples that corrupt us, each person will be his own master in that respect. All the more, then, must we ponder the example of Lot. Now as for drunkenness, we dealt with that when discussing the story of Noah (cf. *Gen.* 9:21), but what Moses says here ought to remind us of what was said at that time: wine was created for man's use, and not only for his nourishment, as necessity requires, but also to make his heart glad, as the psalm says (cf. *Psa.* 104:15). And in that fact we see how bountiful God showed himself to be when he was not content to give us what we required simply for our nourishment, but he added something special to make our hearts glad. Yet that joy had to be tempered, for when we are being glad, we always have to give special consideration to the fact that God opens our mouths to praise him and give thanks for all his benefits (cf. *Psa.* 71:17; 75:1). So let us be even better disposed to honour him and dedicate ourselves to him.

Now since we have the instruction that wine was created for men to make their hearts glad and also so that they will be all the more cheerful in giving themselves to God's service, that is how they will be able to use it permissibly. But if all that is perverted, does it not appear that people want to disregard God in the things he has created and in the good things he has ordained for their use? If we seek after an animal-like joy, one which is particularly exuberant and would make us go against God's will, would it not seem that we want to upset the order of heaven and earth? That, then, is the first thing we have to note about drunkenness.

And then there is the matter of our being created in the image of God (cf. *Gen.* 1:26-27). And when we go and deliberately make ourselves like brute animals, so overcome by wine that we lose all sense of judgment and reason, do we not deface God's image? Is that not rank sacrilege? Consequently, when we realize the kind of vices drunkenness brings with it, it is certain we will condemn it more than we are accustomed to do. So let us always be advised when it comes to eating and drinking, that we keep our eyes fixed on God, who is our sustaining Father, and let us realize that he has ordained foods for our use and that each of us must regulate his appetite. And even if there had been no regulation or prohibition, may it be enough for us to know that God, who gives us food and drink, wants us to use them temperately. May that be our practice.

And since we know his paternal bounty toward us, let us be even more enthusiastic to give ourselves fully to him, seeing that he is concerned for these bodies which are only rotting corpses, so to speak, and seeing that he still wants to sustain them and condescend to provide for their needs and even go beyond that with an overabundance that makes them glad. So when we think about that, should we not be delighted to love such a good Father and yield ourselves fully to his will?

Moreover, let us realize that all the foods we enjoy will turn to our condemnation unless they are sanctified for us. Now that means, first, that God's name is invoked and that we ask him for our daily bread (cf. *Matt.* 6:11; *Luke* 11:3), and that we acknowledge that food and drink not only proceed from him, but that they must also be appreciated for sustaining us. For we could overeat a hundred times on bread and wine and other foods, and it would do us no good if God did not give them such vigour that we are nourished by them. However, when we call upon God's name that way, we must also apply the food and drink to the usage that God destined them for. In other words, we must be nourished and refreshed by them, not so stuffed and stupefied that we cannot function.

The contrary is also true. We are obliged to conclude that when men eat and drink without thinking about the one who created all things, they pollute everything they eat and are sacrilegious. Likewise, if you abuse food and drink in gluttony and drunkenness and indulge in excess to the point of going beyond God's regulation, you have an additional pollution of the good things of God. It is as if you wanted to dishonour God in the things he created. For if gluttonous and intemperate men get drunk, it is because they lose their sense of judgment and their memory, and they take in so much wine that they do not know who they are and they lose all discretion. They even scorn God more grievously. For wine was ordained only to strengthen men, to give them some vigour, to make their hearts glad, so that they may know God, bless his name, and yield themselves more freely to his service. If wine turns them into animals and makes them forget God and themselves and every shame, and they become like pigs, where are they going to end up? So let us pay attention to all those things. And instead of being like gluttons and drunkards who say: 'And things turned out well when Lot got drunk,' let us tremble every time we think about such an example. As for how things turned out for Lot, he was punished in a strange way, for God abandoned him to uncommon depravity. He who had been the host of angels of paradise and had lodged God in his house, so to speak, who had been just in the midst of the most wicked people in the world, who became incestuous and depraved, and that is the way he fell precipitously. When such things come to mind, should we not be more deeply stricken with fear? So while the wicked and profane only make jest of what is said here for our instruction, let us learn to walk in greater fear, and let us find drunkenness especially detestable.

And in fact if we tolerate drunkenness, it is like opening the door to every licence and every excess. When the man is given over to wine that way, he is in a daze, stupefied. There is good reason that people say that wine carries with it pride, for there will only be scorn for both God and the world. And from drunkenness will come both wrangling and altercations. And then there will be sexual laxity. For a man, as I said, being thus stupefied, will no longer be able to distinguish between good and evil. Consequently, when drunkenness is permitted, it is the same as wanting to destroy all integrity between men deliberately so that there would no longer be restraints or order and everybody could do as he pleased with abandonment. Therefore, we must enforce an even stricter policy for chastising drunks.

But as for us, we must not be forced to stay sober, and we must not expect laws and edicts to prescribe such punishments as prison and the drinking of water, but everyone must control himself. Let us suppose that magistrates are asleep and do not exercise their responsibility to chastise vices;[2] our Lord knows how to reward drunks according to what they deserve. For there is no one who is not a punisher of self when too much wine is consumed; he will always be transformed in prison! For those who are thus intemperate weaken themselves and in the end corrupt themselves, and there they are half putrefied. The world will not touch them, but, as I said, God takes vengeance on the abuse of the wine which had been created for a different use. And those wretched people who have no shame of gluttony of any kind have to punish themselves and they themselves have to execute God's judgment.

Moreover, let us not get it into our heads that drunkenness is to excuse the evil deeds which are committed, for people will often say: 'Wine got the best of the poor fellow.' It is true, but drunkenness is already a vice of its own. And if on that basis we pardon some evil, it is certain that will always compound the sins. So if a man gives himself over to sexual immorality because of drunkenness or commits murder or blasphemes the name of God, he is far from being spared because of the excuse that wine got the best of him. He receives double punishment. To begin with, he abused the things that God created and polluted and stained what God had dedicated to a good and holy use. And then he defaced God's image in himself. And such ingratitude, or rather sacrilege, he deserves. And if he adds to it some murder or sexual immorality or disgorges some blasphemy, he has committed a twofold sin. And that is because he has given himself over to Satan. And is that excusable? So let us note that because drunkenness brings with it many bad wars, we must all the more avoid it and view it as detestable along with all that results from it. And though that may be pardoned by men, it will still have to be accounted for

2 The first Geneva edicts against drunkenness date from 1549.—*M.E.*

before God. So much for the drunkenness which caused Lot to be stupefied. For God sometimes punishes one sin with another, and there is no doubt, as we have already stated, that God blinded Lot and sent him a spirit of madness and brutishness, such that he had no understanding. When we see that, let us be instructed to keep ourselves on a shorter leash.

Then there is the matter of incest. It is certain that incest will always be naturally imprinted in the hearts of men. Even in the absence of a written law, it is detestable that a father cohabit with his daughter, or a mother with her son, or a nephew with a niece. It is true that some nations are so disordered, so morally reprehensible, that brothers and sisters of the same parents got married without any distinction,[3] and because they did not do it against conscience, that was considered permissible. And on that point we realize how God had abandoned the wretched people who had plunged into idolatries, as Paul notably says that if God is not honoured, those who pervert his worship must be given over to every ignominious act and make themselves a shame and a reproach (cf. *Rom.* 1:24-25). And so it happened. And we see especially that the kings of Egypt and Syria, who were neighbours of the Jews, stooped to that level. It was only a question of marriage between uncles and nieces, nieces and nephews, and brothers and sisters.[4] It is true that mothers and sons gave themselves to that, but it was not looked on as permissible.[5] But still those ignominious acts that I mentioned, as between uncle and niece and brother and sister,

[3] Cf. perhaps Cornelius Nepos, *Cimon* 1, who mentions an Athenian law authorizing these incestuous unions. We know that the Greek pantheon contained several incestuous unions: Saturn and Ops; Oceanus and Tethys; Zeus and Hera; the sons of Aeolus marrying their sisters (cf. perhaps Ovid, *Metamorphoses* IX, v. 497-528). Below, Calvin mentions the kings of Egypt and of Syria.—*M.E.*
[4] Need we be reminded that Isis and Osiris were brother and sister as well as husband and wife? Origen, in his *Against Celsus*, recalls that it was even permitted to certain fathers in Greece to unite with their daughter (IV, 45).—*M.E.*
[5] Cf. the myth of Oedipus.—*M.E.*

were permitted, and they did not think they needed to have scruples about them. Even so, whether they liked it or not, they felt that such was evil and perverse. Be that as it may, we have already pointed out that Lot's daughters were not convinced that it was permissible for them to go to bed with their father, for they deprive him of all awareness and memory because they know he would never have consented to such a base and execrable act. And being convinced, they show that God had already provided them with knowledge that made them inexcusable, as Paul says in the second chapter of Romans (cf. *Rom.* 2:1, 12-15).

Let us return to what we discussed above, which is that today we would be much guiltier and deserve more serious punishment when it comes to defacing what God has engraved from all time in the hearts of natural man, seeing that we have the written law, the prophets and the gospel, because God has declared his will in so many ways. If we are like wild animals and let ourselves go with abandon, it is certain that if the sin was grievous and egregious in Lot's daughters, it would be a much more despicable crime for us. So let us bear that in mind when they say: 'Let us give our father wine,' for they knew very well that their incest was not permitted by God and that they had to hide themselves from their own father. We also see how men become involved in many sins when they turn away from the strict simplicity that God commands. Lot's daughters had only this way to raise up a lineage, but they still realize that the act they are undertaking is wicked. And how do they go about it? They get their father drunk. So that is how people scheme when they have some suitable pretexts when they want to indulge themselves.

Yet there remains some remorse. And what does that remorse mean? It is to get them to make an about-face and say: 'I must not follow this wicked and pernicious path,' but they will try to disguise their steps and seek devious ways, and they think that will erase their sin. Now it is certain they doubled the evil and got themselves tangled up and tightened their noose even more, as we say. That is what happened to Lot's daughters, for they want to hide their base act, which God made them feel nonetheless. And the means? By getting their father drunk. And we see again a second offence they commit, but it is not an act so unusual that we do not see many like it every day. So let us learn not to seek disguises for our sins, but as often as we see something evil, let us be reminded to fear God. And if we are already doing something that is not permissible, let us turn from it as if God had barred the way. That, then, is again what we have to remember.

In addition, let us also realize what it is to open oneself for an attack by evil, for the devil takes possession when men harden themselves; for the same happened to Lot when he lived in Sodom (cf. *Gen.* 19:1-16). We will not say he was a drunkard and an winebibber. He could not be as just and chaste as he was witnessed to be (cf. *2 Pet.* 2:7-8) if he had not been sober and had not practised abstinence in his manner of living. Now he got drunk once. He does a second time. And even though he is not aware of the evil he committed, he is nonetheless aware that his senses were dulled and that he was like a dead man and that his sleep was not normal. As a result, he could know that intoxication had made him senseless. Consequently, we see that sometimes we will be so corrupted by Satan's enticements that a little bit of nothing can harden us and that we will continue our vices, going from bad to worse until we become completely incorrigible. Therefore, let us take preventive steps, and let us not continue our excesses, seeing that they will attract us to another and another. It is true that Lot did not continue in his drunkenness, but to whom did he cling, if not to God, who had pity on him in the end? For there is a pitiable, condemned man. Satan possesses him, as we have said, and he is not excusable for the incest he committed while drunk. But God stupefied him.

As if he had put him in stocks to make him contemptible, and Lot nonetheless returns to his drunkenness. So God had to show him unusual mercy. Yet let us be on guard, if we happen to fall once, not to return to the same offence. And let us always anticipate the dangers, and let us not throw ourselves knowingly into Satan's hands so that he gets the best of us and gains entry, for we cannot allow a slight crack but that he wins the upper hand and carries us where he wills, and we will be completely distanced from God and plunge into perdition. And we will not know how. So all the more must we pay attention to what is said here: that Lot's daughters returned the second time and got their father drunk and that he gave in to such a villainous thing as drunkenness.

Then we are told that they both conceived by their father. The first gave birth and named her son Moab, and the second named hers Benammi. Now it is certain that lineage is numbered among God's blessings, even above riches and many other things which are precious and naturally desired. But here it is certain God wanted to give Lot and his daughters a sign of malediction. It is true that goodness triumphs later, for the earth was made more habitable and two great peoples descended from Lot's two daughters, who conceived by incest. We know that the Moabites were one great people and the Ammonites another.[6] That fact shows us the wondrous goodness of God. Even so, he wanted to put memorable marks on Lot, as if he wanted to curse him. For when Ammon and Moab are spoken of, it is as if to brand them for the egregious act Lot had committed. He has also given us instruction by way of his person that we must be in horror of this egregious deed when we think about it. It is true we must always keep in mind this word

---

[6] Cf. some passages in which it is said that the Moabites and/or the Ammonites defeated the children of Israel or of Judah: Judges 3:12; 11:15; 2 Kings 1:1; 2 Chronicles 20:1. Most of the time God causes the Moabites (cf. Jeremiah 25:21) and the Ammonites to drink more of the wine of his wrath, as Calvin recalls below.

'just,' which is attributed to him (cf. *2 Pet.* 2:7). But in this particular, God marked him with everlasting disgrace, and his daughters more so. So much, then, for one point: even though lineage is a sign and witness of God's blessing, yet Lot felt God's wrath when he fathered two male children and became the father of two great peoples, for the means is always vile, egregious and execrable, since it is in fact against nature and animal-like, and worse than animal-like. That, then, for one point.

But we see how God converted darkness into light (cf. *Amos* 5:8) when he permits two peoples to arise from that incest. So God's goodness triumphs, but Lot is always humbled. As for his daughters, it is true they lose all sense of shame. And that is what happens, as Paul says in the fourth chapter of Ephesians: when men abandoned themselves to evil, they finally stop grieving over it, for their consciences are dead and they are no longer aware of the difference between good and evil (cf. *Eph.* 4:19). That is what happened to Lot's daughters. Did they not have to be filled with the devil for no longer feeling shame and for boasting of what was so despicable? For Ammon means 'of my people,' as if to say that the blood of the father and the blood of the daughter are mingled. And then the name Moab means 'of my father.' Can we not indeed say that these villainous women, these sows who cohabited with their father that way, are appearing again before us to announce the triumph of their enormity and to make public themselves their filthy stench. So, as I have cited from Paul, let us learn to keep a tight hold on fear so that our Lord will not abandon us and blind us and turn us in the direction of the reprobate such that we will no longer have scruples, but let us learn to be deeply concerned morning and evening and groan so that our Lord will cover and eradicate our depravity, which he could reveal and which would be counted against us if it were not for the fact that he has sustained us by his infinite mercy.

Gluttony, Drunkenness, and Incest (Gen. 19:31-38)

Now let us bow before the majesty of our gracious God in acknowledgment of our faults, praying that he will make us so aware of them that we will be led to and drawn to a true repentance, and let us take advantage of it every day, and let us learn to examine ourselves so closely that when we have failed once, we will not do so again, but let us make every effort to return immediately to the right path from which we have wandered. And may he strengthen us in our weaknesses and so govern us by his Holy Spirit that we will not stumble and fall into perdition but always be led and instructed by him. May he grant that grace not only to us but to all the peoples and nations on earth.

96

On Adultery, Prostitution, and Sexual Immorality

Tuesday, 14 May 1560

And Abraham journeyed from thence toward the south country, and dwelled between Kadesh and Shur, and sojourned in Gerar. And Abraham said of Sarah his wife, She is my sister: and Abimelech king of Gerar sent, and took Sarah. But God came to Abimelech in a dream by night, and said to him, Behold, thou art but a dead man, for the woman which thou hast taken; for she is a man's wife. But Abimelech had not come near her (Gen. 20:1-4a).

I N THIS STORY we see how God never shows himself to be so kind and gentle toward his servants that he does not mingle in some afflictions to test their patience. Abraham experienced an almost unbelievable joy when he received the promise of a blessed seed (cf. *Gen.* 15:4-5) in which was the salvation of the world. He had Ishmael, but it was not certain that God had blessed that child, and he especially realized that he had been mistaken in his thought (cf. *Gen.* 17:18-21). But when Isaac was promised (cf. *Gen.* 17:19; 18:10), it is as if he already had the assurance of a pledge of the salvation from which the entire human race had been rejected and excluded because of Adam's fall. That is what can and ought to fill Abraham with joy.

In the meantime, he has to pull up stakes and move elsewhere. Moses does not state the reason, but we learned earlier that Abraham was a determined man, one who would not throw up his hands, as we say. So we are obliged to conclude that he was driven by some great and urgent necessity when he pulled up stakes and moved toward the south. Now he did not do it to set up his tent in another place, for he had to take his livestock and his entire household all across the land of Canaan and withdraw into the region of Gerar. Perhaps he was chased away by the malice of neighbours, by the wrongs he had suffered daily and by the many troubles that assailed him from many sides, as we have already seen and will see again.[1] Nor did he have to find rest in this world, as God makes all believers aware by experience that they are strangers here below (cf. *Heb.* 11:13; *1 Pet.* 2:11). It is true he will often give rest to his children, but they will always experience some unrest which will encourage them to seek for the heavenly inheritance. And if he strengthens the weakness of some and tests the others more keenly, it will all be done in proportion to the measure of their faith. For our Lord always considers our limits when it pleases him to afflict us. And what is that limit? It is certain we are all equal by nature. That is, we are so weak we cannot endure being pricked in the finger. But in proportion as God distributes his gifts more amply to one than to another, he also examines him more rigorously.

So there we have Abraham, who was endowed with the special gifts of patience and all virtues according as God had worked in him. He put to good use the gifts God had put in him, for God's gifts must not be useless, like a fire that has been put out, but they must be active and shining. And yet God, as I have said, according as it pleases him to afflict some more than others, also bestows upon them a more ample measure of patience so they can

---

[1] Cf. Genesis 21:25-27; but the sermon or sermons preached in June of 1560 on this chapter are lost.—*M.E.*

battle more effectually and be victorious in all the struggles they are called to. That was Abraham's situation. For, being the father of all the faithful (cf. *Gal.* 3:7), he had to serve as the pattern so that as we look to him, we will know what can happen to us when we are members of the church and what we must be prepared for.

And yet, if God gives us some liking for his bounty in this world and causes us to be glad, let us be even more patient when it pleases him to stir into our joy some sadness and affliction, and let us realize that his purpose is to keep us from being too satisfied with any felicity we have imagined, as if our paradise were on earth. So, in order to keep us alert, our Lord always sends us some hardships, but he nonetheless softens all our sorrows so that not only do we have times to be consoled but also to be blessed with joy, aware that he pities us in every situation and is not too rigorous but also aware that he moderates his rigour so that we will never lose heart, for we know that he is gracious to us. That, then, is what we have to remember about the present story.

Now even though Abraham pulls up stakes without grumbling and withdraws to a region toward the south and, in so doing, shows how he was disposed to obey God and renounce all his pleasures and conveniences, we still continue to see many weaknesses in him. Even though he was established as an example for all, an example of holiness and perfection, he still fell short in many ways. As a result, we see that he had not yet rid himself of many human vices, and that is so we will take courage and follow him and imitate him in God's service. For there are many who imagine an unpleasant picture when someone explains to them how God's servants lived. They think: 'Oh, they were not like us!' And they provide disinterest and unconcern as a reason as they distance themselves as far as they can from the rank of God's servants, who they thought were like angels and whom they ought to be joined to openly and without pretence. Now when we see that Abraham, whose children we certainly are if we are believers (cf. *Gal.* 3:7), had outstanding virtues and yet was a man who failed, made mistakes, went astray somewhat, and experienced serious fears, did not always make the right decisions, as he should have, and wavered now in one way, now in another, and when we see that, we understand that God sustains his children, even though they are not completely such as they should be.

In addition, let us be even more enthusiastic to follow Abraham when we see that he had to fight against his faults and weaknesses and that he was not made of iron or steel any more than we are. Seeing, then, that there was something lacking in him, we ought to be the more encouraged to walk uprightly and resist all temptations and not to grow weary, even though it takes great effort and hard work to walk where God calls us.

Now here are the wrongs Abraham committed in the story Moses recounts. In the first place, experience did not make Abraham wiser, and it is said that that is the master of fools.[2] That is a great fault in Abraham, for he had the idea in Egypt to say that Sarah was his sister. God had punished him for it, not that he lied, for she was a relative of his (cf. *Gen.* 12:10-20), as we have seen. And this word 'sister' in the language means all kindred of any degree. So Abraham spoke only truth when he says Sarah is his sister. But what is the intention of his statement? He did not want anyone to think she was his wife. That, then, is dissimulation and deceit, which are to be condemned. And what happened to him as a result? God punished him severely by having his wife taken from him. So he should have known that that dissimulation displeased God, and he should have learned to walk in greater simplicity. Now he returns to his old ways as if he knowingly wanted to provoke God again. So much for one point.

Now for the second point. When his wife is taken from him, why does he not object? For he knows how God helped him once

[2] Cf. Erasmus, *Praise of Folly* XXIX.—M.E.

and how his wife was returned to him miraculously, how God also kept her from being violated by Pharaoh. Now when Abraham dissimulates again in the same way and permits his wife to be taken to the king of Gerar, that is inexcusable ingratitude. Why does he not call upon God? Why does he not show himself to be steadfast, seeing that he knew the help which had already been given him in such anguish? And there is also no doubt that Abraham's faith was shaken here and that he did not have the zeal to call upon God and place himself again in his hands, as was required of him. So we see how Abraham failed. But the failures of the holy fathers must not serve as instruction, as we saw earlier, beyond what I have recently touched upon, and we ought to be induced even more to conform ourselves to their virtues, seeing that they were as weak as we are. On the other hand, when they happened to offend God because they did not take him into consideration and when they were surprised by some troubles and some danger, we see that they went astray. When we see that, we see just that many instructions that we must apply to our use so that while God leaves us in peace and we have the leisure to meditate on his promises, we will call upon him often so that he will not abandon us in times of need.

Moreover, when troubles come our way, let us not be overly frightened, for if it happened to Abraham, what can we expect? So let us ponder this: 'There Abraham was, ready to die a hundred times rather than provoke God's wrath. Nonetheless, there remains in him some small residue of unbelief. He does not take refuge in God, as he should.' So when we are thus tested, let us be careful not to be confused and incapable of making a purposeful decision. Consequently, the example of Abraham should, in the first place, teach us that if we have learned from experience that our Lord wanted to chastise us for some sin or other, we should not revisit that situation, and that we should be on our guard against it; and if we should be confronted by some temptation similar to the one that got the best of us, let us always remember it. 'What? I have already felt God's hand once, and that was so I would remember it the rest of my life. So I must resist now.' That is the first thing we have to do.

As for the second, after God has pity on us and extends his hand to afflict us in some way, let us know that for the future it will never fail us. And let us make that our prayer. And when we are confronting some danger that threatens to cause us to turn aside from him, let us know: 'Indeed, the God who helped us once, is he not still living? Has his nature changed? Do his promises not still have the same vigour? Will their effect not be evident?' Therefore, let us always keep before us what we know about God's goodness, and may it so strengthen us in all our struggles that we will conclude: 'My God, I will be confident because I have once realized that you cannot fail those who trust in you and find their rest in you' (cf. *Psa.* 2:12; 32:10; *Prov.* 29:25). And after that? We have to pray to him.[3] And even as God tests our faith, he entreats us at the same time to come to him, and as he does this, he shows us that the hope we put in him is never misplaced or put to shame.

That, then, is what we have to remember about the example of Abraham: that if such a patriarch did not have the perfection of faith he should have had, if he was not aflame with the ardent affection required of him, let us be even more afraid. And let us always persevere, even though we cannot arrive at the goal that we seek with the kind of enthusiasm we should have, but let us proceed by hobbling along, and may our vices not hinder us or cause us to fail under any circumstance, but let us deal with our weaknesses forcefully and violently, knowing that God will still show he is merciful. Even though there is something amiss in our faith, even though we call upon him too nonchalantly and unenthusiastically, he will always be pleased with our faith and

[3] Cf. *Institutes* III, xx, 16; or Psalm 66:8-12.—*M.E.*

our prayers because he deals with us as a father. That, then, is what we have to remember.

Moreover, let us think about how great Abraham's trial was when Sarah was taken from him a second time. We must not only consider here the affections husbands have for their wives, for Abraham knew Sarah was to give birth to Isaac, from whom would come the salvation of the world. Abraham knows that he is cursed and damned, as is Adam's entire lineage. He has but one hope of salvation through a child God wishes to give him. Now that Sarah is taken from him, what do we have here but God's confounding him to say to him: 'The redemption and salvation of yourself and all believers by mercy that you have been expecting thus far is meaningless.' That is Abraham's state of mind. And if he has that strong feeling of a husband, seeing that his wife was taken from him, does he not have even more to pierce his heart? But the two are joined together, and would that not be enough for God to bring him to such a state of distress? Must he revisit that? In addition, where is the promise given to him a short while ago? And here is Sarah, who is to become pregnant; yet she is taken away. And where is that blessed seed? So we see how Abraham is struggling under a horrible weight, as if God had added the weight of his hand to overwhelm him completely and lead him to the depths.

Let us not think that that is an easy trial, like the ones we frequently have, for Abraham's must have been extreme, for he was so disturbed in mind that he found no counsel or discretion. When we see that, let us not find it too unusual, but let us compare the struggles we have to confront. The moment God threatens us from a distance or raises his finger, there we are as distraught as can be, and we do not know what will happen to us. And we think we are unforgivable when we act like stray animals and always lament: 'Alas, what will I do? I am not made of iron or steel. Why is God testing me so harshly?' That will be trifling, in a manner of speaking, in comparison with the trials that God allows us to experience. Therefore, let us realize we have even greater need to ask God to give us wisdom and counsel so we will know what to do when he lets us be trampled on and cast into pits, so to speak; nonetheless, let us always walk in his paths and ask him to guide us and enlighten us with his heavenly light when we are at our wits end in this world. That, then, for one point.

And in addition, whenever it seems that God deals with us unduly harshly, let us consider our father Abraham, and we will find that we are very far from matching him and that we are a long shot from enduring a hundredth of the struggles he had to withstand, and that was not without faltering and going awry, and he fell short in the matters we have mentioned, but he still overcame. And let us not find it strange if God raises up one trial and follows it with another and we have to start all over again. Even if we are assailed so severely that we do not know which way to turn, let us not think that that is anything new. Why not? It happened to the one who is the father of believers, and he endured much more than we. That, then, is what we have to remember.

And let us especially learn to arm and fortify ourselves against the temptations of the spirit as well as of the flesh. I call temptations of the flesh those which afflict the body and this present life, as when one person is stricken with diseases and has to suffer long bouts of weakness and discouragement; another does not have bread to eat; another is harassed by his enemies; another endures cold and heat; another is crushed by humiliation, such as when someone spits in his face. Well, those are the temptations, the trials, of the body since we are wretched as men and our situation is such that it seems God has abandoned us.

And there are the temptations of the spirit, which are worse. It is true we do not always feel them as much, for we are disposed to

satisfy the senses and we are so preoccupied with our earthly concerns that we have a weak disposition in matters of the body. But
the temptations and trials of the spirit are even worse. We confront
them when we think that God has rejected us or that our sins are
warring against us so that it seems Satan has us trapped in his nets
and we are completely cut off from the hope of life because we do
not have the kind of faith we should have, when we do not have
the ardour to call upon God and the dedicated affection to serve
and honour him as we should, when we are aware of many strong
desires within ourselves, when the vanities of this world get the
best of us, when it seems the door of paradise is closed to us, and
when we think it serves no purpose to seek after God. So when
those kinds of battles confronts us, it is certain it would be much
better to endure everything the body is capable of than to have our
poor souls held captive in those ways.

The temptations, the trials, of the body and the spirit are seen
here in Abraham. On the one hand, his wife is taken from him,
whom he loved as a chaste husband of holy life; and, on the other
hand, where is his salvation and all the hope he received from God
and his goodness? For it is as if the promises had been eradicated,
so to speak, and completely wiped out when Sarah was taken from
him. Why? It is she who is to give birth to the one from whom the
salvation of the world is to proceed. So Abraham is deprived of
what he was to desire above all else in the world. That is the only
reward for his faith, and it is taken from him. For in Jesus Christ,
as Paul says, all the promises of God are yes and amen (cf. *2 Cor.*
1:20). What is to become of him now that he no longer has his
wife Sarah, who is to provide the child from whom he was expecting grace and by whom God was to be reconciled with the world?
So when we see all those things, let us learn to fortify ourselves.
And if on occasion our Lord loosens Satan's restraints so that we
are tormented and our sins make war on us, let us remember that

we are people under judgment and that our sins condemn us to the extent that we sense that God is working against us and we dare not approach him, that we have no defence and our hearts are closed (cf. *Rom.* 8:26). That, then, is what we have to remember about what is demonstrated by the example of Abraham.

It is then said that God warns Abimelech that he will die because he took another man's wife, for she was married. As for Abimelech, we must not think he was the king of a great country, for at that time men were called kings if they had authority and were chosen as the most worthy of the people. And in fact his name means that in Gerar he was honoured inasmuch as he was called 'father king.' So he was not a tyrant who dominated by violence, but he was a king, that is, a governor in that area, because the people looked upon him as a father. It is likely he dealt with his people humanely. It is also likely he responded to his name, as we will see later in the excuse he offers to God (cf. *Gen.* 20:4b-5). He takes Sarah and yet God opposes that, even though Abraham is at fault. That is what we have to consider.

In the first place, mockers and profane people say that Sarah, being old and decrepit, could not be as desired as a young girl of great beauty would be. To them we can answer, as we have already seen, that she was of an outstanding beauty (cf. *Gen.* 12:11-14). And then, in the second place, God was able to preserve her as if she were in the flower of her age. Nor do we know whether Abimelech was inflamed by desire, as those who have excessive love affairs in which the visual plays the only role. We saw that earlier when the sons of God, that is, those who ought to be separated from the world's pollutions, looked at the daughters of men (cf. *Gen.* 6:2); that is, they were carried away by their animal-like lust; they had only eyes and did not know what marriage was. As for Abimelech, perhaps he looked upon Sarah not for any beauty she had, but because he sees her in a good way, as a woman worthy of honour, in whom he recognizes excellent qualities because of which he takes her as his wife, thinking that she was not married. That much, then, for Abimelech's affection.

We have to note now that God shows himself to be more than merciful to his servant when he takes his side. Was Abraham worthy of having God correct this evil which he, because of his foolishness and lack of consideration, preferred to choose over doing what he knew to be right? For it is possible Abraham was well enough instructed to entrust himself to God and provide an excuse for his wife, as we will see later when Abimelech, even though a pitiable pagan, rebukes him.[4] 'You have,' he says, 'laid your wife bare here. You should have been a covering for her, but you abandoned her.' Abraham was chastised by the mouth of an ordinary man. Why? Because he had profited badly from God's school. Consequently, as I have said, he indeed deserved to have God allow his wife to be taken from him, and he remained disconsolate, languishing in his distress. He deserved such a reward. No matter, God is willing to take up his servant's cause, whatever his fault. Consequently, what the psalm says is fulfilled where the prophet says that God has always said he would show favour to the fathers of Israel (cf. *Psa.* 105:8-9, 12-14). Our fathers, he says, were wanderers in the land of Canaan. They were strangers; they were chased from one place to another, for they had no relatives or friends. But God was their shield and fortress and always sustained and protected them, not only against the ordinary people, but he chastised kings on their behalf. So since God was willing to chastise kings on behalf of Abraham, a man worthy of contempt, was that not a witness of singular kindness? So we see God did not look upon

---

[4] Cf. Genesis 20:9-10, 16, but Calvin confuses the two passages since, in the first, Abimelech is speaking to Abraham and, in the second (mention of the covering), he is speaking to Sarah. Calvin will take up Genesis 20:7 and the following verses beginning with sermon 98, for Tuesday, 16 May 1560, but that is the first sermon in the lost series of his preaching on Genesis.—*M.E.*

Abraham's many misdeeds, done as much in unbelief as in ingratitude because he had not known how to profit from what he knew from experience.

So since Abraham forgets all that and yet God does not fail to help him, we see how in a mirror God is obliged to sustain us often and to show his mercy, even though we are unworthy of it and give him occasion to abandon us and leave us when we are perplexed. Still he closes his eyes to our offences and does not impute them to us. He chastises us for them for a time because he knows it is good for us to be humbled and to be better aware of his grace and mercy. But, on the other hand, that does not keep him from extending his power to help us and letting us know that he has cared for and protected us. And even though we repulse his mercies by our vices, he finds the means to touch us and show us that he overcomes all the hindrances we set before him. That, then, is what we have to remember.

Now that is not to make us bolder to offend God, for there are scoffers who say: 'Well, since God pardoned our father Abraham of all his faults and continued to help him, when we do the worst we can, the fact is that God will still continue to pity us.' Let us be careful not to abuse his patience that way; rather, let us be warned not to shut the door when he wants to help us this way. Even so, when he helps us, let us realize that it is not because of our merits or because we have done something good to draw him to ourselves, but let us realize that there are faults in us which could distance us from him and cause him to withdraw his hand and leave us in our need, but that he has waged a battle against our vices. We must always come to that conclusion. It is true we will not always know how we have got in the way of God's helping us, but when we examine what is in us, it is certain we will always find faults that God will have to battle against when it pleases him to pity us and have mercy on us. So much, then, for that point.

Now if Abraham, who is the father of believers (cf. *Gal.* 3:7), was helped in time of need, what will happen to us, who have not reached such perfection! Let us come now to what God states when he takes up Abraham's cause. He tells Abimelech that he will die and is already dead, for the word means that: 'You are dead; you are done for, for you have taken the wife of another.' God speaks here matter-of-factly, like a judge. He does not plead long with Abimelech. Why not? Because he does not want to frighten him to bring him immediately to repentance. Now it is true that our Lord will often employ long admonitions and warnings when he wants to move us to fear and correct our vices, but it is a privilege that he does that for us because he has been pleased to accept us as his children. It is then that he acts, not only as judge, but as a teacher who instructs his own children privately, using simple, clear words, and who supports them, knowing their lack of knowledge. That, then, is how God often works in our behalf.

As when we come to hear the word of God, there will not only be specific sentences to condemn all crimes and injustices, but our Lord tells us how we must guard against evil. And then he warns us with gentle words why we must battle against the desires of our flesh, against the devil's and the world's temptations. So God teaches us very gently, little by little, and tries to draw us to himself consistently and by degrees, and that is because he is our Father and our Teacher. Sometimes he speaks vigorously, briefly and emphatically, to show us how his arm is working against us. For there are in Scripture harsh threats to frighten us (cf. *Isa.* 30:30; 51:5). But whatever the situation, God uses those threats when he sees in us such hardness that we abuse his gentleness and intimacy and are incapable of even remotely profiting from anything. Why? To teach. This word 'teach' is emphasized. But does that profit nothing? Immediately following is the word 'reprove,' that is, we have to be prodded, we have to be encouraged, if we are cold and unmotivated. And then if we still do nothing to change, we must be intentionally reproved to the point that we are frightened and astonished by God's wrath so that we will be by all means brought back to the right path, from which we strayed.

Now as for Abimelech, God does not favour him with long comments, but with a single word he pronounces him dead. Why? He took the wife of another. Now that sentence is very harsh, and especially so if we think about Abimelech's response and excuse. For he had not yet touched Sarah. He had taken her as his wife, thinking she was free and marriageable, and yet God declares that he is a criminal and declares it seriously. When a sentence issues from God's mouth, we must not attempt to reply as if he were jesting, for it is God who has spoken. For who is the unfortunate creature who will now dare to challenge that sentence and then plead against it with his admirable reasonings? Are they not just so many blasphemies? Is that not to want to topple God from his judgment seat? So if we find that sentence rigorous, let us realize that it is coming from the fountain of all righteousness (cf. *Jer.* 2:13). And then when God has spoken, men must cease speaking and say only 'Amen' (cf. *Rom.* 3:19), realizing it is a just sentence, an irrevocable decree that is not to be contradicted.

Let us note in addition that it is not without reason that God condemns adulterers as rigorously as he does, for he is the author of marriage (cf. *Gen.* 2:18-24). Also, marriage is called his covenant in the second chapter of Proverbs.[5] If contracts are not to be violated between men and if the one who alters a contract dealing with vintage will be put to death[6] and merit it, and if no contrary argument can be made, what will become of the person who breaks the contract with God, who is separate from all conventions, all the

[5] Calvin must be alluding to Proverbs 2:16-17.—*M.E.*
[6] I can find no trace of such a severe legislation in Geneva dealing with the falsification of a vintage contract.—*M.E.*

promises, and all the dealings that men have among themselves? That, then, is a man who has made a contract in God's name. That is a contract on which God has placed his mark. And if a person breaks it, must that be considered a small and insignificant fault that requires only a sprinkling of holy water? Therefore, let us note that there is good reason for our Lord to speak this way: 'You will die, for you have taken another man's wife,' for when marriages are corrupted this way, it is a manifest act of war against God. For what trust and what faithfulness will there be among men if a wife abandons herself like a prostitute or if the husband prostitutes himself like a dog after God's name has been mocked between both and they say: 'God is our witness that we are joined in his name'? And then let both one and the other admit that: 'I am now only one half of one person, we are now two, but if we are only one person—for Scripture speaks that way (cf. *Gen.* 2:24)—and I then go and profane myself as if I were openly scorning God and tear asunder that union which is to be inviolable, I am breaking the marriage which is the image and figure of the sacred union that we have with our Lord Jesus Christ' (cf. *Eph.* 5:21-33). So if there is such uncertainty, what more remains in all of human life? The greatest treasures that people have are the children that come from marriage (cf. *Psa.* 127:3). And if adultery is permitted, we can no longer know whose children they are. No longer will trust or faithfulness exist, or anything else!

Moreover, when we have thoroughly considered everything, God reproves adulterers to such an extent, that is to say, he abandons them to such an extent that they must always go from bad to worse. Even the pagans said that if a woman is an adulteress, she will at the same time open herself to being poisoned.[7] In fact, if

---

[7] An increase in the severity of punishment for adulterers is observed in the course of the history of the Roman Empire. Cf. Seneca the Elder (the rhetorician), *Controversies* VII, vi, 13; Aulus Gellius, *Attic Nights* X, xxiii, 5. Cf. also *Corpus juris*

there are adulterers, the door will be open to poisonings and mur-
ders, and a wife will cut her husband's throat. And if she cannot
or dares not go that far, she will poison him. That will not always
happen, but we have seen rather obvious examples.[8] And since it
happened once, God showed we must avoid evil and employ preventive measures. But if we had only the single reason that God,
having instituted marriage, wishes to be the protector of mutual
chastity between a husband and a wife, wishes to be witness and
judge, if one of the parties breaks faith, if it should be only that,
it is certain we are not to find that sentence to be excessive. So
when God declares it is a mortal crime when one has committed
adultery and violated such a holy thing as marriage and introduced
the entire human race to uncertainty and broken the trust more
important than all others, we must accept it. And those who object
to that, let them go make their case before God. But, as I have said,
those who argue in favour of adultery and try to maintain it are
depraved. They, I say, show they have not experienced Christianity and do not know either God or his word. Here God has pronounced his sentence on a poor pagan. The law was not yet written; there were no prophets except Abraham, unless Melchizedek
was still alive. That, then, is a world deprived of teachers. They did
not have the instructions or exhortations which we have now. They
had only some order that God placed in nature so that men might

---

civilis, Codex Justinianus 9, 9, '*Ad legem Juliam de adulteriis et de stupru,*' particularly
§ 4 or 27. Adulteries are likewise punished more severely in Geneva from 1540
to 1560. The deliberations of the '*Compagnie des pasteurs*' in 1546 proposed less
severe measures against adulteries than twenty years later, when death would
strike married adulterers (cf. RCP 1, p. 18; Rivoire-Van Berchem, *Sources du droit:*
t. 3, p. 170; cf. also Kingdon, *Adultery,* chapt. 5, 'Death for Adultery,' pp. 116-139;
Seeger, *Nulité de marriage*).—*M.E.*

[8] One example out of a thousand, Agrippina the Younger had her second husband,
the emperor Claudius, poisoned. The ordinances of 1566 'on the crimes of
prostitution and adultery' present an argument identical to that of this sermon...
Cf. Rivoire-Van Berchem, *Sources du droit,* t. 3, p. 167 (17 April 1566).—*M.E.*

not be like brute beasts. Nonetheless, that sentence has been pronounced: whoever takes the wife of another man, that man must die.

We now have the law God gave us. We see in it the condemnation that was placed there for us, a condemnation to death (cf. *Lev.* 20:10).⁹ We have many warnings from the prophets (cf. *Jer.* 3:8; 13:27; *Ezek.* 16:35-38; *Hos.* 4:13-14). We have examples to show how much adulteries displease God, as Paul speaks of them (cf. *1 Cor.* 6:9-10), and especially of acts of venery, showing how God punished them when he once exterminated such a great people (cf. *Judg.* 20).¹⁰ We have living pictures, as it were, in which God shows us his vengeance against adulteries. We have the gospel, in which it is said that marriage is honourable before God (cf. *Heb.* 13:4), but he will punish whoremongers and adulterers. But we even have the laws of pagans, for God was not satisfied to give his law and to confirm the teaching contained in the prophets and to ratify it particularly in the gospel, but he wanted the poor unbelievers who never knew anything about the law or the gospel to have it and talk about it. Where are the Christians now who are steeped in the gospel and come here and 'play the hypocrite,' as they say in the Papacy of those who 'eat the crucifix'? So they will come and do the same thing; they want to devour the entire gospel! And yet, they do not understand the severity of the punishment for adultery, and yet they would gladly find fault with it. Are they worthy of coming here to God's church? All they do is pollute it. Let them learn from the pagans, and the pagans will condemn them, as we see. Since that is true, what remains for us to do but to keep silent and consent to the sentence which God has declared?

It is true this will be interpreted differently. But so? I cannot abandon the text I have to deal with. And then I do not know whether

⁹ By way of contradiction, cf. John 8:3.—*M.E.*
¹⁰ This deals with the twenty-five thousand Benjamites after the violation of the Levite's wife.—*M.E.*

the subject of adultery will come up on Tuesday or Monday. So when I enter the pulpit and have a subject to deal with, depending on the text which is set forth, if I intend only to take back my words and say: 'I will retract what I said so I will not be unjustly criticized,' would that mean I would be doing my duty as I must? Well, let them interpret it anyway they wish, but God must be heard. And if we have to preach today on one subject and tomorrow on another according as the texts appear, let us realize, as I have said, that God wants us to be instructed fully in his teaching.

In the meantime, let us know that what happens will be by his providence, as has often been the case, and we would be aware of it if we had our eyes open to recognize it. So it will sometimes happen that God will put before us a certain subject which will come at the right time; and with the teaching, he will simultaneously add approval by a deed so that we will be taught more clearly and also be more grievously condemned if we do not take advantage of what he says and of what he does. Of what he says, because he is instructing us, and of what he does, when he simultaneously executes his judgments to prove his teaching is not in vain. Now if this was declared to king Abimelech, as we have already said, let us consider that we must all lower our heads.

It is true God judges without respect of persons; he does not distinguish between great and small. In fact, we know what the psalm says, that kings and princes and servants of righteousness are servants of God (cf. *Psa.* 2:10-11). They are called his children (cf. *Psa.* 82:6), but they must die every one of them, and the form of this world must pass away (cf. *I Cor.* 7:31). Therefore, when God condemned Abimelech, it was to show that he judges without respect of persons, but we must nonetheless impress upon our hearts the teaching that that fact does not prevent kings themselves from being chastised; they will not be spared. We see how God demotes them and shows them that their rank does not exempt them from the condemnation which he has pronounced upon adulterers.

It is noteworthy that it is said that Sarah was married. For even though acts of sexual immorality are despicable to God, acts of adultery are much deadlier crimes. Sexual immorality in itself brings pollution to the temple of God. That already ought to horrify us. Now we are the temple of God because he lives in us by his Holy Spirit (cf. *1 Cor.* 3:16). And if we go and soil our bodies with sexual immorality, it is as if we wanted to profane the temple of God and eradicate all its holiness. That much for one point.

So then, we are members of our Lord Jesus Christ (cf. *2 Cor.* 6:15; *Eph.* 5:30). Will Jesus Christ be joined with that filthy act? Can we mingle him with our immoral practices? Certainly not! It is as if we wanted to tear him to pieces. Those are two enormous crimes, pollution of the temple of God and the outrage done to Jesus Christ. For, as Paul says, the other sins are committed outside the body (cf. *1 Cor.* 6:17-19). It is true that we say murderers have blood on their hands (cf. *Isa.* 1:15; 59:3; *Ezek.* 23:37), as do highway robbers, but there remains a stain in sexual immorality which makes life even more detestable, when a man gives himself this way to sexual immorality. That, then, is how those acts bring with them much evil.

But adultery is even worse, for, as we have already argued, our word is given in God's name when marriage is solemnly pledged. God is called as witness and judge in case the man or the woman is a perjurer. And in addition to the fact that God, who protects that holy office he has instituted, is offended, we enter into a state of such confusion that there is no longer a father or a son, that is, there is no longer any order among men. The words 'father,' 'mother,' and 'child' are sacred, and God wants his glory to shine in them. And all is lost and destroyed if adultery has clear sailing, so to speak. So since we see that, in addition to sexual immorality, there are so many other despicable acts, not only in the eyes of God but also in the eyes of the world, must we prolong this discussion? So let us note the reason given us here when God declares that since Sarah was married to another, it was not permissible for Abimelech to touch her, for it was more than if he had taken all of Abraham's goods when he took from him this way his own substance and his honour.

Now let us bow before the majesty of our gracious God in acknowledgment of our faults, praying that he will make us so aware of them that we will truly humble ourselves before him and ask his forgiveness. And in addition, let us find all our refuge in his mercy, and let us also pray that he will so cleanse us by his Holy Spirit of all our infections and uncleanness that we will be able to be true temples dedicated to his service, and may we, in body and soul, make an effort to glorify him. And may he strengthen us in our weaknesses that we will not be rejected by him, and may he remove them from us more and more until he has clothed us in his righteousness and brought us all to that angelic purity to which we aspire, though we are very far from it. May he grant that grace not only to us but to all the peoples and nations on earth.

97

Intentional Sins vs. Inadvertent Sins
and
The Role of Prayer for One Another

Wednesday, 15 May 1560

But Abimelech had not come near her: and he said, Lord, wilt thou slay also a righteous nation? Said he not unto me, She is my sister? and she, even she herself said, He is my brother: in the integrity of my heart and innocency of my hands have I done this. And God said unto him in a dream, Yea, I know that thou didst this in the integrity of thy heart; for I also withheld thee from sinning against me: therefore suffered I thee not to touch her. Now therefore restore the man his wife; for he is a prophet, and he shall pray for thee, and thou shalt live: and if thou restore her not, know thou that thou shalt surely die, thou, and all that are thine (Gen. 20:4-7).

W E SAW YESTERDAY the sentence God pronounced against Abimelech, king of Gerar, because he took Sarah as his wife. Moses here recounts that he made excuses before God, protesting that he had done so with integrity of heart and clean hands, and he gives the reason: because he had heard that Sarah was only Abraham's sister and not his wife. Now it is true God accepts and approves his excuse, but he does not completely absolve him, as we will see later,[1] for he is punished along with his entire household despite his ignorance. So God does not fully justify him, but he does not wish to deal with him rigorously as if he were guilty of a crime. That is why he tells him he knows why he acted the way he did, and for that reason he prevents him from doing worse. He commands him to return Abraham's wife and points out that Abimelech needs mercy, even though the sin he committed was not all that bad, for he had not knowingly taken another's wife, and he adds the rather harsh and bitter threat that he and everything belonging to him would be destroyed unless he returned Abraham's wife pure and untouched.

Now because Abimelech says to God that he, God, will not kill an innocent people, we understand that although he was a poor ignorant man and that all teaching of the truth was withheld from the world at that time, he walked in darkness and even lived in superstition and idolatry; yet he possessed the knowledge that God is just and does not condemn those who have fallen short and transgressed without knowledge. That is how pagans, even though they were blind, have always had imprinted in their hearts some awareness of God's righteousness so they would know that he was a just judge and so they would be made more inexcusable. For if every source of mercy and religion had been dead, men would have taken the liberty to do evil without scruples; but since they realized there was a God before whom they had to give an account, they had something to restrain them, so that when they yielded to evil, they had no excuse and could not claim ignorance, for they were already convinced they had to appear before the judgment seat of the one who rules the world and provided law and governance, even though unwritten.

Now it is not enough that people have the opinion, without being sure, that there is some sovereign majesty we are subject to,

[1] Cf. Genesis 20:7b and the next day's sermon, the first to be missing.—*M.E.*

but they must at the same time be persuaded of the justice and uprightness of God so that they will realize that the responsibility of judging belongs to him because all perfection resides only in him, that he cannot fail and that his will is itself perfect righteousness, and that it is because of that that we must find all our good in him. That was Abimelech's situation.

So much the worse for us today if we do not attribute to God at least the honour of confessing that he is just and if we have the conviction in our hearts that he cannot do wrong when he punishes the world's sins and iniquities. It is true that each person will confess that much about God just as Abimelech did at first, for we would be ashamed, indeed horrified, to blaspheme against God, saying he is iniquitous and maintains no order and is cruel, but even so, the complaints we have show rather well that there is some uncertainty in the thought about that justice which we confess is in God, for if we are not dealt with as we like, we will immediately make known our grumblings and dissatisfactions; and if they are not full throated, some bitter words will still escape our mouths. And what does that mean but that we do not realize that God is just and equitable and that we must yield to what he arranges and thinks best, for he cannot fail? Now if that teaching were imprinted on our hearts, it is certain we would be patient in all our afflictions and be so humble that none of us would complain and that we would always keep our mouths shut, or at least not open them except to glorify our Judge while willingly condemning ourselves. All the more, then, must we adhere to the teaching that a poor unbeliever who has neither law nor prophet to instruct him has nonetheless realized, namely, that God does not act indiscriminately when punishing offences and iniquities, but that he was maintaining an unfailing integrity so that we would bow our heads humbly. If God sometimes punishes us for our sins, let us realize he does so rightly, and let us keep control of all our senses, and may all of our feelings be bridled and held captive so that we will not use our tongues to utter some venomous laments. So that is what we have to remember in the first place.

In the second place, let us note that when someone talks to us about God, we must not enter into clever speculations, as some frivolous-minded people do, for there are those who poke into everything, and their curiosity is insatiable. Consequently, when God is the subject, they want to ask about his incomprehensible counsels. The one who is the most confident will be thought to be the most learned and the sharpest. But let us learn that there is nothing better to know about God than what contributes to his praise and what keeps us in fear of him, things that cause us to revere his majesty and his glory. Not only that, but also his goodness and wisdom, his mercy, and his rigour, especially when he exercises it against the wicked. In summary, in order to know well who God is, we must not flit around above the clouds searching for what is beyond our understanding and is hidden from us, but let us learn that since he is Judge of the world and its Creator, everything good proceeds from him and that it is in him that we must seek everything that is desirable for both the body and the soul, and that we must find our rest in his goodness and aspire to him and turn to him with true faith and repentance, knowing that if he were not merciful, we would be lost people and without hope. That, I say, is the kind of knowledge we need to have about God, knowledge which works itself out in practice, in serving and honouring him, in calling earnestly upon his name and praising him for all the good things we receive from him; otherwise, everything we can imagine about him will be nothing but smoke and will vanish without fruit or usefulness. In a word, let us learn to do what we have learned about God, those things which bring us to what is said in the psalm: 'Lord, just as your renown is upon the entire earth, so is your praise' (cf. *Psa.* 45:17). That is, we will never speak of him except to exalt him and cause the world to submit to him. Let us all, great and small, pay him the homage that belongs to him. In brief, may his name be sanctified,[2] as we pray every day.

Now when Abimelech says he did what he did in the integrity of his heart and with clean hands, it is not because he wants to justify himself totally, as holy Scripture sometimes, when speaking of the perfection of living a good life, mentions these two things: clean hands and a pure heart (cf. *Psa.* 24:4). Abimelech does not justify himself totally, but he opposes that pure heart to a bad conscience and declares it was not out of deliberate malice that he did what he did, and he opposes clean hands to injustice, violence, theft and armed robbery. So that is the way he understands it. In other words, even though he fell short, he did not commit a crime, as someone who willingly commits extortion, knowing that he does wrong and that he was not influenced by sexual desire to take the wife of another. Thinking that the woman was marriageable, he wanted to have her as his wife. That, then, is the pure heart and clean hands Abimelech is speaking out here.

Now because God accepts that kind of response, we can gather a teaching from this passage, namely, that God makes a distinction between sins which are committed out of intentional evil and sins that are committed inadvertently (cf. *Lev.* 4:2; *Acts* 3:17; *1 Tim.* 1:13), for we will be ill-advised sometimes. It is true in general that Scripture will call sins ignorance (cf. *Lev.* 4:2; *Acts* 3:17; *1 Tim.* 1:13), and that is because we have to be half blind, as it were, when we confront God and lose every natural sense of awareness he gave us. It is certain our eyes will be open to consider our duty and seek to know what God approves and what we are permitted to do, so that we will live right. Consequently, ignorance has to play a role when we are people gone astray. So when we lose all discretion and

[2] The first petition of the Lord's Prayer. Cf. Matthew 6:9; Luke 11:2.—*M.E.*

are carried in all directions to offend God, we certainly have to be blind.

And in fact our passions blind us, I say, especially when there is definite evil intention, especially when a lecher is caught up in his lust. Oh, he will be convinced in himself that he is offending God, but he has no reason that guides him, and his mind will be encumbered and clouded. The same is true of avarice, the same is true of gluttony; the same is true of all the other vices: it is as if all reason and intelligence were dead. Without them, there is a madness which carries us away and we will be living in darkness, as it were, and we will not discern between good and evil and we will not be able to feel shame and make distinctions between good and evil. That is how sins are combined with some ignorance. Why? The reason is that all our passions and lusts blind us and are like so many things that obstruct our prudence. Now there is that distinction which is placed in the law between voluntary sins and the sins which are committed out of ignorance in the fourth chapter of Leviticus (cf. *Lev.* 4:2). Voluntary sins are those we commit knowing that God has forbidden an act which we do not hesitate to participate in as if we were willingly breaking the bonds by which God bound us. So if we do not sin in complete ignorance, the sin is then voluntary.

Now there are sins which are committed out of ignorance. How? It is when sometimes, of a sudden, we trip up without thinking about it. True, God makes us aware of the evil after we have committed it, but at the time we knew nothing about it. Especially will it seem to us that we are doing the best that can possibly be done, for zeal will sometimes be imprudent in many people. They will think they are serving God when they are offending him. For there is a blindness in us because of original sin and because of the corruption in our nature which, when we think we are doing good, we fall into evil. That is not to say, however, that we are excused. Sin is to be imputed to us and deserves chastisement and punishment, but even so, it is not as bad as when we go and violate our consciences because of unbridled passion and when we are convicted of what we do but still continue to offend God; it is like the servant, knowing his master's will, who will be punished doubly (cf. *Luke* 12:47). If a servant commits some fault and claims, 'Oh, do not blame me. I thought I was doing the right thing'; his master will say to him: 'Why did you not ask me what I wanted? Did you not know that you are my subject and that you must serve me according to my will? You were supposed to know what was right or wrong, and I would have answered you. And since you went about it without knowing what you were doing, you deserve to be punished.' That is how the servant who does not know his master's will will nonetheless be punished when he does not do his duty. For he was disinterested and hasty. Do not those two vices deserve punishment? In the first place, disinterest is to be condemned since the will of the master is not sought. And then since he does what he wanted to do in accordance with his own will, he is hasty. And that kind of haste always means pride and presumption. And that pride is a kind of rebellion, even though there is no deliberate purpose. So the servant, having failed for lack of knowledge of his master's will, will not avoid punishment; but the servant who knows his master's will deserves to be punished doubly, as our Lord Jesus declares.

Now let us learn to be careful not to fail that way, and especially let us go to the trouble of knowing what God's will is, as Paul also exhorts us, for such is his good pleasure (cf. *Rom.* 12:2). In other words, let us know what is acceptable to him. That is what we are to apply all our attention to and what we are to practise every day of our lives, as Paul advises. When our Lord shows us the way, let us be careful not to wander from it and race around like wild animals, but let us always have pure hearts and clean hands. In other words, let us make an effort to serve God with such integrity that there is no hypocrisy and no hidden evil intention that will cause us to work against or around what God has commanded or forbidden. That much for one point.

And then let our hands be pure and clean. That is, let us attend to dedicating all our members to God's service in such a way that we will be able to assert firmly that we are obligated to, indeed bound to, obey what he has shown us and taught us in his word. That, then, is what we have to do.

But still each of us must hold himself suspect when he has fulfilled every duty according to what people say and will think, just as each will try to serve God in innocence, yet we must not, for all that, think we are upright and innocent. Why not? Many things will happen to us which will deceive us, for in the first place we will never put our sins to death as much as necessary, and there will always be flatteries, for we are drunk with self-love. But let us take the case that we search ourselves thoroughly and make every effort to ponder our sins. Does God not see much more clearly than we, as John says in his letter? (Cf. *1 John* 3:20.) So let us return to what Solomon says in Proverbs, that man will consider his ways right, but God weighs the hearts (cf. *Prov.* 21:2), that is, when we think we are justified in what we do, God will have another set of scales which are more sensitive than our judgment and opinion. So let us learn, as I have already said, to be even more vigilant; and even though we think all is going well, let us know that if God wanted to judge us rigorously, he would always find something to condemn in us. And that is also why David cries out: 'Lord, who will discern his errors? Cleanse me of my hidden sins' (cf. *Psa.* 19:12). When David spoke of God's law and said that those who keep his precepts diligently will not be ashamed (cf. *Psa.* 119:6) or disappointed, he thereupon exclaims: 'Alas, how far I am from acquitting myself.'[3] And then he concludes that we deserve to be condemned, if our Lord wanted to judge us according to the law (cf. *Psa.* 130:3). Why? Who knows his sins? (Cf. *Job* 13:23.) And then he adds: 'Lord, do not call me into account, for I know I need to take refuge in your mercy because of the many hidden sins that I do not know of, but you know them well, Lord, and I will have to be condemned for them unless you cover them with your infinite goodness.'[4] And that is also why God instituted sacrifices in his law as much for sins of ignorance as for voluntary sins. If men deserve no punishment, if they are unaware of their sins, and if their own consciences do not rebuke them, what need would there be to be reconciled? It would be a useless undertaking. God wants sinners to confess that they are worthy of death and need him to receive them in mercy, even though they have not sinned knowingly.

So let us now learn to regulate our lives in such a way that when we walk in fear and anxiety, we will not think about being acquitted unless God has pity on us and sustains us as his children and covers our offences with the merit of our Lord Jesus Christ's death and suffering and washes and cleanses us of all our blemishes by the blood he shed for that purpose. That, then, is what we have to remember.

And we especially see that Paul, after glorying in the truth that he had served God with the greatest integrity possible in his calling, that he had a zeal for building up the church and had spared nothing, that he had sought neither his advantage nor his honour, but that he had completely disregarded himself in order to carry out the charge entrusted to him (cf. *1 Cor.* 3), adds: 'I do not feel guilty in any respect, but I am not justified because of that' (cf. *1*

---

[3] If this exclamation is not exactly Davidic, especially not in 119, we think of Psalm 51:7.—*M.E.*

[4] This passage corresponds to no precise text of David, but we can relate it to Psalm 90:8 (concerning hidden sins).—*M.E.*

Cor. 4:4). He realizes he has to do with a judge who knows many sins we do not understand. Therefore, along with our anxiety, let us be humble. In other words, after being vigilant and keeping close watch to avoid sin, let us learn how not to be deceived by Satan's clever devices, for we can fall into his nets because of our reckless-ness and gullibility. Therefore, let us always be humble and realize that many sins we do not recognize will be accounted for before God unless they are buried in his mercy. That, then, is what we have to remember about this distinction Abimelech faced.

Now we have to note two things in the response God gave him, namely, that God preserved him from going from bad to worse by immediately having him return the wife to her husband; and that he then added threats. As for the first point, that God pre-served him from going from bad to worse, we have to gather a good teaching: that God pities those who reel or stumble or fall because of ignorance, as poorly informed people who are not moti-vated by definite evil intention and rebellion. If a person, by his own will and folly, wants to do evil, it will be very hard to have pity on him. But if we see some poor blind person who is on the verge of breaking his arms and legs, we will quickly hasten to help him. Why? We see his disability. Such are all sins. If a man has failed, and that happened to him by chance, as we say, if he was overcome by some emotion which is so sudden that he did not have time to think about it, that sin is distinguished from malice and manifest rebellion. But if an evil man is indifferent in his malice and has thrown off all fear of God, has become hardened and is incorrigi-ble, will that man be worthy of any mercy? Everyone will condemn him as unworthy.

Thus our Lord declares that he would have pity on those who fail out of innocence, as Abimelech speaks of innocence; it is with-out offence, and the thought of offence holds them back so that they do not act rashly and, if there is some fall, it is not mortal.

And in fact, we need our Lord to spare us that way. What would the situation be otherwise? For if we are the most vigilant people in the world and try to avoid all of Satan's enticements, we will still continue to fall three times, ten times, a day even while being completely involved in God's service, being led in it, and seeking only to please him and govern ourselves in accordance with his will. Even if we possess that devotion and zeal, we will nonetheless fail. What would happen now if our Lord did not hold us back? Our ignorance would soon become customary, and the person who fails once because of inattention will forgive himself and close his eyes, so to speak, so that he will do the same thing three or four times a day. And what if that becomes a habit? We become hardened to it and want it to be considered good,[5] for if someone convinces himself that he has not sinned, he cannot be rebuked. That, then, is how ignorance brings with it obstinacy, and in the end we will have no more scruples about resisting God. Consequently, what would happen to us if we were the most righteous people on earth if we were not restrained by some unseen bridle and God did not keep our times of ignorance from becoming malice and our malice from becoming times of extreme rebellion? It is certain the devil would win us over that way little by little and would finally possess us fully, and every one of us would be destroyed.

So, given the weakness each one of us feels within himself, given the many false ideas and the many opinions and allusions which are ours, why do we still walk in the fear of God and try to follow the right path (cf. *Psa.* 16:11; *John* 14:4-6) and make a great effort to achieve our goal (cf. *Phil.* 3:14), which is why we persevere the way we do, seeing we are very frail and offend God so many times, especially without thinking about it? God, seeing our debility, does

---

[5] This passage can illustrate Calvin's opposition to the legitimacy of custom, which is based on human practices that are not necessarily in accord with God's law.—*M.E.*

not want us to be completely rebellious and places within us a wholesome desire to serve him. He supports us, and when he sees us fall, he lifts us up. When we want to run loose and free, he holds us back. When we wander from the right path, he brings us back and causes us to follow where his word leads us. That, then, is how God preserves us miraculously in many ways. Otherwise, it is certain the devil would be such a great prince of this world that everything would seem to be bound and gagged and he would lead us at will, and we would have no fear of God, no integrity and no ability to distinguish between good and evil. That, then, for one point.

On the other hand, it is said in Scripture that God sends a spirit of madness upon those who become rebellious and continue in their iniquities and puts them in a state of reprobation (cf. *Deut.* 28:15, 28), and as a consequence they can no longer judge anything and can no longer experience shame; they no longer experience lamentation, and they give themselves fully to Satan, as if they had knowingly plotted to seek out their own destruction. Could it be that men were so reduced to madness that they would have devoted themselves to destruction and knowingly provoked God's wrath if God had not exercised that vengeance which Scripture places before us, namely, that he puts in a state of reprobation those who offended him excessively and could not be corrected when he wanted to bring them to repentance? Therefore, let us fear God's horrible judgment when we knowingly sin and when we violate his righteousness by unquestioned malice. Let us fear that he will abandon us completely and, withdrawing his spirit from us, allow Satan to possess us fully and blind us and not only make us pitiable drunkards, but like completely crazed people, possessed by such madness that we go and throw ourselves into that pit without fear. Let us be afraid of that. That, then, is the teaching we have to gather from this passage where our Lord says to Abimelech: 'I have prevented you from doing a greater evil because I knew that you were doing it in ignorance.'

So let us come to a contrary conclusion, namely, that when men despise God with definite malice, when they break all ties, act like horses that have broken free and cannot be tamed, when they have reached that state of boldness, God must place upon them a harsh hand, that is, he must leave them abandoned. And after he removes his grace from them, let the devil possess them; let him drive them; let him motivate them and push them around; and that will be a horrible spectacle to frighten us. Let us fear that. And let us learn better to walk in uprightness and purity of heart.

Moreover, let us realize that it is by the incomprehensible mercy of God that we are not abandoned every time and that the devil does not take us and drag us around at his pleasure. For if we were not preserved by the grace that we do not see, oh, it is certain each of us would trip and fall into the deepest pits. That, then, is what we must continue to remember.

Abimelech is now told to return the wife to her husband at this time, for he is a prophet and will pray for him (cf. *Gen.* 20:7a). Here God orders king Abimelech to make satisfaction for his sin, not such as the papists have forged it, for they think they compensate God in some way for removing their sins, but the satisfaction which is shown us here is that if we have offended our neighbour, we try to repair the offence we have committed against him, and that if we have taken something from him, we make restitution. Those, then, are the satisfactions God approves and commands. If we wrong or injure someone, we try to compensate for it in totality insofar as we can. So it is not enough for someone who has stolen to be moved by some sorrow or other; if he has the means, he must restore to each person what belongs to him and wash his hands of his larceny. For as long as he keeps what belongs to another, it is certain his hands will always be unclean. The same is true for verbal injuries.[6] For even though I have not taken from someone

---

[6] Cf. Matthew 5:22; but Calvin used, if not abused, injurious comments in

what belongs to him, if I have wronged him with words (cf. *Matt.* 5:22), it is only right that I try to make reparation. Those, I say, are the satisfactions God requires. That is, when we go against the rule of love, when we deprive one person of his goods and another of his good name, we must make satisfaction for our offences. That, in general, is what we have to remember here.

In that way we see that penitence always produces its fruits. Many people think they are acquitted before God if they experience some remorse and lament. There will always be hypocrisy unless our hands are joined with our hearts, as it is said here: 'with the purity of my hands and the purity of my heart.' Consequently, if there is no integrity and the heart is wicked and perverse, the hands follow. So what must we do? If we wish to make known that we are truly repentant, our hearts must walk, that is, we must have an integrity of heart; and then the hands must do their duty at the same time, that is, we must show by results and external works that the evil we have committed displeases us, that we condemn it gladly and truly. That, then, is what we have to remember about Abimelech's returning the wife to her husband.

Now if he had done nothing but confess to having done evil and had humbled himself, that would still have been considered a virtue, but before God it would have been only pretence, for, as I have said, these are two requirements that cannot be separated: the inner feeling of the heart and the works that result as its fruits. If a tree has good roots, the fruit will indicate that, but if the roots are bad, the tree will produce nothing of value and be useless (cf. *Matt.* 21:18-19; *Rom.* 11:16-18). Consequently, if we possess a true root of the fear of God, it is certain our lives will testify that we have been restored to the right road and that evil

---

polemic, exactly as the great majority of his contemporaries. The registers of the Consistory are nonetheless filled with admonitions against injurious people, exhorting them to ask pardon for their offences.—*M.E.*

displeases us and that we desire to pursue what is good. That for one point.

Now it is said that Abraham is a prophet and that he will pray for Abimelech. It seems that our Lord is here excluding Abimelech from being able to pray. In fact, he was unable to offer a prayer to God until he had been better instructed. For how will we call upon the one in whom we have not believed, Paul asks? And how will we believe if we have not been instructed (cf. *Rom.* 10:14) and guided by God's word? Consequently, faith must necessarily give us access to God. Consequently, this poor king, being a blind man, being an idolater, was as one rejected and did not have access to God for prayer until he was better instructed. Now it is said that Abraham will pray for him. The reason is added: he is a prophet; as if God were saying that he is an intimate friend of his and that he had deigned to reveal himself to him, for we have seen that Abraham had already had many visions (cf. *Gen.* 15:1ff.). That was not just for his private use, but to condemn the rest of the world, for everywhere he went, his faith had to have a fragrance that would condemn those who would not conform themselves to his example. In short, God states that he will hear Abraham's prayers because he is a prophet and in this way Abimelech's sin will be pardoned.

Now to conclude briefly what is contained here, let us note in the first place that God answers those who are closer to him and whom he has condescended to approach and receive as his servants. We must not find that strange, for it is said that the prayer of a righteous man is pleasing to God (cf. *James* 5:16); but it is not because of the righteousness God finds in his servants, as if the virtue of prayers was based on the merits or holiness of those who call upon God—in no way—but God adds grace upon grace. So when he chose Abraham, he manifested himself to him more privately than to any other. That gave Abraham access, and he was able to pray and be answered. That then is how Abraham had more power in praying to God, I say more effectiveness in obtaining what he asked for in all his requests. Even so, we are not to attribute that to Abraham's holiness as if he had deserved to be answered and thought of God as being obligated. What was the reason then? It is because God accepted him and chose him, for it is said that Abraham's house was like a sanctuary where God lived (cf. *Lev.* 26:11–12). Consequently, we must return to what James says, namely, that the prayer of a righteous man will always have its effect before God (cf. *James* 5:16) and never be without fruit.

And that is why we must greatly value being joined to God's church, for we are participants in all the prayers and discourses of the church. Now what a privilege is ours when we know that we, as members of the church, share in all the prayers of the faithful and that the mouths of the righteous are not opened in prayer without being for our welfare and salvation! And those are the intercessions which the church approves, and not those for the dead, as has been imagined. The papists will say we must have advocates and intercessors, but it is certain that each of us must be an advocate and intercessor for his brothers and that we must be convinced of that if we are to be helped and encouraged by the prayers of those who are joined with us in faith, even if they do not know us. And especially do we see that Paul recommends himself to the prayers of believers and that he desires to be helped in that way and says that when the faithful pray for him, they are fighting as if they were there in the same struggle with him. They, I say, are the real intercessors God answers and approves (cf. *Col.* 4:3, 12). Such are the righteous who are alive in this world. James likewise points out that when we confess our weaknesses to one another, we must also pray for one another (cf. *James* 5:16). James does not say that we must confess our weaknesses to Peter or Paul. That would be absurd. They are not now alive with us here below to share their

886

weaknesses with us. So let us note carefully that the prayers God approves are reciprocal, as we say. In other words, they are offered mutually for one another. When I pray for my neighbours, I also must be assured of being helped by their intercessions, and they by mine. The two go together. That, then, is what we have to practise.

As a matter of fact, Abimelech is not referred to Noah, who had been as just as all others, as God and his Holy Spirit witness. If the intercessions of the dead had been the order of the day, it is certain God would have said to Abimelech: 'Pray to Noah so he will be your intercessor and advocate,' but he does not say that. He proposes Abraham to him, who was with him, for he has given us all that responsibility to pray for one another as long as we live in the world (cf. *1 Thess.* 5:17; *Col.* 4:2-3; *James* 5:16). In a word, we see that when we seek God's mercy, we are not to forget the help he has given us. So let us realize with all humility that we need to be helped by our brothers who are in the world and who pray for us. And the purpose of that is to make us humble ourselves even more before God and offer a more forthright confession of our prayers when we call everyone to our aid, for we are guilty before our God. So if we want everyone to pray for us, the result will be that we will be more moved by true fear to glorify our God and show how much we need his mercy. Each one of us, then, must do that where we are, and we must all do it from the first of the last; yet that does not prevent Jesus Christ from remaining our only intercessor and advocate (cf. *1 John* 2:1). For when I pray for myself and for others, does that mean I set myself up as an advocate who is able to appease God wrath? Far be it from any creature to reach the height of being the advocate for the entire world, and far be it from each person to be one as concerns himself unless he comes in the name of Jesus Christ and through his mediation. But the fact remains that prayers for one another while we are in this world are heard because we follow the teaching our Lord Jesus Christ himself has left us. For when I pray, I do not say: 'Forgive me my sins' (cf. *Matt.* 6:12; *Luke* 11:4), but I ask for the forgiveness of sins for each person as well as for myself, and each person does the same for me. And if we practise that, what audacity and pride we would have if we wanted to take upon ourselves the office of being advocates and intercessors for others and to appease God and reconcile him with the world! But since Jesus Christ is our one and only Advocate and we come in his name to God his Father, our prayers and petitions are acceptable to him. And especially does each of us not only have private access to call upon God for ourselves and for our own particular needs, but we will also be heard when we pray for one another.

Now let us bow before the majesty of our gracious God in acknowledgment of our faults, praying that he will be pleased to cleanse us of them every day and so pardon us that we will not be prevented from being able to present ourselves before him and call upon him, for in that our salvation lies. So let us all say: Almighty God, heavenly Father...

INDEX OF SCRIPTURE REFERENCES

Commentary on Genesis
by John Calvin

Different in tone from his *Sermons on Genesis*, Calvin's commentary on the same book demonstrates his skill as a sound exegete. Indeed, Calvin is recognised by common consent as the greatest biblical commentator of all time. Here, he excels in bringing out the principles of God's dealings with men and in showing faithfully yet tenderly the human weakness and sin all too evident in Genesis.

This is certainly the foundation volume for Genesis. Reads well for devotions. A model commentary.

[TABERNACLE BOOKSHOP REVIEW]

ISBN: 978 0 85151 093 4   523pp.   Clothbound

Songs of the Nativity:
Selected Sermons on Luke 1 & 2
by John Calvin (tr. Robert White)

Calvin's sermons on the nativity are the fruit of 25 years in the ministry. Here we see the faithful pastor, expounding the text with passion and vigour. All four Gospels bear witness to the supernatural work and person of Jesus Christ, but only the first and third explicitly testify to his supernatural conception and birth. These are issues of perennial importance to all Christian men and women.

For all his sophistication as a thinker, the Genevan reformer had a way of dealing with complex issues in a simple way.
[AUSTRALIAN PRESBYTERIAN]

ISBN: 978 1 84871 010 8   258pp.   Clothbound

About the Publisher

THE Banner of Truth Trust originated in 1957 in London. The founders believed that much of the best literature of historic Christianity had been allowed to fall into oblivion and that, under God, its recovery could well lead not only to a strengthening of the church today but to true revival.

Inter-denominational in vision, this publishing work is now international, and our lists include a number of contemporary authors along with classics from the past. The translation of these books into many languages is encouraged.

A monthly magazine, *The Banner of Truth*, is also published and further information will be gladly supplied by either of the offices below or from our website.

THE BANNER OF TRUTH TRUST

3 Murrayfield Road
Edinburgh, EH12 6EL
UK

PO Box 621, Carlisle
Pennsylvania, 17013
USA

www.banneroftruth.co.uk